D1270924

SUICIDE

Understanding and Responding

Harvard Medical School Perspectives

SUICIDE
Understanding and Responding

Harvard Medical School Perspectives

edited by

Douglas Jacobs
Herbert N. Brown

International Universities Press, Inc.
Madison, Connecticut

Library of Congress Cataloging-in-Publication Data

Suicide : understanding and responding : Harvard Medical School
   perspectives / edited by Douglas Jacobs, Herbert N. Brown.
      p.   cm.
   Includes bibliographies and index.
   ISBN 0-8236-6695-6
   1. Suicidal behavior.   2. Suicidal behavior—Epidemiology.
3. Suicide.   I. Jacobs, Douglas.   II. Brown, Herbert N.
   [DNLM: 1. Crisis Intervention.   2. Suicide—psychology.   HV 6545
S9497]
RC569.S938   1989
616.85'8445—dc19
DNLM/DLC   88-13717
for Library of Congress   CIP

Printed in the United States of America

Contents

Contributors

George W. Arana, M.D., Associate Professor of Psychiatry, Tufts University School of Medicine; Lecturer in Psychiatry, Harvard Medical School; Associate Director of Psychiatric Research, Boston VA Medical Center.

Myron L. Belfer, M.D., Professor of Psychiatry, Harvard Medical School; Chief, Department of Psychiatry, The Cambridge Hospital.

Herbert N. Brown, M.D., Assistant Professor of Psychiatry, Harvard Medical School; Senior Supervising Psychiatrist, The Cambridge Hospital.

Dan H. Buie, M.D., Training and Supervising Analyst, The Boston Psychoanalytic Society and Institute.

Lee Chartock, M.D., M.P.P., Kennedy Fellow, John F. Kennedy School of Government.

Paul G. Cotton, M.D., Assistant Clinical Professor of Psychiatry, Harvard Medical School at Massachusetts Mental Health Center; Medical Director, Pembroke Hospital.

Robert A. Dorwat, M.D., Assistant Professor in Psychiatry, Harvard Medical School; Associate Chairman, Department of Psychiatry, The Cambridge Hospital.

Robert E. Drake, M.D., Ph.D., Associate Professor, Department of Psychiatry, Dartmouth Medical School; Medical Director, West Central Community Mental Health Services.

Timothy F. Dugan, M.D., Instructor in Psychiatry, Harvard Medical School at The Cambridge Hospital.

Erik Erikson, Professor Emeritus, Harvard University.

Rohn S. Friedman, M.D., Private Practice; Former Director Psychiatric Inpatient Service, The Cambridge Hospital.

Charlene Gates, M.S., Research Associate, Pembroke Hospital.

Leston Havens, M.D., Professor of Psychiatry, The Cambridge Hospital, Harvard Medical School.

Steven Hyman, M.D., Fellow in Genetics, Harvard Medical School; Fellow in Molecular Biology and Psychiatry, Massachusetts General Hospital.

Douglas Jacobs, M.D., Assistant Clinical Professor of Psychiatry, Harvard Medical School; Supervisor, McLean Hospital; Director, Suicide Education Institute of Boston; Clinical Director, Professional Psychiatric Associates.

Alexandra G. Kaplan, Ph.D., Lecturer in Psychiatry, Harvard Medical School; Administrative Director, Stone Center Counseling Service, Wellesley College; Training and Research Consultant, Stone Center, Wellesley College.

Rona B. Klein, M.D., Clinical Instructor in Psychiatry, Harvard Medical School; Clinical Director, Stone Center Counseling Service, Wellesley College.

Robert Jay Lifton, M.D., Professor of Psychiatry and Law, John Jay College of Criminal Justice, New York.

Robert E. Litman, M.D., Clinical Professor of Psychiatry, University of California at Los Angeles; Formerly Co-Director, Institute for the Studies of Destructive Behaviors, and the Suicide Prevention Center, Los Angeles.

John E. Mack, M.D., Professor of Psychiatry, Harvard Medical School; Staff Psychiatrist, Cambridge-Somerville Mental Health and Retardation Center.

John T. Maltsberger, M.D., Lecturer on Psychiatry, Harvard Medical School; Faculty, The Boston Psychoanalytic Society and Institute.

Ronald W. Maris, Ph.D., Professor and Director, Center for the Study of Suicide, University of South Carolina, Columbia.

Karl Menninger, M.D., Chairman of the Board, The Menninger Foundation, and The Villages, Inc.

Alexander C. Morgan, M.D., Instructor in Psychiatry, Harvard Medical School; Former Medical Director Geriatric Service, The Cambridge Hospital.

Jerome A. Motto, M.D., Professor of Psychiatry, University of California, San Francisco, School of Medicine.

J. Christopher Perry, M.P.H., M.D., Assistant Professor of Psychiatry, Harvard Medical School; Assistant Director Psychiatric Emergency Service, The Cambridge Hospital.

Jenny Potter, M.D., Resident in Anesthesiology, Harvard Medical School.

Sheldon Roth, M.D., Assistant Clinical Professor of Psychiatry, Harvard Medical School; Training and Supervisory Analyst, Psychoanalytic Institute of New England.

Edwin S. Shneidman, Ph.D., Professor of Thanatology, UCLA School of Medicine; Founder and former president of the American Association of Suicidology.

Thomas S. Szasz, M.D., Professor of Psychiatry, SUNY Health Science Center at Syracuse.

Anne Whitaker, M.D., Resident in Psychiatry, Yale University.

Norman E. Zinberg, M.D., Clinical Professor of Psychiatry, Harvard Medical School. (Deceased.)

Foreword: A Dialogue with Erik H. Erikson

Douglas Jacobs: Dr. Brown and I have been working on the problem of suicide for several years. After conducting the Harvard Medical School conferences on the subject of suicide, we decided we would collate the materials from the conferences and coedit a book. Dr. Brown had the idea of viewing the problem of suicide from the perspective of the person's total concept to incorporate some of the ideas that you, Professor Erikson, have talked about, namely biology, psychology, and one's social life. We reviewed your work to see if you had previously addressed the subject. However, we did not find anything. That is why we wanted to ask you your thoughts about the clinical issue of suicide. If you were going to approach the problem of suicide, how would you see it? How would you view it from an Eriksonian perspective?

Erik H. Erikson: Could you say what you mean? Frankly, I have not spoken much about suicide. It has happened in my work with adolescents, of course. The problem has vexed me, but I have not written about it.

Herbert Brown: What we mean is a perspective that does not get polarized and fragmented, that is, a view that avoids looking at suicide only from the perspective of individual psychodynamics or only from a nonlongitudinal social and cultural context. Specifically, we think of a perspective that goes beyond the increasingly prevalent inclination these days that many people can be given only biological treatment such as electroconvulsive therapy (ECT) or antidepressants to make despair better. We do plan to look at different groups of people, such as adolescents, older people, and women. It seems clear that each of these perspectives has some bearing on almost every case, but then there is almost something too large about such an inclusive approach. We wondered how you might integrate these perspectives.

EHE: Adolescents? Old people? Men—not so many women? The suicidal act must first be viewed as a form of total self-destructive action in a *life-situation* in which positive alternatives of action seem to have lost their credence. This came up most recently in my work with old people (Erikson, 1982). The most important overall aspect of life is the certainty that death is coming. The individual has no decision over *when* it is going to take place and *how*. As to the theme of the end of life, there is something almost too large about that inclusive idea, for what is so all-inclusive is a unique action which is putting an *end* to one's *own* life: how, indeed, could one diagnostically blame one or the other: individual psychodynamics or the social and cultural context? All old people simply have to accept approaching death as a daily problem. They see it happen to their relatives and their friends, and know that it is apt to suddenly come from somewhere where it was not expected. Their suicide, thus, is most of all an *active* death: at least they have made the decision and the choice of time and place. In my clinical work, I have noted that the "borderline" condition in adolescence is a parallel to and maybe an anticipation of the corresponding one in old age: namely, a stage of life that imposes an unbearable conflict over one's *choice* of overall *identity,* that must unavoidably end childhood and begin a course of adulthood within a sequence of social roles. There may also be in both these life situations a threatening regression to the total dependence of early infancy. With borderline adolescents as well as the elderly all of the future is out of control. The suicidal idea quite obviously "cures" that. Their psychosocial situation is so undefinable that to become a suicide can be almost a giant *identity decision.*

HB: It is a direction. This seems related to the commonly observed clinical situation when someone is suicidally depressed, and then seems to feel better just before the suicide. It fits with the notion that they have decided: "I'm no longer helpless, hopeless, or out of control; now I've decided to take control and I'm on a course. I've got a direction."

EHE: In adolescence, this decision can combine childhood and old age in a very perverse way. It means "now I know who *I* am," and you *must* believe it. So when it just then seems that they may be over the worst of their condition, they may only appear that way *because* they have come to a decision—even if it is to end it all. Which means it gives them an identity in life, even if it is an identity of one who brought about his own death.

HB: There seem to be people who take this on as an identity that is never fully consummated, as it were. They become professional suicide people who come to emergency rooms with their identity card. They never cash it in entirely, but they unconsciously always carry it around.

EHE: But after a while, they realize it. That is why I have told therapists in this situation to be careful and not make the patients feel that they have the greatest reality for the community—and the doctors—as a potential suicide. The risk increases when the adolescent may feel that he has more reality for everybody as a *patient* than in any other role. And, in that sense, to be suicidal can mean to harbor that more than any other self-definition. Suicidal thoughts happen all the more easily in adolescence when the psychosocial identity is not yet firm.

DJ: Do you think that people, especially adolescents, lose their sense of "I" when they become suicidal?

EHE: I have tried to formulate the "sense of I." It seems to me that all the discussion of the ego and of the self does not quite complete that subject. What we have to add is the sense of I, which is, of course, a sense of existence that every human being has and, in old age, must ripen into some *existential identity*. Younger people, adolescents in particular, can have a philosophical mood and seem to be wandering about, preoccupied very much with the sense of I (Erikson, 1981). They are very much concerned with what it feels like to exist in that time and space. When this is lacking, and when there is a desperate feeling that it can no longer be restored, I am sure that that may lead to an idea of suicide, of "now at least I really know who and where I am."

DJ: I'd be interested in what you think about the concept that suicidologists have developed, namely, that suicide is an escape from pain—the pain of living. Perhaps it is the pain of not knowing who they are or the pain of losing who they were, or perhaps the pain of fearing that they are not going to be.

EHE: That would be identity, some sense of who they are in their own judgment and in that of others. The sense of I would become more experiential. Freud was quite aware of, and tried to formulate this sense of I which is the very *sense* of continuity and activity and thus our centermost consciousness.

DJ: If you were assessing a person's suicide potential, you might ask the following questions: Do they have any sense of continuity? Do they see themselves moving on in life? And that view could be approached from any life stage.

EHE: In assessing suicide potential, one must remember that there is often a mixup in the simplest *and* deepest things. The sense of I would have much to do with, for example, a sense of being *active*. Those are big words. The opposite of that would be to become *inactivated* (not just to be "passive"). If someone feels totally inactivated, suicidal ideas may be inevitable as a way to restore *some* sense of being "in control."

DJ: What is the impact of crisis on suicide potential? Is crisis a disruption in continuity? Although it is a time for a person to go forward, it is so often a time when patients commit suicide.

EHE: It can, I think, also be a cause of suicidal thoughts in old age. Religions try to solve all this by supporting a lifelong sense of having been created with continuity and centrality, and even with an awareness of luminosity.

DJ: When we try to apply what you are saying to mental disorders such as schizophrenia I think it can take on great relevance. One of our colleagues at the hospital studied a small group of schizophrenics who committed suicide. He found that they killed themselves when they realized how chronic they were, when they realized that they were "schizophrenic," and that maybe in your terms did not feel central anymore, they did not feel active. They could not work.

EHE: Schizo means split does it not? "Split personalities." Do not these patients feel that their split is incurable?

DJ: Dr. Brown and I view suicide from our clinical experience. But perhaps we look at it too much in terms of the person as a patient and immediately we get very involved with the system, with the decision to hospitalize; with evaluating the seriousness of the attempt. What you talk about seems to be more crucial in terms of the central issues of a person. But perhaps that can only take place when you get to know somebody.

EHE: When we start with a "case history" so much depends on what we feel must as yet be clarified—theoretically, clinically, and ideologically, and so on. It makes us a little too "technical" in our questions. I happen to feel right now that we can learn much by looking at the simplest dimensions of existence behind those foreign and ancient terms we use to explain what we are talking about.

HB: Is it "pathological" to lose the sense of centralness, that ability to appreciate one's centrality? If so, is there a way to appoach that clinically?

EHE: Can it result in meaningful pathology? That is the question. Yes, because it takes away exactly what we are talking about, one's centrality, one's activity. Finally, what is important about it is that in practice we often permit the patient to depend on us rather than make it clear somehow that everybody has to recover his own sense of actuality.

References

Erikson, E.H. (1981), The Galilean sayings and the sense of "I." In: *Yale Review*, 70/3: 321–362. New Haven, CT: Yale University Press.
———— (1982), *The Life Cycle Completed*. New York: W.W. Norton.

Acknowledgments

Douglas Jacobs, M.D.
Herbert N. Brown, M.D.

This book is truly the result of collective effort. The initial groundwork was laid by Dr. John Mack following his presentation at a Cambridge Hospital Grand Rounds of his work-in-progress on a psychological case study of an adolescent suicide. This presentation prompted one of us (Dr. Douglas Jacobs) to consider the subject as a continuing education program of the department. Dr. Lee Macht, who was then the chairman of the department, encouraged Dr. Jacobs to pursue the idea of a Harvard Medical School suicide symposium. With the cooperation of the Continuing Education Department of Harvard Medical School, including Mr. Norm Shostak, Dr. Stephen Goldfinger, and the addition of Dr. Brown as the co-director, the Harvard Medical School symposia on suicide began.

The Suicide Symposia became a yearly tradition and have continued to attract over 700 participants annually. Experts on suicide around the country responded to the opportunity to present their work to the Harvard community. Their generosity and creativity are reflected in the chapters throughout the book. The support of Dr. Myron Belfer, Chief of the Department of Psychiatry at The Cambridge Hospital, allowed this effort to continue. The staff of the Continuing Education Division at The Cambridge Hospital, including the Associate Director, Denise Brouillette, and Administrative Assistants, Doris Hutchinson and Hilary Palmer, were essential to both the production of the symposia and to the follow through that was necessary to complete the book project. During the book's final phases of production, much of the administrative coordination and typing was handled by Ms. Shelley Truett.

The editors are indebted to the intellectual atmosphere of the Department of Psychiatry at The Cambridge Hospital. Ideas about topics came from many sources, but particularly from Dr. Leston Havens. Other colleagues in the Boston area with special interests in suicide, especially Drs. Terry Maltsberger and Dan Buie, made significant contributions.

No project of this sort comes to fruition without the support of families; our case was no exception. Our loving thanks, therefore, to Mary, Carolyn, Deborah and Betsy, Will, and Peter. We also want to acknowledge the many patients whose life situations are included in this book, particularly the patient who granted permission to be interviewed.

Introduction

Herbert N. Brown, M.D.
Douglas Jacobs, M.D.

Like many before us, our original professional encounter with the problem of suicide was clinical. As our teaching responsibilities grew and our exposure to suicide broadened, we became increasingly interested in how to conceptualize and then to communicate an understanding of suicide to our colleagues and students. Steadily the desire to develop a clinically useful and broad-ranging book about suicide began to take shape, accentuated by strong influences from three additional directions.

First, in 1981 suicide became the focus of a new series of symposia centered in the Department of Psychiatry at The Cambridge Hospital and sponsored by the Harvard Medical School. As we planned and directed these symposia, the challenge of helping others to learn motivated us to become familiar with the viewpoints of many experts in the field and to develop further our own thoughts and interests.

Second, in the summer of 1983 we had the opportunity to discuss suicide with Erik Erikson, who had then become our department's scholar-in-residence. Fortunately we audiotaped this discussion, and it now appears as the Foreword to this book. Erikson's comments, along with portions of his lifelong work, provided an important guiding theme for us. To ourselves we began referring to an "Eriksonian perspective," by which we meant a synthetic view of human nature and behavior (including human suicide) that takes into account biological, psychological, and sociocultural influences. In *Childhood and Society* (1950) Erikson had already expressed this perspective with regard to psychological disturbances in general: ". . . we have come to the conclusion that a neurosis is psycho- *and* somatic, psycho- *and* social, and *inter*personal" (p. 19) and "Our searchlight does not attempt to isolate and hold in focus any one aspect or mechanism of this case; rather it deliberately plays at random around the multiple factors involved, to see whether we can circumscribe the area of disturbance" (p. 21). This perspective is one of the cornerstones of this book.

A third influence—really sources of inspiration and support—came from two senior faculty members in our department, Leston Havens and John Mack, both Professors of Psychiatry at the Harvard Medical School. Dr. Havens is known for his creative and extensive exploration of what he calls the different "schools" in psychiatry (Havens, 1973). We, along with countless students, residents, and colleagues, have benefited from his appreciation of these different approaches, including his tenacious sensitivity to the unique individual aptitudes of different therapists for applying them. His perceptiveness about the "fit" of the different methods with distinct clinical situations is deservedly legend. With more specific regard to the subject of this book, his paper, "The Anatomy of Suicide" (1965), continues to be a classic exposition of the intrapsychic and interpersonal dynamics of suicide. It stands steadfastly as testament to how penetrating his thinking on the subject already was over 20 years ago. We believe his interview in this book (chapter 18) demonstrates an important example of the evolution of his thinking and the realization of his belief that the future of clinical psychiatry lies with refining its methods (Havens, 1973, p. 330). Our personal interactions with Dr. Havens over the years have never failed to further our efforts to understand suicidal people and those (ourselves included) who try to help them.

John Mack was as an enabler (Mack, 1978). The ground work for our department's academic involvement in suicide was laid by Dr. Mack as he shared in a grand rounds presentation his work in progress on a psychological case study on an adolescent suicide (Mack, 1981). The principles set forth in his conception of an architectural model (or systems approach) became a guiding light for clinicians and teachers; he brought to this model his experience as clinician, psychoanalyst, child psychiatrist, psychobiographer, and social scientist.

Our way of bringing these influences together, reflected in the title of the book, naturally evolved into the twin concerns of "understanding and responding." We begin with an Overview and a Public Health Perspective. Then, in Part I, Foundations, we set the stage for an integrated appreciation of suicide. The fundamental building blocks of understanding—psychological, biological, and social—are discussed separately in some detail. While one factor or another may be most influential in an individual case, we emphasize that suicide truly is "the final common pathway of diverse circumstances, of an interdependent network rather than an isolated cause, a knot of circumstances tightening around a single time and place" (Havens, 1965, p. 401). There are, indeed, devastatingly synergistic influences in most cases of suicide. Or, as Professor Erikson puts it: "How, indeed, could one diagnostically blame one or the other."

In Part II, Understanding, we highlight those social, biological, and psychological considerations that affect the general assessment of suicide risk and particular groups. We address some of the revealing gender differences in suicidal behavior by inviting two members of Wellesley's Stone Center faculty to discuss female suicide—even though this subject had not yet been the subject of any of our symposia. Paradoxically (because our department has for years been associated with expertise in this area) we do not directly address the role of alcoholism ("substance abuse" generally) in this section. We do recognize that alcohol, especially, is involved in a large proportion of suicides. The complex questions relating to the direct chemical (biological) effects of alcohol itself, along with the social and psychological elements in the self-destructive use of drugs, warrant the most serious attention. The omission of a specific chapter on this subject should not be construed as our minimizing this very important piece in the unhappy puzzle of suicide.

Part III, Responding, primarily addresses responses to the dilemma of suicide. We focus on particular treatment contexts (such as inpatient units, the emergency room, and outpatient psychotherapy) and, at the end, venture into the less-discussed realm of the aftermath of suicide—specifically the impact on trainees and on inpatient units. We single out a particular approach to interviewing and working with many suicidal patients because we believe it is not widely appreciated, and because it represents the influence of some of the newer schools of psychiatry. Moreover, the cost of "empathic failure" with a suicidal patient can be so much higher than with a nonsuicidal patient: a nonsuicidal patient may respond to a slip in empathy with silence, or with a direct expression of disappointment and anger, or perhaps with lateness for the next meeting, while the suicidal patient may not arrive at all—permanently ending any opportunity for growth or increased understanding. Despite this emphasis, we still recognize that empathy is a particularly complex and even controversial subject. It may, therefore, help to foreshadow three specific empathic dilemmas that appear in our book.

These three dilemmas come into focus around some classic clinical advice (worded in different ways by many, but, according to oral tradition in the Boston area, put memorably by the late Elvin Semrad as): "*Never* do for the patient what the patient can do for himself, but *always* do for the patient what the patient needs and cannot do for himself." The clinical problem of doing too much or doing too little can, and often does, reach excruciating proportions in decisions about suicidal patients because of the life-or-death stakes of miscalculation. Generally a clinician's empathic capacities serve as one of the most valuable guideposts in his or her attempt to apply the Semradian advice. Yet the application of empathy with suicidal patients is especially tricky. Here, then, in abbreviated form, are three dilemmas.

1. It is striking how confused we can get about empathy with suicidal patients. Often clinicians are drawn to feel excessive concern about people who are really not at much risk to kill themselves, while—in a dangerous and all-too-familiar scenario— the genuinely suicidal patient produces a strange lull in our worry and eludes emotional detection. Buie and Maltsberger (chapters 3 and 15) discuss this dilemma from the perspective of emphasizing the *limitations of empathy,* asserting that reliable assessment of suicide risk must come from a psychodynamic formulation that illuminates particular psychological vulnerabilities to suicide. They remind us that, for many clinicians, our empathic capacities can be misleading and/or inadequate.

2. The second empathic dilemma is highlighted by Havens (chapter 18) and discussed by Jacobs (chapter 19). Havens centers on the need to get in touch with the suicidal patient's painful hopelessness and despair. He describes and demonstrates what he calls "going below" or, more formally, the use of "extensions" (Havens, 1986, pp. 67–79). It is important to recognize that Havens' emphasis is different from that of Buie and Maltsberger. He places great weight on the empathic capacities of the therapist and on how to go about actively reaching the patient— establishing rapport with what is sick or hurting or despairing in the patient. For him, empathic contact becomes even more than the most reliable guide to assessing

suicide risk. Such contact provides the critical lasting foundation for the patient's treatment—without which there can be no helpful therapy, no change or growth, and no genuinely free choice about life or suicide. Havens emphasizes the *centrality of empathy*, not its limitations.

3. Zinberg (chapter 16) describes and illustrates a third empathic dilemma. His ego-psychological approach harkens back to the more cognitive, formulative emphasis of Buie and Maltsberger, and it is particularly relevant to outpatient psychotherapy where distinguishing the genuinely suicidal patient from the patient who threatens suicide as part of their characterological style is perhaps the central clinical problem. Zinberg puts emphasis on a precise explication of how the patient functions psychologically, which an empathic stance makes bearable for the patient. This might be seen as stressing an *empathic context* for therapeutic interventions or, simply, objective empathy.

These empathic dilemmas must be acknowledged and, in a sense, wrestled with in most attempts to understand and respond therapeutically to a suicidal patient.

In Part IV, Philosophical and Larger Perspectives, we take up larger themes such as value systems and philosophical and social perspectives as they apply both to clinical work with suicidal patients and to suicidal thinking and behavior viewed from an existential and larger-than-one-person vantage point. Within these themes, typically Eriksonian concerns about identity, culture, and continuity remain distinctly detectable. For example, Dr. Szasz determinedly defends human freedom and its compatriot, human responsibility. These aspects of life are so essential, he argues, that without them there is no real human existence. But it can also be observed that the *will* to live is complexly motivated and the *capacity* to live is variable: astoundingly durable in some of us, frighteningly precarious in others— like a roaring flame at one extreme, like a mere flicker continually in danger of being extinguished at the other. When such differences in constitution, in developmental history, in internal psychological resources, and in environmental support are contemplated, respect grows for the responsibility to help those who are in a currently vulnerable position.

Because politics reflects psychology and values, some of the problems posed by these larger perspectives also appear in the familiar "conservative" versus "liberal" debate in which freedom is weighed against fair and equal opportunity. In the life and death drama of suicide, even if ultimate responsibility for one's life cannot be disowned (and even if it is granted that suicide may under rare and special circumstances be rational and acceptable), active attempts are needed to reach out and to try to save anyone who is really acutely suicidal. This position takes issue with the philosophical assertion that true freedom (and therefore responsibility) is equally available to all individuals at all times. Perhaps the "constriction" of options observed in most seriously suicidal people is the hallmark of genuinely reduced capacity for free choice (Shneidman, 1985). Ultimately, the authors in this part grapple, in one way or another, with the question: Where is the line that marks for us the nature and the limit of responsibility in interactions with suicidal patients? If the line is drawn, as it were, too *far* from the patient, we may be able to defend this stance as profoundly respectful of the person's autonomy—but we may then contribute to losing, literally losing, people who require more of a working apportionment of what they can understand and bear and what they cannot. Such people may be unable, at particular times in their lives, to continue to live without external structure and support in the midst of dreadfully painful relations with others or conflict that is unconscious (and, therefore, that they are powerless to master or take responsibility for). On the other hand, if we draw the line too *close* to the patient, we run the equally enormous risk of stifling growth and fostering only dependent regression, stagnation, and, perhaps, meaningless life—all in the name of "helping." Moreover, in this process, we may so overburden ourselves with untenable rescue fantasies that we begin to resent the patient and thereby possibly contribute to their riddance. Eventually, it may come down to working through the Semradian advice mentioned previously. Our responsibility in that sense, our philosophical or value-related perspective, might be seen as an obligation to contact and treat the patient genuinely, doing what is needed and possible to open him or her to a truly free choice as a whole and self-possessed person. Sometimes, despite our best efforts, this process may be interrupted by or end with suicide. That can never be the therapist's goal or decision, but it may not be preventable. As Shneidman (1985) has said:

> There is never a suicide without some keen need. The fulfillment or resolution of some need(s) answers the question of the *why* of any suicide. There are many pointless deaths, but never a needless suicide [p. 102].

Such a perspective and course of action takes on magnified and even qualitatively different meaning when we shift our focus from the predominantly individual domain to the larger arena of our world and our species. No contemporary discussion of suicide can ignore this new dimension. The self-destructive action of a single individual or group may obviously not be best for the rest of us. Also, we believe (although this is essentially unknowable) that there are individuals who kill themselves without fully intending to achieve that end. In an age of nuclear weapons, we must consider the conditions which could lead to a similar miscalculation for mankind.

We acknowledge that a book that is the collection of the thoughts and styles of multiple authors cannot have the solidly synthetic feel of a single-authored text. Nevertheless, we have designed and developed this book in a way that will make it a source of both information and widely divergent perspectives on suicide while it, at the same time, is organizationally and conceptually integrated enough to hold meaningfully together. We welcome the reader's active involvement with the perspectives that follow.

References

Erikson, E.H. (1950), *Childhood and Society*. New York, W.W. Norton.

Havens, L.L. (1965), The anatomy of suicide. *N. Engl. J. Med.*, 272:401–406.

———— (1973), *Approaches to the Mind*. Boston: Little, Brown.

———— (1986), *Making Contact*, Cambridge, MA: Harvard University Press.

Mack, J.E. and Hickler, H. (1981), *Vivienne: The Life and Suicide of an Adolescent Girl*. Boston: Little, Brown.

Mack, J.E. (1978), *A Prince of Our Disorder: The Life of T.E. Lawrence*. Boston: Little, Brown.

Shneidman, E.S. (1985), *Definition of Suicide*. New York: John Wiley & Sons.

Overview:
A Multidimensional Approach to Suicide

Edwin S. Shneidman, Ph.D.

It is almost banal to say that the topic of suicide is a complicated one. Suicidal phenomena *are* enormously complex. A dozen individuals can end their lives by shooting bullets through their head and *do* twelve different things; that is, arrive at seemingly the same unit of behavior by means of very different routes and histories. In order to understand suicide, one, ideally, has to be a personologist; to understand suicide one must understand human behavior, by which I mean mostly human mentation, what goes on in the mind, and the multiple reasons—biological, sociocultural, dyadic–interpersonal, cognitive, affective, unconscious (to name a few)—that lie behind or accompany a suicidal event.

This brief statement itself contains several implications. One implication, already stated rather directly, is that suicide phenomena can best be understood through multidisciplinary approaches. In suicidology, no one specialty has a stranglehold on truth. We must listen to several voices, each of which may represent legitimate aspects among the relevant specialties. Also, any reasonable scientist is warranted in taking umbrage if an associate in a specialty other than his own states that *his* piece of the action represents the whole field.

Portions of this chapter, in slightly different form, have appeared previously in the following: (1984) Suicide. In: *Encyclopaedia of Psychology*, ed. R. Corsini. New York: John Wiley & Sons; (1985) *Definition of Suicide*. New York: John Wiley & Sons; (1986) Some Essentials of Suicide and Some Implications for Response. In: *Suicide*, ed. A. Roy. Baltimore, MD: Williams & Wilkins; and (1987) A Psychological Approach to Suicide. In: *Cataclysms, Crises and Catastrophes: Psychology in Action*, ed. G. R. VandenBos and B. K. Bryant. Washington, D.C.: American Psychological Association.

APPROACHES TO SUICIDE

The full understanding of "suicide"— the topic of suicide, the etiology of suicide, the mystery of suicide, the subject matter of suicidology—can be visualized as a circle made up of several *sectors*. Thus we would have a circle or a pie with various sectors or wedges or pieces. Whether or not there is a special core or essence at the center of this circle we have yet to conceptualize. There is such a conceptual circle for each instance of suicide. The size and density and importance of the various sectors vary from case to case of individual suicide. The common labels of these several sectors are as follows: (1) literary and personal document; (2) philosophical and theological; (3) demographic, epidemiological, nomothetic; (4) sociocultural, anthropological; (5) sociological; (6) dyadic–interpersonal, familial; (7) psychodynamic; (8) psychological; (9) psychiatric, mental illness; (10) constitutional, genetic; (11) biological, biochemical; (12) legal, ethical; (13) preventive (14) systems theory; and (15) political, global, supranational.

Another implication (still having to do with multiplicity) is that we need both benchwork and field work; we cannot disregard either Virchow or Freud; we should be as precise, scientific, statistical, nomothetical as we can possibly be but we cannot, on the basis of misguided principle, eschew the great power of the idiographic, clinical, intensive, longitudinal single-case approach. It is a mistake to trade specious precision for indispensable relevance.

THE LITERARY AND PERSONAL DOCUMENT APPROACH

If you believe, as I do, that the great novelists and playwrights—Dostoevsky, Melville, Ibsen—offer us enormous insights into the human condition and its vicissitudes (including suicide), then it is to their works that we should go to study and to learn. For example, can you imagine what one could learn about the psychology and sociology of suicide of nineteenth century women by a close study of Edna's drowning in Kate Chopin's *The Awakening* (1899); or, if we can permit male authors on this same topic, by studies of Anna's death in Tolstoy's *Anna Karenina* (1877), or of Emma's poisoning in Flaubert's *Madame Bovary* (1856), or of Lucy's and Isabel's deaths in Melville's *Pierre* (1852), or of Hedda's suicide in Ibsen's *Hedda Gabler* (1890)?

In addition, in this same idiographic and literary tradition, there are those rare personal documents, diaries, by individuals who ruminated and wrote for years about their own suicidal thoughts, and then, in a tragic validation of their own beliefs and urgings, committed suicide. These diaries are "the real thing." They are deposits with nuggets of insight and implication for any careful and patient miner.

There is one diary I would like to mention separately. In 1985 Harvard University Press issued a two-volume edition of *The Inman Diary,* edited by Professor Daniel Aaron from Inman's original 155 volumes. Inman is a conspicuously unattractive character: querulous, acerbic, a pro-Nazi, a child molester, a hypo-chrondriac, but what an undeniably rich document his diary is: perfect grist for a multidisciplinary mill. What a joy it would be someday to conduct an intensive Assessment Council on this one rich and fascinating documentation of a suicide with several experts representing several different specialties—a procedure described by Henry A. Murray in *Explorations in Personality* (1938).

From a somewhat different, but no less interesting angle, A. Alvarez, contemporary English poet, critic, and author (and a failed suicide himself) has written a book, *The Savage God* (1970) about suicide *in* literature: that is, "the power that the act of suicide has exerted over the creative imagination" (p. 141). In this context, Alvarez discusses the impact of the *idea* of suicide on the works of Beckett, Chatterton (who committed suicide), Coleridge, Cowper, Dante, Donne, Dostoev-sky, Eliot, Goethe, Kafka, Mann, Pasternak, and Yeats. [Lester, Sell, and Sell (1980, pp. 113–142), list authors who have committed suicide and literary works dealing with the theme of suicide; Cutter (1983) includes similar information for artists.]

One should not disregard the great power of the Assessment Council to study individuals by having members of a first-rate multidisciplinary team independently examine them in depth. The meaning of any individual suicide is not a sum, or an abstract or a synthesis of these proceedings; it is, rather, everything that all the experts will have said, with multiple wisdoms and multiple insights and multiple implications for the rescue of others in the future.

PHILOSOPHICAL AND THEOLOGICAL APPROACHES

Philosopher Jacques Choron in his book *Suicide* (1972), outlined the position of the major Western philosophers in relation to death and suicide. In general, the "philosophers of suicide" never meant their written speculations to be prescriptions for action, but simply to reflect their own inner intellectual debates on this ubiquitous and fascinating topic.

Many famous philosophers have touched on the topic of suicide: Pythagoras, Epictetus, Montaigne, Descartes, Spinoza, Voltaire, Montesquieu, Rousseau, Hume, Kant, Schopenauer, Nietzsche.

The existential philosophers of our own century—Kierkegaard, Jaspers, Camus, Sartre, Heidegger—have made the pointlessness and meaninglessness of life (and willy-nilly the topic of suicide) a central issue. Camus begins *The Myth of Sisyphus* by saying that the topic of suicide is the central problem for philosophy.

The indispensable reference for anyone who wishes the larger view of philosophic and theological matters is Stephen Pepper's book, *World Hypotheses* (1942). For me, this clarifying book organized my thoughts and answered my questions on these important topics in a totally satisfying way. This book is not at all about suicide, but it is one of the half-dozen most important books in my own career as a suicidologist.

Theologically speaking, neither the Old nor the New Testament directly forbids suicide. Contemporary Western attitudes are highly colored by Christian doctrine. Historically, the excessive martyrdom of the early Christians frightened the church elders sufficiently for them to introduce a serious deterrent; they related suicide to sin. The notion of suicide as sin has taken firm hold since the fourth century, when St. Augustine (A.D. 345–430) stated that suicide violated the Sixth Commandment (relating to killing) and precluded the possibility of repentence; in the seventh century when the Council of Toledo proclaimed that an individual who attempted suicide was to be excommunicated; and in the thirteenth century when St. Thomas (1225–1274) emphasized that suicide was a mortal sin in that it usurped God's power over man's life and death. For hundreds of years it has continued to play an important part in Western man's view of self-destruction. [See Battin (1982), chapter 1, as a source regarding the church's view of suicide.]

The topic of suicide is a lively one to this day in theological circles. In general suicide is condemned, especially in the fundamentalist churches of this country. It can be noted, with approval, however, that in 1986, when a conservative southern United States Senator committed suicide, the eulogies never mentioned the word *sin*.

DEMOGRAPHIC APPROACH

The demographic approach relates to various statistics on suicide. The medieval English coroners—the word *cornor* means the custodian of the Crown's pleas—began to keep "rolls"; that is, documents that incorporated death as well as birth records. In England from the eleventh century on, whether or not the property of a deceased individual could be kept by the heirs or had to be forfeited to the Crown depended on whether or not the death was judged by the coroner to be an act of God or a felony. Suicide was the latter, a felony against the self, felo de se; thus the way in which a death was certified was of enormous importance to the survivors. [A historical consideration of penal laws and suicide may be found in Guernesy (1883).]

In 1662 John Graunt (Shneidman, 1976), a tradesman, published a small book of "observations" on the London bills of mortality (a listing of all deaths) that was to have great social and medical significance. Graunt devised categories of information—sex, locale, type of death—and made mortality tables. He was the first to demonstrate that regularities could be found in mortality phenomena and that these regularities were important data to be used in policy-making and planning by the government and business.

In 1741, the science of statistics (from the Greek word *statistik,* the study of political facts and figures) came into existence with the work of a Prussian clergyman, Johann Süssmilch. He called his efforts "political arithmetic," what we now call "vital statistics." From his studies came the "laws of large numbers," which permitted long-range planning (for food and supplies and potential tax income based on size of population) in Europe as well as in the American colonies. Recently,

Cassedy (1969), writing about colonial America, said that Süssmilch's "exhaustive analysis of vital data from church registers . . . became the ultimate scientific demonstration of the regularity of God's demographic laws" (p. 110). The traditions about statistics on suicide stem from Graunt and Süssmilch.

Turning now to some fairly recent data: during the eleven-year period, 1970 to 1980, 272,322 suicides were recorded in the United States. The suicide rate is around 12 per 100,000 population—it was 12.4 in 1984 (National Center for Health Statistics, 1986). Except for those over 65, it ranks as one of the ten leading causes of death in all age groups. Suicide rates gradually rise during adolescence, increase sharply in early adulthood, and parallel advancing age up to the 75 to 84 age bracket when they reach a rate of 22.0 suicides per 100,000 (in 1984). Male suicides outnumber female suicides by a ratio of three to one (3.4:1 in 1984). More whites than nonwhites commit suicide (27,002 versus 2,284, respectively in 1984). Suicide is more prevalent among the single, widowed, separated, and divorced. The commonest method is firearms.

The suicide activities of youth and young adults have been of particular recent interest. In relation to those data, I quote a few lines from a recent paper by Holinger and Offer (1986) directly on this topic:

> Among the young, 20–24 year olds are at highest risk of suicide, followed by 15–19 and 10–14 year olds. White males have the highest suicide rates in all youthful age groups. However, suicide rates for the young are lower than the adult and older age groups. Time trends for adolescents show high rates during the 1930s, decreases throughout the 1940s and 1950s, dramatic increases from the late 1960s to the late 1970s with a recent levelling off of suicide rates [p. 1].

Nonetheless, suicide among the young is considered to be a special problem, and rightly so. [For reviews of youth suicide see Seiden (1969); Peck, Farberow, and Litman (1985).] As a reflection of this, organizations concerned with suicide, notably the National Institute of Mental Health, the American Association of Suicidology (AAS), and the National Committee for Youth Suicide Prevention, have all made youth suicide a focus for study and concern.

SOCIOCULTURAL APPROACH

On this topic two facts are obvious: that everyone is born into and develops within a sociocultural matrix; and that the act of suicide itself has different integral meanings (for both perpetrator and survivor) among different cultures. In this presentation I am discussing suicide primarily within the United States, although I believe also that my model applies to Western Europe. However, I extrapolate with increasing hesitancy to Latin America, the Arab world, and Asia. There are some universals, some transcultural elements, and many particulars.

This may be as good a place as any to introduce my definition of suicide, stated here to emphasize what I believe to be the essentially relativistic and contextual nature of suicide when considered in global and omnihistorical terms. My definition is (1985): "Currently in the Western world, suicide is a conscious act of self-induced annihilation, best understood as a multidimensional malaise in a needful individual who defines an issue for which the suicide is perceived as the best solution" (p. 203).

The several implications of this definition will be expanded upon as we wind through this paper; namely, its contextualism, the role of intention, its multidimensional nature, the strong belief that suicide is a malaise and not a disease (and should not be confused with affective disorders), that the key is pain attendant to frustrated psychological needs, that this pain is compounded by perceptual constriction.

There are, of course, many sociocultural studies (Hendin, 1964). One especially fine, recent one comes immediately to mind, written by a rare bicultural scholar. I refer to Iga's (1986) *The Thorn in the Chrysanthemum: Suicide and Economic Success in Modern Japan*. It speaks of an ancient culture dramatically transmuted by its foreign victor, of recovery in the context of its old and new values, and of suicide as one especially onerous price of recovery and success.

SOCIOLOGICAL APPROACH

Emile Durkheim's giant book, *Le Suicide* (1897) demonstrated the power of the sociological approach. As a result of his analysis of French data on suicide, Durkheim proposed four kinds of suicides, all of them emphasizing the strength or weakness of the person's relationships with or ties to society. "Altruistic" suicides are literally required by society. Here, the customs or rules of the group "demand" suicide under certain circumstances; hara-kiri and suttee are examples.

"Egoistic" suicide occurs when the individual has too few ties with his community. Demands to live do not reach him.

"Anomic" suicides are those that occur when the accustomed relationship between an individual and his society is suddenly shattered, such as the shocking, immediate loss of a loved one, a close friend, a job, or even a fortune. "Fatalistic" suicides derive from excessive regulation. Examples would be persons such as slaves or prisoners whose futures are piteously blocked.

For years after Durkheim, sociologists did not make major changes in his theory. Henry and Short (1954) added the concept of internal (superego) restraints to that of Durkheim's external restraint, and Gibbs and Martin (1964) sought to operationalize Durkheim's concept of social integration.

In a major break with Durkheim, sociologist Jack Douglas (1967) pointed out that the social meanings of suicide vary greatly and that the more socially integrated a group is, the more effective it may be in disguising suicide; further, social reactions to stigmatized behaviors can themselves become a part of the etiology of the various actions the group seeks to control.

Maris (1981) believes that a systematic theory of suicide should be composed of at least four categories of variables: those concerning the person, the social context, biological factors—there's the new sociology!—and "temporality," a concept that he expands into the fruitful idea, with major psychological underpinnings, of "suicidal careers."

It seems that after an extended hiatus, the sociological theories vis-à-vis suicide, are in a period of development and twentieth century "modernization."

DYADIC, INTERPERSONAL, FAMILIAL APPROACHES

Suicide notes are written by approximately 15 percent of those who commit suicide, and one gets the keenest impression from reading them that, if suicide is anything, it is an interpersonal, literally a two-person, event (Shneidman, 1980). "It was not your fault . . . I love you . . . I hate you . . . Forgive me . . ." (p. 48)—all these words make the dyadic point. The concept of the "significant other" has its sharpest operational meaning in a case of suicide where another person seems to be both the life-sustainer and the last straw, at any rate, the focus of the victim's life and the precipitating reason for the death.

Quite recently, Cynthia Pfeffer (1986) has described the family characteristics that lead to the abandoning of the individual and that even support suicide within the family setting. A few lines from her 1986 book, *The Suicidal Child,* tell us a great deal:

> Studies consistently have reported that families of suicidal children are disorganized by parental separations, divorce, and stresses of living in a one-parent family . . . the suicidal children were distinguishable from [others] . . . by the seriousness of family stresses [where] losses were the predominant type of stress . . . [and by] parental violent and sexual[ly] abusive patterns . . . and [other] parental psychopathology [p. 125].

Arthur Crew Inman's diary, noted earlier, is filled with his fear and hatred of, and then his fantasies of revenge on his father. One can hardly disconnect his suicide from his relationships to his father and, then, to his wife.

PSYCHODYNAMIC APPROACH

As Emile Durkheim detailed the sociology of suicide, so Sigmund Freud fathered the psychodynamic explanations of suicide (Friedman, 1967). To him, suicide was a drama within the mind, mainly of unconscious hostility directed toward the introjected love object.

Karl Menninger, in his important, thoroughly American book, *Man Against*

Himself (1938), delineated the psychodynamics of hostility and asserted that suicide is made up of three strands: (1) the wish to kill; (2) the wish to be killed; and (3) the wish to die.

Gregory Zilboorg (1937) refined Freud's psychoanalytic hypothesis and stated that every suicidal case contained not only unconscious hostility but also an unusual lack of the capacity to love others. He extended the concern solely from intrapsychic dynamics to include the external world, specifically citing the role of the broken home in suicide proneness.

In an important exegesis of Freud's thoughts on suicide from 1881 to 1939, Robert E. Litman (1967) concluded that there is more to the psychodynamics of suicide than hostility. These factors include several emotional states: rage, guilt, anxiety, dependency, as well as a great number of specifically predisposing conditions. Feelings of abandonment and particularly of helplessness and hopelessness are important.

A further word about the locus of blame: The early Christians made suicide a personal sin, Rousseau transferred sin from man to society, Hume tried to secularize and decriminalize suicide entirely, Durkheim focused on societies' inimical effects on people, and Freud—eschewing both the notions of sin and crime—gave suicide back to man but put the locus of action in man's unconscious mind.

PSYCHOLOGICAL APPROACH

The psychological approach can be distinguished from the psychodynamic approach in that it does not posit a set of dynamics or a universal unconscious scenario but, rather, emphasizes certain general psychological features which seem to be necessary for a lethal suicide event to occur. Four have been noted (Shneidman, 1976): (1) acute *perturbation,* an increase in the individual's state of general upset; (2) heightened *inimicality,* an increase in self-abnegation, self-hate, shame, guilt, and self-blame, and overtly in behaviors which are against one's own best interests; (3) a sharp and almost sudden *constriction* of intellectual focus, a tunneling of thought processes, a narrowing of the mind's content, a truncating of the capacity to see viable options which would ordinarily occur to the mind; and (4) the idea of *cessation,* the insight that it is possible to put an end to suffering by stopping the unbearable flow of consciousness. The last is the igniting element that explodes the mixture of the previous three components. In this content, suicide is best understood not as a movement toward death (or cessation) but rather as flight from intolerable emotion—psychological pain.

The psychological approach to suicide cannot afford to ignore psychological needs, especially the needs that are felt to be unacceptably unfulfilled, thwarted, or blocked. We have a lexicon of psychological needs presented to us, like a conceptual feast, in Murray's *Explorations in Personality* (1938). In my own work with suicidal patients, I have found Murray's need system indispensable for my understanding of a particular person's psychological pain, and thus indispensable for my efforts to mollify and reduce the pain and the perturbations that drive the suicidal impulses.

The psychological approach believes that certain human thoughts, feelings, and behaviors, such as a phobia or an irrational prejudice, or a desperate (even lethal) transient feeling that one would be better off dead, are in the *mind* and not in the brain. Of course, the mind is located "in" the brain, but these feelings are functions of the mind and an autopsy reveals no indications of them as structures. There is no question that certain experiences such as a defeat (in an athletic contest or an election), or rejection by or loss of a loved one do produce concurrent changes in blood chemistry and a hundred other physiological processes, but then to convert suicide into "depression" may mix cause and effect. It does not address what the person is hurting from. Many people have been "down," blue, dysphoric, depressed, dispirited, and bereft, but no one dies of these conditions. Many people, however, have died of suicide. Suicide is a human, psychological orientation toward life, not a biological, medical disease. There is no virus or biochemical storm that causes suicide: suicide is not a disease like measles or AIDS. Suicide is a human malaise tied to what is "on the mind," including one's view of the value of life at that moment. It is essentially hopeless unhappiness and psychological hurt—and that is not a medical condition.

THE PSYCHIATRIC, MENTAL ILLNESS, AND DISEASE APPROACH

Of course I am aware of the scores of studies of affective disorders (manic-depressive disease, bipolar depression, unipolar depression, etc.) and of the scores of studies that indicate what percentage of suicides—usually in the 90 percents—have been assigned or could be assigned DSM-III psychiatric diagnostic mental disease labels (Miles, 1977; American Psychiatric Association, 1980). My own belief is that absolutely 100 percent of all suicides are perturbed. But perturbation itself is not a disease. It is usually "just" a state of mind with a concomitant, but usually not causative condition of the brain. Further, it is clear that the vast percentage, I would estimate 99 percent, of individuals diagnosed as schizophrenic do *not* commit suicide; just as the vast majority of individuals diagnosed with a depressive illness lead relatively long, albeit unhappy lives (as, unhappily, do their loved ones).

Accordingly, I shall refrain from citing the plethora of studies relating suicide to psychiatric disorders, except to say that they look formidable, almost overwhelming, until one steps back from them and views them in a broader perspective.

THE CONSTITUTIONAL AND GENETIC APPROACHES

There is a long-standing interest throughout human history in trying to understand man's behavior in terms of his constitution or his inner physiological workings. The ancient Greek physician Galen (A.D. 130–200) posited four humors: sanguine (blood), phlegmatic (phlegm), choleric (yellow bile), and melancholic (black bile). Burton's *Anatomy of Melancholy* is an explication of dysphoria, filled with all sorts of phrases for the word *suicide*. Earlier in this century, Kretchmer and Sheldon independently attempted to link somatic, constitutional body types to temperament and indirectly to suicide. I think it is safe to say that their approach has joined phrenology as a serious competitor in the scientific discussion halls.

But the status of the topic of genetics and suicide is quite different. It is as lively and as current as the 1986 conference at the National Institutes of Health. Alec Roy (1986a) in his paper "Genetics and Suicidal Behavior," reports that there are five lines of evidence about, or relating to, genetic factors in suicide: clinical studies, twin studies, the Iowa-500 study, the Amish study, and the Copenhagen adoption studies. He believes they provide indirect evidence for genetic factors in suicide.

Roy's (1986a) summary reads as follows:

> Suicide like so much else in psychiatry tends to run in families. The question is what is being transmitted. No doubt in some youthful suicide victims what is being transmitted is not a genetic factor but a psychological factor. . . . However, the family, twin and adoption studies show that there are genetic factors in suicide. In many victims there will be genetic factors involved in the genetic transmission of manic-depression, schizophrenia and alcoholism—the psychiatric disorders most commonly associated with suicide. However, the Copenhagen adoption studies strongly suggest there may be a genetic factor for suicide independent of, or additive to, the genetic transmission of psychiatric disorder" [pp. 14–16].

In a similar paper (Roy, 1986a), he cited another possible reason for this conclusion. He suggested that a family member may serve as a role model. He emphasized that it is not clear which of these factors or what combination of them accounts for "suicide running in families."

However, has it been demonstrated that manic-depression, schizophrenia, and alcoholism are genetically transmitted? Are the psychological sequelae of being an adopted child fully understood? Is suicide really a psychiatric disorder? Both the conceptualizations and the evidence in this matter are murky and equivocal.

Kety (1986) stated: "We cannot dismiss the possibility that the genetic factor in suicide is an inability to control impulsive behavior. . . . In any case, suicide illustrates better than any of the mental illnesses . . . the very crucial and important interaction between genetic factors and environmental influences" (p. 44).

Researchers should not dismiss the role of any possible relevant sector. But, I need to add that in my experience with suicidal patients, with suicide diaries, and suicide notes it is quite clear to me that it is not impulsiveness, but rather planned, calculated behavior, and carefully (though admittedly confused) thought-out behavior which we see. It could hardly be impulsiveness that geneticists would claim to be inherited, and then related to suicide. But the major mistake is to conceptualize suicide as a disease in the first place. My reflections may very well be a genetic defect in me, but my inherited skepticism prompts me to say that I doubt it.

THE BIOLOGICAL, BIOCHEMICAL APPROACH

Before we begin to discuss the biology of suicide an introductory note of caution must be sounded. In this paper I am discussing the prevention and treatment of suicide, not the prevention and treatment of depression, or, for that matter, of schizophrenia, of alcoholism, or addiction, or paresis. Suicide and depression are not synonymous. There is much current research and exciting developments, some reported at the 1986 meeting of the American Psychological Association, on depression, but eliminating depression, an enormously important goal in its own right, would not eliminate suicide. In this connection, Ronald Maris's recent volume on the biology of suicide (1986) merits careful study.

The contemporary line of biochemical studies began in the 1950s with reports of observations of the chemical similarity between the putative neurotransmitters serotonin and LSD and the suggestion that schizophrenia might be caused by abnormal serotonin transmission. (This logic reminds me disturbingly of the original rationale for the use of metrozol, insulin, or electric shock to induce epilepticlike seizures for the cure of schizophrenia, based on the absolutely erroneous clinical belief that no schizophrenics had epilepsy and the tortured logic that if one could remit an induced epilepticlike seizure, one might then pull the schizophrenia back with it.) At any rate, in the 1960s it was recognized that the use of reserpine, which depletes levels of serotonin, noradrenaline, and dopamine in the brain, and was administered to reduce blood pressure, could cause severe depression in some patients. At about the same time, pharmacologists discovered that monoamine oxidase inhibitors and tricyclic compounds of the imipramine type labeled antidepressant drugs (e.g., Elavil, Sinequan) also interfered with turnover of the monoamines in the central nervous system. These observations led to two further hypotheses (primarily about depression): the noradrenaline and the serotonin hypotheses, both of which posited a relationship between depression and transmission of the substances at certain key sites in the central nervous system.

Asberg, Nordstrom, and Traskman-Benz (1986) indicate the emergence of two clusters of biological factors that tend to correlate with suicidal behavior; variables associated with a serotonergic transmitter, the monoamine serotonin, 5-hydroxy-tryptamine (5-HT) and certain endocrine functions, particularly the release of cortisol and thyrotropin. Asberg et al. (1986) state that in the period 1958 to 1967 only five among 1,267 titles on the general topic of suicide dealt with biological subjects, whereas in Asberg et al.'s 18-page 1986 report the authors cite 152 references, mostly on biological aspects of depression and suicide. In their résumé of seven postmortem studies of monoamines and their metabolites in the brains of suicide victims, three show no differences and one is equivocal. There are many studies of different chemicals and different methods involving enormous energy and thought, dozens of investigators, and hundreds of subjects, but in summary they are more equivocal than clear, like a murky fluid in a frosted test tube of ambiguous shape.

On a closely related topic, deCatanzaro (1981) has written a sociobiological perspective of suicide from a neo-Darwinian view, attempting to collate evidence from anthropology, sociology, biology, psychology, and psychiatry into a unified sociological–genetical–evolutionary framework. He proposes a study of the social ecology of suicide and suggests that suicide occurs when an individual's capacity to behave toward his inclusive fitness is impaired. I am reminded of Henry Murray's statement in *Explorations in Personality* (1938): "Suicide does not have *adaptive* (survival) value, but it does have *adjustive* value for the organism. Suicide is *functional* because it abolishes painful tension" (p. 216).

LEGAL AND ETHICAL APPROACHES

In the United States, only Alabama and Oklahoma consider committing suicide a crime, but inasmuch as punishments are too repugnant to be enforced, there are no effective penalties for breaking these laws. In several states suicide attempts are misdemeanors, although these laws are seldom, and then rather selectively, enforced. Thirty states have no laws against suicide or suicide attempts, but every state has laws that specify that it is a felony to aid, advise, or encourage another person to commit suicide (see Victoroff, 1983, chapter 15 and appendix B). There are essays and books about the legal aspects of suicide by Silving (1957), Williams (1957), Shaffer (1976), and Engelhardt and Malloy (1982).

Discussion of the ethics of suicide, an omnipresent topic, has had a recent renaissance. Battin and Mayo's edited volume, *Suicide: The Philosophic Issue* (1980) and Battin's book, *Ethical Issues in Suicide* (1982), as well as the 1983 issue on suicide and ethics in the AAS journal *Suicide and Life-Threatening Behavior* (Battin and Maris, 1983) on suicide and ethics provide us with a sufficiency of thoughts on a number of provocative and vexatious issues. The major subtopics in this area seem to be the role of intention in suicide; the morality of suicide; the rationality of suicide; the right to commit suicide; the responsibility not to commit suicide; assisted suicide, and the related topics of active and passive euthanasia. There are a fair number of relatively young scholars writing on these lively topics and I consider these activities a good augury for suicidology.

PREVENTIONAL APPROACH

In this country Shneidman, Farberow, and Litman (1970) are generally associated with approaching suicide from the preventive perspective. The Los Angeles Suicide Prevention Center was established under their direction in the 1950s. Early on, they concluded from their researchers that the vast majority (about 80 percent) of committed suicides have recognizable presuicidal signs, symptoms, manifestations, verbal and behavioral clues. Many people now know what these are—speaking of not being around, giving away prized possessions, and so on (Shneidman, 1965). A special interview procedure was developed at the Los Angeles Suicide Prevention Center along with the County Coroner to help answer the question "What is the most accurate mode of death (natural, accident, suicide, or homicide)?" (Litman, Curphey, Shneidman, Farberow, and Tabachnick, 1963; Weisman and Kastenbaum, 1968; Shneidman, 1969, 1977). In reconstructing the events preceding a death by means of a "psychological autopsy" it was concluded that suicidal behavior is often a form of communication, "a cry for help" born out of pain, with clues and messages of suffering and anguish and pleas for response. If Shneidman, Farberow, and Litman have not unequivocally demonstrated that they single-handedly effected a drastic reduction in the suicide rate of Los Angeles, they have at least convinced themselves and others that they serve thousands of people who are perturbed, have undoubtedly saved some lives, indisputably increased the communication among mental health and other agencies in the community, and directly and indirectly raised the consciousness and lowered the extent of the taboo about the topic of suicide throughout the country. [See outcome/prevention studies regarding suicide prevention centers and suicide rates, Auerback and Kilmann (1977, pp. 1191–1194); Miller Coombs, Leeper, and Bartin (1984).]

THE SYSTEMS THEORY APPROACH

Perhaps a systems theorist might consider that he or she was the crust or the topping of the whole conceptual suicidal pie, holding it together and giving it the overall flavor. Within the last fifty years there have been important advances in theoretical thinking based on the insight that there is an alternative to the mechanistic theories that have dominated physics, biology, and psychology. This alternative, called *general systems theory,* emphasizes the interconnectedness of parts within cells, organism, or collectivity, and the uniqueness of the whole.

I wish to speak especially of James Grier Miller's 1978 book, *Living Systems*. It is a big book, an encyclopedia of twentieth century physical, biological, and social science organized in a masterful fashion in terms of a brilliantly conceived scheme. More than an encyclopedia, it is an empirically testable scientific theory. Miller states:

The general living systems theory which this book presents is a conceptual system concerned primarily with concrete systems which exist in space–time. Complex structures which carry out living processes can be identified at seven hierarchical levels—cell, organ, organism, group, organization, society and supranational system. My central thesis is that systems at all these levels are open systems composed of subsystems which process inputs, throughputs and outputs of various forms of matter, energy and information. I identify nineteen critical subsystems whose processes are essential for life, some of which process matter, energy, or information. Together they make up a living system . . . [p. 1].

Into this framework Miller places 173 hypotheses which he discusses in detail. It seems to me that several of Miller's hypotheses have possible implications for self-destruction in the human organism.

From the suicidological point of view it appears that the main challenge (and the greatest potential) for living systems theory is, after having identified instances of (literal or paradigmatic) self-destruction "above" and "below" the human organism, in cells and organs and human collectivities, to formulate some generalizations about self-destruction that are true and relevant for self-destruction in man. Perhaps our cells and our organs, our groups and our organizations, even, *especially*, in their self-destructive activities can give us fresh insights into ourselves.

What insights and what handles on prevention a systems theory approach might yield! A priori, the implications of this exciting task are enormous (Blaker, 1972).[1]

[1]I shall attempt to formulate a hypothesis in the language of Miller's systems theory approach (1978). This is my hypothsis:

When any living systems—cell, organ, organism, group, organization, community, society, or supranational—manifests or displays the following three features, then the probable result will be the *destruction* of that living system (see section on "Cubic Model," below): (1) *heightened* stress, disorganization, tension, chaos, internal antitheses, pathology, pain (either "organizational pain" or, in the sole case of human beings, subjectively felt and reportable pain); (2) limitation of the range of options (either realistic limitations or perceived ones) that results in a reduction of possible actions; and (3) a fast-growing (chemical, physical, social, psychological, or political) push for precipitous irreversible action.

In the human organism this kind of destruction is called *suicide,* but in other than living systems—from cells to supranational systems—it is necessary to change the concept from *suicide* (which implies motivation) to a more objective term, *self-destruction.* There is a long list of synonyms and near-synonyms for destruction or termination: death, catabolism, decay, deterioration, decline, disintegration, atrophy, decomposition, disappearance, failure, fall, downfall, defeat, bankrupcy, or "the dust of entropy."

One obvious implication of this view is that we shall need *two* models: (1) For human science—those two words have a certain redundancy—a *subjectivist* cube model, as presented below, which features subjectively felt psychological pain, perceptual constriction, and an untoward penchant for action; and (2) for all other living systems, an *objectivist* model, in which reliably reported past or present processes, and events such as chaos, disorganization, decay, pathology, and so on, relating to termination furnish the appropriate data.

Limitations of space do not permit an explication of these ideas, but four brief examples can be given:

THE POLITICAL, GLOBAL, AND SUPRANATIONAL APPROACHES

Henry A. Murray (1981) said: "There will be no freedom for any exuberant form of life without freedom from atomic war . . . nothing is of signal importance today save those thoughts and actions which, in some measure, propose to contribute to the diagnosis and alleviation of the global neurosis which so affects us" (p. 613).

Contemporary (self-disserving) national neuroses (amounting to an international insanity) may very well lead to the self-induced death of human life. We live in a death-haunted time.

Overwhelmingly the most important kind of suicide for everyone to know about and to prevent is the global suicide which threatens us all and which, by the very presence of that threat, poisons our lives. Lifton (1979) appropriately urges on our consciousness the fact that we are in great danger—even if The Bombs do not explode!—of breaking our psychological connections to our own sense of human species continuity and generativity, connections which are necessary to sustain our human relationships.

COMMONALITIES OF SUICIDE: A PSYCHOLOGICAL APPROACH

Given that I am a psychologist, it follows that it is only sensible that I stick to my particular specialty and talk about, among the various legitimate approaches to suicide which I have outlined, the one I know best; namely, the psychological aspects of suicide. Before I do so I say again: I do not mean to imply by my presentation the depreciation or denigration of other approaches to this topic; but I speak now for this psychological approach which I have developed, and I leave it to proponents and spokespersons of the other approaches to make their presentations at other times and in other settings. Here, as I view suicidal acts, are ten common psychological characteristics that accrue to most committed suicides (Shneidman, 1985). They are meant to answer the key question: What are the interesting, relevant, common psychological dimensions of committed suicide (see Table 1.1).

First, a few words about the word *common* may be helpful. Each suicide is an idiosyncratic event. In suicide, there are no universals or absolutes. I am convinced that the search for a universal formulation for all suicide is a chimera. The best that one can reasonably hope to discuss are the most frequent (common) characteristics

One at the level of the cell—"If too much water enters a red cell, it swells up, the internal osmotic equilibrium is destroyed, and the cell membrane ruptures" (Miller, 1978, p. 100); a second example, at the level of an organization, specifically the failure (termination) of a microcomputer company because of breakdowns within the "system" of the company (Reynolds, 1987); the third at the societal–national level, namely the recent (1986) downfall (destruction) of the Marcos regime in the Phillipines; and finally, touching on possible international self-destruction, what Karl Menninger (1983) calls the "exhibitionistic drunken gesturing of two suicidal giants."

Table 1.1

The Ten Commonalities of Suicide

---

1. The common purpose of suicide is to seek a solution
2. The common goal of suicide is cessation of consciousness
3. The common stimulus in suicide is intolerable psychological pain
4. The common stressor in suicide is frustrated psychological needs
5. The common emotion in suicide is hopelessness-helplessness
6. The common cognitive state in suicide is ambivalence
7. The common perceptual state in suicide is constriction
8. The common action in suicide is egression
9. The common interpersonal act in suicide is communication of intention
10. The common consistency in suicide is with life-long coping patterns

---

that accrue to most suicides, and to make this discussion in as common sense and ordinary language as possible.

The Common *Purpose* of a Suicide Is to Seek a *Solution*

First of all, suicide is not a random act; it is never done pointlessly or without purpose. It is a way out of a problem, a dilemma, a bind, a challenge, a difficulty, a crisis, an unbearable situation. It has an inexorable logic and impetus of its own. It is the answer, seemingly the only available answer, to a real puzzler: How to get out of this? What to do? Its purpose is to solve a problem; to seek a solution to a problem generating intense suffering.

The well-known English novelist and essayist, John Fowles, early in his career, wrote a brilliant set of aphorisms, called *The Aristos* (1964). The Greek word *aristos* means the best possible solution to a given situation. The dozen or so individuals whom I have talked to, who, in one way or another, actually committed suicide and fortuitously survived—immolating, jumping, shooting—have all, to paraphrase them, said something like this: It was the only thing I could do. It was the best way out of that terrible situation; it was the answer to the problem I had to solve; I could not see any other way.

In this sense every suicide is an *aristos;* every suicide has as its purpose the seeking of a solution to the perceived problem. To understand what a suicide was about, one has to know the problem it was intended to solve. All this is tied to my definition of suicide.

The Common *Goal* of Suicide Is *Cessation* of Consciousness

In a curious and paradoxical way, suicide is both a moving toward and a moving away from something; the something that it is moving toward, the common practical goal of suicide, is the stopping of the painful flow of consciousness. Suicide is best understood not so much as a moving toward the idea of a reified Death, as in terms of the idea (in the mind of the suicidal person) of "cessation," specifically when cessation—the complete stopping of one's consciousness of unendurable pain—is seen by the suffering individual as the perfect solution to life's painful and pressing problems. The moment that the idea of the possibility of stopping consciousness occurs to the anguished mind as *the* answer or *the* way out—in the presence of the three essential ingredients of suicide, elevated perturbation, unusual constriction, and high lethality—then the igniting spark has been added and the active suicidal scenario has begun.

The Common *Stimulus* (or Information Input) in Suicide Is Psychological *Pain*

If cessation is what the suicidal person is moving toward, pain is what that person is seeking to escape. In any close analysis, suicide is best understood as a combined movement toward cessation and a movement away from intolerable emotion, unendurable pain, unacceptable anguish. No one commits suicide out of joy; no suicide is born out of exaltation. The enemy to life is pain. It is psychological pain of which we are speaking, metapain; the pain of feeling pain. Suicide is a human response to psychological pain. The clinical rule is: Reduce the level of suffering, often just a little bit, and the individual can choose to live.

The Common *Stressor* in Suicide Is Frustrated Psychological *Needs*

Suicide is best understood not so much as an unreasonable act—every suicide seems logical to the person who commits it given that person's major premises, styles of syllogizing, and constricted focus—as it is a reaction to frustrated psychological needs. A suicide is committed because of thwarted, blocked, or unfulfilled needs.

In order to understand suicide in this kind of context, we need to ask a much broader question, which, I believe, is the key: What purposes do most human acts, in general, intend to accomplish? The best nondetailed answer to that question is that, in general, human acts are intended to satisfy a variety of human needs. There is no compelling a priori reason why a typology (or classification or taxonomy) of suicidal acts might not parallel a classification of general human needs. Indeed, such a classification of needs exists. It can be found in Murray's *Explorations in Personality* (1938). There, in Murray's list of human needs—they include the need for achievement, affiliation, autonomy, counteraction, defendance, harm-avoidance, inviolacy, and succorance—is a ready-made, viable, useful taxonomy of suicidal behaviors.

Most suicides represent combinations of various needs, so that a particular case of suicide might properly be subsumed under two or more different need categories.

There are many pointless deaths, but there is never a needless suicide. Address the frustrated needs and the suicide will not occur.

The therapist's function is to help the patient in relation to the thwarted needs. Even a little bit of improvement can save a life. In general, the goal of psychotherapy is to increase the patient's psychological *comfort*. One way to operationalize this task is to focus on the thwarted needs. Questions such as "What is going on?" "Where do you hurt?" and "What would you like to have happen?" can usefully be asked by a therapist who is helping a suicidal person.

The Common *Emotion* in Suicide Is *Hopelessness–Helplessness*

At the beginning of life the common emotion is probably randomized general excitement. In the suicidal state it is a pervasive feeling of helplessness–hopelessness. "There is nothing that I can do (except to commit suicide), and there is no one who can help me (with the pain that I am suffering)." I believe that this formulation permits us somewhat gracefully to withdraw from the (sibling) rivalry among the various emotions, each with the proponents to assert that *it*—hostility, shame, guilt, depression, and so on—is the central one of them all. Historically, in the twentieth century, that is, hostility was the eldest brother. Stekel said so in the 1910 meeting of the Psychoanalytic Society in Vienna (Friedman, 1967). No man kills himself except as he fantasizes the death of another. And then, in a somewhat more ornate phrase: Suicide is essentially hostility directed toward the ambivalently viewed introjected love object. One would plunge a knife into one's chest in order to expunge or kill the internalized homunculus of the loved–hated father within—what I once called murder in the 180th degree.

But today we suicidologists know that there are other deep basic emotions. The early psychoanalytic formulations are seen as a brilliant hypothesis, more pyrotechnic than universal.

But underlying all of these, and others that might be mentioned, is that emotion of active, impotent ennui, the feeling of hopelessness–helplessness.

The Common *Cognitive State* in Suicide Is *Ambivalence*

One does not ordinarily think of Freud as a giant in the history of logic but, in a way, he made as enormous an impact in extending our understanding of our cognitive maneuvers as perhaps Bacon, Mill, and Russell. Western logic is Aristotelian. Aristotle's logic is dichotomous, it is binary; a term is either A or non-A. An inference is either true or false; a mood of the syllogism is either valid or invalid; an idea is either logical or illogical.

Freud brought to our attention in unforgetable fashion the psychological truth (that transcends the Aristotelian appearance of the neatness of logic) that something can be *both* A and non-A. We can both love and hate the same person. It is an Aristotelian response to say: Make up your mind! The answer is that we are of two minds, at least. We can now assert that the prototypical suicidal state is one in which an individual cuts his throat and cries for help at the same time, and is genuine in both of these acts. This non-Aristotelian accommodation to the psychological realities of mental life (ambivalence) is the common cognitive state in suicide: To feel that one has to do it and, simultaneously, to yearn for rescue and intervention.

No one univalently wishes to commit suicide. Individuals would be happy not to do it, if they didn't "have to."

It makes more sense to discuss this all too human conflict in concrete and effective terms and to answer the cruel question: "Why not let him?" by asking the practical counterquestion: "Why not reduce the level of his unbearable stress?" In effect, why not be a good Samaritan and *do* some things, quite simple things, inexpensive things—like talking to some people, making some arrangements, contacting some agencies, persuading some intransigent people—all on behalf of a suicidal person. The suicidal person's life can be saved by the efforts of a benign person, a helper, a compassionate friend, an ombudsman, a champion.

The Common *Perceptual State* in Suicide Is *Constriction*

I am one who believes that suicide is not best understood as a psychosis, a neurosis, or a character disorder. I believe that it is much more accurately seen as a more-or-less transient psychological constriction of affect and intellect. Synonyms for constriction are a tunneling or a focusing or narrowing of the range of options usually available to *that* individual's consciousness when the mind is not panicked into dichotomous thinking: either some specific (almost magical) total solution *or* cessation; all *or* nothing; *Caesar aut nihil,* to quote from Binswanger's (1958) famous case of Ellen West.

The usual life-sustaining images of loved ones are not disregarded; much worse, they are not even within the range of what is in the mind. A person who commits suicide turns his or her back on the past, declares bankruptcy, and declares memories to be unreal. Memories can no longer help or save; one is beyond their reach. Any attempt at rescue or remediation has to deal from the first with the psychological constriction.

This fact, that suicide is committed by individuals who are in a special constricted condition, leads us to suggest that no one should ever commit suicide while disturbed. It is not a thing to do while one is not in one's best state of mind. Never kill yourself when you are suicidal. It takes a mind capable of scanning a range of options greater than two to make a decision as important as taking one's life. Dichotomous slogans like Death Before Dishonor, Live Free or Die, Give Me Liberty or Give Me Death, or Better Dead than Red, all have some patriotic appeal, but they are not sensible or wide-ranged enough to be prescriptions for making it through life.

It is vital to counter the suicidal person's constriction of thought by attempting to reduce the extent of the mental blinders and to increase the number of options, certainly beyond the two options of either having some magical resolution *or* being dead.

An example may be useful. A teenage college student, demure, rather elegant (and somewhat wealthy) was encouraged to come to see me. She was single, pregnant, and suicidal, with a formed suicide plan. Her challenge to me was that I somehow magically had to arrange for her to be the way she was before she became pregnant, virginal in fact, or she would have to commit suicide. Her being pregnant was such a mortal shame to her, combined with strong feelings of rage and guilt, that she simply could not "bear to live." At that moment suicide was the *only* option for her.

I did several things. For one, I took out a sheet of paper and, in order to begin to widen her vision, I said something like: "Now, let's see: You could have an abortion here locally." ("I couldn't do that.") (It is precisely the "can'ts" and "won'ts" and "have to's" and "nevers" and "alwayses" and "onlys" that are negotiated in psychotherapy.) "You could go away and have an abortion." ("I couldn't do that.") "You could bring the baby to term and keep the baby." ("I couldn't do that.") "You could have the baby and adopt it out." ("I couldn't do that.") "We could get in touch with the young man involved." ("I couldn't do that.") "We could enlist the help of your parents." ("I couldn't do that.") And "You can always commit suicide, but there is obviously no need to do that today." (No response.) "Now, let's look at this list and rank them in order of your preference, keeping in mind that none of them is optimal."

The very making of this list, my nonhortatory and nonjudgmental approach, already had a calming influence on her. Within a few minutes her lethality had begun to deescalate. She actually rank-ordered the list, commenting negatively on each item. What was of critical importance was that suicide was now no longer ranked first or second. We were then simply "haggling" about life—a perfectly viable solution.

The point is not how the issue was eventually resolved or what interpretations were made as to why she permitted herself to become pregnant, or about other aspects of her relationships with men. What is important is that it was possible to achieve the assignment of that day: To lower her lethality by reducing her perturbation by widening her range of "logical" and realistic options from only the choice between suicide and one other untenable choice to a wider range of possibilities.

In addition, it is important to keep in mind that there is a latent syllogism in every suicide. In working with a suicidal person it is vital not to "buy into" his major premise (because all his suicidal solutions flow from that), though I certainly do not mean that one should argue or dispute the premise directly. Still, the key lies in not accepting the person's suicidal syllogism, his premises, and his lethal conclusion.

Just as one does not collude with a suicidal person in fact, one should not collude with a suicidal person in thought and logic.

The Common *Action* in Suicide Is *Escape* (Egression)

Egression is a person's intended departure from a region of distress. Suicide is the ultimate egression, besides which running away from home, quitting a job, deserting an army, leaving a spouse, are relatively pale actions. Erving Goffman spoke of "unpluggings": having a good read, darting into a movie, going for a weekend to Las Vegas or Atlantic City, benign egressions all. But we must distinguish between the wish to get away and the need to stop it for good. The point of suicide is a radical and permanent change of scene; the action taken to effect it is to leave.

Here is an excerpt from a letter, dated March 26, 1921, from Violet Keppel Trefusis to her lover Vita Sackville-West, then in the eighth year of her marriage to Harold Nicolson, both spouses being bisexual (Nicolson, 1972): "I am dead with grief. I am utterly alone. You cannot want me to suffer so. You had to choose between me and your family, and you have chosen them. I do not blame you. But you must not blame me if one day I seek for what escapes I can find" (p. 179).

That passage is an operational definition of what, at rock bottom, from the suicidal person's point of view, suicide is: ". . . what escape I can find." In that brief quotation from the letter, one can see intimations of several common characteristics of suicide: the wish for cessation, the need to stop pain, the sense of hopelessness, the presence of constriction, and the search for escape, as well as the communication of the intent.

The Common *Interpersonal Act* in Suicide Is *Communication of Intention*

One of the most interesting findings from large numbers of psychological autopsies of unequivocal suicidal deaths was that there were clues to the impending lethal event in approximately 80 percent of the cases (Shneidman, Farberow, and Leonard, 1961). Individuals intent on committing suicide, albeit ambivalent about it, consciously or unconsciously emit signals of distress, whimpers of helplessness, pleas for response, in the usually dyadic interplay that is an integral part of the suicide drama. It is a sad and paradoxical thing to note that the common element in the interpersonal act of suicide is not hostility, not rage or destructiveness, not even withdrawal, not depression, but communication of intention.

Everyone in suicidology now knows the usual clues, verbal and behavioral (Shneidman, 1965). The verbal statements are tantamount to saying I am going away (egression), you won't be seeing me, I cannot endure the pain any longer; the behavioral signs are such unusual acts as putting affairs in order, giving away prized possessions, and, more generally, behaving in ways that are different from usual behaviors, ones that betoken a bubbling thermal in a perturbed psyche.

The communication of suicidal intention is not always a cry for help. First, it is not always a cry; it can be a shout or a murmur or the loud communication of unspoken silence. And it is not always for help; it can be for autonomy or inviolacy or any of a number of other needs. Nonetheless, in most cases of suicide, the common penultimate act is some interpersonal communicative exchange related to that intended final act.

The Common *Consistency* in Suicide Is with *Lifelong Coping Patterns*

People who are dying of a disease, say cancer, over a period of weeks or months, are very much themselves, even exaggerations of their normal selves. Contrary to some currently popular notions in paperback thanatology, there is *not* any standard set of stages in the dying process through which individuals are marched in lockstep to their deaths (Shneidman, 1973). In terms of emotions displayed (rage, acceptance, etc.) or mechanisms of psychological defense manifested (projection, denial, etc.) one sees a full panoply of both of these arranged in almost every conceivable number and order. However, what one does see in almost every case, I believe, are certain patterns: displays of emotion and uses of defense mechanisms that are consistent with *that* individual's microtemporal, mesotemporal, and macrotemporal reactions to pain, threat, failure, powerlessness, and duress in previous earlier episodes of that life. People who are dying are emotionally enormously consistent with themselves; so are suicidal people, and so are people who are neither dying nor suicidal.

In cases of suicide, we are initially thrown off the scent because suicide is an act, by definition, that that individual has never done before; so there is no precedent. And yet there are some consistencies with lifelong coping patterns. We must look to previous episodes of disturbance, to the capacity to endure psychological pain, to the penchant for constriction and dichotomous thinking, for earlier paradigms of egression. Examples would lie in the details and nuances of *how* jobs were quit and spouses divorced.

I speak with a tiny bit of experimental authority on this general issue, at least with a sense of conviction that flows from some data I examined (Shneidman, 1971). I was involved in a bite-sized study of a group of men who were about 55 years old, each of whom had been studied rather intensively on a continual basis since they were about six years old.[2] Other than the demonstration that it was possible in a blind study (beyond chance expectation) to select the five subjects who had committed suicide from a group of thirty cases, the main finding was that working

---

[2] I am referring here to the well-known Terman longitudinal study of the gifted, begun in 1920, with 1,528 young male and female subjects and continuing to this day at Stanford University under the direction of Professor Robert Sears.

as I did from a detailed life-chart, which I constructed for each individual, the determination that the person would (or would not) commit suicide at around age 55 could be made *before the thirtieth birthday* in each man's life. There were already certain psychological consistencies within the life, certain characteristics or habitual patterns of reactions for that person to threat, pain, pressure, and failure which made dire predictions of a tragic suicidal outcome at 55 an almost straightforward psychological extrapolation from the earlier years.

In light of the enormous unpredictability of life, what impresses and excites me as a psychologist is how much of a person's life, in some of its more important aspects, is reasonably predictable. In general, I feel this way about suicide. It is enormously complicated, but it is not totally random and it is amenable to some prediction. That is our main handle on individual prevention.

THE CUBIC MODEL OF SUICIDE

What are some of the implications of this approach for a possible overarching theoretical model of suicide; for theory building as a guide for future research; for a framework into which data collection on a large range of variables might be placed to build up an empirical science of suicidology? I shall attempt to outline a proposal.

We have talked about a circle and its various sectors. Now imagine a cube made up of 125 cubelets with 25 cubelets on each plane or surface, and five cubelets in each row and each column. As we look at the cube (and clearly see its three dimensionality), we see three planes, surfaces, or sides, each with 25 small squares. I call these three factors or components: press, pain, and perturbation (see Figure 1.1).

Press

Henry Murray (1938) might have had the word *pressure* in mind when he decided to use the word *press* to represent those aspects of the inner and outer world, or environment that move, touch, impinge on, or affect an individual and make a difference to his life. *Press* is the word for those events that affect the individual and to which he reacts. There is positive press (good genes and happy fortune) and negative press (conditions and events that perturb, stress, threaten, or harm the individual). It is the latter, even success if it is threatening, that are relevant to suicide. Press includes both actual and imagined (or interpreted) events. There are all sorts of negative press: belittlement by an insult, being rejected or humiliated, a real or imagined slight, the loss of a loved one, failure (realistic or magnified), a diagnosed cancer, powerlessness, humiliation, loss of control, poverty, bigotry, oppression, persecution. But what we are talking about mostly is the press that comes as the mind mediates (or exaggerates or even imagines) the negative press that it perceives or misperceives.

Edwin S. Shneidman

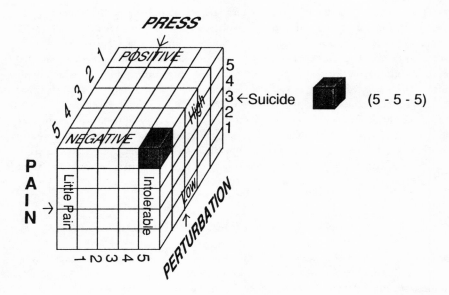

Figure 1.1 A theoretical cubic model of suicide.

In this cubic model, press ranges from positive (in the back row of the top plane) to bad luck, ill-fortune, unfavorable chance, malignant fate, persecution, torture, in the front row of the top plane.

Pain

Pain refers to psychological pain tied to thwarted psychological needs. It is close to *dolor*, the Latin word for pain. Let us imagine pain as the front plane of our macrocube. The left column of cubelets represents little or no pain; the next column over, some bearable pain, and so on, until the extreme right column, which represents unbearable, intolerable, unacceptable psychological pain.

The psychological pain is conceptualized as clearly related to psychological needs, specifically frustrated, blocked, or thwarted needs. Murray's list of psychological needs (1938) includes the following, which are especially relevant in suicide: achievement, autonomy, recognition, succorance, avoidance of humiliation, shame, and pain. To repeat our basic dictum: There are many pointless deaths but never a purposeless suicide. Redress the throbbing needs and the willingness to live resurges.

Perturbation

Perturbation—arbitrarily the *side* plane of the large cube—means the state of being perturbed, upset, disturbed, stirred up, disquieted, discomposed. On a nine-point rating, perturbation includes everything in and out of DSM-III (1980). Perhaps very low or mild perturbations, one to three, do not belong in any diagnostic manual; DSM-III is the catch-all for all perturbations, including both mania (excessive activity) and catatonia (absence of overt activity), that might be rated four through nine.

In relation to suicide, perturbation includes especially (1) constriction and (2) the self-harmful penchant for precipitous or ill-advised action. Let us look at these separately.

Constriction   Constriction refers to the reduction of the individual's perceptual and cognitive range. At its worst, the individual cuts the viable options down to two, or one; there is dichotomous thinking: Either everything I want (total surcease from pain) *or* death. On this plane, the bottom row reflects open-mindedness, wide mentational scope, clear syllogistic and uncontaminated reasoning. As we climb the rows of this plane, the top row reflects constriction of thought, tunnel vision, a narrowing of focus to one or two options, with cessation, death, egression as one, and, at its ultimate, as the *only* solution to the problem of pain and frustrated needs.

The Penchant for Action   The penchant for action relates to the tendency to *do*. The relevant needs are for inviolacy and autonomy. The farthest row of cubelets reflects tolerance for ambiguity, capacity for patience, comfort with the Zeigarnik incomplete circle. As we move on this plane from one to five, we come closer to this penchant for consummatory action, the push to *do* something—even an irreversible action that is inimical to one's self. That is what the nearest top row represents.

In this imaginary cube of 125 cubelets, there is but *one* shaded cubelet that represents a committed suicide. The upper right-hand corner (5-5-5 in this example) is the only cubelet that contains the concatenation of maximum pain, maximum perturbation, and maximum press. When egression, leaving the scene, death as escape, is added, the suicidal cubelet has come into being.

Although most (but not all) aspects of press represent the outer world, the 5-5-5 cubelet represents a totally intrapsychic experience. Suicidal individuals are in an autistic state; that is what suicide is, a closed world. They feel totally alone; they may know or vaguely remember that there are others somewhere in their lives, but they are, at that moment, simply not connected with them. For the connections to be reestablished, there must first be some diminution, however slight, of the crippling pain, the incapacitating negative press, and/or the blinding constriction.

If we call the three planes or aspects of this cubic model A (pain), B (perturbation), and C (press), then three sets of correlations or relationships are possible: A-B, A-C, and B-C. Examples related to A (pain) might include studies of pain thresholds; studies of levels of psychological disturbance, including anxiety. Examples related to B (perturbation) might include studies of perceptual sharpeners and levelers; studies of intense concentration; tunnel vision; styles of scanning; dichotomous thinking; impulsiveness; or acting out. Examples of C (press) might include studies of traumatic life events, studies of disaster, defeat, and death. I hope to examine the literature of psychiatry and psychology (sensation, perception, emotion, learning, personality, etc.) to find nonsuicide studies that have related one of these aspects with another (A-B, A-C, or B-C), and then ponder the possible implications of those general findings for this suicide model. Of course, I invite others to do the same.

These three aspects of suicide, press, pain, and perturbation, are closely interconnected. The cube twirls in conceptual space; one can address either the topic of suicide or an individual case of suicide by beginning with any of the three faces of the cubic model. Conceptually, the three separate aspects are, in some ways, synonymous: pain grows out of perturbation; perturbation makes for pain; there is neither pain nor perturbation without negative press; some negative press grows out of perturbation. If there is any one "natural order" in suicide it is press, pain, perturbation, but one can come in on the concatenating suicidal drama during any one of its three linked acts. Even so, I believe the central feature of suicide is *pain* and the key to suicide prevention lies in the reduction of that individual's felt psychological pain. All else is peripheral: demographic variables, family history, previous suicidal history, except as they themselves bear on the currently felt pain. Address the pain. The critical question to ask is: Where do you hurt? But ultimately, suicide occurs when there is the coexistence of intolerable pain, intense negative press, and extreme perturbation with perceptual constriction and an irresistible penchant for life-ending action.

I see it as the future task of a scientific suicidology to explicate, with empirical studies on intrapsychic variables (thoughts, feelings, bodily sensations), on interpersonal aspects of suicide, on a range of situational stressors—the several cubelets of this larger model.

TREATMENT IMPLICATIONS

One can hardly fail to infer the implications for treatment from the foregoing in the real life-and-death situation of a suicidal crisis. They follow logically from the explication of the suicidal state of mind. Thus, psychologically speaking, the simply stated prescriptions run something like this: *Reduce the hurt* and/or *widen the vision* and/or *pull back from action* and/or *lighten the pressure*—even just a little bit. (Get the person out of the 5-5-5 cubelet.) Any of these actions can save a life. In terms of this model, that is how suicide is prevented. The underlying rule is: Lower the intensity of the pain–perturbation–press and the lethality will come down with it.

Following this model, a "questionnaire" for potential suicide would include some commonsense, open-ended queries: Where do you hurt? What is going on? What do you feel that you have to solve or get out of? Do you have any formed plans to do anything harmful to yourself and what might you do? What would it take (to keep you alive)? Have you ever been in a situation similar to this before, and what did you do and what happened and how was it resolved? And, not a question, because the suicidally constricted mind usually cannot formulate an answer, but a statement: Let me help you generate more possibilities, first to rethink (and restate) the problem, and then look at possible courses of action other than the only one that you have in mind. While these new ideas might not totally solve the problem the way you had conceptualized it, they will provide some solution that you can live with. (Of course, the statement to a patient will be in less formal terms, and in shorter sentences.)

An example can be given: A senior at a university who made straight A's for three-and-a-half years received a B and was determined to kill himself. Friends around him pointed out to him that he was still Phi Beta Kappa and had a 3.98 grade average. That did not "cut any ice." They were attempting to dissuade him by talking about grades. That was on the phenotypic level and missed the genotypic point. He could better be addressed by saying that you understand his anguish, his need for a *perfect* performance, this blemish on his academic record, and his problem was how to *live* with a major blemish or lack of perfection—like the man who committed suicide attendant to having lost the tip of a finger in an industrial accident. The student's pain, perturbation, and press all related to the push of his inner standards (which, at this point, threatened his life). A would-be rescuer cannot leave a would-be suicide with his notions undiscussed, lest he remain suicidal. A highly suicidal state indicates that the time has come, unfortunately, for the standards themselves to be touched. Simply put, the rule is: change the patient's *aufgabe;* change his lesson plan. Change them a little bit and the pain and press will then, one hopes, be redefined, and as a result, the perturbation, which drives the lethality, is reduced and the person can live.

Suicide (in Melville's terms) is much more like "a damp and dismal November of the soul" than it is like an earthquake in the brain. Earthquakes are manifestations of the inexorable forces of Nature. But with suicide, "human nature" and potential victims are one and the same. Both the etiology and the remediation are intrapsychic, interpersonal, and sociocultural; one need not look to larger geological, meteorological, cosmic, or divine factors.

If you think about it, there is no suicide (except possibly jumping) that does not involve the hand. In a figurative sense, suicide is always held within the hand of the individual (which linguistically is a way of saying it is within the mind). But also, in this figurative way, the intervention of a suicidal plan (that is to say, prevention) is clearly in the hands of others. But we are talking here not only of helping hands but of alert minds. Minds (everyday, ordinary minds will do nicely) that are attuned to signals, or symptoms of lethally oriented perturbation in a distressed fellow human being.

REFERENCES

Aaron, D., ed. (1985), *The Inman Diary*, 2 vols. Cambridge, MA: Harvard University Press.

Alvarez, A. (1970), *The Savage God*. New York: Random House.

American Psychiatric Association (1980), *Diagnostic and Statistical Manual of Mental Disorders*, 3rd ed. Washington, DC: American Psychiatric Press.

Asberg, M., Nordstrom, P., & Traskman-Benz, L. (1986), Biological factors in suicide. In *Suicide*, ed. A. Roy. Baltimore: Williams & Wilkins.

Auerback, S.M., & Kilmann, P.R. (1977), Crisis intervention: A review of outcome research. *Psycholog. Bull.*, 84:1189–1217.

Battin, M.P., & Mayo, D.J., eds. (1980), *Suicide: The Philosophical Issues*. New York: St. Martin's Press.

———— (1982), *Ethical Issues in Suicide*. Englewood Cliffs, NJ: Prentice-Hall.

———— & Maris, R. (1983), Special issues: Suicide and ethics. *Suicide & Life-Threat. Behav.*, 13:7–129.

Beauchamp, T.I. (1978), What is suicide? In: *Ethical Issues in Death and Dying*, eds. T. Beauchamp & S. Perlin. Englewood Cliffs, NJ: Prentice-Hall.

Bertalanffy, L. (1969), *General Systems Theory*. New York: Braziller.

Binswanger, L. (1958), The case of Ellen West. In: *Existence*, ed. R. May. New York: Basic Books.

Blaker, K.P. (1972), Systems theory and self-destructive behavior: A new theoretical base. *Perspec. Psychiat. Care*, 10:168–172.

Cassedy, J.H. (1969), *Demography in Early America: Beginnings of the Statistical Mind*. Cambridge, MA: Harvard University Press.

Cavan, R. (1928), *Suicide*. Chicago: The University of Chicago Press.

Chopin, K. (1899), *The Awakening*. New York: Gordon Pr. Pubs., 1974.

Choron, J. (1972), *Suicide*. New York: Scribner.

Cutter, F. (1983), *Art and the Wish to Die*. Chicago: Nelson-Hall.

deCatanzaro, D. (1981), *Suicide and Self-Damaging Behavior: A Sociobiological Perspective*. New York: Academic Press.

Douglas, J.D. (1967), *The Social Meaning of Suicide*. Princeton, NJ: Princeton University Press.

Durkheim, E. (1897), *Suicide*. Glencoe, IL: The Free Press, 1951.

Engelhardt, H.T., Jr., & Malloy, M. (1982), Suicide and assisting suicide: A critique of legal sanctions. *SW Law J.*, 36:1003–1037.

Flaubert, G. (1856), *Madame Bovary*, trans. P. de Man. New York: W.W. Norton, 1965.

Fowles, J. (1964), *The Aristos*. Boston: Little, Brown.

Friedman, P. (1967), *On Suicide*. New York: International Universities Press.

Gibbs, J.P., & Martin, W.T. (1964), *Status Integration and Suicide*. Eugene, OR: University of Oregon Press.

Guernesy, R.S. (1883), *Suicide: A History of the Penal Laws in Reflection to It and Their Legal, Social, Moral, and Religious Aspects in Ancient and Modern Times*. New York: Strouse, 1963.

Hendin, H. (1964), *Suicide and Scandinavia*. New York: Grune & Stratton.

Henry, A.F., & Short, J.F. (1954), *Homicide and Suicide*. Glencoe, IL: The Free Press.

Hill, T.E. (1983), Self-regarding suicide: A modified Kantian view. *Suicide & Life-Threat. Behav.*, 13:254–275.

Hollinger, P.C., & Offer, D. (1986), Sociodemographic, Epidemiologic, and Individual Attributes of Suicide. Bethesda, MD: Department of Health and Human Service, USPHS. Unpublished paper.

Isben, H. (1890), Hedda Gabler. In: *Hedda Gabler and Three Other Plays*. Garden City, NY: Doubleday/Anchor, 1961.

Iga, M. (1986). *The Thorn in the Chrysanthemum: Suicide and Economic Success in Contemporary Japan*. Berkeley & Los Angeles: University of California Press.

Kety, S.S. (1986), Genetic factors in suicide. In: *Suicide*, ed. A. Roy. Baltimore, MD: Williams & Wilkins.

Lester, D., Sell, B.H., & Sell, K.D. (1980), *Suicide: A Guide to Information Sources*. Detroit: Gale Research Company.

Lifton, R.J. (1979), *The Broken Connection*. New York: Harper & Row.

Litman, R.E., Curphey, T.J., Shneidman, E.S., Farberow, N.L., & Tabachnick, N.D. (1963), Investigations of equivocal studies. *J. Amer. Med. Assn.*, 184:924–929.

———— (1967), Sigmund Freud on suicide. In: *Essays in Self-destruction*, ed. E.S. Shneidman. New York: Science House.

Maris, R. (1981), *Pathways to Suicide*. Baltimore: Johns Hopkins University Press.

———— ed. (1986), *Biology of Suicide*. New York: Guilford Press.

Melville, H. (1851), *Moby Dick*. New York: New American Library, 1961.

———— (1852), *Pierre, or the Ambiguities*, ed. H.A. Murray. New York: Farrar Straus, 1949.

Menninger, K. (1938). *Man Against Himself*. New York: Harcourt, Brace.

———— (1983), The suicidal intentions of nuclear disarmament. *Bull. Menn. Clin.*, 47/4:322–353.

Miles, C.P. (1977), Conditions predisposing to suicide: A review. *J. Nerv. & Ment. Dis.*, 164:231–246.

Miller, H.L., Coombs, D.W., Leeper, J.D., & Barton, S.N. (1984), An analysis of the effects of suicide prevention facilities on suicide rates in the United States. *Amer. J. Pub. Health*, 164:340–343.

Miller, J.G. (1978), *Living Systems*. New York: McGraw-Hill.

Murray, H.A. (1938), *Explorations in Personality*. New York: Oxford University Press.

———— (1981), *Endeavors in Psychology: Selections from the Personology of Henry A. Murray*. New York: Harper & Row.

National Center for Health Statistics (1986), Advance report of final mortality statistics, 1984. NCHS Monthly Vital Stat. Rep., 35, 6:Supplement 2.

Nicolson, N. (1972), *Portrait of a Marriage*. New York: Atheneum.

Peck, M.L., Farberow, N.L., & Litman, R.E. (1985), *Youthsuicide*. New York: Springer.

Pepper, S. (1942), *World Hypotheses*. Berkeley & Los Angeles: University of California Press.

———— (1967), Can a philosophy make one philosophical? In: *Essays in Self-destruction*, ed. E.S. Shneidman. New York: Science House.

Pfeffer, C. (1986), *The Suicidal Child*. New York: Guilford Press.

Reynolds, P. (1987), Imposing a corporate structure. *Psychol. Today*, March:33–38.

Rosenblatt, P.C. (1983), *Bitter, Bitter Tears: Nineteenth-Century Diarists and Twentieth-Century Grief Theories*. Minneapolis: University of Minnesota Press.

Roy, A. (1986a), Genetics and suicidal behavior. Paper presented at HHS Task Force on Youth Suicide, National Institute of Mental Health, Bethesda, Maryland, May 8.

———— (1986b), Genetic factors in suicide. *Psychopharmacol. Bull.*, 22:666–668.

———— (1986c), *Suicide*. Baltimore: Williams & Wilkins.

Seiden, R.H. (1969), *Suicide among Youth: A Review of the Literature, 1900–1967*, Pub. Health Serv. Pub. No. 1971. Washington, DC: U.S. Government Printing Office.

Shaffer, T. (1976), Legal views of suicide. In: *Suicide: Contemporary Developments*, ed. E.S. Shneidman. New York: Grune & Stratton.

Shneidman, E.S. (1965), Preventing suicide. *Amer. J. Nursing*, 65/5:111–116.

———— (1969), Suicide, lethality and the psychological autopsy. In: *Aspects of Depression*, eds. E.S. Shneidman & M. Ortega. Boston: Little, Brown.

———— (1971), Perturbation and lethality as precursors of suicide in a gifted group. *Suicide & Life-Threat. Behav.*, 1:23–45.

———— (1973a), *Deaths of Man*. New York: St. Martin's Press.

———— (1973b), Suicide. *Encyclopaedia Britannica*. Chicago: William Benton.

———— ed. (1976), *Suicidology: Contemporary Developments*. New York: Grune & Stratton.

———— (1977), The psychological autopsy. In: *Guide to the Investigation and Reporting of Drug Abuse Death*, ed. L.I. Gottschalk. Washington, DC: U.S. Government Printing Office.

———— (1980), *Voices of Death*. New York: Harper & Row.

———— (1984), Suicide and suicide prevention. In: *Encyclopaedia of Psychology*, ed. R. Corsini & B.D. Ozaki. New York: John Wiley.

———— (1985), *Definition of Suicide*. New York: John Wiley.

———— Farberow, N.L., & Leonard, C. (1961), *Some Facts About Suicide: Causes and Prevention*, NIMH Pub. No. 852. Bethesda, MD: National Institute of Mental Health.

————, ————, Litman, R.E. (1970), *Psychology of Suicide*. New York: Science House.

Silving, H. (1957), Suicide and law. In: *Clues to Suicide*, eds. E.S. Shneidman & N.L. Farberow. New York: McGraw-Hill.

Tolstoy, L. (1877), *Anna Karenina*, trans. R. Edmonds. Harmondsworth, UK: Penguin Books, 1954.

Tyler, L. (1984), *Thinking Creatively*. San Francisco: Jossey-Bass.

Victoroff, V.M. (1983), *The Suicidal Patient: Recognition, Intervention, Management*. Oradell, NJ: Medical Economic Books.

Weisman, A.D., & Kastenbaum, R. (1968), *The Psychological Autopsy: A Study of the Terminal Phase of Life*, Community Mental Health Journal Monogr. 4. New York: Behavioral Publications.

Williams, G. ed. (1957), *The Sanctity of Life and the Criminal Law*. New York: Alfred A. Knopf.

Windt, P. (1980), The concept of suicide. In: *Suicide: The Philosophic Issues*, eds. M.P. Battin & D.J. Mayo. New York: St. Martin's Press.

Zilboorg, G. (1937), Considerations on suicide, with particular reference to that of the young. *Amer. J. Orthopsychiat.*, 7:15–31.

2

Suicide: A Public Health Perspective

Robert A. Dorwart, M.D., M.P.H.
Lee Chartock, M.D., M.P.P.

Suicide is both a public health and a clinical problem. From a public health perspective, all mental health professionals, including clinicians, have a responsibility for reducing the risk of suicidal behavior in their communities. In this chapter, therefore, we describe some of the available public mental health strategies and interventions. In order to highlight the psychosocial context of suicide, we focus on the importance of the "psychological sense of community" in planning public mental health approaches to the prevention of suicide (Sarason, 1974). While some observers remark that suicide rates reflect an overall increase in the level of violence and trauma in society, such as the use of firearms and homicide, we are especially interested in suicide as a potentially preventable cause of death through organized public health efforts.

First, we briefly review the magnitude of the problem of suicide, especially among adolescents. Next, we present the public mental health model of primary, secondary, and tertiary prevention and relate it to existing suicide prevention programs. Then we consider predisposing factors and, by way of illustration, the social context of adolescent suicide, as well as some interventions that have been proposed or attempted and some ways in which public policy may affect suicide rates. We describe how one mental health center, the Cambridge–Somerville Mental Health Center in Cambridge, Massachusetts, exemplifies the public mental health approach to preventative interventions (Glasscote, Kohn, Beigel, Raber, Roeske, Cox, Raybin, and Bloom, 1980). The rationale for this approach is the linking of prevention efforts with existing services and treatment programs, rather than creating separate, freestanding programs as proposed by some suicidologists. Finally, we review several ways in which mental health professionals may use their knowledge and clinical skills as part of public mental health efforts to reduce the risk of suicide in their communities through consultation, education, media, and self-help programs.

THE MAGNITUDE OF THE PROBLEM

In 1982, suicide was reported to be the ninth leading cause of death in the United States, and among adolescents it ranked second (U.S. Department of Health and Human Services, 1984). Put differently, although suicide accounts for roughly 2 percent of all deaths, it accounts for more than 15 percent of deaths among adolescents. This means that in terms of life-years lost, suicide ranks among the first five causes in the United States. These figures are all the more alarming when we realize that for a variety of reasons it is widely believed that (1) completed suicides represent only 2 to 5 percent of attempts; (2) suicide is statistically underreported; and (3) the rates of suicide in industrialized countries are increasing, especially among the young ages 15 to 24 and the elderly over age 65 (Eastwood, 1980; Robins, 1985).

Adolescent suicide rates have been increasing at especially alarming rates. Over the past 30 years, the rate of adolescent suicide in the United States has tripled; in Massachusetts it reportedly increased by one-third in 1984 alone. Mark Rosenberg, chief of the violence epidemiology unit of the Center for Disease Control (CDC), has stated that there is a risk of "epidemics" in schools related to the rapidly rising incidence of adolescent suicides (Rosenberg, Mercy, and Smith, 1984). Recently, a paperback science fiction book described an invasion of the United States by alien forces bent on creating a suicide epidemic, and at one point in the book 50 young persons per week jumped to their death. In fact, the current adolescent suicide rate in the United States is approaching 100 per week, with increasing reports of clusters in communities (Naha, 1982; *New York Times*, 1984). And it has been estimated that worldwide more than 1,000 persons commit suicide daily (World Health Organization, 1968). Adolescent suicide has received increasing attention in newspapers, magazines, radio and television, and professional journals and books. Also important, however, is our understanding of predisposing factors for suicide and the way in which data about incidence may be useful to clinicians and public health officials.

Other populations of interest from a public health perspective on the problem of suicide include the elderly, psychiatric patients, and individuals with alcoholism or major or chronic illness or medical conditions such as pregnancy. Several of these special clinical populations are described in other chapters of this book. Data on trends in suicide rates in the United States are available from the National Institute of Mental Health (NIMH, 1985).

PUBLIC HEALTH MODEL

In public health, *primary prevention* refers to programs designed to reduce rates of illness before any signs or symptoms have appeared; in other words, to "prevent" illness from occurring (Last, 1980). Traditional examples include sanitation or immunization programs. *Secondary prevention* aims to detect illness at an early stage and to prevent the worsening of illness. An example is hypertension screening and treatment; thus, early detection and treatment are closely linked. *Tertiary prevention* refers to efforts to reduce the severity, duration, complications, and other sequelae of illnesses already diagnosed and treated. This public health model of prevention has been found effective in efforts involving infectious, genetic, or environmentally induced diseases, such as tuberculosis, phenylketonuria, and lead poisoning, to name only a few.

In public mental health, Caplan has elaborated these principles of prevention (Caplan, 1964). Primary prevention often involves making basic socioenvironmental interventions designed to prevent mental illness from occurring at all; for instance, genetic counseling, prenatal education, and supplemental care programs aim to reduce the risk of infant morbidity or environmental insult. Another example of primary prevention is suicide centers. Secondary prevention involves the early diagnosis and treatment of emotional disturbances before they reach serious proportions; examples of well-established programs are child guidance clinics to evaluate and treat children with early emotional disorders and developmental problems. Tertiary prevention involves services for emotional disturbance after it has been treated or become chronic, with the aim of preventing increased impairment; the most widespread examples involve programs of rehabilitation for patients with chronic schizophrenia or mental retardations, such as a day treatment and residential programs. Recently, federally funded centers were created to conduct research on the rehabilitative aspects of schizophrenia and other chronic mental illnesses. Another example is programs that ensure availability of lithium carbonate for patients with diagnosed manic-depressive illness; it has been estimated that the risk of suicide for patients with manic-depressive illness is reduced by 20 percent if treated with lithium.

Besides the three-tiered approach to prevention, the public mental health model addresses the needs of a target population or a defined community, not specific individuals. This model was the basis for the federal community mental health center (CMHC) programs of the past twenty years in the United States. Programs derived from this model included 24-hour emergency services, crisis and consultation programs, and suicide prevention centers (Klein and Goldston, 1977). Often these programs were developed in the context of a network of established community health and social services. Such programs have identifiable capabilities regarding intervention with suicidal patients (Jacobs, 1983). The effectiveness of emergency services is increased by having specialized resources and techniques available, such as multilingual counselors, home visits, emergency medical services, and liaison to police. In addition to the clinical subpopulations already mentioned, CMHCs may target other high-risk groups, such as disaster victims, immigrant populations, or individuals or families in crisis, including the homeless mentally ill (Lamb, 1984). Thus, in thinking about programs of suicide prevention, it is useful to keep in mind that prevention efforts may be linked to already existing services, thereby potentially reducing costs and increasing the effectiveness of these programs. Let us briefly review how primary, secondary, and tertiary prevention programs relate to suicidal behavior.

Primary Prevention: Suicide Prevention Centers

Suicide prevention centers are one of the most extensively investigated means of primary prevention (Miller, Coombs, Leeper, and Barton, 1984), especially the Samaritan Centers. The Samaritans grew from a movement started in England in 1953 with the goals of providing "help, advice, and friendship" to those contemplating suicide (Varah, 1964). The centers are staffed by lay persons who "befriend" and sometimes refer people who call with thoughts of suicide. In 1977 there were 154 Samaritan centers in the British Isles staffed, on average, by 120 volunteers and serving approximately 200,000 new clients each year (Fox, 1977). It is difficult to measure the success of these centers. Although they provide a needed service, it is unclear what population they serve; for instance, Sawyer and Jameton (1979) found that 51 percent of 67 chronic callers to a prevention center in Cleveland, Ohio, were alcohol or drug dependent and that 37 percent made suicide attempts in the course of the year.

The effect of suicide centers on suicide rates is also unclear. Bagley (1971) analyzed Samaritan efforts in Britain, matching communities with and without centers on 57 variables. He found significant differences with reductions of 6 percent in counties with centers compared with increases in control locales. However, Barraclough and Jennings' (1977) reanalysis did not confirm these original differences. In the United States, studies by Weiner (1969) and by Bridge, Potkin, Zung, and Soldo (1977) found little effect in rates attributable to centers. A recent study by Miller et al. (1984) found an association of centers with a reduction of suicides only for young white females and on this basis extrapolate that the presence of centers might "prevent" more than 600 suicides per year in the United States. They conclude that "Evidence of a reliable effect, of whatever size, suggests that future research can now attempt to analyze the factors that are responsible for this reduction and extend the principles to other populations which, while not reached by prevention centers, are at greater risk for suicide" (p. 343).

Secondary and Tertiary Prevention

Secondary and tertiary prevention more closely resemble traditional clinical models of intervention. Secondary prevention may involve evaluation and therapy with children or high-risk individuals or groups. Education of primary health care providers concerning the signs and symptoms associated with risk of suicide is another important aspect of secondary intervention, as is the example of the recent work of Deykin, Perlow, and McNamarra (1985). She and her co-workers designed and carried out an education and intervention program in which patients aged 13 to 17 were tracked and services offered following visits to a general hospital emergency room for documented parasuicide (suicide attempts). This method illustrates the features of secondary prevention wherein there is clearly a disorder of some sort that is by design detected early (e.g., first attempts) and services offered in a timely fashion. By identifying a high-risk subpopulation and offering outreach and treatment, it is theoretically more likely that intervention will reduce the risks of suicide.

This study by Deykin of suicidal behavior in emergency room admissions among 13- to 17-year-olds showed that females predominated over males by almost two to one. The authors distinguished three types of behavior: "life-threatening" events, which did not occur at different rates by sex; and "suicide attempts" and "suicide gestures" that occurred two to four times as often among females. Repeat admissions were most common among attempters (.24), then life-threatening events (.18), followed by "gestures" (.10). Further work by these investigators has shown a link between exposure to child abuse or neglect and suicidal behavior in adolescence, with three to six times as many prior contacts with the state social services department among attempters over controls (Deykin, 1983).

Tertiary prevention often involves therapeutic work with patients who are being treated for major mental illness, such as manic-depressive illness or paranoid schizophrenia. The public health focus of such work often lies in ensuring access to adequate treatment of after-care programs to maintain levels of functioning outside the hospital. An example of such a program is the Ambulatory Community Services program of the Cambridge–Somerville Mental Health Center. This program for former patients has been described by Cotton, Bene-Kociemba, and Cole (1979). The program provides after care, case management, crisis intervention, social club functions, home visits, and supportive psychotherapy for patients following discharge from catchment area hospitals. The goal of the service is to maintain levels of functioning, detect impending relapse, decrease the likelihood of isolation and inadequate monitoring in the community, and generally to provide access to medical and mental health services (see chapter 21 by Cotton et al.). The need for and benefits of such services for patients with chronic mental illness has been documented repeatedly (Freedman and Moran, 1984). Apart from organized public health programs, public policy changes may also influence rates of suicide in the society, although causal relationships are difficult to prove.

ADOLESCENT SUICIDE: EXAMPLE OF A TARGET POPULATION

Despite increasing knowledge about the population of people who commit suicide, we still lack adequate predictive and preventive knowledge for treating individuals. Using the problem of adolescent suicide as an example, it is important for the mental health professional to look beyond the statistics or publicized cases for clues to clinically helpful interventions. One approach to understanding suicide is the intensive case study example of the account of *Vivienne: The Life and Suicide of an Adolescent Girl,* which attempts to put the act of suicide in the perspective of personal biography, the life cycle, and social context (Mack and Hickler, 1981). Their book demonstrates the critical role that may be played by teachers in the lives of their students and the opportunities to detect early signs of depression and other symptoms of serious maladjustment (see chapter 4).

Another approach is the careful study of specific subpopulations at risk. In March 1983, newspapers across the United States carried the story of a 14-year-old, 9-month-pregnant girl from Edgewood, Maryland, who committed suicide by kneeling in front of a speeding train near her school where her mother worked, killing herself and her near-term male fetus (Kraft, 1983; Hartford *Sun,* 1983). As tragic as this story is, especially in light of the denial and absence of help-seeking from family or outreach by school counselors, this is only one instance of a larger public health problem—namely, suicide in pregnancy. A recent clinical book by Kleiner and Greston (1984) addresses this special problem from several perspectives and suggests the important role of obstetricians and primary care physicians as well as mental health professionals in relation to this complicated group of patients at risk.

Still another approach is that of epidemiology. Besides the population-oriented approach of the CDC mentioned above, some prevention–intervention studies have been undertaken, such as those of Deykin and associates at the Harvard School of Public Health (Deykin, 1983). These investigators have undertaken a prevention–intervention study not only to assess the rates of suicide attempts and self-destructive behavior in an emergency room setting but also to evaluate which interventions are effective in maintaining and facilitating follow-up treatment, reducing the recurrence of such behavior or reducing the risk of suicide.

Numerous factors have been adduced to explain the rise in suicide among the young. Holinger and Offer (1982) describe a population model pointing to the baby boom as the critical factor because it led to a high ratio of persons aged 15 to 24 relative to the whole population. The tasks of adolescence—separation and establishing independence and identity—have been espoused logically as contributing factors (Konopka, 1983). A related complicating factor is the breakdown of the nuclear family and rising rates of marital separation and divorce (McArnarvey, 1979); a popular account is to be found in the book and movie *Ordinary People* (Guest, 1976). The increase in availability of weapons and the glamorization of violence have already been mentioned as contributing factors. A commonly cited contributing factor to rates of major mental illness is economic stress and unemployment, which is as high as 40 percent for black male adolescents in some locales (Brenner, 1973; Boor, 1980). Klerman (1985) has also noted sociological factors such as decreasing religious values and increasing geographic mobility as sources of stress and strain on adolescent adjustment. Others note the high rates of drug and alcohol use among adolescents and increasing attention to early sexual activity.

Public Policy and Suicide Rates

Another form of primary prevention arises from planned changes in public policy, such as reduction in the availability or lethality of the means for attempting suicide. One example of this type of effect of public policy on the rate of suicide is the reduction of the carbon monoxide concentration in coal gas in Great Britain. The change of gas regulation by which carbon monoxide content of coal gas went from 12 to 0 percent was followed by reduced suicide rates nationally. In 1963, there were 144 suicides per million in England; in 1970 there were 64; 60 percent of those in 1963 were by domestic coal gas, but in 1970 there were only 12 by this means, a statistically significant change. Importantly, during the same period, the rate of death from suicide by other means did not change significantly (Hassall and Trethowan, 1972; Malleson, 1973). A paper by McClure (1984) suggests an upturn in suicide rates in Great Britian by other means, which the author attributes to worsening economic conditions, such as inflation and unemployment.

Another example of public policy affecting suicide rates is in altering availability of the means of suicide. Looking at the suicide rates by method in Australia between 1910 and 1971, Oliver and Hetzel (1973) saw a dramatic increase in the early 1960s followed by a subsequent decrease after 1967. Most of the differences in these rates may be accounted for by changes in rates of drug suicides, defined as deaths due to ingestion of therapeutic substances. A careful analysis of changes in the laws regulating prescription drugs demonstrates that increased availability of lethal drugs after 1960 was related to an increase in drug suicides and that a subsequent decreased availability after 1967 was related to a marked decline. Again there was no increase in suicides by other methods, suggesting that people are not indifferent to the choice of method. The clear implication of these findings is that by altering availability of means, one can reduce the overall suicide rate.

A more politically controversial and methodologically thorny issue is the link between firearms and suicide rates. In the United States, firearms were the method of 53 percent of male suicides and 25 percent of female suicides (*Vital Statistics,* 1977). From 1962 to 1975 suicide by firearms was the only method for committing suicide to show a statistically significant increase in the United States with 92 percent of suicide attempts with firearms ending in death (Card, 1974; Boor, 1981). Studying the relationship of availability of firearms to suicide rates is difficult. Markush and Bartolucci (1984) collected data on the proportion of households in the United States that had obtained guns for several different years, and, using multiple regression, found that the prevalence of guns in a region was significantly correlated with suicide rates. Lester and Murrel (1980) established a scale for determining the strictness of gun control legislation in the various states in the United States and found a significant inverse relationship between strictness of gun control laws and suicide rates by firearms. Boyd (1983) analyzed policy concerning manufacture and importing of guns and claims that rising suicide rates can be explained by those related to firearms. More importantly, he further notes that while the overall suicide rate by firearms rose by about 10 percent from 1953 to 1978, the rate for suicide by firearms for people under 40 more than doubled, suggesting the need for research to focus more on high-risk groups rather than on total population rates. This is consistent with the findings of Miller et al. (1984) cited earlier concerning the selectivity of effects of Samaritan Centers on suicide rates. Even though research is only one basis for public policy-making, it is clear that more thorough and rigorous research is needed in this area, such as that proposed by the CDC.

PUBLIC HEALTH AND POLICY INTERVENTIONS: TARGET POPULATIONS

Although suicide is becoming increasingly prevalent in our culture, epidemiologic research to delineate groups of people who are at highest risk of suicide now offers clinicians and policymakers a more realistic opportunity to exert higher yield efforts to curb this trend. Distressingly, there are insufficient resources to begin to mount a serious assault against this pervasive problem. We begin by briefly reviewing this need for further research data. We then focus on three examples of target populations at extremely high risk of suicide. These include (1) those who suffer from psychiatric illnesses; (2) substance abusers; and (3) pregnant teenagers. For each target population, we consider selected primary, secondary, and tertiary prevention strategies and highlight areas in which intervention techniques are lacking. Each section offers examples of what physicians, parents and families, teachers and human service professionals, peers, or members of the target populations themselves can do to reduce the number of suicides. We also offer an example of the development of one community's public mental health program in order to illustrate the importance of the psychological sense of community and the concurrent availability of clinical services for prevention. We conclude with a more general discussion of large-scale initiatives that can serve as models for better program coordination, data collection, and dissemination of information.

Research Issues

The major policy issue of our time, regarding primary prevention and suicide, is the shortage of funds for research on mental illness and addictive disorders. Psychiatric illnesses and addictive disorders contribute to the overwhelming majority of suicides, particularly among adolescents. The Institute of Medicine/National Academy of Sciences report to the Alcohol, Drug Abuse, and Mental Health Administration (ADAMHA) indicates that support for research on mental and addictive disorders is inadequate compared with research support for physical disorders (Institute of Medicine, 1985). Indeed, mental disorders rank third among the ten most expensive medical conditions in the United States, behind diseases of the circulatory and digestive systems and above injuries, diseases of the nervous, respiratory, and musculoskeletal systems, and cancer (National Center for Health Statistics, 1984). Yet, the real purchasing power of federal research allocations for mental and addictive disorders has declined in recent years. For example, by the mid-1980s inflation-adjusted research allocations for the National Institute of

Mental Health (NIMH) had decreased to about half of those for 1966. This decline is not a result of an overall deemphasis on research, as allocations for the National Institutes of Health (NIH) have kept pace with inflation; nor is it a product of any single administration or Congress—Democratic or Republican. It may reflect a lack of awareness of the problems of mental disorder and their treatment. The Institute of Medicine (IOM) report recommends a greatly increased national commitment to research on mental and addictive disorders and calls for almost a doubling of the ADAMHA research budget, to $500 million a year in constant 1983 dollars. The recommendation singled out mental disorders of children and adolescents, and alcohol research as areas that merit particular support and expansion. Both program areas are vital to reducing the disturbing suicide rates.

Mental health professionals can play an important role in lobbying for increased funding. Organizations that focus on suicide, such as the American Association of Suicidology should cooperate with other professional associations to ensure that adequate research funding is available. By reducing splintering of interests among mental health professionals, research efforts can be focused and directed toward the most pressing problems and promising solutions. Psychiatric patients comprise a population who are both at risk of suicide, and who frequently come in contact with medical and mental health care professionals.

Psychiatric Patients

Depression, either diagnosed or unrecognized, is the most important risk factor for suicide. Fifteen percent of depressed individuals die by suicide (Blumenthal, 1984). At present, affective disorders are disrupting the lives of over 10 million Americans. About 15 percent of the population, or 30 million people, will experience at least one serious bout of depression during their lifetime (Institute of Medicine, 1985). Over the past 25 years treatment of depression has improved radically, with the discovery of effective antidepressant drugs. Despite their success, antidepressant medications have an inherent problem: their toxicity. Their lethality in overdosage makes these drugs especially dangerous for those who need them most urgently— people with depression and suicidal ideation. Psychiatrists need to educate primary care physicians, who routinely prescribe these medications, of the adverse risks of antidepressant medications. Research to develop new medication with higher thresholds for lethality are needed. Until safer antidepressants are discovered, warning labels on bottles and better informed consent and monitoring could serve to prevent accidental overdose among depressed patients. Inpatient treatment may be the best alternative for those whose illness cannot wait for therapeutic effect.

Jamison and Akiskal followed 9,000 affective disorder patients over the course of nine years in three major affective disorder clinics in university-affiliated medical centers. They showed that intensive treatment of affective disorders yielded a decrease in the suicide rate in the population (Jamison and Akiskal, 1982).

Unfortunately, many people who suffer from affective disorders remain untreated. While appropriate use of medication and psychotherapy can help about 80 percent of those afflicted, less than one-third of these people receive treatment. Further investigation into the reasons for this underutilization would elucidate ways to prevent suicide among depressed people.

The federal government recently has been taking an increasingly larger role in targeting the relationship between affective disorders and suicide. In 1982 NIMH sponsored a workshop entitled "Prevention Research—Suicide and Affective Disorders Among Adolescents and Young Adults." Now, NIMH has underway a major public and professional education campaign on depression. Entitled "Depression/Awareness, Recognition, Treatment (D/ART)" it is designed to increase the recognition, early detection, diagnosis, and treatment of affective disorders. Their initiative is based on the findings that the presence of an affective disorder is the most common precursor of suicide.

In 1983 NIMH established a Suicide Research Unit (SRU) within its Center for Studies of Affective Disorders. The SRU coordinates NIMH's program in suicide research, conducting research projects, conferences, and workshops, and making scientific presentations about suicide to professional groups and to the public. These federal funds, however, are not targeted for prevention programs or research on prevention models through this unit. Those projects that are funded generally support biochemical research and clinical searches for physiological causes of suicide, not research on prevention.

Schizophrenics have about a 10 percent lifetime chance of committing suicide. Furthermore, about 20 percent of schizophrenics make a suicide attempt (Drake, Gates, and Cotton, 1985). Because one percent of the U.S. population suffers from schizophrenia at any one time, the number of deaths related to this illness is staggering. A recent study has identified those schizophrenics who are most likely to kill themselves (Cotton, Drake, and Gates, 1985). The profile of two-thirds of the patients was consistent with the literature on suicide among schizophrenic patients, namely that the victims tend to be young males, usually in their thirties, who had been ill for five to ten years. They had experienced courses of illness characterized by many exacerbations and remissions, and they averaged more than six hospitalizations. Despite histories of good premorbid adjustment that included attending college, working, or establishing relationships outside the family of origin, they were functioning poorly at the time of the suicide. They were unmarried, unemployed, and living alone. Nevertheless they maintained expectations of high performance for themselves that were congruent with their previous experiences but not with current abilities. The overall picture was one of collapsed self-esteem and overwhelming despair in the context of severe, chronic mental illness.

A recent finding (Drake et al., 1985) serves as an example for how secondary prevention techniques can be used to curtail suicide attempts. Schizophrenic patients who are burdened by their own internal expectations and their inability to live up to them need someone to share the burden of despair while they look for new sources of hope. Contrary to standard treatment of schizophrenia, which emphasizes high expectations, performance skills, and mastery, these patients need protection and support while reconstructing their own expectations and self-esteem. Recruiting families to serve as allies in their treatment can minimize the type of sudden, precipitous family losses that often precede suicide. Thus, early detection of schizophrenic patients who manifest these risk factors for suicide can be coupled with supportive and protective therapy. This approach not only benefits the patient, but can decrease the family's guilt about their role in the patient's predicament and increase their coping skills. To implement this treatment approach successfully requires educating physicians and mental health professionals to be aware of the characteristics that place a schizophrenic at high risk, educating therapists about this new treatment, and educating families and friends on methods of offering support.

The best predictor for subsequent suicide attempts and completions is previous suicide attempts. Over 80 percent of those who take their own lives have made previous attempts (U.S. Department of Health and Human Services, 1979). This is the group, therefore, to whom intervention strategies should be most heavily directed. Although the incident immediately preceding a suicide attempt is a critical factor in the adolescent's action, a troubled history of many months or even years duration usually precedes the suicidal behavior. Thus, only treating a patient immediately after the event ameliorates the symptoms while not addressing underlying issues. Patients who come to an emergency room for treatment due to complications from suicidal behavior should not be discharged from the hospital until a social worker and physician are assigned to long-term follow-up. Hospital personnel are not the only ones who can intervene. Anyone who has contact with patients at high risk of suicide can help. For instance, workers at departments of social services who treat child abuse–neglect victims should ensure that these youths receive similar follow-up care to those who have attempted suicide.

Alcohol and Substance Abuse

Alcohol and substance abuse commonly play a role as a precipitant to the act of suicide itself. The actual decision to kill oneself, although it may have been incubating for many months or years, is, nevertheless, strongly affected by the situation or setting that immediately precedes the suicidal act. Powerful affects, especially intense feelings of sadness, hopelessness, and rage, can acutely impair judgments regarding the future and the permanence of circumstances that seem, at the time, to be utterly without the possibility of change for the better. Alcohol can exaggerate these feelings and unleash one's impulses. As many as 80 percent of those who attempt suicide have been drinking at the time (Alcohol, Drug Abuse and Mental Health Administration, 1983). Although the relationship between substance abuse and suicide is less well documented, it is known that drug overdose is the leading method of attempted suicide among females, and that the problem is especially acute during adolescence. Adolescents account for about 15 percent of drug-related suicide attempts seen in hospital emergency rooms. Preliminary results from a study of recent teenage suicide victims in New Jersey, New York City, and western Connecticut show that substance abuse was a factor in 45 percent of the cases studied (Shaffer, 1985).

Many communities have responded to the problems of youth alcohol and drug abuse by focusing on educational efforts, warning of their dangers, beginning in elementary school. The most comprehensive programs have staged a five-pronged strategy. These include (1) direct student education; (2) training teachers who teach in grades five to twelve to develop and implement alcohol and drug prevention programs in their classrooms; (3) training selected high school seniors to become alcohol and drug educators for their peers; (4) training and consulting with staff of other youth serving agencies; and (5) making the community sensitive to these issues through public lectures and information dissemination. These educational programs are timely for inclusion of the dangers that alcohol and drugs play in complicating the adolescent suicide problem. Moreover, it is estimated that those with alcoholism commit suicide from six to fifteen times more frequently than the general population. It is important for hospital units and shelters that have contact with alcoholics to alert their personnel, especially physicians, to the warning signs and symptoms of suicide because early intervention could reduce the suicide rate among this population. For example, ADAMHA has undertaken a program to improve primary care physician awareness of alcohol and drug abuse and psychiatric disorder.

Pregnant Teenagers

In recent years, teenage pregnancy, especially in large urban centers in the United States, has assumed epidemic proportions (*New York Times*, 1984). The pregnant teenager is often socially and emotionally handicapped and especially prone to medical complications of pregnancy. Suicide in association with pregnancy in adolescence is a serious reality (*British Medical Journal*, 1971). Otto (1972), in a follow-up study of attempted suicide among 1,226 girls and women under 21 years of age, states that 75 or 6.1 percent were pregnant. Gabrielson, (1970) revealed that fourteen of 105 pregnant teenagers under eighteen years of age, admitted to the Yale–New Haven Hospital over a two-year period, were subsequently known to have made one or more self-destructive attempts or threats that were serious enough to require care or to be reported to the physician at the hospital. They concluded that adolescent pregnancy may have a direct effect on the future potential for suicidal behavior. Very little has been done to address this problem.

Current public policies in the United States mitigate against advocating birth control measures even in the face of evidence that adolescent pregnancy is increasing at a rapid rate. Sex education in the schools to prevent and warn against the hazards of teenage pregnancy has met widespread resistance. Furthermore, counseling services for pregnant adolescents is limited by funding. These trends also bring an increased risk of suicide. Peer counseling by women who had teenage pregnancies and successfully dealt with their related problems offers one short-term intervention. In addition, mutual help groups may provide the emotional support to adolescents who feel isolated and in need of help.

PREVENTIVE INTERVENTIONS AND STRATEGIES

Consultation

There is a role for mental health professionals in a consultation capacity regarding suicide. Psychiatrists and psychologists have been consulting for many years for clients as varied as the military, the Peace Corps, private industry, and schools. Self-help groups, while not employing professionals to lead meetings, can utilize their experience in structuring certain ways of coping that would be beneficial to the participants. In addition to helping a group itself, mental health professionals could consult to individuals who lead help groups.

Gerald Caplan (1969) has written about the role of consultation by mental health professionals to agencies and institutions in the community. His approach is pertinent to the role that mental health professionals can play in helping agencies which deal with suicide and those agencies which could be working on suicide at the present time but do not have the resources or knowledge base. He believes consultation to be an effective tool for building a mental health network. He recommends choosing to work with highly visible agencies, so that information about the mental health program will be widely disseminated, and with care givers who occupy key positions in the community service network, so that improved procedures have a better chance of being copied by others. His fundamental principle is to create proximity and establish a reputation for trustworthiness, competency, and eagerness to help without infringing on the rights of other agencies or endangering their programs. He advises that a single worker be assigned to a particular target institution so that he or she can build a personal knowledge of its social system and of its staff. However, he warns that a consultant may become so integrated within the structure of a consultee agency that he or she ceases to be effective. Rotating consultants among two or three similar agencies is one solution to this problem.

Three target areas for agency consultation regarding suicide are the hospital, especially the emergency room, schools, and places of employment. Many medical or surgical patients in the hospital suffer from depression or demoralization. While it is well documented that physical illness is a precipitant to suicide among the elderly, there is evidence that suicide rates among adolescents with chronic diseases (e.g., leukemia) is much higher than among healthy adolescents. These patients are already known to the health care system and, thus, provide a population that is easily accessible and in great need of mental health care. Physicians trained in consultation–liaison (C–L) psychiatry could initiate contact with a patient while in the hospital and periodic follow-up could provide an outlet for suicidal impulses. The emergency room should be the entrance to the mental health network for those who appear there after a suicide attempt.

As mentioned earlier, schools are a place where adolescents at risk are in contact with teachers and one another. In instances where school administrators and teachers need assistance in planning programs to warn of and teach about adolescent suicide, mental health professionals should be consultants. Likewise, mental health professionals have a critical role to play in the aftermath of completed suicide.

There is growing evidence that fluctuations in the economy of a society contribute to the changing rates of mental illness and related conditions. Four studies have shown a positive association between economic fluctuations, as indicated by changes in the annual unemployment rate, and concomitant changes in the male suicide rate at different time periods (Brenner, 1973; MacMahon, Johnson, and Pugh, 1963; Hamermesh and Soss, 1974; Vigderhous and Fishman, 1978). A recent study shows a positive association between unemployment rate and female suicide rates among certain age groups in Canada (Cormier and Klerman, 1985). Durkheim's concept of anomie has been useful to understand how changing social conditions may contribute to suicide rates (Durkheim, 1897). He defines anomie as a state of societal normlessness that results from rapid social changes that produce loss of social control, disconfirmation of expected social contingencies, and a decreased sense of community affiliation.

Employers, unions, and government unemployment programs could undertake employment counseling, whereby workers who are laid off get skilled counseling to prepare them for the psychological trauma of unemployment. Counselors would help the employee to strengthen the surrounding human as well as financial resources, and see to it that mental health care could be provided in the lapse between jobs. Employee assistance programs could sponsor periodic lectures and symposia on the stresses related to unemployment and offer strategy sessions for coping with this life-style change. This process could also screen candidates who are at highest risk for suicide and intervene to see that they are referred for appropriate mental health treatment.

Education

Education, as a tool for preventing suicides, can be effective at the primary, secondary, and tertiary modes. Generally, there has been inconclusive evidence that education programs have been effective. A recent study evaluated an intervention program designed to reduce suicidal, self-destructive behavior among high-risk adolescents (Deykin, Perlow, and McNamarra, 1985). The intervention consisted of two separate but theoretically linked endeavors. These included (1) direct service to identified at-risk adolescents by means of a community outreach social worker who acted as a primary resource for psychological and social needs in addition to acting as an advocate for the adolescent with his or her family, school, the courts, and other community agencies; and (2) an education program to increase the participant's knowledge of adolescent depression and suicidal behavior in addition to informing them of relevant community resources. The results indicate that this two-pronged intervention program was effective in increasing subjects' compliance with a medical regimen. To a lesser extent, the intervention facilitated early help-seeking among adolescents with suicidal thoughts and slightly reduced the overall occurrence of emergency room admissions for suicidal behavior. The program, however, had no effect on the occurrence of repeat suicide episodes.

The results indicate that physicians may play an even greater role than they may realize, especially for adolescents who suffer from concurrent medical or psychiatric disease. They also support the hypothesis that the educational component of the program, a primary prevention technique, was effective. This was substantiated by the fact that many more adolescents came to the emergency room with recurrent, obsessional, suicidal thoughts *without* self-inflicted injuries. The failure to curb repeat episodes of suicidal behavior may be due to the unacceptability or ineffectiveness of direct service. This, in turn, may be due to a population who commit repeat acts, the ones who are most difficult to reach and involve. Importantly, the authors conclude that the combined effect of both components is greater than either individually, and thereby document an effective primary prevention intervention. Similar studies that seek to substantiate the validity of suicide intervention programs would be extremely useful.

One of the most comprehensive models of primary prevention using education is the Suicide Information and Education Centre (SIEC), administered by the Canadian Mental Health Association of Alberta in Calgary. The SIEC is a computer-assisted resource library containing written and audiovisual materials specific to the topic of suicidal behaviors. The aim of the Centre is to collect all of the literature regarding suicidal behaviors that has been published in the English language since 1955, create a data base of these bibliographic references, and make this collection available to all interested persons. The Centre is funded by a grant from the province and although primarily intended for use by Albertans, there are no geographical restrictions placed on those wishing to use and contribute to the SIEC. Users of the data base include researchers, health care professionals, educators, social service agency staff, students, librarians, and members of the general public. To ensure the highest level of service, the Centre uses all possible resources, including providing referrals where appropriate. Their resources include literature searches; a newspaper clippings service; a listing of training programs, organizations, associations, institutes, funding sources, research being conducted, consultants and upcoming events; photocopies of publications; an index of video materials and services; loans of video materials; and a service which connects people with others who share common suicide interests.

In the United States, the American Association of Suicidology provides resources to anyone regardless of membership. They have a directory of suicide prevention centers, a file of statistics, and educational pamphlets. They also act as a clearinghouse for information. There is an interest in creating a national centralized computer bank to monitor and collect suicide data. Also, there is the Youth Suicide National Center in Washington, DC, a nonprofit organization that also acts as a clearinghouse for youth suicide prevention efforts.

The NIMH has recently started an educational campaign directed toward physicians; they recently released a Suicide Monograph and a Black Suicide Monograph. A videodisc on adolescent suicide, targeted to medical students and residents, has been prepared. This innovative program is needed since currently there is very little time in most medical school curricula devoted to educating future physicians about suicide, especially adolescent suicide, despite its prevalence. And the education is especially relevant for trainees in pediatrics, adolescent medicine, obstetrics, and primary care and family physicians. This training in recognition of the patient at highest risk of suicide and in referrals to mental health professionals should be included in these postgraduate training programs in these specialties. Continuing medical education courses to reach practicing physicians are necessary, too.

The Media

Television, a potentially powerful source for primary prevention, can act as a conduit to reduce suicidal behavior. A recently released Nielsen Study revealed that the average household with children watches 49 hours of television per week. Violent television entertainment encourages aggressive behavior among young viewers (Comstock, 1981) and thus plays an important role in changing adolescents' behavior patterns, particularly regarding violent suicidal behavior.

Efforts to increase the public's awareness of the prevalence of adolescent suicide and its surrounding issues have been advanced by the television film *Silence of the Heart,* a portrayal of the pain, aloneness, and individual nature of adolescent suicide. Public figures, such as Art Linkletter, who have had a suicide in their family, can do a tremendous public service by increasing awareness of the problem, and acceptability of open discussion. Even those who have not been affected directly by this trauma can offer greater exposure to the warning signals of impending disaster. There is a role for more athletes, musicians, entertainers, politicians, and physicians to do public service announcements to generate greater awareness of the magnitude of the problem.

Suicide prevention centers and hot-line telephone numbers and the services they provide need to be widely disseminated. It is crucial that adolescents in particular know about available services and that these services are truly accessible in terms of location and hours of operation. Local networks and the federal government could cosponsor these ads in the form of public service announcements. Proliferative air time would ensure that adolescents and others at risk know these telephone numbers as well as they know the number of directory assistance.

Many local television stations have aired health-oriented features in their regular programming. For example, in Boston, one network affiliate has focused on raising public awareness about emergency medical care by providing viewers with emergency telephone numbers and weaving emergency care information into regularly scheduled programming. The campaign is cosponsored by the Metropolitan Boston Hospital Council, the Department of Public Health, the Red Cross, and the Medical Foundation. Another network affiliate in Boston has launched a year-long campaign called, "To Your Health," which includes five prime time specials, four Saturday children's specials, 107 public service announcement-type health tips, and regular programming emphasizing "positive stories" about "prevention, cure, and hope." Sponsors include Boston University Hospital, the four Boston Archdiocesan hospitals, the Affiliated Neighborhood Health Centers, the Visiting Nurse Association Coalition of Massachusetts, and Bay State Health Care. These are just two examples of the positive influence that public and private partnerships can play in improving health attitudes and behavior patterns. They represent good opportunities in which local suicide organizations can involve themselves in order to raise community awareness.

Self-help Groups

Mutual self-help groups, a form of tertiary prevention, can be very effective in helping people undergoing a transition that requires a shift in social roles—whether they are pregnant adolescents, recovering alcoholics or substance abusers, former mental patients, or previous suicide attempters. Some groups are devoted mainly to helping their members directly and personally like Alcoholics Anonymous (AA). Others, however, serve the purpose of consciousness raising, even changing public attitudes and laws that affect their membership. Examples include women's rights and homosexual groups. Most groups, including these, have many purposes and serve many functions. As Silverman (1985) writes: "The support provided by mutual help organizations has a special meaning. The helper and the beneficiary are peers, and everyone in the group can be both. Not being bound to the role of either helper or recipient may in itself have therapeutic value. Discovering that others have the same problem, members of mutual help groups no longer feel alone. Their feelings and experiences are legitimated, and they are provided with a framework for coping" (p. 5).

Suicide and parasuicide have a painful legacy of effects. The burden of guilt, suppressed anger, sadness, shame, and hurt can be devastating to the surviving family and friends, particularly to a young victim's parents. Survivors' groups, recently established in a few major cities, have provided greatly needed support to their members. In Boston and elsewhere, support groups called Safe Place have been established for survivors who have lost an immediate family member to suicide. The organization, founded in 1982, is affiliated with the Samaritans. It is not run by professionals, and is restricted only to survivors of suicide. Meetings are unstructured and take place twice monthly. There is no fee to attend. Although not evaluated, their role in preventing more family suicides, illnesses, and psychological deterioration is potentially great. An advocacy group, similar to the increasingly vocal National Alliance for the Mentally Ill, and the recently established groups for families with members who suffer from Alzheimer's and other degenerative diseases, could be an outgrowth of these mutual help groups. They could, and presumably would, act as a watchdog to see that initiatives to curb adolescent suicide in particular would be followed through. This active role as advocate for the yet unrecognized suicide victim is vitally needed.

Community Organization

According to Klerman (1985), mental health policy is strongly influenced by three factors other than epidemiology. These are (1) the influence of political and economic conditions; (2) the traditions of psychiatric thinking and practice; and (3) the public perception of epidemiologic trends. In general, public mental health policy has emphasized the expansion of direct services over prevention, and management approaches over community psychology. We believe that the meaning and importance of what Sarason (1974) has called the "psychological sense of community" is also crucial to understanding public health programs and strategies. Indeed, the federal community mental health center programs of the past twenty years have incorporated many public health concepts and have often developed in the context of a network of established community health services (Macht, Scherl, and Sharfstein, 1977). But the very development of the community mental health center depends fundamentally on a shared sense of community which is important for the creation of effective local public mental health programs. We will briefly illustrate the historical and psychosocial dimensions of this concept in the community of Cambridge, Massachusetts.

In overview, four phases in the development of ideas about community in Cambridge can be described. The first phase is the colonial period wherein the word "community" referred to a small group phenomenon best described as a "communion of individuals" from about 1641 to 1785. The second phase involved community in the commonwealth period of development in Massachusetts when "communitarian" values held sway and charity prevailed in the town. In terms of mental health services, these earlier periods lead into the institutional period when community increasingly became the context for diverse developments and reforms, from hospitals to urban renewal of the progressive era from 1786 to 1912. The "mental hygiene" period from 1913 to 1962 preceded the community mental health center era and introduced many ideas about prevention as the influence of psychoanalysis and child guidance clinics spread throughout the country. In the modern community era, people and their institutions are virtually interdependent and the distinction of public versus private is becoming complex if not blurred (Starr, 1982; Schlesinger and Dorwart, 1984). One theme that runs through all of these periods is that of the importance of the community as a psychosocial basis for health and human service programs.

In colonial America there were both religious and political connotations to the idea of community, but there was also a sense of community as "communion" with shared spiritual values and small, compact, relatively homogeneous communities similar to the villages and towns of Elizabethan England (Demos, 1970). Some commentators trace the development of community mental health programs to the early English poor laws of that time. Early settlements in colonial times were characterized by their sense of a communal experience. A dramatic example is reported by William Bradford in his journal. Of the Pilgrims' experience at Plymouth there survives the legendary tale of the tragic first winter in New England that became an ordeal for survival of the community. Bradford's wife drowned, possibly an act of suicide, shortly after their arrival. In his diary he described the gruesome condition reminiscent of a hospital ward: "There died sometimes two or three a day . . . there was but six or seven sound persons who to their great commendations, be it spoken, spared no pains night nor day, but with abundance of toil and hazard of their own health, fetched them wood, dressed them meat, made their beds, washed their loathesome clothes, clothed and unclothed them . . . showing herein their true love unto their friends and brethren" (Brown, 1978, p. 30). Such a sense of group survival and spiritual mission must have remained an enduring psychological basis of community identity at least for this first generation in one early settlement.

In the institutional period of the nineteenth century the idea of commonwealth as a public welfare state developed with the creation of jails, almshouses and state mental hospitals—then called lunatic asylums. During this time private and church charity, the communicare of colonial times, gave way to demands for public and state-sponsored care, the precursors of modern Medicaid and Medicare in our time. As the town of Cambridge grew larger and national developments lead to the emergence of the State as the major political entity, the period of community as commonwealth emerged. The commonwealth period was characterized by industrialization, large-scale immigration, the growth of state bureaucracy, and the building of institutions, among them the insane asylums. Links to the earlier colonial period of the moral treatment philosophy of the early to midnineteenth century is remarked on by Greenblatt. He points out that earlier moral treatment sprang from the warm regard of the early settler for his neighbor. It depended on small-group living, was nourished by close interpersonal contact, and included by its very nature, a concern with continuity of care (Greenblatt, 1984).

Community in general then forms a continuous theme running throughout

American urban history and the development of its institutions. The institutions related to public mental health in Cambridge can be identified at this early period. In 1886, when Westborough State Hospital opened and the new Cambridge (general) Hospital treated its first patient, America according to Wiebe (1967), was in the throes of one of its recurrent crises of community. Confidence in the reigning mythology of community sovereignty and the capacity of each community to govern itself and care for its own people was crumbling under the weight of economic distress and technological progress. The reality if not the ideal of the "island community" was dissolving. Community it seemed would once again need to be redefined. Community as personalized, informal local autonomy was under pressures of social change and transformation that required a new identity, a new sense of community, and that preserved the basic desire for self-governance. Public mental health programs arise within particular communities—states, cities, and towns— and these social structures greatly affect the scope and effectiveness of prevention efforts. Indeed, the nature of these efforts can often be tailored to the needs and resources of particular communities. One example is described here.

In 1922 a division of mental hygiene was established in Massachusetts and "traveling clinics" and outpatient departments of state hospitals were opened. The state's Department of Mental Health was officially created in 1938. Progress toward community mental health services in Cambridge was gradual with an outpatient clinic of Westborough State Hospital begun at Mt. Auburn General Hospital in 1947, the founding of the Cambridge Child Guidance Clinic in 1955, and a Day Care Center in 1963. The events of this period are important for an understanding of the community mental health period that followed, growing out of the passage of the federal Community Mental Health Center Act of 1963.

In particular in Cambridge, the events of the past ten years may be seen against the background of earlier periods. The 1960s included affiliation of the Cambridge City Hospital with Harvard Medical School, the building of a new general hospital facility and primary care clinics, the growth of neighborhood health centers, and the growth and expansion of the Cambridge–Somerville Mental Health Center. Of special interest is the creation and development of the Cambridge Hospital Department of Psychiatry and its role in promoting university–community relations in mental health and in contributing to the concept of the community mental health center as an educational institution.

To illustrate the relationship between community and programs, the early development of the city of Cambridge around three separate and distinct zones of settlement recognized prior to incorporation of the city in 1846—known traditionally as East Cambridge, Old Cambridge, and Cambridgeport—later provided a basis for neighborhood health services. The three early settlements within the city also represent different elements of this city's social structure: the cosmopolitan, Harvard-dominated Old Cambridge; the polyglot, industrial population of East Cambridge; and the diverse, commercialized urban residential section of Cambridgeport. These relationships are not merely lines on the map or organizational charts, but represent important elements of a complex network of human services with concomitant social, political, and cultural meaning and implications. They form a community of health, mental health, and human services for the city with a definable structure. In the 1970s, these divisions became the basis for the development of "neighborhood psychiatry" programs based in geographically distinct neighborhood health centers.

Similarly, the tertiary relationship of the university, general hospital and mental health center has a superimposed and congruent set of relationships among Harvard Medical School, the city government of Cambridge (municipal hospital) and the state's Department of Mental Health (administrator of the community mental health center). The ways in which these groups of people and institutions have developed their relationships with one another over the past several years represent the structuring within the community of the expression of concern for public health and welfare. In contemporary thinking about community psychiatry, we often seem to underestimate how fundamental, immediate, and tangible is our sense of community and family to the psychological and social health of individuals. To some extent, the effective promotion of community health has as a prerequisite the existence of an identifiable community.

Programs of public mental health prevention, such as suicide prevention, do exist both for individuals and for identified subpopulations, in such a historical and social context that influences the resources available for therapeutic and public policy intervention. Many of the clinical strategies of intervention described in this book for defined populations would not be feasible without the support provided by community hospitals and mental health centers. However, even where community support and a well-established network of services exists, it is still necessary to conceptualize and implement a strategy for prevention based on what is known about the clinical problem, in this instance suicidal behavior.

Legislation and Federal Initiatives

As a part of the federal response to suicide as a public health problem, the Center for Disease Control has established within its Center for Health Promotion and Education a new organizational unit, the Violence Epidemiology Branch. This branch has the responsibility for assessing the magnitude of mortality and morbidity related to suicide and suicide attempts; identifying population groups at highest risk of suicide-related morbidity and mortality; and suggesting intervention and prevention strategies to be implemented by public health, social service, and education agencies.

Currently (1987) there are several pieces of legislation before Congress that address the problem of suicide, such as the bills by Rep. Charles E. Bennett (D-Fla) for increased dissemination of materials by the NIMH (HR 57); by Rep. Gary L. Ackerman (NY) for grants to local education boards (HR 1099). Some of the provisions of the proposed legislation concerning suicide prevention were incorporated in the Omnibus Drug Enforcement Education and Control Act in 1986 (PL 99-570).

Another program is the establishment of a temporary three-year grant program to aid states, local governments, and private nonprofit agencies to implement programs for the prevention of suicide among children and youth. The act authorized $10 million per year for the next three fiscal years for this purpose. Programs eligible for funding under the bill include youth education programs; training personnel who work with youth to recognize signs of self-destructive behavior; establishing community suicide-prevention resources such as 24-hour teen hotlines; providing educational materials, including public service announcements for radio and television; and holding appropriate national conferences on youth suicide. Both programs are short term in order to encourage expansion and dissemination of information on existing programs which have been shown to be effective in preventing youth suicide so that a longer term national agenda for action on youth suicide can be set.

CONCLUSION

In this chapter we have described and illustrated a public health perspective on suicide. This viewpoint emphasizes primary, secondary, and tertiary prevention designed to reduce rates of suicide in high-risk or target populations and in identified communities. The strategies commonly available to most mental health professionals include consultation, education, media, and self-help groups. Often overlooked in thinking about prevention is the role of existing services, such as community mental health centers and hospitals. Besides local efforts, state and federal support is needed especially to support large-scale research and prevention programs.

REFERENCES

Alcohol, Drug Abuse and Mental Health Administration (1983), *Alcohol and Health: Fifth Special Report to the U.S. Congress.* Washington, DC: U.S. Government Printing Office, Serial # 017-024-01199-1.

Bagley, C.R. (1971), The evaluation of a suicide prevention method by an ecological method. *Soc. Sci. & Med.*, 2:1–14.

Barraclough, B.M., & Jennings, C. (1977), Suicide prevention by the Samaritans. *Lancet*, 237–238.

Blumenthal, S.J. (1984), Prepared Statement on Suicide and Suicide Prevention: A Briefing by the Subcommittee on Human Services of the Select Committee on Aging, House of Representatives, Comm. Pub. No. 98–497. Washington, DC: U.S. Government Printing Office.

Boor, M. (1980), Relationship between unemployment rates and suicide rates in eight countries, 1962–1976. *Psychol. Rep.*, 47:1095–1101.

——— (1981), Methods of suicide and implications for suicide prevention. *J. Clin. Psychol.*, 37:70–75.

Boyd, J.H. (1983), The increasing rate of suicide by firearms. *N. Eng. J. Med.*, 308:872–874.

Brenner, H. (1973), *Mental Illness and the Economy*. Cambridge, MA: Harvard University Press.

Bridge, T.P., Potkin, S.G., Zung, W.W., & Soldo B.J. (1977), Suicide prevention centers. *J. Nerv. & Ment. Dis.*, 164:18–24.

Brit. Med. J. (1971), Suicide risk in teenage pregnancy (editorial). 2:602.

Brown, R.D. (1978), *Massachusetts*. New York: W.W. Norton.

Caplan, G. (1964), *Principles of Preventive Psychiatry*. New York: Basic Books.

———— (1969), *The Theory and Practice of Mental Health Consultation*. New York: Basic Books, pp. 43–47.

Card, J.J. (1974), Lethality of suicidal methods and suicide risk: Two distinct concepts. *Omega*, 5:37–45.

Centers for Disease Control (1985), *Suicide Surveillance, 1970–1980*. Washington, DC: U.S. Government Printing Office.

Comstock, G. (1981), Influences of mass media on child health behavior. *Health Ed. Quart.*, 8:32–38.

Cormier, H.J., & Klerman, G.L. (1985), Suicide, economie et environment social au Quebec, 1950–1981. *L'Union Med. Can.*, 14/5:1–5.

Cotton, P.G., Bene-Kociemba, A., & Cole, R. (1979), The effect of deinstitutionalization on a general hospital's inpatient psychiatric service. *Hosp. & Commun. Psychiat.*, 30:609–612.

———— P.G., Drake, R.E., & Gates, C. (1985), Critical treatment issues in suicide among schizophrenics. *Hosp. & Commun. Psychiat.*, 36/5:534–535.

Demos, J. (1970), *A Little Commonwealth: Family Life in Plymouth Colony*. New York: Oxford University Press.

Deykin, E. (1983), Teenage suicide: Can it be prevented? *Focus*, 11:1–3.

———— Perlow, R., & McNamarra, J. (1985), Non-fatal suicidal and life-threatening behavior among 13 to 17 year old adolescents seeking emergency medical care. *Amer. J. Pub. Health*, 75:90–92.

Dietz, J. (1984), Dealing with teen suicides. *Boston Globe*, November 12, p. 39.

Dorwart, R.A., & Meyers, W.R. (1981), *Citizen Participation in Mental Health: Research and Social Policy*. Springfield, IL: Charles C Thomas.

Drake, R.E., Gates, C., & Cotton, P.G. (1985), Suicide among schizophrenics: A review. *Comprehen. Psychiat.*, 26:90–100.

Dumont, M.P. (1968), *The Absurd Healer: Perspectives of a Community Psychiatrist*. New York: Viking Press.

Durkheim, E. (1897), *Suicide: A Study in Sociology*, trans. J.A. Spaulding & G. Simpson. New York: Free Press, 1951.

Eastwood, R. (1980), Suicide and parasuicide. In: *Public Health and Preventive Medicine*, 11th ed., ed. J.M. Last. New York: Appleton-Century-Crofts.

Fox, R. (1977), Suicide prevention in Great Britain. *Ment. Health Soc.*, 4:74–79.

Freedman, R., & Moran, A. (1984), Wanderers in a promised land: The chronically mentally ill and deinstitutionalization. *Med. Care* (Suppl.), 22 (2).

Gabrielson, I.W., Klerman, L.B., Currie, J.B., Tyler, N.C., & Jekel, J.F. (1970), Suicide attempts in a population pregnant as teenagers. *Amer. J. Pub. Health*, 60:2289–2301.

Glasscote, R.M., Kohn, E., Beigel, A., Raber, M.F., Roeske, N., Cox, B.A., Raybin, J.B., & Bloom, B.L. (1980), *Preventing Mental Illness: Efforts and Attitudes*. Washington, DC: Joint Information Service.

Greenblatt, M. (1984), The future of community psychiatry: The therapeutic society. In: *Current Themes in Psychiatry*, Vol. 3, eds. T. Gaind & F. Fawzy. New York: Spectrum Publications.

Guest, J. (1976), *Ordinary People*. New York: Ballantine Books.

Haitch, R. (1985), Follow-up on the news. *New York Times*, January 20, p. 33.

Hamermesh, A.S., & Soss, N.M. (1974), An economic theory of suicide. *J. Polit. Ec.*, 82:83–98.

Hassall, C., & Trethowan W.H. (1972), Suicide in Birmingham. *Brit. Med. J.*, March:717–718.

Holinger, P.C., & Offer, D. (1982), Prediction of adolescent suicide: A population model. *Amer. J. Psychiat.*, 139:302–307.

Institute of Medicine (1985), Research on mental illness and addictive disorders: Progress and prospects. *Amer. J. Psychiat.* (Suppl.), 142:7.

Jacobs, D. (1983), The treatment capabilities of psychiatric emergency services. *Gen. Hosp. Psychiat.*, 5:171–177.

Jamison, K.R., & Akiskal, H.S. (1982), Medication compliance in patients with bipolar disorder. *Psychiat. Clin. N. Amer.*, 6:175–192.

Klein, D.C., & Goldston, S.E. (1977), *Primary Prevention: An Idea Whose Time Has Come*, DHEW Pub. No. (ADM)77-447. Washington, DC: U.S. Government Printing Office.

Kleiner, G.J., & Greston, W.M., eds. (1984), *Suicide in Pregnancy*. Boston: John Wright PSG Inc.

Klerman, G.L. (1985), Trends in utilization of mental health services: Perspectives for health services research. *Med. Care*, 23:1–14.

——— (1986), Epidemiology and mental health policy. In: *Epidemiology and Health Policy*, eds. S. Levine & A. Lilienfeld. New York: Methuen.

Konopka, G. (1983), Adolescent suicide. *Except. Child.*, 49:390–394.

Kraft, S. (1983), Mom . . . I am taking the easy way out. *Boston Globe*, March 22, pp. 1 & 10.

Lamb, H.R., ed. (1984), *The Homeless Mentally Ill*. Washington, DC: American Psychiatric Association Press.

Last, J.M., ed. (1980), *Public Health and Preventive Medicine*, 11th ed. New York: Appleton-Century-Crofts.

Lester, D., & Murrel, M.E. (1980), The influence of gun control laws on suicidal behavior. *Amer. J. Psychiat.*, 137:121–122.

Macht, L.B., Scherl D.J., & Sharfstein, S. (1977), *Neighborhood Psychiatry*. Lexington, MA: Lexington Books.

Mack, J.E., & Hickler, H. (1981), *Vivienne: The Life and Suicide of an Adolescent Girl*. New York: New American Library.

MacMahon, B., Johnson, S., & Pugh, T.F. (1963) Relation of suicide rates to social conditions. *Pub. Health Rep.*, 78:285–293.

Malleson, A. (1973), Suicide prevention: Myth or mandate. *Brit. J. Psychiat.*, 122:238–239.

Markush, R.E., & Bartolucci, A.A. (1984), Firearms and suicide in the United States. *Amer. J. Pub. Health*, 74:123–127.

McArnarvey, E.R. (1979), Adolescent and young adult suicide in the U.S. A reflection of societal unrest? *Adolescence*, 14:765–773.

McClure, G.M.G. (1984), Trends in suicide rate for England and Wales 1975–80. *Brit. J. Psychiat.*, 144:119–126.

Miller, H.L., Coombs, D.W., Leeper, J.D., & Barton, S.N. (1984), An analysis of the effects of suicide prevention facilities on suicide rates in the United States. *Amer. J. Pub. Health*, 74:340–343.

Naha, E. (1982), *The Suicide Plague*. New York: Bantam Books.

National Center for Health Statistics (1984), *Health: United States*. PHS 84-1232. Washington, DC: U.S. Government Printing Office.

National Institute of Mental Health (1985), *Mental Health: United States*, eds. C.A. Taube and S.A. Barrett, DHHS Pub. No. (AOM) 85–1378. Washington, DC: U.S. Government Printing Office.

New York Times (1984), When children bear children (editorial). August 1.

Oliver, R.G., & Hetzel, B.S. (1973), An analysis of recent trends in suicide rates in Australia. *Internat. J. Epidem.*, 2:91–101.

Otto, U. (1972), Suicidal acts by children and adolescents (a follow-up study). *Acta Psychiat. Scand.*, (Suppl.) 233:1–123.

Robins, E. (1985), Suicide. In: *Comprehensive Textbook of Psychiatry*, 4th ed., Vol. 2, eds. H.I. Kaplan & B.J. Sadock. Baltimore, MD: Williams & Wilkins.

Rosenberg, M.L., Mercy J.A., & Smith, J.C. (1984), Violence as a public health problem: A new role for the CDC and a new alliance with educators. *Ed. Horiz.*, 62/4:124–127.

Sarason, S.B. (1974), *The Psychological Sense of Community: Prospects for a Community Psychology*. San Francisco: Jossey-Bass.

Sawyer, J.B., & Jameton, E.M. (1979), Chronic callers to a suicide prevention center. *Suicide & Life-Threat. Behav.*, 9:97–104.

Schlesinger, M., & Dorwart, R. (1984), Ownership and mental-health services: A reappraisal of the shift toward privately owned facilities. *N. Eng. J. Med.*, 311:959–965.

Shaffer, D. (1985), Adolescent suicide. Paper presented at the National Conference on Youth Suicide, Washington, DC, June 19–20.

Silverman, P. (1985), Mutual help groups. *Harvard Ment. Health Letter*, 1/11:4–6.

Starr, P. (1982), *The Social Transformation of American Medicine*. New York: Basic Books.

The Sun, Hartford County Bureau (1983), Pregnant girl kneels down on railroad tracks and meets her death. March 17, p. D14.

U.S. Department of Health and Human Services (1979), *Healthy People*, Serial # 017-001-00416-2. Washington, DC: U.S. Government Printing Office.

———— (1984), *Health: United States*. Washington, DC: Government Printing Office, PHS 84-1232.

Varah, E.C. (1965), *The Samaritans*. London: Constable Press.

Vigderhous, G., & Fishman, G. (1978), The impact of unemployment and familial integration on changing suicide rates in the USA. *Soc. Psychiat.*, 13:239–248.

Vital Statistics of the United States Government, 1961–1975: Mortality (1977). Washington, DC: U.S. Government Printing Office.

Wiebe, R.H. (1967), *The Search for Order: 1877–1920*. New York: Hill & Wang.

Weiner, I.W. (1969), The effectiveness of a suicide prevention program. *Ment. Hyg.*, 53:357–363.

World Health Organization (1968), *Prevention of Suicide*. Geneva: World Health Organization, Public Health Paper No. 35.

Youth Suicide Prevention Act of 1985. Presented April 2, 1985 in the House of Representatives before the 99th Congress by Representative Tom Lantos.

Part **I**

Foundations

3

The Psychological Vulnerability to Suicide

Dan H. Buie, M.D.
John T. Maltsberger, M.D.

SUICIDE VULNERABILITY AND THE USE OF SELF OBJECTS

There are three motives for suicide: two involve murder, and one an escape from pain. Murder meant for another individual may be carried out on the person of the self. Murder also may be meant for the self or a component of the self. Suicide for relief from suffering is not psychologically a murder because it is not meant to induce death. Caught up in the illusion that death offers escape into a timeless place of peace and rest, a miserable patient may kill himself. Attempts at suicide may aim to accomplish one purpose predominantly. Various forms the motives take have been described elsewhere and need not be detailed here (Maltsberger and Buie, 1980). What must occupy us is the nature of psychological vulnerability that predisposes to suicide. Consider first the incapacity to endure solitude.

Normal psychological development from infancy through adolescence through middle age gradually increases the capacity for emotional autonomy. It is not that a mature adult chooses always to live independently of the emotional nourishment of mutually loving and esteeming relationships; sometimes he may elect to do so, or necessity may compel it. Such a person will tolerate degrees of loneliness, depression, anxiety, and anger. Individuals who have achieved less autonomy do not have this option. By virtue of their incomplete development they must depend on resources external to themselves to sustain their psychological integrity. The defects in their development and their imperative dependency are the subject of wide-ranging studies and researches. We cannot review them here but can present only a generalized summary of our understanding as it pertains to assessment of persons who are suicide prone. We have studied clinical suicide intensively for the past 15 years and have been aided especially by the contributions of certain authors (Winnicott, 1960; Fraiberg, 1969).

Two threats underlie suicide vulnerability. One is loss of the psychological self through mental disintegration. The other is overwhelming negative self-judgment. The sense of worthlessness and the sense of guilt can both be more than the mind can sustain. The threat of psychological disintegration arises from an intolerably intense experience of aloneness (Adler and Buie, 1979). Aloneness is to be distinguished from loneliness. Loneliness is the bearable experience of being by oneself and yearning for companionship. A lonely man is able partially to recapture the subjective well-being that human proximity has previously brought him through remembering and imagining experiences of companionship. The capacity in fantasy to feel as if one is present with someone desired is possible only for those individuals who have the capacity to form introjects. For this discussion we define introjects as memories composed not only of ideas and images but also of feelings that have impact on the affective state of the self. To remember the well-being arising from actual companionship while having to "make do" with an introject gives rise to the unpleasant if endurable aspect of loneliness.

From the earliest months of life psychological survival requires adequate comforting and love from others. True separation–individuation becomes possible only to the degree that emotional resources for self-soothing develop internally. Soothing introjects are a means of gaining internal security: they develop through the confluence of neuropsychological maturation processes and the experience of consistent caring, soothing, and holding. With further maturation certain parts of the self, such as a solid sense of identity, progressively add to the internal resources of security. A large proportion of persons vulnerable to suicide have acquired few such resources, and they are especially deficient in soothing introjects. They must look to resources external to themselves for a sense of comfort, and without them they experience aloneness.

By the subjective experience of aloneness we do not refer to the sadness of ordinary solitude. Aloneness is a subjective state of vacant, cold isolation without hope of comfort from within or without; it is accompanied by varying degrees of fear and horror that may amount to terror. It may be felt in lesser degrees as an agitating sense of disquiet, but essentially it is akin to the panic of the screaming infant overwhelmed with separation anxiety. It involves to some degree the sense of dying.

Suicidal persons are vulnerable to the extremes of aloneness, and at the extreme it is experienced as impending annihilation, as loss of the self. Frightening if lesser degrees of aloneness permeate the mental content of these patients, but its extreme is rarely seen because it is modulated by medications or avoided through suicide attempts, psychotic defenses, perversions, or addictions.

It is usually other persons who supply the aloneness-vulnerable individual with the soothing security he cannot supply himself. So long as external resources are available to supplement the meager internal resources, aloneness is not a problem and suicide is not a threat. When external resources fail, or the capacity to use them is fouled by fears of closeness (as in borderline conditions), or internal resources are lost beyond the level that can be replenished from without, suicide becomes a risk. Let us set aside the matter of solitude and the effect of aloneness for a moment and take up the other difficulty that can predispose to suicide—negative self-judgment.

In recent years Kohut (1971) has drawn attention to the need for feeling valuable if self-cohesion is to be maintained. He has outlined the ways in which children and narcissistically immature persons must use other people to maintain a sense of worth, that is, through idealizations (perfection can be shared if one is close to a perfect friend) and through "mirroring" from others of some reflection of value (without such mirroring some people cannot affectively value their own good qualities). Others who, as idealized or mirroring objects, enable the immature person to feel narcissistically valuable Kohut calls *self objects*. The availability of adequate narcissistic self objects during the formative years makes possible the evolution of those internal resources needed to maintain a realistic sense of self-value. Introjects derived from experiences with these self objects (self object introjects) as well as parts of the self (such as the ego ideal) come to constitute such internal resources and make possible increasing autonomy in maintaining narcissistic equilibrium. When they lose their self objects, persons who lack such internal resources are vulnerable not only to the fragmentation that Kohut describes, but also to a particular kind of depressive affect related to feelings of personal worthlessness. (Loss of cohesiveness of the self, fragmentation, is much less traumatic than the threat of annihilation that aloneness can bring. Fragmentation only affects the quality of functioning and integration of functioning of the components of the self. For example, the integration of various self-images that allows a sense of coherent personal identity may be lost so that the individual's sense of himself becomes uncertain as it shifts among various seemingly disparate self-images. But the survival of the self is not brought into question.) It is the depressive experience, not self fragmentation, that can promote suicide. The depression brings intolerable feelings of worthlessness and arouses harsh, sadistic self-contempt. A person may feel loved and comforted but at the same time utterly worthless. So painful may the sense of worthlessness be and so great may be the self-contempt that the wish to be rid of oneself can prompt suicide. This motive can be reinforced by hostile contemptuous introjects or expressions of contempt by real external objects.

We have mentioned that suicide becomes a risk when the vulnerable individual is deprived of the external holding—soothing necessary to the psychological survival of the self. It is reasonable to apply Kohut's term self object to any object that performs any function for maintaining the self which in maturity the self does for the self. It follows that in some individuals self objects to support a sense of self-value are vital, and self objects to ward off aloneness are sometimes essential also. When self objects are lost, vulnerable people fall prey to dangerous affects of worthlessness or aloneness (sometimes to both at once). Their survival is then in danger.

When faced with threat to survival human beings are ready to fight and are animated by hate and rage. Self objects that threaten abandonment or actually go away become the objects of such fury, whether the threatening loss is actual or is the result of the subject's momentary incapacity to use the self object. A self object that fails to meet a vital need becomes the object of murderous hate; this is one of the sources of a suicide's drive to kill.

Should the homicidal fury be turned around against the self suicide may occur, and the self object will be spared. The person of the self often becomes the target of attack because the self object is not only hated but loved. Sometimes the self object is inaccessible. Sometimes the self object may not be a person at all but rather an institution or a group. Where this motive predominates, the balance of choice between suicide and homicide may be narrow.

Sometimes suicide is the psychological equivalent of killing someone else. This was the circumstance described by Freud in "Mourning and Melancholia" (Freud, 1917). The lost self object (Freud referred to an object invested with ego libido) may be introjected and felt to reside within the person of the self. Hate for the self object introject predominates over love, and it becomes the target of attack. That killing it requires self-injury is overlooked or denied; the death of the self is incidental to the act. Some psychotic patients make suicide attempts of this sort in the belief that they will not die and that only the hated person within will be destroyed.

Suicidal individuals are profoundly aggressive. Because of the harshness of superego forerunners that comprise their primitive conscience (Kernberg, 1970), they are also characteristically profoundly intolerant of their murderous drives. The self object that threatens abandonment is hated, but because it is also loved and often highly idealized, the primitive superego often demands punishment according to the Talion principle (he who wishes to kill must die). The primitive conscience dictates turning some of the aggression against the self, just as it does in the negative therapeutic reaction (Freud, 1923). It may inexorably sentence the patient who wishes to kill a loved one to death by his own hand. The influence of the primitive conscience may be augmented by hostile punitive introjects as well as by harshly judgmental real external objects.

The murderous motives for suicide have now been covered. Self objects vital to ward off annihilatory aloneness or to sustain a sense of self-worth make survival seem impossible when they appear to threaten abandonment or in fact become unavailable, and homicidal rage is aroused. Instead of acting it out on the self object, it is turned against the self. Directly motivated killing of the self may be set in motion when the primitive superego demands a Talion death. Feeling worthless and self-contemptuous may also compel self-extermination. Let us now examine the circumstances of suicide carried out to achieve peace.

Sometimes people kill themselves in the illusion that the psychological or physical self will survive the act (Maltsberger and Buie, 1980). No corpse is expected to result—suicide is magic. It transforms existence into a setting of warmth and peace. The content of such illusions varies. Some patients anticipate the grave as a womb of eternal holding by mother earth. Some believe they can rejoin a dead self object by dying themselves. In some psychotic cases such ideas occur as delusions.

Many suicidal patients not obviously deluded are very attached to such fantasies, which at moments of crisis may operate with delusional force. Patients subject to annihilatory aloneness whose self objects are vital for comfort are especially prone to such delusional thought in circumstances of loss. Death promises to restore the lost external holding resource, and to restore it permanently.

Other people may abet suicide committed for such a motive. "At least if he killed himself it would relieve his suffering," they may say. From those moved by the plight of a wretched patient one sometimes hears that suicide is a right, an appropriate exercise of self-determination with which others should not interfere. In another paper we have described the varieties of countertransference therapists experience with suicidal patients (Maltsberger and Buie, 1974). A brief allusion to countertransference participation in suicide must suffice here, but it is certainly clinically commonplace that suicidal patients, consciously or unconsciously, provoke and invite others to collaborate in their deaths. They do so by generating in others pity, hate, rejection, and devaluation that set the stage for a deadly scenario.

CLINICAL ASSESSMENT OF SUICIDE RISK: THE PSYCHODYNAMIC FORMULATION

A patient continuously suicidal for years will be found to suffer from a chronic psychosis or severe character disorder. Prominent in such a personality is a serious limitation in the capacity to use self objects. For such patients close relationships arouse a sense of danger. Schizoid patients may achieve stability through reliance on fantasy relationships or by contriving work or social conditions that support a sense of worth and provide enough but not too much comforting human company. So long as the fantasy resources function, suicide is not a threat. Should reality deprivations intrude too much and dislodge the sustaining fantasy, or should a real relationship develop that upsets the equilibrium, suicide becomes a possibility unless psychosis intervenes to prevent it.

With this example of character formulation let us turn to the matter of clinical evaluation of suicidal patients. We are concerned here with assessment of acutely suicidal patients. The first principle to note is that vulnerability to suicide is found at all levels of descriptive psychopathology and normalcy. The outwardly manifest adjustment of an individual will not necessarily betray extreme dependency on self objects. A successful surgeon may appear well adjusted. When the mirroring of his success and the holding provided by his hospital position are lost due to hand injury, however, hidden dependency may emerge in the form of reactions other than ordinary sadness, anger, and pain. Instead he would be dominated by starker fears, murderous rage, violent self-derision, hopelessness, and the idea that he would be better off dead. Were these reactions sufficiently intense, he might do away with himself. If he developed delusions, a thought disorder, or hallucinations, he would also qualify for a diagnosis of one of the psychoses. If his ego functioning remained more intact and he developed some other symptom, such as intractable pain without evidence of organic disturbances, he would be diagnosed as suffering a neurotic depression with a psychophysiological reaction.

A careful psychiatric history and mental status examination will ordinarily yield enough information about a patient's autonomy and dependency on self objects to permit an accurate appraisal of suicide potential. The history from patient and family plus observations of the patient's behavior with the examiner and others must be refined into a disciplined psychodynamic formulation (Whitehorn, 1944; E. V. Semrad, personal communication).

Formulation of the premorbid personality requires special attention to sectors of the patient's adaptation before breaking down. The examiner appraises what the patient derived from relationships with people, what he derived from his work and other pursuits in his life, what the nature and sources of his self-esteem and self-confidence have been. He assesses the role of the patient's sexual life in his sense of being effective and securely appreciated. He studies the qualities of the patient's guilt and the issues that evoke it. He studies the stability of the patient's identities, both sexually and in various life roles, the psychological mechanisms of defense habitually used, and the capacity for reality testing, at peace and under stress.

From this survey a schema of the sources of strength in the patient's life can be constructed. The formulation can describe the patient's autonomous capacities to maintain self-soothing and self-worth, his solid identity formations and areas of self-confidence, his reality relatedness to the environment, his capacity to use healthy defenses that involve little compromise with reality relatedness, and his capacity for object love. One can also point to potential suicide vulnerability. Does the patient rely on self object relationships? Does the patient idealize objects unrealistically? Must he obtain mirroring admiration from others in order to keep a somewhat grandiose view of himself puffed up? Are his identity formations shallow, is his self-confidence weak, does he habitually use primitive defenses that compromise reality relatedness? Does he rely on fantasy to maintain self-equilibrium? The formulation of the personality prior to the acute illness allows the psychiatrist to estimate what specific losses in the patient's life could promote suicide and what resources are available in his personality and object world to oppose it.

When a patient's personality has been studied in this way the development of a suicidal crisis, how dangerous it may be, and its resolution will be readily intelligible. The patient will have become suicidal because external resources or fantasies vital for a sense of inner comfort and self-value have been lost and because his internal resources are inadequate to replace them. As part of the psychodynamic formulation the critical loss or losses are indentified as precipitating stresses, and the nature of the reaction to these losses is set down in specific detail. The various motives to suicide can be observed as they occur in the individual patient. Does he struggle with the advent of terror, self-worthlessness, self-derogation, murderous rage, primitive guilt? Does he evolve fantasies of eternal peace through death? Does he maintain the capacity to tell fact from fantasy?

It is especially important to determine whether a patient's anger with self or others is of murderous quality. Not to inquire into this possibility (in the case of a genteel old lady in an agitated depression for instance) can mean failure to grasp an essential clue for differentiating a potential suicide from a nonmalignant form of anger. The functional state of the patient's defenses, the degree of ego regression, and the presence of psychotic elements are also essential to note in the formulation.

The psychodynamic formulation is essential to the ongoing assessment and treatment of suicide risk because it tells the psychiatrist what resources for self-soothing or self-value must be restored or replaced, and it clarifies whether the patient needs help to understand and work through a murderous rage with a disappointing self object or to resist the forces of primitive conscience or self-contempt, or assistance in recognizing the false lure of fantasied peace through death. Furthermore, the formulation allows the psychiatrist to think out ahead of time what subsequent events in the patient's life, perhaps in the course of his illness, might heighten suicide hazard. The prudent psychiatrist will be on the lookout for further losses of external resources of soothing or self-worth, further losses of fantasy serving the same ends, or mental status deterioration with loss of reality testing, personality integration, or impulse control. Ongoing occurrences in the patient's life are monitored, then, in the light of this formulation.

In this regard, close awareness and monitoring of important events in the patient's environment is essential. The psychiatrist must know the ongoing realities of a family's disposition toward a suicidal member; to what extent they care, to what extent they are exhausted, to what extent they want him dead. It is vital to know whether an important job or other position is assured or in jeopardy. Sometimes the cooperation of a colleague working closely with the patient's self objects can be lifesaving.

Similarly important is the monitoring of the mental status for signs of weakening self-control, psychosis, or emergence from psychosis. Without alteration of psychodynamic configurations a patient may be more likely to kill himself when psychotic than when sane. This is the case when psychosis brings terror of ego disintegration (Sachar, Kanter, Buie, Engle, and Mehlman, 1970). Delusions and hallucinations may lend more concrete force to introjects or parts of the self which urge murder or death. On the other hand, when psychosis is dominated by ego disorganization, catatonic immobilization, or psychomotor retardation, the patient may be safer from acting on his suicidal dynamics while psychotic and in greater danger of self-destruction when the psychosis recedes. Rage projected onto others in a paranoid state may be turned against the self as the psychosis clears.

ERRORS AND DANGERS IN ASSESSMENT

These comments about assessment of suicide are well known and would not deserve emphasis were it not for the fact that in our experience as consultants we have so frequently observed failures by well-trained psychiatrists and hospital staffs consistently to formulate and plan treatment accordingly. Preventable suicides have followed, and several of these invite more extended comment.

A common error is to sequester the history and case formulation. As treatment proceeds over weeks or months they get relegated to a file drawer and are forgotten as vital tools for accurate assessment of the impact of day-to-day events. It is an error to take for granted family attitudes and job availability. Mild fluctuations in mental status may be observed but their implications for suicidal action overlooked.

Too often clinicians rely on the patient's mental state as an index to suicide hazard, perilously overlooking the current constellation of events and relationships in the perspective of the case formulation. It is well known that psychotically depressed patients are especially in danger of suicide when they begin to improve clinically. It is not sufficiently recognized that patients carrying any diagnosis can likewise grow suicidal when they are clinically improved, even markedly improved. There are two pitfalls here. One is that suicide proneness is primarily a psychodynamic matter; the formal elements of mental illness only secondarily intensify, release, or immobilize it. *The urge to suicide is largely independent of the observable mental state, and it can be intense despite the clearing of symptoms of mental illness.* The other pitfall lies in the caretaker's failure to appreciate that the psychotherapeutic relationship or the hospital environment are important supports. They may replace lost self object resources sufficiently to ameliorate the suicidal drive. While with the therapist or in the hospital the patient really is not suicidal, and with the operation of defenses of denial, repression, and rationalization, the patient may appear to himself as well as others as successfully treated. Discharge this patient from therapy or the hospital into circumstances without restored or replaced self objects, however, and he will again become acutely suicidal. He may be more dangerously suicidal than before. Disappointed and discouraged by exacerbation of his illness, he may conclude he is hopeless and beyond the help of psychiatry. With the current trend toward brief hospitalization this pitfall becomes all the more dangerous. It is essential that discharge of the suicidal patient from hospital or the interruption of other treatment not take place until it is demonstrated that the psychodynamic propensity to suicide particular to the individual patient has been adequately diminished by virtue of restoration or replacement of the vital resources. Otherwise he will likely be overwhelmed with aloneness, worthlessness, or rage, and he may die.

There is a corollary to be stated in regard to all psychotherapeutic treatment, individual, group, or milieu. The initial phase of treatment for acutely suicidal patients (which may be prolonged and may be the only phase) consists of support. The crucial losses must be identified and if restoration cannot be made, replacement must be attempted through involvement in individual or group relationships, in activities, training, or pursuits that are meaningful in context with the individual patient's needs. Psychotherapeutic efforts to work through irretrievable losses by promoting grief are often essential, but they cannot be conducted without adequate ongoing support.

Somatic therapies also are vitally important in lessening or relieving intense pathological affects and may provide life-saving support. They do nothing to alter the underlying vulnerability to suicide, however, and are primarily useful as measures that provide temporary comfort.

A common source of error in suicide assessment is the overreliance on the empathic reactions of the examiner. Empathy is vital in our work, but it has limitations.

Empathy is the process by which one person can know the inner experience of another person in the absence of overt, direct expression of it. Empathy is the single most useful capacity we possess for our professional work, and mental health professionals are accustomed to using it in their moment-to-moment efforts to assess and treat patients. In the course of professional growth the capacity for empathy expands considerably, and its workings occur largely automatically on a preconscious level. It is natural that clinicians develop high levels of competence in empathically derived understanding of patients. Very often they come to regard empathy as if it were a mode of perception in itself independent of ordinary communication. Apart from whether a patient says he is or is not suicidal, the tendency is to weigh empathic impressions heavily in arriving at an assessment. If suicide proneness is felt empathically by the examiner, he is inclined to believe the patient is suicidal whether the patient says he is or not. If suicide proneness is not felt empathically, or if the examiner empathically feels the patient not to be suicidal, he is inclined to assess the patient as not suicidal, especially if the patient claims not to be (sometimes even if he claims he is). By and large empathy is weighted much more heavily in assessing suicide potential than the psychodynamic formulation.

The limitations of empathy have been examined in detail by Buie (1979). On reflection it seems obvious that empathic impressions must be gained through ordinary sense perceptions of visual and auditory cues provided by the patient. A most significant finding in our clinical study of suicides is that many suicidal patients can conceal their suicidal state totally through providing no cues to it. Indeed such patients may manifest instead behavior bespeaking investment in life, interest in the future, engagement with others. This they do in empathically convincing ways. Sometimes they do it with conscious intent; some suicide notes reveal what in life had been intentionally concealed. In other instances the patient is unconscious of the suicidal force at work within him. Suicide impulses can be conscious, preconscious, or unconscious. So can the concealment of the impulses from the careful, empathic examiner. Empathy is an unreliable tool for assessment of suicide.

If the clinician empathically senses a patient is suicidal, and if the patient provides confirmation for the hunch, the empathic reaction was correct. If empathically a patient feels suicidal to the examiner and there is no other corroborative evidence for it (perhaps the patient may even disclaim it), the empathic assessment may or may not be correct. Certainly it must be taken seriously, and one way to estimate its validity is to search for perceived cues the patient unwittingly provided and the examiner had preconsciously registered. When the therapist can recover conscious awareness of such cues, he has good reason for confidence in his empathic assessment. If, however, the patient claims not to be suicidal, is not psychotic, and seems empathically indeed not to be suicidal, it is essential that no confidence be placed in the empathic judgment, and that assessment rest strictly on the case formulation.

Repetitive experience in reviewing cases of suicide and attempted suicide have proven a vital principle in the assessment of suicide potential: the mental status examination and empathic judgment are untrustworthy guides, especially if they suggest that a patient is safe from suicide. The only reliable instrument of assessment is the psychodynamic formulation, through which the current sufficiency or insufficiency of self object resources for soothing and self-worth can be estimated.

The following case helped us formulate this principle; later suicidal deaths have confirmed it. The light such an example gives may help in future suicide prevention.

Case Example

A middle-aged executive was highly successful in his work and family life. He was quiet, confidence inspiring, and often consulted about problems of both a business and personal nature. His relationship with his wife was well-adjusted, and his four adolescent children were developing well. Though socially popular he preferred spending his leisure time alone, pursuing a hobby of designing and building architectural models. He appeared to be a hard-working, obsessional man whose personality was within the range of normal.

Early life had been difficult. His mother had spent time in a sanitorium for tuberculosis; late in her pregnancy with him she relapsed and returned to a sanitorium, where the patient was born. There she remained while the baby was taken home by his father to be cared for by a capable, loving paternal aunt. When he was a year-and-a-half old, his mother returned. Very soon she became intolerant of her sister-in-law, who in response left the house. For the patient this experience seems to have been tantamount to changing mothers at a time when libidinal object constancy (Fraiberg, 1969) had not yet been achieved. His aunt was allowed little contact with him thereafter, although they established a relationship of some warmth late in his adolescence. He and his father, a laborer, were never close.

From late childhood on the patient was a diligent worker. His school performance was outstanding, his peers liked him. But he shared few personal thoughts and feelings with them. He worked after school; there was no time for sports. He seems to have felt secure at home (his mother idolized him), and he was much gratified by the acclaim he received as a student and effective worker.

He supported himself through college, living at home and working part time. Soon after the patient began college his father suffered a series of strokes, became bedridden, and for a full year lay dying in the next room, where his babbling and crying distracted the overworked son. The mother was forced to go to work. After the father died his mother developed severe complications of diabetes. Progressively she approached blindness, and a series of amputations almost immobilized her. Within two years she, too, began having strokes, and the patient, still working and going to school, vowed he would not see her suffer further. He procured a poison, which he planned to administer to her if she became more "gorked out." She died suddenly without his taking that step. As soon as he finished his schooling he moved across the country, vowing never to return to the city where he had suffered so much. For several years he carried the poison meant for his mother in his left pocket because it gave him a comfortable feeling; he did not feel so alone.

While he could to some degree care about people, he could not allow himself fully to love. He married his wife because she expressed her love for him directly but asked no more than quiet affection in return. He was solidly reliable as husband and father, but she took the major responsibility for running the household and raising the children. He was especially invested in work, and he advanced rapidly. To each advancement in school or work he reacted with severe anxiety, which would abate as he proved to himself that he could excel at the new level as he had before. Eventually he was transferred to a large city, where he had no ties, to become manager of a branch of his corporation.

The promotion meant he was ultimately in line for a very high position. A month before the move the aunt who cared for him in infancy died. Breaking his vow, he returned to the city where he grew up to attend her funeral and to settle her affairs. In his new job the patient now became exceedingly anxious; his work performance suffered. Deprived of the gratification of work success he needed to sustain his self-confidence, he became depressed. To discover he was emotionally so vulnerable was a further blow to his tenuous self-esteem. The depression deepened to the point that hospitalization was required.

Upon admission the patient was in a state of severe psychomotor retardation. He felt deeply hopeless. There was no evidence that he was suicidal, nor of psychotic thinking. His wife was very supportive and competent. He was placed on a partial hospitalization program, therefore, to spend nights and weekends at home. Antidepressant drugs were administered and psychotherapy was attempted. Months went by; improvement was very gradual. The patient resisted talking about himself in therapy and maintained a moderately friendly distance from everybody.

He was aware, as was the staff, that his disability insurance was about to end. The corporation had filled his job in the intervening months and it was uncertain what work he could resume with them once he had recovered. The patient's wife tried to be supportive but confided to the social worker that her love for him was getting exhausted. These circumstances moved the staff to consider administering electroshock therapy despite the fact that he was clinically improved. The patient worried whether electroshock would make him "gork out." He was asked whether he was suicidal, and he convincingly said he was not.

At this point the senior ward psychiatrist sought consultation with other colleagues. None of these examined the patient, but they were given the clinical information provided above. They were unanimous in the opinion that he was a high suicide risk and advised he be hospitalized full time. Retrospectively, the reasons for their opinions were clear.

The patient was a man with inadequate intrapsychic capacity to feel secure, worthy, and confident. He was seriously limited in being able to use direct relationships with people other than his wife for supportive purposes. The tone of his life was darkened by the unresolved losses of his aunt (in late infancy as well as recently), his father, and his mother. He was increasingly concerned about his personal stability and safety and was afraid electroshock treatment would make him "gorked out" too. He had long before developed the feeling that through death a person could be afforded peace from suffering. He had carried the intended instrument for killing his mother as a source of personal comfort, much as if it were a transitional object. In adult life he relied heavily on self object resources—his wife and his ever-advancing job positions—for the holding–soothing, esteem, and confidence he needed for self-equilibrium. Now he was beginning to lose his wife's caring, had lost his high-level corporate position, was realistically doubtful about his job future, and was, moreover, facing imminent financial insecurity with the loss of disability pay. By psychodynamic formulation one would expect severe anxiety and hopelessness, even though he did not show evidence of it. One would also expect violent rage against fate, against his corporation, against the hospital staff for not curing him, or with himself for failing, though none of these was observable. The only concrete indication of suicide potential was his veiled hint that he would consider joining his parents in death rather than lose his mind through treatment the hospital might administer.

The senior ward psychiatrist reexamined the patient in the light of this consultation. Although he felt his consultants reasoned plausibly, this crisis had arisen before the psychodynamics of suicide had received intensive systemic study. The consultants had not examined the patient as he had, and he was deeply impressed with his empathic sense that the patient was not suicidal. The examiner's empathic understanding coincided with the patient's stated view of himself, and it was clear that the patient's clinical condition had improved. Other members of the ward staff examined the patient, and on the basis of empathic impressions and in the absence of observable evidence of suicide readiness, they came to similar conclusions. The patient was judged not to be a suicide risk and full-time hospitalization was not instituted.

A few days later the patient became uncharacteristically loving with his family and was solicitous about his wife's difficulty getting to sleep. She was worried about his sudden change but did not call the hospital, as she had been asked to do in the event she developed any concerns. After she fell asleep he got out of bed, put his coveralls on over his pajamas, and drove his car to a gas station where his tank was filled. Then he proceeded to a well-known cliff several miles away. There he killed himself by driving his car at great speed through the metal guard rails and over the side, plunging to the bottom where his car was smashed and burned.

We have observed repeatedly the same error in the assessment of suicide risk. Psychodynamic formulation illuminates this patient's lifelong overdependence on self objects for self-survival, the precipitation of overt mental illness through loss of persons or situations serving self object functions, and the mobilization of particular dynamic motivations for suicide. So it is in other fatal cases. Mental status examination and empathic assessment may suggest the lessening or absence of suicide potential; the patient seems clinically better and positively motivated to live. The patient is discharged, returned to work, or otherwise deprived of the self object support afforded by the treatment situation. In the face of worsening life circumstances, which would by psychodynamic formulation signal increased suicidal danger, more extensive treatment efforts and safeguards are not instituted. Suicide follows.

REFERENCES

Adler, G., & Buie, D.H. (1979), Aloneness and borderline psychopathology: The possible relevance of child development issues. *Internat. J. Psycho-Anal.*, 60:83–96.

Buie, D.H. (1981), Empathy: Its nature and limitations. *J. Amer. Psychoanal. Assn.*, 29:281–307.

Fraiberg, S. (1969), Libidinal object constancy and mental representation. *The Psychoanalytic Study of the Child*, 24:9–47. New York: International Universities Press.

Freud, S. (1917), Mourning and melancholia. *Standard Edition*, 14:237–258. London: Hogarth Press, 1957.

———— (1923), The ego and the id. *Standard Edition*, 19:3–66. London: Hogarth Press, 1961.

Kernberg, O. (1970), A psychoanalytic classification of character pathology. *J. Amer. Psychoanal. Assn.*, 18:800–822.

Kohut, H. (1971), *The Analysis of the Self*. New York: International Universities Press.

Maltsberger, J.T., & Buie, D.H. (1974), Countertransference hate in the treatment of suicidal patients. *Arch. Gen. Psychiat.*, 30:625–633.

———— (1980), The devices of suicide: Revenge, riddance, and rebirth. *Internat. J. Psycho-Anal.*, 7:61–72.

Sachar, E.J., Kanter, S.S., Buie, D.H., Engle, R., & Mehlman, R. (1970), Psychoendocrinology of ego disintegration. *Amer. J. Psychiat.*, 126:1067–1078.

Whitehorn, J.C. (1944), Guide to interviewing and clinical personality study. *Arch. Neurol. & Psychiat.*, 52:197–216.

Winnicott, D.W. (1953), Transitional objects and transitional phenomena. In: *Through Paediatrics to Psycho-Analysis*. New York: Basic Books, pp. 229–242, 1968.

———— (1958), The capacity to be alone. In: *The Maturational Process and the Facilitating Environment*. New York: International Universities Press, pp 29–36, 1965.

———— (1960), Ego distortion in terms of the true and false self. In: *The Maturational Process and the Facilitating Environment*. New York: International Universities Press, pp. 140–152, 1965.

4

Biological Contributions to Suicide

George W. Arana, M.D.
Steven Hyman, M.D.

EVOLUTIONARY PERSPECTIVES

It remains a significant puzzle from an evolutionary perspective that an organism would intentionally commit suicide. Certain species aside from humans manifest suicidal behavior and quasi-suicidal behaviors, usually under stressful circumstances such as threat to individual survival, threat to survival of the social set, or lack of nutrition which threatens survival of the social set. Self-injurious behavior also has been seen in certain animals while in captive states as well as in natural settings. It is not known whether animals suicide in natural settings when confronted with overwhelming stress. A behavior that may be better understood by employing a sociobiological view is the apparently "suicidal" behavior of the Arctic lemming. There is a substantial literature comprised of both folklore and scientific observation regarding the lemming, an Arctic rodent, which occasionally has been noted to migrate in large numbers in an apparently willful, suicidal course (Marsden, 1964). Although their apparently intentional self-injury can be easily interpreted as suicidal behavior, there is little to support this hypothesis. It is generally held that the large-scale migration of lemmings is in response to overpopulation, which results in intense competition for mates and nutrition.

There is evidence that certain butterflies, in the presence of predators, will approach the predator as if to be intentionally destroyed (Blest, 1963; Shapiro, 1976). Rats have been known to die suddenly without obvious physiological cause when faced with inescapable death; also, wild rats occasionally die when handled gently by humans (Richter, 1957, 1958). Primates and rodents have been known to exhibit self-injurious behaviors such as head-banging, self-scratching, and self-biting when reared in complete or partial social isolation (Cross and Harlow, 1965; Harlow and Griffin, 1965). In the face of inescapable pain, horses have been known to bang their heads against the stalls and kill themselves. Dogs and horses have been reported to die in the absence of their masters, often by not caring for themselves

(Einsidler and Hankoff, 1979). Further investigations are necessary to better understand the origins of this seemingly intentional self-injury, sometimes leading to death, which mimics suicidal behavior.

Physiological manipulations such as temporal lobe lesions (Kluver and Bucy, 1939), interventions of the caudate nuclei (Korten, VanDorp, Hustinx, Scheres, and Rutten, 1975), as well as treatment with various drugs including clonidine, a drug known to affect adrenergic mechanisms in the brain (Razzak, Fujiwara, and Ueki, 1975), caffeine (Peters, 1967), and amphetamines (Melzack and Scott, 1957), have been known to elicit self-injury in nonhuman species and has raised the question of whether there are neurobiological factors involved in intentional self-injury.

SUICIDE AMONG PRIMITIVE CULTURES

Suicide is evident in humans at approximately similar rates both in primitive and highly developed cultures, even at times where there are no apparent, life-threatening stresses. Therefore, there is evidence that aside from cultural and social parameters, there are factors unique to humans that may be important as determinants of suicidal behavior. Table 4.1 has figures compiled from three reports in more traditional cultures in which a total of 523 suicides were documented (Elwin, 1943; Bohannan, 1943; Asuni, 1962). When examining the totals among the three reports, it is apparent that causes for suicides seem to be evenly divided between disease (27 percent), psychosis and grief (23 percent), quarrels (28 percent), and other causes (22 percent) (see Table 4.1). It is difficult to know in what manner the diagnosis of psychosis and grief are related to these disorders as described today, or as known in the present nosology of clinical or research criteria, but one

Table 4.1

Apparent Cause of Suicide in Various Cultures

Apparent Cause	India[b]		African Tribes[c]		Nigeria[d]		Totals	
Psychosis	20	(8)	15	(9)	54	(49)	89	(17)
Disease	58	(24)	63	(38)	20	(18)	141	(27)
Grief	17	(7)	6	(4)	6	(6)	29	(6)
Quarrels	109	(45)	26	(16)	14	(13)	149	(28)
Other	41	(17)	58	(35)	16	(15)	155	(22)
Totals	245	(100)	168	(100)	110	(100)	523	(100)
		101		102		101		

Suicides[a]

[a]Percentage calculated for each column of figures appears in parentheses.
[b]Elwin (1943).
[c]Bohannan (1943).
[d]Asuni (1962).

assume it generally describes a certain degree of emotional or psychological turmoil. There are some differences between the three cultures such as a higher rate of suicide in (1) Nigerian tribesmen because of psychosis (49 percent); (2) African tribes (Soga and Gisu) secondary to disease (38 percent); (3) Indians because of quarrels with family or spouse (45 percent). Also, grief as a cause of suicide remains quite constant among the three distinct groups (7, 4 and 6 percent).

A SOCIOBIOLOGICAL SYNTHESIS OF SUICIDE

A common thread in the biological, cross-cultural, and psychiatric literature with regard to suicide is that the individual is in some severely stressful situation that is found to be unbearable and inescapable (deCatanzaro, 1981), which renders the individual debilitated, either in a physical sense (illness, injury, or old age), a social sense (having lost status with tribesmen or kin), or in a perceived sense (psychosis and/or grief following loss of a loved one). The individual then finds himself impaired with regard to ability for survival, and thus is impaired for fitness to survive. From a strictly sociobiological perspective in which individual motives, feelings, and drives are not considered, in this state of reduced fitness, the individual does not possess the capacity to promote the dissemination of his genes, and thus his loss from the gene pool will have little or no impact. To the extent that suicide may occur in such a situation, the death of the individual does not extract from the population residual reproductive capacity or a capacity to promote fitness in other individuals of the species. Hence, suicide under these circumstances removes an individual whose fitness for survival or for facilitating the survival of others in the species is impaired.

The sociobiological argument would view suicide in more developed cultures as consistent with this hypothesis. When suicide occurs in persons who are in their reproductive years, they have often been socially isolated or have become convinced that they will not find a partner to form a family. The sociobiologist also would cite the fact that the group at highest risk to suicide are elderly males living alone, chronically ill, unemployed, and without significant social ties. Similarly, most epidemiologic data shows that those who are single, separated, or divorced are at highest risk for suicide. Those with families tend not to suicide at as high a rate as those without, again, lending credence to the hypothesis that being in a procreative position, or in a situation in which an individual feels that offspring need to be protected, in itself protects from suicide.

Although the sociobiological model is of interest and heuristically relevant, one would not conclude that this hypothesis could explain such a complex behavior as suicide.

HERITABLE FACTORS OF SUICIDE

General Considerations

In examining and reviewing the literature on suicide, it is important to consider the manner in which the data were generated. Although investigators in the field acknowledge the difficulties that are inherent in gathering data on suicide from interviews with relatives, hospital records, death certificates, newspaper clippings, and coroners' reports, it is generally held that suicide figures probably are higher than reported. Thus, in one report, of 30 deaths that were confirmed as suicide, only 26 were reported as such on the death certificate (Tsuang and Woolson, 1978). Another report has presented data in which the real incidence of suicide may be 30 percent higher than the figures given by coroners (Jacobson and Jacobson, 1972). In a related report, it was found that 60 percent of accidental deaths were in persons having a history of mental illness, and the major causes of death were self-poisoning, solitary drowning, and fall from heights (Holding and Barraclough, 1977).

The majority of studies that have examined the relationship between psychiatric illness and suicide have found that there is an increased incidence of suicide among people with certain disorders, particularly affective disorders, alcoholism, and schizophrenia (Tsuang and Woolson, 1978). However, it is understood that suicide can occur in individuals who do not carry a psychiatric diagnosis. Certain twin studies would suggest that a proportion of those who successfully suicide may have inherited this vulnerability independent of psychiatric diagnosis.

Table 4.2

Risk of Suicide Among Relatives of Psychiatric and Control Patients

Diagnostic Group	Morbidity Risk (%)[a]		
	Patients (N)	All Relatives (N)	Relatives of Suicides (N)
Schizophrenia	6.4 (200)	1.2 (1,261)	0.0 (41)
Mania	9.7 (100)	1.5 (844)	9.4 (53)
Depression	8.7 (225)	3.4[b] (2,967)	10.2 (99)
Control	1.0 (150)	0.3 (1,549)	0.0 (0)

Source: M.T. Tsuang (1983), Risk of suicide in the relatives of schizophrenics, manics, depressives, and controls. *J. Clin. Psychiat.*, 44:396.

[a]Suicides $= \dfrac{(N)}{(n + Rm)}$, where N = number per group; n = age-adjusted N; RM = % suicide risk middecade.

[b]Depression vs. schizophrenia, $p < .01$; depression vs. mania, $p < .05$.

Family, Twin, and Genetic Studies of Suicide

In a series of epidemiologic studies on the rate of suicide among a group of carefully diagnosed and traced psychiatric patients, it was found that relatives of patients known to have suicided were at greater risk for suicide than control populations (Tsuang, 1977, 1983; Tsuang and Woolson, 1978). Table 4.2 shows that in affectively ill patients (mania and depression), the morbid risk of suicide among relatives of patients who suicided was approximately 10 percent as compared to zero percent morbid risk in the relatives of schizophrenics and control subjects who suicided (Tsuang, 1983). In a study of 243 patients with a family history of suicide, 48.6 percent had attempted suicide, 91 percent of whom had a form of affective disorder (Roy, 1983). Among the remaining patients with other diagnoses including schizophrenia, depressive neurosis, and personality disorder, a family history of suicide was found to increase significantly the risk for attempted suicide, supporting the hypothesis that suicide may be a heritable behavior.

A powerful method to examine the etiology of a particular behavior that may be influenced both by genetic and environmental factors is to analyze the concordance rate for these behaviors among pairs of twins (Kallman and Anastasio, 1947; Kety, Rosenthal, Wender, and Schulsinger, 1968). In one such review of suicide among 149 twin pairs, of whom 60 were identical (monozygotic) twins, and 98 were fraternal (dizygotic) twins, it was found that nine of the 60 identical twins were concordant for suicide, whereas none of the 98 fraternal twins were concordant for this behavior (Haberlandt, 1967). Statistical analysis revealed that this was significant at the $p < .001$ level (Fisher's exact, one tailed) suggesting that suicide could be influenced by genetic factors (Table 3.3). Of the nine twin pairs concordant for suicide, four were known to have had affective illness in both twins, although not all of the twin pairs had known psychiatric diagnoses (Haberlandt, 1967). Although this finding is evidence that genetic factors play a role in this complicated behavior, the fact that 82 percent of the monozygotic twin pairs were discordant for suicide shows that other factors play strongly into an individual's decision to suicide.

In a series of studies taken from the Danish Twin Adoption series, it was found that the incidence of suicide in the biologic parent predicted clearly and convincingly the incidence of suicide among twin adoptees, whereas suicide in adoptive relatives poorly predicted suicide behavior (Table 4.4; Schulsinger, Kety,

Table 4.3

Suicide in Twins

Type	Number of Pairs[a]	Both Suicided
Monozygotic	51	9
Dizygotic	98	0

From: Haberlandt (1967), *Folia Clinica Inter.*, 17:319.

[a]One member of each pair suicided

Rosenthal, and Wender, 1979). This series of studies stands as the most convincing evidence that heritable factors play a role in suicide. This method of studying twins who are adopted, each into separate homes of nonbiologic parents, is a powerful method for separating environmental from genetic aspects of a behavior as complex as suicide that could be influenced strongly by learning. With this evidence for the influence of heritable factors in suicide, the search for factors involved in biologic suicide is made far more compelling. The question that presents itself is: What gene product or products can produce a vulnerability to suicidal behavior? Although pathophysiologic mechanisms are the eventual goal of biologic research in psychiatric illness, much attention has initially been focused on biologic markers that can aid in diagnosis.

Table 4.4

Suicide in Relatives of Adopted Subjects Who Suicided versus Control

Adoptees (N)	Biologic Relatives		Adoptive Relatives	
	N	Suicides	N	Suicides
Suicide (57)	269	12*	148	0
Control (57)	269	2	150	0

Source: F. Schulsinger, S. S. Kety, D. Rosenthal, and P. H. Wender (1979), In: Origins, Prevention and Treatment of Affective Disorders, eds. M. Schou & E. Stromgren. New York: Academic Press.

*$p < .01$

BIOLOGICAL MARKERS ASSOCIATED WITH SUICIDE

Pituitary–Adrenocortical Axis

The earliest reports in the early 1950s associating suicide with a biochemical abnormality derived from the observations made in patients with Cushing's syndrome among whom emotional disturbances were frequent (Trethowan and Cobb, 1952). Preclinical studies at the time described experiments in animals that found that glucocorticoids mediated electrolyte changes in brain cells and exerted significant effects on intracellular sodium levels (Woodbury, 1958; Swingle, DaVanzo, Glenister, Wagle, Osborn, and Rowen, 1960). A report in the endocrine literature cited seven cases of nervous and mental disorders associated with Cushing's syndrome of which one female experienced a remission of suicidal ideation and risk after she received "deep X-ray therapy to the pituitary gland" (Spillane, 1954). In a more recent report, a study of 35 individuals with Cushing's syndrome revealed that six (17 percent) patients had recurrent suicidal thoughts and two (7 percent) of these had made suicide attempts since the onset of their hypercortisolism (Starkman, Schteingart, and Schork, 1981). Although endocrine profiles with ACTH and urinary free cortisol (UFC) levels are not presented for the subjects who had suicidal ideation or had made suicide attempts, those with the most severe depressive clinical presentations had persistently and significantly elevated ACTH levels (Starkman et al., 1981). The authors highlight that these patients did not present a typical clinical picture of endogenous depression but rather manifested mood and cognitive disturbances that lasted one to two days, rarely exceeding three days' duration. This finding suggests that depressive mood and cognitive symptoms with attendant suicidal thoughts (in 17 percent of the patients) and attempts (in 7 percent of the patients) were not associated with a major depressive syndrome, but rather had a distinct clinical profile and course. This would support a hypothesis that suicidal behavior, at last in a subgroup of patients with hypercortisolism, may not necessarily be associated with a major depressive disorder, and that suicidal behavior may be associated with a dysregulation of the pituitary–adrenal axis.

A 1963 study attempted to explore the relationship between the 24-hour production of adrenal glucocorticoids as measured by urinary output of 17-hydroxycorticosteroids (17-OHCS), an indirect measure of daily cortisol production, and suicide attempts, to assess whether this biochemical test could serve as a predictor of suicide (Bunney and Fawcett, 1965). Of 36 patients admitted for depression, three subsequently suicided; these patients had among the highest levels of mean 17-OHCS as compared to the group as a whole (Bunney and Fawcett, 1965). These authors completed a longitudinal steroid analysis on an additional six patients who subsequently committed suicide and found that the mean urinary 17-OHCS levels in both male and female subjects were significantly elevated when compared to mean levels of 134 controls (Bunney, Fawcett, Davis, and Gifford, 1969). This pattern of urinary 17-OHCS elevation was seen both for an extended period of time prior to the suicide and in the ten days immediately prior to the suicide. This suggested to the authors that repeated elevations of urinary 17-OHCS in at-risk patients should "raise the index of concern" of clinicians (Bunney et al., 1969). In a related study, adrenocortical measures were analyzed in 205 patients admitted because of suicide attempts, threats, or ideation; the six cases who suicided within two years of admission had higher levels of plasma cortisol at 8:30 A.M. (Krieger, 1970). The mean plasma cortisol in the six who suicided was 22.45 μg/dl, whereas the mean plasma cortisol in those who were at risk but did not suicide was 19.53 μg/dl (Krieger, 1970). A subsequent report by this same investigator presented 52 patients with similar clinical presentations and risk for suicide; 13 suicided within 24 months of having body-surface-area-adjusted plasma cortisol levels measured and were found to have significantly higher levels than the nonsuicide group (Krieger, 1974). Table 4.5 shows both the plasma cortisol levels and the adjusted plasma cortisol levels from this report by Kreiger; although both achieve levels of significance, the body surface area adjusted cortisol levels of 11.34 μg/dl for suicide versus 8.51 μg/dl for nonsuicide patients, predicts suicide with greater precision. This led the author to recommend that a patient who is thought to represent a suicide risk with a plasma cortisol level >20 μg/dl in the absence of

Table 4.5

Plasma Cortisol in Suicide versus Nonsuicide Patients

	Suicide[a] $N = 13$	Nonsuicide[a] $N = 39$
8:30 A.M. Plasma cortisol[b]	$21.08 \pm 5.56*$	16.54 ± 2.44
8:30 A.M. Plasma cortisol adjusted for body surface area	$11.34 \pm 3.55**$	8.51 ± 1.22

Source: G. Krieger (1974), *Dis. Nerv. System*, 35:237.

[a]As determined within 2 years of plasma cortisol determination
[b]Mean of 4 values taken at weekly intervals: μg/dl ± S.D.
*$p = 0.025$
**$p = 0.01$

other possible causes for such a high level, should be monitored more closely, have more contact with his therapist, and be followed for a longer period of time in an after-care program (Krieger, 1974). *This in no way implies that an 8:30 A.M. plasma cortisol level less than 20 μg/dl would exclude suicide risk or that a level this high is indicative of suicide.*

More recently, the dexamethasone suppression test (DST), used in endocrinology to aid with the diagnosis of hypercortisolemic states, has been proposed as highly specific for melancholia, which is often associated with suicidal ideation (Carroll, Feinberg, Greden, Tarika, Albala, Haskett, James, Kronfol, Lohr, Steiner,

Table 4.6

DST, Suicide, and Primary Endogenous Depression[a]

	Suicide		
DST[b]	+	−	Total
+	4	92	96
−	0	109	109[c]
Total	4	201	205

Source: W. Coryell, and M. A. Schlesser, *Amer. J. Psychiat.*, 138:1120, 1981.

[a]Feighner Criteria (13).
[b]Criteria after Carroll et al. (1981).

deVigne, and Young, 1981). In a study of 243 inpatients with unipolar depression, four of 205 patients with primary endogenous depression, and one of 38 patients with secondary depression, successfully suicided (Coryell and Schlesser, 1981). Of the 205 with primary endogenous depression, all four patients who suicided were nonsuppressors postdexamethasone (DST[+]), whereas none of this subgroup who were DST[−] subsequently suicided (see Table 4.6). Although preliminary, this study yielded a negative predictive power of 100 percent for suicidality and shows that a DST [+] result in primary endogenous depression *doubles* the chances of suicidality, i.e., from 2 percent (4/205) to 4 percent (4/96) (see Table 4.6). Although there has been a suggestion in the literature that the actual administration of dexamethasone may predispose to suicide in patients that are at risk, this claim has not been substantiated when carefully reviewed (Coryell, 1982).

Another study examined both cortisol and urinary catecholamine levels in 22 psychiatric inpatients with a variety of diagnoses including schizophrenia ($N = 11$), schizoaffective disorder ($N = 7$), manic-depressive disorder ($N = 2$), and unipolar depressed disorder ($N = 2$) (Ostroff, Giller, Bonese, Ebersole, Harkness, and Mason, 1982). These authors reported that two patients successfully suicided and a third made a very serious attempt; these three patients were found to have significant elevations ($p < .01$) of 24-hour urinary free cortisols as compared with 19 control patients (98.0 µg/day versus 51.1 µg/day, respectively), and additionally were found to have significantly lower ($p < .001$) urinary norepinephrine/epinephrine ratios than controls (1.23 vs. 3.12, respectively) (see Table 4.7). Although an intriguing biological finding, the clinical utility and etiologic significance of urinary catecholamines for psychiatric disorders is unclear.

Most recently suicide victims have been found to have reduced binding of corticotropin releasing factor (CRF) in frontal cortex (Nemeroff, Owens, Bissette, Andorn, and Stanley, 1988). CRF hypersecretion is thought to be the basis for cortisol dysregulation in depression. In this study of 26 suicide victims and 29 controls, CRF binding sites were decreased by 23 percent in the brains of those who suicided. This result is consistent with the hypothesis that CRF is hypersecreted in depression with resulting receptor downregulation.

Biogenic Amine Metabolites

Serotonin (5-HT) is a biogenic amine neurotransmitter postulated to be involved in specific CNS functions including sleep and affective regulation. 5-Hydroxyindole-acetic acid (5-HIAA) is the major metabolite of 5-HT and measurement of this metabolite has been used by many investigators as a measure of 5-HT turnover. Several reports have suggested that 5-HIAA may be a useful marker in identifying potential suicide victims. Thus, one group has reported that six of 68 depressed inpatients who attempted suicide by violent means (hanging or drowning) had cerebrospinal fluid (CSF) 5-HIAA levels below 15 ng/ml which differed significantly ($p = .006$) from the mean of nine patients who overdosed with sedative drugs or the mean of the entire inpatient sample (Asberg, Traskman, and Thoren, 1976). Of the 15 patients who attempted suicide, two were successful and both had CSF 5-HIAA levels below 15 ng/ml, suggesting to the investigators that this biological marker may be of utility in predicting suicidality (Asberg et al., 1976). In a follow-up study

Table 4.7

Neuroendocrine Profiles of Suicidal versus Nonsuicidal Psychiatric Patients

Determination	Suicidal (3)[a]	Nonsuicidal (19)[a]
Norepinephrine/Epinephrine Ratio (Mean ± SE)	1.23 ± 0.68*	3.12 ± 0.79
24-Hour Urinary Free Cortisol (μg/day)	98.0 ± 33.1**	51.1 ± 26.4

Source: Ostroff (1982), *Amer. J. Psychiat.*, 139:1323.

[a]Number of patients: Schizophrenic (11), manic-depressive (2), schizoaffective (7), or unipolar depression (2).
*p < .001
**p < .01

in which the investigators profiled CSF 5-HIAA as well as CSF 3-methoxy-4-hydroxyphenyl glycol (MHPG), and CSF homovanillic acid (HVA) in suicidal subjects and normal controls, they confirmed their original finding, although their comparison group now was normal, paid volunteers (Traskman, Asberg, Bertilsson, and Sjostrand, 1981). Violent suicide attempters were found to have markedly lower CSF 5-HIAA ($p < .001$) and moderately lower CSF HVA ($p < .05$) levels than controls (Traskman et al., 1981). In addition, depressed suicide attempters had marked reductions of both CSF 5-HIAA and HVA ($p < .001$); surprisingly, nondepressed suicide attempters also had significant reductions of CSF 5-HIAA, suggesting that suicide behavior, aside from depressive disorders, may have a biological substrate (Traskman et al., 1981). One group has examined CSF 5-HIAA in a group of nondepressed borderline patients with a history of aggressive and suicidal behavior finding a significantly lower level of this serotonin metabolite. They hypothesized that altered serotonin metabolism may be a contributing factor in both aggressive and suicidal behaviors regardless of a diagnosis of depression (Brown, Ebert, Goyer, Jimerson, Klein, Bunney, and Goodwin, 1982). Although a total of ten reports from six separate groups have found a relationship between 5-HIAA and suicidal behavior (Asberg et al., 1976; Brown, Goodwin, Ballenger, Goyev, and Major, 1979; Agren, 1980; Traskman et al., 1981; Banki, Molnar, and Vojnik, 1981: Oreland, Wiberg, Asberg, Traskman, Sjostrand, Thoren, Bertilsson, and Tybring, 1981; van Praag, 1982) another group has found in a series of 45 depressed inpatients of which eight made suicide attempts, that there was no correlation between suicidality and reduced levels of CSF 5-HIAA (Roy-Byrne, Post, Rubinow, Linnoila, Savard, and Davis, 1983). Furthermore, these investigators saw no association between the severity of the suicide attempt and the level of CSF 5-HIAA (Roy-Byrne et al., 1983). This study and another similar report (Vestegaard, Sorenson, Hoppe, Rafaelson, Yates, and Nicolaou, 1978) have been the only negative findings with regard to decreased 5-HIAA in suicidal patients, and in both of these, the patient sample was comprised in large part of bipolar depression. This has raised speculation that bipolar depression may be biochemically distinct from unipolar depression.

It has been postulated on the basis of preclinical studies that serotonergic mechanisms in the CNS may subserve modulation of aggressive behavior (Eichelman, 1979). A clinical correlate of this hypothesis has found support in a report in which a strong negative correlation has been found between CSF 5-HIAA levels and a lifetime history of aggressive behavior in military men with personality disorders (Brown et al., 1979). Many of the patients found to suicide successfully or to make serious attempts in the reports of Asberg (Asberg et al., 1976; Traskman et al., 1981) apparently did so in an impulsive, unpremeditated fashion, suggesting that this behavior might represent a deficiency in control of aggressive impulses with a corresponding dysregulation of central serotonergic mechanisms that may manifest in decreased levels of 5-HIAA. Consistent with decreased 5-HT turnover among suicidal patients, 5-HT receptor binding and β-adrenergic receptor binding were found to be increased in the brains of suicide victims (Mann, Stanley, McBride, and McEwen, 1986), consistent with compensatory upregulation.

CSF magnesium levels have also been studied in suicidal patients and were found to be significantly lower in both depressed and adjustment disorder patients than other patients; these decreased levels of magnesium were correlated with CSF 5-HIAA (Banki, Vojnik, Papp, Bolla, and Arato, 1985). In light of the known relationship between magnesium and serotonin biosynthesis, the authors speculate that magnesium may be necessary to maintain normal serotonin metabolism and that magnesium may be dysregulated as a function of suicide behavior rather than of depression (Brown et al., 1982).

CONCLUSIONS

If genetic predisposition plays a role in determining suicide behavior independent of psychiatric illness (as suggested by several lines of evidence presented here), it is plausible that a biological factor independent of psychiatric diagnosis may be identified in individuals who may be at risk for suicide. Such a marker might prove extremely useful in suicide prevention by helping identify individuals at risk. The independent factors which predispose to suicide might act synergistically with affective disorders and other high-risk states (e.g., alcoholism) to further increase suicidal risk. Although the most promising independent factor investigated to date is serotonin turnover, the evidence is, as yet, far from compelling. Indeed the pharmacology of serotonergic systems in the brain is still quite poorly understood. Given the apparent genetic input into suicide, traditional pharmacologic studies may soon be supplemented by DNA linkage studies, allowing investigators to converge on the biologic factors involved in suicide.

Clinical Implications

Insofar as clinically useful material could be derived from the evidence reviewed here, it would seem reasonable to recommend that a psychiatric evaluation for suicide would not be complete without a thorough family history for suicide. Although family history of suicide certainly should alert the clinician to a higher risk for this behavior, the search for a biological marker to predict more accurately patients likely to suicide would further aid clinicians in their efforts to reduce mortality from this temporary but lethal condition.

REFERENCES

Agren, H. (1980), Symptom patterns in unipolar and bipolar depression correlating with monoamine metabolites in the cerebrospinal fluid: Suicide. *Psychiat. Res.,* 3:225–236.

Asberg, M., Traskman, L., & Thoren, P. (1976), 5-HIAA in the cerebrospinal fluid: A biochemical suicide predictor? *Arch. Gen. Psychiat.,* 33:1193–1197.

Asuni, T. (1962), Suicide in Western Nigeria. *Brit. Med. J.,* 2:1091–1097.

Banki, C.M., Molnar, G., & Vojnik, M. (1981), Cerebrospinal fluid amine metabolites, tryptophan and clinical parameters in depression: Psychopathological symptoms. *J. Affect. Dis.,* 3:81–89.

———— Vojnik, M., Papp, Z., Bolla, K.Z., & Arato, M. (1985), Cerebrospinal fluid magnesium and calcium related to amine metabolites, diagnosis, and suicide attempts. *Biol. Psychiat.,* 20:163–171.

Blest, A.D. (1963), Longevity, palatability, and natural selection in the species of New World saturniid moth. *Nature,* 197:1183–1186.

Bohannon, P. (1943), *African Homicide and Suicide.* Princeton, NJ: Princeton University Press, 1960.

Brown, G.L., Ebert, M.H., Goyer, P.F, Jimerson, D.C., Klein, W.J., Bunney W.E., & Goodwin F.K. (1982), Aggression, suicide, and serotonin: Relationship to CSF amine metabolites. *Amer. J. Psychiat.,* 139:741–746.

———— Goodwin F.K., Ballenger J.C., Goyer, P., & Major, L. (1979), Aggression in humans correlates with cerebrospinal fluid amine metabolites. *Psychiat. Res.,* 1:131–139.

Bunney, W., & Fawcett, J. (1965), Possibilities of a biochemical test for suicide potential. *Arch. Gen. Psychiat.,* 13: 232–239.

———— Fawcett J.A., Davis J.M., & Gifford S. (1969), Further evaluation of urinary 17-hydroxycorticosteroids in suicidal patients. *Arch. Gen. Psychiat.,* 21:138–150.

Carroll, B.J., Feinberg, M., Greden, J.F., Tarika, J., Albala, A.A., Haskett, R.F., James, N.M., Kronfol, Z., Lohr, N., Steiner, M., deVigne, J.P., & Young, E. (1981), A specific laboratory test for the diagnosis of melancholia. *Arch. Gen. Psychiat.,* 38:15–22.

Coryell W. (1982), Suicidal behavior and the DST: Lack of association. *Amer. J. Psychiat.,* 139:1214.

———— Schlesser M.A. (1981), Suicide and the dexamethasone suppression test in unipolar depression. *Amer. J. Psychiat.,* 138:15–22.

Cross, H.A., & Harlow, H.F. (1965), Prolonged and progressive effects of partial isolation on the behavior of Macaque monkeys. *J. Experiment. Res. Pers.,* 1:39–49.

deCatanzaro, D. (1981), *Suicide and Self-Damaging Behavior, A Sociobiological Perspective.* New York: Academic Press.

Eichelman, B. (1979), Role of biogenic amines in aggressive behavior. In: *Psychopharmacology of Aggression,* ed. M. Sandler. New York: Raven Press, pp. 61–93.

Einsidler, B., & Hankoff, L.D. (1979), In: *Suicide Theory and Clinical Aspects,* eds. L.D. Hankoff & B. Einsidler. Littleton, MA: PSG Publishing Company.

Elwin, V. (1943), *Muria Murder and Suicide*. London: Oxford University Press.

Guze, S.B., & Robins, E. (1980), Suicide and primary affective disorders. *Brit. J. Psychiat.*, 117:437–438.

Haberlandt, W.F. (1967), Aportación a la genética del suicidio. *Folia Clin. Int.*, 17:319–322.

Harlow, H.F., & Griffin, G. (1965), Induced mental and social deficits in rhesus monkeys. In: *The Biological Basis of Mental Retardation*, eds. S. Olser & R. Cook. Baltimore, MD: Johns Hopkins Press.

Holding T.A., & Barraclough B.M. (1977), Psychiatric morbidity in a sample of accidents. *Brit. J. Psychiat.*, 130:244–252.

Jacobson, J., & Jacobson, D.M. (1972), Suicide in Brighton. *Brit. J. Psychiat.*, 121:369–377.

Kallman, F., & Anastasio, M.M. (1947), Twin studies on the psychopathology of suicide. *J. Nerv. & Ment. Dis.*, 105:40–55.

Kety, S.S., Rosenthal, D., Wender, P.H., & Schulsinger, F. (1968), The types and prevalence of mental illness in the biological and adoptive families of adopted schizophrenics. *J. Psychiat. Res.*, 6:Suppl. 1, 345–362.

Kluver, H., & Bucy, P.C. (1939), Preliminary analysis of functions of the temporal lobe in monkeys. *Arch. Neurol. & Psychiat.*, 42:979–1000.

Korten, J.J., VanDorp, A., Hustinx, Th.W.J., Scheres, J.M.J., & Rutten, F.J. (1975), Self-mutilation in a case of 49, XXXY chromosomal constitution. *J. Ment. Def. Res.*, 19:63–71.

Krieger, G. (1970), Biochemical predictors of suicide. *Dis. Nerv. System*, 31:479–482.

———— (1974), The plasma level of cortisol as a predictor of suicide. *Dis. Nerv. System*, 35:237–240.

Mann, J.J., Stanley, M., McBride, P.A., & McEwen, B.S. (1986), Increased serotonin$_2$ and β-adrenergic receptor binding in the frontal cortices of suicide victims. *Arch. Gen. Psychiat.*, 43:954–959.

Marsden, W. (1964), *The Lemming Year*. Toronto: Clarke, Irwin.

Melzack, R., & Scott, T.H. (1957), The effects of early experience on the response to pain. *J. Compar. & Physiolog. Psychol.*, 50:155–161.

Nemeroff, C.B., Owens, M.J., Bissette, G., Andorn, A.C., & Stanley, M. (1988), Reduced corticotropin releasing factor binding sites in the frontal cortex of suicide victims. *Arch. Gen. Psychiat.*, 45:577–579.

Oreland, L., Wiberg, A., Asberg, M., Traskman, L., Sjostrand, L., Thoren, P., Bertilsson, L., & Tybring, G. (1981), Platelet MAO activity and monoamine metabolites in cerebrospinal fluid in depressed and suicidal patients and in healthy controls. *Psychiat. Res.*, 4:21–29.

Ostroff, R., Giller, E., Bonese, K., Ebersole, E., Harkness, L., & Mason, J. (1982), Neuroendocrine risk factors of suicidal behavior. *Amer. J. Psychiat.*, 139:1323–1325.

Peters, J.M. (1967), Caffeine induced hemorrhagic automutilation. *Arch. Internat. de Pharmacodynamie et de Therapie*, 169:139–146.

Razzak, A., Fujiwara, M., & Ueki, S. (1975), Automutilation induced by clonidine in mice. *Europ. J. Pharmacol.*, 30:356–359.

Richter, C.P. (1957), On the phenomenon of sudden death in animals and man. *Psychosom. Med.*, 19:191–197.

———— (1958), The phenomenon of unexplained sudden death in animals and man. In: *Physiological Bases of Psychiatry*, ed. W.H. Gantt. Springfield, IL: Charles C Thomas.

Roy, A. (1983), Family history of suicide. *Arch. Gen. Psychiat.*, 40:971–974.

Roy-Byrne, P., Post, R.M., Rubinow, D.R., Linnoila, M., Savard, R., & Davis, D. (1983), CSF 5-HIAA and personal and family history of suicide in affectively ill patients: A negative study. *Psychiat. Res.*, 263–274.

Schulsinger, F., Kety, S.S., Rosenthal, D., & Wender, P.H. (1979), A family study of suicide. In: *Origins, Prevention and Treatment of Affective Disorders*, eds. M. Schou & E. Stromgren. New York: Academic Press, pp. 277–287.

Shapiro, A.M. (1976), Beau geste? *Amer. Nat.*, 110:900–902.

Spillane, J. (1954), Nervous and mental disorders in Cushing's syndrome. *Brain*, 74:72–93.

Starkman, M.N., Schteingart, D.E., & Schork, M.A. (1981), Depressed mood and other psychiatric manifestations of Cushing's syndrome: Relationship to hormone levels. *Psychosom. Med.*, 43:3–18.

Swingle, W.W., DaVanzo, J.P., Glenister, D., Wagle, G., Osborne, M., Rowen, R. (1960), Effect of mineralo- and glucocorticoids on fasted adrenalectomized dogs subjected to electroshock. *Proc. Soc. Exp. Biol. Med.*, 104:184–188.

Traskman, L., Asberg, M., Bertilsson, L., & Sjostrand, L. (1981), Monoamine metabolites in CSF and suicidal behavior. *Arch. Gen. Psychiat.*, 38:631–636.

Trethowan, W.H., & Cobb S. (1952), Neuropsychiatric aspects of Cushing's syndrome. *AMA Arch. Neurol. Psychiat.*, 67:283–309.

Tsuang, M.T. (1977), Genetic factors in suicide. *Dis. Nerv. Sys.*, 38:498–501.

———— (1983), Risk of suicide in the relatives of schizophrenics, manics, depressives, and controls. *J. Clin. Psychiat.*, 44:396–400.

———— Woolson, R.F. (1978), Excess mortality in schizophrenia and affective disorders: Do suicides and accidental deaths solely account for this excess? *Arch. Gen. Psychiat.*, 35:1181–1185.

van Praag, H.M. (1982), Depression, suicide and the metabolism of serotonin in the brain. *J. Affect. Dis.*, 4:275.

Vestergaard, P., Sorenson, T., Hoppe, E., Rafaelson, O.J., Yates C.M., & Nicolaou, N. (1978), Biogenic amine metabolites in cerebrospinal fluid of patients with affective disorders. *Acta Psychiatra Scand.*, 58:88–96.

Woodbury, D.M. (1958), Relation between the adrenal cortex and the central nervous system. *Pharmacol. Rev.*, 10:275–357.

5

The Social Relations of Suicide

Ronald W. Maris, Ph.D.

At least since Esquirol's *Maladies Mentales* (1838) there has been a tendency to assume that suicide is always, and perhaps only, associated with affective mental disorder (Robins, 1981). For example, the French psychiatrist de Fleury (1924) contended that the morbid anxiety into which depressive individuals periodically lapse "is, in the immense majority of cases the only cause of suicide." Throughout its history suicide also has been thought to be related to heredity, temperament, insanity (especially melancholia), alcoholism, and even cosmic factors like the phases of the moon or climate (Lester, 1983, p. 70ff.). However, to some suicidologists it has seemed eminently reasonable to question whether psychological, psychiatric, or biophysical factors alone could adequately explain individual suicides or, especially, account for variations in suicide rates. Put positively, it is argued that social and cultural factors are also related to suicide and suicide rates. Even the most isolated suicides do not take place in an interpersonal or social vacuum (Shneidman, 1985). Clearly, different norms and values of social groups and cultures have been associated with variations in the prevalence of suicide (Farberow, 1975; Bankston, Allen, and Cunningham, 1983; Headley, 1984).

One founder of the sociological study of suicide, Emile Durkheim, went even further. He claimed that since the suicide rate of a group is a social fact, that even individual suicides are usually products of human association or "interaction," explanations of suicide must themselves be social, that is, *not* psychological or psychiatric.[1] Accordingly he wrote:

> Sometimes men who kill themselves have had family sorrow or disappointments to their pride, sometimes they have had to suffer poverty or sickness, at others they have had some moral fault with which they reproach themselves, etc. But we have seen that these individual peculiarities could not explain the social suicide rate; for the latter varies in considerable proportions, whereas the different combinations of circumstances

[1]For a social perspective that is more sympathetic to the concerns of psychiatry, see the work of Durkheim's student Halbwachs (1930).

which constitute the immediate antecedents of individual cases of suicide retain approximately the same relative frequency. They are, therefore, not the determining causes of the act which they precede. Their occasionally important role in the premeditation of suicide is no proof of being a causal one [1897, p. 297].

For Durkheim, structural patterns of human behavior, like suicide rates, required a different, nonpsychological, level of explanation than did the behavior of a particular individual or that of a small group of individuals (Mayhew, 1981). Elsewhere we have gone into great detail expounding Durkheim's theory of society and suicide (Maris, 1969, 1981). Thus, we will spare you yet another exegesis of "Durkheim on suicide." Nevertheless, it will be necessary to highlight a few of Durkheim's major claims. To begin with, Durkheim exaggerated his theoretical perspective, in part in an attempt to help legitimate sociology as an aborning discipline (Alpert, 1939; Giddens, 1971, pp. 36–54, on the Durkheim–Tarde debates). First, the differences between individuals and the social were not as great as Durkheim sometimes made them appear to be. Second, Durkheim emphasized that suicide rates were negatively related to social integration. The less social integration, the higher the suicide rate. Durkheim argued that society gave order and "moral support" to individuals. Like Hobbes, Durkheim believed that without the external constraint and cohesiveness ("solidarity") of social forces, individuals lacked the ability to live together.

> First of all, it can be said that, as collective force is one of the obstacles best calculated to restrain suicide, its weakening involves the development of suicide. When society is strongly integrated, it holds individuals under its control, considers them at its service and, thus, forbids them to dispose willfully of themselves. Accordingly, it opposes their evading their duties to it through death [1897, p. 209].

> Irrespective of any external regulatory force, our capacity for feeling is in itself an insatiable and bottomless abyss. But if nothing external can restrain this capacity, it can only be a source of torment to itself. Unlimited desires are insatiable by definition and insatiability is rightly considered a sign of morbidity [1897, p. 247].

Third, society was thought to be transcendent (as, for example, in the more abstract connotation of the word *institution*) and superior to individuals in much the same way that many religions conceive God to be (Durkheim, 1912). Lack of involvement in society (egoism), or social deregulation (anomie), could leave individuals vulnerable and spawn many types of deviant behavior, including suicide. Durkheim thought that social factors like egoism and anomie could explain high suicide rates.

With the notable exception of Phillips's work (1974, 1979, 1980), most investigations of the social relations of suicides or of the social structure of suicide subsequent to Durkheim's have continued to emphasize the role of social disintegration, social isolation, and status loss in suicide (Henry and Short, 1954; Breed, 1963; Gibbs and Martin, 1964, 1981; Maris, 1969, 1981; Stack, 1980a; Wasserman, 1984). For example, as seen in Table 5.1, Sainsbury (1955) showed that

Table 5.1

Incidence of Social Isolation, Mobility, and Social Disorganization in Each Quartile of the Population of London When Boroughs Are Ranked in Order of Suicide Rate and Their Correlation with Suicide

Quartiles of Population	Isolation				Mobility				Social Disorganization		
	% Persons Living Alone	% Persons Living Alone in One Room	% Persons in Lodgings and Hotels	% Lodging-house Keepers	% Immigrants	% In and Out of Borough Daily	% Foreign-born	% London-born	% Divorced	% Illegitimate	% Delinquent
Upper ¼	35.1	36.1	64.8	57.2	34.9	37.4	37.8	19.0	48.8	36.7	—
2nd ¼	25.2	27.5	12.8	17.2	20.7	21.8	20.8	27.4	19.9	25.6	—
3rd ¼	22.0	21.9	14.1	16.1	23.4	23.4	34.4	26.1	18.9	21.8	—
Lower ¼	17.7	14.5	8.3	9.5	21.0	17.4	7.3	27.5	12.4	15.9	—
Coefficient of correlation (τ) and whether significant (1% level)	0.56 yes	0.43 yes	0.50 yes	0.44 yes	0.37 yes	0.35 yes	0.52 yes	-0.33 yes	0.56 yes	0.57 yes	0.07 no

Source: Peter Sainsbury (1955), Suicide in London. London: Chapman & Hall, p. 41.

when London boroughs with the highest suicide rates were compared with boroughs
with the lowest suicide rates, significant associations emerged among suicide rates
and social isolation, mobility, and social disorganization. Generally speaking, the
higher the suicide rate, the greater the percentage of people living alone, the higher
the percentage of immigrants, and the greater the percentage of divorces.[2] As with
Durkheim's *Suicide,* Sainsbury's data should be interpreted to apply not to individual
suicides in particular areas but rather to *areas* that have high suicide rates (see
Robinson [1950] on "the ecological fallacy").

Post-Durkheim social suicidologists have made numerous methodological
advances in particular, as well as theoretical ones (Stack, 1982). Some have claimed
that Durkheim's concept of "social integration" was not operationally defined and,
thus, was untestable. In an attempt to meet this objection, Gibbs and Martin
introduced that concept of "status integration" (1964) and tried in a series of
empirical tests to demonstrate that suicide rates are negatively related to status
integration (Gibbs and Martin, 1981; Stafford and Gibbs, 1985). The heart of their
theory is that less-frequent occupancy of status sets implies more unstable or
disrupted social relationships, more role conflicts, more incompatible statuses, and
thus, higher suicide rates. For Gibbs and Martin, "status integration" is measured in
three different ways: by the simple proportion of individuals occupying a status set
(the fewer the occupants, the lower the status integration); by the proportions of
status sets squared and summed to give a measure for a more general status set
(usually a column in a table); and by the sum of sums of squares to give a measure for
an entire table. Gibbs and Martin predict that measures of association between status
integration measures and suicide rates for those statuses tend to reveal significant
negative coefficients. For example, in Table 5.2 of the 1964 study, white males have

Table 5.2

Mean Annual Suicide Rates, 1949–1951, and Measures of Occupational Integration, 1950, for Six
Race–Sex Status Configurations, United States

Race–Sex Status Configuration	Occupational Integration Measure	Rank	Suicide Rate	Rank
White Male	.1295	5	18.5	2
Negro Male	.1588	3	6.1	3
Other Male	.1243	6	21.3	1
White Female	.1828	2	5.3	5
Negro Female	.2473	1	1.5	6
Other Female	.1416	4	5.9	4

Source: Jack P. Gibbs and Walter P. Martin (1964), *Status Integration and Suicide.* Eugene, OR: University
of Oregon Press, p. 62.

[2]This is consistent with the theory of Durkheim, according to whom divorce was an indicator of
anomie.

low status integration and a high suicide rate, but black females have high status integration and a low suicide rate. Overall in Table 5.2 the status integration and suicide rates for six race–sex status configurations display a rank-order correlation of −.94, which is highly significant and in the direction predicted.

Unfortunately for status integration theory, the results have not proved to be uniform. Chambliss and Steele (1966) contended that when one of the statuses is not ascribed or when achieved statuses are placed in columns rather than rows, then Gibbs and Martin's results often are not replicated. Additionally, Hagedorn and Labovitz (1966) argued that there are status configurations in which actual occupancy and role conflict could *both* be low. Furthermore, between 1940 and 1950 in the United States the occupational integration of females decreased but female suicide rates also decreased.[3] In short, although Gibbs and Martin's status integration theory of suicide rates is a methodological advance over Durkheim, the evidence to date for status integration theory has been equivocal at best. It should also be noted that even if Gibbs and Martin (1964) were to prove the truth of a derived proposition concerning status integration, this says nothing about the truth of the more general proposition concerning social integration from which it was derived. A valid argument is defined as follows: *if* its premises are true, then its conclusion must also be true. However, there can be a valid argument whose conclusion is true but whose premises are all false. Logical validity is completely independent of the truth of propositions (Copi, 1968). It is noteworthy that Gibbs's later work (1968) mentions only disrupted social relations—the first premise in his original status integration argument.

In fact, in his most recent publication (Stafford and Gibbs, 1985), Gibbs himself concedes that 1970 data simultaneously testing four dimensions of status integration (occupation, marriage, residence, and household) does *not* support status integration theory. Hope is held out only for occupational status integration, which alone still shows significant negative associations with suicide rates. Marshall (1981) has concluded that occupational status confounds many presumed relations, such as the alleged negative association of "great" wars and suicide. When unemployment is held constant, the effect of war on suicide rates is insignificant.

Andrew Henry and James Short (1954) examined "external restraint" and suicide by looking in great detail at variations in business cycles and suicide and homicide rates [see Durkheim's concept of social facts as "external and constraining" (1897); "Locus of control theory," Lefcourt (1976)]. Although they agreed with Durkheim that high social status and low external restraint are associated with high suicide rates, Henry and Short went further by adding what George Homans (1974, chapter 16) might call the subinstitutional variable of "internal restraint" and the concepts of "frustration" and "aggression." Their basic proposition was that suicidal behavior was determined by both external and internal forces operating conjointly. Henry and Short assumed that aggression is often, but not always, a consequence of

[3]Recent data seem to indicate that this trend may be reversing (see *Slater*, 1973; and Maris [1981, Figure 4.3]).

frustration, that business cycles produce variations in the hierarchical ranking of persons and groups, and that frustrations can be generated by interfering with the "goal response" of maintaining a constant or rising position in a status hierarchy relative to the status position of others in the same system. For them, "external restraint" included the notions of vertical restraint (restraint deriving from one's position in a status hierarchy) and horizontal restraint (restraint deriving from the degree of relational involvement with others). Henry and Short claimed that (1) the reactions of both suicide and homicide rates to the business cycle could be interpreted as aggressive reactions to frustration generated by the flow of economic forces (Wasserman, 1984; Stack and Haas, 1984); and (2) frustration varied in its intensity and consequences depending upon sets of institutional and subinstitutional pressures. For example, they suggested that when people are subjected to strong external restraint and weak internal restraint, by virtue of either subordinate social status or intense involvements in social relationships, it is easier for them to blame others when frustration occurs; that is, circumstances favor externally directed aggressions like homicide or assault. But when external restraints are strong, then the self has to bear primary responsibility for frustration; that is, circumstances favor internally directed forms of aggression such as suicide and related types of self-destructive behavior.

Although Henry and Short and Gibbs and Martin used more sophisticated correlational and regression techniques to analyze their data, they essentially supported Durkheim's claim of a direct relationship between social status and suicide rates. Other research on social status and suicide rates has raised serious questions about the claim of a direct relationship between status and suicide rates. Sainsbury (1955), Yap (1958), Breed (1963), Lalli and Turner (1968), Maris (1969, 1981), Breed and Linden (1976), and Stack (1980b) have all found an inverse relationship between social status and suicide. If the lower social classes do have higher suicide rates the possibility exists that strong external restraint causes high suicide potential in conjunction with certain subinstitutional variables, since the lower classes are highly restrained vertically. For example, our Chicago data indicate that when interaction is negative, having significant others may actually increase suicide potential (Perlin and Schmidt, 1975).

Beginning in the 1960s some sociologists began to express fundamental doubts about the adequacy of the Durkheimian approach to the study of suicide. Following in the tradition of Max Weber (1925), George Herbert Mead (1934), and Harold Garfinkel (1967), Jack Douglas (1967, 1970) investigated the "subjective meanings" of suicide and questioned the reliability and validity of "official statistics" on suicide (Jacobs, 1971; Atkinson, 1978). Douglas believed that Durkheim's explanation of the suicide rate was neither operationally defined nor based on data with common social meanings. His three major points were (1) "suicide" has many meanings, (2) suicide cannot be explained until we ascertain what it is we are trying to explain, and (3) the way to arrive at the meanings of suicide is to observe the statements and behavior of individuals engaged in suicidal behaviors. Douglas claimed that the meanings of suicidal actions are "problematic." Indeed suicide has at least cognitive, moral, and affective meanings. The usual procedure in sociology had been to assume that the definitions of suicide are nonproblematic and then to analyze the official statistics (death certificates, coroner's reports, medical records, police files, and so on), as Durkheim, Gibbs and Martin, Henry and Short, Maris, and Stack did. Unfortunately, contended Douglas, there are about as many official statistics as there are officials (Nelson, Farberow, and McKinnon, 1978). It follows, Douglas believed, that official statistics are inadequate data for the study of suicide. According to Douglas, the best way to proceed is by "trying to determine the meanings [of suicide] to the people actually involved, i.e., the meanings to the labeled rather than . . . taking as the definitions the unknown but assumed definitions of officials." Many of the labelers of suicide could not agree among themselves just what "suicide" means. The story has been told of one medical examiner who would certify a death as suicide only if a suicide note was left. Contrary to Durkheim, Douglas argued that there is a need to consider the internal meanings of the external association of suicide and abstract social characteristics like anomie and egoism; that is, he was pleading for what Max Weber called *Verstehen* (1925).

Douglas claimed that it is not possible to predict specific types of social events such as suicide in abstract terms like *anomie* or *egoism*. If the labelers of suicide did not have a common meaning for the word, "official statistics could not be expected to have any significant value in constructing or testing sociological theories of suicide." For example, one could easily argue against Durkheim that the more socially integrated an individual is, the more he and his significant others will try to avoid having his death categorized as a suicide, assuming that suicide is judged negatively (i.e., it follows that upper status suicides will be underrepresented in the official statistics). Douglas emphasized the need to get at the "situated meanings" of suicide rather than their abstract meanings. He advocated a basic reorientation of sociological work in suicide in the direction of "intensive observation, description, and analysis of individual cases of suicide" (cf. Light, 1972). At this point Douglas seemed to be advocating a medical model of intensive examination of particular cases, for to him the most important sources of information on suicidal phenomena were the transcriptions and reconstructions of what individuals who made suicidal statements or committed suicidal actions said or did, and in what sequence. Clearly Douglas was influenced by Garfinkel's (1967) "ethnomethodology"; namely, uncovering the unstated, implicit, commonsense perceptions held and acted upon by participants in a situation (Douglas, 1970). [For a critical review of Garfinkel, see Coleman (1968); for a critical review of Douglas, see Maris (1975).]

Still other sociologists have contended, in effect, that Durkheim in his reductionistic zeal did not fully explore the implications of this theory of suicide for some types of social phenomena. Most notably, Durkheim underestimated the roles of imitation, suggestion, contagion, and modeling in influencing suicide rates. The most interesting pieces of work in this genre have been done by demographer David

Phillips. First in his Princeton doctoral dissertation (1970) and later in the *American Sociological Review* (1974), Phillips argued that people routinely postpone their deaths (regardless of cause) until just after important social occasions in which they have been meaningfully involved, such as their own birthdays, presidential elections, or Yom Kippur. For example, after constructing a matrix of birthdays and deathdays for 400 famous Americans, Phillips discovered there was a statistically significant dip in deaths (compared with what was expected) in the month before their birthdays, while there was a significant rise in deaths (compared to expected frequencies) in the four months consisting of the birth month and the three months afterward. Phillips speculated that persons who are highly integrated into society and involved with its ceremonies tend to die "postmaturely" in order to participate in those important social ceremonies. [For criticism of Phillips, see Schulz and Bazeman (1980); Kessler and Stripp (1984).]

In a series of later papers (Phillips, 1974, 1979, 1980; Phillips and Bollen, 1985), Phillips introduced evidence that Durkheim did not fully appreciate the impact of suggestibility or contagion upon suicide. As seen in Table 5.3, which reiterates some of Phillips's data, the actual incidence of suicide increased significantly over the expected incidence following the front-page coverage of suicides in *The New York Times* (especially after the suicides of actress Marilyn Monroe and psychiatrist Stephen Ward, who was involved in the British Profumo scandal). Durkheim had claimed that suggestion has only a local effect. In the cases of Monroe and Ward the effect was international. According to Phillips, Durkheim had also contended that suggestion merely precipitates suicides that would happen later anyway. Phillips stated that if that were the case, then we should see a dip in the number of suicides occurring in the months following a front-page story. No such dip was observed, but the time frame might have to be longer than a few months in order to record such dips. Finally, Phillips thought Durkheim was probably right that the effects of suggestibility are relatively small. For example, in Phillips's *New York Times* data overall, the suicide level increased only about 2 to 3 percent after the suicide stories were publicized. In spite of these refinements to Durkheim's claims, Phillips ends up sounding very much like Durkheim when he concludes that "anomic individuals may be particularly susceptible to suicide when the notion of suicide has been heavily publicized" (1974, p. 351). [But see Phillips's later work on suggestibility (1979), Phillips and Bollen (1985).]

In the last ten to fifteen years the sociological study of suicide rates has been curiously obsessed with the influence of imitation. This is curious because imitation is such a small part of the total dynamics of suicide and, most importantly, it is obvious that imitation can never explain why those who are imitated themselves suicide (logically there must be an original suicide who did *not* copy). No doubt part of this preoccupation with imitation or suggestion derives from the sheer tenacity and publication success of David Phillips. Another part comes from the basic challenge suggestibility offers to the heart of Durkheimian explanations of suicide. In a real sense, with imitation those who are most (not least, as Durkheim assumed) socially integrated are most at risk of suicide.

Table 5.3

Rise in the Number of U.S. Suicides after Suicide Stories Are Publicized on the Front Page of *The New York Times*, 1948–67

Name of Publicized Suicide	Date of Suicide Story	Observed No. of Suicides in Mo. after Suicide Story	Expected No. of Suicides in Mo. after Suicide Story	Rise in No. of U.S. Suicides after Suicide Story
Lockridge (author)	Mar. 8, 1948	1,510	1,521.5	−11.5
Landis (film star)	July 6, 1948	1,482	1,457.5	24.5
Brooks (financier)	Aug. 28, 1948	1,250	1,350	−100.0
Holt (betrayed husband)	Mar. 10, 1949	1,583	1,521.5	61.5
Forrestal (ex-secretary of defense)	May 22, 1949	1,549	1,493.5	55.5
Baker (professor)	Apr. 26, 1950	1,600	1,493.5	106.5
Lang (police witness)	Apr. 20, 1951	1,423	1,519.5	−96.5
Soule (professor)	Aug. 4, 1951	1,321	1,342	−21.0
Adamic (writer)	Sept. 5, 1951	1,276	1,258.5	17.5
Stengel (N.J. police chief)	Oct. 7, 1951	1,407	1,296.5	110.5
Feller (U.N. official)	Nov. 14, 1952	1,207	1,229	−22.0
LaFollette (senator)	Feb. 25, 1953[a]	1,435	1,412	23.0
Armstrong (inventor of FM Radio)	Feb. 2, 1954	1,240	1,227	13.0
Hunt (senator)	June 20, 1954	1,458	1,368.5	89.5
Vargas (Brazilian president)	Aug. 25, 1954	1,357	1,321.5	35.5
Norman (Canadian ambassador)	Apr. 5, 1957	1,511	1,649.5	−138.5
Young (financier)	Jan. 26, 1958	1,361	1,352	9.0
Schupler (N.Y.C. councilman)	May 3, 1958	1,672	1,587	85.0
Quiggle (admiral)	July 25, 1958	1,519	1,451	68.0
Zwillman (underworld leader)	Feb. 27, 1959	1,707	1,609	98.0
Bang-Jensen (U.N. diplomat)	Nov. 27, 1959	1,477	1,423	54.0
Smith (police chief)	Mar. 20, 1960	1,669	1,609	60.0
Gedik (Turkish minister)	May 31, 1960	1,568	1,628.5	−60.5
Monroe (film star)	Aug. 6, 1962	1,838	1,640.5	197.5
Graham (publisher) Ward (implicated in Profumo Affair)	Aug. 4, 1963	1,801	1,640.5	160.5
Heyde & Tillman (Nazi officials)[b]	Feb. 14, 1964	1,647	1,584.5	62.5

Table 5.3 *(continued)*

Name of Publicized Suicide	Date of Suicide Story	Observed No. of Suicides in Mo. after Suicide Story	Expected No. of Suicides in Mo. after Suicide Story	Rise in No. of U.S. Suicides after Suicide Story
Lord (N.J. party chief)	June 17, 1965	1,801	1,743	58.0
Burros (KKK leader)	Nov. 1, 1965	1,710	1,652	58.0
Morrison (war critic)	Nov. 3, 1965			
Mott (American in Russian jail)	Jan. 22, 1966	1,757	1,717	40.0
Pike (son of Bishop Pike)	Feb. 5, 1966	1,620	1,567.5	52.5
Kravchenko (Russian defector)	Feb. 26, 1966	1,921	1,853	68.0
LoJui-Ching (Chinese army leader)	Jan. 21, 1967	1,821	1,717	104.0
Amer (Egyptian field marshal)	Sept. 16, 1967	1,770	1,733.5	36.5
Total				1,298.5

Source: David P. Philips (1974), The influence of suggestion on suicide, *American Sociological Review*, 39:344.

[a]All February statistics have been normed for a month of 28 days.
[b]The suicides of Heyde and Tillman were discussed in the same suicide story.

Since the early 1970s Phillips has extended and replicated his first results. He now argues that not only do general suicide rates rise after celebrity suicides, but also that homicide rates rise after heavyweight championship fights, suicide rates rise after soap opera television suicides, airline crashes rise after publicized murder–suicides, and single driver vehicle fatalities rise after publicized suicides. Of course, his findings are much more precise than has been indicated here (e.g., they vary by race, amount and region of newspaper coverage, do not vary with television coverage, and so on).

Phillips's research has generated a host of critics and many nonreplications. For example, Wasserman (1984) using a multivariate time series analysis and controlling for unemployment found that the national suicide rate rose significantly only after publicity of highly celebrated suicides. He also contends that Phillips must control for the confounding influence of the business cycle. Kessler and Stripp (1984), using more accurate data (i.e., daily data) and more sophisticated methods found no evidence of a link between soap opera suicides and subsequent real-life fatalities. Finally, Baron and Reiss (1985)—see Phillips and Bollen's reply (1985)—claimed that imitative effects attributed to mass media events are statistical artifacts of the mortality data, the timing of media events, and the methods of Phillips's research. Most damning, however, is the fact that the *theory* of imitation and suicide rates is seriously underdeveloped. The only theory Phillips advances is a feeble analogy of six possible linkages to biological infection (1980).

Other sociologists (Rushing, 1968; Robins, 1981; Maris, 1981, 1986) have maintained that Durkheim should have incorporated the relationships of suicide with alcoholism and mental illness into his theory. Given what we now know about suicide, alcoholism, and mental illness, Durkheim was certainly wrong to exclude them from a general theory of suicide rates. (Clinard, 1964, pp. 128–157; 189–212). Finally, although Durkheim focused on static status categories, contemporary social suicidologists [especially Breed (1963); Maris (1967, 1971, 1981); Breed and Linden (1976); Wasserman (1984), and Stack (1980a)] have increasingly turned their attention to social mobility and suicide. We should also mention the recent rise of suicide rates in the young (Sudak, Ford, and Rushford, 1984; Maris, 1985) and the decline of suicide rates in the aged (Marshall, 1978). Today sociologists are giving more attention to both age and race as factors in suicide (Swanson and Breed, 1976; Hendin, 1982). For other reviews of work on the social relations of suicide, the reader is referred to Gibbs (1968), Maris (1975, 1981), and Stack (1982).

In the remaining sections of this chapter we will present data from our Chicago studies (Maris, 1969, 1971, 1981) that show that, in terms of at least some of our indicators, suicide completers were more socially isolated than either the nonfatal suicide attempters or natural deaths we studied. Furthermore, both the completers and nonfatal attempters were more anomic and egoistic than the natural deaths, although there were some important differences between the completers and attempters as well. To this extent we tend to agree with Durkheim. However, unlike Durkheim, our "suicidal-careers" concept allows us to ask how our self-destructive samples *became* egoistic or anomic. For the most part, the quality of early social interaction of our suicidal individuals was negative. Self-destructive individuals are not merely people whose social surrounds are disintegrated, anomic, and the like; rather they are people who come to be unregulated and alone through negative, rejecting, angry social relations, and many of them want revenge for these past and present negative interactions. Thus, our theoretical approach will attempt to meld Gibbs's notion of "disrupted social relations," Henry and Short's (1954) conjoint emphasis on social psychology and structural analysis, and Douglas's (1967) plea for getting at the situated meanings of suicide. Focusing on negative interaction, we will review some data on marital and sexual problems, especially among young female suicide attempters. Finally, a case presentation of the poet Sylvia Plath will be made to illustrate our findings and theory.

SOCIAL ISOLATION AND SELF-DESTRUCTIVE BEHAVIORS

What, if anything, is suicidogenic about being alone? It has been argued that suicide is enhanced by the loss of necessary social supports; by increases in levels of hostility and aggressiveness accompanied by a reduction of targets of aggression other than oneself; by greater impulsivity resulting from less external constraint; and by heightened depression, sleep loss, and hopelessness. Durkheim was one of the chief advocates of the "social support" hypothesis (1897). As we have just noted, he saw excessive individuation as giving rise to "egoistic suicide" and emphasized that deviance of all sorts was more likely to occur when the external and constraining influence of society was diluted ["anomic suicide" is considered in Maris (1981, chapter 6)]:

> But society cannot disintegrate without the individual simultaneously detaching himself from social life, without his goals becoming preponderant over those of the community, in a word without his personality tending to surmount the collective personality. The more weakened the groups to which he belongs the less he depends upon them, the more he consequently depends only on himself and recognizes no other rules of conduct than what are founded on his private interests. If we agree to call this state egoism, in which the individual ego asserts itself to excess in the face of the social ego and at its expense, we may call egoistic the special type of suicide springing from excessive individualism [1897, p. 209].

Other investigators have commented that isolated individuals often tend to go along with group judgments, even when they believe the group judgment to be erroneous (Asch, 1955). Assuming that suicide is judged negatively in the society at large, to the degree that one is isolated from these group constraints the probability of suicide might increase. Of course, other kinds of deviance short of suicide might increase as well (Fleck, 1960; Lidz, Fleck, Alanen, and Cornelison et al., 1963). Thus, we must ask whether or not isolation predisposes individuals to *self-destructive deviance.*

There is evidence from both natural and laboratory experiments that social isolation does tend to raise levels of hostility and aggression. For example, as seen in Table 5.4 a summary of reactions to "wintering over" in the Antarctic, small groups of men living in close proximity to one another for periods of six to eight months, but isolated from other people and from the usual amenities of group life, tended to become intellectually inert, insomniac, depressed, covertly hostile, and aggressive in their eating patterns (weight gains of 20–30 pounds were not unusual). A similar natural experiment including both men and women crossing the Atlantic Ocean in a raft (Genoves, 1974) also revealed high levels of irritability and aggression. As we have shown elsewhere (Maris, 1981) depression, irritability, sleep loss, and intellectual impairment are all factors related to suicidal behaviors. In a laboratory experiment, Zimbardo (1969) [see Milgram (1974)] found that subjects who thought they were anonymous were more aggressive than their individually conspicuous peers in another treatment (generally pressing a shock button twice as long). Thus, it does appear that the more alone we are, other things being equal, the more likely we are to behave aggressively *toward others.* And, if Menninger is right, the ego suffers in direct proportion to the aggression it vents upon others (1938). Nevertheless, there are situations of social isolation in which aggression seems less prominent than apathy, disorganization, and simple loss of the will to live. One illustration that readily comes to mind is the behavior of Jews in Nazi concentration camps during World War II (Bettleheim, 1943). Bettleheim reports that there were

Table 5.4

Reactions to "Wintering Over" in the Antarctic[a]

Problems related to the individual's adjustment to close group interdependence, monotony of environment, and absence of accustomed sources of emotional gratification have been studied among groups of volunteers subjected to Antarctic living for six to eight months at isolated U.S. bases. Scientists, officers, and enlisted personnel lived in groups of 12 to 40; each man was assigned a specific job and hence was dependent on every other man. Technical competence, responsibility, and stability in job performance thus became key factors in determining group acceptance and status. Reactions such as those cited below are of special interest in terms of their possible relationship to reactions to the conditions of space travel.

Symptoms Observed

Intellectual inertia	Lack of energy for intellectual pursuits, especially during winter. Earlier plans to catch up on reading or learn a foreign language rarely realized.
Impaired memory and concentration	Varied from absent-mindedness and poor concentration to marked lowering of intellectual acuity and periods of amnesia. Most pronounced during winter months.
Insomnia	Varying degrees of sleeplessness, again mostly in winter. Individual felt tired but unable to relax.
Headaches	Frequent headaches, more common among officer-scientist group than among enlisted men. Appeared to be of psychogenic origin and possibly related to repression and control of hostility.
Hostility	Relatively little overt hostility expressed, probably because of the tremendous need for relatedness and group acceptance in these small, isolated groups. Social censure, in the form of the "silent treatment," inflicted on the occasional troublesome individual; resulted in "long-eye" syndrome—varying degrees of sleeplessness, crying, hallucinations, deterioration in personal hygiene, and a tendency to move aimlessly about or to lie in bed staring blankly into space until again accepted by group.
Depression	Low-grade depression prevalent, particularly during winter months. Of six men who became psychiatric casualties, three diagnosed as cases of relatively severe neurotic depression.
Appetite	Appetite for food greatly increased, possibly because of absence of other gratifications. Weight gains of 20 to 30 pounds not unusual.

Source: Ronald W. Maris (1981), *Pathways to Suicide*. Baltimore, MD: Johns Hopkins Press, p. 112.

[a]This program was initiated during the International Geophysical Year, 1957–1958, and is still continuing on a reduced scale.

almost no suicides in these camps [however, see Steiner (1967) and Ryd (1987)]. In their study of brainwashing by Chinese Communists, Hinkle and Wolff also do *not* accentuate the presence of aggressiveness:

> When the initial period of imprisonment is one of total isolation . . . the complete separation of one prisoner from the companionship and support of others, his utter loneliness, and his prolonged uncertainty have a further disorganizing effect upon him. Fatigue, sleep loss, pain, cold, hunger, and the like augment the injury induced by isolation. . . . With the passage of time, the prisoner usually develops the intense need to be relieved of pressures put upon him and to have some human companionship.

He may have a very strong urge to talk to any human and to be utterly dependent on anyone who will help or befriend him. At about this time he also becomes mentally dull and loses his capacity for discrimination. He becomes malleable and suggestible [1956, p. 173].

In sum, it seems that social isolation produces somewhat different effects depending upon the context of the situation. Aggressiveness and irritability seem to be higher when one is isolated with a few other people, especially when the confines are small and unchanging (Gove and Hughes, 1983). Listlessness or hopelessness seem to be more prevalent when one is totally isolated or confined with others but with no hope of removal. The former situation would appear to be related primarily to relatively low-lethality suicide attempts, whereas the latter situation seems more typical of completed suicide or suicidal equivalents. In both types of social isolation there is increased depression, sleep irregularities, and impairment of intellectual functioning.

In our preliminary review of the suicide outcomes accounted for by the major predictors of the Chicago study (Maris, 1981, Tables 2.2 and 2.3), we saw that Chapin's Social and Organizational Participation Scale and the number of friends who visited the subject in the last month before the suicidal event were moderately strong predictors of suicide attempts and completed suicides. Sainsbury (1955) discovered that the correlation between families living alone in a single room in London and the suicide rate was .43, which was statistically significant at the .01 level. In a related study in Cook County, Illinois, we found that the population per household and the suicide rates in 76 community areas were inversely related ($-.72$), and when age was controlled for, there was still an inverse relationship ($-.60$) (Maris, 1969). In general, then, the greater number of people living in a dwelling unit, the lower the suicide rate in the community area. Apparently, having more people around promotes suicide prevention and intervention. Ganzler (1967) found that not only did suicidal subjects experience more social isolation than controls but they were also less optimistic about any future change in their isolation. As we will see in the next section, perhaps part of their lack of optimism was related to their perception that they were in fact unable to overcome their social isolation. For example, Lester reports that Fawcett and Bunney (1969) discovered that high suicidal-risk subjects were isolated because of their lack of interpersonal skills.

Fawcett *et al.* (1969) studied completed, attempted, and threatened suicides retrospectively. They were divided into high and low risk groups. Those who were judged to be high risks were more likely to have shown a lifelong inability to maintain warm and mutual interdependent relationships. They tended to be interpersonally isolated and disengaged in spite of overtly conventional marriages. They showed an inability to express dependency needs and to obtain support and gratification [Lester, 1972, p. 163].

Finally, Stengel (1963) has pointed out that it may not be social isolation that is the critical factor but rather *changes* in the state of isolation. We know that some people suicide shortly after being put into isolating circumstances such as solitary confinement in jail or prison, but interestingly, it is also the case that suicide often occurs just after release from a highly structured, total institution like a mental hospital.

In our own data we attempted to measure social isolation by the extent of the subject's participation in so-called voluntary organizations,[4] by the number of close friends[5] the subject had in the last year before the suicide attempt or death, and by the marital status of the subject (Maris, 1981). Stuart Chapin's Social Participation Scale (1936) was a Guttman-type scale which measured organizational membership, how often the organization was attended, whether or not the subject made a financial contribution to the organization, whether the subject served on a committee of the organization, and whether or not the subject was an elected officer of the organization. The score for each of the five items was 1 for an affirmative answer, zero for no. The affirmative answers were summed for each item. These totals were multiplied by constants of one, two, three, four, and five, respectively, and then summed to give a total social and organizational score varying from a low of zero to an undetermined high (usually not much more than 20). The actual question asked was, "Please tell me the names of all the organizations in which [name of deceased or suicide attempter] was member, etc." No special effort was made to limit the time reference to recent participation. The data for our three study groups are presented in Table 5.5. Of particular bearing on our argument was the percentage of zero scores on social and organizational participation by suicide completers (54 percent) and nonfatal suicide attempters (43 percent) versus that by natural deaths (30 percent). More than half of the suicide completers did not belong to any organizations.[6] Overall, the natural-death sample was the most active in organizations, but this difference was not statistically significant.[7] The mean organizational participation for all three study groups was less than the mean for normative groups of professionals, managers, and clerical workers, although about 10 percent of the natural death and completed-suicide samples scored in the highest organizational participation category.

Of course, Table 5.5 measures social isolation in the sense of lack of participation in more formally organized, institutionalized social structures. All sociologists are aware that informal organizations—usually interpersonal networks based on friendship, common values, or sometimes opposition to the prescriptions and goals of formal organizations—tend to coexist with formal organizations. Thus,

[4]Church or synagogue, Moose Lodge, Rotary Club, Jaycees, political party, hobby groups, ethnic clubs, professional unions, and so on.

[5]Persons he or she saw frequently and confided in about highly personal matters.

[6]See the bottom of Table 5.5 for *t* tests for significant differences in means. None of the three study groups showed significant differences.

[7]Natural deaths were on the average 20 years older than suicide completers.

Table 5.5

Chapin's Social and Organizational Participation Scale Scores by Sample

Social & Organizational Participation Scores	Natural Deaths	Suicide Attempters	Suicide Completers
0 (low)	30	43	54
1–5	21	17	7
6–10	22	14	13
11–15	14	6	6
16–20	3	9	4
20$^+$ (high)	9	5	10
DK	1	6	6
Total	100%	100%	100%
	(71)	(64)	(266)
X̄ Scores[a]	7.6	5.8	6.5

Source: Ronald W. Maris (1981), *Pathways to Suicide.* Baltimore, MD: Johns Hopkins Press, p. 209.

[a]The Chapin Social Participation scores for selected occupational categories were: professionals and managers, 20; clerical, 16; skilled, 12; semiskilled, 8; unskilled, 4.

t tests for difference of means were

	t	significance
natural deaths versus suicide completers	0.8	n.s.
natural deaths versus suicide attempters	1.2	n.s.
suicide attempters versus suicide completers	−0.5	n.s.

it is possible that someone could score low on Chapin's Social Participation Scale and yet not be socially isolated. One way of doing this would be to have a number of meaningful relationships outside the workplace or voluntary associations. Accordingly we asked: "How many close friends did [the subject] have in the last year; that is, persons [he or she] saw frequently and confided in about highly personal matters?" Table 5.6 reveals that about one-half the suicide completers had no close friends in the final year before their deaths compared with about one-third of the natural deaths and one-fifth of the nonfatal suicide attempters. On the average, natural deaths had about twice as many close friends as suicide completers, even though they were usually much older than the suicide completers. Notice that while the distribution of close friends for natural deaths tends to be bimodal, for suicide completers the distribution is skewed in the direction of having no close friends. In general, then, suicides tend to be the most interpersonally isolated of the three study groups and to experience the highest degree of total nonparticipation (i.e., 0 scores in Table 5.5) in organizations and social groups. This could be in part a function of their relatively advanced age, although the natural deaths were 20 years old, on the average.

One final indicator of social isolation is the degree of involvement in marital and familial relationships, an amalgam of institutional involvement and potentially close personal companionship and support. Durkheim claimed that being married

Table 5.6

Number of Close Friends Subject Had in the Last Year before Suicide Attempt or Death by Sample (percentages)

Number of Close Friends	Natural Deaths	Suicide Attempters	Suicide Completers
0	33	22	49
1	11	11	18
2	13	27	11
3 +	29	35	11
DK	14	5	11
Total	100%	100%	100%
	(71)	(64)	(266)
X̄ Scores[a]	2.4	2.0	1.0

Source: Ronald W. Maris (1981), *Pathways to Suicide*. Baltimore, MD: Johns Hopkins Press, p. 115.

[a]*t* tests for significance of means were:

	t	significance
natural deaths versus suicide completers	3.8	$p < .001$
natural deaths versus suicide attempters	0.9	n.s.
suicide attempters versus suicide completers	4.8	$p < .001$

and having children combated egoism and anomie and, thus, were associated with lower suicide rates (Maris, 1969, pp. 107–114, 1981). Gibbs and Martin (1964) predicted a negative relationship between marriage and the suicide rate that was based on higher status integration among the married. However, they cautioned that

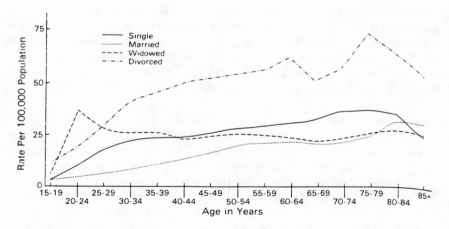

Figure 5.1 Suicide rates by marital status and age, 1959–1961 (three-year averages). Source: National Center for Health Statistics, 1967, p. 7. Cf. Centers for Disease Control (1985) Suicide Surveillance, 1970–1980, April, p. 31.

Table 5.7

Number of Marriages of Subjects by Sample (percentages)

Number of Marriages	Natural Deaths	Suicide Attempters	Suicide Completers
0	6	38	17
1	77	49	65
2	14	8	15
3 +	3	3	3
DK	0	2	0
Total	100%	100%	100%
	(71)	(64)	(266)
X̄ Scores[a]	1.2	0.7	1.1

Source: Ronald W. Maris (1981), *Pathways to Suicide*. Baltimore, MD: Johns Hopkins Press, p. 117.

[a]*t* tests for significance of means were:

	t	significance
natural deaths versus suicide completers		n.s.
natural deaths versus suicide attempters	1.0	*p* < .001
suicide attempters versus suicide completers		*p* < .01

there is nothing inherent in any status that provides immunity to suicide. One must always consider the context of the status. For example, the comparative immunity of married persons to suicide is relative to age. Figure 5.1, from the National Center for Health Statistics, reveals that in general, marriage does protect against suicide. The highest suicide rates are among the divorced except in the 20 to 24 age group, where widowhood has the highest rates (Stack, 1980a). Being single is more suicidogenic than being widowed after the ages 40 to 44. In our own data there was no significant difference in the total number of children born to natural deaths and suicide completers; the mean for both groups was 2.5 children. However, in Table 5.7 there is some evidence that more suicide completers than natural deaths never married (17 percent and 6 percent respectively). In considering similar data, Warren Breed refers not to social isolation but rather to loss of social interaction.[8]

> [T]he loss can take many forms but . . . three forms predominate. These are job ("position"—mostly among men); person (usually the mate, and most frequently among women); and something more general that I will call "mutuality." One or more of these kinds of losses occurs, but the process is not over. Many persons—perhaps all of us—encounter such losses. Two further steps seem to be taken by the person who eventually kills himself. First, he must become aware of the loss and feel it, in the sense of being embarrassed or humiliated by it. This involves the awareness that other people notice the loss . . . and the awareness (whether acute or not) that other people

[8]However, there are parallels in loss of job, mutuality, and spouse to isolation in a formal organization, informal organization, and marriage.

recognize the failure. Second, the individual's particular structure must impel him to suicide rather than some less final course of adaptation [Breed, 1967, pp. 190–191].

This raises the important issue of the role of the *quality* of interaction in suicide (rather than the sheer absence of interaction) and leads us to an examination of what we have chosen to designate "negative interaction."

NEGATIVE INTERACTION

Perhaps the most novel claim of this chapter is not the relative social isolation of suicide completers and nonfatal attempters vis-à-vis natural deaths, but rather the *negative* quality of social relations among many self-destructive individuals. Unlike most investigators, who for the most part restrict their analysis to one point in time, we use suicidal–career data, and, thus, we can see how self-destructive groups and individuals *came to be isolated*. We argue that simply being alone or unregulated is qualitatively different from being rejected, experiencing early trauma in social relationships, being "driven to suicide," and so on. As Perlin and Schmidt have suggested:

> The dynamics maybe more akin to the scapegoating of a given family member, earmarking him as "sick"; in some families that the authors have studied, a member seems to have been pushed toward suicide as a means of resolving a familial conflict.
>
> In one case of known suicide that could be rated on a passive-to-active pressure continuum, the history was obtained from a husband who had cared for his chronically bedridden wife for 20 years. Although the wife suffered chronic pain from severe arthritis and was bitter at her circumstances, she bore the situation in a tenacious manner. Gradually, the husband began to express his distaste for his own care-giving role, to blame his wife more and more for the constriction imposed on his own activities, and to voice barely disguised antipathy toward her for continuing to live. He verbally projected the picture of what he would be "robbed of" in the future, but at the same time expressing concern for her very real physical pain and continued his nursing activities. As the neighborhood deteriorated over the years, he began to talk of burglaries and purchased a gun which he discharged in a "how to work it" session; he then left the loaded gun within arm's reach of his bedridden wife. After the demonstration and a particularly bitter soliloquy, the husband went to work. The wife killed herself shortly afterwards [1975, pp. 156–157].

"Negative interaction" means essentially, interpersonal relationships that are painful, unpleasant, rejecting, and/or isolating (Stephens, 1985). It encompasses Durkheim's concepts of egoism and anomie but goes beyond them. Suicides do not simply lack involvement or experience social surrounds that are deregulated. Suicides and especially nonfatal suicide attempters are often rejected by significant others, feel anger toward and from them (Naroll, 1965); want revenge (Freud, 1917; Menninger, 1938; Jeffreys, 1952; Douglas, 1967, pp. 310–319); look on suicide as murder or revenge (Baechler, 1979). Sociologist Gibbs begins (1968) to build a bridge from Durkheim's concept of social disintegration to our concept of negative interaction by considering the role of "disrupted social relations" in the etiology of suicide:

> An attempt is made in this volume by postulating disruptions of social relations as the etiological factor in suicide, whether variation in the rate or the individual case. The general thesis is stated formally as two propositions: (1) the greater the incidence of disrupted social relations in a population, the higher the suicide rate of that population; and (2) all suicide victims have experienced a set of disrupted social relations that is not found in the history of non-victims.
>
> Unfortunately, neither proposition can be subjected to a specific kind of test, because the concept disruption of social relations does not indicate exactly what evidence would be relevant and also because several qualifications are attached to the propositions. No claim is made that a particular type of disruption is crucial. Instead, the referent is all kinds of disruptions, that is, any instance where a regular pattern of social interaction between two or more persons is interrupted. As such, the concept embraces a wide range of events—the death of a parent, spouse, or child; separation; divorce; termination of employment; some types of residential changes; the termination of a love affair; and some changes in employment situations, to mention only a few possibilities [1968, p. 17].

Clearly, we wish to go further than Gibbs, and when possible to accentuate and specify the traits (other than mere "disruption") and the time sequences of the social relations of suicides and nonfatal attempters. Events like the death of a spouse, separation, divorce, job loss, and so on, are not *merely* disruptions; they are inextricably bound up with certain feeling states, affects, and sentiments and occur in definite patterns in one's life history. Negative interaction, as we define it, includes early separation, lack of feeling close to one's mother and/or father, having parents and siblings with major personal problems, having problems in marriage and with sex, social isolation, job or work troubles, problems with the police (e.g., being arrested), low self-esteem, and wanting to die or to punish someone. The concept encompasses both social–structural and social–psychological variables.[9] What Durkheim and his successors tended to leave out—largely as a consequence of their data base (death certificates and official records), but partly as a consequence of what Mills (1959) might have called their "methodological inhibition" or professional blinders—were subjectively meaningful social processes, such as an individual's social–psychological development.[10]

---

[9]Note, too, that "negative interaction" has some definitional overlap with other Chicago study predictors, such as early trauma and depression.

[10]Socioeconomic status, anomie, and changes in SES and work patterns are different and important enough to warrant special consideration in Maris (1981).

Table 5.8

Negative Interaction Scores by Sample (percentages)

Negative Interaction Scores	Natural Deaths	Suicide Attempters	Suicide Completers
0 (low)	1	0	4
1–10	36	3	20
11–20	34	11	43
21–30	17	27	17
31$^+$ (high)	10	56	14
DK	2	3	2
Total	100%	100%	100%
	(71)	(64)	(266)
$\bar{X}$ NI Scores[a]	18.5	34.6	20.5

Source: Ronald W. Maris (1981), Pathways to Suicide. Baltimore, MD: Johns Hopkins Press, p. 119.

[a]t tests for significance of means were:

	t	significance
natural deaths versus suicide completers	-1.3	n.s.
natural deaths versus suicide attempters	-8.0	$p < .001$
suicide attempters versus suicide completers	8.8	$p < .001$

Turning to our data on negative interaction, in Table 5.8 we observe that high negative interaction differentiates nonfatal suicide attempters from natural deaths, but not suicide completers from natural deaths. This is not surprising, since on many indicators[11] suicide attempters were less isolated than suicide completers, and thus had more opportunities for interactions to be negative. Also, some of the items on the negative interaction scale—notably sexual activity and early family disruption—are either more appropriate for younger people or more easily recalled by them. However, the differences between nonfatal attempters and suicide completers on negative interaction should not be exaggerated. There were moderate-to-strong relationships between early trauma, sexual deviance, depression, and negative interaction for both suicide attempters and suicide completers (Maris, 1981, Table 2.2).

Perhaps these subtleties in the data can best be illustrated by examining some of the subitems that comprise the negative interaction index. Elsewhere we presented the distributions for "closeness to father and mother" from birth until about age sixteen for the subjects in our three study groups (Maris, 1981, Table 4.6). We speculated that self-destructive individuals—especially female attempters—tend to have authoritarian, distant, rejecting fathers, and thus find it difficult to feel close to them or to develop normally as adults:

[11]For example, number of close friends. Tests for significant differences are given at the foot of Table 5.8.

Some researchers have inferred that females whose marital problems contribute to their suicides have unresolved Oedipal problems (or "Electra" problems, if you will). That is, the difficulty of suicidal females with marital relationships both stems from an earlier rejection or abandonment by their fathers, producing feelings of low self-esteem, and symbolizes a larger problem in sustaining any meaningful (i.e., demanding) interpersonal relationships. Women with such early deprivations are seen as excessively dependent, dissatisfied, and demanding of others in an effort to resolve their identity crises (especially the need for validation as a worthwhile human being) and sex-role distortion (excessive instrumental sexual acting-out) (Bowlby, 1960; Spitz, 1946, pp. 224–62) [Maris, 1971, p. 114].

Our research in Chicago revealed that both nonfatal attempters and completers were less close to their parents (especially less close to their fathers) than were natural deaths (Maris, 1981). For example, about 56 to 57 percent of our nonfatal attempters and completers reported that they were "very or fairly close" to their fathers compared with 71 percent of the natural deaths. However, 41 percent of the nonfatal attempters compared with 29 percent of the completers said they were "not very or not at all close" to their fathers. (The response of "closeness to mother" was roughly the same.) Thus, although distance from father and mother does distinguish nonfatal attempters and completers from natural deaths, the negative interaction score on this subitem (especially when applied to fathers) is somewhat higher for attempters than for completers. This finding is consistent with what we discovered earlier about early trauma.

We had speculated that since there appeared to be at least two types of social isolation, (1) being confined with a few others, which tends to generate anger and irritability, and (2) being alone, which tends to generate apathy and listlessness, there might also be at least two types of negative interaction. For example, hate and guilt[12] deriving from negative interaction might be more characteristic of nonfatal suicide attempters, while hopelessness[13] deriving from negative interaction might be more characteristic of suicide completers. Unfortunately, further analysis of subitems in the negative interaction index confounds this interpretation (Table 5.9). For example, 57 percent of *both* nonfatal attempters and completers lost interest in other people in the two months just prior to their deaths compared with only 21 percent of the natural deaths. This indicates higher levels of isolation and probably a greater reaction to prior negative interaction among *all* self-destructive individuals. Hopelessness does not clearly differentiate nonfatal suicide attempters from suicide completers, at least not in our data (Maris, 1981, chapter 8). The hypothesis that nonfatal suicide attempters feel more anger and act more aggressively toward others than completers do, and thus conceive of their attempts as revenge or manipulation, whereas suicide completers are simply hopeless, tired, and wish to die [a hypothesis

[12]Hate and guilt correspond to Menninger's (1938) "wish to kill" and "wish to be killed."
[13]"Hopelessness" corresponds to the "wish to die."

Table 5.9

Percentage Distribution of Negative Interaction Scale Items for Three Study Groups[a]

Scale Items	Natural Deaths	Suicide Attempters	Suicide Completers
S *not* at home until age twenty-five	77	89	70
Very or fairly close to			
Mother	84	75	74
Father	71	56	58
Mainly physical discipline by			
Father	6	25	20
Mother	4	29	8
Multiproblem family of orientation	7	41	9
Reaction of R to S's suicide attempt or death			
Resignation	26	37	58
Relief	73	27	66
Anger	74	48	57
Married two or more times	17	11	21
Multiproblem family of procreation	16	3	3
Marital or dating problems			
Incompatibility	—	8	2
Adultery	1	3	—
Alcoholism	3	3	2
Finances	1	3	1
S ever raped or molested	—	13	2
S has sex-oriented occupation			
(e.g., cocktail waitress)	1	10	2
S frigid	6	25	6
Two or more friendships broken			
within last year	16	5	3
Lost interest in other people	21	57	57
S ever arrested	7	33	13
S's main ambition was happy marriage	33	48	41
S's main ambition was respect	13	6	13
Death seen as definitely or probably			
a way to get even	3	21	47
Total Negative Interaction $\bar{X}$ Score			
(not a percentage)	18.5	34.6	20.5

Source: Ronald W. Maris (1981), *Pathways to Suicide*. Baltimore, MD: Johns Hopkins Press, p. 122.

[a]S = subject; R = respondent.

put forward by Menninger (1938), Shneidman and Farberow (1957, pp. 41–57) and numerous others] is contradicted by some of our data. Almost one-half of the suicide completers (47 percent) were seen as definitely or probably conceiving of their deaths as "a way to get even with someone." Only 21 percent of the nonfatal attempters felt the same way. Thus, at least in our data, self-destruction and revenge, hate, or a disguised wish to kill are not more characteristic of nonfatal attempters than of completers. It does seem to be the case that revenge is a more common motive among nonfatal attempters than among natural deaths (21 and 3 percent respectively).

Table 5.9 summarizes the percentage distributions of individual scale items comprising the negative interaction index. Of the items we have not yet discussed we see that nonfatal suicide attempters are somewhat more likely than the other two study groups to leave home before age twenty-five. This is not surprising, since nonfatal attempters are also much more likely to come from a multiproblem family of origin. There was significantly more physical disciplining of the subject in the two self-destructive groups than in the natural-death group (roughly 30 percent versus 5 percent), with the father doing more of the physical disciplining than the mother in the families of suicide completers. Respondents for suicide completers were much more resigned to the deaths of the subjects than were those for natural deaths. Nonfatal attempters and completers appear to have been more concerned about having a happy marriage than the natural deaths. Finally, sexual problems seem to occur primarily among nonfatal suicide attempters. In considering negative interaction as a whole, it is apparent that the index is not unidimensional. Although negative interaction in general is higher for both self-destructive groups than for natural deaths, it does not clearly discriminate or rank-order nonfatal attempters and completers. On a few items (e.g., closeness to mother or father, loss of interest in people, and having as one's main ambition to be happily married) nonfatal attempters and suicide completers score about the same and are both different from natural deaths. However, on other items (e.g., resignation of the respondent to the subject's death and death being seen as revenge), suicide completers score higher than nonfatal attempters, who in turn score higher than natural deaths. Finally, early separation, multiproblem family of orientation, sexual difficulties, and problems with arrest seem to be relatively unique traits of nonfatal attempters. In order to have a chance to be truly predictive of completed suicide, negative interaction would have to be further specified. Care would have to be taken to delineate the various contexts and types of negative interaction. All social interaction has some negative components. However, it is clear that self-destructive groups experience a greater degree of certain types of negative interaction than do non-self-destructive groups.

SEXUALITY, SUICIDE, AND DEATH

It has always seemed noteworthy that several well-known suicidologists[14] have also been seriously interested in sexual adjustment and maladjustment. In a few cases these same suicidologists have turned from the study of suicide to a primary concern with sex education and couples counseling. Superficially, sexuality and suicide seem

---

[14]For example, two former presidents of the American Association of Suicidology, Robert Litman and Avery Weisman; a former director of the National Center for the Studies of Suicide Prevention, H. L. P. Resnik; and the former coadministrator of the Johns Hopkins University Postdoctoral Fellowship Program in Suicidology, Chester Schmidt, Jr.

like strange bedfellows. Are not sexually active individuals living full, healthy lives? And are not would-be suicides "burned-out craters," ready to renounce life altogether? The answer to both questions is a qualified "no." Sexuality and suicide display a number of similarities.

First, several authors have argued that both suicide attempts and sexual activity serve important ego-defensive purposes. According to Ernest Becker, one of the most common and basic of the purposes of sexuality is to attempt to deny the finitude and decay essential to being human:

> We are witness to the new cult of sensuality that seems to be repeating the sexual naturalism of the ancient Roman world. It is a living for the day alone, with a defiance of tomorrow; an immersion in the body and its immediate experiences and sensations, in the intensity of touch, swelling flesh, taste and smell. Its aim is to deny one's lack of control over events, his powerlessness, his vagueness as a person in a mechanical world spinning into decay and death [Becker, 1973, p. 84].

Or, as psychiatrist Avery Weisman puts it, many so-called "perversions" are only efforts to maintain a semblance of "normality" (1967, p. 272, 1984).

However, both Weisman and Becker leave no doubt that they believe that many sexual defenses are not wholly adaptive. As Becker claims, we cannot expect metaphysical answers from physical bodies:

> No wonder that man is impaled on the horns of sexual problems, why Freud saw that sex was so prominent in human life—especially in the neurotic conflicts of his patients. Sex is an inevitable component of man's confusion over the meaning of his life, a meaning split hopelessly into two realms—symbols (freedom) and body (fate). No wonder, too, that most of us never abandon entirely the early attempts of the child to use the body and its appendages as a fortress or a machine to magically coerce the world. We try to get metaphysical answers out of the body that the body—as a material thing—cannot possibly give [1973, p. 44].

Weisman expressed his doubts about sexual defenses even more crisply: "Some people can adapt to inner problems and impairments only by calling upon methods that actually prevent wholly successful adaptations" (1967, p. 290). Both Weisman and Becker maintain that sexuality can be a risky defense. In fact, some commentators maintain that what is being risked is no less than life itself. Greenwald, for example, contends that at best, sex is a temporary removal activity of limited use in grappling with basic issues of death, hopelessness, and depression (1970). At worst it may also be a form of chronic self-destruction (Harry, 1983). Part of every sexual act is aggressive and narcissistic. Even when sex is tempered and motivated by mature love, its pleasures are still ephemeral and transitory. Nevertheless, Becker and Greenwald (not Weisman) are probably overly harsh in failing to give sufficient credit to the positive aspects of sexual defenses. Even if sexuality is a feeble attempt to deny death or to remove oneself temporarily from anxiety and stress, sexual adaptations and even low-lethality suicide attempts can be life-preserving in the short run:

> [T]he argument is that female suicide attempts (and antecedent behavior) are most appropriately conceived of as partial self-destruction to the end of making life possible—not ending it. The majority of self-destructive women are engaging in forms of ego-defensive risk-taking, which may prove fatal but are intended to be problem solving. The evidence for this assertion is the positive correlations of a cluster of variables with each other and suicide attempts, and the negative correlations of this cluster and attempted suicide with completed suicide. . . . These women's persistent self-destructive coping assumes the character of "life-work," or "achievement in a vocation." The "job" is to stay alive through a kind of psychic surgery; cutting themselves off from pathological families of origin, evolving a narcissistic personality to fend off labels of "worthless" and "inadequate," deviating from prescribed sexual behavior in a maneuver to find warmth and affection, withdrawing from time to time into a subcommunity of drug users, even attempting suicide—a dramatic *communiqué* and a plea to a public that has stigmatized and ostracized them. Although this is not the best of all possible worlds, it seems to work [Maris, 1971, p. 123].

Thus, both sexual acts and low-lethality suicide attempts can be conceived of as psychic defenses, perhaps not the best defenses, but defenses nonetheless.

Second, Weisman argues that "disposition toward suicide is, at times, like sexual desire, because both are preemptory, primitive forces that are difficult to deny" (1967, p. 266). Although we do not have a solid empirical base for this assertion, the claim is being made that nonfatal suicide attempts and sexual acts are both products of drives or needs (e.g., the need to reduce tension). By implication, suicide attempts and sexual acts are affective, nonrational, impulsive, even passionate. There has always been a genre of art and literature in which death and dying are eroticized. Samuel Klausner (1968) argues that too little or too much arousal is painful. People take chances—climb mountains, skydive, hang glide, shoot white-water rapids, and so on—to avoid boredom and experience pleasure (Farberow, 1980). Unfortunately, some of our "arousal jags," sexual as well as nonsexual, get out of control and reach a point of no return in which one's life is not only threatened [and thereby validated and infused with energy, if we are to believe author James Dickey (1970)] but actually lost in the gamble to find it. For some the ultimate high appears to be a composite experience of sexuality, aggression, and death. The popular James Bond novels of Ian Fleming, often provide exactly this mesh except that others die, while the hero Bond and his heroine are constantly dying but are never dead. A prime example occurs in the novel *Live and Let Die*. There a young white woman is captured by black Caribbean islanders and tied between two posts as a sacrifice. With the entire black community assembled on the remote island, the witch doctor dances sensually in rhythm with the writhing movements of his victim. Near the climax of the ritual a chest of poisonous snakes is opened. The witch doctor picks out an exceptionally big one and dances with it around the woman. There is an increasing frenzy to the music with the mounting emotions of the crowd simulating an approaching collective orgasm in which the deadly snake is to be allowed to bite the young woman on the breast, but of course Bond does not allow the woman to be killed.

Third, both sexual acts and nonfatal suicide attempts can be seen as manipulation, control efforts, revenge, a special kind of communication (Fawcett and Bunney, 1969; Stephens, 1984). Erwin Stengel (1964) has commented on the "appeal" nature of attempted suicide. Shneidman and Farberow tap the same dynamic when they speak of suicide as a "cry for help" (1961). Obviously, if you are willing to die, then this fact alone gives you great control over others who prize life highly and emphatically are not willing to die. Just witness the terror that is engendered by the escaped death-row felon. Such an individual has nothing to lose and thereby gains great power. George Homans says somewhat the same thing about "socially dead" individuals: "If a group has done its worst to a member, and the worst has failed, it has effectively lost control over him. It has nothing more to take away from him, and so he has nothing more to lose by not conforming. The cost of his not conforming has vanished" (1974, p. 107). What happens most commonly with nonfatal suicide attempters is that they do not directly jeopardize the significant others' lives but rather make them feel guilty or responsible for the attempt. However, the other people involved are generally not willing to assume the guilt and responsibility for the would-be suicide's death. In a similar manner, sexual acting out can be conceived of as a partial sacrifice of self that relatively few others are willing or emotionally and physically able to make and that therefore helps the sexual deviant to gain control over more timid people and their resources. These people and resources are thought to enhance other aspects of the sexual deviant's life, and thus to be "worth the sacrifice."

If the above reasoning is sound, then self-destructive populations ought to be more sexually active than non-self-destructive populations, such as natural deaths, other things such as age being equal.[15] Furthermore, these sexual activities ought to serve as ego defenses, as drives leading to more arousal, and as a means of manipulation for those attempting suicide. Now, we must admit at the beginning that our methods and survey data are not wholly adequate to test our hypotheses about sexual behaviors, suicide, and death. A relatively nonstructured clinical interview probably would have been much more appropriate. Furthermore, the difference in the ages of the samples confounds some of the interpretations we wish to make. For example, is it the youth of suicide attempters or the fact of having attempted suicide which is related to sexuality among nonfatal attempters? Since the natural deaths and completers are on the whole much older populations, it is hard to

---

[15]This should be true of both deviant and nondeviant sexual activities. Another logical consequence is that sexually deviant populations would tend to be more self-destructive than less sexually deviant populations.

control for age effects. Unfortunately, we were able to establish norms for the routine sexual activities of our three study groups only indirectly. To illustrate, the Beck Depression Inventory does ask if the subject was less interested in sex recently than he or she used to be. About 25 percent of both the nonfatal attempters and suicide completers answered this question in the affirmative compared with about 40 percent of the natural deaths. However, this does not tell us very much, since we do not know how interested in sex the groups were at some prior time. Be all this as it may, our data do take us part way in attempting to answer the questions posed.

Table 5.10 presents sexual deviance scores for our three samples—suicides, nonfatal attempters, and natural deaths. [See Maris (1981, Appendix A, item 30), for an operational definiton of "sexual deviance."] Two major conclusions can be drawn from Table 5.10. First, most *deviant* sexual activity occurs among nonfatal suicide attempters, who are primarily young women. The percentages for "some sexual deviance" from our natural death, nonfatal suicide attempters, and suicide completers were 9 percent, 49 percent, and 11 percent, respectively. Other data suggest that our attempters were more active than natural deaths and completers in a *nondeviant* sexual activity too. Consider that 44 percent of the attempters had sexual intercourse before marriage, while only 15 percent of both the natural deaths and completers had. Also, 29 percent of the attempters admitted to being adulterous at least once, compared with 3 percent of the completers and 1 percent of the natural deaths.[16] When asked if they had "ever had an abortion," 13 percent of the suicide attempters said "yes," but only 5 percent of the completers and less than 1 percent of the natural deaths said "yes." Second, for the most part, sexual activity, deviant or otherwise, did not differentiate natural deaths from completers, although there was a small but consistent trend for completers to be somewhat more sexually active. (However, this could simply be a product of the suicide completer's younger average age.) To pursue the possibility of slightly greater sexual activity among suicide completers than among natural deaths a bit, we do have data that show that the only prostitutes in all three samples were suicide completers; that suicide completers scored higher than natural deaths on adultery, number of abortions, and receiving "bad sexual publicity"; and that on "other unusual sexual habits," completers exceeded even nonfatal attempters by a slight margin.

Thus, excepting a small percentage of suicide completers, sexuality appears to be a factor in self-destruction primarily among nonfatal suicide attempters. We cannot be certain that this relative hyperactivity among suicide attempters has anything to do with their self-destructiveness, although we believe it is an important part of their suicidal careers. One check on our hunch was to inspect Kinsey, Pomeroy, Martin, and Gebhardt (1953) sexual behavior data on nonsuicidal women of about the same age as out attempters (Hunt, 1974). For example, Kinsey et al. found that 18 percent of normal females had been adulterous at least once by age 30 (26 percent by age 40), 25 percent of normal females in their first year of marriage

---

[16]Of course, some of this variation may be attributed to the fact that our data came primarily from the subjects themselves (attempters) and from third-party informants (for completers and natural deaths).

Table 5.10

Sexual Deviance Stories by Sample (percentages)

Sexual Deviance	Natural Deaths	Suicide Attempters	Suicide Completers
None	91	46	87
Some	9	49	11
DK	0	5	2
Total	100%	100%	100%
	(71)	(64)	(266)

Source: Ronald W. Maris (1981), *Pathways to Suicide.* Baltimore, MD: Johns Hopkins Press, p. 127.

were "frigid" (i.e., experienced no orgasm during coitus), and about 1 percent were "promiscuous" before marriage (i.e., had had more than 20 sexual partners before marriage) (1953, pp. 416, 408, 683). In sum, frigidity does not seem to distinguish suicide attempters from normals, but attempters do seem to be somewhat more sexually active before and during marriage with partners other than their spouses than are normal controls. Recalling the three hypotheses posited earlier in this section, we argue (1) that nonfatal suicide attempters and some suicide completers are seeking higher levels of arousal; (2) that a large part of this heightened concern with sex is really an attempt to bolster sagging and fragmented egos resulting from other aspects of their suicidal careers (e.g., early trauma, depression, rejection and isolation, low self-esteem, etc.)—that is, sex is used to reduce tension and the products of stress, to deny hopelessness, to fight depression, loneliness, and loss of love, etc; (3) that suicide attempters use sexuality to control or manipulate significant others, especially lovers and spouses who may be symbolic of earlier parent–child (usually father) conflicts. Especially for suicide completers, the suicide attempt is often perceived as an act of revenge, which not altogether incidentally ends marital and sexual supports to the spouse or lover at least in empirical consequence, if not in actual intention. In short, sexuality often serves social, emotional, or existential ends that have little or nothing to do with eroticism in its usual connotations.

THE SOCIAL RELATIONS OF SYLVIA PLATH

As many readers already know, Sylvia Plath was a bright female poet who suicided at age 30 after a tortured young adulthood. We have elected to consider Ms. Plath to illustrate the concepts of social isolation, negative interaction, and sexual deviance. Along the way we will also comment on Plath's early trauma, subjective inadequacy, rigidity, depression, and hopelessness. We are aware that in presenting "gifted suicides" (Shneidman, 1971) like Plath, the very fact of their talent and celebration may be thought to contribute to their being unlike more inconspicuous and uncelebrated suicides. However, less celebrated suicides are not by that fact alone different from celebrated suicides. Moreover, Plath wrote very well. She said clearly what others have felt but usually did not articulate. We know a great deal about Plath from her poetry (1960, 1965, 1972), her novel *The Bell Jar* (1963), Harriet Rosenstein's critical biography of Plath (1972a), the initial chapter of A. Alvarez's *The Savage God* (1970), and more recently from friend and biographer Lois Ames, who also knew and wrote about poet-suicide Anne Sexton (for Ames, see Plath, 1963). Sylvia Plath was raised in Winthrop and Wellesley, Massachusetts, the daughter of a distinguished Boston University biology professor, an expert on bees, and a woman who taught shorthand and typing. Sylvia herself was an excellent student, graduating Phi Beta Kappa and summa cum laude from Smith College in 1955. After her junior year at Smith, Sylvia received a guest editorship award from *Mademoiselle*. This experience seemed to trigger serious suicidal episodes and resulted in mental hospitalization and electroshock treatments [reported in *The Bell Jar* (1963)]. In 1956 Plath received a Fulbright Fellowship to Cambridge University, where she met and married poet Ted Hughes. In 1957 the Hugheses moved to the United States and Sylvia accepted a position as an instructor in English at Smith College. The following year (1958) they moved to Beacon Hill in Boston, where they both continued to write. In December 1959, they returned to England, where in the spring of 1960 Sylvia met A. Alvarez, poetry editor of *The Observer*. A daughter was born to the Hugheses in April 1960; a son in the summer of 1962. About the time their son was born Sylvia finished *The Bell Jar*. Sylvia suffered repeated illnesses, and for reasons that are not entirely clear she and her husband separated in 1962.[17] The children remained with Sylvia. Finally, after a bitterly cold winter in London and a frenzy of writing poems, including some of the *Ariel* poems, Sylvia Plath suicided by gassing herself in her kitchen. She had been depressed, lonely, burdened by the care of two small children, and periodically ill with the flu. But of course, there is much more to Sylvia Plath's suicidal career than the superficial account just given.

To back up as far as we can, Sylvia Plath had a significant love-hate relationship with her father. He died of a long and difficult illness when Sylvia was eight years old. She never worked through her feelings about her father and did not mourn his death until she was an adult (Plath, 1963, pp. 135–137). Some of this ambivalence was captured in her well-known poem "Daddy," which is partially excerpted here:

> Daddy, I have had to kill you.
> You died before I had time—
> Marble-heavy, a big, full of God,
> Ghastly statue with one grey toe
> Big as a Frisco seal.

[17]There is some hint that she and Alvarez may have become romantically involved.

And a head in the freakish Atlantic
Where it pours bean green over blue
In the waters off beautiful Nauset.
I used to pray to recover you.
Ah, du . . .

If I've killed one man, I've killed two—
The vampire who said he was you
And drank my blood for a year.
Seven years. If you want to know.
Daddy, you can lie back now.

There's a stake in your fat black heart
And the villagers never liked you.
They are dancing and stamping on you.
They always knew it was you.
Daddy, daddy, you bastard, I'm through.

It seems likely that what psychiatrist Robert Litman calls "ego-splitting" was a fundamental byproduct of Sylvia's relationship with her father. Litman (1967) contends that ego-splitting occurs when a hated external object is internalized (cathected, identified with, etc.), then that death wish for the hated external object is turned back upon the ego. Of course, Freud (1917) and Menninger (1938) argued along much the same lines. Menninger called this phenomenon "murder in the one-hundred-and-eightieth degree." Plath also had very negative feelings toward her mother, feelings verging on hatred (1963, p. 166). Rosenstein (1972a) believed that these early traumas later generalized into dislike and contempt for people in general. In describing Esther Greenwood (see Sylvia Plath), the central character in *The Bell Jar*, Rosenstein observed:

> While Esther is still pursuing the American Dream, is, indeed, its paragon, her great pleasures are hot baths and anchovy paste. But beyond that, what? Does she like anything? Not men, not children, few, if any women. . . . Esther cherishes her inexplicable rage at arrangements—one cannot call them relationships—she herself has acquiesced in, even initiated [1972a, p. 48].

What Rosenstein failed to notice with sufficient clarity and compassion was Plath's ultimate contempt *for herself* (Plath, 1963, pp. 61–62). Sylvia's early trauma led to a very basic and tenacious subjective inadequacy. All of her achievements, straight-A grades, prizes, fellowships, and awards could not substitute for her loss of early love and noncontingent approval. Respect and love are very different emotions. "Mother love" is freely given, or withheld, without regard to merit; and later achievements, no matter how grand, can never substitute for early noncontingent acceptance.

This inability to accept self and others led almost inexorably to social isolation. Plath became intensely, even painfully, critical, compulsive, perfectionistic, and rigid (Neuringer, 1961). Unlike Doreen, her roommate during the *Mademoiselle* adventure described in the early pages of *The Bell Jar*, Sylvia lacked animal vitality. Often she could not do anything, became virtually paralyzed (Plath, 1963, p. 85; hysteria?). In one of the more poignant metaphors of *The Bell Jar*, Plath pictured herself as sitting in the crotch of a fig tree starving, but unable to choose which fig to pick:

> I saw my life branching out before me like the green fig tree in the story.
>
> From the tip of every branch, like a fat, purple fig, a wonderful future beckoned and winked. One fig was a husband and a happy home and children, another fig was a famous poet and another fig was a brilliant professor, and another fig was Ee Gee, the amazing editor, and another fig was Europe and Africa and South America, and another fig was Constantine and Socrates and Attila and a pack of other lovers with queer names and offbeat professions, and another fig was an Olympic lady crew champion, and beyond and above these figs were many more figs I couldn't quite make out.
>
> I saw myself sitting in the crotch of this fig tree, starving to death, just because I couldn't make up my mind which of the figs I would choose. I wanted each and every one of them, but choosing one meant losing all the rest, and, as I sat there, unable to decide, the figs began to wrinkle and go black, and one by one, they plopped to the ground at my feet [Plath, 1963, pp. 62–63].

Men were not tolerable once Plath got to know them (1963, p. 67). Of course, the ultimate isolation and logical conclusion of her rigidity was the closed world of the "bell jar." Plath was shut off and shut herself off from other people, new experiences, reality, and finally from life itself. Thus, the symbolism of the bell jar was closure of the unborn child in the jar of formaldehyde, of a life that had never been fully lived, of psychosis, and finally of death. As Plath wrote: "To the person in the bell jar, blank and stopped as a dead baby, the world itself is a bad dream" (1963, p. 193).

Plath's early trauma and rigidity as a child and adolescent led to further negative interaction and sexual problems as a young adult. Rosenstein notes correctly that Plath's sexual repression was closely related to her general difficulty with human relationships: "that sexuality contaminates is merely an extension of Esther's notion of human relatedness. It's not just kisses that stick. It's people. Her horror of male domination, the freedom she thinks she's won with her diaphragm— laudable in the abstract—remain tragically only that. Abstractions, little bell jars, shielding Esther from intimacies odious when she is sane, lethal once she is mad" (Rosenstein, 1972a, p. 49). Plath entered into a series of doomed, often sadomasochistic relationships with men. Her high school sweetheart, Buddy Willard, was safe; he was a relatively nonaggressive, well-mannered Yale premedical student, a kind of all-American boy who never seemed to have much in common with Plath. It was clear that Plath believed that Buddy would never understand her. Later on, Plath turned to more sadomasochistic affairs with men. For example, she decided to be "relieved" (sic) of her virginity and chose a Harvard math professor (Plath, 1963, pp. 197–98). When the episode went awry Plath blamed the seduced professor and demanded that he pay the hospital emergency-room bill for treatment of her hemorrhaging. Sex and children were conceived of as "experiences" that might make her a better writer rather than as gratifying ends in themselves (Plath, 1963, p. 99). Even an initially positive, nonsexual therapeutic interaction with a female psychiatrist, Dr. Nolan, turned out negatively. Plath felt betrayed when she was given unanticipated electroshock treatment. Her final involvement with someone who might have saved her life was negative too. Just prior to her death, A. Alvarez confessed that he was unable to help her even though he anticipated her suicide:

> She must have felt I was stupid and insensitive. Which I was, but to have been otherwise would have meant accepting responsibilities I didn't want and couldn't in my own depression, have coped with. When I left about eight o'clock to go to my dinner party, I knew I had let her down in some final and unforgiveable way. And I knew she knew. I never again saw her alive [1970, p. 33].

Of course, it would be a disservice to Alvarez and to our own knowledge of Plath's complex suicidal career to even suggest that Alvarez was responsible for Plath's suicide. Still, it is not difficult to imagine countless other human beings who might have been able to help Plath, at least in the short run. Once again, Plath had become involved with someone who seemed to contribute to her undoing, rather than to her growth and continued well-being.

Plath's early trauma, rigidity, isolation, and lack of positive human interaction (of which sexual problems were just one facet) meant that her life had become unacceptable—not just unsatisfying, but intolerable. It was not long before the depression that had hounded her all her life turned irreversibly into hopelessness. As Plath herself wrote in *The Bell Jar,* "Only my case was incurable" (p. 130). Rosenstein comes to essentially the same conclusion in her critical biography of Plath:

> Plath's late poetry is full of mouths, open, demanding, never satisfied. Those of children, of flowers, of animals, of other women, of men, and of her speakers. One's sense always is that the universe is insatiable because the speaker herself is insatiable. No amount of food, real or symbolic, can fill the emptiness within. And every demand from outside threatens to deplete her still further, provocations thus to terror or rage. Her fate—her dissolution—has in this and many other poems the ring of inevitability [Rosenstein, 1972b, p. 99].

Of course, there had been suicide attempts all along. One of the earliest had probably been when Sylvia skied down a mountainside totally unprepared and unskilled, with the clear thought that such risk-taking might kill her; she "only" broke her leg. In fact, in thinking about her descent and possible death, Plath openly observed: "This is what it is to be happy" (1963, p. 79). As she became more agitated, depressed, and hopeless, the attempts became more lethal. In the grip of psychotic depression at age 20, Plath took about 50 barbiturates and then misled potential rescuers into believing that she had gone for a "long walk." She could very easily have died from this attempt. It is worth noting that her description of mourning for her father is followed immediately by the overdose (1963, p. 137). That these two events were linked in Plath's mind is clear from an exerpt from *Lady Lazarus:*

> The first time it happened I was ten.
> It was an accident.
> The second time I meant
> To last it out and not come back at all.
> I rocked shut
>
> As a seashell.

As described by Alvarez (1970, pp. 33–41) and Ames (Plath, 1963, pp. 215–216), the final attempt with gas had a kind of quiet desperation about it. It was cold, there were two young children to care for, Sylvia had been ill, she was recently separated from her husband and very lonely, and Alvarez had been unable to help. Yet all of Plath's attempts were also acts of ambivalence. Like most suicides, she wanted to die *and* to live. Plath left a note for her au pair girl to call her doctor; she even gave the phone number in the note. When the au pair could not get in, and no neighbors could be roused (the gas had also knocked out Sylvia's neighbor) the young woman left for a few hours before trying again. By then Plath was already dead. Although Plath's suicidal career is complex, it is clear that she suffered from an impoverishment of supportive human relationships. There are so many relational "ifs." If her father and mother had been different, if Plath had been able to form deeper friendships, if her marriage had been more gratifying, if she had been able to receive and accept better psychiatric care, if someone had just been there when she gassed herself, then she might have had a chance. To be fair to those who tried to help Plath, we must admit that there were other nonsocial (e.g., biological, chemical, genetic, hormonal, etc.) factors operating and that suicides often reject the very nurturance that might save their lives. Nonetheless, each needless death diminishes us all. We share Rosenstein's tribute to Plath:

> The final notes. First, a profound sense of loss that a woman of genius, capable of such uncanny beauties and such inspired furies that her work has measurably extended the range of English poetry, abandoned her art at 30. *Winter Trees* attests that loss. Its title poem, "Event," "Mystic," "Child," and "The Other," a poem of great complexity and brillance, are superb works. Second, an overwhelming compassion for the anguish the woman must have experienced at the end of her life. Of those who write vengefully

about Plath's lifelong love affair with death, one can only ask whether their hypothesis renders her suicide any less terrible, her suffering any less real, or their resources of pity any the less impoverished. Her loss is, simply, a tragedy [Rosenstein, 1972b, p. 99].

SUMMARY

Most of the early studies of the social relations of suicides and of the social context of suicide rates have emphasized the importance of external and constraining social forces that help to reduce social disorganization and social isolation and thereby minimize all deviant behaviors, including suicide (Durkheim, 1897; Cavan, 1928; Henry and Short, 1954; Gibbs and Martin, 1964). Glossing over some of the important differences among these studies, most have asserted that the individual, without the restraining and directing force of social structures and human interaction, lacks the capacity to be satisfied, happy, and hopeful. Henry and Short (1954) added that suicide is most likely when one's culture cultivates a punitive superego (a high degree of internal restraint) in combination with weak or low external constraints. More recent thinking (Garfinkel, 1967; Douglas, 1967; Jacobs, 1971; Sacks, 1976; Atkinson, 1978) has shifted attention to the situated meanings of suicide (usually of nonfatal suicide attempts) and away from more abstract considerations of concepts like "anomie" and "egoism." There has also been a concomitant call for closer attention to the particularistic dynamics of suicidal acts, to detailed descriptions or accounts of the microinteractions of suicides with others. The subjective-meanings approach has its roots in the work of Weber (1925), and the symbolic-interaction approach in the lectures and writings of Mead (1934) and Blumer (1969). Still other social-suicidologists (e.g., Phillips and Feldman, 1973; Phillips, 1974, 1979, 1980; Stack, 1980a; Wasserman, 1984; Stack and Haas, 1984; Phillips and Bollen, 1985) have not so much broken with Durkheim as they have refined, critically analyzed, and extended his work; for example, in order to include new data about the influence of suggestibility on the suicide rate.

Several authors (Sainsbury, 1955; Fawcett and Bunney, 1969; Maris, 1981; Gove and Hughes, 1983) have argued that relative social isolation tends to raise levels of hostility and aggression and at the same time reduces targets of external aggression. Total isolation, such as solitary confinement in a prison setting, tends to result in apathy and hopelessness rather than in irritability. On three major indicators of social isolation in our data (participation in formal organizations, number of close friends in the last year before the suicide attempt or death, and divorce or never having been married) the suicide completers generally scored higher than the nonfatal suicide attempters and natural deaths (Maris, 1981). For example, suicide completers were the most likely of the three study groups to score zero on the Chapin Social Participation Scale. Fifty percent of the completers had no close friends compared with 33 percent of the natural deaths and 20 percent of the nonfatal attempters. In general the highest suicide rates were among divorced persons. Finally, more suicide completers than natural deaths never married at all.

However, it is not just social isolation that characterizes the social relationships of self-destructive individuals. More of the interaction *prior to* social isolation was *negative* among the two self-destructive samples than among the natural death sample. Negative interaction was highest for the nonfatal suicide attempters, next highest for the suicide completers and natural deaths, in that order. This was not surprising, since among other influences, the suicide attempters were less isolated than the suicide completers and thus had more occasion for interaction of all kinds, including negative interaction. Furthermore, some of the negative interaction items were more often present in younger people (as the suicide attempters were). Looking at a few of the particular items that make up the negative interaction scale, we saw that both the suicide completers and nonfatal attempters were less close to their fathers when they were growing up than were the natural deaths. Also, there was more physical disciplining of suicide attempters and completers by their parents than was the case for natural deaths. Feelings of revenge toward significant others were stronger among suicide completers, and respondents for completers were more resigned to the suicidal deaths than respondents were to the natural deaths. When asked about their main life ambitions, nonfatal attempters and suicide completers were more concerned than natural deaths about having a happy marriage, which we interpreted as meaning they had more problems with marriage. Finally, sexual problems seemed to exist primarily for nonfatal suicide attempters.

In examining the role of sexuality in suicide and death, we observed that we often learn to use our bodies to defend ourselves emotionally. Also, sex can function to "remove" us from depression, pain, and boredom. Psychiatrist Samuel Klausner (1968) contends that we seek arousal—and take chances in doing so—that can be life-threatening, although usually death does not result (Farberow, 1980). Sexuality, especially among nonfatal suicide attempters, can be thought of as control, appeal, or manipulation of others. In our data, suicide attempters were somewhat more sexually active and sexually deviant than normal controls and much more active and deviant than completers and natural deaths (both of whom tended to be older). We closed the chapter with an illustration of its three main subthemes—social isolation, negative interaction, and sexual deviance—as they affected the life of the late poet Sylvia Plath.

REFERENCES

Alpert, H. (1939), *Emile Durkheim and His Sociology*. New York: Columbia University Press.

Alvarez, A. (1970), *The Savage God*. New York: Random House.

Asch, S.E. (1955), Opinions and social pressure. *Sci. Amer.*, November: 31–35.

Atkinson, J.M. (1978), *Discovering Suicide: Studies in the Social Organization of Sudden Death*. Pittsburgh: University of Pittsburgh Press.

Baechler, (1979), *Suicides*. New York: Basic Books.

Bankston, W.B., Allen, H.D., & Cunningham, D.S. (1983), Religion and suicide. *Soc. Forces*, 62: 521–528.

Baron, J.N., & Reiss, P.C. (1985), Mass media and violent behavior. *Amer. Sociol. Rev.*, 50/3:347–373.

Beck, A.T. (1967), *Depression*. New York: Harper & Row.

———— Resnick, H.L.P., & Lettieri D.J., eds. (1974), *The Prediction of Suicide*. Bowie, MD: The Charles Press.

Becker, E. (1973), *The Denial of Death*. New York: Macmillan.

Bettleheim, B. (1943), Individual and mass behavior in extreme situations. *J. Abnorm. Psychol.*, 38:417–452.

Blumer, H. (1969), *Symbolic Interactionism*. Englewood Cliffs, NJ: Prentice-Hall.

Bowlby, J. (1960), Separation anxiety. *Internat. Lib. Psychoanal.*, 41:89–113.

Breed, W. (1963), Occupational mobility and suicide among white males. *Amer. Sociol. Rev.*, 28:179–188.

———— (1967), Suicide and Social Interaction. In: *Essays in Self-destruction*, ed. E.S. Shneidman. New York: Science House.

———— Linden, L. (1976), The demographic epidemiology of suicide. In: *Suicidology: Contemporary Developments*, ed. E.S. Shneidman. New York: Grune & Stratton.

Cavan, R.S. (1928), *Suicide*. New York: Russell & Russell, 1965.

Chambliss, W.J., & Steele, M.F. (1966), Status integration and suicide: An assessment. *Amer. Sociol. Rev.* 31:524–532.

Chapin, F.S. (1936), The effects of slum clearance on family and community relationships in Minneapolis in 1935–1936. *Amer. J. Sociol.*, March: 744–763.

Clinard, M.B., ed. (1964), *Anomie and Deviant Behavior*. New York: Free Press.

Coleman, J. (1968), Review of *Studies in Ethnamethodology* by H. Garfinkel. *Amer. Sociol. Rev.*, 33:126–130.

Copi, I.M. (1968), *Introduction to Logic*. New York: Macmillan.

de Fleury, M. (1924), *L'Angoisse humaine*. Paris: Editions de France.

Dickey, J. (1970), *Deliverance*. New York: Houghton-Mifflin.

Douglas, J.D. (1967), *The Social Meanings of Suicide*. Princeton, NJ: Princeton University Press.

———— (1970), *Understanding Everyday Life*. Chicago: Aldine.

Durkheim, E. (1897), *Suicide*. New York: Free Press, 1951.

———— (1912), *The Elementary Forms of the Religious Life*. New York: Free Press, 1954.

Esquirol, E. (1838), *Maladies Mentales*. Paris.

Farberow, N.L., ed. (1975), *Suicide in Different Cultures*. Baltimore, MD: University Park Press.

———— (1980), *The Many Faces of Suicide*. New York: McGraw-Hill.

Fawcett, J., & Bunney, W.E. (1969), Suicide. *Arch. Gen. Psychiat.*, 21:129–137.

Fleck, S. (1960), Family dynamics and origin of schizophrenia. *Psychosom. Med.*, 22:337–339.

Freud, S. (1917), Mourning and melancholia. *Standard Edition*, 4:237–258. London: Hogarth Press, 1953.

Ganzler, S. (1967), Some interpersonal and social dimensions of suicidal behavior. *Diss. Abstr.*, 28B:1192–93.

Garfinkel, H. (1967), *Studies in Ethnomethodology*. Englewood Cliffs, NJ: Prentice-Hall.

Genoves, S. (1974), The acali experiment. *Human Behav.*, January.

Greenwald, H. (1970), *The Elegant Prostitute*. New York: Ballantine Books.

Gibbs, Jack P., ed. (1968), *Suicide*. New York: Harper & Row.

———— & Martin, W.T. (1964), *Status Integration and Suicide*. Eugene, OR: University of Oregon Press.

———— ———— (1981), Still another look at status integration and suicide. *Soc. Forces*, 59/3:815–823.

Giddens, A., ed. (1971), *The Sociology of Suicide*. London: Frank Cass and Co.

Gove, W.R., & Hughes, M. (1983), *Overcrowding in the Household*. New York: Academic Press.

Hagedorn, R., & Labovitz, S. (1966), A note on status integration. *Soc. Prob.*, 14:79–84.

Halbwachs, M. (1930), *The Causes of Suicide*, trans. H. Goldblatt. New York: Free Press.

Harry, J. (1983), Parasuicide, gender, and gender deviance. *J. Health & Soc. Behav.*, 24/4:350–361.

Headley, L.A., ed. (1984), *Suicide in Asia and the Near East*. Berkeley: University of California Press.

Hendin, H. (1982), *Suicide in America*. New York: W.W. Norton.

Henry, A.F., & Short, J.F. (1954), *Suicide and Homicide*. New York: Free Press.

Hinkle, L.E., Jr., & Wolff, H.G. (1956), Communist interrogation and indoctrination of enemies of the state. *Arch. Neurol. & Psychiat.*, 76:115–174.

Homans, G.C. (1974), *Social Behavior: Its Elementary Forms*. New York: Harcourt, Brace & Jovanovich.

Hunt, M. (1974), *Sexual Behavior in the 1970s*. Chicago: Playboy Press.

Jacobs, J. (1971), *Adolescent Suicide*. New York: Wiley Interscience.

Jeffreys, M.D.W. (1952), Samsonic suicides: Or suicides of revenge among Africans. *African Stud.*, 2:118–122.

Kessler, R.C., & Stripp, H. (1984), The impact of frictional television stories on U.S. fatalities: A replication. *Amer. J. Sociol.*, 90/1:151–167.

Kinsey, A.C., Pomeroy, W.B., Martin, C.E., & Gebhard, P.H., (1953), *Sexual Behavior in the Human Female*. Philadelphia: W.B. Saunders.

Klausner, S.Z. (1968), *Why Man Takes Chances*. Garden City, NY: Doubleday/Anchor Books.

Lalli, M., & Turner, S.H. (1968), Suicide and homicide. *J. Crim. Law & Police Sci.*, 59:191–200.

Lefcourt, H.M. (1976), *Locus of Control: Current Trends in Theory and Research*New York: John Wiley.

Lester, D. (1972), *Why People Kill Themselves*. Springfield, IL: Charles C. Thomas, 1982.

Lidz, T., Freck, S., Alanen, U.O., Cornelison, A. (1963), Schizophrenic patients and their siblings. *Psychiatry*, 26:1–18.

Light, D.W., Jr. (1972), Psychiatry and suicide: The management of a mistake. *Amer. J. Sociol.*, 77:821–838.

Litman, R.E. (1967), Sigmund Freud on suicide. In: *Essays in Self-destruction*, ed. E. Shneidman. New York: Science House, pp. 324–344.

Maris, R.W. (1967), Suicide, status, and mobility in Chicago. *Soc. Forces*, 46:246–256.

——— (1969), *Social Forces in Urban Suicide*. Homewood, IL: Dorsey Press.

——— (1971), Deviance as therapy: The paradox of self-destructive females. *J. Health & Soc. Behav.*, 12:114–124.

——— (1975), Sociology. In: *A Handbook for the Study of Suicide*, ed. S. Perlin. New York: Oxford University Press.

——— (1981), *Pathways to Suicide*. Baltimore: Johns Hopkins University Press.

——— (1985), The adolescent suicide problem. *Suicide & Life-Threat. Behav.*, 15/2:91–109.

——— (1986), *Biological Aspects of Suicide*. New York: Guilford Press.

——— Slater, J. (1973), Suicide: A growing menace to black women. *Ebony*, 27:152–160.

Marshall, J.R. (1978), Changes in aged white male suicide: 1948–1972. *J. Gerontol.*, 35/5:763–768.

——— (1981), Political integration and the effect of war on suicide: United States, 1933–1976. *Soc. Forces*, 59/3:771–785.

Mayhew, B. (1981), Structuralism versus individualism: Part II. *Soc. Forces*, 59/3:627–648.

Mead, G.H. (1934), *Mind, Self, and Society*. Chicago: University of Chicago Press.

Menninger, K. (1938). *Man Against Himself*. New York: Harcourt, Brace & World.

Milgram, S. (1974), *Obedient to Authority*. New York: Harper & Row.

Mills, C.W. (1959), *The Sociological Imgination*. New York: Oxford University Press.

Naroll, R. (1965), Thwarting disorientation and suicide. Unpublished manuscript, Northwestern University.

Nelson, F., Farberow, N., & Mackinnon, D.R. (1978), The certification of suicide in eleven western states. *Suicide & Life-Threat. Behav.*, 8:75–88.

Neuringer, C. (1961), Dichotomous evaluations in suicidal individuals. *J. Consult. Psycho.*, 25:54–58.

Perlin, S., & Schmidt, C.W., Jr. (1975), Psychiatry. In: *A Handbook for the Study of Suicide*, ed. S. Perlin. New York: Oxford University Press.

Phillips, D.P. (1970), *Dying as a Form of Social Behavior*. Unpublished doctoral dissertation. Princeton University, Princeton, NJ.

——— (1974), The influence of suggestion on suicide. *Amer. Sociol. Rev.*, 39:340–354.

——— (1979), Suicide, motor vehicle fatalities, and the mass media. *Amer. J. Sociol.*, 84:1150–1174.

——— (1980), Airplane accidents, murder, and the mass media. *Soc. Forces*, 58:1001–1024.

——— Bollen, K.A. (1985), Same time, last year: Selective data dredging for negative findings. *Amer. Sociol. Rev.*, 50/3:364–371.

———— Feldman, K.A. (1973), A dip in deaths before ceremonial occasions. *Amer. Sociol. Rev.*, 38:678–696.

Plath, S. (1960), *Colossus*. London: William Heinemann.

———— (1963), *The Bell Jar*. New York: Harper & Row.

———— (1965), *Ariel*. London: Faber & Faber.

———— (1972), *Winter Trees*. New York: Harper & Row.

Robins, E. (1981), *The Final Months*. New York: Oxford University Press.

Robinson, W.S. (1950), Ecological correlations and the behavior of individuals. *Amer. Sociol. Rev.*, 15:351–357.

Rosenstein, H. (1972a), Reconsidering Sylvia Plath. *Ms*: 1:44–57.

———— (1972b), Unpublished doctoral dissertation. Brandeis University, Massachusetts.

Rushing, W. (1968), Individual behavior and suicide. In: *Suicide*. ed. J.P. Gibbs. New York: Harper & Row, pp. 96–124.

Ryd, Z. (in press), Suicides in Nazi concentration camps. *Suicide & life-Threat. Behav.*, 17/1.

Sacks, H. (1976), The search for help: No one to turn to. *Essays in Self-Destruction*, ed. E.S. Shneidman. New York: Science House.

Sainsbury, P. (1955), *Suicide in London*. London: Chapman & Hall.

Schulz, R., & Bazeman, M. (1980), Ceremonial occasions and mortality. *Amer. Psychologist*, 35:253–261.

Shneidman, E.S. (1971), Perturbation and lethality as percursors of suicide in a gifted group. *Suicide & Life-Threat. Behav.*, 1:23–45.

———— (1985), *Definition of Suicide*. New York: John Wiley.

———— Farberow, N.L., eds. (1957), *Clues to Suicide*. New York: McGraw-Hill.

———— ————, eds. (1961), *The Cry for Help*. New York: McGraw-Hill.

Spitz, R.A. (1946), Anaclitic depression. *The Psychoanalytic Study of the Child*, 2:313–342. New York: International Universities Press.

Stack, S. (1980a), The effects of marital dissolution on suicide. *J. Marr. & Fam.*, 42:83–91.

———— (1980b), Occupational status and suicide: A relationship reexamined. *Agg. Behav.*, 6:243–244.

———— (1982), Suicide: A decade review of the sociological literature. *Deviant Behav.*, 4:41–66.

———— Haas, A. (1984), The effect of unemployment duration on national suicide rates: A time series analysis, 1948–1982. *Sociol. Focus*, 17/1:17–29.

Stafford, M.C., & Gibbs, J.P. (1985), A major problem with the theory of status integration and suicide. *Soc. Forces*, 63/3:643–660.

Steiner, J.F. (1967), *Treblinka*. New York: Simon & Schuster.

Stengel, E. (1963), Attempted suicide: Its management in the general hospital. *Lancet*, 1:233–

———— (1964), *Suicide and Attempted Suicide*. Middlesex, U.K.: Penguin Books.

Stephens, J.B. (1984(, Vocabularies of Motive and suicide. *Suicide & Life-Threat. Behav.*, 14/4:243–253.

———— (1985), Suicidal women and their relationships with husbands, boyfriends, and lovers. *Suicide & Life-Threat. Behav.*, 15/2:77–90.

Sudak, H.S., Ford, A.B., & Rushtard, N.B., eds. (1984), *Suicide in the Young*. Boston: John Wright.

Swanson, C.S., & Breed, W. (1976), Black suicide in New Orleans. In: *Suicidology: Contemporary Developments*, ed. E.S. Shneidman. New York: Grune & Stratton, pp. 99–130.

Wasserman, I.M. (1983), Presidential elections, suicide, and mortality patterns. *Amer. Sociol. Rev.*, 48/5:711–720.

———— (1984), Imitation and suicide. *Amer. Sociol. Rev.*, 49/3:427–436.

Weber, M. (1925), *Wirtschaft und Gesellschaft*. Tubingen: J.C.B. Mohr.

Weisman, A. (1967), Self-destruction and sexual perversion. In: *Essays in Self-destruction*, ed. E.S. Shneidman. New York: Science House.

———— (1984), *The Coping Capacity*. New York: Human Sciences Press.

Yap, P.M. (1958), *Suicide in Hong Kong*. London: Oxford University Press.

Zimbardo, P.G. (1969), The human choice: Individuation, reason, and order versus reindividuation, impulse, and chaos. In: *Nebraska Symposium on Motivation*, eds. W.J. Arnold, & D. Levine. Lincoln: University of Nebraska Press, pp. 237–307.

Part **II**

Understanding

A. General Assessment Considerations

6

Problems in Suicide Risk Assessment

Jerome A. Motto, M.D.

The need to estimate the likelihood of suicide arises in all settings in which one person tries to help another who is in distress. In the field of medicine, concern about suicide risk is intensified by the would-be helper feeling responsible for the physical well-being of those being treated. Though suicide is traditionally regarded as a "psychiatric" problem, all clinical specialities share the burden of recognizing and evaluating self-destructive states, just as all share the painful experience of losing patients to suicide. Greater attention to this task is now emerging among social workers, nurses, and psychologists as well, in view of the trend toward clinicians in allied health disciplines assuming increased responsibility for patient care.

That the assessment of suicide risk is, indeed, a problem, is attested to by the fact that to date we have no established and generally accepted procedure to guide us in this task. Innumerable decisions regarding risk are made and implemented every day—the job gets done—but how it is done is determined primarily by the skills and philosophy of the individual clinician.

Available statistics on suicide in the United States are not reassuring from a preventive point of view. The overall suicide rate persists, with a troubling shift in relative frequency toward younger age groups and minority populations. Yet we can only focus on one individual at a time for the task at hand. The present discussion considers the means of accomplishing this, and the obstacles that must be dealt with in order to do so. The term *suicide,* as used here, refers to a self-inflicted, self-intentioned, noncoerced death. We are not addressing the related issues of suicide attempts, or indirect self-destructive behaviors such as alcohol abuse or a deleterious life-style.

THE NATURE OF THE ASSESSMENT PROBLEM

The basic obstacle to accurate risk assessment is the uniqueness of each individual to be considered. The clinical knowledge and experience of an examiner is of unquestioned value, but that value is remarkably limited unless it is provided with full details about the person being examined. It is as though we must start our learning all over again with each assessment task. If we do not, our prior experience can be a handicap unless we hold the implications of that experience firmly in abeyance until we can determine its applicability to the task at hand. Failure to do so leads to our making assumptions, consciously or unconsciously, which is a common prelude to disaster. We must say to our patient, in effect, "I don't know anything about you that you don't tell me," and hope that our experience and clinical sensitivity will help us to ask the right questions.

That each subject possesses a unique set of risk indicators, accounts for the bewildering number of such variables that have appeared in the literature on suicide. Baechler (1979) observes that, "the number of facts that can be introduced to explain a suicide is practically infinite" (p. 4), and points out that the primary clinical problem is, thus, "to sort out the irrelevant from the pertinent" data. He goes on to assert that doing so assumes a theory of suicide, and that such a theory does not yet exist in a scientific sense.

This basic obstacle, individual uniqueness, is compounded by an array of well-known issues that further complicate risk assessment. These include the relative infrequency of completed suicide, which limits any prospective study, the large number of determinants that tend to operate in each case, the uncertain validity of available data, the numerous unpredictable and uncontrollable intervening influences that contribute to outcome, and the lack of opportunity for retrospective study with the patient after a suicide (in contrast, for example, to other forms of behavior such as homicide, assault, or substance abuse). In an individual case, we are also unable to verify the accuracy of the estimated risk, regardless of outcome. Lastly, we recognize the confounding effect on validation that is introduced by special interventive measures made necessary by a high-risk situation.

Given this formidable set of obstacles, it is understandable that suicidal patients are not always welcome additions to a caseload. In spite of the known handicaps, however, a systematic approach to risk assessment can still be used with reasonable confidence as the basis for a treatment and management plan.

APPROACHES TO THE ASSESSMENT PROBLEM

Direct Clinical Inquiry (Initial Assessment)

The most straightforward way to determine how probable it is that a person will commit suicide is to ask—directly and simply. This method, or some form of it, is a standard mode of operation for the large majority of clinicians. The emphasis is on matter-of-factness, clarity, and freedom from implied criticism. Outspoken candor and concern on the examiner's part will generally evoke the same qualities in the response. Whatever the examiner's language and style, a typical sequence using this approach might run as follows: Does the person have periods of feeling low or despondent about how things are going? How long do these times last? How frequent are they? How severe do they get? Do they produce crying spells or interfere with daily activities, concentration, sleep, or appetite? Are there feelings of discouragement, hopelessness, or self-criticism? Are these feelings ever so severe that life doesn't seem worthwhile; that thoughts of suicide come to mind? How persistent are such thoughts; how strong have they been; did it require much effort to resist them? Have there been any impulses to carry them out? Were any plans made? How detailed were they? Have any tentative or preliminary actions been taken, such as collecting pills or obtaining a gun? What deterred the person? Could these feelings be managed if they recur? If not, is there anyone the person could turn to for help at such times?

This brief inquiry, carried out in an empathic and understanding way, will provide the clinician with a preliminary estimate of risk. The wording and content will vary somewhat, reflecting individual circumstances. It is generally appropriate in settings where rapid decisions must be made, such as an emergency room, or when a brief screening device is needed, as in routinely determining the mental status of a medical–surgical patient. If other sources of information are available (e.g., family or friends), they would be used as well. This approach is based primarily on the premise that going directly to the heart of the issue is a practical and effective clinical tool, and that patients and collaterals will usually provide valid information if an attitude of caring concern is communicated to them. The fact that such is not always the case does not reduce its clinical usefulness.

Indirect Clinical Inquiry (Extended Assessment)

When time and setting permit, a more inferential approach is also appropriate if our direct inquiry gives us reason for concern. In practice, these approaches tend to overlap to some extent, as the clinician responds to the information elicited. The focus of the indirect approach continues to reflect the clinician's experience and style, but several specific areas have emerged as deserving special attention. These are derived from a number of sources, primarily descriptive studies of completed suicides, clinical experience, and common sense.

A history of prior suicide attempts is an important clue to the person's resistance to self-destructive action. Something akin to facilitation, as used in neurophysiology, seems to occur in suicidal behavior. A first suicide attempt appears to meet with most psychological resistance, with subsequent attempts requiring progressively less intensity of motivation to find overt expression. In the balance of forces that ultimately determine a suicidal act, the demonstrated breaching of this resistance at a prior time must be considered an indication of potential vulnerability. Some patients who make a second attempt express surprise and dismay that the second one was so easy to carry out, sensing that a protective element was less effective than expected. A single prior attempt, especially during adolescence, appears to be less ominous than two or more and the seriousness of a prior attempt is positively related to the risk of subsequent suicide. In any case, a detailed review of such past experience can be of great value in assessing current risk.

The extent of feelings of hopelessness is another useful area of indirect inquiry. Minkoff, Bergman, Beck, and Beck (1973) found that suicidal intent is more closely related to hopelessness than to the syndrome of depression, and Beck (1967) showed that in his Depression Inventory, suicidal wishes correlated more highly with hopelessness than with any other item. Yufit and Benzies (1973) also emphasized this element, and developed an instrument for its measurement in terms of "time perspective."

The specificity of a suicide plan has been recognized as another indirect indicator of risk that can be readily assessed. Litman (1974) first emphasized this observation, based on experience with callers to the Los Angeles Suicide Prevention Center.

The presence of "termination behavior" provides invaluable indirect data, usually obtained from family members or other collaterals. Making or revising a will, checking insurance, giving away valued possessions, or any actions that appear to negate the future, can speak as eloquently to the level of suicide risk as any verbal statements.

The presence of a lethal weapon in the home of a suicidal person is clearly a factor in risk assessment. The obviousness of this can diminish its impact, especially with hunters, gun collectors, and persons with experience in the military or law enforcement, who tend to keep firearms readily available. Similarly, ready access to medicines or chemicals, as is common in health care occupations, increases the risk in vulnerable persons.

Although diagnostic categories are generally of limited value in suicide risk assessment, the presence of a psychotic state or of drug or alcohol abuse continue to demand attention as indirect indicators of vulnerability. The traditional association of depressive states with suicide is well known, but the absence of depression has little significance in assessing risk.

Lastly, the presence or threat of an extremely painful experience, usually involving the loss of an important person or a stabilizing element in the person's life, needs no explication to be recognized as an important consideration in assessing suicide risk. Even if no suicidal issue can be discerned initially under such circumstances, repeated assessment is indicated until the situation is resolved.

Scales of Suicide Risk

A third approach to suicide risk assessment is the use of a clinical instrument to provide a quantifiable indication of risk. Methodological and practical problems have plagued the development of this approach to the point of discouraging even devoted and experienced workers in the field of suicide prevention. Overlapping with the clinical issues noted above, these obstacles have been small samples, limited data, a low base rate, nongeneralizability of critical stressors, the individual uniqueness of suicidal persons, unknown and uncontrollable variables that contribute to outcome, ambiguity of outcome (e.g., "suicidal behavior"), and problems of demonstrating reliability and especially validity.

For many years, the only generally known measure was the little-used suicide risk scale of the Minnesota Multiphasic Personality Inventory (MMPI). Contemporary efforts at scale construction were introduced in 1963, when the Los Angeles Suicide Prevention Center devised a special scale for assessing callers to that Center (Farberow, Heilig, and Litman, 1968). In spite of some difficulties with it, the subsequent proliferation of suicide prevention and crisis centers led to wide use of this scale, usually in a simplified form, as it was the only one readily available. Though a number of alternate instruments were developed over the next decade (Cohen, Motto, and Seiden, 1966; Poeldinger, 1968; Weisman and Worden, 1972; Yufit and Benzies, 1973; Beck, Schuyler, and Herman, 1974; Zung, 1974), their use remained primarily as research tools rather than aids for the front-line clinician.

A review by Brown and Sheran in 1972 suggested that the search for generalizable indicators of high risk had severe inherent limitations, and that a more useful approach might be the study of precisely defined populations and settings. The resulting scales would then be appropriate for use in those "situation-specific" circumstances from which they were derived.

This challenge had been anticipated by a number of investigators who were already developing scales applicable to specific populations, such as male Veterans Administration psychiatric inpatients being considered for discharge (Farberow and McKinnon, 1974), inpatients in a community mental health facility (Braucht and Wilson, 1970), specific age–sex groups (Lettieri, 1974; Motto, 1979), and various defined clinical patterns (Wold, 1971). Litman (1975) provided an estimate of risk for nineteen different patient populations, such as "suicide attempters seen in hospitals" (moderate risk), "depressed alcoholic middle-aged male caller to Suicide Prevention Center" (high risk), and "young female suicide attempters" (low risk). Subsequent work continued to focus on "clinical models," defined in terms of personality characteristics or clinical picture, for example, "stable with forced change," "alienated," "nice person," "alcohol abuse," "drug abuse" (Motto, 1977, 1979, 1980a, 1980b), or "suicide attempter" (Pallis, Barraclough, Levey, Jenkins, and Sainsbury, 1982; Pallis, Gibbons, and Pierce, 1984). As with earlier studies, these reports generated interest among researchers but did not have a demonstrable impact on clinical practice. One probable reason for this is that little attention was paid to providing clinicians with a simple, brief procedure that could be quickly translated into a clear indication of suicide risk.

An effort to respond to this practical need led to the development of the California Risk Estimator for Suicide (Motto, Heilbron, and Juster, 1985), an easily administered, fifteen-item, paper-and-pencil scale for persons ages eighteen to seventy who are known to be at some risk for suicide. This instrument addresses several of the major problems of "objective" risk assessment. It is derived empirically from a large, broad-based sample with a wide range of data, the outcome criterion is clear (the estimated risk of completed suicide within two years). It addresses special individual qualities by recognizing stress unique to the person being assessed; it provides validation information by its performance on independent samples; and it avoids the specter of "false positives" and "false negatives" by estimating the degree of risk rather than predicting a specific outcome in individual cases. This last issue has been the most troublesome aspect in examining assessment scales and has generated the most negative observations about their potential value (Pokorny, 1983; Murphy, 1983, 1984).

Some inherent problems of the empirical approach are still evident. For example, the scale is not a screening device to identify "suicidal" and "nonsuicidal" individuals. Rather it requires a preceding recognition of suicide risk, from which it separates the highest risk persons from the less high risk, which is the situation usually faced by clinicians. It also demonstrates some "paradoxical" risk factors, that is, indicators of high risk that are contrary to intuition, such as risk increasing with amount of sleep. Though this is not rare in empirical studies, it can understandably diminish confidence in a measuring instrument. Maximum confidence would be achieved by using traditional risk indicators, which provide comfort for the rater, but often contradict what many completed suicides teach us. One such rating scale (Patterson, Dohn, Bird, and Patterson, 1983) suggests ten risk factors, six of which have appeared, paradoxically, as low risk indicators in empirical studies (Motto, 1984).

The use of scales is at best a supplement to clinical judgment. No matter how carefully developed a scale may be, and how conveniently structured for easy use, the special characteristics of each individual remain the most critical determinants of risk assessment.

Dynamic Approaches

It appears self-evident that an accurate assessment of suicide risk is facilitated by a full understanding of the mechanisms that generate the suicidal impulse. Efforts to achieve that understanding have not been lacking, but no generally accepted formulation has emerged to "explain" the phenomenon of self-destruction.

Most widely known in Western cultures is Freud's discussion in his paper "Mourning and Melancholia" (Freud, 1917), which postulates identification with a lost object toward which strong ambivalent feelings exist. The suicide serves to express rage by destroying the object, express guilt by punishing the ego for its murderous wish, and provide surcease from pain. Menninger (1938) later developed this as a wish to kill, be killed, and to die. Though Freud specifically disclaimed any general validity for this formulation, even when limiting it to melancholia, his statement that suicide starts with a death wish against others has been so emphasized it "has become a cliche" (Litman, 1967).

Freud saw each suicide as multiply determined. First, a *general human vulnerability* is determined by the inherent characteristics of (1) aggression, both outwardly and inwardly directed, derived from the death instinct, (2) splitting of the ego into good and bad components, and (3) guilty compliance required by family and society for continued acceptance. Second, there are many *individual predisposing conditions,* such as ego disorganization under high levels of stress or a chronically self-destructive living pattern. Finally, a *specific suicide mechanism* leads to a breakdown of defenses and release of destructive energy, as with loss of a love object, narcissistic injury, or an overwhelming affect, for example, rage, guilt, or anxiety (Litman, 1967).

The absence of a scientific dynamic explanation for suicide has been treated harshly by some contemporary scholars. Expressions are found such as, "the astonishing weakness [and] laughable simplicity . . . of the proposed explanations" (Baechler, 1979, p. vxiii), or "fallacies, hunches, guesses, conjectures and inferences that have often proved to be counter-productive, sometimes farcical and pathetic, sometimes exercises in futility—and sometimes fatuous in their simplistic naivete" (Wekstein, 1979, p. 68). Such statements may have some truth in them, but our limited understanding of the suicidal act reflects the problem of understanding, in a scientific sense, any specific pathological behavior.

Additional dynamic elements reported by clinicians as leading to suicide include a number of fantasies: of rebirth or reunion with a deceased loved one, of revenge, of inducing guilt in a rejecting object, of achieving subsequent reconciliation, and of simple relief from pain (Furst and Ostow, 1979). Ringel (1976) postulates a "presuicidal syndrome," in which unresolved stress leads to a gradual process of psychological constriction, followed by inhibited aggression, and finally, suicidal fantasies and dreams. The intensity, specificity, and degree of volition of the last stage are suggested as an indicator of the degree of suicidal risk.

Berent (1981) postulates a basic depressive state and a rescue fantasy, to which the suicidal person provides clues for would-be rescuers. This is similar to a number of current sociological approaches which emphasize the "appeal function" of the suicidal act (Stengel, 1964). Baechler (1979) adds to these the classic motivations of sacrifice (Durkheim, 1951, "altruistic") and transfiguration (Motto, 1975, "symbolic"), as well as the "ludic suicide"—proving one's self by gambling with death.

Litman's (1975) dynamic model for suicide focuses on the fragmentation of the personality under stress, loss of one's usual coping patterns, feeling helpless, hopeless, and abandoned, and with a great deal of unexpressible aggressive tension.

When thinking becomes stereotyped and constricted, alternate coping measures cannot be imagined, and suicide risk becomes high.

Buie and Maltsberger (1983) present the most detailed argument for the value of a dynamic formulation in assessing suicide risk. Their focus is on the function of the suicidal act as a means of (1) restoring or attaining a perfect union, (2) killing the hated object, and (3) killing the self in anger (at one's inadequacy which caused the loss) or guilt (atonement for murder of the hated object). Suicidal persons are characterized as being vulnerable to "aloneness," a specific, terrifying sense of isolation. This state seems very similar to what Hellmuth Kaiser (1965) referred to as a loss of the "delusion of fusion," which all persons require as a stabilizing element in emotional life.

Buie and Maltsberger (1983) postulate that when the external elements that provide a person's sense of self-worth are lost, such vulnerable individuals are prone to experience severe depressive affect with feelings of personal worthlessness or aloneness. This signals the onset of a suicidal state.

Buie and Maltsberger suggest further that the appraisal of suicide risk requires a careful psychiatric history and mental status examination, to clarify the person's *degree of autonomy* and degree of *dependency on external sources of emotional support* ("self-objects"). The appraisal, including input from the family and others, as well as observation of the patient's behavior, takes the form of a "disciplined psychodynamic formulation." This process is said to make the development, risk, and resolution of a suicidal crisis "readily intelligible." It is especially important to determine whether the person's anger is of a "murderous quality." These authors point out that special precautions with this approach include the need to (1) continuously use the formulation as a working tool (rather than simply as "paperwork"), (2) recognize the potential for increased risk at a time of clinical improvement, (3) appreciate the importance of the supports offered in treatment, maintaining them until they are replaced, and (4) if empathic assessment is negative for suicide risk, let the risk assessment "rest strictly on the case formulation", that is, whether "self-object resources" are sufficient to sustain the person.

The dynamic approach to risk assessment has the advantage of going directly to more basic causes of the suicidal state at the time that the level of risk is determined. It also provides a clearer picture of critical personality strengths as well as vulnerabilities. Asking a person, "Can you stand what you are going through?" generally elicits more superficial data than a careful review of prior coping patterns under similar stresses. This approach also provides the examiner with a sense of understanding, as well as measuring the level of suicide risk, which may permit more confidence in subsequent planning and monitoring. There is likewise a smoother transition to the treatment phase of patient care, and when this type of assessment is done thoroughly, it can be said to constitute the initial stage of a treatment program.

For many front-line workers (e.g., in emergency rooms, crisis clinics, medical–surgical wards, telephone crisis-intervention centers, social service facilities, college student health clinics, pastoral counselors' and nonpsychiatric physicians' offices), that is, where most potentially suicidal persons are encountered, an approach requiring extensive study of personality structure has severe limitations. The necessary time, training, and experience are not always available to front-line staff, and the cooperation of patients cannot be counted on. On the other hand, after a person has reached a treatment setting, or even an experienced psychiatric consultant, the dynamic approach may be not only appropriate, but required, for sound clinical practice.

Buie and Maltsberger's (1983) presentation of the psychodynamic approach might be said to artificially dichotomize the use of "empathic" or "intuitive" understanding as contrasted with "dynamic" formulation in the assessment procedure. Both processes are continually involved. For example, the extent to which a given resource provides emotional support to the patient is not an objective decision, nor is the decision whether "sufficient" resources are available to consider the suicide risk diminished, nor whether anger is of "murderous quality." Writing the dynamic formulation on paper does not make it other than the clinician's subjective, "intuitive" impression. Relying solely on a written formulation, as recommended in certain circumstances, could be a handicap, by screening out much supplemental information. And suggesting that this approach is the only reliable means for assessing suicide risk must itself be an intuitive judgment.

BIOLOGICAL APPROACHES

Attempts to develop biological measures of suicide risk stemmed from the early recognition of increased levels of biogenic amines in states of internal agitation or turmoil (Bunney and Fawcett, 1965). Stimulated by remarkable advances in the technology of identifying and measuring biological compounds, a vigorous search for chemical "markers" of various emotional disorders—including suicidal behaviors— has taken place over the past decade. Areas of biological study related to suicide risk include: urinary 17-hydroxycorticosteroids, plasma and cerebrospinal fluid cortisol, dexamethasone suppression, cerebrospinal fluid 5-hydroxyindoleacetic acid, thyroid-stimulating hormone response to thyrotropin-releasing hormone, urinary norepinephrine: epinephrine ratio, 3-methoxy-4-hydroxyphenylglycol, homovanillic acid, tritiated imipramine binding, cerebrospinal fluid magnesium, electroencephalography, genetics, and symptomless autoimmune thyroiditis.

Though new reports are seen almost daily in this active area of study, biological markers of suicide risk now constitute an area of continuing research rather than practical clinical tools. None of them has a clear application for risk assessment at this time.

THE FINAL DECISION: A WORKING HYPOTHESIS

The final decision as to suicide risk is an intuitive judgment. Whatever approach or combination of approaches taken, the data that we use are based on a subjective interpretation of both our conscious and unconscious perceptions. Only the most superficial criteria (age, race, sex, occupation, religion, presence of suicide note, and so on) are "objective," and even these are often perceived incorrectly. We are obliged to accept that no matter how much information is gathered, sooner or later all the data must be weighed together and an intuitive estimate of risk recorded. That it is only an educated guess does not diminish its importance or its value as a consideration in management and treatment planning.

The method used to arrive at the final decision varies with the clinical situation, the patient, and the clinician. The author tries to use all the approaches discussed above, if the circumstances permit, emphasizing direct inquiry at first and gradually including indirect data and dynamic material as he becomes better acquainted with the patient. There is invariably some combining of these areas, as the patient responds so often to a direct inquiry with dynamic material, and provides direct information in reply to dynamic probing. In any case, the author tries never to omit asking directly about the person's own estimate of his or her ability to survive.

The author's final decision is based on what he considers a universal model, specifically, that every individual has a threshold beyond which pain (physical or psychic) cannot be tolerated. This takes into consideration the person's pathology, strengths, and available defensive patterns, such as obsessive or intellectual defenses, alcohol, drugs, and psychotic decompensation. If the pain level exceeds the pain threshold, even briefly, suicide is imminent.

The clinical task is to determine and monitor the pain threshold, and continually estimate how close the pain level comes to it. The better we know the patient, the more sensitive we can be to the influences that can alter these two critical determinants of a suicidal act. Treatment aims ideally at both raising the threshold by maturational development, and decreasing the pain level by providing emotional support and by resolution of pain-generating conflicts.

PITFALLS IN RISK ASSESSMENT

The Clinician's Feelings

If we set aside the inherent difficulties in assessing suicide risk, the greatest handicap to overcome is our own feelings. Anxiety is most common, and its manifestations (or our defenses against it) range from denial of risk to anxious preoccupation with the suicide issue. A secondary handicap is generated when the patient senses the anxiety, and responds by falsely reassuring the clinician, or conversely by trying to fulfill the perceived expectations of a suicidal act. In any case, free and open communication is compromised, as is the potential for optimal psychotherapeutic work.

Another feeling that can hinder risk assessment is hostility toward the patient. This is most apparent and most often commented on in the emergency room setting, though it exists in various forms wherever suicidal persons are seen. Maltsberger and Buie (1974) developed this observation in the psychiatric treatment setting through the concept of "countertransference hate." They point out the need for the therapist to gain comfort with these feelings by acknowledging them, bearing them, and putting them into perspective, and to exercise "loving self-restraint."

Another view of this issue is that self-restraint, though desirable, does not go far enough. A mature clinician strives to accept the reality of human limitations—patient and therapist alike—and must be prepared for any of the possible manifestations of the patient's emotional state. With suicidal patients this includes coping not only with the usual narcissistic wounds that patients can inflict, but also with the disturbing social, professional, and legal implications of unrelenting suicidal threats and behaviors. It is incumbent on training centers to prepare trainees for this task by focusing on therapists' limitations as well as their skills. Specifically, if a therapist is not prepared to lose a patient to suicide, that therapist is not fully prepared to treat suicidal patients. The presence of anger toward a patient reflects the immaturity of the therapist rather than the pathology of the patient. It is coming to terms with this reality that we must strive for, in order to minimize distortion in assessing risk.

Strengths of the Patient

Pathology in a person's emotional life is observed through a screen of strengths, thus patients with a great deal of strength may experience severe disruption before it becomes evident to an observer. Especially when obsessive and intellectual defenses continue to function, recognition of the seriousness of a suicidal state can be severely handicapped. Terms such as *hidden depression* usually apply to such circumstances.

Limited View of Etiology

The pathway to a suicidal state has so many configurations that if the clinician has the expectation of any given clue to a high-risk situation (e.g., depressive phenomena, agitation, personality changes, or a serious loss), such an expectation would be a severe handicap. "But he seemed so cheerful . . . had so much to live for . . . was looking forward to . . . was doing so well . . ," are too frequent indications of this pitfall.

Cultural Disparity

If the patient and clinician live in essentially different worlds, with different value systems, a serious obstacle to empathic understanding and trust is clearly present. This dilemma seems obvious in the recognized minority cultures, but less obvious in subcultures, such as the young, the elderly, or drug users.

Failure to Document

This is included as a legal note, but is frequently closely related to the anxieties and frustrations experienced by clinicians. In short, the assessment of risk should be carefully documented. This serves both to provide a correct medical record and to attest to the attention paid to the issue of suicide risk. It also serves as the basis for suicide prevention measures. When such measures (e.g., obtaining consultation) and their implementation are likewise documented, a therapist has done all that can be done regarding legal vulnerability, and all available energy can then be directed into the process of therapy.

SUMMARY AND CONCLUSIONS

The problem of suicide risk assessment is basically the same as other evaluative procedures in medicine and in behavioral science. Data are gathered from the patient, from the family, and other collaterals, from the history, from specific tests, and from direct observation. All information is tinged with intuitive elaboration of a nature and degree that is unique to each clinician. Though the available information at a given time may be incomplete, ambiguous, contradictory, or of questionable validity, a decision is made, primarily on intuitive grounds, as to the estimated level of risk. As new data become available, and circumstances change, the estimate of risk is modified accordingly.

In arriving at a decision, each clinician will apply the available information to his or her own unique theoretical model and experience as regards self-destructive behavior. This precludes any single set of criteria being established as having preference. The risk assessment issue is analogous to Murphy's (1972) characterization of optimal treatment for suicidal persons, specifically, that each therapist has the responsibility to do it "as best he knows how."

The problem is greatly intensified by the specters of social stigma, professional embarrassment, and legal liability in the event of suicide. These can impose such pressures on the clinician that he adopts defensive maneuvers, such as denial of risk, making assumptions, clinging to a rigid and doctrinaire approach, or regressing to emotional states that further compromise effectiveness.

As we approach the limits of our potential for assessing suicide risk, our efforts can be more fully focused on the challenge of treatment. Whether a more accurate estimate of risk will reduce unnecessary and preventable suicides has yet to be shown. Yet that prevention is the purpose of our efforts at improving risk assessment, and the end toward which we must constantly strive.

REFERENCES

Baechler, J. (1979), *Suicides*. New York: Basic Books.

Beck, A. (1967), *Depression: Clinical, Experimental and Clinical Aspects*. New York: Hoeber/Harper & Row.

Beck, A., Schuyler, D., & Herman, I. (1974), Development of suicidal intent scales. In: *The Predication of Suicide*, eds. A. Beck, H. Resnick, and D. Lettieri. Bowie, MD: Charles Press.

Berent, I. (1981), *The Algebra of Suicide*. New York: Human Sciences Press.

Braught, G., & Wilson, N. (1970), Predictive utility of the revised suicide potential scale. *J. Consult. Clin. Psychol.*, 34:426.

Brown, T., & Sheran, T. (1972), Suicide prediction: A review. *Suicide & Life-Threat. Behav.*, 2:67–98.

Buie, D., & Maltsberger, J. (1983), *The Practical Formulation of Suicide Risk*. Cambridge, MA: Firefly Press.

Bunney, W., & Fawcett, J. (1965), Possibilities of a biochemical test for suicide potential. *Arch. Gen. Psychiat.*, 13:232–239.

Cohen, E., Motto, J., & Seiden, R. (1966), An instrument for evaluating suicide potential. *Amer. J. Psychiat.*, 122:886–891.

Durkheim, E. (1951), *Suicide*. Glencoe, IL: Free Press.

Farberow, N., Heilig, S., & Litman, R. (1968), *Techniques in Crisis Intervention: A Training Manual*. Los Angeles: Suicide Prevention Center, Inc.

———— McKinnon, D. (1974), Prediction of suicide in neuropsychiatric hospital patients. In: *The Psychological Assessment of Suicide Risk*, ed. C. Neuringer. Springfield, IL: Charles C Thomas.

Freud, S. (1917), Mourning and melancholia. *Standard Edition*, 14: 237–258. London: Hogarth Press, 1957.

Furst, S., & Ostow, M. (1979), The psychodynamics of suicide. In: *Suicide: Theory and Clinical Aspects*, eds. L. Hankoff and B. Einsidler. Littleton, MA: PSG Publishing.

Kaiser, H. (1965), *Effective Psychotherapy*, ed. L. Fierman. New York: Free Press.

Lettieri, D. (1974), Suicidal death prediction scales. In: *The Prediction of Suicide*, eds. A. Beck, H. Resnik, and D. Lettieri. Bowie, MD: Charles Press.

Litman, R. (1967), Sigmund Freud on suicide. In: *Essays in Self-Destruction*, ed. E. Shneidman. New York: Science House.

———— (1974), Prediction models of suicidal behaviors. In: *The Prediction of Suicide*, eds. A. Beck, H. Resnik, and D. Lettieri. Bowie, MD: Charles Press.

———— (1975), The assessment of suicidality. In: *Consultation-Liaison Psychiatry*, ed. R. Pasnau. New York: Grune & Stratton.

Maltsberger, J., & Buie, D. (1974), Countertransference hate in the treatment of suicidal patients. *Arch. Gen. Psychiat.*, 30:625–633.

Menninger, K. (1938), *Man Against Himself*. New York: Harcourt Brace & World.

Minkoff, K., Bergman, E., Beck, A. & Beck, R. (1973), Hopelessness, depression and attempted suicide. *Amer. J. Psychiat.*, 130:455–459.

Motto, J. (1975), The recognition and management of the suicidal patient. In: *The Nature and Treatment of Depression*, eds. F. Flash and S. Draghi. New York: John Wiley.

———— (1977), Estimation of suicide risk by the use of clinical models. *Suicide & Life-Threat. Behav.*, 7:236–245.

———— (1979), The psychopathology of suicide: A clinical model approach. *Amer. J. Psychiat.*, 136:516–520.

————— (1980a), Suicide risk factors in alcohol abuse. *Suicide & Life-Threat. Behav.*, 10:230–238.

————— (1980b) Suicide risk factors in drug abuse. *Crisis*, 1:8–15.

————— (1984), Paradoxic aspects of suicide risk assessment. In: *American Family Physician, Family Practice Annual 1984.* Kansas City, MO: American Academy of Family Physicians.

————— Heilbron, D., & Juster, R. (1985), Development of a clinical instrument to estimate suicide risk. *Amer. J. Psychiat.*, 142:680–686.

Murphy, G. (1972), Clinical identification of suicidal risk. *Arch. Gen. Psychiat.*, 27:356–359.

————— (1983), On suicide prediction and prevention. *Arch. Gen. Psychiat.*, 40:343–344.

————— (1984), The prediction of suicide: Why is it so difficult? *Amer. J. Psychother.*, 38:341–349.

Pallis, D., Barraclough, A., Levey, A., Jenkins, J., & Sainsbury, P. (1982), Estimating suicide risk among attempted suicides: The development of new clinical scales. *Brit. J. Psychiat.*, 141:37, 44.

————— Gibbons, J., & Pierce, D. (1984), Estimating suicide risk among attempted suicides: Efficiency of predictive scales. *Brit. J. Psychiat.*, 144:139–148.

Patterson, W., Dohn, H., Bird, J., & Patterson, G. (1983), Evaluation of suicidal patients: The SAD PERSONS scale. *Psychomatics*, 24:343–349.

Poeldinger, W. (1968), *Zur Abschatzung der Suizidalitat.* Bern: Hans Huber.

Pokorny A. (1983), Prediction of suicide in psychiatric patients. *Arch. Gen. Psychiat.*, 40:249–257.

Ringel, E. (1976), The presuicidal syndrome. *Suicide & Life-Threat. Behav.*, 6:131–149.

Stengel, E. (1964), *Suicide and Attempted Suicide.* Baltimore, MD: Penguin.

Weisman, A., & Worden, W. (1972), Risk-rescue rating in suicide assessment. *Arch. Gen. Psychiat.*, 26:553–560.

Wekstein, L. (1979), *Handbook of Suicidology.* New York: Brunner/Mazel.

Wold, C. (1971), Subgroupings of suicidal people. *Omega*, 2:19–29.

Yufit, R., & Benzies, B. (1973), Assessing suicide potential by time perspective. *Suicide & Life-Threat. Behav.*, 3(4):270–282.

Zung, W. (1974), Index of potential suicide. In: *The Prediction of Suicide*, eds. A. Beck, H. Resnik, and D. Lettieri. Bowie, MD: Charles Press.

7

Suicides: What Do They Have in Mind?

Robert E. Litman, M.D.

THE VITAL BALANCE

Karl Menninger has always emphasized that suicide holds a central position in psychiatry. The concept of a "vital balance" provides a model of the mind that explains the first question, "Why do people stay alive, considering that all lives are a struggle, that human beings are vulnerable and helpless, and in the end, everyone dies?" According to Dr. Menninger (1963), people stay alive because they are in a vital balance in their own selves. In this concept, the self is an assemblage of component subselves comprising various attributes and characteristics and ways and habits of interacting drawn from past relationships and experiences, especially with important people, so-called "objects." Weakness in the ability to integrate these subselves and balance them is one of the measures of vulnerability to suicide.

In this concept, the mind is organized in levels or hierarchies of adaptational complexity. At times, in some people's lives, due to stress and disease, the organization falters. The vital balance is upset or perturbed and the person regresses to less complex, more primitive levels of adaptation. Suicide, then, is the result of a regression to the deepest level of adaptational disintegration or more accurately, suicide is the choice of death rather than suffering disintegration.

This is an "illness" concept of suicide. According to this model, suicide is intimately associated with mental disorders. There are, of course, other points of view, for example, sociological, ecological, religious, and forensic. There are some advantages both for the patient and the doctor for the concept of suicide as a disorder closely related to disease. For example, the Vatican, impressed by the illness metaphor, has ruled that no suicides shall have burial restrictions or other religious penalties. Similarly, insurance programs are more willing to pay to repair cut wrists. When suicidal persons call a telephone counseling service, the counselor can say, "Wait a minute, you're not yourself. The reason you feel this way is that you're ill. You can recover from the way you feel. There is help through treatment." Psychotherapists think in terms of "presuicidal syndromes" and "high risk" mental disorders.

PRESUICIDE SYNDROMES OR THE SUICIDE ZONE

While nonlethal suicide attempts are often impulsive and unplanned, that is not true of most highly lethal suicide attempts and completed suicides. Suicide is an ever present option as the answer to problems in living. Surveys indicate that 10 to 15 percent of the population have considered suicide fairly seriously at some time in their lives. Usually, at first, the suicide solution arouses feelings of anxiety and is rejected. Other options and potential solutions are sought and tried, both in imagination and in reality. However, if other possibilities fail to bring relief, the fantasy of death as a final solution to life's problems becomes more vivid and more compelling and more attractive. A method is chosen, a means is identified and rehearsed in imagination and in behavior. At this point, the person is well within what we may call the suicide zone. Clinically, we say they are at risk. This does not mean they are inevitably going to commit suicide; quite the opposite. For every 100 persons who enter the suicide zone, only one or two actually complete the act of suicide and die. Whether or not they actually kill themselves depends on a multiplicity of factors, including possibilities of rescue and the availability of treatment. A well-delineated presuicidal syndrome has been described by a number of investigators. The emphasis is on constriction of choices, constriction of preception, a tunnel vision of the world as hopeless, combined with tension and perturbation, and relieved by a fantasy of death. There is a hopelessness, combined with help-rejection and distrust. Often, in the background, there is a long-term disposition toward impatient action, an all or nothing approach to problems, and the characterological attitude, "my way or no way."

An example of constriction is the case of a 21-year-old woman who jumped off the Golden Gate Bridge in San Francisco and survived. Some months later, she was referred to me in Los Angeles because she was depressed, somewhat suicidal again, and she was addicted to drugs. The suicide attempt, she said, followed an abortion, which left her depressed and feeling disassociated, even from her boyfriend. With the idea of jumping off, she walked out on the bridge looking over the railing and thinking, "No one loves me. . . . My mother didn't love me, my father left me, my boyfriend doesn't care, no one cares." At this point, a guard drove up, took her by the elbow and said to her, "I think you're considering jumping off, aren't you, miss." When she nodded, yes, he drove her back to her hotel, back into the care of her fiancé. The next day, she came back to the bridge, and this time, all that was on her mind was, "I don't want the guard to catch me and stop me." So she dashed out on the bridge, ran a few steps, and grabbed the rail and vaulted over without looking. She landed in the water next to a footing of the bridge, surrounded by a concrete casing that protects the bridge footing. She broke all the ribs on one side, broke an arm, broke a leg, but she found herself in quiet water. A few feet away was an iron ladder, which she grasped and soon she was rescued. Incidentally, all the way down, she thought she would survive.

Several years ago, the author tried to answer the question of why people commit suicide by obtaining and personally reading all of the suicide notes discovered in Los Angeles over a period of two consecutive years. During that time, there were almost 3,000 committed suicides and almost 1,000 suicide notes. The task turned out to be a peculiarly distressing and disappointing one—distressing because there was so much human misery recorded in the coroner's files and in the suicide notes, disappointing because the notes failed to provide an explanation for the question, Why suicide? Suicide notes tend to be stereotyped and uncreative. The most typical note says: "I am sorry. I love you. Please forgive me. I have to do this." The next most common item in notes are instructions: "My car is parked across the street"; "Please pay back Stan the $20 I borrowed"; "Police, this is a suicide."

Some persons give reasons for the act of suicide. They express regret over a lost lover, apprehension about sickness, unwillingness to be a burden. Often, the communications describe fatigue, exhaustion, and a need to escape. "I just can't stand it any more, I am too tired to go on." The notes seldom (less than 10 percent) express anger or reproach. Humor is absent. The general mood of those notes that express feelings is one of hopelessness. However, there are those exceptional messages that convey a confident religious faith in a happy after-life.

Behavioral scientists have studied retrospectively the lives and circumstances surrounding individual suicides by interviews with surviving relatives and friends, a method sometimes called "psychological autopsies." After collecting these materials, psychiatrists have no great difficulty in making retrospective psychiatric diagnoses on 95 percent of those committed suicides. Typically, about 40 percent of the committed suicides are given the diagnosis of "affective disorder"; 20 to 25 percent of the committed suicides suffered from chronic alcoholism; 10 to 15 percent were schizophrenic; 20 to 25 percent could be diagnosed as chronic behavior disorder or personality maladjustment. Psychiatrists feel that these individuals should have consulted psychiatrists. The general public recognizes a moderate degree of association or relationship between suicide and madness, although, of course, most psychotic persons do not commit suicide and most persons who committed suicide were not psychotic. Slightly less than half of the persons who committed suicide have ever had some contact or connection with the mental health system, including psychiatrists.

SUICIDE PREDICTION

My colleague Carl Wold and I (Wold and Litman, 1973) once classified the persons who were in touch with the Suicide Prevention Center (SPC) in Los Angeles according to their presenting problems: persons who were old and sick; men and women who were suicidal in relation to a separation and divorce; young persons in turmoil; persons with continuing malignant masochism who dream about death as erotic fulfillment; middle-aged and older men and women with major affective disorders. By far the most dangerous were depressed persons with alcoholism as the presenting condition. Follow-up studies of suicide prevention center callers indicate that in general, 1 to 2 percent of them commit suicide within two years after their first contact with the center. This is pretty much the same rate as that of persons who have made suicide attempts sufficiently injurious to bring them to a hospital facility for medical treatment. That is understandable since about 50 percent of the callers to the SPC have made a previous suicide attempt. Only 20 percent of the callers are primarily alcoholics, but 80 to 90 percent of the completed suicides were alcoholics. Our experience over the years illustrates, on one hand, the high suicide rate in alcoholics, and on the other hand, the fact that treatment was not effective for depression or suicide ideation until the problem of alcoholism was first faced and solved.

Besides alcoholism, there were other differences between persons who committed suicide and persons who did not. Suicides tend to be male, older, not in crisis when they were first in touch with the Center, and very importantly, they tended to be treatment rejecting. One would think that when people call a telephone counseling service they want help. Their calling is a cry for help, but they want help on their own constricted terms. Many times they refuse an offer of face-to-face treatment or referral for face-to-face treatment. Nor is treatment refusal limited to SPC callers. Recently, a friend, Dr. O., a psychiatrist in treatment for manic-depressive disorder, repeatedly rejected the recommendation of the treating doctor that Dr. O. be hospitalized because he said that would destroy his image of himself as a practicing psychiatrist. When his therapist was away on vacation, Dr. O. shot himself. Apparently, preserving his image was more important than preserving his life.

Efforts to predict suicide by means of signs or symptoms or clusters of variables or psychiatric diagnoses have not been successful for two reasons. The first reason is the low base rate of suicide. For any patient, even the most lethal suicide risk (e.g., an elderly, sick man living alone, who has made a suicide attempt), the chance that he will commit suicide within a given period of time, say, a year, is much less than the chance that he will not have committed suicide within that time. That fact is used as a basic element in the author's long-term treatment of chronically suicidal persons. "I recognize that there is a possibility that you'll commit suicide in the next two or three years, but in my experience, the odds are very much in favor of your survival, and that helps me to be optimistic about the treatment."

The second problem in prediction of suicide is the extremely important distinction between suicidal crises and suicidal careers. Suicide prediction studies follow the careers of persons identified by certain traits or clusters of traits. Those who committed suicide are compared with those who survived. But these are outcome studies that measure suicide over a given period of time, one year, two years, five years. What clinicians want to know is how to evaluate the patient for committing suicide within the next 24 hours or the next two weeks, that is, short-term, rather than long-term prediction. For short-term suicide risk prediction we depend on clinical judgment and our empathic understanding of the patient based on taking sufficient time to build a therapeutic alliance and asking the appropriate questions to reveal suicidal trends.

MOTIVES, GOALS, AND INTENTIONS

Recognizing that suicide has many different motives and purposes, we search for evidence to help us understand the meaning of each suicide. We reconstruct persons' life-styles and life activities, what they said and wrote and did.

In general, people who commit suicide understand quite well that their particular action will lead to death and that death is final, and will end their earthly existence. Within their constricted viewpoints, they understand who they are, where they are, and what is going on around them. They state that suicide is the solution. Well then, what are the problems? Many suicides seem to be precipitated by a loss, for instance, of health or love or money, but motivations are various and multiple. Karl Menninger (1938) specified three major motivations as the wish to die, that is, to escape; the wish to kill, that is, anger and revenge; and the wish to be killed, which is guilt or atonement. Baechler (1975) developed a different classification with eleven types of motivation, including death and rebirth and transfiguration. There are usually complex combinations of motives for suicide.

Take, for example, the case of D.S., age 40, who killed himself with carbon monoxide in Los Angeles several years ago when investigators were closing in on his collapsing financial empire. He left a 40-minute tape recording of his last thoughts, which included many routine dispositions of possessions, recognition that his investors were out about $60 million, and a number of statements to the effect that, "I know a thousand ways to leave this country and never be found." But he repeated over and over again that he simply could not do that because that would not be his way, and, instead, he would commit suicide because that was the only way for him to go now. Mainly, the taped record was a last statement to his wife. He ended it by saying, "I love you, but it's too difficult for me to go on. I made up my mind a long time ago, and it has nothing to do with you." Beyond loss of money and guilt, there is a sense of *identity confirmed by suicide*. If my life can't be my way, then it will be no way.

SIGMUND FREUD ON SUICIDE

Some twenty years ago (1967), the author reviewed all of Freud's experience with
suicide, both personal and professional. Based on that, it is the author's opinion that
Freud never solved the "enigma of suicide," even to his own satisfaction, for more
than a few months at a time. The unsolved problem of suicide had a tremendous
influence on his instinct theory, which, of course, underwent a succession of
revisions. For the last decade of his life, Freud was totally convinced of the merit of
his concept of a primary self-destructive instinct, in conflict with Eros, so that in
theory, he searched for pockets of unfused destructive energy as the theoretic origin
of suicidal behaviors. The quotations from "Mourning and Melancholia" are familiar
in which "The shadow of the object fell upon the ego and thereafter, . . ." (Freud,
1917). Freud's dictum that suicide starts with a death wish against others, which is
then redirected toward an identification within the self, has been overly accentuated
among some psychotherapists, in the author's opinion, and has become a cliché.
Freud is quoted in support of a relative overemphasis on aggression and guilt as
components of suicide, with underemphasis of the elements of helplessness and
paranoia, and the erotic. Often, the suicidal drama reproduces not so much guilt for
the unconscious wish of the child to murder the parent but rather an abandonment
reaction on the part of the child to the parent's unconscious wish for the child's
death. The mechanism of regression and the themes in suicide of helplessness,
constriction, and paranoid distrust have made the deepest impression on the author.

Freud pointed out that infantile helplessness is the essential circumstance that
creates masochism, but Freud was accustomed to using his concept of the oedipal
complex as his reference point for psychopathology. From that viewpoint, guilt over
rivalry with parents, especially the father, looms large. At the Suicide Prevention
Center, the mother–child preoedipal relationship is used as a reference concept.
Freud, like many other clinicians who deal with suicide regularly in practice, came
to adopt a pragmatic treatment attitude. In 1926, in discussing a young patient,
Freud wrote, "What weighs on me in his case is my belief that unless the outcome is
very good, it will be very bad indeed. What I mean is that he would commit suicide
without any hesitation. I shall therefore do everything in my power to avert that
eventuality" (letter to Oskar Pfister in 1926, quoted by Meng and Freud, 1963).

DREAMS AND SUICIDE

In recent years, with increased attention to the problems of narcissistic, borderline,
and psychotic persons, psychoanalysts (e.g., Stolorow) have tried to designate more
clearly two different classes or categories of dreams. One class of dreams could be
termed classic neurotic dreams. The psychological structures involved are firm and
well integrated. The dream represents conflict and the manifest dreams are

considerably disguised. These are the dreams of neurotic persons or well-integrated persons. There is, however, a second class of dreams in which concrete symbols serve, not so much to actualize specific configurations of experience, but rather, to maintain psychological organization per se. The dreams of persons trying to recover from traumatic experiences and often the dreams of borderline, narcissistic, and suicidal persons have this quality. With these dreams, the distinction between manifest and latent content is much less germane because the aim of disguise has not been prominent. Kohut (1977) called these "self-state" dreams.

The dreams of suicidal persons are not identical with dreams of depressed persons, although there may be considerable overlapping, since some depressed persons are also suicidal persons. According to Beck and Ward (1961), the dreams of depressed persons are characterized by the following themes: being deprived, disappointed, mistreated; being thwarted, exploited, disgraced; being rejected and abandoned; being blamed, criticized, or ridiculed; being punished or injured; being lost or losing. The author's experiences are in agreement with Beck. Mostly, the author's depressed patients have reported unpleasant dreams. "I planted flowers but they wouldn't grow"; "I told my wife to find another man because I couldn't take care of her"; "You scheduled me for brain surgery. All of the patients were having brain surgery"; "The police took me away. No one believed me." The special themes that characterized my suicidal patients were dreams of violence, of destruction, of death and dead persons, and of giving up and merging with death. Examples in the literature come from Raphling (1970), Hendin (1982), Gutheil (1948), and Mintz (1971). Here it must be cautioned that dreams of death and destruction do not always, necessarily, or even usually, indicate suicidal situations. A physician dreamed, "My sister died." His first association involved a cousin who shot herself. He was not suicidal, but he was in the process of recognizing that he was immobilized in an untenable working situation with a female colleague.

A woman's dream of lying dead in a coffin referred to her sexuality without implying suicide. Another woman's dreams of tidal waves referred to passion, which she feared.

ILLUSTRATIVE DREAMS

Case Example 1

A 50-year-old male lawyer was referred for psychiatric treatment because of depression, sleep disorder, inability to concentrate, deep pessimism, alcoholism, and suicidal ideation. His first dream was the following: "There lay a piece of meat, laid out and revealed. Somehow, I felt that piece of meat was me." Shortly thereafter, there was a second dream: "This dream is similar to many other dreams I have had. I was inside a walled building. There was a gate with the door ajar. I felt anxious, I stepped out and slammed the door shut and started away. Then I became frightened and tried to get back." The dreams indicated low self-esteem, masochism, and great indecision about staying or leaving the treatment and his home and his whole style of life, but he was not seriously suicidal.

Most of the time, he was angry and dissatisfied with his work and with his home life. In fact, he was poorly regarded both by his wife and his business associates, and it became obvious that he needed to reorganize both these aspects of his life, but he felt incompetent to take action in either regard. Then he became highly suicidal. He dreamed he fell into a lake with terrible rough waves, became exhausted, and drowned. Another dream: "Things on the roof. The house was falling apart. The whole thing collapsed. I was standing in the middle of dead bodies. Was I responsible?" These dreams vividly picture self dissolution and images of death.

Earlier, he had done service work in a rural community and he came to dwell on this experience as the one ideal time in his life. As he became more certain of his decision to kill himself, he began to dream regularly of returning to that community with a feeling of peace and resolution. His death, by gunshot, represented an escape by merging with that idealized time and place.

Case Example 2

The author reviewed this case because there was litigation. The patient walked out of a psychiatric hospital and jumped to his death from the Bay Bridge. That same morning, the patient had reported a dream to his psychiatrist, who entered it into the hospital records. "I am in a car by the harbor. There is a military jet plane, barely above, and then a fiery plane crash. I am driving with someone else. We turn off the rocky road and see where the accident was. No one knew who was the mechanic who had been working on this plane." Information from various sources led the author to the clear inference that the patient identified himself with the malfunctioning aircraft. The dream presented a concrete image of the dissolution of his self.

Case Example 3

A woman who survived jumping from a great height reported: "The night before, I dreamed my dog was dead, and I thought, that's me."

Case Example 4

In potential suicide situations, dreams may be useful as guides to treatment measures. Unexpectedly, a young engineer volunteered the following: "Last night I had a vivid dream. In my dream, there were two of me sitting in the driver's seat holding a gold-plated gun to my head. Then the passenger (who was also me) put his hand on the gun and pulled the trigger spattering stuff all over. The one in the driver's seat said, 'oh no!'" The dream report caused the therapist to alter substantially his therapeutic stance. Note especially the imagery of splitting of the self.

Case Example 5

A manic-depressive woman who was going through a stressful divorce almost died in a suicide attempt. Later, she became depressed again and she dreamed: "My husband's grandmother was dying in a beautiful room. She looks better but she's really dying. We need to put her out of her misery, but how? Someone tells me this thin needle will do it, she won't feel a thing and it will be all over." Associations are that the patient wants to die and feels suicidal. At this point, there was a psychiatric consultation with the recommendation of antidepressant medication and a more supportive psychotherapy.

Case Example 6

An outstanding feature of many final dreams before suicide is the image of death as merging into a state of peace or beauty or erotic fulfillment. The following cases are examples: The day before she committed suicide by taking an overdose of sleeping pills, a 50-year-old woman dreamed: "I was walking down a street with my brother and we said goodbye to each other. I turned and walked off the road into a beautiful meadow with flowers and sunshine, peaceful and lovely. He, on the other hand, walked on into the dirty, dark, dangerous alley filled with garbage and filth." Her brother was the only person with whom she had a consistently supportive relationship, and in the dream, she was bidding goodbye to him and the therapist. The dream image of the beautiful meadow symbolizes her wish to regain her own youth and beauty; the alley into which she sends her brother–analyst, symbolizes the current feeling about herself as ugly, old, and dirty.

Case Example 7

The night before a party to honor his fortieth birthday, a research professor lay in bed restlessly wondering what to do with his life. Finally, sleeping, he dreamed of a large black cube which lay in his way as he tried to walk along a path. No matter how hard he tried to move it, the cube moved with him, so he could not proceed. Finally, in the dream, he gave up and merged with the black cube. The dream feeling was one of resignation and peace. That day, he went to the party but was unable to face his colleagues, and, instead, drove to a nearby motel and made a suicide attempt by turning on the gas. The symbolism of the large black cube had to do in part with the type of work he did, and his unique modes of thought. The cube reminded him of black holes, entropy, the destiny of the universe. Giving up and merging with the powerful cube symbolized the end of his efforts to try to cope and his acceptance of death. He had felt completely powerless and helpless. In the concrete symbol of the dream, and in the enactment of suicide, the patient preserved his self-esteem by merging completely with a powerful object.

In summary, the dreams of persons who are at high risk for suicide consistently present images of being trapped and helpless, images of impending dissolution of self, or images of attaining freedom through merging with representations of death as peace and healing power. These dreams portray the situation of the dreamer and the solutions he has in mind: the destruction and elimination of the painful and unworthy self, and the preservation of the ideal self by merging with death as peace and healing power.

TREATMENT

To the extent that these dream images represent typically the psychological state of persons about to take suicidal action, they provide some guidelines for treatment. The goal here is to heal or bring together the split in the self in which one important part is felt as an impossible ideal and the other part is destined for destruction.

In planning treatment, it is important to assess the time dimension; that is, how long a person has had it in mind to commit suicide. For suicidal patients in a true short-term crisis, most of the therapeutic activity of the therapist is aimed at reinforcing ego defenses, renewing feelings of hope, love, and trust, and providing emergency scaffolding to aid in the eventual repair and healing of the splits in the patient's self. Such patients may require protective custody and security observation for short periods of time (48 hours to a week). The special precautions are justified by the expectation that acute patients will tend to make a complete recovery in a reasonably short period of time. On the other end, there are many patients who are involved in careers of suicide with histories of repetitive suicide attempts or recurrent depressive episodes or self-destructive life-styles, including alcohol abuse and drug addiction. Many of these patients remain at high risk for suicide over long periods of time—months or years. Their suicidal behaviors do not represent crises so much as repetitive behavior patterns in a person with a serious personality disorder or major psychiatric disorder. For these patients, the treatment plan should emphasize the gradual amelioration of their self destructive life-styles, with rather less emphasis on active intervention to insure the safety of the patient. We noted, in one study, (Litman and Wold, 1976) that continuing psychotherapeutic interventions with depressed and suicidal substance abusing patients were not helpful and were possibly harmful. They were harmful because many of the therapists found that they could not adequately deal with the destructive and hateful attitudes of the clients. The therapists developed various counterreactions of discouragement and rejection.

Under the heading of countertransference hate, some of these problems have been well discussed by Maltsberger and Buie (1974). For those therapists who have countertransference problems with their borderline and psychotic suicidal patients (we all do), the author strongly recommends sharing the problem through supervision, consultation, through case presentations, and best of all, through planned team approaches. In Los Angeles, about 7 or 8 percent of the suicides occur in persons who were in therapy at the time they killed themselves. Since suicide often occurred when the therapist was away on vacation, it is advisable to have an ancillary therapist, someone who is still there when the primary therapist goes away. It is advisable, at times, especially after a nonfatal suicide attempt, to transfer the patient to another therapist. Although it is unethical to abandon suicidal patients, it is often good technique to transfer the patient. To use a sports metaphor, the therapy of a chronically suicidal person does not necessarily have to be a marathon. Often, successful therapy is a relay. The concept of the expendable therapist is offered, that is, the therapist who encounters the patient's transference and hate and does the best he or she can, resolves some of it, and passes the patient along to the next therapist. It is something like the function of the defensive end trying to tackle O. J. Simpson. The end is doing well enough to knock down the blockers and let the linebacker make the tackle. In a more morbid metaphor, cancer is often treated by sequences of therapists: surgery then radiation, then chemotherapy.

It is heuristically worthwhile to consider suicide as the end point of a widespread mental disorder with symptoms of almost universal malaise and a consistent noticeable mortality (i.e., 1 to 2 percent of U.S. deaths are by suicide). Recently, the Center for Disease Control in Atlanta has activated a section for epidemiologic research on suicide. It is fair to report, however, that so far no health-oriented development has affected the rate of suicide. No effect has been seen due to the increase in psychiatrists and other mental health personnel; no change due to shorter or longer stays in psychiatric hospitals; no reduction due to electric shock treatment, antidepressant drugs, antipsychotic drugs, or the Centers for Crisis Intervention.

We have not yet devised educational or treatment strategies that consistently reach the core of the problem and resolve it. Indeed, one cannot be sure that such resolution is possible. Many investigators in various disciplines concur with Freud's concept that self-destructiveness is carried in the human genes and encouraged by the repressive aspects of civilization so that a certain minimal suicide rate is to be expected as part of the human condition.

Our present antisuicide therapy is pragmatic. Recognizing clearly the reality of our own limitations as therapists, we do for the patients "everything in our power." Usually, that is enough to help them survive.

REFERENCES

Baechler, J. (1975), *Suicides*. New York: Basic Books.
Beck, A.T., & Ward, C.H. (1961), Dreams of depressed patients. *Arch. Gen. Psychiat.*, 5:462–467.
Freud, S. (1917), Mourning and melancholia. *Standard Edition*, 14:237–258. London: Hogarth Press, 1957.

Gutheil, E.A. (1948), Dreams and suicide. *Amer. J. Psychiat.*, 2:283–294.

Hendin, H. (1982), *Suicide in America*. New York: W.W. Norton.

Kohut, H. (1977), *The Restoration of the Self*. New York: International Universities Press.

Litman, R.E. (1967), Sigmund Freud on suicide. In: *Essays in Self Destruction*, ed. E.S. Shneidman, New York: Science Press.

————— (1980), Dreams in the suicidal situation. In: *The Dream in Clinical Practice*, ed. J. Natterson. New York: Jason Aronson.

————— Wold, C.I. (1976), Beyond crisis. In: *Suicidology: Contemporary Developments*, ed. E.S. Shneidman. New York: Grune & Stratton.

Maltsberger, J.T., & Buie, D.H. (1974), Countertransference hate in the treatment of suicidal patients. *Arch. Gen. Psychiat.*, 30:838–842.

Maris, R.W. (1981), *Pathways to Suicide*. Baltimore, MD: Johns Hopkins University Press.

Meng, H., & Freud, E.L. (1963), *Psychoanalysis and Faith*. New York: Basic Books, p. 101.

Menninger, K. (1938), *Man Against Himself*. New York: Harcourt Brace.

————— (1963), *The Vital Balance*. New York: Viking Press.

Mintz, R.S. (1971), Basic considerations in the psychotherapy of the depressed suicidal patient. *Amer. J. Psychother.*, 25:56–73.

Raphling, D.L. (1970), Dreams and suicide attempts. *J. Nerv. & Ment. Dis.*, 151:404–410.

Shneidman, E.S., Farberow, N.L., & Litman, R.E. (1970), Sigmund Freud on suicide. In: *The Psychology of Suicide*. New York: Science House.

Stolorow, R.D. & Lachmann, F.M. (1980) *Psychoanalysis of Developmental Arrests*. New York: International University Press.

Wold, C.I., & Litman, R.E. (1973), Suicide after contact with a suicide prevention center. *Arch. Gen. Psychiat.*, 28:735–739.

B. Specific Assessment Considerations

8

Personality Disorders, Suicide, and Self-destructive Behavior

J. Christopher Perry, M.P.H., M.D.

Like murder, suicide is the ultimate unleashing of destructive aggression. Whatever the circumstances, individuals who commit suicide or murder could be expected to differ from the general population in the belief that their options for coping are less effective, more limited in scope, and beyond their control. These features are also characteristic of individuals with personality disorders.

THE ASSOCIATION BETWEEN SUICIDAL BEHAVIORS AND PERSONALITY DISORDERS

There are no population-based surveys that delineate the relationship between personality disorders and suicidal behaviors. However, studies of suicide attempters in treatment settings suggest that there is a substantial association. Helgason (1964) examined causes of death among 247 individuals with personality disorders in Iceland. Four of the 67 deaths (6 percent) were attributed to suicide. Pokorny (1964) examined follow-up data of several psychiatric disorders and found a suicide rate among personality disorders of 130 per 100,000 per year. Miles (1977) reviewed these studies among others and estimated that the proportion of deaths by suicide among personality disorders is about 5 percent, a smaller proportion than for depression, alcoholism, schizophrenia, and opiate addiction.

A study by Black, Warrack, and Winokur (1985) examined cause of death among former psychiatric inpatients. The proportion of deaths in each diagnostic group due to suicide was as follows: affective disorder (32.3 percent); schizophrenia (20.5 percent); personality disorder (10.3 percent); alcohol and drug abuse (8.8 percent). The standard mortality ratio (i.e., proportion of observed deaths to expected deaths) for suicide was 11.91 for males and 16.67 for females with personality disorders. Seventy-nine percent of the suicides occurred within two years

157

of the index admission. In addition, the incidence of accidental death was 26.3 percent among personality disorders (standard mortality ratios of 3.15 for males and 5.76 for females). Because this study assigned personality disordered individuals with concurrent major psychiatric syndromes to the concurrent diagnosis, these figures may actually underestimate the risk of suicide and accidental death attributable to personality disorders.

Montgomery and Montgomery (1982) conducted controlled studies of the pharmacological prevention of suicide in multiple suicide attempters with personality disorders. Of 37 patients on placebo, 49 percent had made a subsequent attempt within three months of follow-up, and 65 percent had made an attempt within six months, giving a suicide attempt rate 650 times that for the general population.

Overall, personality disorder should be considered a substantial risk factor for suicide, accidental death, as well as for nonlethal suicide attempts. Furthermore, the risk rises given a history of previous attempts.

SUICIDE AND SPECIFIC TYPES OF PERSONALITY DISORDERS

The *Diagnostic and Statistical Manual of Mental Disorders* (DSM-III) personality disorders can be divided into three groups. These are discussed in ascending order of the risk for suicide and self-destructive behavior.

Schizophrenic Spectrum

The schizophrenic spectrum includes paranoid, schizoid, and schizotypal personality disorders. To date, no study has reported an association between these three diagnoses and suicidal phenomena. Although diagnoses were not noted, Kiev (1976) found a cluster of socially isolated adults in a study of suicide attempters. They were characterized by many interpersonal conflicts, unusual thoughts and behaviors, and high suicide potential. Their suicide attempts were usually done in isolation, without attempt to elicit rescue. The author was unable to locate these subjects for follow-up, which parallels the finding of the high treatment dropout rate in this group.

Anxiety Spectrum

The anxiety spectrum includes the compulsive, dependent, passive–aggressive, and avoidant personality disorders. The revision of DSM-III also adds masochistic personality disorder. Anecdotally, compulsive traits are often found in middle-aged individuals who make suicide attempts, but there is no documented association with compulsive personality disorder. In a sample of 40 adolescent suicide attempters

(Crumley, 1979), only one patient had a compulsive personality disorder. Similarly there is no evidence that dependent or avoidant personality disorders are at risk for suicide. In theory, these two disorders might be associated with a decreased risk for suicide, because they tend to express attachment needs and rejection-sensitivity by taking care of others, while they are generally inhibited in expressing anger.

In contrast, the passive–aggressive personality disorder is associated with the expression of anger, often directed inward. Crumley (1979) found passive–aggressive personality disorder in only one of 40 adolescent suicide attempters. In an eleven-year follow-up of 100 inpatients with the passive–aggressive diagnosis, Small, Small, Alig, and Moore (1970) found that only one patient had committed suicide (during a depressive episode), although symptoms of alcohol abuse, anxiety, depression, and suicidal ruminations were common. There does appear to be a significant risk for suicide attempts in the passive–aggressive personality disorder, but less so than among the impulsive spectrum of personality disorders noted below.

The Impulsive Spectrum

Narcissistic, histrionic, antisocial, and borderline personality disorders constitute the impulsive spectrum, the third group of personality disorders. These disorders—especially the latter two—constitute by far the greatest risk for suicide and self-destructive behavior.

Narcissistic Personality Disorder   The relationship between narcissistic personality and suicide potential is unexplored. Theoretically, the extreme vulnerability to loss of self-esteem coupled with dysphoria in response to failure, criticism, and humiliation should put these individuals at high risk for suicide attempts. The overlap between narcissistic and borderline personality disorders (Adler, 1981) may be responsible for this apparent increased suicide risk, especially in males (Vaillant and Perry, 1985).

Histrionic Personality Disorder   Histrionic traits are common in suicide attempters. Among 22 adolescent suicide attempters, Crumley (1981) found histrionic traits in 32 percent, while borderline personality disorder was present in all cases. In another series of forty adolescent suicide attempters, only one (3 percent) had histrionic personality disorder without borderline personality disorder (Crumley, 1979). Confusion between these two disorders is possible when the dramatic, attention-seeking features of the histrionic patient overshadow the borderline features. To aid this discrimination, the revision of DSM-III is removing the criterion "prone to manipulative suicidal threats, gestures, or attempts" from the definition of histrionic personality disorder.

Antisocial Personality Disorder   Antisocial personality disorder has been associated with suicide attempts and self-destructive behavior. In a follow-up of a community-based sample of antisocial adults, Robins (1966) found that 11 percent had a history of a suicide attempt. In a psychiatric study of imprisoned male felons, Guze (1976) found that 78 percent had antisocial personality by Feighner criteria, but only 5 percent had ever made a suicide attempt. Virkkunen (1976) examined criminals with antisocial personality sent for evaluation by the court to a special psychiatric ward, 24 percent of whom had a history of wrist-slashing. The context of the slashing is important since 87.5 percent of them occurred in prison or during other confinement. The reasons given for slashing included finding solitary confinement oppressive, wanting to create some diversion, wanting tranquilizers, or attempting to get transferred to a psychiatric unit, which was seen as more desirable than a cell.

When studies examine antisocial individuals seen in psychiatric settings, the figures rise. Woodruff, Guze, and Clayton (1971) found 23 percent of antisocial psychiatric outpatients had a history of a suicide attempt, while Spalt (1974) found a figure of 34.6 percent. When they examined antisocial psychiatric patients—half of whom were inpatients—Garvey and Spoden (1980) found that 72 percent had made at least one suicide attempt. The incidence of attempts was the same for men and women. Most attempts were nonserious (i.e., of low lethality) and manipulative, since they usually followed a breakup or problems in a relationship.

The presence of depressant type drug abuse may increase the risk for suicide attempts. A study of polydrug abusers (Ward and Schuckit, 1980) demonstrated that those with a history of serious suicide attempts were more likely to have sociopathy (47 percent), to prefer alcohol and other depressant type drugs (27 percent), and to have a history of barbiturate withdrawal (48 percent).

The present author has been conducting a study of antisocial and borderline personality disorders, and bipolar type II affective disorder, that is, depression with hypomania (Perry, 1985; Perry and Cooper, 1985). Only 29 percent of fourteen individuals with DSM-III antisocial personality disorder gave a history of a suicide attempt, and none had made five or more attempts. However, among eleven individuals with both antisocial and borderline personality disorder, 82 percent had made at least one suicide attempt, and 27 percent had made five or more. Thus, suicide attempts in antisocial individuals may indicate a concurrent borderline personality disorder, especially when occurring outside of a correctional facility.

These studies suggest several conclusions about antisocial personality disorder. First, a higher proportion of antisocial individuals with histories of suicide attempts is found in more intensive psychiatric settings, such as inpatient wards. Second, most suicide attempts are nonserious and often have a manipulative intent. Third, more serious attempts may be associated with depressant drug use. Fourth, the more serious and repeated suicide attempters are found in patients with concurrent borderline personality disorder.

Borderline Personality Disorder   Gardner and Dowdry (1985a) defined four constellations of suicidal and self-destructive behaviors in borderline patients. The first type in which melancholia and despair lead to true suicidal acts, has the highest risk. In their evaluation of 40 borderline patients at the National Institute of Mental Health (NIMH), the three patients who subsequently suicided did so several months into classical endogenomorphic depressive episodes. Impulsive, nihilistic rage constitutes the second type. The patient's perception that others have wronged him or her or failed to offer support leads to a narcissistic rage. This may result in impulsive violence toward others or the self. Communicative parasuicidal gestures, the third type, are manipulative suicide gestures that occur in proximity to others in order to convey a message. Rescue is usually intended, although sometimes these gestures are practice attempts leading up to a more serious attempt. The fourth type is characterized by self-mutilation or overdose, which are attempts to relieve dysphoria, often precipitated by rejection. The self-mutilation includes wrist-cutting, burning, scratching or hitting oneself, or overuse of medications. The patient often goes through several phases: ruminating over a real or perceived rejection, feeling anxiety and depression mount, and finally reaching a state of emptiness and depersonalization, which the self-destructiveness then relieves. This typology of self-destructive behavior may have important etiological and therapeutic implications.

There is a significant association between suicide attempts and borderline personality disorder. Crumley (1979) found that 55 percent of adolescent suicide attempters had borderline personality disorder. Friedman, Aronoff, Clarkin, Corn, and Hurt (1983) examined 53 depressed adolescent and adult inpatients and found that suicide attempts were significantly more common among borderline (92 percent) than nonborderline (59 percent) inpatients. This association increased when they examined suicide attempts rated at least mildly serious in lethality (borderline 86 percent, other personality disorders 30 percent, nonpersonality disorders 29 percent.

The converse is also true: studies of borderline personality disorder find that a high proportion of these patients have a history of suicide attempts and other self-destructive behaviors. In the present author's sample of twenty subjects with borderline personality disorder, 80 percent have made at least one suicide attempt, while 45 percent have made five or more attempts. The most characteristic attempt in 42 percent was done with precautions to prevent discovery, while fewer attempts were done with others nearby who were likely to discover the subject (21 percent), while alone followed by going for help (16 percent), or done while in an institution (5 percent). The modal attempt therefore demonstrates some lethal intent. Wrist-cutting was found in 80 percent, while other forms of self-mutilation were found in 65 percent of the borderline subjects. Taking pills or alcohol to the point of passing out (excluding suicide attempts) was found in 60 percent of borderline subjects, although this was less than for the subjects with antisocial personality (86 percent) or both antisocial and borderline personality disorders (100 percent). When Schaffer,

Carroll, and Abramowitz (1982) examined fourteen self-mutilators, they diagnosed all as borderline, using Gunderson's DIB.

As expected, borderline patients with a history of repeated suicide attempts are at special risk for future attempts. In their study of the efficacy of medications for decreasing the incidence of suicide attempts among repeat attempters without melancholia, Montgomery and Montgomery (1982) found that 65 percent of borderline and histrionic patients in the placebo control groups had made a subsequent suicide attempt by six months of follow-up. Among the active medication groups, the incidence of attempts was not significantly lower (47 percent) for those taking low dose mianserin (30 mg q.h.s.), an antidepressant. However those taking the depot neuroleptic flupenthixol (20 mg q. 4 weeks) made significantly fewer attempts (21 percent).

Coexisting depression, alcohol, and substance abuse probably predispose to suicide attempts or the loss of control over self-destructive urges. Rigorously conducted studies have found major depressive disorder in from 50 to 90 percent of borderline patients (Perry, 1985; Gunderson and Elliott, 1985). In addition, the present author (Perry, 1985) found chronic depression in 100 percent of his borderline subjects. Alcohol abuse or dependence and drug use or dependence was diagnosed respectively in 43 and 87 percent of the same sample of borderline personality disorder (Perry and Cooper, 1985). Symptoms of alcohol and drug abuse were not significantly associated with borderline psychopathology on follow-up, whereas they were with antisocial personality disorder. Nace, Saxon, and Shore (1983) found that suicide attempts were significantly more common in alcoholics with borderline personality (60 percent) than in nonborderline alcoholics (13.6 percent).

Treatment studies offer some intriguing evidence that the risk of suicide attempts and self-destructive behavior can be ameliorated in some cases. As noted above, Montgomery and Montgomery (1982) found that a depot neuroleptic decreased the subsequent incidence of suicide attempts by two-thirds compared to placebo. No effect was found for a low dose antidepressant. Gardner and Cowdry (1985b) reported a NIMH study of four active drugs and placebo in outpatients with borderline personality disorder. There were no changes in self-destructive behavior either on placebo or the neuroleptic trifluoperazine. There was a pronounced improvement in depression and secondarily in self-destructive behavior with the MAO inhibitor tranylcypromine. The anticonvulsant carbamazepine demonstrated significant improvement in global self-control and control of self-destructiveness, with only modest improvement in depression. Finally the benzodiazepine drug, alprazolam, was associated with increased episodes of dyscontrol (Gardner and Cowdry, 1985b) in 58 percent of the cases. Despite this, 17 percent of the patients showed good clinical improvement without loss of control on alprazolam. Frankel (1984) noted that ECT is rarely effective in treating suicidal individuals with personality disorders, except in the presence of a major depression. It is safe to conclude that medications may play an important part in helping ameliorate depression, as well as suicidal and self-destructive behavior in borderline patients, although no single class of drugs helps all patients.

Behavioral and dynamic treatments have also proved efficacious. Rosen and Thomas (1984) devised a substitute behavior to reduce emotional tension for three chronic wrist-cutters with borderline personality disorder. They had the patients squeeze a rubber ball beyond the point of producing ischemic muscle pain whenever they felt like cutting themselves. All three patients remained free of wrist-cutting on follow-up. Liberman and Eckman (1981) compared behavior and dynamic therapies in an intensive eight-day inpatient treatment of repeated suicide attempters, most of whom had personality disorders. The behavior therapy used anxiety management techniques (relaxation and imagery), social skills training, and contingency contracting with family members to improve family relationships. On 36-week follow-up both treatment groups remained less depressed and suicidal than prior to hospitalization. There was a trend for those treated with behavior therapy to show more improvement.

PSYCHODYNAMIC FACTORS

The present author has examined psychodynamic conflicts in a sample of borderline and/or antisocial personality disorders compared with bipolar type II affective disorder (Perry and Cooper, 1985; Perry and Cooper, 1986). Each subject was rated on the Borderline Personality Disorder Scale (BPD Scale) (Perry and Cooper, 1986). Subscale two of the BPD Scale, self-destructive dyscontrol of impulses and anger, consists of the following items: general impulsiveness, physically self-destructive acts, intentional drug overdoses, repetitive impulses, and suicide attempts. Psychodynamic conflicts were rated from videotaped interviews of thirty-two subjects using a two-stage procedure that yielded scores on eleven conflicts measured by the Psychodynamic Conflict Rating Scales (Perry and Cooper, 1986). Three conflicts correlated significantly with the patient's history of self-destructive dyscontrol as measured by the BPD subscale.

Separation–abandonment conflict demonstrated the highest correlation with self-destructiveness (spearman $rs = .57$, $p < .001$, $n = 32$). Individuals with separation–abandonment conflict become strongly attached and they are painfully prone to separation and abandonment feelings. They experience significant others as necessary parts of their emotional lives. Whenever rejection is threatened or occurs, the individuals feel anxious and helpless and they try to bargain or manipulate to preserve the attachment bond. Because they cannot rely on inner resources for soothing themselves, these individuals get overwhelmed by feelings of emptiness and despair. This conflict is highly associated with borderline psychopathology ($rs = .70$, $p < .001$, $n = 27$) and negatively associated with antisocial symptoms ($rs = -.33$, $p < .10$, $n = 27$).

Object hunger correlated next highest with self-destructiveness ($rs = .47$,

$p < .01$, $n = 32$). Individuals with this conflict experience an emotional void in their lives and believe that they are endangered without attachment to someone most of the time. This need is not specific to one individual, and the subject fears that one object can never suffice. Individuals with this conflict are often indiscriminate so that many attachments are short-lived. The capacity to be alone is diminished. Any circumstance that isolates the individual from known attachments might increase the risk for self-destructiveness. This conflict correlated significantly with borderline psychopathology ($rs = .49$, $p < .01$, $n = 27$) but not with antisocial symptoms ($rs = -.13$, n.s.).

The global conflict over the experience and expression of emotional needs and anger correlated third highest with self-destructiveness ($rs = .37$, $p < .05$, $n = 32$). Individuals with this conflict are usually inhibited from clearly experiencing their own needs and anger. They generally believe that both are unacceptable to others. A pervasive sense of self-loathing, anxiety, and dysphoria commonly arise whenever they become aware of their own needs or anger. In addition they are generally blocked in expressing themselves except when feeling desperate, at which times they may act in very entitled and aggressive ways, or become self-destructive. This conflict was found in 100 percent of the borderline and 63 percent of the antisocial subjects. This conflict predisposes individuals to experience themselves as trapped and limited in their options to get their needs met.

The finding that all three of these conflicts are associated with borderline personality disorder whereas only the third conflict is associated with antisocial personality disorder helps explain why borderline patients are at higher risk for suicide and self-destructive behavior than antisocial patients are. Individuals with borderline personality disorder are prone to suicide attempts because they crave attachments, are unable to express their needs and anger adequately in relationships, and are prone to extreme anxiety when threatened with rejection. Serious suicide attempts occur when despair attends real or perceived loss of close attachments. Manipulative suicide gestures occur when anger is turned against the self instead of toward the attachment figure for fear of rejection. Paradoxically, such an attempt often promotes closeness by inducing a sense of guilt in the significant other as if he or she should have done something to prevent the subject from feeling so overwhelmed. When alone, self-destructive behavior sometimes relieves tension and dysphoria whenever the subject feels increasingly out of touch with needs and anger building up inside. There may also be an element of communication in these acts, when the subject later relates his or her actions to others.

PSYCHODYNAMICS AND THE MANAGEMENT OF SELF-DESTRUCTIVENESS

While the long-term treatment of suicidal and self-destructive individuals with personality disorders is beyond the scope of this chapter, there are some useful principles that can help the clinician manage episodes of acute risk. These are based on identifying which of the preceding psychodynamic conflicts underlie the patient's acute presentation. Some patients—especially those with borderline personality disorder—may have more than one of these conflicts. The management principles apply across the DSM-III personality disorder types. They should be used in concert with a thorough assessment of the risk for self-harm, and they should not be viewed as a substitute for hospitalization should the clinician judge serious self-harm likely.

Separation–Abandonment

The patient with separation–abandonment presents during periods of high risk with feelings of panic, despair, and a pronounced sense of helplessness, following a real or perceived rejection. The patient may request concrete help with coping, but refusal to help himself or herself parallels the patient's disorganized responses. Instead there is a temporary conviction that only the constant presence of a helping figure will allow him or her to survive the crisis. The end of the interview occasions increased anxiety, tears, and threats of potential harm, inviting the therapist to lose objectivity.

After identifying the presence of separation–abandonment conflict, the clinician should inquire about stressors that have triggered the potentially self-destructive crisis. The overall aim of the interview then is to calm the separation panic and find other less destructive ways to handle the crisis at hand.

The therapist should limit the emotional outpouring by being active. Questions, clarifications, and empathic comments can help the patient contain his or her pain. On the other hand, extended passive listening may paradoxically increase the patient's conviction that there is no escape from painful feelings apart from self-harm, and the patient may regress during the interview. Asking about areas of the patient's life undisturbed by the crisis may identify strengths that will subsequently play a part in the restitution of emotional control.

The therapist should find ways to comfort and soothe the patient. This diminishes anxiety and panic. In some settings it may be possible to offer coffee, tea, or a cold drink, which the patient can hold and take in as a symbol of help. Small gestures of concern, such as letting the patient make a phone call from the office, may help. It is also useful to diminish the pressure of time. In emergency settings, this may involve talking with the patient several brief times over a longer period of time than the traditional hour. In office settings, it may require scheduling a short check-in appointment before the next regular session. For those cases in which the patient feels unable to leave the office at the close of a session, simply suggesting that the patient sit in the waiting room until calmed down may suffice. This may forestall the resurgence of separation–abandonment panic. The therapist should not push for closure on all of the problems at hand because the patient may get more anxious.

Rather, temporizing on large problems while seeking alternatives for the management of the immediate crisis is preferable.

The patient may have many potentially self-defeating and self-destructive responses to the crisis. In weighing alternative ways to cope, the therapist should not convey rejection of the patient's views. Including them as alternatives along with more effective suggestions obviates a struggle with the patient. Instead, the therapist can help the patient think through the consequences of all of the alternatives, urging him or her to pursue these actively. "What do you think would happen if you did . . ." may elicit a realistic appraisal of the consequences from the patient. If not, then the therapist may offer one. Finally, the therapist should understand that acceptable alternatives require some fulfillment of attachment needs or repair of the threatened attachment bond. When this is not the case, the patient is at higher risk for self-harm.

The session should not end without some concrete plans. In emergency settings, this may include a list of activities to help weather the crisis, arrangements to stay with a friend or relative, and active follow-up plans. In most cases, the next visit should be scheduled within several days. The availability and proximity of the appointment matter more than its duration. It helps create the expectation that adequate help will be available, and allows the patient to direct some attachment feelings toward help givers.

Global Conflict over the Experience and Expression of Emotional Needs and Anger

Although generally submissive and unexpressive, in a crisis the person with this global conflict usually presents differently. Any events that make the patient aware of mounting unmet needs or anger may precipitate the feeling of being overwhelmed. This may be complicated by feeling guilty about what is finally expressed, or feeling blamed by significant others. The patient may appear angry and demanding, while exaggerating the situation that produced the crisis. The patient defends against fears of being ignored or put down by acting as if he is entitled to have any request fulfilled. This aggressive self-assertion covers up the patient's usual inability to assert himself. Finally, when the patient's wishes meet with frustration, he may manipulate others by inducing some disaster to make others assume responsibility. Self-destructive behaviors have the same intent. Unfortunately, the patient's way of demanding action from the clinician, while rejecting the help offered as too little, invites the therapist to respond with countertransference hate (Maltsberger and Buie, 1974) and blame the patient for the crisis.

After the clinician has determined that the potentially self-destructive crisis is related to the underlying global conflict over experiencing and expressing emotional needs and anger, the following principles in management should help. The clinician should avoid any statement that might be interpreted as criticism or blame. Similarly, confronting the patient early about maladaptive choices or behavior should be avoided, because of the patient's sensitivity to criticism. The therapist should respect the patient's entitlement. In the context of a crisis, it is best construed as a sign of a will to survive despite a painful sense of deprivation. Allying with this entitlement to survive may be the first step in reaching a conclusion to the crisis that is not self-destructive.

If the patient defensively denies personal responsibility, the therapist should accept this. Going along with the denial may facilitate the patient eventually becoming less defensive and more open to accepting a positive role in solving the crisis at hand. The therapist should handle projection of blame the same way. By not challenging the patient, the clinician can make the interview seem safer. The patient will reveal his or her more vulnerable concerns when safety from blame is assured.

When the clinician has established some rapport and helped the patient ventilate some anger and distress, he or she can begin to explore alternatives with the patient. The patient's angry statements that suicide is the best solution should be accepted as only one of the possible alternatives. The therapist may mobilize the patient to think of healthier actions by fully delineating the consequences of the self-defeating alternatives. The patient then needs to explore multiple alternatives with the therapist. Opening up new options relieves the hopeless and trapped feeling better than trying to foreclose bad options.

Finally, helping the patient select ways to handle the crisis requires acknowledging what is lacking in the chosen solutions. After the crisis is settled the basic context of the patient's life remains the same, as do the patient's psychological conflicts. For instance, the patient may decide that it is necessary to express something important to a significant other, but one cannot guarantee an understanding response.

By the end of the interview, the clinician should try to do something concrete for the patient based on understanding his needs. If the patient is conflicted over asking for help, then spontaneously offering a follow-up visit, a prescription, or even writing down some of the suggestions from the interview will be welcomed. If the patient is overburdened with responsibilities, a written medical excuse for missing work may give him permission to begin taking better care of him or herself.

By the interview's end, the clinician should again inquire whether the patient feels that he can promise to put aside self-destructive solutions in favor of the others arrived at. Some uncertainty is common here, and the clinician should weigh the importance of letting the patient handle things and develop a sense of efficacy against the likelihood of self-harm. One cannot avoid taking some risk in the service of emotional growth.

Object Hunger

The patient with object hunger often has only transitory relationships and no one to rely on at times of crisis. Despair may rapidly develop as the patient looks for nonexistent external supports. A common precipitant is the loss of some involvement that has helped emotionally stabilize the patient, even if it has been superficial and transitory. Rather than simply feeling abandoned, the patient feels an emotional void and believes that he or she lacks the internal resources to go on. Self-destructive behavior may be viewed as an escape from this state.

Patients with object hunger often respond dramatically to the clinician's attention and interest. The interview supplies the very elements that the patient continually seeks from others. In this case it is important to give the attention freely and supportively. As the interview progresses, the patient will feel less anxious and more able to follow the clinician's lead in coming up with ways to fulfill some of the needs for human contact. For instance, talking with others in the waiting room may often provide emotional relief and a sense of connectedness.

The goal of the interview is therefore twofold. First, one should help restore the patient's sense of emotional connectedness in the interview. Second, the clinician needs to explore how the patient can fill these needs in the short term until his or her usual resources are available again. This will involve going over the patient's usual activities, friends, social involvements, and so on, and helping him to make a concrete choice as to what to do over the next several days. More rapid follow-up may be necessary if the usual therapy appointment time is too distant. At the end of the interview the clinician should discuss with the patient whether the object-related activities the patient has decided on are enough to prevent him or her from becoming self-destructive. Hospitalization is not usually required.

REFERENCES

Adler, G. (1981), The Borderline-narcissistic personality disorder continuum. *Amer. J. Psychiat.*, 138:46–50.

Black, D.W., Warrack, G., & Winokur, G. (1985), The Iowa record-linkage study. I. Suicides and accidental deaths among psychiatric patients. *Arch. Gen. Psychiat.*, 42:71–74.

Crumley, F.E. (1979), Adolescent suicide attempts. *J. Amer. Med. Assn.*, 241:2404–2407.

———— (1981), Adolescent suicide attempts and borderline personality disorder: Clinical features. *South. Med. J.*, 74/5:546–549.

Frankel, F.H. (1984), The use of electroconvulsive therapy in suicidal patients. *Amer. J. Psychother.*, 38:384–391.

Friedman, R.C., Aronoff M.S., Clarkin, J.F., Corn, R., & Hurt, S.W. (1983), History of suicidal behavior in depressed borderline inpatients. *Amer. J. Psychiat.*, 140:1023–1026.

Gardner, D.L., & Cowdry, R.W. (1985a), Suicidal and parasuicidal behavior in borderline personality disorder. *Psychiat. Clin. N. Amer.*, 8:389–403.

———— ———— (1985b), Alprazolam-induced dyscontrol in borderline personality disorder. *Amer. J. Psychiat.*, 142:98–100.

Garvey, M.J., & Spoden F. (1980), Suicide attempts in antisocial personality disorder. *Compreh. Psychiat.*, 21:146–149.

Gunderson, J.G., & Elliot, G.R. (1985), The interface between borderline personality disorder and affective disorder. *Amer. J. Psychiat.*, 142:277–288.

Guze, S.B. (1976), *Criminality and Psychiatric Disorders.* New York: Oxford University Press.

Helgason, T. (1964), Epidemiology of mental disorders in Iceland. *Acta Psychiat. Scand.*, 40:1.

Kiev, A. (1976), Cluster analysis profiles of suicide attempters. *Amer. J. Psychiat.*, 133:150–153.

Liberman, R.P., & Eckman, T. (1981), Behavior therapy vs. insight-oriented therapy for repeated suicide attempters. *Arch. Gen. Psychiat.*, 38:1126–1130.

Maltsberger, J.T., & Buie, D.H. (1974), Countertransference hate in the treatment of suicidal patients. *Arch. Gen. Psychiat.*, 30:625–633.

Miles, C. (1977), Conditions predisposing to suicide: A review. *J. Nerv. & Ment. Disord.*, 164:231–246.

Montgomery, S.A., & Montgomery, D. (1982), Pharmacological prevention of suicidal behavior. *J. Affect. Dis.*, 4:291–298.

Nace, E.P., Saxon, J.J., & Shore N. (1983), A comparison of borderline and non-borderline alcoholic patients. *Arch. Gen. Psychiat.*, 40:54–56.

Perry, J.C. (1985), Depression in borderline personality disorder: Lifetime prevalence and longitudinal course of symptoms. *Amer. J. Psychiat.*, 142:15–21.

———— Cooper, S.H. (1985), Psychodynamics, symptoms and outcome in borderline and antisocial personality disorders and bipolar type II affective disorder. In: *The Borderline: Current Empirical Research,* ed. T. McGlashan. Washington DC: American Psychiatric Press.

———— ———— (1986), A preliminary report on defenses and conflicts associated with borderline personality disorder. *J. Amer. Psychoanal. Assn.*, 34:863–893.

Pokorny, A.D. (1964), Suicide rates in various psychiatric disorders. *J. Nerv. & Ment. Dis.*, 139:499–506.

Robins, L.N., (1966), *Deviant Children Grow Up.* Baltimore, MD: Williams & Wilkins.

Rosen, L.W., & Thomas M.A. (1984), Treatment technique for chronic wristcutters. *J. Behav. Ther. & Exp. Psychiat.*, 15:33–36.

Schaffer, C.B., Carroll, J., & Abramowitz, S.I. (1982), Self mutilation and the borderline personality. *J. Nerv. & Ment. Dis.*, 170:468–473.

Small, I.F., Small, J.C., Alig, V.B., & Moore, D.F. (1970), Passive-aggressive personality disorder: A search for a syndrome. *Amer. J. Psychiat.*, 126:973–981.

Spalt, L. (1974), Death thoughts in hysteria, antisocial personality and anxiety neurosis. *Psychiat. Quart.*, 48/3:441–444.

Vaillant, G.E., & Perry, J.C. (1985), Personality disorders. In: *Comprehensive Textbook of Psychiatry,* 4th ed., eds. H.I. Kaplan & B.J. Sadock. Baltimore: Williams & Wilkins, pp. 958–986.

Virkkunen, M. (1976), Self-mutilation in antisocial personality disorder. *Acta Psychiat. Scand.*, 54:347–352.

Ward, N.G., & Schuckit M.A. (1980), Factors associated with suicidal behavior in polydrug abusers. *J. Clin. Psychiat.*, 41:379–385.

Woodruff, R.A., Guze, S.B., & Clayton, P.J. (1971), The medical and psychiatric implications of antisocial personality (sociopathy). *Dis. Nerv. Syst.*, 32:712–714.

9

Suicide and Affective Disorders

Steven Hyman, M.D.
George W. Arana, M.D.

The importance of studying the relationships between suicide and specific psychiatric disorders lies in the possibility of (1) improved prediction of suicide risk; (2) better clinical management aimed at reducing suicide risk; and (3) better understanding of the biological and psychological mechanisms that predispose to suicide. In this chapter we will (1) attempt to define the affective disorders and briefly review the evidence that they are valid diagnostic categories; (2) review the findings of the major studies linking suicide with the affective disorders; and (3) discuss the problems of treating affective disorders with a view to suicide prevention. The pathophysiological mechanisms that may be common to affective disorders and suicide are discussed in chapter 2. The term *suicide,* as used in this chapter, refers to the completed act rather than to suicide attempts. A study of unsuccessful suicide attempters would not illuminate the relationship between depression and completed suicide because it is well established that, despite overlap, the populations that attempt suicide and those that complete suicide are different (Pallis, Barraclough, Levey, Jenkins, and Sainsbury, 1982).

While an association between suicide and the affective disorders (primarily depression) has long been appreciated, many studies have been performed during the last three decades that have provided quantitative information about suicide in this group of patients. Above all, the risk of suicide conferred by the state of depression has been well documented. Despite this progress, the exact relationship between suicide and affective disorders is not fully understood. For example, suicide risk cannot be equated simply with severity of depression. Further, in recent years there has been a trend toward increasing incidence of suicide among younger white males. The role of affective disorders, other psychiatric disorders, and psychosocial factors in this trend has not yet been adequately studied. The role of treatment of affective disorders in suicide prevention has also not been well studied. A major obstacle to understanding these problems is that the vast majority of clinical studies have been retrospective, introducing the possibility of bias, based among other things on the poor reliability of suicide reporting. Moreover, the methodology of many older studies did not include the use of clearly defined, clinically validated diagnostic criteria, further confounding interpretation. Finally, many of the classic studies of suicide were performed before affective antidepressant medications were widely employed. Clearly, further studies are needed.

DIAGNOSTIC CONSIDERATIONS

Affective disorders are common and have a wide variety of manifestations. Thus it is not surprising that many systems of classification have been suggested none of which has met universal approval. However, valid and reliable diagnoses are necessary if studies are to be replicated or compared. Without valid and reliably applicable diagnostic criteria, studies of the same putative diagnostic entity may report on a least partially dissimilar groups, resulting in confusion rather than the accumulation of knowledge (Goodwin and Guze, 1979). The need for reliable diagnosis both for clinical purposes and research has led to the formulation of sets of diagnostic criteria that are operationally defined and tested for validity by patient follow-up (Feighner, 1972; Spitzer, 1978; American Psychiatric Association, 1980). Verifiable diagnostic criteria in psychiatry are based on most or all of the following: symptoms and signs, clinical course (natural history), family history studies, and studies of treatment response (Pope and Lipinski, 1978; Goodwin and Guze, 1979). In addition, there is currently a vast amount of research attempting to discover biological markers of psychiatric disorders including depression (Carroll, Feinberg, Greden, Tarika, Albala, Haskett, James, Kronfol, Lohr, Steiner, de Vigne, and Young 1981; Loosen and Prange, 1982). Although no markers have yet been found that are sensitive and specific enough to be included as a diagnostic criterion for any disorder, abnormalities of the hypothalamic–pituitary–adrenal axis occur in approximately one-half of neurovegetatively depressed patients and have become an important area of investigation.

In attempts to classify the affective disorders, the unipolar–bipolar distinction is the most widely accepted. Although further study may yield subdivisions of bipolar disorder, its validity as a diagnostic entity is well attested to by numerous studies of course, family history, and treatment response (Winokur, Clayton, and Reich, 1969; Carlson, Kotin, Davenport, and Adland, 1974; Goodwin and Jamison, 1984). In addition to the unipolar–bipolar distinction, the other fundamental distinction is between primary and secondary disorders (Woodruff, Murphy, and Herjanic, 1967). This distinction separated out as "secondary" those affective disorders that might be attributable to either an organic cause (e.g., medication effect or neurologic disorder) or to a major nonaffective psychiatric disorder (e.g., alcoholism, drug abuse, schizophrenia). This distinction appears to increase the homogeneity and validity of diagnostic groups (Coryell and Winokur, 1984). The primary affective disorders include bipolar (or manic-depressive) disorder and a heterogeneous group of unipolar depressive disorders.

The primary–secondary distinction among unipolar depressive disorders does not, however, fully solve certain difficult diagnostic problems: specifically, it does not clarify the relationship between depression and substance abuse. As will be seen below this is a critical issue in the study of suicide since depression and alcoholism rank first and second, respectively, as the psychiatric diagnoses associated with suicide. Thus it is important to know whether depression and alcoholism are distinct entities, or whether there is some biological or psychological commonality between the two that increases the risk of suicide.

It is well known that there is a high prevalence of depression among alcoholics and that alcoholism and depression appear to be linked by family studies (Pottenger, McKennon, Patrie, Weissman, Ruben, and Newberry, 1978; Coryell and Winokur, 1984). On the other hand, several studies suggest that depression in alcoholics is due to direct toxic effects of alcohol on the brain and that these effects dissipate within a year of abstinence (Carlen, Wortzman, Holgate, Wilkinson, and Rankin, 1978; Hatsukami and Pickens, 1982). The controversy remains unsettled, however. A recent study (Behar, Winokur, and Berg, 1984) suggests that in the long term there is a 15 percent rate of serious depression after a mean of 35 months of sobriety. Those authors who stress the link between depression and alcoholism from family studies (Winokur, Cadoret, Dorzab, and Baker, 1971; Winokur, 1972; Coryell and Winokur, 1984) consider alcoholism to be part of a depressive spectrum disorder. Pending further clinical, genetic, and biological studies, however, current standard practice as reflected in DSM-III (1980) is to consider alcoholism as a separate diagnostic category not related to the primary affective disorders. This chapter will follow DSM-III usage; a discussion of the relationship of alcoholism to suicide may be found in chapter 2. The issue of relatedness to depression is also unsettled for other substance abuse disorders including cocaine and opiate abuse.

CURRENT DIAGNOSTIC CLASSIFICATION

Of the current consensus on primary affective disorders, both bipolar disorder and major depressive disorder as described by DSM-III appear to be valid diagnostic entities based on clinical presentation, natural history, and family and genetic studies including studies of mono- and dizygotic twins (Gershon, Bunney, and Leckman, 1976; Bertelsen, Harvald, and Hauge, 1977; Pope and Lipinski, 1978; Goodwin and Guze, 1979). *Bipolar disorder* is the DSM-III term for manic-depressive illness. The diagnosis is made if there is a history of a manic episode, even if a depressive episode has not occurred. The depressive episodes are not clinically different from those that occur in major depression. In the major studies of suicide and psychiatric diagnosis (Robins, Murphy, Wilkinson, Gassner, and Kayes, 1959; Dorpat and Ripley, 1960; Barraclough, Bunch, Nelson, and Sainsbury, 1974) the manic state did not appear to be a significant contributor to suicide; however, the patients, when in their depressed phases, appear to be subject to essentially the same risks of suicide as unipolar patients. In a 30- to 40-year follow-up of 76 manic patients, 182 depressed patients, and 170 schizophrenic patients in Iowa (Winokur and Tsuang, 1975) 8.5 percent of those who had presented as manic and 10.6 percent of the depressives who were deceased had committed suicide. The phase of illness of the initially manic patients when they committed suicide was not reported. It is the clinical experience of the authors that patients may commit suicide while in the manic state when they are delusional, when dysphoric or effectively labile, or accidentally because of imparied judgment of danger.

DSM-III uses the term, *major depression*, for serious episodic depression that is accompanied by neurovegetative symptoms. This term is synonymous with most usages of the older terms *unipolar* or *endogenous depression*. The clinical picture is usually dominated by a persistently dysphoric mood. In addition, the criteria require that the individual have at least four of the following eight symptoms for at least two weeks (DSM-III): appetite disturbance, insomnia, psychomotor retardation or agitation, anhedonia, loss of energy, feelings of worthlessness or guilt, decreased cognitive functioning, or suicidal thoughts. Patients with major depression also may develop psychotic symptoms. When the criteria for major depression are met, the history or absence of a precipitating event is not relevant to the diagnosis. At least one-half of all patients with major depression have recurrent episodes. Family studies suggest a significant genetic component in this disorder (Gershon et al., 1976). Clinically, however, it is not always possible to obtain a positive family history even in clear-cut cases. DSM-III does not separate out patients who meet criteria for major depression who are delusional. Some authors (Glassman and Roose, 1981), however, have argued that on the basis of presentations and treatment response (poor response to tricyclics alone; better response to tricyclics plus neuroleptics or to electroconvulsive therapy) these patients represent a separate diagnostic entity. Roose, Glassman, Walsh, Woodring, Vital-Herne, (1983) retrospectively analyzed all suicides among inpatients at a major psychiatric hospital from 1955 to 1980 and rediagnosed patients according to both DSM-III and Research Diagnostic Criteria. They found that there were 39 suicides of whom 22 had a major affective disorder; eight had what they termed minor depression; four had schizophrenia; two had personality disorder; and three were undiagnosed. Of the 22 with a major affective disorder 14 had unipolar (major) depression. Ten of these 14 (71 percent) were definitely or probably delusional. They concluded that at least in their population, delusionally depressed patients had a fivefold greater risk of suicide than nondelusional depressives. Although delusional depression may carry a higher risk of suicide, further study of the natural history and epidemiology of these patients and of their familes is needed.

Dysthymic disorder is the DSM-III term for chronic depression. Symptoms are less severe than those of major depression, and the neurovegetative symptoms are minor and/or absent. Patients complain of chronic dysphoria and often develop irrational patterns of negative thinking. Prior to DSM-III, such patients were often termed *characterologically depressed*. Attempts have been made to subclassify chronically depressed patients according to age at onset, prior psychiatric and family history, and response to pharmacologic agents (Akiskal, King, Rosenthal, Robinson, and Scott-Strauss, 1981). Given the criteria outlined for this disorder in DSM-III it probably encompasses a heterogeneous group of individuals including (1) incompletely recovered major depression, (2) personality disorders, and (3) true chronic mild or attenuated depression. Since this is a new classification, older studies of suicide and affective disorder cannot easily be applied. In addition, since it probably lumps patients with different long-term outcomes and treatment responses, it may not survive further refinements in psychiatric diagnosis.

The most common type of depression is reactive or situational, described in DSM-III as adjustment disorder with depressed mood. It occurs following a significant life stress and resolves when the stress is removed or if improved coping skills are developed. Neurovegetative symptoms are neither severe nor prolonged. This should not be considered one of the primary affective disorders from the point of view of natural history, family history, or treatment response.

STUDIES RELATING SUICIDE TO AFFECTIVE DISORDERS

The association of affective disorders and suicide has been studied from a variety of perspectives. These include (1) the percentage of all deaths among affectively ill patients attributable to suicide (Guze and Robins, 1970; Winokur and Tsuang, 1975); (2) the percentage of all suicides diagnosed with major affective disorder (Robins et al., 1959; Dorpat and Ripley, 1960; Barraclough et al., 1974); (3) the relative risk of suicide in those with major affective disorders (Pokorny, 1964; Guze and Robins, 1970; Miles, 1977); (4) the suicide risk factors other than diagnosis among those with affective disorders (Roy, 1982; Roose et al., 1983; Roy 1983); (5) the risk of suicide among first-degree relatives of probands with affective disorders (Tsuang, 1983). These analyses clearly establish that among psychiatric diagnoses depression conveys the highest risk of suicide, although the relationship of the various subtypes of depression to suicide has not been clearly established. In addition, it has not been established whether aggressive treatment of primary depressive disorders leads to a decrease in the rate of suicide. This issue is complicated by the fact that the most effective treatments for primary depressive disorders include medications (heterocyclic antidepressants and monoamine oxidase inhibitors) with a low therapeutic index. Thus, paradoxically, the depressed patient with increased risk of suicide might be armed with a lethal drug making the clinician reluctant to prescribe effective treatment.

According to Guze and Robins (1970), the percentage of patients with primary affective disorders who die by suicide is a striking 15 percent. This diagnostic group is presumably equivalent to the sum of major depression and bipolar disorder, depressed phase, as delineated in DSM-III. They reviewed 17 reports on the course and outcome of affective disorders which included a total of 4,983 patients with a mean follow-up of 7.9 years. Although the percentage of patients who died by suicide in these studies ranged between 12 percent and 60 percent, their analysis showed that the percentage of all deaths among affectively ill patients attributable to suicide reached an asymptote of 15 percent as the study population approached 100 percent mortality. The higher relative risk of suicide found earlier in the course of illness derived from the fact that overall mortality rates are lower among younger patients making suicides a greater precentage of those who die in this age group. Overall the authors calculated that the risk of dying by suicide is 30-fold higher among patients with primary affective disorders than among the general populations.

Clinical factors involved in suicide, including psychiatric diagnosis, were examined in three major studies. The earliest of these reported on 134 consecutive suicides in St. Louis, 1956–1957 (Robins et al., 1959); 94 percent of these individuals had a psychiatric disorder at the time of their death with 47 percent diagnosed as depressed. Other diagnoses in the sample included the following: (1) alcoholism 25 precent, (2) organic brain syndromes 4 percent, (3) schizophrenia 2 percent, (4) drug abuse 1 percent, (5) undiagnosed psychiatric disorder 15 percent, (6) no psychiatric disorder 6 percent. Of those who were depressed (63/134), the group had typical symptoms of the disorder (36). The most common symptoms were insomnia 80 percent, weight loss 77 percent, loss of interest 73 percent, anorexia 71 percent, and sadness 70 percent. The mean age of the depressed males was 58.4 years, and for the females was 54.9 years. In contrast, the alcoholic group had a mean age of death of 45.8 years for males and 44.4 years for females. In these three large studies the percentage of suicides attributable to a particular psychiatric disorder varied, but the rank order of the first two, depression and alcoholism, remained the same (see Table 9.1). Only in the St. Louis group is the information available to rediagnose the patients (Robins, 1981), but variable diagnostic criteria may account for some of the disparity. In particular, schizophrenia represented a more inclusive diagnostic group among many clinicians prior to the current decade (Pope and Lipinski, 1978), which may account for some of the discrepancies among the reports (Robins et al., 1959; Dorpat and Ripley, 1960; Barraclough et al., 1974). In addition, the study which reported the lowest percentage of depressed patients among suicides reported 18 percent of their sample as undiagnosed (Dorpat and Ripley, 1960). Despite these variations the studies cited confirm that more than 90 percent of suicides are associated with mental illness and that depression is the leading diagnosis among those who successfully suicide. If alcoholism is considered as part of an affective disorder spectrum, as favored by some authors, three out of four suicides is the result of an affective disorder according to two of the studies cited (Robins et al., 1959; Barraclough et al., 1974).

Studies that have calculated the relative risk of death by suicide according to psychiatric diagnosis also have found depression and alcoholism to be leading diagnostic risk factors. A review of patients in an urban general veterans hospital (not primarily psychiatric) in 1964 (Pokorny, 1964) found a higher rate of suicide among male veterans than in the general population (22.7 per 100,000 as opposed to

Table 9.1

Percentage of Suicides Attributable to Various Psychiatric Disorders[a]

	Study 1 (%)	Study 2 (%)	Study 3 (%)
Depressive Illness	47	28	70
Alcoholism	25	26	15
Schizophrenia	2	11	3
Organic Brain Syndrome	4	4	—
Personality Disorders	—	9	—
Drug Dependence	1	—	1
Other or Undiagnosed	15	22	4
No Psychiatric Illness	6	—	7

[a]Based on the studies of (1) Robins et al., 1956–1957, St. Louis, 134 cases; (2) Dorpat and Ripley, 1957–1958, Seattle, 108 cases; and (3) Barraclough et. al., 1966–1968, West Sussex County, England, 100 cases.

10). Within the veterans population the calculated risk of suicide for patients with depression was 566 per 100,000 or 25 times the overall risk. A more recent study (Miles, 1977) found a calculated rate of suicide of 230 per 100,000 for patients said to have endogenous depression and 270 per 100,000 for alcoholism. Differences from the earlier study may have been due to a shorter follow-up period in the veteran's hospital study and a more inclusive concept of schizophrenia.

The foregoing amply illustrates the increased risk of suicide associated with depression. However, it also illustrates the wide variation from study to study in the percentage of all suicides attributed to depression and in the relative risk of suicide said to exist for depressed patients. These variations certainly reflect differences in populations studied and in methodology employed (e.g., time of follow-up), but they also probably reflect differences in diagnosis. Although in the clinical study reported by the St. Louis group (Robins et al., 1959; Robins, 1981) it is possible for the reader to rediagnose the patients in terms of current criteria from adequate clinical vignettes, it is impossible to do so for the other studies. In the St. Louis study it can be said that virtually all of the suicides classified as having a "primary affective disorder" would fulfill current DSM-III criteria for major depression. In the other studies it is quite possible that diagnoses were not based on replicable and valid criteria, so that the relative contributions of what would now be termed *major depression, personality disorders,* and *reactive depression* to deaths by suicide is not clear. In addition at least some of the patients classified as schizophrenic in older studies would now be diagnosed as having an affective disorder.

Given the diagnosis of depression, additional factors that compound the risk of suicide have been studied. Among depressed patients, further risk factors for suicide appear to be similar to those for patients with other psychiatric disorders. These include living alone, being unmarried, being unemployed, and history of a prior attempt (Roy, 1982, 1983).

Significant physical illness also increases the risk (Robins et al., 1959). It is unfortunately clear that no combination of risk factors provides the sensitivity and specificity to allow an algorithm for predicting suicide. Thus clinical decisions can only be made on an individual basis. Nonetheless, the combination of depression with other known epidemiological risk factors for suicide (e.g., white males, unmarried, living alone, chronic physical illness, etc.) or the history of a previous attempt must be taken extremely seriously as indicating a high risk of suicide. It must be noted, parenthetically, that one of the classic epidemiologic risk factors for completed suicide, advancing age, is rapidly changing (Centers for Disease Control, 1985). Since 1970 there has been a large percentage increase in rates for males between the ages of 15 and 34. During the period 1970–1980 suicide rates for white males increased 60 percent within the 15- to 19-year-old group and 44 percent in the 20- to 24-year-old group. Thus, although older white males are still at the highest risk, the risk appears to be increasing rapidly among younger white males.

The risk of suicide in the relatives of psychiatrically ill probands has also been studied. Tsuang (1983) has analyzed the risk of suicide in the first-degree relatives of 315 affectively ill patients and 195 schizophrenics, compared with surgical controls. For probands who presented with depression, the risk of suicide among first-degree relatives was 3.4 percent; among relatives of manics 1.5 percent; among relatives of schizophrenics 1.2 percent; and among relatives of controls 0.1 percent. In this sample, the male relatives of the probands had a higher risk than female relatives. Rates of suicide in relatives was even higher if the proband had also committed suicide. This study revealed a particularly high risk of suicide in relatives of patients with affective disorders, especially unipolar depression. Further, it suggests a familial component to suicide risk that is twofold: (1) risk is increased by inheritance of a psychiatric disorder, particularly an affective disorder; and (2) a positive family history of suicide is an additional risk factor independent of the diagnosis of the proband.

THERAPEUTIC CONSIDERATIONS

The treatment of patients with major affective disorders centers on pharmacotherapy. Major depression is treated with tricyclics, monoamine oxidase inhibitors, or electroconvulsive therapy (ECT). In bipolar disorder lithium is usually added. Chronically depressed (dysthymic) patients who have neurovegetative symptoms or who appear to have incompletely resolved major depression may also benefit from antidepressant drugs. As noted earlier in this chapter all of the drugs used in the treatment of depression are potentially fatal in overdose. Thus the physician is faced with a difficult problem; whether or not to prescribe these drugs to potentially suicidal patients. Unfortunately, the question of whether antidepressant treatment alters the suicide rate in depressed patients has not been well studied. In the experience of one large clinic treating affective disorders, energetic treatment of depression decreased the rate of suicide; in an ongoing study at the Memphis Mood Clinic, as of 1983, 0/600 patients with primary affective disorders had committed suicide, whereas 4/200 with secondary disorders had suicided (Khuri and Akiskal, 1983). However, an earlier study did not document improvement in the suicide rate of depressed patients treated with antidepressants or ECT (Avery and Winokur, 1976). Two British studies, one using Mianserin (Montgomery and Montgomery, 1982), and the other Mianserin and Nomifensin (Hirsch, Walsh, and Draper, 1982) showed no significant effect on attempts (rather than completed suicide), but lack of reported diagnostic criteria, short duration of treatment, and small numbers of patients in both reports makes it impossible to draw conclusions. Additionally, one of the British groups (Montgomery and Montgomery, 1982), reported that depot neuroleptics were helpful in decreasing the number of suicide attempts among patients with personality disorders who were chronic suicide attempters. The overall clinical benefit versus the risks of such treatment remains to be studied; moreover the authors do not suggest that this finding is applicable to patients with affective disorders.

Clearly, a more definitive prospective study of suicide prevention by vigorous treatment of affective disorders remains to be accomplished. Such a study would require a well-diagnosed population, adequate length of follow-up, and documentation of the adequacy of treatment. The relative rarity of completed suicide and the problems of long-term follow-up makes any such prospective study difficult to undertake. Nonetheless, without such a study many clinicians may continue to be timid about treating affective disorders with effective doses of antidepressants, especially if they fear that patients have suicidal tendencies. Although such a reassuring study has not been done, it is possible to draw several conclusions from the current literature. (1) There is no evidence that use of antidepressants in depressed patients increased the risk of suicide. (Of course patients at high suicide risk should be treated initially in an inpatient setting, and all medications must be prescribed with care.) (2) There is ample evidence that pharmacologic treatment is effective in the acute treatment of affective disorders and in prophylaxis against recurrence (Prien, Klett, and Caffey, 1973; Klerman, DiMascio, Weissman, Prusoff, and Paykel, 1974; Weissman, Kasl, and Klerman, 1976; Hirsch et al., 1982). (3) The failure of several studies to show the benefit of pharmacotherapy in reducing suicide rates may be due in part to contamination of the study population with patients who are personality disordered and in part to inadequate use of antidepressant therapies (e.g., low doses of tricyclics or failure to administer a prophylactic pharmacologic agent after a successful course of ECT.)

Overall it can be concluded that affective disorders must be recognized and treated. The risk of suicide in acutely depressed patients and lifetime risk of suicide in patients with recurrent affective disorders is clear. Depressed patients with high clinical risk of suicide should be handled with the utmost care; even given our current state of knowledge, this requires not only hospitalization and observation, but also effective treatment of the underlying affective disorder, with adequate long-term prophylaxis if indicated by the clinical course.

REFERENCES

Akiskal, H.S., King, D., Rosenthal, T.L., Robinson, D., & Scott-Strauss, A. (1981), Chronic depressions. Part 1. Clinical and familial characteristics in 137 probands. *J. Affect. Disord.*, 3:297–315.

American Psychiatric Association (1980), *The Diagnostic and Statistical Manual of Mental Disorders*, 3rd ed. Washington, DC: American Psychiatric Press.

Avery, D., & Winokur, G. (1976), Mortality in depressed patients treated with electroconvulsive therapy and antidepressants. *Arch. Gen. Psychiat.*, 33:1029–1037.

Barraclough, B., Bunch, J., Nelson, B., & Sainsbury, P. (1974), A hundred cases of suicide: Clinical aspects. *Brit. J. Psychiat.*, 125:355–373.

Behar, D., Winokur, G., & Berg, C.J. (1984), Depression in the abstinent alcoholic. *Amer. J. Psychiat.*, 141:1105–1107.

Bertelsen, A., Harvald, B., & Hauge, M.A. (1977), Danish twin study of manic-depressive disorders. *Brit. J. Psychiat.*, 130:330–351.

Carlen, P.L., Wortzman, G., Holgate, R.C., Wilkinson, D.A. & Rankin, J.G. (1978), Reversible cerebral atrophy in recently abstinent chronic alcoholics measured by computed tomography scans. *Science*, 200:1076–1078.

Carlson, G.A., Kotin, J.L., Davenport, Y.B., & Adland. (1974), Follow-up of 53 bipolar manic-depressive patients. *Brit. J. Psychiat.*, 124:134–139.

Carroll, B.J., Feinberg, M., Greden, J.F., Tarika, J., Albala, A., Haskett, R., James, N., Kronfol, Z., Lohr, N., Steiner, M.. de Vigne, J.P., & Young, E. (1981), A specific laboratory test for the diagnosis of melancholia. *Arch. Gen. Psychiat.*, 38:15–22.

Centers for Disease Control (1985), *Morbid. & Mort. Weekly Rep.*, 34:353–357.

Coryell, W., & Winokur, G. (1984), Depression spectrum disorders: Clinical diagnosis and biological implications. In: *Neurobiology of Affective Disorders*, ed. R.M. Post & J.C. Ballenger. Baltimore, MD: Williams & Wilkins, pp. 102–106.

Dorpat, T.L. & Ripley H.S. (1960), A study of suicide in the Seattle area. *Comp. Psychiat.*, 1:349–359.

Feighner, J.P., Robins, E., Guze, S.B., (1972), Diagnostic criteria for use in psychiatric research. *Arch. Gen. Psychiat.*, 26:57–63.

Gershon, E.S., Bunney, W.E., Jr., Leckman, J.F., (1976), The inheritance of affective disorders: A review of data and of hypotheses. *Behav. Genet.*, 6:227–261.

Glassman, A.H., & Roose, S.P. (1981), Delusional depression: A distinct clinical entity? *Arch. Gen. Psychiat.*, 38:424–427.

Goodwin, D.W., & Guze, S.B. (1979), *Psychiatric Diagnosis*, 2nd ed. New York: Oxford University Press.

Goodwin, F.K., & Jamison, K.R. (1984), The natural course of manic-depressive illness. In: *Neurobiology of Affective Disorders*, eds. R.M. Post & J.C. Ballenger. Baltimore, MD: Williams & Wilkins, pp. 20–37.

Guze, S.B., & Robins, E. (1970), Suicide and primary affective disorders. *Brit. J. Psychiat.*, 117:437–438.

Hatsukami, D., & Pickens, R.W. (1982), Posttreatment depression in an alcohol and drug abuse population. *Amer. J. Psychiat.*, 139:1563–1566.

Hirsch, S.R., Walsh, C., & Draper, R. (1982), Parasuicide. A review of treatment interventions. *J. Affect. Disord.*, 4:299–311.

Khuri, R., & Akiskal, H.S. (1983), Suicide prevention: The necessity of treating contributory psychiatric disorders. *Psychiat. Clin. N. Amer.*, 6:193–207.

Klerman, G., DiMascio, A., Weissman, M., Prusoff, B., & Paykel, E. (1974), Treatment of depression by drugs and psychotherapy. *Amer. J. Psychiat.*, 131:186–191.

Loosen, P.T., & Prange, A.J. (1982), Serum thyrotropin response to thyrotropin-releasing hormone in psychiatric patients: A review. *Amer. J. Psychiat.*, 139:405–416.

Miles, C.P. (1977), Conditions predisposing to suicide: A review. *J. Nerv. Ment. Dis.*, 164:231–246.

Montgomery, S.A., & Montgomery, D. (1982), Pharmacological prevention of suicidal behaviour. *J. Affect. Disord.*, 4:291–298.

Pallis, D.J., Barraclough, B.M., Levey, A.B., Jenkins, J.S., & Sainsbury, P. (1982), Estimating suicide risk among attempted suicides. *Brit. J. Psychiat.*, 141:37–44.

Perry, A., & Tsuang, M.T. (1979), Treatment of unipolar depression following electroconvulsive therapy. *J. Affect. Disord.*, 1:123–127.

Pokorny, A.P. (1964), Suicide rates in various psychiatric disorders. *J. Nerv. Ment. Dis.*, 139:499–506.

Pope, H.G., & Lipinski, J.F., Jr. (1978), Diagnosis in schizophrenia and manic-depressive illness. *Arch. Gen. Psychiat.*, 35:811–828.

Pottenger, M., McKernon, J., Patrie, L.E., Weissman, M.M., Ruben, H.L., & Newberry, P. (1978), The frequency and persistence of depressive symptoms in the alcohol abuser. *J. Nerv. & Ment. Dis.*, 166:562–570.

Prien, R.F., Klett, C.J., & Caffey, E.M., Jr. (1973), Lithium carbonate and imipramine in the prevention of affective episodes: A comparison of recurrent affective illness. *Arch. Gen. Psychiat.*, 29:420–425.

Robins, E. (1981), *The Final Months. A Study of the Lives of 134 Persons Who Committed Suicide*. New York: Oxford University Press.

———— Murphy, G., Wilkinson, R., Gassner, S., & Kayes, J. (1959), Some clinical considerations in the prevention of suicide based on a study of 134 successful suicides. *Amer. J. Pub. Health*, 49:888–899.

Roose, S.P., Glassman, A.H., Walsh, B.T., Woodring, S., & Vital-Herne, J. (1983), Depression, delusions, and suicide. *Amer. J. Psychiat.*, 140:1159–1162.

Roy, A. (1982), Risk factors for suicide in psychiatric patients. *Arch. Gen. Psychiat.*, 39:1089–1095.

———— (1983), Suicide in depressives. *Comp. Psychiat.*, 24:487–491.

Spitzer, R.L., Endicott, J., & Robins, E. (1978), Research Diagnostic Criteria, 3rd. ed. New York: Biometrics Research. New York State Department of Mental Hygeine.

Tsuang, M.T. (1983), Risk of suicide in the relatives of schizophrenics, manics, depressives, and controls. *J. Clin. Psychiat.*, 44:396–400.

Weissman, M., Kasl, S.V., & Klerman, G. (1976), Follow-up of depressed women after maintenance treatment. *Amer. J. Psychiat.*, 133:757–760.

Winokur, G. (1972), Types of depressive illness. *Brit. J. Psychiat.*, 120:265–266.

———— Cadoret R., Dorzab, J., & Baker, M. (1971), Depressive disease: A genetic study. *Arch. Gen. Psychiat.*, 24:135–144.

———— Clayton, P.J., & Reich, T. (1969), *Manic Depressive Illness*. St. Louis: Mosby.

———— Tsuang, M. (1975), The Iowa 500: Suicide in mania, depression, and schizophrenia. *Amer. J. Psychiat.*, 132:650–651.

Woodruff, R.A., Murphy, G.E., & Herjanic, M. (1967), The natural history of affective disorders. I. Symptoms of 72 patients at the time of index hospital admission. *J. Psychiat. Res.*, 5:255–263.

10

The Suicidal Schizophrenic

Robert E. Drake, M.D., Ph.D.
Charlene Gates, M.S.
Anne Whitaker, M.D.
Paul G. Cotton, M.D.

Suicidal behavior among schizophrenics constitutes an enormous clinical problem. According to Bleuler (1950), "The most serious of all schizophrenic symptoms is the suicidal drive" (p. 488). Suicidal behavior leads to a large proportion of hospital admissions (Planansky and Johnston, 1971; Solomon, 1981) and complicates discharge for many others (Dorwart, 1980). Although lifetime prevalence is difficult to estimate, two long-term follow-up studies of large numbers of schizophrenics found that 12.9 percent and 10.1 percent of deaths were due to suicide (Bleuler, 1978; Tsuang, 1978). Miles (1977) reviewed 34 studies of suicide among schizophrenics and estimated that 10 percent of all schizophrenics will kill themselves. Approximately 20 percent of schizophrenics make suicide attempts (Planansky and Johnston, 1971; Niskanen, Lonnquist, and Achte, 1973). Several clinicians have observed that the rate of suicide among schizophrenics is increasing under the stress of brief hospitalizations and community treatment (Cohen, Leonard, Farberow, and Shneidman, 1964; Lindelius and Kay, 1973; Arieti, 1974; Yarden, 1974).

Despite the clinical significance and prevalence of suicide among schizophrenics, little consensus exists regarding prediction and understanding. Traditional suicide risk scales are not predictive for schizophrenics (Shaffer, Perlin, Schmidt, and Stephens, 1974). Few guidelines are available to help the clinician in the difficult task of assessing suicide risk among these patients.

Because risk factors that are predictive for the general population are often irrelevant when applied to a specific high-risk group (Pokorny, 1983), this review focuses exclusively on suicidal risk among schizophrenics. The term "risk" refers here

Acknowledgment. An earlier version of this chapter was published in *Comprehensive Psychiatry*, (1985) 26:90–100.

to antecedent factors that increase the likelihood of suicide. The purposes of this chapter are (1) to review the empirical evidence regarding risk factors associated with suicide among schizophrenics, and (2) to summarize the existing literature for clinicians.

SAMPLES AND DESIGNS

This review includes empirical studies of the clinical features of schizophrenics who attempt or commit suicide. Case studies are excluded. Studies are classified according to design into three categories: descriptive, poorly controlled, and well controlled.

We assume that schizophrenics without suicidal behavior (or with less severe suicidal behavior) constitute the most appropriate comparison group for schizophrenics who do manifest suicidal behavior. This design not only obviates the problem of diagnostic heterogeneity but also replicates the clinical, decision-making situation.

"Descriptive" studies, summarized in Table 10.1, identify various features of schizophrenics who attempt or commit suicide, but do not provide a comparison group. The identified features in these studies could be characteristic of schizophrenics in general rather than of those at high risk for suicide. Studies in Table 10.2 are designated "poorly controlled" because of the limitation of diagnostic heterogeneity. Findings from these studies could be due to diagnostic differences within the samples. The "well-controlled" studies, summarized in Table 10.3, either focus exclusively on schizophrenics or provide a separate analysis of results for schizophrenics. Although limited by other methodologic problems, such as the lack of blind ratings, these eleven studies provide the most dependable data available and will therefore be emphasized throughout this review.

FINDINGS

Demographic

Schizophrenics who kill themselves tend to be young and male. Suicide usually occurs before age 45 (Levy and Southcombe, 1953; Banen, 1954; Cohen et al., 1964; Yarden, 1974; Virkkunen, 1974). Males predominate in most studies in proportions ranging from 60 percent to 90 percent (Warnes, 1968; Roy, 1982; Breier and Astrachan, 1984; Drake, Gates, Cotton, and Whitaker, 1984). Male schizophrenics also tend to kill themselves at a younger age than females (Yarden, 1974; Roy, 1982).

Few data are available regarding race and socioeconomic status. Sletten, Brown, Evenson, and Altman (1972) found among inpatients of a mental hospital that the suicide rate for whites was twice that of blacks. Breier and Astrachan (1984) also

Table 10.1

Descriptive Studies

Author	Number of Suicides (percentage schizophrenic)	Number of Attempters (percentage schizophrenic)	Diagnostic Criteria[a]	Method and Design
Achté et al. (1966)	57 (44%)	0	NS	Inpatients; case records, parish records, & physician interviews
Banen (1954)	23 (78%)	0	NS	Inpatients; hospital records
Chapman (1965)	18 (78%)	0	NS	Hospitalized male veterans; VA records
Corton et al. (1985)	20 (100%)	0	DSM-III	Boston patients; therapist interviews
Levy & Southcombe (1953)	58 (50%)	0	NS	Inpatients; hospital records
Lindelius & Kay (1973)	18 (100%)	—	Diverse clinical criteria	5- to 20-year follow-up of first admission male schizophrenics
Niskanen et al. (1973)	7 (NS)[a]	56 (NS)[a]	NS	5- to 15-year follow-up of hospitalized schizophrenics & paranoid psychotics; patient interviews & hospital records

Table 10.1 *(continued)*

Author	Number of Suicides (percentage schizophrenic)	Number of Attempters (percentage schizophrenic)	Diagnostic Criteria[a]	Method and Design
Niskanen et al. (1974)	71 (55%)	0	NS	Inpatients; hospital records
Planansky & Johnston (1973)	0	52 (100%)	NS	Hospitalized male veterans; patient interviews, VA records
Yarden (1974)	20 (100%)	—	DSM-III	Maximum 5-year follow-up of hospitalized schizophrenics; clinical records; interviews with family, therapists, social workers & others; visits to patient's living quarters

[a]NS = Nor specified.

Table 10.2

Poorly Controlled Studies

Authors	Number of Suicides (percentage schizophrenic)	Number of Attempters (percentage schizophrenic)	Number of Controls (percentage schizophrenic)	Diagnostic Criteria[a]	Methods and Design	Control Characteristics
Beisser & Blanchette (1961)	71 (45%)	0	61 (24%)	1952 Diagnostic Nomenclature	Inpatients; hospital records	Diagnostically heterogeneous matched for race & sex
Bolin et al. (1968)	27 (48%)	0	61 (49%)	NS	Suicides during hospital leave; hospital records: 18 item checklist	Random sample of patients on leave at same time as suicides
Noreik (1975)	48 (44%)	325[b] (33%)	1918 (31%)	NS	5-year follow-up of first admission functional psychotics: hospital records; interviews with physicians, patients, family; patient questionnaire	Functional psychotics who had not killed themselves or attempted suicide on follow-up of 5 years
Pokorny (1960)	44 (30%)	0	44 (23%)	NS	VA records & interviews with ward physician	Matched for age, race, psychiatric versus nonpsychiatric diagnosis
Sletten et al. (1972)	97 (51%)	0	97 (NS)[a]	NS	Inpatients or patients discharged within 1 year; case records, questionnaire sent to family	Control group selected from "same population"
Wilson (1968)	17 (59%)	0	29 (41%)	NS	Inpatients or patients discharged within 11 months; hospital records; 5-factor psychosocial evaluation	Patients put on suicide precautions during hospitalization who had not killed themselves on follow-up

Table 10.2 (continued)

Authors	Number of Suicides (percentage schizophrenic)	Number of Attempters (percentage schizophrenic)	Number of Controls (percentage schizophrenic)	Diagnostic Criteria[a]	Methods and Design	Control Characteristics
Virkkunen (1974)	82 (90%)	0	82 (0%)	10 typical symptoms present	Paranoid, psychotic and schizophrenic inpatients & outpatients; questionnaires to physicians & hospital staff; interviews with family & friends	Suicides with other diagnoses
Virkkunen (1976)	58 (NS)[a] (all cases included in Virkkunen, 1974)	0	40 (NS)[a]	10 typical symptoms present	Paranoids, psychotics, and schizophrenics who had been in contact with medical personnel within 2 months of suicide; questionnaires to physicians & other treatment personnel	Suicides with other diagnoses who had been in contact with medical personnel within 2 months of suicide matched for age

[a]NS = Not specified.
[b]This figure includes the 48 completed suicides.

Table 10.3

Well-Controlled Studies

Authors	Number of Suicides	Number of Attempters	Number of Controls	Diagnostic Criteria	Methods and Design	Control Characteristics
Beck et al. (1975)	0	98[a]	—	NS[b]	Hospitalized attempters; data analyzed separately for 98 schizophrenics; patient interviews, Suicide Intent Scale, Beck Depression Inventory, Hopelessness Scale	Less serious attempters used as control group for serious attempters
Breier & Astrachan (1984)	20	0	a = 81 b = 20	DSM-III	Mental health center patients; non-blind review of all clinical data	Two schizophrenic control groups: (a) nonsuicided schizophrenics (b) nonsuicided schizophrenics matched for age
Cohen et al. (1964)	40	0	40	NS	White, male veterans; blind review of comprehensive chart abstracts by panel of psychiatrists & psychologists; includes 30 suicides & 30 controls from Farberow et al. (1961) study	Nonsuicided schizophrenics matched for age, sex, race, years of hospitalization, & religion
Drake et al. (1984) Drake & Cotton (1986) Drake et al. (1986)	15	19	70	DSM-III	Hospitalized schizophrenics; blind review of chart data	Nonsuicided "high-risk" schizophrenics of similar age, sex, & illness history
Farberow et al. (1961)	30	0	30	NS	White, male veterans suicides; selected randomly; chart abstracts, blind psychological autopsy	Nonsuicided schizophrenics matched for sex, age, race, religion, & marital status
Minkoff et al. (1973)	0	23[a]	—	DSM-III	Hospitalized attempters data analyzed separately for 23 schizophrenics; patient interviews, Suicide Intent Scale, Beck Depression Inventory, Generalized Expectancies Scale	Less serious attempters used as control group for serious attempters

Table 10.3 (continued)

Authors	Number of Suicides	Number of Attempters	Number of Controls	Diagnostic Criteria	Methods and Design	Control Characteristics
Planansky & Johnston (1971)	3	49	153	NS	Male veterans; patient interviews, VA records	Hospitalized schizophrenic veterans who had not made attempts
Roy (1982)	30	0	30	DSM-III	Chronic & subchronic schizophrenics; chart data, review method not described	Nonsuicided chronic and subchronic schizophrenics matched for sex, age, & type of schizophrenia
Roy et al. (1984)	0	70	57	RDC & DSM-III	Hospitalized chronic schizophrenics who attempted suicide; hospital records	Hospitalized chronic schizophrenics who had not made attempts
Shaffer et al. (1974)	12	0	75	NS	5-year follow-up of hospitalized schizophrenics; chart data rated blindly on clinical grounds by two psychiatrists and on two suicide scales	Random sample of previously hospitalized schizophrenics who had not killed themselves on follow-up
Warnes (1968)	16	0	16	NS	Data, source, & methods not described	Chronic schizophrenics with past suicidal behavior matched for sex & age

[a]These numbers refer to schizophrenics only, for whom results were analyzed separately.
[b]NS = Not specified.

found that suicides were more likely to be white. However, Shaffer and colleagues (1974) found similar racial proportions in suicide and control groups. Schizophrenics who kill themselves tend to have more education than controls (Farberow, Shneidman, and Neuringer, 1966; Sletten et al., 1972; Drake, et al., 1984).

Schizophrenics are typically unemployed and unmarried at the time of suicide (Wilson, 1968; Yarden, 1974; Niskanen, Lonnquist, Achte, and Rinta-Manty, 1974). Because functional deterioration characterizes chronic schizophrenia, these features are not clear predictors of suicide. Three controlled studies (Shaffer et al., 1974; Breier and Astrachan, 1984; Drake et al., 1984) found no significant differences in marital or employment status between suicides and controls. Roy (1982) found that suicides were more likely than controls to have been unemployed, but not more likely to have been unmarried.

Type of Schizophrenia

Several studies suggest that paranoid schizophrenics have higher suicide risk than other diagnostic types (Levy and Southcombe, 1953; Achte, Stenback, and Teravainen, 1966; Virkkunen, 1974). There are, however, no controlled studies to support this association.

Premorbid Adjustment

Patients with a history of good premorbid functioning may be predisposed to suicide because they experience greater disruption of performance and have more difficulty accepting chronic illness. Sletten et al. (1972) observed that schizophrenics who kill themselves tend to have higher levels of education. Among well-controlled studies which address this question, Farberow et al. (1966) found that suicides had more education and higher military rank than controls. These findings were interpreted as reflecting a tendency to be "overstrivers" with a strong need to succeed. Drake and colleagues (1984) found that suicides had more education and higher performance expectations that were congruent with previous educational attainments but not with current functional abilities.

Course of Illness

Unexplained suicides in young people are often attributed to incipient psychosis (Lehman, 1975). Such individuals, it is speculated, become aware of the disintegration of their thinking capacity and choose to end their lives. Since the diagnoses in these cases are uncertain, no firm data support this theory.

Diagnosed schizophrenics who kill themselves have typically experienced a severe, chronic illness (Niskanen et al., 1974) characterized by many exacerbations and remissions (Yarden, 1974). Their treatment history is marked by numerous relapses and hospitalizations (Pokorny, 1960; Sletten et al., 1972; Yarden, 1974). Roy's (1982) well-controlled study confirmed that suicides are more likely than other schizophrenics to have had a chronic illness with exacerbations and remissions (80 versus 50%). Drake and colleagues (1984), however, found no differences in number of hospitalizations or number of exacerbations between suicides and hospitalized controls.

Within the overall context of a chronic, relapsing illness, vulnerability to suicide is maximal during the early years of illness (Banen, 1954; Virkkunen, 1974; Noreik, 1975) The well-controlled studies confirm that most completed suicides occur during the first ten years of schizophrenic illness (Warnes, 1968; Roy, 1982; Drake et al., 1984). Three studies (Planansky and Johnston, 1971; Roy, Mazonson, and Pickar, 1984; Drake, Gates, and Cotton, 1986) also found that suicide attempts tend to occur early in the course of illness.

Although the overall clinical course shows deterioration, a large proportion of these patients show clinical improvement just prior to suicide (Sletten et al., 1972). Consistent with this finding, the majority of inpatient suicides are committed soon after the patient has been granted a pass (Farberow et al., 1961; Cohen et al., 1964; Chapman, 1965; Warnes, 1968; Niskanen et al., 1974); and many outpatient suicides occur soon after discharge (Pokorny, 1960; Warnes, 1968; Bolin, Wright, Wilkinson, and Lindner, 1968).

Precipitants

Loss is frequently cited as a precipitant to suicide. Losses may be threatened, real, or imagined (Bolin et al., 1968). They include the death of a relative (Chapman, 1965; Achte et al., 1966); separation from a spouse, parent, or lover (Yarden, 1974); loss of physical health, job, money, or home (Bolin et al., 1968); loss of a therapist (Cotton, Drake, and Gates, 1985); or loss of hospital supports (Farberow et al., 1961). Breier and Astrachan (1984) and Cotton and colleagues (1985) found that loss of familial support was the most frequent precipitant to completed suicide. However, not all studies have confirmed the importance of loss. In Planansky and Johnston's (1973) interviews of suicide attempters, only a small minority mentioned losses. In a well-controlled study, Shaffer and associates (1974) found that a minority of schizophrenics who killed themselves had experienced losses during the six months prior to suicide and that suicides were no different from controls in this respect.

Changes in the course of illness—relapses, hospitalizations, and discharges—are more clear precipitants to suicide. The majority of inpatient suicides occur during the first six months of hospitalization, with the greatest frequency during the first month (Levy and Southcombe, 1953; Beisser and Blanchette, 1961; Achte et al., 1966; Sletten et al., 1972). Among outpatients, the risk of suicide is greatest immediately following discharge (Bolin et al., 1968). In Roy's (1982) well-controlled study, 30 percent of the suicides among discharged schizophrenics occurred within one month of discharge and 50 percent within three months.

Social Isolation

Suicide among schizophrenics has been related to social isolation in general and to lack of familial support in particular. Like other schizophrenics, these patients have few close interpersonal contacts and tend to live alone (Yarden, 1974; Niskanen et al., 1974). In a poorly controlled study, Wilson (1968) found that only 29 percent of suicides, compared to 59 percent of controls, were involved in at least one meaningful or therapeutic relationship.

The well-controlled studies support the association between a lack of familial support and suicide but not the more general hypothesis regarding social isolation. Warnes (1968) found a lack of familial support or ties among suicides. Cohen and associates (1964) noted that clinically improved patients who committed suicide lacked familial support. Drake and colleagues (1984) found that suicides were more likely to live alone (60 versus 27%), but three other controlled studies (Shaffer et al., 1974; Roy, 1982; Breier and Astrachan, 1984) reported that similar proportions of suicides and controls lived alone. None of the well-controlled studies measured social isolation in a more global sense.

Behavior

A large proportion of schizophrenics who kill themselves—usually more than half—have made previous suicide attempts. Among well-controlled studies, Cohen et al. (1964) found that 70 percent of suicides, compared to 32 percent of controls, had made previous attempts. Shaffer et al. (1974) found that number of previous attempts was the most important predictor of subsequent suicide; no other variables increased the predicted variance. Breier and Astrachan (1984) also found that prior suicide attempts were the strongest predictor of suicide. On the other hand, Roy (1982) found that suicides (40%) and controls (37%) had similar histories of suicidal behavior. Drake and colleagues (1984) also found similar histories of attempts.

Antisocial behavior and substance abuse have been associated with suicidal behavior in several studies (Achte et al., 1966; Sletten et al., 1972; Noreik, 1975). Two well-controlled studies (Shaffer et al., 1974; Drake et al., 1984), however, found that neither antisocial behavior nor alcohol abuse was related to suicide.

Just prior to suicide, schizophrenics manifest signs of increased agitation, such as irritability and assaultiveness (Achte et al., 1966; Yarden, 1974). The well-controlled studies support these descriptions. Planansky and Johnston (1971) found that psychomotor restlessness and agitation typically preceded suicide attempts. Warnes (1968) reported agitation, hostility, restlessness, and "severe persecutory anxiety." Farberow and associates (1961) found that hospitalized schizophrenics were "extremely tense, restless, and impulsive" prior to suicide. Drake and colleagues (1986) found that this was true for attempters but not for completed suicides. They also noted that increased agitation among attempters was sometimes due to akathisia (Drake and Ehrlich, 1985).

Withdrawn, passive behavior may precede a minority of suicides among schizophrenics (Achte et al., 1966; Sletten et al., 1972). In a well-controlled study, however, Cohen and associates (1964) found that withdrawn behavior was more characteristic of controls than suicides.

Thoughts

A controversy has long existed as to whether schizophrenics commit suicide at the peak of intense and frightening psychotic activity or during periods of symptomatic remission. According to the former view, schizophrenics kill themselves either in direct response to psychotic thoughts or in order to escape them (Levy and Southcombe, 1953; Wilson, 1968; Yarden, 1974). Planansky and Johnston (1973) found that a majority of attempters experienced intense psychotic activity—defined as observable excitement and reported "mental anguish"—immediately prior to their attempts. However, the well-controlled studies do not support this link between intense psychotic activity and completed suicide. Roy (1982) found that only a small proportion of suicides, no more than controls, had command hallucinations. Breier and Astrachan (1984) and Drake and colleagues (1984) also found that command hallucinations and increased psychosis were rare among completed suicides. Warnes (1968) reported that over twice as many controls as suicides struggled with frightening hallucinations. Exacerbations of psychosis may more commonly precede suicide attempts rather than completed suicides (Drake et al., 1986).

According to the view that schizophrenics commit suicide when relatively nonpsychotic, vulnerability increases during remissions when these patients become realistically aware of the effects of their psychopathology. The well-controlled studies support the importance of awareness of illness as a risk factor. The majority of suicides in Farberow et al.'s study (1961) realized they were ill. Warnes (1968) found that 75 percent of the suicides, versus 44 percent of the controls, showed hopeless awareness of pathology. More of the suicides also expressed feelings of inner disintegration (31 versus 13%). Drake and colleagues (1984) confirmed the importance of awareness of illness (47 versus 11%) and fears of mental disintegration (33 versus 1%).

Mood

Depression is one of the most frequently cited features of schizophrenic patients who commit suicide (Beisser and Blanchette, 1961; Achte et al., 1966; Sletten et al., 1972; Niskanen et al., 1974). Because patients with affective illness typically manifest depression, this finding is particularly susceptible to the effects of diagnostic heterogeneity. The well-controlled studies do, however, support this relationship. Cohen and associates (1964) found that 70 percent of the suicides, compared with 38 percent of the controls, had moderate to severe depression, but they did not use a standardized measure of depression. Using DSM-III criteria (American Psychiatric Association, 1980), Roy (1982) found that 53 percent of suicides and only 25 percent of controls met the criteria for major depressive episode. Drake and Cotton (1986) found that suicides were more likely to have persistent depressed mood (80 versus 48%), feelings of worthlessness, hopelessness, and suicidal ideation, but did not typically meet DSM-III criteria for a major depressive episode. Results for attempters are more mixed. Minkoff, Bergman, Beck, and Beck (1973) and Beck, Kovacs, and Weissman (1975) found that seriousness of suicidal intent was not significantly related to severity of depression. Drake and colleagues (1986) found that attempters were less likely to be depressed than were completed suicides. Roy et al. (1984), however, found that attempters had high levels of depression compared with controls.

One possible explanation of these divergent findings is that suicidal schizophrenics experience hopelessness rather than typical depressive symptoms. Yarden (1974) and Virkkunen (1976) reported that a majority of schizophrenics expressed hopelessness about the future prior to suicide. In well-controlled studies, Minkoff et al. (1973) and Beck et al. (1975) established that, for suicide attempters, severity of suicidal intent was more strongly related to level of hopelessness than to level of depression. In Beck et al.'s (1975) study with a larger sample of schizophrenics, controlling for the effect of hopelessness completely eliminated the relationship between suicidal intent and depression. Drake and Cotton (1986) found that hopelessness also eliminated the effect of depression among completed suicides.

Treatment

The use of antipsychotic medications has often been cited as contributing to suicides among schizophrenics by removing psychotic symptoms prematurely, increasing depression, and falsely suggesting stable improvements (Beisser and Blanchette, 1961). Although suicide is more likely during nonpsychotic periods, the well-controlled studies do not support a direct medication effect. Warnes (1968) found that schizophrenics who killed themselves were taking significantly lower doses of medications than controls. Cohen and associates (1964) found that equal numbers of suicides and matched controls were receiving medications. They also noted that a significant number of suicides occurred soon after abrupt discontinuance of medications. The side effects of antipsychotic medications, such as akathisia, may be associated with impulsive suicide attempts (Shear, Frances, and Weiden, 1983; Drake and Ehrlich, 1985).

Another clinical view holds that brief hospitalizations and community treatment increase the suicide risk for these patients (Lindelius and Kay, 1973; Arieti, 1974; Yarden, 1974). According to this view, suicide is related to decreased monitoring, increased social isolation, and increased expectations of performance. No data are available to support these clinical impressions. Curiously, Bleuler (1950) felt that the surveillance of institutional treatment was responsible for suicide.

Problems in the treatment relationship are associated with subsequent suicide. Virkkunen (1976) found that, compared to other schizophrenics, those who killed themselves had negative attitudes toward medications and treatment in general. Giving up on treatment seemed to be one aspect of the hopeless withdrawal that preceded suicide. In well-controlled studies Farberow et al. (1961) and Cohen et al. (1964) linked excessive dependence on psychiatric services to subsequent suicide. Excessive dependence, manifested by demandingness, neediness, and fears of discharge, characterized 60 percent of the suicides and only 15 percent of controls (Cohen et al., 1964).

DISCUSSION

There has been no clear understanding of suicide risk among schizophrenics. The usual problems of studying suicide are partially responsible. Suicide is a low base rate phenomenon, and subjects are not available for study after identification. Several additional methodologic problems have impeded progress. First, diagnostic heterogeneity in many studies has obscured issues that are specific to schizophrenics. Only eleven controlled studies specifically address suicide among schizophrenics. Second, a lack of standardized measures and blind ratings further reduces the comparability of studies. Only four of the well-controlled studies utilize blind ratings. Third, studies usually focus on behavior during hospitalization and ignore other perspectives so that immediate behavioral antecedents are the only possible findings. This perspective overlooks the patient's history, attitudes, and relationships in the community, among other things. Fourth, most studies have focused on either attempters or completed suicides, although the relationship between the two groups is unclear. It seems likely that for schizophrenics, as for others, attempters and completed suicides form overlapping but largely distinct groups (Stengel, 1962). Fifth, the absence of consensually agreed upon risk factors has made the identification of high-risk patients for a prospective study difficult.

CONCLUSIONS

Despite the methodologic limitations of existing studies, several clinical implications can be drawn from the literature. Suicide is a common outcome of schizophrenic illness. Young male patients, particularly those with a history of good premorbid functioning, are the most vulnerable. A clinical course characterized by exacerbations and remissions increases risk because patients maintain a painful awareness of their functional deterioration. Suicide is most likely during the early years of illness and around the time of hospitalizations.

Suicide is relatively uncommon during psychotic episodes. Contrary to clinical wisdom, command hallucinations are not strongly associated with suicide. Harbingers of suicide in the mental status exam are those features associated with depressive episodes. Presuicidal patients are likely to report depression, worthlessness, suicidal ideation, and hopelessness about the future. They may be specifically hopeless about fulfilling expectations in the context of chronic illness and may express fears of further mental deterioration.

Many young schizophrenics make suicide attempts, often in the context of interpersonal conflict, but completed suicides are likely to be preceded by hopeless withdrawal from family, friends, and caregivers. The progression of despair about overcoming illness and constructing a personally meaningful future is the best barometer of suicide potential at any particular time.

Although this review addresses risk assessment rather than treatment, a more accurate understanding of suicide risk among schizophrenics should allow clinicians to increase structure and supports at appropriate times for high-risk patients. The identification of high-risk patients should also facilitate the development of prospective studies of treatment.

REFERENCES

Achte, K., Stenback, A., & Teravainen H. (1966), On suicides committed during treatment in psychiatric hospitals. *Acta Psychiat. Scand.*, 42:272–284.

American Psychiatric Association (1980), *The Diagnostic and Statistical Manual of Mental Disorders*, 3rd ed. Washington, DC: American Psychiatric Press.

Arieti, S. (1974), *An Interpretation of Schizophrenia*, 2nd ed. New York: Basic Books, p. 309.

Banen, D.M. (1954), Suicide by psychotics. *J. Nerv. & Ment. Dis.*, 120:349–357.

Beck, A.T., Kovacs, M., & Weissman, A. (1975), Hopelessness and suicidal behavior: An overview. *J. Amer. Med. Assn.*, 234:1146–1149.

Beisser, A., & Blanchette, J. (1961), A study of suicides in a mental hospital. *Dis. Nerv. Sys.*, 22:365–369.

Bleuler, E. (1950), *Dementia Praecox or the Group of Schizophrenias*. New York: International Universities Press, p. 488.

Bleuler, M. (1978), *The Schizophrenic Disorders: Long-term and Family Studies*. New Haven, CT: Yale University Press.

Bolin, R.K., Wright, R.E., Wilkinson, M.N., & Lindner, C.K. (1968), Survey of suicide among patients on home-leave from a mental hospital. *Psychiat. Quart.*, 42:81–89.

Breier, A., & Astrachan, B.M. (1984), Characterization of schizophrenic patients who commit suicide. *Amer. J. Psychiat.*, 141:206–209.

Chapman, R.F. (1965), Suicide during psychiatric hospitalization. *Bull. Menn. Clin.*, 29:35–44.

Cohen, S., Leonard, C.V., Farberow, N.L., & Shneidman, E.S. (1964), Tranquilizers and suicide in schizophrenic patients. *Arch. Gen. Psychiat.*, 11:312–317.

Cotton, P.G., Drake, R.E., & Gates, C. (1985), Critical treatment issues in suicide among schizophrenics. *Hosp. Commun. Psychiat.*, 36:534–536.

Dorwart, R. (1980), Deinstitutionalization: Who is left behind? *Hosp. Commun. Psychiat.*, 31:336–338.

Drake, R.E., & Cotton, P.G. (1986), Depression, hopelessness, and suicide in chronic schizophrenia. *Brit. J. Psychiat.*, 148:554–559.

———— Ehrlich, J. (1985), Suicide attempts associated with akathisia. *Amer. J. Psychiat.*, 142:499–501.

———— Gates, C., & Cotton, P.G. (1986), Suicide among schizophrenics: A comparison of attempters and completed suicides. *Brit. J. Psychiat.*, 149:784–787.

———— ———— ———— Whitaker, A. (1984), Suicide among schizophrenics: Who is at risk? *J. Nerv. & Ment. Dis.*, 172:613–617.

Farberow, N.L., Shneidman, E.S., & Leonard, C.V. (1961), Suicide among schizophrenic hospital patients. In: *The Cry for Help*, eds. N.L. Farberow & E.S. Shneidman. New York: McGraw-Hill, pp. 78–109.

———— Neuringer, C. (1966), Case history and hospitalization factors in suicides of neuropsychiatric hospital patients. *J. Nerv. & Ment. Dis.*, 142:32–44.

Lehman, H. E. (1975), Schizophrenia: clinical features. In: *The Comprehensive Textbook of Psychiatry*, 2nd ed., eds. A. Freeman, H. Kaplan, & B. Sadock. Baltimore, MD: Williams & Wilkins, pp. 909–910.

Levy, S., & Southcombe, R. (1953), Suicide in a state hospital for the mentally ill. *J. Nerv. & Ment. Dis.*, 117:504–514.

Lindelius, R., & Kay D.W.K. (1973), Some changes in mortality in schizophrenics in Sweden. *Acta Psychiat. Scand.*, 49:315–323.

Miles, C. (1977), Conditions predisposing to suicide. *J. Nerv. & Ment. Dis.*, 164:231–246.

Minkoff, K., Bergman, E., Beck, A.T., & Beck, R. (1973), Hopelessness, depression and attempted suicide. *Amer. J. Psychiat.*, 130:455–459.

Niskanen, P., Lonnquist J., & Achte, K. (1973), Schizophrenia and suicide. *Psychiat. Fennica*, 223–227.

———— ———— ———— Rinta-Manty, R. (1974), Suicides in a Helsinki psychiatric hospital: 1964–1972. *Psychiat. Fennica*, 275–280.

Noreik, G. (1975), Attempted suicide and suicide in functional psychoses. *Acta Psychiat. Scand.*, 52:81–106.

Planansky, K., & Johnston, R. (1971), The occurence and characteristics of suicidal preoccupation and acts in schizophrenia. *Acta Psychiat. Scand.*, 47:473–483.

———— (1973), Clinical setting and motivation in suicide attempts in schizophrenics. *Acta Psychiat. Scand.*, 49:680–690.

Pokorny, A.D. (1960), Characteristics of forty-four patients who subsequently committed suicide. *Arch. Gen. Psychiat.*, 2:314–323.

———— (1983), Prediction of suicide in psychiatric patients: Report of a prospective study. *Arch. Gen. Psychiat.*, 40:249–257.

Roy, A. (1982), Suicide in chronic schizophrenia. *Brit. J. Psychiat.*, 141:171–177.

———— Mazonson, A., & Pickar, D. (1984), Attempted suicide in chronic schizophrenia. *Brit. J. Psychiat.*, 144:303–306.

Shaffer, J.W., Perlin, S., Schmidt, C.W., & Stephens, J.H. (1974), The prediction of suicide in schizophrenics. *J. Nerv. & Ment. Dis.*, 159:349–355.

Shear, M.K., Frances, A., & Weiden, P. (1983), Suicide associated with akathisia and depot fluphenazine treatment. *J. Clin. Psychopharmacol.*, 3:235–236.

Sletten, I., Brown, M., Evenson, R., & Altman, H. (1972), Suicide in mental hospital patients. *Dis. Nerv. Sys.*, 33:328–334.

Solomon, P. (1981), The admissions process in two state psychiatric hospitals. *Hosp. Commun. Psychiat.*, 32:405–408.

Stengel, E. (1962), Recent research into suicide and attempted suicide. *Amer. J. Psychiat.*, 118:725–727.

Tsuang, M.T. (1978), Suicide in schizophrenics, manics, depressives and surgical controls. *Arch. Gen. Psychiat.*, 35:153–154.

Virkkunen, M. (1974), Suicide in schizophrenia and paranoid psychoses. *Acta Psychiat. Scand.* (suppl.), 250:1–305.

—— (1976), Attitude toward psychiatric treatment before suicide in schizophrenia and paranoid psychoses. *Brit. J. Psychiat.*, 128:47–49.

Warnes, H. (1968), Suicide in schizophrenics. *Dis. Nerv. Sys.*, 29 (suppl.) 5:35–40.

Wilson, G. (1968), Suicide in psychiatric patients who have received hospital treatment. *Amer. J. Psychiat.*, 25:752–757.

Yarden, P. (1974), Observations on suicide in chronic schizophrenics. *Compreh. Psychiat.*, 15:325–333.

11

Suicide in Children: Diagnosis, Management, and Treatment

Timothy F. Dugan, M.D.
Myron L. Belfer, M.D.

> I am very hungry.
> I bite people and try to eat them up.
> I am a bad girl and I should die.

This is the opening statement offered by a 6-year-old girl brought into the clinic for an emergency consultation by her mother. Over the prior three weeks, the child had been threatening to throw herself out of a moving car. On the day preceding the consultation, the patient's mother had to stop her moving car on a major highway to restrain the child who was leaning out of the back window, holding on with her hands with only her lower extremities remaining inside the window. The mother was angry, called the suicidal threat "attention-seeking," was worried enough to seek consultation, but continued to dismiss the psychiatrist's use of the word *suicide*. Hearing this material in an accepting, nonchallenging manner, which includes the child's feelings of despair, and the desirability of death, constitutes a diagnostic and therapeutic challenge.

Children commit suicide. For most of us this very thought is difficult to comprehend; it is especially so for clinicians involved in saving lives and parents who feel responsible for their children and their maladies.

The clinician's resistance to acknowledging the child's despair subtly tends to undercut efforts toward definitive emergency treatment and this can have dire consequences. The suicidal child seen in crisis along with his or her family or responsible caretakers is at the optimal point for definitive intervention since the motivation for treatment on the part of the patient or family significantly decreases following the acute crisis.

Parents and caretakers deny serious childhood diagnoses out of a sense of guilt, responsibility, and rage. "Countertransference hate" is a concept put forth by

Maltsberger and Buie (1974) to explain the rage induced in clinicians by the hopelessness of a suicidal individual. This disavowed rage of the clinician (or parent) leads to an avoidance of the suicidal patient and can be a factor precipitating suicide.

EPIDEMIOLOGY

The frequency of suicide attempts increases with chronologic age, with a rapid rise at ages 13 to 14 (Mattson, Hawkins, and Seese, 1969; Weissman, 1974). Shaffer (1974), in a study of completed suicides under age 12, found the report of psychiatric symptoms in 27 of 31 cases. Connell (1972), in a report on 15 children over the age of 8 years who were admitted to a general hospital for treatment of accidental overdosing, noted that numerous children's deaths reported as accidents may be unrecognized suicides. In general, frequent or suspect accidents should be investigated by the physician for possible suicidal intent, especially in the family contexts likely to engender that behavior. The unexplained, too frequent, or unusual presentation of a child to a physician should be viewed with suspicion. Guggenheim (1982) noted that 15 percent of suicidal completers have seen a physician within six weeks prior to their death.

Approximately 70 percent of all children admitted to a Child Psychiatry Inpatient Unit exhibit suicidal ideation, whereas 10–33 percent of children referred for outpatient evaluation exhibit suicidal indeation (Kashani, Ray, and Carlson, 1984; Pfeffer, Conte, Plutchik, and Jerrett, 1979, 1980). In a review of completed suicides of children and adolescents by Shafii, Carrigan, Whittinghill, and Derrick (1985), suicidal ideation had been communicated by the patient 85 percent of the time in the instance of completed suicide, whereas suicidal ideation was seen in 20 percent of a matched control group. The authors go on to state: "We believe a close relationship exists between suicidal wishes, threats, attempts, and completed suicide. In our study frequently the 'talkers' become the 'doers'" (p. 1063). Depression is a major symptom present in suicidal children (McArney, 1975; Pfeffer et al., 1979, 1980). Otto (1972) discovered that 38 percent of the subjects in his study had been depressed three months before attempting suicide. Mattson et al. (1969), found 40 percent of suicidal children they studied were depressed one month before being seen compared with only 13 percent of 95 nonsuicidal disturbed children. Pfeffer (1981) demonstrated that depression, feelings of hopelessness and worthlessness, and the child's wish to die, significantly differentiated nonsuicidal and suicidal children. These data compare with interview data taken from children admitted to a pediatric ward where 7 percent met *Diagnostic and Statistical Manual of Mental Disorders* (DSM-III) criteria for depression.

In administering to the emergency needs of the child there is no value in attempting to distinguish between a suicidal gesture and a suicidal attempt. Since the word *gesture* may be used to minimize the severity of the episode, we do not permit its use in our clinic. The statistics have no meaning in assessing the severity of an attempt in any individual case. Any concern for possible secondary gain for the patient is outweighed by the consequences of a failure to respond adequately.

ANTECEDENTS AND PRECIPITANTS

Suicidal behavior typically occurs in a context of intensely stressful, chaotic, and unpredictable family events. Children who feel incapable of making an impact on these circumstances use suicide as a desperate, last-ditch effort to affect or coerce those who threaten their well-being (Cohen-Sandler, Berman, and King, 1982). Suicidal behavior may function as an interpersonal coping strategy for children to gain revenge, to punish or be punished, or to end their plight with a fantasy of rebirth (Asch, 1980; Maltsberger and Buie, 1980). Self-esteem is considerably diminished in these children (Malmquist, 1983). School grades that are viewed as unsatisfactory, the existence of punishment, and ostracism may lead to suicidal thoughts and action. Subjective discontent with one's personal identity may lead to a sense of inadequacy or badness. Children who complete a suicide have had contact with a friend or relative who has threatened or attempted suicide at a rate five times greater than a matched control group (Shafii et al., 1985). The final precipitating factor is actual or perceived loss of human contact in the context of a prevailing sense of loneliness and isolation during the months prior to suicide (Shafii et al., 1985; Mack and Hickler, 1981, p. 55).

The families of these children will show a high incidence of parental affective disorder and alcoholism (Beardslee, Bemporad, Keller, and Klerman, 1983; Shafii et al. 1985; Famularo, Stone, and Popper, 1985). The parents have a higher rate of marital discord as well and seem to model and foster the use of impulsive, ineffective coping styles in their children (Shaffer, 1974). Preliminary data has pointed to the development of problems of early attachment behavior in children 12 months of age in families where at least one parent has manic-depressive illness (Gaensbauer, Harman, Cytryn, and McKnew, 1984). Also, the most socially and intellectually competent children of psychotic parents are more likely to have schizophrenic mothers, while the least competent children are likely to have severely depressed mothers (Kaufman, Grunebaum, Cohler, and Gamer, 1979). Affective illness in families extracts a considerable toll from all members. The cost of untreated, denied affective illness extracts a developmental cost socially and intellectually, and may result in the literal loss of life.

Case Example

The 6-year-old presented above had a three-month decline in her school performance. She was reported to be angry, irritable, and difficult to get along with. Her perception of herself as being angry with claws is depicted in Figure 11.1. The child's body image is quite distorted

Figure 11.1

for a 6-year-old girl by virtue of her depressed mood and self-directed anger. Though she had above average intelligence, her school papers showed a plethora of errors, sloppy work, and evidence of impaired concentration. Her peer relationships had deteriorated and scapegoating by peers had become the norm. The acute precipitant was related to the separation of her parents. This child had minimal access to her father, and her mother was quite angry and resentful.

ASSESSMENT AND DIAGNOSIS

Much has been written concerning the controversy about the existence of depression in prelatency and early latency children. Earlier discussions in the psychoanalytic literature debated the existence of childhood depression prior to the age of 7 or 8 because of the theoretical necessity for the existence of an established or punitive superego in the genesis of a clinical depression (Freud, 1917) and the belief that such a psychic structure could not exist prior to resolution of the oedipal conflict (Bowlby, 1961; Rochlin, 1965). However, when these papers are read carefully, it is clear that these authors are describing children with profound mood disturbances and behavioral alterations. For theoretical reasons, these children are not called depressed, and yet descriptively it is clear that these children would fall under the contemporary nomenclature describing depression. This debate is now used as a "strawman" by more biologically influenced thinkers to dismiss psychoanalytic formulations of depression in children, to highlight the "biological imperative," and to dismiss the clinical utility and efficacy of thoughtful individual child evaluations, psychotherapy, and family therapy in favor of premature recommendations for biological therapies, still not proven to be more efficacious than placebo (Poznanski, 1985; Elkins and Rapoport, 1983, p. 368). It is more clear now that children have cognitive abilities to distinguish right and wrong and establish a primitive moral purpose at quite early ages, and such concepts are used in punishing ways by depressed children who suffer defects in self-esteem (A. Freud and Sandler, 1985, p. 414; Malmquist, 1983). It is also true that infants and toddlers suffer disorders thought to be consistent with depression, as in the studies of hospitalism by Spitz (1945) or of orally deprived infants by Engel and Reichsman (1956) and Dowling (1977), and the manifestations of such symptoms as apathy, disinterest, self-stimulation, and resistance to attachment are consistent with earlier psychoanalytic formulations of the primacy of oral conflicts in depression (Abraham, 1911). However, Kashani et al. (1984) report that only 4 percent of a preschool population selected for behavioral symptoms and referred to a child development unit met DSM-III criteria for childhood depression. This raises the question about whether childhood depression is a rare disorder or whether the DSM-III criteria are not specific for this developmental population and underestimate the incidence.

It is now quite clear that childhood depression and suicide do exist as clinical entities, can be thoughtfully diagnosed, and successfully treated. Depressive disorders can be diagnosed by established research criteria as shown by Kovacs, Feinberg, Crouse-Novak, Paulauskas, and Finkelstein (1984a); Kovacs, Feinberg, Crouse-Novak, Paulauskas, Pollock, and Finkelstein (1984b); Cytryn, McKnew, and Bunney (1980); and Kashani et al. (1984). It has also been shown by Carlson and Cantwell (1980) that the earlier conceptualizations of "masked depression" by Cytryn et al. (1980), while drawing attention to significant childhood depression underlying significant behavioral disturbances, cognitive difficulties, and conduct disorders, can be "unmasked" by using DSM-III criteria for depression and direct interviewing techniques.

The clinician who sees a child presenting with an overt or suspected self-destructive act should have as the first goal the protection of the child, and if necessary, the appropriate medical or surgical treatment of the child. Proper attention to the child's physical condition should increase rapport with both child and family and aid in an understanding of the context in which the gesture or attempt has occurred (Belfer, 1977). In this history, acute family disruption, the loss of a significant person or object, or the threat of abandonment should be sought as critical factors. Declining school performance, withdrawal, neglect of dress or self-care, or alienation from friends may be antecedents of suicidal behavior and should be sought in the history. It is particularly important to determine if there has been a familial history of suicide or major difficulties in the expression of anger, both of which increase the suicidal risk in these patients. A history of current or past psychiatric intervention will be helpful in evaluating the degree of psychopathology that is present, the response to treatment, and the possible resources for disposition.

It is important to secure the family's cooperation in reestablishing some meaningful communication with the patient. This process begins in the emergency room, where the clinician's attitude and approach should avoid the fostering of conflict by inadvertantly making a pejorative judgment as to the contribution of the family to the event or the merits of the child's act. It is best to meet with the parents or custodial agent separately, the child individually (Robbins and Alessi, 1985), and then see the family together. One should avoid undue reassurance to the parents that the episode was transient and not likely to progress to further symptomatology, because in most instances the data will not be at hand at this time to support any conclusion. Rather, recognition and acknowledgment of the child's and family's distress are needed. These are features of the "empathic method" of alliance espoused by us and articulated in other chapters of this book, and constitute the first phase of working with a suicidal child.

The clinician should aim to establish rapport with the young patient and avoid a judgmental or dismissive attitude. The patient needs to be engaged. If the child or adolescent appears hostile, then a calm, nonintrusive approach that emphasizes the desire to understand what has happened and what may be going on is most useful. The reinforcement of the alliance is important through statements that assure the patient of your desire to help. If the patient fails to relate, or the relatedness fails to evolve over the interview, then the clinician should be concerned that a more pervasive psychiatric disturbance is present and not assume simply a heightened degree of withholding or negativism.

When there is evidence that the child is not coherent a medical and neurological evaluation of the child is essential even though psychological issues appear most prominent. The physician must be satisfied that there is no head trauma, postingestion toxic psychosis, metabolic disorder, or postictal phenomena. A toxic screen should be done on all children where there is the slightest suspicion of an ingestion. In the presence of a normal medical evaluation and persistent incoherence, the physician should proceed to determine if there is the presence of a thought disorder. If the patient does not make sense, seems preoccupied with bizarre or irrelevant thoughts, has a shifting mental status without relation to meaningful stimuli, and if there is a history of psychosis, then a disturbance of thought must be considered. If hallucinations or delusions are present this is further evidence.

Familiarity with DSM-III criteria for major affective disorder, dysthymic disorder, uncomplicated bereavement, and adjustment disorder with depressed mood is necessary for accurate diagnostic assessment. These diagnoses serve as a useful discriminator when predicting prognosis of the depression and relapse rates (Kovacs et al., 1984a,b).

MENTAL STATUS EXAM

Of particular importance in the evaluation of childhood depression and suicidality are the recent recommendations by Puig-Antich, Chambers, and Tabrizi (1983) for the direct questioning of children. It is important always to ask children about suicide: their ideas, thoughts about death, and the wish to die. These in conjunction with familial suicidal tendencies constitute major risk factors for childhood suicide (Pfeffer et al., 1979, 1980; Pfeffer, 1984). The time course of the child's symptoms and behavioral changes is best elicited from the parents; while the existence of suicidal ideation, hopelessness, and sadness are best elicited from an individual interview with the child (Puig-Antich et al., 1983). The direct questioning of children, analogous to the mental status examination of an adult, while of benefit in eliciting important and defended-against information, can be misunderstood as suggestions to disrespect existing and necessary latency-age defenses. Standard play therapy interviews continue to be the mainstay of the childhood psychiatric evaluation, though now augmented by the methods of direct questioning. It is within the play therapy interviews that disavowed affects of oral hunger and rage, hopelessness, and futility can be delineated within the necessary defensive structure and symbolic function of the stage of latency. Too-quick abandonment of the standard play-therapy method, such as play in displacement, can fracture an empathic alliance, inhibit the development of a long-term relationship with these ill children and dysfunctional families, and may outweigh the gains made by incorporating direct questioning of children within the initial psychiatric interview.

Incorporating direct questioning into the standard play interview provides the most useful information in the evaluation of content of thought.

Standard issues of affect, mood lability, stream of thought, and looseness of association, which may be the only indicator of severe ego impairment or thought disorder, need assessment. Also, some screen for cognitive functioning is necessary, including orientation, time sense, impulsivity, and judgment. Diminished cognitive capacity has implications for understanding the child's comprehension of the consequences of his act, the capacity to develop an alliance, and the capacity to participate in treatment.

Of particular importance in the diagnosis of depression and prediction of suicidality is the assessment of mood. By DSM-III criteria a sad facial expression in a child less than the age of six can substitute for the verbal description of dysphoric mood. This incorrectly assumes that a latency-age child has the cognitive capacity to describe such affects as dysphoria or rage. By inference, this criteria also devalues the empathic method of evaluating mood by a thoughtful clinician, which is so necessary when evaluating a suicidal individual, particularly one who is silent and hostile (Havens, 1967). This issue has been addressed in recent research by Poznanski, Mokros, Grossman, and Freeman (1985), where they address inaccuracies in the diagnosis of prepubertal childhood depression when a verbal expression of dysphoric mood is a necessary criteria for the diagnosis. The nonverbal assessment of mood is an indispensable component to the diagnosis.

TREATMENT AND DISPOSITION

Pfeffer (1981) provides a useful governing statement for the treatment of suicidal children: "All intervention efforts with suicidal latency age children must aim at enhancing communication between parent and child. As a result, the clinician's role is mainly a facilitator of change sufficient to increase the safety of the child and to promote his or her appropriate developmental advances" (p. 158). Suicidal children require intensive therapy that may include psychiatric hospitalization, outpatient psychiatric therapy, psychopharmacology, school consultation, and academic remediation. In addition, a follow-up procedure with the possibility of rapid intervention is necessary since a study of suicide attempts in subjects 10 to 21 years of age found that the greatest risk for completed suicide continued for two years after the attempt (Pfeffer et al., 1979).

Disposition planning for suicidal children and their families should reflect the following hierarchy. If a child manifests psychosis and is suicidal, hospitalization is required. It is dangerous to attempt to treat the psychosis as an outpatient with the hope that its resolution will diminish suicidal risk. If a child is an abuser of drugs or alcohol in the context of a disruptive home situation, then hospitalization is indicated. If the parents give a suicidal child a message of rejection that is unmodified then a return to the home is contraindicated. Of particular importance is the existence of a communication from parent to child that the child is "expendable" or that the parent would be better off without the burden that the child represents (Sabbath, 1969; Browning, 1981). This type of angry and rejecting communication is frequently cited as a precipitant of acute suicidal ideation or attempt in children. In this case the child may be placed in a shelter, an emergency foster home, or a hospital. If the family is supportive but the child rejects the parents, then an alternative, temporary live-in situation should be sought, such as a shelter or a family relative.

The child who takes an overdose where the lethality is low and there was an immediate outreach for help to parents, friends, or others, can be treated as an outpatient, especially if a statement equivalent to, "I wanted to commit suicide, but I don't now," is made. If the child makes a serious attempt with an overdose or otherwise, if depression is present, and there is overt or covert family conflict, then the disposition presents more of a problem. If in the course of the interview with the patient the clinician feels a good alliance with the patient, the patient has a future orientation, and the family is compliant, then outpatient treatment can be pursued. If there is not a sense of an alliance, then hospitalization is indicated. If there is a history of impulsivity and/or history of acting out or "accidents," then possible referral to juvenile court may be indicated for a court-sanctioned hospitalization.

In the acute outpatient management of the suicidal child, the use of psychotropic medication including antidepressants is *not* indicated. Its use may give the patient and the family a false sense of security, the impression that the problem has been solved, or that the answer lies outside the patient and the family (Pfeffer, 1981). This may thwart definitive intervention. Current methods of psychotherapeutic intervention are clinically efficacious. Routine inclusion of psychotropic medications in the management of depressed or suicidal children must await further research; though in children refractory to the usual psychotherapeutic interventions, the use of antidepressants should be considered (Petti, 1983).

INDIVIDUAL PSYCHOTHERAPY

The treatment of a suicidal child and his family is a long-term proposition (Toolan, 1984). Whether the communication of suicidal ideation or a frank suicide attempt by a child is correlated with the diagnosis of depression, in the majority of cases (as described by Carlson and Cantwell, 1982), or, as in the minority of cases, is a vehicle for the expression of anger or resentment, the fact remains that both child and family are experiencing severe stress and disorganization at the time of presentation. The presentation of suicidal ideation or suicide attempt also connotes a process that has been ongoing over a considerable length of time and frequently is associated with developmental delays in areas of affect development, cognition, peer relationships, language processes, identifications, and/or object relations. To sort these out takes time and a well-functioning alliance that will permit the child to divulge issues of importance and for the parents or other caretakers to be able to convey a meaningful history. It is preferable to have the same clinician working with the child and family, as it facilitates a thorough understanding and diminishes the possibility of communicational difficulties arising between clinicians (Toolan, 1984).

A brief description follows of the psychotherapy of the 6-year-old girl, whose case has been briefly described above. The case vignette and accompanying drawings are meant to demonstrate the psychodynamics of depression in this 6-year-old girl, the curative aspects of individual and family therapy (though the individual sessions will be highlighted), and the articulation of phases that the authors have observed in their clinical work.

Phase I consists of developing an empathic alliance with the child and family. Figure 11.1 shows a girl with a prominent mouth, large outstretched arms with claws for hands. This graphically depicts the girl who told me at the first meeting, "I am very hungry. I bite people and try to eat them up. I am a bad girl and I should die." An alliance had to be forged with this girl that would permit her to express this rage in a safe manner and convince her that the clinician could hear and understand her and would not become critical of her, dismiss her, succumb to her rage, or abandon her. So too, with the mother, an alliance had to be forged that allowed for the investigation of her shame and guilt feelings and that gradually allowed the mother to hear and bear the despair conveyed in her daughter's behavior and statements.

Phase II occurs as the child's symptoms abate, the child and the family experience a sense of relief, and higher level defenses, including reaction formation, again begin to function to ward off the unbearable affects. Within two months of initiating psychotherapy, this child was no longer suicidal and she drew a picture of a "love forest" (Figure 11.2) with a flowering vine meant to encircle her recently separated parents. She was less provocative to her mother, and mother and child again began to communicate. While the patient's academic work had improved, her peer relationships were still quite dysfunctional. As Blos (1983) describes "the romantic concept of therapy, so widespread today, is simply being 'made to feel good' . . . [yet] such expectations brush aside the fact that therapy not only resolves old conflicts but introduces by its very nature new conflicts which—by their continual resolution—lift psychic functioning onto a higher, more complex level" (p. 577). This level, Blos calls "maturity." Reaction formation avoids contending with these conflicts, but does permit some respite from the overwhelming, self-destructive affects. Adaptationally, reaction formation does permit the child and family to begin to "approach" each other again in an intimate fashion.

In *Phase III* more of the affect is able to be experienced, expressed, and tolerated. Here old conflicts are described and experienced. At eight months of psychotherapy, the child drew a picture of a "devil being burned in hell for being a bad girl" (Figure 11.3) and a picture of the execution, by fire, of an assassin who "had killing feelings toward the President" (Figure 11.4). The issue of "the hidden executioner" seen in suicidal patients is described by Asch (1980). Within one month of this drawing, the child told of being aware of "killing feelings toward my

Figure 11.2

Figure 11.3

Figure 11.4

mother" that occurred while driving on the same highway as the initial precipitant for psychiatric care. However, these feelings occurred in the absence of her feeling suicidal. More direct affect expression occurred as she began to explore angry and competitive feelings toward her sister, and this included the realization that she and peers of hers had "swearing feelings" (Figures 11.5, 11.6). Use of displacement of affects in play became less necessary as the patient began to own her own affect states. They became more "real" to her and directed at people within her family and life.

In *Phase IV,* intrapsychic conflicts continued to be explored and the impact such conflicts had on her self-esteem. The work focused in the second year on her sense of

Figure 11.5

herself as a person, daughter, and girl and her self-loathing and self-esteem. In addition to modulation of the severity of the superego as occurs in Phase III, her current identifications as a bad or undesirable girl were challenged and new

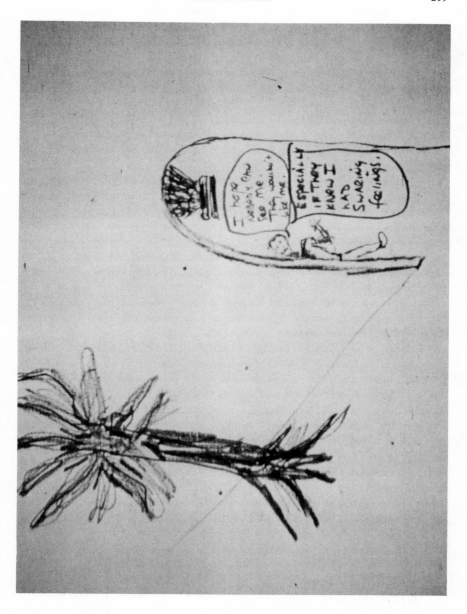

Figure 11.6

identifications as a good, interesting girl began to emerge. The child's transference to the therapist as a man and as another potentially abandoning father could now be explored. Her feelings of being a bad, hungry, biting girl were periodically focused on her therapist and interpreted. Also, the therapist functioned as a "real object," and a new "good object" to help her master her conflicts and begin to feel better about herself (Cohen, 1980; Ritvo, 1978). At this time, the family meetings focused on helping the mother recall her own childhood and her unresolved conflicts with her mother. Additionally, the mother arranged for some athletic experiences for her daughter with other girls and female coaches so as to facilitate her feminine identifications.

It was at this stage that this child's distorted body image, as presaged within her drawings, became directly discussable. As further evidence that mechanisms of displacement, externalization, and isolation of affects were less necessary, this girl began to discuss her own feelings of disgust toward her own body and talk of the desirability of being a boy.

In *Phase V,* the patient felt more connected to others. Even with the acknowledgment of low self-esteem came the feeling of being a valued person within the treatment and by her mother. She was no longer a bad person who was abandoned because of her rage and vengeful feelings and sentenced to die. She had friends, a supportive mother, a psychiatrist who valued her even if her father abandoned her and her family.

The final phase, *Phase VI,* involved termination. The termination occurred after two years of individual psychotherapy and monthly family therapy meetings conducted by the same therapist. The termination included her reexperiencing her rage at abandonment now directed toward her therapist. Her characterological defenses having to do with avoidance of painful affects and avoidance of disappointing objects could now be handled face-to-face within the therapy and allowed her to leave with the sense of ongoing connection even at a distance. The picture (Figure 11.7) of a switchboard with geographic locations symbolized this sense of connection. The picture demonstrates the intactness of good latency-aged defenses. She valued her intellectual accomplishments and used symbolic and creative thought. She felt better about herself and her self-esteem was more stable. She had many friends, felt comfortable with her mother and sister, and exhibited no developmental delays.

Unfortunately the therapy had to be ended for external reasons at the end of two years. The child's conflicts about her body and castration themes were left unresolved. While it is predictable that this child may again need and seek out psychotherapy during her adolescence, her depression and suicidality were absent at the time of her ending therapy. It was also felt that many of the psychodynamic conflicts associated with depression had also been successfully addressed.

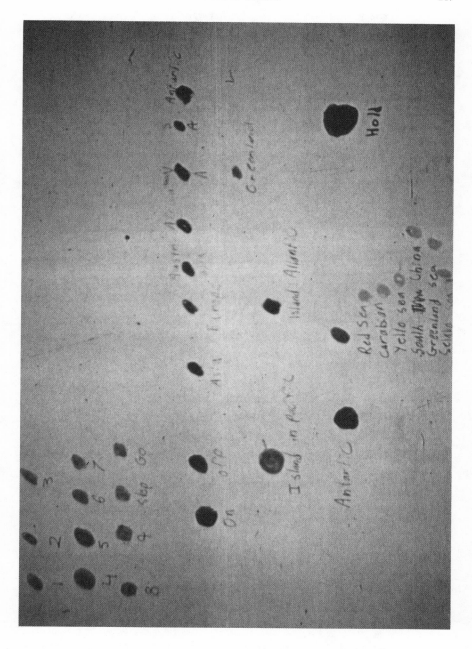

Figure 11.7

SUMMARY

The diagnosis and treatment of children is very challenging. Suicidal ideation can be heard by clinicians and families. As precise a diagnosis as possible is critical to the appropriate treatment. The dilemma confronting all clinicians is how to encounter these hopeless, helpless, isolated children in similarly traumatized and depressed families and convey a sense of hope and possibility and yet avoid inhibiting our inquiry and investigation at the phase of reaction formation (Phase II, above; Toolan, 1984, p. 336). This process is essential and life-saving; as stated in the work of Shafii et al. (1985), "The suicidal idea of yesterday becomes the suicidal threat or attempt of today and the completed suicide of tomorrow" (p. 1064).

REFERENCES

Abraham, K. (1911), Notes on the psycho-analytic investigation and treatment of manic-depressive insanity and allied conditions. *Selected Papers on Psychoanalysis*. London: Hogarth Press, 137–156.

American Psychiatric Association (1980), *Diagnostic and Statistical Manual of Mental Disorders*. Washington, DC: American Psychiatric Press.

Asch, S. (1980), Suicide and the hidden executioner. *Internat. Rev. Psychoanal.*, 7:51–60.

Beardslee, W., Bemporad, J., Keller, M., & Klerman, G. (1983), Children of parents with major affective disorder: A review. *Amer. J. Psychiat.*, 140:825–832.

Belfer, M.L. (1977): Psychiatric emergencies. In: *The Critically Ill Child: Diagnosis and Management*, ed. C.S. Smith. Philadelphia: W.B. Saunders, pp. 341–351.

——— (1979), Psychotropic medication in acute psychiatric disturbances in children. *J. Fam. Pract.*, 8:503–507.

Blos, P. (1983), The contribution of psychoanalysis to the psychotherapy of adolescents. *The Psychoanalytic Study of the Child*, 38:577–600. New Haven, CT: Yale University Press.

Bowlby, J. (1961), Childhood mourning and its implications for psychiatry. *Amer. J. Psychiat.*, 118:481–498.

Browning, N. (1981), The barren ground: A study of suicidal behavior in children. Unpublished manuscript.

Carlson, G., & Cantwell, D. (1980), Unmasking childhood depression in children and adolescents. *Amer. J. Psychiat.*, 137:445–449.

——— ——— (1982), Suicidal behavior and depression in children and adolescents. *J. Amer. Acad. Child Psychiat.*, 21/4:361–368.

Cohen, D. (1980), Constructive and reconstructive activities in the analysis of a depressed child. *The Psychoanalytic Study of the Child*, 35:237–266. New Haven, CT: Yale University Press.

Cohen-Sandler, R., Berman, A.L., & King, R.A. (1982), A follow-up study of hospitalized suicidal children. *J. Amer. Acad. Child Psychiat.*, 4:398–403.

Connell, H.M. (1972), Attempted suicide in school children. *Med. J. Austral.*, 1:686–690.

Cytryn, L., McKnew, D., & Bunney, W. (1980), Diagnosis of depression in children: A reassessment. *Amer. J. Psychiat.*, 137:22–25.

Dowling, S. (1977), Seven infants with esophageal atresia: A developmental study. *The Psychoanalytic Study of the Child*, 32:215–256. New Haven, CT: Yale University Press.

Elkins, R., & Rapoport, J. (1983), Psychopharmacology of adult and childhood depression: An overview. In: *Affective Disorders in Childhood and Adolescence: An Update*, eds. D. Cantwell & G. Carlson. Jamaica, NY: Spectrum, pp. 363–374.

Engel, G., & Reichsman, F. (1956), Spontaneous and experimentally induced depression in an infant with a gastric fistula. *J. Amer. Psychoanal.*, 4:428–452.

Famularo, R., Stone, K., & Popper, C. (1985), Preadolescent alcohol abuse and dependence. *Amer. J. Psychiat.*, 142:1187–1189.

Freud, A., & Sandler, J. (1985), *The Analysis of Defense: The Ego and the Mechanisms of Defense Revisited.* New York: International Universities Press.

Freud, S. (1917), Mourning and melancholia. *Standard Edition,* 14:237–258. London: Hogarth Press, 1957.

Gaensbauer, T., Harman, R., Cytryn, L, & McKnew, D. (1984), Social and affective development in infants with a manic-depressive parent. *Amer. J. Psychiat.*, 141:223–229.

Guggenheim, F.G. (1982), Recognition and treatment of suicide. Harvard Medical School Department of Continuing Education Course, Emergency Psychiatry, 1978. Cited in McKenry, P.C., Tishler, C.L., & Kelley, C. (1982), Adolescent suicide. *Clin. Pediat.*, 21:266–270.

Havens, L. (1967), Recognition of suicidal risks through the psychologic examination. *N.Eng. J. Med.*, 276:210–215.

Kashani, J., Ray, J., & Carlson, G. (1984), Depression and depressive-like states in preschool-age children in a child development unit. *Amer. J. Psychiat.*, 141:1397–1402.

Kaufman, C., Gruenbaum, H., Cohler, B., & Gamer, E. (1979), Superkids: Competent children of psychotic mothers. *Amer. J. Psychiat.*, 136:1398–1402.

Kovacs, M., Feinberg, T., Crouse-Novak, M., Paulauskas, S., & Finkelstien, R. (1984a), Depressive disorders in childhood, I. *Arch. Gen. Psychiat.*, 41:229–237.

——— ——— ——— Pollack, M., & Finkelstein, R. (1984b), Depressive disorders in childhood, II. *Arch. Gen. Psychiat.*, 41:643–649.

Mack, J.E., & Hickler, H. (1981), *Vivienne: The Life and Suicide of an Adolescent Girl.* Boston: Little, Brown.

Malmquist, C. (1983), The functioning of self-esteem in childhood depression. In: *The Development and Sustaining of Self-Esteem in Childhood,* eds. J.E. Mack & S.L. Ablon. New York: International Universities Press.

Maltsberger, J.T., & Buie, D. (1974), Countertransference hate in the treatment of suicidal patients. *Arch. Gen. Psychiat.*, 30:625–633.

——— (1980), The devices of suicide: Revenge, riddance, and rebirth. *Internat. Rev. Psychoanal.*, 7:61–72.

Mattson, A., Hawkins, J.W., & Seese, L.R. (1969), Suicidal behavior as a child psychiatric emergency. *Arch. Gen. Psychiat.*, 20:100–109.

McArney, E.R. (1975), Suicidal behavior of children and youth. *Pediat. Clin. N. Amer.*, 22:595–604.

Otto, V. (1972), Suicidal acts by children and adolescents. *Acta Psychiatr. Scand. Suppl.*, 233:5–117.

Petti, T. (1983), Imipramine in the treatment of depressed children. In: *Affective Disorders in Childhood and Adolescence: An Update,* eds. D. Cantwell & G. Carlson. Jamaica, NY: Spectrum, pp. 375–416.

Pfeffer, C.R., Conte, H.R., Plutchik, R., & Jerrett, I. (1979), Suicidal behavior in latency age children: An emprical study. *J. Amer. Acad. Child Psychiat.*, 18:679–692.

——— ——— ——— ——— (1980), Suicidal behavior in latency age children: An empirical study: An outpatient population. *J. Amer. Acad. Child Psychiat.*, 19:703–710.

——— (1981), Suicidal behavior of children: A review with implications for research and practice. *Amer. J. Psychiat.*, 138/2:154–159.

——— (1984), Clinical assessment of suicidal behavior in children. In: *Suicide in the Young,* eds. H. Sudack, A. Ford, & N. Rushforth. Littleton, MA: John Wright PSG, Inc., pp. 171–182.

Poznanski, E. (1985), Depression in children and adolescents: An overview. *Psych. Annals,* 15:365–367.

——— Mokros, H., Grossman, J., & Freeman, L. (1985), Diagnostic criteria in childhood depression. *Amer. J. Psychiat.*, 142:1168–1173.

Puig-Antich, J., Chambers, W., & Tabrizi, M.A. (1983), The clinical assessment of current depressive episodes in children and adolescents: Interviews with parents and children. In: *Affective Disorders in*

Childhood and Adolescence—An Update, eds. D. Cantwell & G. Carlson. Jamaica, NY: Spectrum, pp. 157–179.

Ritvo, S. (1978), The psychoanalytic process in childhood. *The Psychoanalytic Study of the Child,* 33:295–305. New Haven, CT: Yale University Press.

Robbins, D., & Alessi, N. (1985), Depressive symptoms and suicidal behavior in adolescents. *Amer. J. Psychiat.* 142:588–592.

Rochlin, G. (1965), The loss complex. In: *Griefs and Discontents.* Boston: Little, Brown, pp. 35–62.

Sabbath, J.C. (1969), The suicidal adolescent—The expendable child. *J. Amer. Acad. Child Psychiat.,* 8:272–289.

Shaffer, D. (1974), Suicide in childhood and early adolescents. *J. Child Psychol. Psychiat.,* 15:275–291.

Shafii, M., Carrigan, S., Whittinghill, J., & Derrick, A. (1985), Psychological autopsy of completed suicide in children and adolescents. *Amer. J. Psychiat.,* 142:1061–1064.

Spitz, R. (1965), Hospitalism. *The Psychoanalytic Study of the Child,* 1:53–74. New York: International Universities Press.

Toolan, J. (1984), Psychotherapeutic treatment of suicidal children and adolescents. In: *Suicide in the Young,* eds. H. Sudak, A. Ford, & N. Rushforth. John Wright, PSG Inc., pp. 325–343.

Weissman, M. (1974), Epidemiology of suicide attempts, 1960–1971. *Arch. Gen. Psychiat.,* 30:737–746.

12

Adolescent Suicide:
An Architectural Model

John E. Mack, M.D.

INTRODUCTION

For every human being the question of whether to live or die presents a profound philosophical choice to be confronted many times in the course of one's life. Camus wrote: "There is but one truly philosophical problem, and that is suicide" (Camus, 1955, p. 3). The decision to commit suicide is a statement not only that one's own life is not worth living but may express as well a view that life has no value. In working with individuals who are confronting the choice of whether to live or die, as clinicians we are most interested in the balance of forces that influence, or may influence, the decision in the direction of life. As physicians we are committed to protecting and enhancing life.

A completed suicide, although generally occurring in the context of psychopathology, can at the same time be a highly elaborate and creative, even artistic, phenomenon. In *The Myth of Sisyphus* Camus wrote, "An act like this is prepared within the silence of the heart, as is a great work of art" (1955, p. 4). Suicide traverses many human realms. The theme is important in sociology, literature, art, and, of course, in religion. In this chapter, I will consider suicide as a major clinical challenge. Although I plan to discuss suicide at the individual level, the aggregate nature of the problem will also be borne in mind. There are debates in the scientific literature about the incidence of adolescent suicide, whether its apparent marked statistical increase in recent decades is actual, or an artifact of naming and reporting (Eisenberg, 1980; Offer, Ostrov, and Howard, 1981; Bassuk,

A version of the material in this chapter was first presented at the Research Workshop on Preventive Aspects of Suicide and Affective Disorders Among Adolescents and Young Adults, Boston, December 3–4, 1982. It has also appeared in *Suicide and Depression Among Adolescents and Young Adults*, ed. G.L. Klerman, Washington, DC: American Psychiatric Press, 1986, pp. 55–76.

Schoonover, and Gill, 1982). There does, however, appear to have been an actual two- to threefold increase in the incidence of completed suicides in the 15 to 19 age group in the past quarter of a century (National Center for Health Statistics, 1978). It is possible, as Eisenberg (1980) suggests, that when one considers the underreporting of suicide, the incidence may be even higher.

I wish to suggest a particular approach to adolescent suicide, a way of looking at the problem. Although this approach was developed in relation to teenagers, and grew out of the intensive study of a single adolescent, Vivienne, it is my hope that it may have applicability for our understanding of the problem of suicide in adults as well (Mack and Hickler, 1981).

I will describe an architectural model, which might also be looked on as a contextual, structural, or systems approach. In our effort to provide a complete understanding of adolescent suicide from a clinical point of view it is not sufficient to consider only the individual teenager's private conflicts, however essential a part these may play in the outcome. The elements or parts which comprise the model can be grouped under the following headings:

1. The macrocosm; the sociopolitical context
2. Biological vulnerability; the genetic predisposition to suicide
3. Earliest developmental influences and experiences
4. Personality structure or organization, especially the regulation of self-esteem
5. The individual's object relationships and the state of those relationships as the suicidal preoccupation developed
6. Clinical depression and other psychopathology
7. The ontogeny or developmental relationship to death
8. The contemporary clinical situation or circumstances of the individual's life at the time of assessment.

Since beginning my study with Mrs. Hickler of Vivienne's life and suicide, I have applied this model to a number of other adolescent cases.

Vivienne Loomis lived in Melrose, Massachusetts. She was 14 years and 4 months old when she hanged herself in December 1973 in her mother's silversmithing shop with rope that she obtained from her mother. She was a bright, sensitive, artistic girl who was an excellent writer. In her voluminous journal entries, letters, compositions, and poetry she gave us a rare look into the inner world of an adolescent struggling with questions of life and death. Adolescents tend not to be very willing to share their deepest thoughts, feelings, and conflicts with other people, especially adults. For this reason diaries, journals, letters, and other writings, such as poems and school compositions, represent a particularly rich source for understanding the inner life of teenagers.

THE MACROCOSM

The macrocosm is the larger world, or the society as a whole, as it affects the individual adolescent. What, for example, is the impact of events, values, and sociopolitical trends and phenomena on a particular child or adolescent? What effect do societal patterns of drug taking, alcoholism, and violence in our society, including the constant threat of death in a nuclear war, have on adolescents, especially those who are vulnerable to suicide for other reasons? What do these cultural phenomena mean to teenagers and how do they affect the choices of life and death? I was recently consulted by the parents of an 11-year old girl who was afraid of nuclear war. They said that their daughter had wanted to know whether she would have time to commit suicide, if she knew that nuclear bombs were on the way, before they actually exploded.

There are examples in which several suicides occur in the same school, like small epidemics (*New York Times*, 1979; *Time*, 1980). What is the role of the school system in promoting or preventing suicide? Freud, as you may recall, once remarked that a school ought to do something more "than not driving its pupils to suicide" (Friedman, 1967, p. 61). There have been epidemics of student suicide in Japan and Germany that seem related to the rigidities of their competitive school systems (*Newsweek*, 1976, 1978). There are also trends about suicide within the adolescent culture. My 18-year-old son, during a talk we had several months ago about the fact that there seemed to be more suicides among teenagers nowadays, remarked: "It's an option that's opened up." Sociopolitical and economic influences may increase the number that actually do commit suicide out of the pool of those who, for other reasons, may be suicide prone.

Changing sexual mores, and the breakdown of structure and guidance in relation to sexual choice and behavior, may place particular stresses on those teenagers who are less able to handle the emotional challenges or threat of increased freedom in this area. Vivienne, who was one such child, made this clear in several letters she wrote to an important schoolteacher, about whom more will be said shortly. In one such letter five months before her death she wrote:

> I myself have managed to stay unattached, thanks to my unfailing lack of charm. Only one guy tried to rape me five days ago, and I haven't seen him since. Mommy and Daddy would have a fit if they knew, but I didn't find it as traumatic as everybody seems to make it. The fact is that this particular fellow had already had a few six packs too many. It had nothing to do with me. Well, so much for the "Dirt of the day" [Mack and Hickler, 1981, p. 82].

A month later she wrote:

> I don't think that I can follow the nation's trend; now the average girl puts down the last good book in the house and says, Shit. Nothing else to do. I guess I'll go over to

the stone wall on the corner and get picked up. I don't know. Three times, three people in the last 2½ weeks, have tried to fuck me. Twice I was good and stiff. But each time, I just thought to myself—God! Is this all there is? Not only is there no true love, no giving—but this is all as routine as taking your vitamins in the morning. I don't see how you get Saturday night fun out of it. So I'll probably keep my ideals for the time being. Of course, I don't have, and never had had, any hang-ups about marriage. I just require a deep and caring love [Mack and Hickler, 1981, p. 13]..

This passage tells a lot, of course, about Vivienne as an individual, of her personal ideals and conflicts. But it also says something about what is going on in the larger society that a barely 14-year-old girl, in a middle-class family, could be such an acceptable target, an easy prey for any boy or young man who chooses to approach her. She does not feel that she can turn to her parents, nor do her parents act as if they have a sanction from the society for setting limits.

Vivienne, it is true, had more than average sensitivity to events in the outside world. Her parents described how upset she would become when she would see something on television, such as the Arab-Israeli War of 1973, or the immoral behavior of political leaders. She would sometimes express her thoughts and feelings in poems. One of them was called "Joys of Living."

> The Stock Exchange,
> Neon Signs,
> Traffic jams,
> Indo China,
> Another exam and the Watergate.
> New train tables,
> inflation, highway repairs,
> Nixon,
> His dog "Checkers,"
> Your new Bugged home . . .
> It's all too late!
> [Mack and Hickler, 1981, p. 74]

Vivienne was also troubled about the conditions in prisons. "Wasn't that horrible about the prisons?" she asked in her journal. "A man doesn't have any rights or respect or anything! I knew it was *really* bad in prisons, but I didn't know it was that bad. I guess the general public really doesn't know because they are told stories that they like to hear about, and *not* the truth. What should I do!" (Mack and Hickler, 1981, p. 51).

I would ask if teenagers now are confronted more overwhelmingly with these disturbing realities and what part this confrontation plays in suicide and other adolescent disturbances. Did Emily Dickinson at 14 write poems about political events and social problems in the America of the 1840s?

For a particular child there is a specific family and societal context. Vivienne's family was Protestant in a strongly Roman Catholic neighborhood. They were liberals in a politically conservative town. They stood out. Her father, who was a minister in a Universalist church, was being criticized in the community and was losing his ministry. There was a poor "fit" between Vivienne's family and the local community. Her mother would dress Vivienne in clothes that somehow were not right—handmade smocks, for example—and she would be ridiculed by her elementary school classmates.

BIOLOGICAL VULNERABILITY

The Denmark studies by Frank Schulsinger and Seymour Kety and their coauthors demonstrated twelve suicides among 269 biological relatives of 57 adoptees who had committed suicide (Schulsinger, Kety, Rosenthal, and Wender, 1979) Among the group of 148 adopted relatives (nonbiological relations, including the parents who raised the children who had committed suicide) there were no suicides. Recent work on the biochemistry of suicide has shown that there are low cerebrospinal fluid levels of the serotonin metabolite 5-hydroxyindolacetic acid in patients who have tried to kill themselves (Brown, Ebert, Goyer, Jimerson, Klein, Bunney, and Goodwin, 1982). It will be interesting to see if this finding can be corroborated and will lead to other discoveries.

The question of constitutional sensitivity was brought into focus by the work of Paul Bergman and Sibylle Escalona published in 1949 (Bergman and Escalona, 1949). They demonstrated that there are children who show unusual sensitivities from the beginning of life. These children react differently to noise, colors, or changes in temperature or light. It is uncertain whether such observations can be correlated with later tendencies to be overwhelmed by everyday stresses or tied to vulnerability to suicide and depression. Applebaum and Holzman examined Rorschachs of individuals who had made suicide attempts, or who later killed themselves, and found that in the color-shading responses there was a tendency for the suicidal individuals to go beyond the given, to read their own ideas and fantasies into the material (Applebaum and Holzman, 1962). The authors concluded that these individuals would have been "better served if they were buffered by the refuge of greater generality, less involvement, and an increased ability to 'let it go at that'" (Applebaum and Holzman, 1962, p. 160).

EARLY DEVELOPMENTAL INFLUENCES AND EXPERIENCES

After her death Vivienne's mother wrote a kind of narrative for the family. It was clear that from the time of her birth Vivienne was special. Even the delivery was unusual. "I was determined," her mother wrote, "to use natural childbirth and I decided to be part of an experiment using music. All the time I was in labor I had on earphones. Vivienne's arrival was watched by as many hospital personnel as could crowd into the delivery room in their interest in the effects of music heard through earphones in lieu of anesthesia. Vivienne arrived, a chubby, purple baby whose tiny apricot tongue revealed the jaundice she had contracted when our incompatible blood types mixed" (Mack and Hickler, 1981, p. 7). Throughout her infancy the mother felt this incompatibility. Mrs. Loomis had two other active, more difficult, children—a son nearly 4 years and a daughter 2 years older than Vivienne. Vivienne was different. She was quiet. She could be left in the playroom. Vivienne tended to react to early separations by "tuning out" the family, showing another kind of early sensitivity.

At quite an early age Vivienne expressed responses to loss that were unusual. When she was in her fifth year both of her grandfathers died. She demonstrated a special empathy, an intense involvement and identification, especially with her mother's grief at the time of the death of Vivienne's maternal grandfather. Two months before her death Vivienne wrote in a composition for school about one of her grandfathers:

> My grandfather comes back to me now, with his intensely gentle eyes and a strangely distorted face. An unconquered mind; I remember he always used to tell me that my dear you must never forget in all your life that eyes are for seeing and *dreams* were for pursuing. He is with me now, and he paints me his pictures of flat-tailed doves that glide purposefully over black and scrawny ravens who fight over death. And he shows me carefully the valley where the two mountains of reason and emotion meet and twine their efforts together in winding streams that quietly defy your logic. But just as I relinquish my power to fight this strange current, and I feel the waters rush through my veins, my grandfather is leaving me . . . to remember [Mack and Hickler, 1981, p. 7].

Vivienne's sensitivity at four or five presaged the way she would react all her life to separations and loss.

PERSONALITY STRUCTURE AND ORGANIZATION

In discussing "personality organization" I have in mind especially the narcissistic dimension, the development of self and self-esteem. Vivienne had a strong sense of identity, which needs to be distinguished from the uncertain or low level of her self-regard. She could write in the seventh grade:

I am the youngest in my family.
I am one out of twenty in the seventh grade.
I am the minister's daughter.
I am a pretender of moods.
I am a New Englander.
I am a person who plays the flute.
I am very polite.
I am a girl.
I am me—because everyone is "me" inside
Everything else.
[Mack and Hickler, 1981, p. 7]

This strong sense of self, of identity, did not protect her from suffering a great deal as a result of disturbances of self-esteem. Interestingly, Vivienne was "on to" the narcissistic sector of development in general, especially the aspect of self-love, even though conflicts in the domain of self-regard played such an important role in her depression and suicide. She wrote the following story, which she called *On Vanity*, when she was in the eighth grade:

Once upon a time there lived a ravishing princess named Prunelda. Prunelda was an extremely vain creature and very hard to please. She dabbled in the arts a bit, but only to the extent of painting self-portraits. She spent days on end in her rooms, which consisted almost solely of mirrors, and this caused her father, King Kong, to indulge in quite a bit of worrying. Prunelda had to get married off soon, or he'd never be rid of her.

Well, not far off in a near-by kingdom lived a dazzling prince named Prince Hector. He, too, was vain and hard to please. One of the most vain things about him was the fact that he wore mirror glasses—the wrong way 'round. Prince Hector did this because he liked to gaze into his eyes and marvel at their beauty. Hector had heard stories of Prunelda and her room of mirrors, and so he decided that he would be allowed to frequent her rooms as often as he wished, and that meant that he would be able to gaze at himself as frequently as he wished by merely looking into her mirrors.

At 3:50 Tuesday afternoon, Prunelda and Hector could be found sitting back to back gazing into the mirrors, entranced in themselves. Soon the compliments came gushing out for themselves: "Splendid! . . . Magnificent! . . . Ah!!" Each thought that the other's compliments were for himself and so they took a great liking to each other (not that they ever actually saw each other!).

King Kong knew a sure thing when he saw one, and so he had them married right away. Hector and Prunelda spent many fun-filled years staring into mirrors and what turned out to be flattering each other. So *everyone* lived happily ever after.

The moral to this story is that if you're extremely vain, what you don't know can only help you [Mack and Hickler, 1981, pp. 58–59].

Vivienne begins in her twelfth year to reflect great concern with the problem of self-worth. On April 8, 1971 when she was 11 years and 8 months old she wrote in her journal:

> Do you understand me? Do you love me? Do you know the things I know? Do you feel the way I feel? . . . I bet nobody knows the things I know or feels the things I feel. Does anyone admire things the way I do? I don't think so, but maybe, no, it couldn't be. Does anyone experience things the way I do? Does anybody take remarks or words the way I do?
>
> Did anybody ever wonder how close they were to their ideal? I do. Does anybody ever wonder how they looked in the eyes of friends? Do people admire me? Does anybody admire me? I hope so. I care what people say to me and what people think about me. I want to set an example that is good. I wish everybody had a healthy grin and I hope I have one anyway. I don't mean to sound stupid or anything, but that's how I really and truly feel. Anyway no one will ever read this anyway so it's OK. [Mack and Hickler, 1981, p. 15].

Early in adolescence the ego-ideal, which is a crucial agency in the regulation of self-esteem, begins to take form, as can be seen in the above example. Anais Nin wrote in the first volume of her diary when she was in her late twenties: "This image [the ideal] is always a great strain to live up to. Some consider the loss of it a cause for suicide" (Nin, 1966, p. 128).

The ego-ideal is a structure in the personality that connects the self with other human beings, as well as providing a link between self and society. It contains the internalized expectations of the individual. It is distinguished from the superego (in some psychoanalytical writings it is part of the "superego system") in that it is more deeply tied to narcissism and early hurts, representing the projecting forward into the future of the possibility of a kind of "second chance." For we may repair or redeem early hurts and disappointments if we can create a world for ourselves which approximates a model of the visions contained in the ego-ideal. Vivienne's ego-ideal was so exalted and rigid as to be incompatible with daily reality, close to what Edith Jacobson has called "the wishful ego-ideal" (Jacobson, 1964). Before she was twelve, Vivienne already gave evidence of this rigidity. In June 1971, she wrote in her journal:

> I don't love life, I just love the little bit of life that touches my ideal one. It's my ideal life I love and try to live and introduce into the lives of others. All I can do is hold my stand and not give up until I've accomplished what I want to and not give up or out with exhaustion or with depression and disappointment. I just won't. I'll just stick with it. I will. No matter how hopeless it seems right now. I'll be persistent. [Mack and Hickler, 1981, pp. 27–28].

The ability to "bounce back" from disappointment or injury is an important aspect of personality strength. Vivienne identified this quality and wrote about it.

She would say that she *would* bounce back. At times she did. But she did not work through the meaning of major losses and disappointments, whose impact seemed to accumlate.

Another dimension of personality strength which is difficult to categorize but closely connected to the vulnerability to suicide, might be called "the management of affect and disappointment," the ability to bear pain (Zetzel, 1965, pp. 82–114). Although this capacity seems quite specific to the predisposition to suicide, we understand relatively little about what determines the ability to tolerate depressive or other painful affects. This was clearly a major problem for Vivienne.[1] Finally, when we speak of personality structure in relation to suicide we need to include a broader matrix than individual personality. We have also to consider the availability of family and community supports, as these contribute an important element in the ongoing capacities of the self, what the author has called elsewhere "self-governance" or "the governance of the self" (Mack, 1978, pp. 97–109; 1981).

OBJECT RELATIONS

In considering the individual's object relationships I am including those ties that complete the sense of self [self objects (Kohut, 1971, 1977)], as well as more autonomous relationships with others. We are concerned here, for example, with relationships with parents, the degree to which separation from them has occurred, the quality of the involvement, identifications with them, ties to other adults, competition and intimacy with siblings, relationships with and availability of friends. Vivienne was closely tied to her parents. But the relationship with her mother was so conflicted that she could not confide in her and felt burdened by her demands. Her father felt that he could not understand this daughter, and with her sister, to whom she was close, Vivienne developed a kind of pact in which Laurel would look away from Vivienne's flirtation with suicide if Vivienne would not betray to the parents the things Laurel was doing, especially sexual activities, of which they would not approve. Vivienne had a few intimate friends but had difficulty making friends with a broad representation of her classmates at school or with neighborhood peers.

Teachers play a critical role at this time of life and can protect a child from suicide or contribute to its likelihood. When Vivienne was 11 and in the sixth grade,

---

[1]Psychoanalytic theorists and clinicians have developed a sophisticated understanding of the mechanisms of internalization and externalization of object representations which seem to characterize the personality organization of suicidal adults (Meissner, 1977; Asch, 1980; Maltsberger and Buie, 1980; Maltsberger, 1983). In particular, the identification with a "victim object"; that is, the introjection of the victim aspect of a parent or other figure to whom the patient is closely attached, seems to be a frequent finding in suicide-prone individuals (Orgell, 1974; Meissner, 1983).

having had several very difficult years in public schools, she was transferred to the Cambridge Friends School, a private school where she met a teacher, John May, who was very sensitive to her situation. He was a conscientious objector to the Vietnam War. He saw correctly that Vivienne suffered from injured self-regard. He brought to her a great deal of caring, warmth, and compliments. For example, he would tell her over and over that she should think better of herself. What he did not realize was the degree to which he was functioning, in Kohut's sense, as a kind of self object for Vivienne, in that he completed something that was missing in her own sense of self-worth. For this reason, when he finally had to leave it was devastating for Vivienne. This loss played a major role in the tailspin that culminated in her suicide. Therapists also need to be sensitive to this aspect of their relationship with teenagers. They too may function, without being aware of it, as a self completing kind of object. Thus, slights, separations, or losses in relation to the therapist can become highly amplified in meaning for teenagers, particularly for those who have disturbances in the domain of self-esteem. In one of her diary entries when she was 12 years and 3 months Vivienne shows how central Mr. May was for her self-esteem, the devastating impact of his announced departure, and the importance of this loss in precipitating her preoccupation with death and suicide:

> I wish Mr. May wouldn't go next year. And I wish Dad and Mummy wouldn't keep reminding me that he is.
> A weaker, more immediate wish is that Mr. May would invite us to dinner like he said he would.
> An impossible wish, though strongest, is that he would invite *me* (alone). Because I love him.
> He is going to leave me.
> Forever????
> He's going to leave me behind as he goes on his merry way. But if he leaves me what way will I have to go? Why won't he stay? When will I die? It seems like I ought to die now while the going's good. While life has still got some joy. That joy will be gone in a year. Maybe I will be too—Oh, ah, silver tears appearing now. I'm crying, ain't I? [Mack and Hickler, 1981, p. 34].

CLINICAL DEPRESSION AND OTHER PSYCHOPATHOLOGY

Eli Robins found in his study of the last months in the lives of 134 suicides that at least 47 percent of these individuals could be diagnosed as having had a major affective illness (Robins, 1981). Possibly more had serious depressions but were difficult to diagnose. Another major diagnostic category was alcoholism. In many alcoholics, depressive feelings of suicidal intensity may surge up during intoxicated states and upset the precarious balance between life and death.

Vivienne sensed that she suffered from depression. In a poem which she called *Patterns of My Lifetime* she showed her awareness of the connection between her depression and egoism:

Crossing over, then down
Falling over, then under:
Down through egotistical
Patterns made in my lifetime.

Emotional depression
Existing, at first unobserved:
An old forgotten sword . . .
Suddenly glistening and sharp!

Eternal hope alternating
From blind, whimsical dependence
To strong, resounding salvation:
A bright candle in the night.

Sentiment weaving its way
Through hope in depression,
Depression in hope:
An amazing grace in itself.

Crossing over, then down.
Falling over, then under:
Down through egotistical
Patterns made in my lifetime.
[Mack and Hickler, 1981, pp. 41–42]

In her writings Vivienne demonstrated repeatedly the close connection between the loss of important relationships, especially with John May, and her depression. After he left for California she wrote in her journal:

April 11, 1973

I am worthless, I am of no use to anyone, and no one is of any use to me. What good to kill myself? How can you kill nothing? A person who has committed suicide has had at least something to end. He must know joy to know misery. I have known nothing. Why live? Why die? One is an equal choice to the other. What do I do? I wonder if love would change anything. I don't know anymore. To know that the future looks worse doesn't help me any. I need people and there aren't any who care. It takes tolerance not to give in to death [Mack and Hickler, 1981, p. 63].

THE DEVELOPMENTAL ORIENTATION TOWARD DEATH

Lifton (1979), Becker (1973), Rochlin (1965) and others (Yalom, 1980) have called to our attention that the relationship with death has its own developmental sequences, or ontogeny, and its own set of meanings for particular individuals. Each person carries inside his or her own personal relationship to death. A variety of personifications of death exist in Western literature.

It is possible that suicide-prone individuals may have had a particularly intimate relationship with death during their lives. In assessing suicide proneness or risk it is important to trace this relationship, especially to discover if it has undergone a recent change in the direction of greater familiarity, intimacy, and acceptability. A tendency to romanticize death may be a dangerous sign of suicidal risk for a particular adolescent. Some shift in the relationship to death is probably a necessary precondition to suicide, at least of the premeditated type, which is what I am primarily considering here.

Vivienne showed a strong interest in and relationship with death throughout her life. Vivienne's writings, especially the essay she wrote about her grandfather, reveal rich death imagery and her close relationship to death. In an essay about Elie Wiesel's book, *The Accident,* she commented on how she regarded death:

> I have come to consider death an emotional, deep and poetical fact of life . . . I look forward to dying, but I will live my life to the fullest first. Death will befall me; I will not befall death [Mack and Hickler, 1981, pp. 52–53].

In a rewritten version of this essay she wrote:

> [R]eading the book made me realize that now, if someone should live for death or in it willingly, I would understand them perfectly . . . I have often thought of death as a retreat, myself, but somehow I always have had the guts to find the truth in life, along with the bitter . . . I believe that the difference between life and death (by will) is having the strength to stand up (again?) [Mack and Hickler, 1981, pp. 53–54].

As her depression deepened death itself became for Vivienne a kind of self object with which she developed a personal relationship. She would personify death in various images. Following her first serious suicide attempt, five months before she died, Vivienne wrote in her journal:

> Death comes as an increasingly darkening face and unstrained thin breathing, which I am sure would soon die away altogether. Your head pounds painfully and in the mirror I had the privilege to see for myself what my dead face will look like immediately after the killing. Somehow this effect is much less upsetting than the first. Perhaps this is a sign that my prayers are being considered [Mack and Hickler, 1981, p. 72].

This idea of suicide as a kind of self-murder recurs in the suicidal ideation of other adolescents. The following passage was written by a 16-year-old girl who made several suicide attempts which brought her near to death. She kept a journal in the form of letters to her devoted therapist:

> I am struggling with the thoughts of seeing you again. You see one day I'm afraid that you'll turn me away—I think it will be better to leave good than bad. But I know if I leave now I would surely do murder on myself . . . I swear I feel so trapped and I don't know what to do. When I got home today the least little thing put me in tears [This example provided through her therapist, Dr. Elinor Weeks].

With the sensitive and heroic work of her therapist this girl was alive and doing well two years later.

By the end of her life Vivienne had come to be on intimate terms with suicide. She had transformed death from being a scary, dangerous threat into an image of something beautiful, with which she was on a friendly basis. Through increasingly dangerous suicidal experiments she overcame the fear of death and the natural barriers that most of us have to killing ourselves. The following passages are from a letter she wrote to John May 10 days before her death, which was received too late to save her:

> Even though I have gone over and over suicide in the last three months or so and developed what I would consider a logical and socially acceptable attitude on the matter, it all seemed to leave me in a second. I happened to be standing by my mirror. I looked at myself with a sort of wince, and then, almost mechanically, my hands stretched round my throat and centered in for what seemed a long while. And then the ringing in my ears stopped and everything became soft and hazy and I could just make out my head in the mirror, like a separate, bloated object. I started swaying (with no rhythm to it) and I fell into my bedpost and boxes on the floor etc. Unconsciously, I put out my hand to steady myself, and in so doing, started up my circulation. This in turn started me jolting uncontrollably, while still swaying I caught hold of the mirror and my jolts sent the mirror crashing against the wall. KRSHSH KRSHSH! again and again. As soon as I could I stopped it because it was so loud. Then I went through my sister's drawers til I found a long silk scarf. I tucked it up my sleeve so you couldn't tell that it was there and left a note by my bed that said something like "I didn't want you to think that it was because of you when it was only me all the time. . . ." Then I walked three blocks to a public park . . . I took out the scarf and wrapped it tightly around my neck and pulled as hard as I could—I was standing in the shade in case car headlights should pick me up from the road. The first couple of times were like with the mirror (everything soft and hazy—the traffic would slowly fade away to nothing) and I would eventually fall. It was weird because I could see the glass on the ground, but I couldn't feel it at all. And then I would try to get up, but I would be jerking too

spasmodically and it would take me several minutes—while at the time I was afraid somebody would come by.

Finally I got it so I was cutting off the air completely and not just the blood. But then my lungs would just about burst and I would let go. After a while I knew the whole thing was useless and rather despairingly resigned myself to all the many tomorrows looming up ahead of me. I said "goodnight" to the trees and ground around me and walked back home. My father asked me, "How was your walk—feel any better?" "Sure." "Yuh . . . Sometimes a little fresh air helps. . . ." I could have screamed if I'd had the energy [Mack and Hickler, 1981, pp. 115–116].

THE CONTEMPORARY CLINICAL SITUATION
PRECIPITATING FACTORS

In the contemporary clinical situation or context the author would include recent disturbing events, such as family moves, disappointments or hurts in relationships, and school failures. Vivienne's family was in the process of moving when she died. Furniture had been taken out and the old house looked empty and barren. Jacobs (1971) writes that some form of school failure or disappointment precedes a suicide in a high percentage of cases, especially in school systems that are harsh and provide a minimum of support.

The current clinical situation would also include specific biological influences, such as alcohol or drug intake. One 12-year-old boy killed himself after rejection by a girl. He had also been taking unknown amounts of mind-altering drugs under the influence of a group of older children. Viral illnesses can have a strong depression-inducing effect, though the mechanism of this is not well understood.

The balance or status of existing relationships affects the likelihood of suicide. Vivienne wrote often about how she felt under great emotional pressure from her parents, especially her mother, who turned to Vivienne with *her* problems. Several months before her death she wrote in a letter:

Mommy came to me for help. And I really have helped her whenever I could. But it puts a certain pressure on me; I'm not even fourteen yet, and Mommy's forty-eight. All the pressure and tension mounted up and I snapped. I decided that I couldn't be as perfect as I wanted and I had to have some outlet. I've been smoking grass since around January. I've gotten stoned often enough, but I never really enjoyed it. Usually I just get high enough to relax [Mack and Hickler, 1981, p. 83].

The availability of supports is of crucial importance, as, conversely, are minor hurts, rejections, and slights that occur in the days prior to the suicidal event. Small things can make a difference. Criticisms, or words taken as criticisms in passing encounters, can have a devastating effect out of proportion to their actual importance. Psychotherapy can, of course, be helpful, but ineffectual treatment can be undermining, especially if the teenager and the family are led to believe that something useful is being done when it is not. Vivienne was receiving counseling, but it was a group approach that was not working. She came to feel herself to be friendless. Three weeks before her suicide she wrote to Mr. May:

> We are having counseling for the family. I know that I am probably the most destructive factor, but it's a little late for me to say that. Once you said you were glad I was born. Now I have my doubts about the whole thing. If I didn't have to worry about Mommy and Daddy, I wouldn't bother finishing this letter before I hung myself. But I have to stick with them. Sort of like one burden holding up another, which isn't too stable a thing to begin with. For one thing, I haven't got a single friend nearby. As a matter of fact, I have only one friend to speak of at all, and she lives in Belmont. With the gas shortage I see her solely at school [Mack and Hickler, 1981, p. 111].

IMPLICATIONS FOR EVALUATION AND TREATMENT

The architectural model described here has implications for the evaluation and treatment of a suicidal adolescent. It would lead us to place particular stress on the current life situation. Recent events, such as a move or a disappointment at school, may affect the balance of the teenager's emotional economy. We look especially for warning signals or clues—changes in the child's behavior, such as withdrawal from familiar interests, somatic complaints, changes in habits, expressions of suicidal ideation, and the other indicators that have been so often described in relation to adolescent suicide.

The psychodynamics of depression and suicide need to be evaluated, especially conflicts relating to self-esteem, which are demonstrated when the teenager focuses on injuries to self-regard and expresses a feeling of low self-worth. We are learning to recognize a pesonality organization that may contribute to low self-regard. We look for overly hard superego elements, unrealistically exalted idealization, or ego-ideal expectations, and evidence of an unusual degree of sensitivity to hurt and disappointment. The assessment of available supports has to be made carefully. The most crucial support comes from people who are not only available but sensitive to the teenager's distress. These can include parents, family members, friends, neighbors, and, frequently, teachers. Family dynamics that would disturb the teenager's psychic balance need to be assessed, such as, in Vivienne's case, the burdening of the child with problems that the parents are facing. It is important to assess whether parents are living out psychological needs of their own in relation to the teenager and failing, thereby, to see the child's distress.

The relationship of the family with its community, the "fit" or alienation that is experienced, can play a role in the balance of psychological forces that may lead to suicide. Finally, the degree to which the case is known to the evaluator, or to the clinic or agency undertaking the evaluation, needs to be considered. If a patient is unknown then greater caution and care needs to be taken to see that appropriate intervention takes place. If the case is known to the evaluator, or to another physician or mental health professional, assessment needs to be made of the degree to which a holding relationship exists and the teenager can be relied on to report changes in his or her emotional state.

The choice of treatment grows out of the evaluation described above. It is important in prescribing treatment for a suicidal adolescent to pay attention to the total life context. It is crucial to involve the family, as Edward Shapiro and his group at McLean Hospital have described (Shapiro and Freedman, 1982). The object of therapy should be first to protect the child from the immediate risk of suicide. Sometimes this requires hospitalization, especially if the patient is unknown to the clinic. Outpatient treatment should be focused not only on struggles of the individual teenager. It is important to work with parents and other crucial adults so that distressing or emotionally hurtful forces in the child's key relationships can be offset and family dynamics which undermine the adolescent's self-esteem can become understood. It is often important to involve the school, and for mental health professionals to work with teachers so that they can become more sensitive to the distress signals that their pupils communicate.

Whether or not to hospitalize an adolescent is a particularly difficult decision. In addition to its protective function, the hospital environment can provoke regressive responses in teenagers. In the hospital many weeks or months may be required to discover what is "going on" in a suicidal adolescent, which can be intensely disruptive to the child's ongoing life experience. Nevertheless, hospitalization may be necessary in order to protect the teenager's life and to initiate a comprehensive treatment plan. When there are resources available for skilled psychodynamically oriented psychotherapy, work should be aimed at achieving significant personality change—a modification of superego harshness and unrealistic ego-ideal expectations, the development of greater ego capacity to bear emotional pain and disappointment, and an effort to repair, through the therapeutic relationship the developmental injuries that underlie the vulnerability to suicide.

SUMMARY

An architectural model has been proposed comprising the elements to be considered in seeking to understand suicidal individuals. Although derived initially from the biographical study of an adolescent girl who killed herself, the model has been helpful in examining other adolescent and adult suicidal cases and may have wider utility in the understanding and treating of suicidal patients in the total context of their lives.

The elements of the model or system comprise the macrocosm or sociopolitical context; genetic–biological vulnerability; early developmental influences; personality organization and self-esteem regulation; object relationships past and current; evidences of clinical depression and other psychopathology, the ontogeny of the relationship to death; and the contemporary situation and circumstances at the time of clinical assessment.

Some of the implications of this model for evaluation and treatment have been discussed. It is hoped further that by linking the sociopolitical or broader contextual elements, which affect the incidence of suicide, with the biological and psychological forces that create the vulnerability to suicide, this model may prove to have applicability to the understanding of its epidemiology and to the challenge of its prevention.

REFERENCES

Applebaum, S.A. & Holzman, P.S. (1962), The color-shading response and suicide. *J. Project. Techniques,* 26:155–161.

Asch, S.S. (1980), Suicide and the hidden executioner. *Internat. Rev. Psychoanal.,* 7:51–60.

Bassuk, E.L., Schoonover, S.C.; & Gill, A.D. (1982) *Lifelines: Clinical Perspectives on Suicide.* New York: Plenum Press.

Becker, E. (1973), *The Denial of Death.* New York: Free Press.

Bergman, P., & Escalona, S.K. (1949), Unusual sensitivities in very young children. *The Psychoanalytic Study of the Child,* 3/4:333–352. New York: International Universities Press.

Brown, G.L., Ebert, M.H., Goyer, T.S, Jimerson, D.C., Klein, W.J., Bunney, W.E., Jr., & Goodwin, F.K. (1982), Aggression, suicide and serotonin: Relationships to cerebrospinal fluid amine metabolites. *Amer. J. Psychiat.,* 139:741–746.

Camus, A. (1955), *The Myth of Sisyphus: And Other Essays.* New York: Alfred A. Knopf.

Eisenberg, L. (1980), Adolescent suicide: On taking arms against a sea of troubles. *Pediat.,* 66:315–320.

Friedman, P., ed. (1967), *On Suicide: Discussions of the Vienna Psychoanalytic Society—1910.* New York: International Universities Press.

Hanley, R. (1979), Series of Mendham student deaths troubles classmates. *New York Times,* June 16.

Jacobs, J. (1971), *Adolescent Suicide.* New York: John Wiley.

Jacobson, E. (1964), *The Self and the Object World.* New York: International Universities Press.

Kohut, H. (1971), *The Analysis of the Self.* New York: International Universities Press.

——— (1977), *The Restoration of the Self.* New York: International Universities Press.

Lifton, R.J. (1979), *The Broken Connection: On Death and the Continuity of Life.* New York: Simon & Schuster.

Mack, J.E. (1978), Psychoanalysis and biography: A narrowing gap. *J. Phila. Assn. Psychoanal.,* 5/3 & 4:97–109.

——— (1981) Alcoholism, A.A. and the governance of the self. In: *Dynamic Approaches to the Understanding and Treatment of Alcoholism,* eds. M.H. Bean & N.E. Zinberg. New York: Free Press.

——— Hickler, H. (1981), *Vivienne: The Life and Suicide of an Adolescent Girl.* Boston: Little, Brown.

Maltsberger, J.T. (1983), Certain disturbances of reality sense in suicidal patients. Paper delivered at course on suicide, The Essence of Dynamic Clinical Work, Department of Psychiatry, The Cambridge Hospital and the Cambridge-Somerville Mental Health and Retardation Center, Harvard Medical School, January 28.

——— Buie, D.H. (1980), The devices of suicide: Revenge, riddance, and rebirth. *Internat. Rev. Psychoanal.,* 7:61–72.

Meissner, W.W. (1977), Psychoanalytic notes on suicide. *Internat. J. Psychoanal. Psychother.,* 6:415–447.

———— (1983), Suicide and the paranoid process. Paper delivered at course on Suicide: The Essence of Dynamic Clinical Work. Department of Psychiatry, The Cambridge Hospital and the Cambridge-Somerville Mental Health and Retardation Center, Harvard Medical School, January 28.

National Center for Health Statistics (1978), *Deaths and Death Rates for Suicide.* Washington, DC: Mortality Statistics Branch, Division of Vital Statistics.

Newsweek (1976), West Germany: Suicide course. March 8:28.

———— (1978), Teenage suicide. August 28:74, 76, 78.

Nin, A. (1966), *The Diary of Anais Nin,* Vol. 1 [covers the period 1931-1934]. New York: Harcourt, Brace & World.

Offer, D., Ostrov, E., & Howard, K.I. (1981), *The Adolescent: A Psychological Self-Portrait.* New York: Basic Books.

Orgell, S. (1974), Fusion with the victim and suicide. *Internat. J. Psycho-Anal.,* 55:531–538.

Robins, E. (1981), *The Final Months.* New York: Oxford University Press.

Rochlin, G. (1965), *Griefs and Discontents: The Forces of Change.* Boston: Little, Brown.

Schulsinger, F., Kety, S.S., Rosenthal, D., & Wender, P.H. (1979), A family study of suicide. In: *Origin, Prevention and Treatment of Affective Disorders,* eds. M.Schou & E. Stromgren. London & New York: Academic Press.

Shapiro, E.R., & Freedman, J. (1982), Family dynamics of adolescent suicide. Paper presented at interdisciplinary seminar, The Function of the Family in the Adolescent Individuation Process, American Psychoanalytic Association, December 1982.

Time (1980), Suicide belt: Rates up for affluent teenagers. September 1.

Yalom, I.D. (1980), *Existential Psychotherapy.* New York: Basic Books.

Zetzel, E.R. (1965), On the incapacity to bear depression. In: *The Capacity for Emotional Growth,* ed. E.R. Zetzel. New York: International Universities Press, 1970, pp. 82–114.

13

Special Issues of Assessment and Treatment of Suicide Risk in the Elderly

Alexander C. Morgan, M.D.

At 6:30 A.M. the night nurse in a reputable nursing home found 79-year-old Mr. Delgado dead in his bed with a gunshot wound of the head inflicted by a pistol he held in his right hand. No one had known Mr. Delgado to be mentally ill, and at the time of his death his only active physical illness was a 24-hour-long, severe, unremitting case of diarrhea, which had caused him the unusual embarrassment of soiling his bed. Mr. Delgado had been rather isolated and irritable throughout the four years he had been in the nursing home, but the nursing home psychiatrist had never been asked to consult regarding him. The most notable aspect about his time in the nursing home was that he had vehemently refused to let anyone help him remove the prosthetic leg he wore after an amputation due to a gunshot wound to that leg 30 years previously. It was in that prosthesis that the gun had been kept all this time.

The startling features of the above case highlight the difficulties in assessing and treating suicide risk in the elderly. The combination of social isolation and drastically experienced physical illness must have given Mr. Delgado a sense of hopelessness that eventually overwhelmed him. Additionally, the extreme lethality of his method of suicide made intervention impossible for the health care personnel working with him. The social isolation, physical illness, and highly lethal attempt are some of the factors that will be reviewed in this chapter as requiring special attention in assessing suicide risk in the elderly. The emphasis of this chapter will be on the special clinical problems confronted in assessing and treating elderly suicide risk, and readers are referred elsewhere for complete reviews of the literature on the demographics of elderly suicide (Payne, 1975; Charatan, 1979; Stenback, 1980; Osgood, 1985).

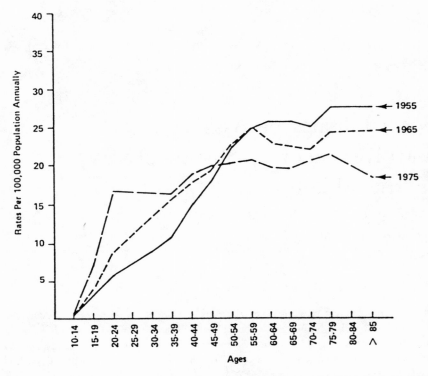

Figure 13.1 Age specific suicide rates by five-year age groups 1955, 1965, 1975. (From Fredericks, 1978.)

OVERVIEW OF THE ELDERLY
SUICIDE RATE IN THE UNITED STATES

Perhaps the best known fact about suicide among the elderly in the United States is that the rate in this age group is higher than at any other time in the life cycle. Figure 13.1 shows that the suicide rate rises to its highest point in the 75- to 79-year age group where it is 42 per 100,000 (Fredericks, 1978; Murphy and Wetzel, 1980). While increased age is an important determinant of suicide risk, sex and race are probably more telling, with the male suicide rate continuing to climb with advancing age, but the female suicide rate leveling off at 65. Also, whites historically have had higher rates of suicide than nonwhites. Thus, the older white males have the highest risk.

While the high rate of elderly suicide is alarming relative to other causes of death in this age group, death by suicide is not as common a cause of death as it is at other ages. Heart disease, malignancies, and cerebrovascular diseases are only a few causes of death in the elderly that are more common than suicide (National Center for Health Statistics, 1978). In many ways, suicide risk is a more treatable potential cause of death than the more common potential causes of death in the elderly such as heart disease, cancer, and so on. The fact that suicide is less common than other causes of death in the elderly, however, may influence people working with them to be inattentive to elderly suicide risk.

An additional, clinically meaningful statistic to be considered in working with elderly potential suicides is that it appears that those elderly who attempt suicide succeed more often than persons attempting suicide in the younger age groups (Rachlis, 1970; Sendbuehler and Goldstein, 1977). The means of suicide chosen by the elderly is also more violent and lethal (hanging, drowning, gunshot wound) (Murphy and Wetzel, 1980). These findings, coupled with the old saw that suicide is a permanent solution for a temporary problem, are in fact the strongest arguments for suicide risk detection and assessment in the elderly.

Before leaving the subject of suicide rate statistics in the United States, it is important to note that the U.S. pattern of a higher suicide rate in the older population is not universal, though it probably is the most common (Ruzicka, 1976). For instance, statistics for Finland show that the suicide rate for males peaks at age 50 and then declines, in contrast to the statistics for U.S. males. In comparing rates from a variety of countries there is the general, though not definitive, impression that societies in which the elderly hold a more valued position have lower rates of elderly suicide. One clear validation of this phenomenon was studied in Hong Kong when the elderly suicide rate in 1922 was compared to rates in 1950 and found to be substantially lower (Yap, 1963). In the three decades between the two sets of statistics the older Hong Kong citizens had lost some of their social–cultural prominence due to changes away from the traditional reverence toward the elderly.

There has, interestingly, been a small decrease in the elderly suicide rate in the United States over the last 20 years (Figure 13.1), and some studies have shown that this regression can be almost entirely explained by the increase that has occurred in the level of elderly income over this time period (Robins, West, and Murphy, 1977). These data underscore a point that will become more clear in the course of discussing the treatment of elderly suicide risk: close attention must be paid to socioeconomic factors in the treatment of such patients.

DEMOGRAPHICS OF SUICIDAL ELDERLY IN THE UNITED STATES

Before discussing assessment of suicide risk in the elderly it is necessary to pay attention to the ways in which suicidal elderly persons differ from the nonsuicidal elderly. The primary features will be summarized and pertinent studies described, but the reader is referred elsewhere for a complete review of the literature (Miller, 1977; Stenback, 1980; Osgood, 1985). It is important at this point to make it clear that, while this chapter deals with old people as a group, the clinician comes to know elderly patients as unique individuals. It is hoped that by learning in general about elderly people and their suicide risk the technique and art of learning about them as individuals will be made easier.

Mental Illness and Emotional State

Hopelessness is the most common feeling state of older persons committing suicide (Minkoff, Bergman, and Beck, 1973), and it often includes the sense that there is absolutely no other resolution to the suffering that the person faces. Diagnostically, depression, alcoholism, and organic brain syndrome are the most common mental disorders of the suicidal elderly population. However, depression is by far the most common, ranging from 48 to 80 percent of elderly suicides (O'Neal, Robins, and Schmidt, 1959; Charatan, 1979). In a cross-section of the elderly, primary depression was present in only 3.7 percent, with a total of 14 percent complaining of some kind of dysphoric state (Blazer and Williams, 1980). The high percentage of elderly suicides who were depressed is in sharp contrast to the low of 3.7 percent of depression in the general population of the elderly, giving clear testimony to the fact that depression is a primary feature of elderly suicide.

Alcoholism clearly is associated with an increased risk of suicide in the elderly, but the exact importance of this concurrent prevalence of alcoholism and suicide risk is not entirely clear. In some views of elderly suicide, alcoholism has been subsumed under the category of depression, whereas in other views it has been treated as a separate entity. What appears to be the case is that intoxication with alcohol is the factor that most increases the risk of suicide in the elderly. The intoxication acts by lowering the elderly person's control over self-destructive behavior that has its genesis in the depression and hopelessness discussed previously. Some confirmation of this view comes from a study that showed that following the liberalization of the drinking laws in Sweden, there was a rise in the elderly suicide rate (Hartelius, 1967).

Organic brain syndrome has been diagnosed at a rate of 10 to 26 percent in elderly suicides, depending on the individual study (O'Neal et al., 1959). But a number of studies are beginning to show that, while people with organic brain syndrome may have suicidal intent, they make fewer truly serious suicide attempts (Farberow and Moriwaki, 1975; Robins et al., 1977). It may be that their cognitive deficits prevent them from performing the actions necessary to kill themselves. The one type of organic brain syndrome, however, which is associated with an increased ability to complete suicide successfully is an acute delirious state. The risk in these patients is that they may react impulsively in a despairing panic and successfully kill themselves.

Physical Illnesses

A large percentage of people over 65 have chronic illnesses, so that it is not surprising that a high proportion (50 to 60 percent) of elderly suicides are reported to have physical illnesses (O'Neal et al., 1959; Sainsbury, 1962). However, what seems to be more clinically significant is the psychological meaning of the physical illness to the older person. If the illness is seen as a direct blow to the person's means of maintaining self-esteem, such as the unremitting diarrhea for Mr. Delgado described in the introductory vignette, then there is indeed an increase of suicide risk.

Socioeconomic Status

There is some uncertainty as to the exact impact social and economic class have on the elderly suicide rate. However, it is abundantly clear that a negative change in socioeconomic class is associated with an increased risk of suicide. As with physical illnesses, it appears that it is the meaning of the socioeconomic variable to the individual person that causes increased risk. In the Great Depression of the 1930s the increased risk of suicide was largely in classes that lost a great deal of money rather than among people who were already moderately poor prior to the Depression (Henry and Short, 1957). The difficulties of continuing on a fixed income in the face of inflation are very much part of some older people's despair about themselves. Other social factors associated with loss such as death of a spouse, retirement, and sense of isolation are also correlated with higher rates of suicide in some studies (Stenback, 1980). It very much depends on the meaning of the specific sociocultural factor to the individual person. For instance, elderly widows do have a slightly higher suicide risk (increased 1.3 times) after the husband's death. However, this rise in suicide rate is less than the rise for younger widows. This imples that as women age there is an increase in their ability to tolerate their husband's death, and this finding perhaps bears upon age-related changes in women's social support network. The true importance of social variables in suicide evaluation of the elderly probably lies in the extent to which the elderly person feels integrated into the society to which he or she belongs.

EVALUATION OF INDIVIDUAL SUICIDE RISK

Before discussing problems of evaluating and treating elderly suicide risk, it is necessary to review briefly the general principles of suicide risk assessment as applied to the elderly. The reader is referred to other chapters in this volume for comprehensive coverage of the topic of risk evaluation. There have been attempts to establish statistical procedures for suicide risk evaluation in the elderly (Letteri,

1973), and these efforts have considerable merit, especially for research. However, for purposes of organizing one's thoughts in the clinical setting the author has found it more useful to divide suicide risk evaluation into sequential steps, beginning with rather statistical demographic factors and moving to more personal, affective, and at times solely empathic factors involved with the potentially suicidal elderly person. The outline of this process is listed below:

I.   Demographic features

    A.   Personal (sex, age, previous attempts, etc.)
    B.   Health
        1.   Emotional health (symptoms of depression, alcoholism, delirium, etc.)
        2.   Physical health (debilitating illnesses, failures of previous therapy plans, etc.)
        3.   Presence or absence of help-seeking behavior for problems (e.g., quality of communication with other people)
    C.   Relations with others
        1.   Family history of suicide
        2.   Extent of social isolation (especially recent losses)
        3.   Reactions of others who know the person (e.g., the level of their concern)

II. Affective factors

    A.   Completeness of planning for suicide (place, violence of the method, other preparations for death such as wills, etc.)
    B.   Meaning of the suicide (e.g., rejoining a dead relative)
    C.   Degree of comfort the person has with the thought of suicide
    D.   Level of the person's hopelessness (including current and anticipated causes of stress)
    E.   Empathic response of the evaluator (e.g., degree of uncomfortableness with any of the suicidal person's assurances of life preservative efforts)

In addition to using this outline as one would for a younger person, with an elderly person there are particular areas to be emphasized. Among the demographic features, the issue of the meaning of the physical illness to the person and the success or failure of treatment attempts is very important. A significant percentage of all older people have some chronic illness. It is the feeling that nothing is being done about the progression of an illness that often has more impact on suicide risk than the presence of the illness itself. Also, the amount of help-seeking behavior is often lessened by the amount of isolation seen in the elderly. If there have been recent losses, there will be more isolation and less help-seeking behavior. Together, these two features of isolation and little help-seeking behavior may make the elderly person contemplating suicide rather invisible to health care deliverers. The only realistic countermeasure to this problem is to have a high index of caution whenever an older person gives any kind of hint about suicidal thinking.

In using the portion of this outline dealing with affective factors, there are several additional comments to be make regarding the elderly. There is, of course, increased risk with both greater completeness of the planning for the suicide and also enhanced degree of comfort with the idea of suicide. However, it is an appropriate life stage task for older persons to be planning for death by writing wills, and so on. It is also stage appropriate to be coming to some kind of an acceptance of the inevitability of one's death. It is therefore important in evaluating older persons to distinguish between planning and feeling comfortable about death, and planning and feeling comfortable about suicide. This distinction is best made by trying to get a comprehensive view of the person's intentions. If the writing of wills or buying of insurance policies has an air of urgency about it, or if it is being carried out with feelings of secrecy or defensiveness, then concern that the planning is about suicide rather than simply death itself is warranted. Likewise, whether the sense of comfort an older person has is about suicide or about dying can be estimated by how much the other people in the older person's world are apprised of his thoughts about death. The more relatives and friends are aware of the older person's thinking about dying the less chance there is that the thinking is about suicide. The other specific affective factors in the outline can only be reviewed by directly discussing the older person's feelings. It is hoped that the older person will be candid and genuine in discussing these feelings. In order to achieve this, it is extremely important that the person evaluating the elderly person's suicide risk be equally candid and genuine. The older person requires a sense of safety in exposing suicidal thinking and interviewers must be neither cloyingly sympathetic nor aggressively intrusive in order to establish such a climate of safety.

SPECIAL PROBLEMS IN ASSESSING SUICIDE RISK IN THE ELDERLY

Frequency of Crisis Presentation

Some of the problems in establishing the sense of safety described above are related to specific issues raised in the caregivers' minds and the health system by the suicidal feelings of elderly persons. A common difficulty is that older people's suicidal thinking often presents itself as very much of a crisis. This means that the person evaluating the elderly patient's suicidal risk often has little past experience with that particular older patient. That is quite a different situation from suicide risk that comes up in the context of an ongoing therapy relationship. Moreover, the elderly person presenting with suicide intent often has been leading a fairly isolated life. It sometimes appears as though it is only in a passing way that the elderly person reveals that their despair has reached life-threatening proportions. On the one hand, this may lead some people to fail to take the suicidal intent seriously. On the other hand, the shocking nature of this revelation can cause people around the older person to withdraw and not be available to the patient throughout the crisis.

For the person evaluating the suicide risk, the combination of the older person's isolation and the dynamics set up in the people around the patient may make it very difficult to get an accurate history and understanding of the older person. It is as if the older person had simply "popped up" with no prior history. This means that one must pay particular attention to getting a full picture of the elderly person from as many people as possible. Some might object that this would cause interference with the alliance between the evaluator and the elderly patient. However, it rarely does so if the contacts with other people are candidly explained as being related to concern for the patient's safety. Family contacts are an obvious place to start, but it is often a multitude of social service personnel interacting with the elderly patient who have a closer view of his state. This is especially true when a patient is depressed and has withdrawn owing to feelings of being unwanted by the family. For the elderly with a lifelong history of isolation, the outreach approach used by community workers may be the only way to obtain a clear picture of the extent of the elderly person's suicide risk.

In one memorable case, the couple who ran the corner magazine and grocery store were the only ones who could give a clear story of a behavior change in a withdrawn, retired elderly woman bookkeeper. The item listed in the risk evaluation outline as "reactions of others" is what needs to be considered in getting history from a variety of sources. The attitude of the retired bookkepper and of her family was rather blasé when inquiries were first made about suicide intent. The seriousness of the suicide risk was learned only when the couple in the corner store were subsequently told of the clinician's concern and came forward. They had noted that the woman had first stopped buying her newspapers and then began to turn away the usual weekly grocery delivery. Recently she had tried to give to the couple some antique magazines of great emotional value to her. With this insight, further inquiries revealed that the patient had been hoarding medicine in preparation for a very serious suicide attempt.

Atypical Presentation of Depressions in the Elderly

This case illustrates the importance of never accepting withdrawal as simply "normal" to old age. Depression is not normal at any age, and it is important to keep in mind the statistics mentioned earlier in this chapter that 85 percent of a community survey of elderly had no symptoms at all of depression or dysphoric mood (Blazer and Williams, 1980). When confronted with a suicidal elderly person, the attitude with which to start the evaluation is that depression is probably present and significant for that particular person. However, there is the additional problem that depression may be more difficult to detect in the elderly because it presents in a masked form. Masked depression presents itself typically in the elderly as (1) indirect self-destructive behavior, (2) somatic concerns masking the person's feeling state, and (3) a falsely deficient cognitive ability (often labeled "pseudodementia").

Indirect self-destructive behaviors are probably most common in the institutionalized settings where others are caring for the elderly person. Control struggles begin to occur over whether the patient will take part in activities, take medication, and so on. (Kastenbaum and Mishara, 1971; Farberow and Moriwaki, 1975; Nelson and Farberow, 1976). The problem of evaluation is that the affects around autonomy and control, such as pride and anger, may be more noticeable than the affect of depression. Staff caring for a patient refusing their help often are so embroiled in their own feelings of irritation at the patient that the patient is felt as someone who is simply "trying to get our goat." Only if the clinician looks behind the control struggle will the patient's depression be apparent.

The fact that there is an increased bodily concern with advancing age is what may obscure the depression of older persons who present with depression masked by *somatic complaints*. It is the exacerbation of chronic bodily concern that should alert the clinician to the possibility of depression in an elderly person. For instance, if a person's persistent concern about constipation and bowel movements begins to prevent them from going to public places, then it is an indication to look carefully for other signs of depression such as tearfulness, sleep changes, appetite changes, and so on. In addition, when the concerns about the body reach the level of extreme but unfounded fearfulness of a fatal illness such as cancer, then the clinician should begin to investigate the possibility of a somatic delusion, which often accompanies depression in the elderly.

In a similar manner, when an elderly person abruptly appears demented, the clinician should consider whether a depressive *pseudodementia* is present. Differentiation of the mixed picture of dementia and depression is extremely difficult, and the subject has been reviewed in some depth elsewhere (Wells, 1982; McCallister, 1983). For the purposes of this chapter, however, it is important that when evaluating suicide risk, the clinician should never accept the dementing process as the sole pathology present in the elderly patient. Depression must be looked for with the variety of methods available. In addition to exploring the vegetative signs and thoughts of death noted previously, the sense of hopelessness must be inquired about in such a way as to enable the elderly person to expose the despair that is being experienced. In recent years, certain pharmacologic and hormonal tests have also been developed, such as the Amphetamine Response Test (Van Kammen and Murphy, 1978) and the Dexamethazone Suppression Test (Carroll, Feinberg, Greden, Tarika, Albula, Haskett, James, Kronfol, Lohr, Steiner, de Vigne, and Young, 1981), that may be helpful in delineating the presence of a depression. While these tests are helpful, they are no substitute for the interviewer sitting with the elderly person and helping him explore the way his life feels. Often it will be the interviewer's own affective response to the patient that will provide the most important information about whether the patient in fact is experiencing a sense of hopelessness that makes suicide appear as the only alternative.

Gerontophobic Attitudes in Caregivers

While the use of one's own affective response to the patient can be useful in the evaluation of suicide risk, unconscious negative attitudes toward the elderly may create another set of problems in evaluating suicide risk in this population. Negative stereotyping of old persons being less worthwhile than young people is abundant (Butler, 1975). In one study involving review of printed case material, the quality of treatment offered to the patients was of poorer quality when the patients were described as elderly than when the same patients were described as younger (Ford and Sbordone, 1980). These negative, or gerontophobic, attitudes toward the elderly impact on elderly suicide evaluation in that there may be an unconscious tendency to fail to take seriously suicide risk in older persons. The best counterforce to these attitudes is to understand their genesis. One source may be that clinicians while working with older persons may not be comfortable with the thoughts of their own aging process. Dealing with suicidal elderly, in particular, may stir up feelings about one's own aging because it is painful to consider old age as possibly being beset with isolation and despair.

An additional reason that caregivers avoid close contact with elder patients is their wish to protect themselves against thoughts of their parents aging and death. It is common that when clinicians work with patients who are the age of their parents, the parents somehow seem younger than the patient of the same age. This frequently holds true regardless of the health of the patient and the parent. Clinicians often find themselves saying, "My mother doesn't seem *that* old!" The ambivalent feelings of affection and anger present in all parent–child relationships may have specific effects on evaluating suicidal elderly. A self-destructive older person may arouse in the clinician a host of feelings including anger, sadness, guilt, and so on, that have as their basis feelings about the clinician's parents, in addition to any relationship to qualities belonging to the particular suicidal older person. Statements such as, "You'll be OK, old girl, just don't pay so much attention to your worries about a tumor," are clearly not helpful to suicidal patients. To a certain extent these comments have their roots in the combined wishes to avoid thinking about the clinician's own aging and to distract the clinician's attention from feelings about the aging of his parents.

Age-Related Differences in Perspective on Death

At all stages of the life cycle, suicide evaluation obviously raises issues about the clinician's feelings about death. With the elderly, this is not markedly different.

Thoughts of death threaten all ages with a sense of aloneness, but there may be age-related differences in the perspective with which death is viewed. From the point of view of the younger caregiver working with the elderly, death represents primarily a taking away of hopes and expectations for the future. For older persons, on the other hand, death represents an end mark, stimulating consideration of the extent to which one has been able to satisfy one's hopes and expectations. The presence of thoughts of death in the older person is part of the stimulus for the dynamic between ego integrity and the despair of which Erikson writes (Erikson, 1950) and also the process Butler (1963) has referred to as the life review. It can be said that people are moving toward death from birth onwards, but while young people face toward death, older people often look away from death and back over their past lives.

In talking with suicidal elderly people, the differing perspectives about death held by the younger evaluator in comparison to the older patient have to be taken into account. Talking with suicidal patients of all ages can arouse strong feelings of countertransference hate, as Maltsberger and Buie (1974) have pointed out. This is so because, among other reasons, the patient's self-destructiveness can express such denigration of the therapist's intention to "help." These interactions may arouse in the therapist either malice or aversion for the patient. The therapist's response may range from repression with mild rejection of the patient to a total disorganization of the therapist into flight from the therapeutic situation. In dealing with suicidal elderly, aversion is probably a more common response than is malice because elderly suicides seem to represent more often a wish to die than a wish to kill or be killed, although this, of course, is not universally true (Farberow and Shneidman, 1957; Lester and Hummel, 1980). Thus, evaluators of suicidal elderly persons must be particularly cognizant of the life review aspects of the older years. It may be more important to talk to the older person about what he has done in his life, for good or for ill, than to talk about what may or may not lie ahead. The understanding of the clinician that the patient, perhaps even via the suicidal thinking, is struggling to put his life into perspective may be very important in assisting the patient to move away from his wish to die.

Suicide as a Symptom or as Life's Resolution

A fifth and final problem to be discussed as specific to evaluating elderly suicide is the issue of whether the suicidal thinking is a symptom to be treated and excised or a resolution that represents the older person's only option (Beckwith-Burnhan, 1979). This is a topic of discussion concerning younger patients also, but because the older person is at the end of the life cycle the dilemma presents particular problems. Especially in institutional patients with indirect self-destructive behavior, the patient's sense of being totally miserable may make suicide appear as truly the only option. When determining whether a suicidal death resolves issues or flees from them, an understanding of the entire experience and background of the suicidal person becomes extremely important. It is only in cultures and religions sanctioning suicide that the strongest case can be made for accepting suicide as resolution rather than pathology. It is intresting that according to some studies religious intensity is somewhat preventative for indirect self-destructive behavior. In Western culture it is unusual to find much congruence between suicidal thinking and patients' adherence to a religion.

It is the opinion of the author and others (Payne, 1964) that suicide as a rational act of resolution is very rare in the elderly of the United States. In the author's experience, the number of cases of persons who feel at one time that suicide truly represents a solution for them and who later, after treatment for depression, view their suicidal thoughts as aberrant are much more common. There is one quite telling case report of a suicide pact between an elderly husband and wife that was aborted at the wife's suggestion; subsequently the couple had an excellent response to treatment for depression (Mehta, Matthew, and Mehta, 1978). Without excluding the possibility that some suicidal thinking may represent a resolution for the person involved, it seems much more important to emphasize that, regardless of the rational intent expressed by the suicidal person, the signs and symptoms of depression should be diligently looked for and treated before the caregiver stands aside and allows the suicide to occur. One clinical indication of how much resolution is involved in the suicidal thinking is the extent to which suicide has been openly discussed with friends and relatives. If the thoughts of suicide have not been shared and accepted by all the people close to the suicidal elderly person, then that would be an indication that the person's suicidal thinking failed to take into account the total effect of a death by suicide. The failure to share suicidal intent with one's emotional contacts highlights a failure to have the suicidal thinking truly become a resolution for the entirety of one's existence. Therefore, it is the author's opinion that such cases deserve not agreement with the suicidal wishes, but, instead, firm and understanding intervention and treatment.

TREATMENT OF SUICIDE RISK IN THE ELDERLY

The treatment of suicide risk in the elderly does not differ substantially from suicide treatment of other age groups. The prime issue at all ages is to increase the safety of the patient. Any substantial risk in an older person means that they should be hospitalized in a psychiatric unit. Because of physical problems, there may be an inclination to hospitalize elderly people on regular medical units. It may represent some wish of the caregivers to deny the emotional distress presented by the suicidal thinking. This is not in fact a reasonable solution for the emotional aspects of the suicide risk.

After the person's safety has been assured, the treatment must aim at decreasing the hopelessness of the patient. The depression that lies behind the hopeless feeling should be aggressively treated, because it is usually the depression that prevents the person from seeing the alternatives to suicide (Patterson, Abrahams, and Baker, 1974; Miller, 1977). The life-saving factor in suicide treatment is often the meaningful presence of a real working therapeutic alliance, or, in other words, a "confidante" (Lowenthal and Haven, 1968). With this relationship, the painful feelings behind the depression may be able to be tolerated in such a way as to help the patient feel worthy of staying alive. The full treatment regimen for depression should of course be used with depressed suicidal elderly. The treatment of depression in the elderly is a topic covered in detail elsewhere (Zung, 1980; Salzman and van der Kolk, 1984), but for the purposes of this chapter, certain aspects should be emphasized. In general, the first medications used are usually the tricyclic antidepressants. For a certain variety of depressive patients, the "atypical depressions," monoamine oxidase inhibitors may be more helpful than tricyclic antidepressants (Davidson, Miller, Turnbull, and Sullivan, 1981; Sovner, 1981). For patients with manic-depressive illness, lithium carbonate is useful, more for the prevention of affective cycling than for the treatment of the acute affective symptoms of depression and mania. Where there are special considerations in treating elderly people with lithium, age is no contraindication to the use of lithium carbonate when it is warranted. Antipsychotic agents may be used in treating the agitation associated with depression in the elderly, but in general they are not as helpful with the depressive symptoms themselves as are the antidepressant agents. The decision as to which medication to use should rest on a thorough knowledge of both the patient and the medications. With any of the psychotropic agents, the special problems elderly people experience with medication side effects must of course be kept in mind. In fact, in a number of patients, particularly those with problems of cardiac irritability, electroconvulsive therapy (ECT), particularly unilateral ECT, will be a safer and more effective treatment than can be offered by either class of antidepressant medication. Electroconvulsive therapy is very much the treatment of choice when the suicide risk is so high that there is no time to wait for the delayed effect of an antidepressant. Neither the stigma that ECT often carries nor the feeling that someone is "too old" for ECT should prevent the clinician from using it when it is called for.

With suicidal elderly people the cause of the patient's depression almost always has some relationship to the realities of his or her life. Thus treatment should include "real" help when it is called for. Physical illness should be aggressively treated. Attention should be paid to maintaining the person's social surroundings as much as possible. Hospitalizations, especially psychiatric ones, often result in friends and relatives distancing themselves from the hospitalized patient. This is particularly true with elderly people and must be countered. In fact, there should be strong efforts to increase the number and availability of people involved with the patient. Family members, neighbors, visiting nurses, homemakers, welfare workers, day care center staff, medical care personnel such as the family doctor and his nurse, should all be involved both in helping the patient and also in communicating to each other the status of their individual work with the patient. The patient should be encouraged to allow this kind of open communication between the caregivers. The intersystemic connection between the multitude of caregivers usually involved with the elderly is particularly important in preventing individual caregivers from feeling unnecessarily responsible and burdened by the patient and then withdrawing their availability for the patient. In increasing the contact between the patient and the people available to him, it is important that the contact be concrete and reality oriented when appropriate. Help with housekeeping and other daytime activities such as shopping may be as necessary as psychotropic medication in helping elderly patients regain their sense of self-worth and ability to manage their lives.

The contact with a suicidal elderly person should, from the beginning, incorporate as much continuity as possible. There are two periods of increased suicidal risk that occur in all ages but can be particularly dramatic with the elderly. The first period is just as help is beginning to be organized for the patient. Thus, it is important that, as soon as the decision has been made to provide assistance to the elderly person, there be no time when the patient could change his mind and successfully kill himself. The second period of increased risk takes place during the course of the treatment of the patient's depression, when the energy level has begun to rise but the patient's mood is still one of despair. There is at that time sufficient energy to go through with a suicide that the anergic state of the depression had previously prevented. With elderly patients there is a third period of high risk, though it is not so much an increase in risk as a dramatic return of the risk. That period occurs when, after a successful treatment and discharge from the hospital, the patient suffers some new, unanticipated blow to what maintains his self-esteem. This is true at all ages, of course, but the elderly person's financial, health, and social situation makes him more vulnerable to the usual inconsistencies of life. The failure to receive a Social Security check due to a bureaucratic oversight, the exacerbation of a chronic physical illness, or the closing of an elderly drop-in center can each have a serious negative effect on the elderly person's recovery from the despair that produced the suicidal thinking. For this reason, after-care planning for the elderly must be very comprehensive and must consider the large variety of supports the patient uses. The treatment must also be very responsive so that the support can be readily available if the feelings of hopelessness return.

PREVENTION OF ELDERLY SUICIDE

Because of the high lethality of most elderly suicide attempts, the best treatment for elderly suicide risk is prevention. It will clearly be helpful if increased attention is paid to elderly people, both by clinicians and by society. There are particular problems, however, in that elderly people tend to underutilize suicide crisis centers (Atkinson, 1971; Fox, 1976). With the introduction of community mental health programs, there is mixed evidence about decreases in the elderly suicide rate (Nielsen and Videbeck, 1973; Sainsbury and Grad de Alarcon, 1973), but the presence of outpatient treatment centers may have protected some elderly patients (Walk, 1967).

Primary prevention, that is, elimination of causes of illnesses, is really the most significant form of prevention of elderly suicide. Much of the suicidal thinking in the elderly arises after the individual experiences personal losses. Attempts at early detection and replacement of an older person's losses might have significant success in preventing the despair that produces suicidal thinking (though it is, of course, impossible to replace some losses, such as that of a spouse). However, if such an irremediable loss occurs and is detected, then other persons and services can at least make up for some of the feeling of deficit. At present the data about the success of such interventions show mixed results. Processes such as retirement preparation, widow-to-widow groups, or postfuneral follow-ups of mourners are the kind of social–psychological interventions that might have some impact on suicidal thinking following losses.

Essentially, suicide prevention in the elderly relates to improving the self-esteem of older persons and has wide social, financial, and political ramifications. While all depression and suicide thinking in the elderly is clearly not related to sociocultural issues, the demographics of elderly suicide show how important these factors truly are. Improving older persons' financial security, housing conditions, health care, and social isolation would have a real impact on their view of themselves within the society. Data have already been mentioned (Robins et al., 1977) that show total statistical correlation between the slight decrease in the U.S. elderly suicide rate over the last three decades and the concurrent rise in elderly income separate from other social variables such as unemployment, divorce rates, and so on. With the well-publicized rising proportion of elderly in the United States population, improvement of older people's financial security is, of course, not without difficulty. However, more attention is now being paid to the condition of the nation's older citizens, including their high suicide rate. With this increased notice, it is becoming increasingly clear that it is necessary to develop improved ways of helping the growing number of elderly people maintain their feelings of self-worth within the society.

A FINAL WORD

While most of this chapter has dealt with the suicidal elderly as if they belong to a homogeneous group, it is necessary to end this chapter with a reminder of the inherent clinical uselessness and lack of validity of too strong an adherence to such a view. The most important aspect of paying attention to older people is to see them as individuals. It is the intention of this chapter to draw attention to older people in general, and then as individuals. Older people are just as unique and varied, one from the other, as people at any other age. In short the message is first to begin to recognize that older people, and their heightened suicide risk, are very much present with us in our clinical work. After that, getting to know and appreciate the individual nature of each older person's own life story is no different from learning the life story of a person of any age. Because the older person's life story is, of course, longer, there may be added richness to the process of that clinical involvement with the elderly patient. It is hoped that readers will be encouraged to find out for themselves the special quality of the therapeutic relationship that develops when working with older patients.

REFERENCES

Atkinson, M. (1971), The Samaritans and the elderly: Some problems in communication between a suicide prevention scheme and a group with a high suicide rate. *Soc. Sci. & Med.*, 5:483–490.

Beckwith-Burnhan, P. (1979), On the right to suicide by the dying. *Dissent*, 26:231–233.

Blazer, D.G., & Williams, C.O. (1980), The epidemiology of dysphoria and depression in an elderly population. *Amer. J. Psychiat.*, 137:439–444.

Butler, R.A. (1963), The life review: An interpretation of reminiscence in the aged. *Psychiat.*, 26:65–75.

——— (1975), Psychiatry and the elderly: An overview. *Amer. J. Psychiat.*, 132:893–900.

Carroll, B.J., Feinberg, M., Greden, J.F., Tarika, J., Albula, A.A., Haskett, R.F., James, N.M., Kronfol, Z., Lohr, N., Steiner, M., de Vigne, J.P., & Young, E. (1981), A specific laboratory test for melancholia. *Arch. Gen. Psychiat.*, 38:15–23.

Charatan, F.B. (1979), The aged. In: *Suicide: Theory and Clinical Aspects*, eds. L.D. Hankoff & B. Einsidler. Littleton, MA: John Wright PSG, pp. 253–262.

Davidson, J.R.T., Miller, R.O., Turnbull, C.O., & Sullivan, J.L. (1981), Atypical depression. *Arch. Gen. Psychiat.*, 39:527–534.

Erikson, E.H. (1950), *Childhood and Society*. New York: W.W. Norton, pp. 268–274.

Farberow, N.L., & Moriwaki, S.Y. (1975), Self-destructive crises in the older person. *Gerontol.*, 15:333–337.

——— Shneidman, E.S. (1957), Suicide and age, In: *Clues to Suicide*, eds. E.S. Shneidman & N.L. Farberow. New York: McGraw-Hill.

Ford, C.V., & Sbordone, R.J. (1980), Attitudes of psychiatrists toward elderly patients. *Amer. J. Psychiat.*, 137:571–557.

Fox, R. (1976), The recent decline in suicide in Britain: The role of the Samaritan suicide prevention movement. In: *Suicidology: Contemporary Developments*, ed. E.S. Shneidman. New York: Grune & Stratton, pp. 449–524.

Fredericks, C. (1978), Current trends in suicidal behavior in the United States. *Amer. J. Psychother.*, 32:172–201.

Hartelius, H.A. (1967), A study of suicides in Sweden 1951–63, Including a comparison with 1925–1950. *Acta Psychiat. Scand.*, 43:121–143.

Henry, A.F., & Short, J.F., Jr. (1957), The sociology of suicide. In: *Clues to Suicide*, eds. E.S. Shneidman & N.L. Farberow. New York: McGraw-Hill.

Kastenbaum, R., & Mishara, B.L. (1971), Premature death and self-injurious behavior in old age. *Geriat.*, 26:71–81.

Lester, D., & Hummel, H. (1980), Motives for suicide in elderly people. *Psycholog. Rep.*, 47:870.

Letteri, D.J. (1973), Empirical prediction of suicide risk among the aging. *J. Geriat. Psychiat.*, 6:17–42.

Lowenthal, M.F., & Haven, C. (1968), Interaction and adaptation: Intimacy as a critical variable. *Amer. Sociol. Rev.*, 33:414–420.

Maltsberger, J.T., & Buie, D.B. (1974), Countertransference hate in the treatment of suicidal patients. *Arch. Gen. Psychiat.*, 30:625–633.

McCallister, T.W. (1983), Overview: Pseudodementia. *Amer. J. Psychiat.*, 140:528–533.

Mehta, O., Matthew, P., & Mehta, S. (1978), Suicide pact in a depressed elderly couple: Care report. *J. Amer. Geriat. Soc.*, 26:136–138.

Miller, M. (1977), A psychological autopsy of a geriatric suicide. *J. Geriat. Psychiat.*, 10:229–242.

Minkoff, K., Bergman, E., & Beck, A.T. (1973), Hopelessness, depression, and attempted suicide, *Amer. J. Psychiat.*, 130:455–459.

Murphy, G.E., & Wetzel, R.D. (1980), Suicide risk by birth cohort in the United States, 1949 to 1974. *Arch. Gen. Psychiat.*, 37:519–523.

National Center for Health Statistics (1978), *Vital Statistics Report for the United States.* Washington, DC: U.S. Government Printing Office.

Nelson, F.L. & Farberow, N.L. (1976), Indirect suicide in the elderly, chronically ill patient. *Psychiat. Fennica* (Helsinki), 7 (Suppl.):125–139.

Nielsen, J., & Videbeck, T. (1973), Suicide frequency before and after introduction of community psychiatry in a Danish island. *Brit. J. Psychiat.*, 123:35–39.

O'Neal, P., Robins, E., & Schmidt, E.H. (1959), A psychiatric study of attempted suicide in persons over sixty years of age. *Arch. Neurol. Psychiat.*, 75:275–284.

Osgood, N.J. (1985), *Suicide in the Elderly.* Rockville, MD: Aspen Systems Corporation.

Patterson, R.O., Abrahams, R., & Baker, F. (1974), Preventing self-destructive behavior. *Geriat.*, 29:115–118, 121.

Payne, E.C. (1964), Teaching medical psychotherapy in special clinical settings. In: *Psychiatry and Medical Practice in a General Hospital*, ed. N.E. Zinberg. New York: International Universities Press.

Payne, E. (1975), Depression and suicide. In: *Modern Perspectives in the Psychiatry of Old Age*, ed. J.G. Howells. New York: Brunner/Mazel, pp. 290–312.

Rachlis, D. (1970), Suicide and loss: Adjustment in the aging. *Bull. Suicidol.*, Fall, 23.

Robins, L.N., West, P.A., & Murphy, G.E. (1977), The high rate of suicide in older white men: A study testing ten hypotheses. *Soc. Psychiat.*, 12:1–20.

Ruzicka, L.T. (1976), Suicide, 1950 to 1971. *World Health Stat. Rep.*, 29:396–413.

Sainsbury, P. (1962), Suicide in later life. *Gerontol. Clin.*, 4:161–170.

———— Grad de Alarcon, J. (1973), Evaluating a service in Sussex. In: *Roots of Evaluation*, ed. J.K. Wing & H. Hafner. London: Oxford University Press.

Salzman, C., & van der Kolk, B. (1984), Treatment of depression. In: *Clinical Geriatric Psychopharmacology*, ed. C. Salzman. New York: McGraw-Hill, pp. 77–131.

Sendbuehler, J.M., & Goldstein, S. (1977), Attempted suicide among the aged. *J. Amer. Geriat. Soc.*, 25:245–248.

Sovner, R. (1981), The clinical characteristics and treatment of atypical depression. *J. Clin. Psychiat.*, 46:285–289.

Stenback, A. (1980), Depression and suicidal behavior in old age. In: *Handbook of Mental Health and Aging*, eds. J.E. Birren & R.B. Sloane. Englewood Cliffs, NJ: Prentice-Hall, pp. 616–652.

Van Kammen, & Murphy, O. (1978), Prediction of imipramine antidepressant response by a one day amphetamine trial. *Amer. J. Psychiat.*, 135:1179–1184.

Walk, O. (1967), Suicide and community care. *Brit. J. Psychiat.*, 113/505:1381–1391.

Wells, C.E. (1982), Refinements in the diagnosis of dementia. *Amer. J. Psychiat.*, 139:621–622.

Yap, P.M. (1963), Aging and mental health in Hong Kong. In: *Process of Aging*, Vol. 2, ed. R.H. Williams. New York: Atherton Press.

Zung, W.K. (1980), Affective disorders. In: *Handbook of Geriatric Psychiatry*, ed., E.W. Busse & D.G. Blazer. New York: Van Nostrand Reinhold.

14

Women and Suicide

Alexandra G. Kaplan, Ph.D.
Rona B. Klein, M.D.

Our own clinical experiences and those of our colleagues have indicated that a thorough understanding of the psychodynamic and social factors operating in a suicidal woman can be gained only by understanding women's relational core self-structure and by delineating the interpersonal conditions that either foster or impede women's relational mode of development. Such an endeavor seems an essential step toward gaining an understanding of why women kill themselves so much less frequently than do men, or of what differentiates those women patients who do choose to kill themselves from those who, for example, may be depressed, but choose to live.

In this chapter, we will apply new conceptions of women's relational mode of development, as viewed by the Stone Center at Wellesley College, to begin to clarify these important issues in the psychodynamics of suicide in women. Our discussion will differentiate typical suicide attempters who "in the majority of cases . . . are moving toward others in the course of the act" from suicide completers and those serious suicide attempters who instead are withdrawing from relational connections (Pokorny, 1965, p. 490).

In addition, we will examine key intrapsychic and interpersonal factors that appear to be characteristic for those women who successfully complete suicide, as well as those women who make unsuccessful attempts that, however, reflect predominant, clear intentions to die. Indeed, those women who do survive serious suicidal action, often as a result of medical technology, present valuable opportunities for learning about the psychology of suicide, especially when the path of inquiry lies within a framework that seeks to answer the question as to: "What is it that gives meaning to women's lives?" or, alternatively, "what is the nature of the female self?"

A RELATIONAL PATH OF DEVELOPMENT

In this exploration, the choice of a particular developmental model, or framework is central. All the major developmental theories (e.g., Freud, Sullivan, Erikson) contain notions of women's development. Yet, as Miller (1984) has pointed out, these theories were implicitly or explicitly written with men in mind. As a result, not surprisingly, women do not fit, and are commonly found to be deficient. Either they lack something they should have, such as a fully developed superego or an identity before marriage, or they have something they shouldn't have, such as neediness or overly enmeshed relationships. Within these phallocentric frameworks, women's strengths and the positive, growth-enhancing aspects of their developmental trajectories remain obscure. For this reason, researchers at the Stone Center (Jordan, 1984; Kaplan, 1984; Miller, 1984, 1986; Stiver, 1985; and Surrey, 1985) have begun to evolve a model of women's psychological development that derives from women's own experience, and does not build on a deficit mode. In essence, this model posits a continuous path of relational development that begins in infancy and evolves in complexity, strength, nuance, and meaning throughout life. Rather than seeing maturity as equated with increasing levels of separation, the Stone Center researchers posit that growth is fostered by action-in-relationship.

As compared to other theories that identify the growth-enhancing aspects of relationships as need-gratification, provision of supplies, or mirroring of the self, the Stone Center model stresses the growth-enhancing quality of relationship as that of a synergystic process. In this model, all participants can be enhanced as they participate in the creation of an evolving mutual connection. Each member is both reaching out and being reached, understanding and feeling understood. While members of both sexes can and do engage in such an exchange, our society especially supports this model for women.

THE FEMALE SENSE OF SELF AND MORAL ISSUES IN SUICIDE

The Stone Center model of women's relational self-development leads us to a revised conception of the actual nature of the self in women. Unlike theories that imply that a woman's most fundamental wish and need is to be passively loved and taken care of (Deutsch, 1944), the relational view of development clarifies that what gives meaning and value to a woman's sense of self is to be actively engaged in relationships characterized by a mutuality of care and of relational responsibility. It is through active participation in a relational connection that is mutually grounded and empathically based that a woman's core self-structure becomes articulated. This growth, in turn, fosters increased self-esteem, enhanced capacities for action and empowerment, and the wish for further connection (Miller, 1986).

This mode of growth leads to a sense of self that has been defined by Miller (1984) as an "interacting sense of self." From the earliest moments of life, beginning with the dynamic of the early parent–child relationship, the girl develops internal relational images of a "self which is in active interchange with other selves" (Miller, 1984, p. 2).

Early identifications with the mother's caretaking activities, that is, with the mother as one who tunes in and responds empathically to her infant's emotional core, become integrated into the very core of the young girl's interacting self-structure. This aspect of female self-development and its divergence from male development has been evocatively described by Miller: "The beginning of mental representations of the self, then, is of a self whose core—which is emotional—is attended to by the other(s); and who begins to attend to the emotions of the other(s). Part of this internal image of oneself includes feeling the other's emotions and acting on the emotions coming from the other as they are in interplay with one's own emotions" (Miller, 1984, p. 4). Miller goes on to note that this "interacting sense of self" is present initially for both sexes. However, infants are immediately subject to powerful cultural norms that tend to reinforce relational development in girls to a greater extent than in boys.

Within this developmental framework, the nature of the female sense of self must be viewed as part of a larger relational whole. This vision contrasts markedly with traditional definitions of the self as derived from the study of men as the model. Kohut, for example, discussed the nature of the self as "a center of productive initiative—the exhilarating experience that I am producing the work, that I have produced it" (1977, p. 18). For women, however, it is not the quality of "productive initiative," nor the quality of a separate "I" apart from others that is central to the sense of self. Rather, what is central is a sense of an "I" that includes an inner perception of the self as part of an emotional process with attention to that process and to a mutuality of relational exchange.

Women come to experience a sense of aliveness, of empowerment, and of zest in a context of ongoing mutual relationships to the extent that their circumstances allow them to develop, express, and experience an interacting sense of self. Indeed, what women live for, what keeps them alive, are the opportunities to experience themselves in this way. Conversely, when a woman's relational priorities and needs are so blocked or distorted that she perceives no further possibilities for growth within relationships her vulnerability to suicide will be great.

Because they experience action-in-relationship as their primary source of growth, women will take major steps to avoid breaking a connection. This involves taking responsibility for the relationship, including responsibility for relational difficulties (Miller, 1984). Fairbairn and Winnicott have said that people are "object seeking"; we would say that women are "seeking a relational process." It follows from this particular developmental perspective that women will act so as to preserve a relationship, not because of dependency on the other or inadequacy in other realms, but because connection provides them with the fullest context for their own active participation in a growth enhancing situation.

This dynamic of women striving to maintain connection even in psychologically damaging situations has been noted in the histories of depressed women (Kaplan, 1984), in battered women (Kaplan, 1988), and in women with eating disorders (Surrey, 1984). We propose that much of women's suicidal behavior can also be understood in this perspective. Suicidal action, then becomes a mode by which the patient is making a desperate plea for mutual engagement in which she can make herself known to others, and others will respond so as to make their feelings known to her. The level of extremity of the action may reflect, in part, the extent of the difficulty in creating this process. The relational context in which suicidal action occurs (i.e., the patient's experience of her own actions-in-relationship and of the other's reactions to her) are central aspects of suicidal behavior for women, both as precipitants and as aspects of the suicidal behavior itself.

The key to understanding the psychological experience of suicidal women is to acknowledge that, for a woman, a decision to kill herself and to therefore abandon and destroy all relatedness (Maltsberger and Buie, 1974) stands in direct opposition to the values most central to her core identity as a relational being. Gilligan's (1982) findings regarding gender and moral development demonstrate that the sense of self in women is closely tied to a sense of morality based on principles of interdependence, mutuality of caretaking, and responsibility for the well-being of others. Women experience and define themselves in terms of a moral imperative to avoid hurting others and to take responsibility for maintaining the continuity of relationships. Thus, the nature of women's most basic ethics, needs, and aims would tend to direct them away from the choice of ending their lives.

Gilligan found that for men, on the other hand, the sense of self is generally connected to a "morality of rights." When faced with ethical dilemmas, men tend to base the choices they make upon universal principles and rules of fairness that are construed apart from and above any relational context (Gilligan, 1982).

These gender distinctions in concepts of self and morality can influence the thought and behavior of suicidal patients. For example, in our own clinical work with seriously suicidal individuals, we have observed that a suicidal man is more likely than a suicidal woman to be highly invested in an intellectualized belief in his fundamental right to kill himself. This kind of patient is usually very insistent on the fairness and logic of his own position and the unfairness of any plans on the therapist's part to interfere with the patient's freedom to choose to kill himself. A case example illustrating this view follows.

Case Example 1

A depressed young professional who was struggling with feelings of failure, shame, and humiliation, revealed in the course of therapy that he had a suicide plan which was clearly a very serious one. When the therapist enquired about the patient's thoughts of how his parents or girl friend might react if he killed himself, the patient replied: "I really don't care. Their response has no bearing on my right to do as I please with my life." Further discussion with the patient revealed that he truly could not imagine or empathize with how his friends or family would feel if he were to commit suicide.

This lack of empathy with the probable impact of suicide on others is, in our experience, not typically found in suicidal women. Instead, a suicidal woman will usually express a vivid awareness and deep concern for how other people might be affected by her suicide. For example, an adolescent who survived a serious suicide attempt expressed in her journal her dread of the pain that her death would cause others: "I hate receiving pain, and giving it to someone else is just as painful for me" (Mack and Hickler, 1982, p. 126). We agree with Mack and Hickler's interpretation that "Perhaps this conflict, her ability to imagine and to identify with the pain of others who loved her, acted as a restraining force in Andrea's case and contributed to the failure of her attempt to kill herself" (Mack and Hickler, 1982, p. 126). Moreover, we would argue that this conflict, rooted in the nature of female morality and the relational sense of self, is experienced by most suicidal women.

Clinical observations indicate that the psychological experience of a seriously suicidal woman often includes feeling torn by an anguished struggle between a sense of responsibility to herself—to alleviate her own unbearable pain—and her sense of responsibility to avoid hurting those who would be affected by her death. Any interaction or experience that tips the scales of this conflict one way or the other can move a woman away from or toward the act of suicide. This dynamic is one that, when recognized and respected within the treatment situation, can be crucial in getting beyond a suicidal crisis. The motivation not to abandon those who need her or who would suffer by her death can form the basis of a strong therapeutic alliance aimed at preserving the patient's life.

Case Example 2

A 36-year-old depressed woman, Anne, was brought by her college's counseling service for evaluation. Anne was a divorced, single mother who had recently moved to the area and had no close friends or family available to her. Although initially silent and withdrawn, Anne eventually responded to direct questions about suicide by admitting that she did have a definite plan, along with the means of executing it. Anne said that she had not acted on her plan because she had not yet determined what arrangements she would make for the care of the five-year-old son she would leave behind. Anne had no prior history of suicide attempts, but she did have a history of hospitalization for major depression, and she had recently noticed herself again getting very depressed. Anne stressed that she could not go through "that kind of pain and torture again" that she "would rather be dead." The evaluting clinician found Anne to be at great risk and in need of hospitalization. At first, because of Anne's unwillingness to go to a hospital, it seemed that Anne would have to be committed to a closed ward, an experience that might have further lowered this patient's already low self-esteem. However, a strategy was evolved of helping Anne to verbalize and more fully appreciate not

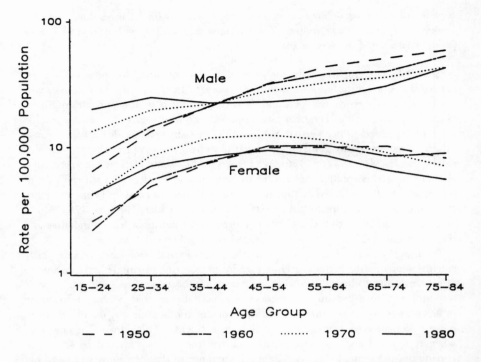

Figure 14.1 U.S. suicide rates by age group and sex for selected years. *Source:* Centers for Disease Control, *Suicide Surveillance*, 1970 to 1980, April 1985, Figure 3, p. 25.

only her own unbearable pain, but also the strength and caring contained in her active concern for the welfare of her son. The resulting sense of affirmation and self-empathy decreased Anne's sense of hopelessness and helplessness sufficiently to enable her to enter the hospital voluntarily. Follow-up information indicates that Anne was able to use her hospitalization to resolve the acute suicidal crisis successfully and to continue working in therapy with a commitment to staying alive.

KEY GENDER-RELATED TRENDS IN SUICIDE STATISTICS

One of the most solidly established areas of factual knowledge concerning suicide is that of the differences found between the sexes in rates and types of suicidal behaviors. For example, it is widely reported that more men commit suicide than women in a ratio of approximately three to one, whereas women make three out of four of the suicide attempts. Women are more likely to ingest pills, while men are more likely to use violent means such as firearms or hanging. Even though the incidence of suicide by gunshot is increasing for both men and women, it is still proportionately higher for men than women. The existence of these gender-related distinctions in the nature of suicidality in women and men strongly suggests that

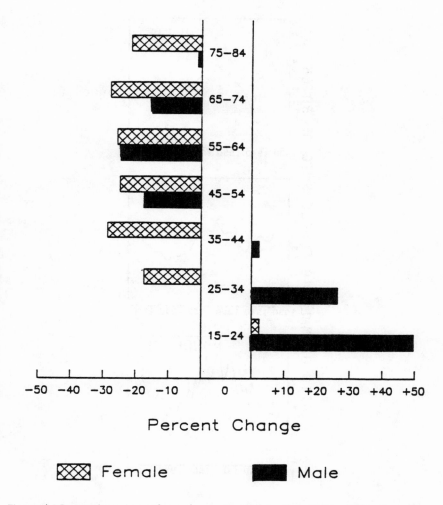

Figure 14.2 Percent change in suicide rates by age group and sex, U.S., 1970 and 1980. *Source:* Centers for Disease Control, *Suicide Surveillance*, 1970–1980, April 1985, Figure 6, p. 28.

gender differences in psychological development must underlie key aspects of suicide.

When examined from the perspective of gender in combination with age, suicide data for the past 30 years reveals several important trends. For example, the pattern of suicide rates by age group has changed differently for men than for women (Figure 14.1). For women, the shape of the age distribution curve for suicide rates was relatively stable between 1950 and 1980, with the highest rates consistently appearing in the forties and fifties, and the lowest rates in the youngest and oldest age groups. In contrast to this, the age group patterns for male suicide have demonstrated a considerable downward shift. In 1950, rates for male suicide were

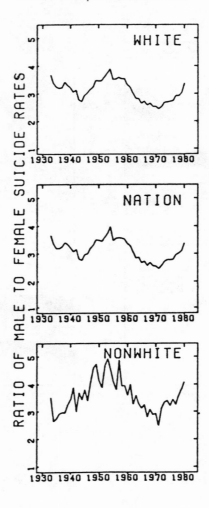

YEARS

Figure 14.3 Ratio of male/female suicide rates, 1933–1980. *Source:* McIntosh and Jewell (1986).

lowest for the youngest ages and increased with each successive age group. By 1980, the increased rates of suicide for men younger than 44, along with the decreased rates for older men, produced a relatively flat curve for all age groups below 65.

The suicide figures for the period 1970 to 1980 also indicate important sex and age differentiated trends, one of the most dramatic being the striking increase in suicide rates for young males under age 35 (see Figure 14.2). Thus, between 1970 and 1980, suicide rates increased by 50 percent for males aged 15 to 24 years and increased almost 30 percent for males aged 25 to 34. During the same decade, female suicide rates increased only slightly for the 15- to 24-year-old age group and decreased by almost 20 percent or more for women in all other age groups. In addition, Petersen and Craighead (1986) have reported an alarming sex differentiated increase (from 1.1 to 1.7 per 100,000) in the rate of completed suicides among 10- to 14-year-old males, while the rate for female completers remained stable.

An important perspective on sex differences in suicide rates can be gained by looking at the ratios of male-to-female annual suicide rates. In a recent study, McIntosh and Jewell (1986) compiled the male-to-female ratios for the years 1933 to 1980. They found that the ratios for both white and nonwhite populations declined from the mid-1950s through 1971, but that from 1971 on the ratios consistently increased (Figure 14.3). The authors note that these fluctuations in male-to-female suicide ratios are based on the fact that, whereas male suicide rates remained relatively stable through the 1950s and 1960s and then increased from 1971 to 1980, female suicide rates increased from the mid-1950s through 1971 and then decreased from 1971 to 1980. As indicated in Table 14.1, the data for 1981 to 1983 continue the trend of increasing suicide rates for males and decreasing suicide rates for women. The experience of the 1950s through the early 1970s of diminishing sex differences in suicide rates led a number of suicide investigators (Shneidman, 1975; Hirsch, 1981; Neuringer, 1982) to erroneously predict that the ratios for suicide would move toward a greater similarity between the sexes, with increasing rates of suicide for women. However, as depicted in Table 14.2, ratios calculated from National Center for Health Statistics data for 1970 to 1983 indicate the opposite;

Table 14.1

Age-Adjusted Suicide Rates by Race, Sex, and Year, United States, 1970–1983

Year	White Male	White Female	White Total	Black and Other Male	Black and Other Female	Black and Other Total	All Races Male	All Races Female	All Races Total	Unadjusted Rate
1970	18.2	7.2	12.4	10.3	3.3	6.5	17.3	6.8	11.8	11.6
1971	18.0	7.4	12.4	10.1	3.8	6.7	17.2	7.0	11.8	11.6
1972	18.4	7.3	12.6	11.8	3.6	7.4	17.8	6.9	12.1	11.9
1973	18.6	7.0	12.5	11.5	3.3	7.1	17.8	6.6	11.9	11.9
1974	18.9	7.0	12.7	11.6	3.2	7.1	18.1	6.6	12.1	12.0
1975	19.6	7.3	13.2	11.9	3.5	7.4	18.8	6.8	12.5	12.6
1976	19.0	7.0	12.7	12.1	3.4	7.4	18.3	6.6	12.1	12.3
1977	20.3	7.1	13.5	12.2	3.6	7.6	19.4	6.7	12.8	13.1
1978	19.0	6.6	12.5	11.9	3.2	7.2	18.2	6.1	11.9	12.3
1979	18.6	6.3	12.2	12.7	3.3	7.7	17.9	5.9	11.7	12.1
1980	18.9	5.7	12.1	11.3	2.8	6.7	18.0	5.4	11.4	11.9
1981	18.9	6.0	12.2	11.2	3.0	6.8	18.0	5.7	11.5	12.0
1982	19.4	5.8	12.4	10.8	2.6	6.4	18.3	5.4	11.6	12.2
1983	19.3	5.6	12.2	10.7	2.6	6.4	18.2	5.2	11.4	12.1

Sources: Centers for Disease Control, *Suicide Surveillance*, 1970–1980, April 1985, Table 3. National Center for Health Statistics, unpublished data.

Table 14.2

Male/Female Suicide Ratios,[a] 1970–1983

Year	White	Black & Others	All races
1970	2.53	3.12	2.54
1971	2.43	2.66	2.46
1972	2.52	3.28	2.58
1973	2.66	3.49	2.7
1974	2.7	3.63	2.74
1975	2.69	3.4	2.76
1976	2.71	3.56	2.77
1977	2.86	3.39	2.9
1978	2.88	3.72	2.98
1979	2.95	3.85	3.03
1980	3.32	4.04	3.33
1981	3.15	3.73	3.16
1982	3.35	4.15	3.39
1983	3.45	4.12	3.5

[a]Computed from age-adjusted suicide rates reported by the National Center for Health Statistics (see Table 14.1).

that is, sex ratios have consistently increased rather than decreased since 1971, reflecting even greater disparity between male and female rates of suicide.

An exception to this pattern is found in age-specific sex ratios. McIntosh and Jewell (1986) point out that decreased male-to-female ratios have occurred for the 45 to 54, 55 to 64, and 64 plus age groups. The authors stress, however, that, even among these groups, the decline in sex ratio is related not to more rapid increases in suicide rates for women over age 45, but to more rapid declines in suicide rates for men over age 45 as compared to the declines found for women over 45.

Thus, contrary to the expectations of many experts in the field, suicide rates for women have not increased to approach those for men. Between 1970 and 1980, the age-adjusted female suicide rate decreased by 20.6 percent, while the rate for men increased by 4.0 percent. Furthermore, the 1970 to 1980 trend of a small increase in suicide rates for women aged 15 to 24 has reversed itself in the years between 1979 and 1983 (Table 14.3), when the rates for 15- to 19-year-old women were stable and rates for 24-year-olds decreased. The highest suicide rates for women occur in white females in their forties and fifties. But even these rates are lower than the suicide rates for men of any age. Suicide attempt statistics are particularly relevant to the topic of suicidal behavior in women. It is estimated that there are at least eight attempts for every completed suicide and that 70 to 80 percent of these attempts are made by women (Farberow and Shneidman, 1961; Weissman, 1974; Tishler, McKery, and Morgan, 1981; Fieldsend and Lowenstein, 1982; Adams, Bouckomo, and Streiner, 1982), most typically by women under the age of 30 (Clayton, 1983). Thus, the frequency of suicide attempts in the female population is much higher than the frequency of completed suicides. The rate of completed suicide is, however,

Table 14.3

Suicide Rates per 100,000 Population, by 5-year Age Groups, 1979–1983

Cause-of-Death Code, Color, Sex, and Year	Total	Under 1 Year	1–4 Years	5–9 Years	10–14 Years	15–19 Years	20–24 Years
Suicide (E950–E959)							
Total, Both Sexes							
1983	12.1	. . .	. . .	0.1	1.1	8.7	14.8
1982	12.2	. . .	. . .	0.0	1.1	8.7	15.1
1981	12.0	. . .	. . .	0.0	0.9	8.7	15.6
1980	11.9	. . .	. . .	0.0	0.8	8.5	16.1
1979	12.1	. . .	. . .	0.0	0.8	8.4	16.4
Total, Male							
1983	19.2	. . .	. . .	0.1	1.6	14.0	24.3
1982	19.2	. . .	. . .	0.0	1.7	14.1	25.1
1981	18.7	. . .	. . .	0.0	1.2	13.6	25.6
1980	18.6	. . .	. . .	0.0	1.2	13.8	26.8
1979	18.6	. . .	. . .	0.0	1.1	13.4	26.5
Total, Female							
1983	5.4	. . .	. . .	0.0	0.6	3.2	5.2
1982	5.6	. . .	. . .	0.0	0.4	3.2	5.1
1981	5.8	. . .	. . .	-	0.5	3.6	5.6
1980	5.5	. . .	. . .	-	0.3	3.0	5.5
1979	6.0	. . .	. . .	-	0.5	3.2	6.3

Source: Excerpted from National Center for Health Statistics, Trend C, Table 292A, January 1985, p. 665.

35 to 100 times higher for those who have made a suicide attempt than for the general population (Clayton, 1983), so that women who have made previous attempts are at high risk.

Many possible questions flow from the consistent statistical differences between male and female suicide completion and suicide attempt rates. For example: (1) Why do more men die by suicide than women? (2) Why are women more vulnerable to suicide attempts than to completed suicide? (3) Given that the incidence of depression is consistently at least twice as high in women than in men (Weissman and Klerman, 1982) and that depressive illness and alcoholism are the diagnoses most frequently associated with suicidal behavior (Robins, 1981; Clayton, 1983; Hirschfeld and Blumenthal, 1986), why is it that the rates of completed and attempted suicide in women are not *higher* than they are? Perhaps the most revealing question to look at, especially in terms of future suicide prevention, is "What keeps women alive?" We believe that to answer these questions, one must explore the meaning of suicidal behavior within the context of women's relational mode of development.

LABOR FORCE PARTICIPATION AND SUICIDE IN WOMEN

In 1978, Stack offered an hypothesis, based on status integration theory (Gibbs and Martin, 1958), in which he predicted that overall rates of suicide in our society would increase in proportion with women's increasing participation in the labor force. Furthermore, Stack asserted that this would be particularly true for married working women who would kill themselves in greater numbers as a result of higher levels of role strain and lower levels of status integration. A study by Davis (1981) reported partial support for Stack's prediction. In this study, female suicide rates were found to follow the hypothesis during the 1960s, when they increased along with the increased rates of female employment. However, in the 1950s, increased rates of female employment were correlated with decreased female suicide rates.

To explain this difference in pattern from one decade to the next, Davis argued that employed women of the 1950s were mainly from lower socioeconomic groups and were in the labor force for a reason deemed acceptable for women of their social stratum, that of economic necessity. He felt that these women did not, therefore, experience the social disintegration that would lead to increased suicide rates. He speculated that by the 1960s the employed women were from more affluent circumstances and working for reasons other than economic need. He asserted that for these women, paid employment did run counter to the social norms for their class and that they did, therefore, experience increased role strain and status disintegration, along with increased suicide rates.

Bourque, Kraus, and Cosand (1983) found that, for women aged 25 to 64 in Sacramento County, California, female suicide rates did increase along with increasing female paid labor through 1969, but that from 1970 to 1979 the rates of completed suicides for 25- to 64-year-old women varied inversely with their rates of employment. This finding led to the conclusion that the higher suicide rate found for the sample of employed women aged 25 to 64 years old during the 1960s was related to an inability on the part of these women to cope with the conflicting demands of wife, mother, and employee, leading to family disruption and thence to suicide. According to these researches, working women in the 1970s experienced greater acceptance of and support for their role in the labor force, producing a decline in those female suicides that result from social disintegration and role strain.

Despite the reported inconsistency in patterns of correlation between female labor force participation and female suicide, there is still considerable speculation in the suicide literature that as women gain greater access to educational, occupational, and economic opportunities, they will inevitably pay a serious price; namely, that of increasing suicide rates.

However, several important bodies of evidence oppose the prediction that women will kill themselves more frequently as they become more fully involved in the world of work. First, one of the most consistent findings in reviews of psychiatric epidemiology is that, for both men and women, the prevalence of mental illness is strongly linked, not with employment, but with conditions of poverty and unemployment (Brenner, 1973; Guttentag, Salasin, and Belle, 1980; Carmen, Russo, and Miller, 1981). In a landmark study of psychosocial factors and depression in women, Brown and Harris (1975) concluded that employment protected women from depression by improving their economic resources, improving self-esteem, and increasing social supports. Further evidence for this is found in Mostow and Newberry's (1975) study, which concluded that women in the labor force were doing and feeling significantly better than those who only worked in the home. These studies indicate that paid employment can be personally enhancing for women and can act as a buffer against other sources of stress.

Second, a number of studies comparing the suicidality of employed versus nonemployed women have demonstrated a protective effect for the employed. Kessler and McRae (1983), for example, compiled suicide attempt data for the period 1940 to 1980 and found a positive correlation between female labor force participation and decreasing female-to-male suicide attempt ratios through the 1960s and 1970s. They stressed an enhancement of women's coping styles as the modus by which increased female employment levels were connected with a decrease in female suicide attempts.

These results are further supported by Cumming and Lazar's (1981) interesting analysis of Canadian suicide rates for five particular years between 1951 and 1971. They found that marriage served a protective function for men, while employment served a protective function for women. The authors believe that women have a "kin-keeper" role in our society and hypothesize that marriage protects men from suicide by enabling them to gain from the network of kinship affiliations maintained by their wives. In regard to women, Cumming and Lazar propose that employed women further expand their own relational networks, thereby decreasing vulnerability to suicide.

The suicide literature clearly contains considerable research data indicating that paid work is generally beneficial to women. Why then does the literature also contain so many predictions that female labor force participation will lead to dire consequences for women? This is a very complicated question about which we can only speculate. One possible factor may be that psychological assumptions about women's behavior are often based on the study of male behavior. Thus, since research has identified the workplace as "the primary stressor for men" (Baruch, 1986. p. 3), as well as a frequent precursor of male suicide (Robins, 1981), it is not surprising that women were expected also to be affected negatively by work.

It is likely that this line of thought has contributed to the unfortunate delay in the field's recognition that women are really far more at risk for a whole range of disorders at home than in the workplace (Gove and Geer, 1977, Gove, 1979; Carmen et al., 1981; Pearlin, Lieberman, Menaghan, and Mullen, 1981). This is underscored by the realization that it is within the institution of marriage that women are "most likely to be slapped and shoved about, severely assaulted, killed or raped" (Carmen et al., 1981, p. 1328). The facts point to a pressing need for the mental health field to at least balance the concern about work stress with a focus on the problem of family violence, an important etiological factor in the suicidality of girls and women (Pfeffer, 1982).

Perhaps another possible element contributing to the overemphasis on work as a risk factor is the one-sided focus on "role strain" that evolved in psychological research without adequate delineation of the important benefits of multiple role involvements and adequate explanation of the vulnerability of groups. What about the vulnerabilities, for example, of women who are single parents, many of whom fall in the age group at greatest risk for female suicide?

In sum, new statistical data and research findings over the past several years show that female employment is correlated with decreased female vulnerability to suicide. The field seems to be gradually moving from thinking of paid work primarily as a risk factor to considering the ways in which it enhances and expands women's options. The evidence suggests that increased female labor force participation will not lead to increased suicide among women, but that it may, in fact, contribute to its prevention.

THE MULTIPLE MEANING OF SUICIDE ATTEMPTS

A primary issue in the discussion of suicidality is whether or not self-destructive behavior that is not consciously linked to a wish to die should be classified as a suicide attempt. Birtchnell (1981) and Sifneos (1978) believe that any self-injurious behavior, whether or not intentionally suicidal, should be considered a suicide attempt. By contrast, Simpson (1976) argues that the failure to differentiate between nonsuicidal self-mutilation and genuine suicide attempts results in inaccurate clinical understanding, which, in turn, results in poor clinical treatment.

One of the qualities that stands out is the relatively greater interpersonal embeddedness of women attempters as compared to male completers. The women are deeply connected to others, albeit conflictfully, while the men appear much more isolated. The women seem to be reaching out, the men to be pulling back. This distinction may be a function not so much of the differences between attempters and completers, but more basically between qualities that differentiate men and women.

Arieti and Bemporad (1978) identify a similar distinction between injury to the self and injury to aspects of relational connection in descriptions of common patterns of the depressive personality in men and women. In the personality pattern identified by the authors as being primarily found in depressed women, "the necessity to please others and to act in accordance with their expectations makes him [sic] unable to get really in touch with himself. He does not listen to his own wishes; he does not know what it means to be himself. When he experiences feelings of unhappiness, futility, and unfulfillment, he tends to believe that he is to be blamed for them" (p. 139). This is essentially a description of an individual who has subordinated her own wishes and impulses so as to facilitate connection through pleasing others. By contrast, their description of the depressive dynamics more typical of men does not contain this motive. Rather the male pattern is pursuit of an omnipresent achievement-oriented goal, which then becomes the means by which love is sought.

Evidence for women's suicide attempts being embedded within relational disappointment or disruption runs consistently through the literature. Many authors cite relational loss, rupture, or conflict as the most common immediate precipitant (Weissman, 1974; Sifneos, 1978; Stephens, 1985). Cassem (1978) points out that for inpatients, a relational rupture on the ward is the most reliable sign of impending suicide attempts. Simpson (1976) noted that suicide attempts are often precipitated by threat of loss, abandonment, or a relational impasse. Birtchnell (1981) concluded that quarreling and hostility in current marital relationships were the predominant characteristics distinguishing depressed suicide attempters.

While interpersonal stress as a factor in women's suicide attempts is relatively well documented and commonly recognized, the dynamic portrayals of underlying motives for the attempts are not as widely agreed upon. One common dynamic configuration of women attempters focuses on wishes for control and/or manipulation of a relationship so as to get needs met. There is an assumption of inappropriate neediness on the part of the receiver, and the use of undue power and coercion to get these needs met. However, within the Stone Center view of relationship as a synergystic process, a different dynamic emerges. In this view, the emphasis is not on what one receives from another, but rather on action-in-relationship as an avenue for growth. If the relationship is grounded in mutual empathy, then everyone gains from their participation, regardless of whoever may be labeled the "needy" one. However, we would speculate that women attempters are seeking connection with others in a context that is neither mutual nor empathic. Their behavior is often experienced as controlling by those who, for their own reasons, need to resist it. In fact, women attempters may indeed become controlling as their attempts to reach out consistently fail. Control, however, is not a primary motive, but a more desperate attempt to make and maintain reciprocal contact.

Suicide attempters cannot act on their wish to seek connection and understanding directly, in part because their low self-esteem creates a barrier to constructive action, and in part because past attempts at some form of contact have undoubtedly not been responded to. Instead, they use the more indirect method of a suicide attempt. This distinction between control as an end in itself and as a means to connection is central. With the former formulation (control as an end in itself), the therapist would be likely to stress the negative, more destructive implications, while minimizing the more affirming underlying wish. The patient's worst fears about her destructiveness and incompetence would thus be reinforced, her self-esteem decreased, and her capacities for more effective communication inhibited. By contrast, the therapist who sees control as a means of connection would promote the patient's valuing of her own relational capabilities (although not necessarily their mode of expression) and hence support a stronger sense of self.

Stiver (1985) provides a clear portrayal of "manipulation" as a search for connection. She sees psychiatric descriptions of women patients, such as the ones reflecting manipulation and control, as indications of the fact that

. . . women's efforts to be heard and truly listened to are often experienced as intensely frustrating when the other person seems emotionally impervious. The result for women is often an escalation of intense feelings with increased loss of focus and defusion of intense affective expression. There is a tendency for women to present a kind of self which often feels unreal. This presentation may take the form of an exaggerated expression of affect in order to be heard and attended to [p. 11].

What Stiver is implying is that not only do suicide attempts emerge out of interpersonal conflict, but also the behavior of the attempter needs to be interpreted in terms of *relational process* rather than strictly in terms of intrapsychic dynamics. Such labels as "manipulating" and "controlling" may reflect more the way the receiver feels than the more realistic nature of the behavior. Because of her sense of helplessness, the female attempter may have to take such extreme measures as a suicide attempt in order to feel heard and maintain connection.

SUICIDE ATTEMPTERS AND SELF-MUTILATORS

Although there is some dispute in the literature as to whether self-mutilators are a subcategory of suicide attempters or a group unto themselves, certain apparent differences between the two groups make their separate consideration reasonable.

Statistics on the sex ratios of self-mutilators (the majority of whom are wrist-cutters) vary widely, partly because many incidents are not reported, and partly because the ratios seem to depend on the specific population studied. The composite picture of a wrist-cutter, according to Simpson, is that of a 16- to 24-year-old woman with a history of school problems and difficulties with the police. Many talk of "hating their own bodies and feeling forced into their fantasies and the acts of mutilation" (Simpson, 1976, p. 290). Many are substance abusers and either very sexually active or deny sexual experience.

According to Simpson's excellent review, many cutters have a history of inadequate parenting. Many researchers and clinicians more specifically identify the mother–daughter relationship as a major causal factor in cutting behavior. Again, as summarized by Simpson (1976), Waldenberg notes that they came from "cold, distant mothers," with a "strident history of maternal deprivation."

In general the literature describes a history of seriously disturbed early family relations and emotional deprivation, with more specific portrayals of domineering mothers and distant fathers (especially in the clinical, as compared to the research literature). In some ways, this portrayal is not distinctly different from the historical accounts of women with a whole range of psychopathology. However, it masks etiological factors. For example, there is a growing awareness in the psychiatric literature of the frequency of physical and sexual abuse in families in general and in the history of psychiatric inpatients in particular. As summarized by Simpson (1976), Grunebaum and Klerman (1967) point out that in many cases cutters had fathers who were "seductive and unable to set limits, intermittently indulgent, often inadequate at his occupation, and frequently alcoholic" (p. 528), and that the most "striking features of parental behavior are the open display of sexuality and aggression" (p. 528).

Recent studies of the incidence of childhood physical and sexual assault among inpatients indicate that the numbers are far higher than previously assumed, and that an abuse history should be considered within a range of diagnostic categories. B. Brooks (unpublished) found that 75 percent of the borderline patients with whom she had been working in an inpatient setting had a history of incestuous involvement.

These data suggest the importance of asking about abuse in any inpatient situation, and especially with women patients. In particular, one is likely to find evidence of self-mutilation among a population of sexually abused women. Conversely, Simpson (1976) has noted that, in his study of self-destructive women, many revealed the hatred of their bodies, sexual confusion, antisocial problems, and a history of substance abuse that is often found in abused women. A link between sexual abuse and self-mutilation is not surprising, especially in view of the Stone Center's recognition (Miller, 1986), that women take responsibility for the quality of a relationship and tend to blame themselves (or accept the blame that others put on them) for relational difficulties.

RELATIONAL DEVELOPMENT AND THE DYNAMICS OF SUICIDE IN WOMEN

Psychodynamic thinking about suicide has, in recent years, been characterized by the increasing recognition of the complex and multidetermined nature of the suicidal act (Havens, 1965; Shneidman, 1975; Warren, 1976). Warren, for example, has described suicide as "dependent upon many ego functions and capacities, especially in reality testing and object relations, superego pressures, and, often, on the social matrix of the person at the time of intense suicidal drive manifestations" (Warren, 1976, p. 202), while Mack (see chapter 12), has delineated a systems approach to understanding suicide potential in adolescents that takes into account the influence of world and community trends, family influences, biological factors, personality organization, and early developmental experiences. These perspectives broaden the traditional psychoanalytic view, which for many years narrowly focused on the role of aggressive components in suicide.

A further addition to the psychodynamic understanding of suicide has been the evolution of object relations theory and self psychology, which provide a useful basis for thinking about the developmental roots of suicide. Several authors have postulated that the act of suicide is a phenomenon of disturbed introjective development with subsequent distortions or deficiencies in the inner representational world. Meissner (1977), for example, postulated that it is the formation of a false self organized around a central victim introject that "forms the basic root and underlying motivation of the suicidal tendency" (p. 438). Buie and Maltsberger (1983), in their contributions toward understanding suicidal patients, stress failures in the development of sufficient internal resources for self-soothing along with "developmental failures specifically in the phase of separation" from the caretaking parent (Maltsberger and Buie, 1980, p. 70).

These formulations have been useful in pointing out that defects in the developing sense of self and in the associated development of the inner representational world can be etiologically related to the adult's later vulnerability to suicide. However, the extent to which these notions can describe the actual experiences of suicidal women is limited by the fact that they are derived from conceptions of the self that equate maturity with sequentially increasing levels of separation and disconnection from family bonds. As we described earlier in this chapter, self-development for a woman follows a different path, one marked by a continuity of affective connection and an expansion of the woman's inner sense of her capacities to understand and to be understood within progressively complex relations (Miller, 1984).

This relational mode of growth involves an evolution of mental images of the self and of others. These psychological representations cannot, however, be accurately thought of as the discrete, static, unidimensional self and object images described by current separation–individuation based theories. Instead, we would argue that what must develop are images of the self in dynamic interaction with others, and images of others that likewise include images of the dynamic interaction between people. Thus, the development of a woman's inner psychological world involves a process of maturation of interacting relational images of self and others in increasingly complex configurations, rather than a process of increasing separation.

Current object relational models of suicide fail to take into account this development of the relational sense of self in women. We believe, however, that the Stone Center conception of women's more relational and empathic lines of development provides an essential context for understanding the psychodynamic forces at play in a seriously suicidal woman and moves us closer to being able to answer the question raised earlier: What keeps women alive?

In considering the psychodynamics of suicidal women at this point, we will be drawing from our own clinical work with female patients who have fortuitously survived serious suicide attempts or have grappled with strong intentions to die. These women, who may be viewed as "failures to complete suicide" (Robins, 1981, p. 421), represent a different group than the suicide attempters discussed earlier.

Internalized Interactive Experience and Predisposition to Suicide

Given that there are complex forces within the very core of the female sense of self that mitigate against suicide as a viable choice, we need to address the question: What then are the psychological forces that act within those women who do kill themselves? Our hypothesis is that what compels these women is a "reality conclusion" (Shein and Stone, 1969) that there is and will be no hope for them of engaging with others in this life in the sort of relational exchange that women need to obtain a sense of meaning and authenticity. Such a perception of personal reality is then accompanied by intolerable feelings of annihilatory aloneness or isolation, and an overwhelming sense of self-hate, the painfulness of which further tips the scales toward death.

The statements made by a patient, Laura, during an acute suicidal crisis capture the issues involved. Her suicidality had been precipitated by a growing conviction that she would never be able to express her innermost passions and values in a way that would allow others to truly know her:

"I am alone, so alone, like falling into an endless blackness. I can't find the words—no words are big enough to express the intensity of my life—so no one will ever be able to understand and I'll be alone forever. All they will be able to see is a dirty, repulsive little girl. It's too much to bear, like a sentence. I feel trapped inside a dead gray skin. It's like a walking death anyway!"

These themes of relational disconnection, intense aloneness, and seriously disturbed self-esteem have been consistently present in most psychodynamic interpretations of suicide. However, when development is defined, as it is here, as a dynamic, relational process—as opposed to a process occurring within a discrete, bounded self—states of aloneness and negative self-esteem and of connection or disconnection take on different nuances. For example, in evaluating these psychological states in a suicidal woman, our attention will shift from assessing the extent to which she has achieved separation to considering the extent to which her relational history and current interpersonal situation fosters an inner sense of meaningful connection.

Aloneness and negative self-esteem are discussed in the current suicide literature in terms of deprivation of "internal introjective resources" (and of "external human resources") for the comfort and sustenance of the self (Buie and Maltsberger, 1983). Thus, the emphasis has been on failure of the self to be ministered to by others. However, within a relational model of development, aloneness and low self-esteem imply deprivation of opportunities to feel affirmed as a person who responds effectively to the emotional state of the other and who is responded to in a reciprocal manner.

The life experiences of those suicidal women we have studied clinically, as well as those discussed in the literature (Hurry, 1977; Mack and Hickler, 1982; Bosworth, 1984), indicate that the internalization of earlier disturbances in parent–child relatedness can set the stage for later vulnerability to suicidal states of aloneness, particularly when they are reinforced by subsequent relational experiences. These disturbances are internalized over time and incorporated into the structure of the core self and reflected in the girl's, and later the woman's, disturbed sense of self and self-regard. A woman who has been affected in this way and who, therefore, has been able to internalize only fleeting images of herself in competent interaction with others may then become seriously suicidal in the context of later disaffirming relationships.

This was played out in the circumstances of Penny, an adolescent woman who began therapy shortly after recovery from a dangerous overdose.

Case Example 3

The suicide attempt had been precipitated by Penny's failure to establish with her boyfriend a relationship in which she could feel needed and respected for her capacity to be giving. She was the youngest child of somewhat older parents who, in general, tended to relate to others in a distant and unemotional style and who, for various reasons, had little emotional energy to give to this particular daughter, whom they experienced as "overly sensitive" and "difficult to understand." Penny experienced the emotional void between herself and her parents as proof of her lack of worth and inability to be of interest to anyone. At parochial school, where her teachers misinterpreted Penny's dyslexia as laziness and negative behavior, she was treated with hostility and disdain. From these childhood interactions she internalized an image of herself as "bad and clumsy" and "undeserving." Her early sense of herself as defective and worthless was expressed in her secret childhood belief that she was adopted, as well as by her plaintive protestation "too 'spensive" that began at age four and became for her a kind of relational theme.

Recent research findings from a study by Tronick and Gianino (1986) lend support to the notion that understanding a woman's early interactive experience and associated internalizations will contribute to understanding her predisposition to choose to withdraw from relational pain through death. Based on their detailed observations of interactive mother–infant pairs, Tronick and Gianino conclude that the critical process in early development is that of "interactive mutual regulation," described as a process of coping with and repairing the many mismatches in behavioral and psychological states that normally occur over the course of daily life between any infant and its interactive partner. In addition, the authors identify and describe the particular coping behaviors found to be available in infancy. These range from higher level strategies, such as signaling, which are aimed at preserving social engagement through the repair of mismatch, to less integrated strategies increasingly aimed at social disengagement and self-regulation, such as withdrawal or averting.

This study demonstrated that the kind of behavior an infant uses to cope with the "interactive stress" of a mismatch is related to the infant's usual degree of success or failure in repairing mismatches. Thus, the repeated experience of successful matching seems to encourage the development of higher level, socially aimed coping strategies, while repeated lack of success encourages reliance on a mechanism aimed at withdrawal from social connection. Furthermore, it was noted that the particular pattern of interactive coping used by an infant begins to stabilize at around six months of age.

Tronick and Gianino postulate that psychopathology may develop as an "outcome of repeated unsuccessful efforts to repair mismatches" (1986, p. 5). They explain that when an infant's attempts to change mismatches into matches are repeatedly met by failure, the infant feels helpless, and in order to control its own sense of helplessness, begins to focus on coping behaviors aimed at self-regulation. Over time, this infant then "internalizes a pattern of coping that limits engagement with social environment and establishes a negative affective core" (p. 2). The authors note that when this infant utilizes these coping behaviors in potentially normal interactions they distort those interactions as well, "leading to a cycle that may eventually become pathological" (p. 2).

The data and conclusions from this study are significant for our discussion in that they suggest that women (and possibly men as well) who decide to end their lives are individuals who have had the developmental experience of chronic mismatches in their early social interactions, leading them to learn to rely on the less integrated coping behaviors, which sacrifice human connection for the regulation of the self. This formulation is further supported by an additional finding from Tronick and Gianino's study. Their observations of mother–infant pairs at six months and nine months showed that "mother/daughter pairs were much more likely to be in match states than were mother/son pairs" (p. 6). Based on this finding, one can predict that females would be more likely than males to internalize coping patterns aimed at maintaining interaction with others. This would be consistent with the reality that women are less likely to choose to kill themselves than men and more likely to engage in desperate attempts to form or to restore connections. The question of when a history of repeated mismatches predisposes to suicide versus when it predisposes to other forms of pathology is also pertinent and in need of further study.

TREATMENT ISSUES

Our developmental emphasis on action-in-relationship as a major contributor to self-esteem and empowerment can be used to suggest ways that therapy can bolster patients' positive sense of their capacity for relational action, and hence their capacity for growth.

The first consideration concerns the nature of the therapy process, and specifically the nature of the therapist–patient relationship. We agree fully with Havens (1965) and others that the first priority in working with a suicidal patient is to form a relationship. The questions then emerge: What does a therapy-enhancing relationship consist of? How does the relationship work to facilitate growth in therapy?

It is generally agreed that the patient–therapist relationship with a potentially suicidal patient has three primary functions: (1) to serve as a reliable vehicle for monitoring suicidality and reaching contractual agreements; (2) to create a supportive, life-affirming patient–therapist connection; and (3) to foster the patient's connection to a sustaining social support system. Comparing these three primary functions, one notes that much more is discussed about the former than the latter two. The recognition that reflection and interpretation were not sufficient with suicidal patients led quickly to careful discussion and some debate on ways to assess suicidality.

For example, Havens (1965) sees empathy as a primary vehicle in assessing suicide potential, while Buie and Maltsberger (1983) argue against empathy as a form of assessing suicidality and caution clinicians that "the mental status exam and empathic judgments are untrustworthy guides of a patient's suicidality especially if they suggest that a patient is safe from suicide" (p. 16). They have found that many suicidal patients hide their suicidal intent to such an extent that the therapist cannot empathically perceive it.

While the above authors all stress the life-sustaining aspect of an empathic relationship with a patient, we focus more specifically on the fact that women grow in a relational context characterized by mutual empathy. While the therapy situation will never be mutual in the form possible between peers, therapy can be used to help the patient appreciate her role in enhancing the work; that is, the mutuality of the patient and therapist's commitment to the process of change. At a more subtle level, there can also be mutuality of gain, not equivalent gain but ways in which both participants have grown through their shared experience.

Admittedly, it may challenge credibility at times to find ways to identify mutuality of effort with a patient who may be angry, stubborn, rebellious, and risking her own life and the therapist's peace of mind. It is the responsibility of the therapist, however, to recognize and share with her the ways in which the patient is also acting to further the work. Even if these communications are expressed via "acting out" or forms of "resistance," their *message* can be of crucial dynamic importance to the therapist, and the patient needs to know that. Thus, at the same time that the therapist might need to set limits or contract around suicidal behavior, she can also share with the patient the value of the patient's contribution. This then invites the patient to work more collaboratively, perhaps with an empathic attunement to the therapist's position, and greater empathy (Jordan, 1984) for her own dilemma. It is therefore extremely important, as Simpson (1976) warns, not to use such labels as "manipulative" or "resistant" in characterizing self-destructive or suicidal patients. This can prompt a worsening of self-esteem and an augmentation of the patient's sense of her own destructiveness.

One additional factor in working with self-destructive and suicidal women is the exploration of possible physical or sexual abuse. It is now acknowledged that questions along these lines should be a regular part of history taking. If a history of abuse emerges, then therapeutic sensitivity is required to respect the patient's reaction, believe her fears, and value her perception, even while working toward change. Too quick a push to challenge the patient's feeling can have damaging results.

In light of our earlier discussion of the psychological consequences of physical or sexual abuse, it is especially important that these patients be taken seriously, and that therapy serve as a place where they can reaffirm their sense of self as a caring and contributing relational being. They, as much as anyone, need to feel their contributions to the therapy process, and their capacity for empathic connection with others.

FUTURE DIRECTIONS

This chapter highlights some of the ways in which men and women differ in their expressions of suicidality. We are suggesting that the impact of these differences is pertinent to research and policy directions that will influence treatment and prevention programs. For women, epidemiological data suggest a specific need to identify factors that will decrease the incidence of suicide attempts and more generally to study and make more accessible those conditions that are most likely to decrease risk of completed suicide.

Among etiological factors that put women at risk for suicide attempts and self-destructive behavior, the topic of physical and sexual abuse in childhood is prominent. At the levels of research, policy, treatment, and prevention, attention first needs to be paid to the multiple levels contained in the psychodynamic link between early abuse and later self-abuse. This will in turn provide guidelines for steps that could contribute to decreasing the incidence of early abuse, better identifying those women with an abuse history, and working clinically with them toward healing. Our work suggests that the theme of women's relational core self-structure will be central in conceptualizing the transformation of earlier experiences of abuse into later self-destructive behaviors.

Therapists can gain from understanding the particular aberrations in relational self-structure that are likely to evolve in women who have been abused or who have been subjected to repeated experiences of relational disconfirmation. While knowledge in this area is sketchy to date, clinical evidence suggests that abused women see themselves as active agents in destroying relationships, blame themselves for participating in socially unacceptable behavior, and feel undeserving of mutually caring connection.

The therapist–patient relationship can thus become a central forum for redressing some of these distortions. Following the Stone Center model of relational growth in women, it would be important that therapists identify and support the growth enhancing aspects of women's steps toward action-in-relationship, while separating those steps from an assumption that they are primarily responsible for relational problems that ensue. Therapists can further demonstrate the patient's essential relational worthiness by establishing a relationship built on empathic understanding, including the possibilities for the patient to contribute empathically to the clinical process.

Preventive efforts could focus on decreasing those conditions that provide increased suicidal risk for adult women. Epidemiological findings suggest that women are at great risk who are unemployed, poor, and feel disconnected from others. Again, steps to redress these factors are complex and reach into the very heart of the present-day social structure. While major policy changes, such as national implementation of a comparable wage structure are probably steps of the distant future, researchers and clinicians can further their understanding of the relationship between poverty, disempowerment, and suicidality. Work in this area should especially focus on conditions affecting middle-aged women, those most at risk for suicide. Surprisingly, despite the vulnerability of this population, little attention has been paid to understanding the conditions that can aggravate or alleviate their high-risk status. Again, using the Stone Center model, the key concept remains connection, or more specifically empowerment through connection. It is central, whether in the therapy hour, at home, or in the workplace, to feel that there are those with whom you can share and by whom you feel understood, whose own needs incorporate, build on, and enhance your needs. Such mutuality of affect and effort produces hope, if not change, but hope can then encourage further efforts at growth through connection and less likelihood of the feeling of disconnection which fuels suicidal behavior in women.

REFERENCES

Adams, K., Bouckomo, A., & Streiner, D. (1982), Parental loss and family stability in interrupted suicide. *Arch. Gen. Psychiat.*, 39:September.
Arieti, S., & Bemporad, J. (1978), *Severe and Mild Depression*. New York: Basic Books.
Baruch, G. (1986), Integrating the study of women and gender into research on stress. Wellesley College Center for Research on Women Research Report, Vol. 5. Wellesley College, Wellesley, MA.
Beck, A., Lester, D., & Kovacs, M. (1973), Attempted suicide by males and females. *Psycholog. Rep.*, 33:965–966.
Birtchnell, J. (1981), Some familial and clinical characteristics of female suicidal psychiatric patients. *Brit. J. Psychiat.*, 138:381–390.
——— Alacon, J. (1971), Depression and attempted suicide. *Brit. J. Psychiat.*, 118:289–296.
Bosworth, P. (1984), *Diane Arbus*. New York: Avon Books.
Bourque, L.B., Kraus, J.F., & Cosand, B.J. (1983), Attributes of suicide in females. *Suicide & Life-Threat. Behav.*, 13:123–138.
Brenner, H.M. (1973), *Mental Illness and the Economy*. Cambridge, MA: Harvard University Press.
Brown, G.W., & Harris, T. (1978), *The Social Origins of Depression*. New York: The Free Press.
——— Nibhrolchain, M., & Harris, T. (1975), Social class and psychiatric disturbance among women in an urban population. *Sociol.* 9:225–254.
Buie, E.H., & Maltsberger, J.T. (1983), *The Practical Formulation of Suicide Risk*. Somerville, MA: Firefly Press.
Carmen, E.H., Russo, N.F., & Miller, J.B. (1981), Inequality and women's mental health: An overview. *Amer. J. Psychiat.*, 138:1319–1330.
Cassem, E.T. (1978), Treating the person confronting death. In: *The Harvard Guide to Modern Psychiatry*, ed. A.M. Nicholi. Cambridge, MA: Harvard University Press.
Centers for Disease Control (1985), *Suicide Surveillance, 1970–80*. April. Atlanta, GA: U.S. Department of Health and Human Services.
Clayton, P.J. (1983), Epidemiologic and risk factors in suicide. In: *Psychiatry Update*, Vol. 2, ed. L. Grinspoon. Washington, DC: American Psychiatric Press.

Cumming, E., & Lazar, C. (1981), Kinship structure and suicide: A theoretical link. *Can. Rev. Sociol. & Anthropol.*, 18:271–281.

Davis, R.A. (1981), Female labor force participation: Status integration and suicide, 1950–1969. *Suicide & Life-Threat. Behav.*, 11:111–123.

Deutsch, H.J. (1944), *The Psychology of Women*. New York: Grune & Stratton.

Edinburgh, G.M. (1982), Women and aging. In: *The Woman Patient*, Vol. 2, eds. C. Nadelson & M. Notman. New York: Plenum Press.

Farberow, N.L., & Shneidman, E.S., eds. (1961), *The Cry for Help*. New York: McGraw-Hill.

Fieldsend, R., & Lowenstein. E. (1981), Quarrels, separations and infidelity in the two days preceding self-poisoning episodes. *Brit. J. Med. Psychol.*, 54:349–352.

Gibbs, V.P., & Martin, W.T. (1958), A theory of status integration and its relationship to suicide. *Amer. Sociol. Rev.*, 23:140–147.

Gilligan, C. (1982), *In a Different Voice*. Cambridge, MA: Harvard University Press.

Gove, W.R. (1979), Sex differences in the epidemiology of mental illness: Evidence and explanations. In: *Gender and Disordered Behavior*, eds. E.S. Gomberg & V. Franks. New York: Brunner/Mazel.

———— Geer, K. (1977), The effects of children and employment on the mental health of married men and women. *Soc. Forces*, 56:66–76.

Grunebaum, H. & Klerman, G. (1967), Wrist slashing. *Amer. J. Psychiat.*, 124:4.

Guttentag, M., Salasin, S., & Belle, D. (1980), *The Mental Health of Women*. New York: Academic Press.

Havens, L. (1965), The anatomy of a suicide. *N. Eng. J. Med.*, 272:401–406.

Hirsch, M.F. (1981), *Women and Violence*. New York: Van Nostrand Reinhold.

Hirschfeld, R.M.A., & Blumenthal, S.J. (1986), Personality, life events, and other psychosocial factors in adolescent depression and suicide. In: *Suicide and Depression Among Adolescents and Young Adults*, ed. G.L. Klerman. Washington DC: American Psychiatric Press.

Hurry, A. (1977), My ambition is to be dead. *J. Child Psychother.*, 4:66–83.

Jordan, J. (1984), *Empathy and Self Boundaries*. Stone Center Working Paper Series. Wellesley, MA: The Stone Center, Wellesley College.

Josselson, R. (1973). Psychodynamic aspects of identity formation in college women. *J. Youth & Adol.*, 2:3–51.

Kaplan, A.G. (1984), *The "Self-in-Relation": Implications for Depression in Women*. Stone Center Working Paper Series. Wellesley, MA: The Stone Center; Wellesley College.

———— (1988), How normal is normal development? Some connections between adult development and the roots of abuse and victimization. In: *Abuse Victimization: A Life-Span Perspective*, ed. M.B. Strause. Baltimore, MD: Johns Hopkins University.

Kessler, R.C., & McRae, J.A. (1982), The effect of wives' employment on the mental health of married men and women. *Amer. Sociol. Rev.*, 47:216–227.

———— ———— (1983), Trends in the relationship between sex and attempted suicide. *J. Health & Soc. Behav.*, 24:98–110.

Kohut, H. (1971), *The Analysis of the Self*. New York: International Universities Press.

———— (1977), *The Restoration of the Self*. New York: International Universities Press.

Mack, J.E. (1986), Adolescent suicide: An architectural model. In: *Suicide and Depression Among Adolescents and Young Adults*, ed. G.L. Klerman. Washington, D.C: American Psychiatric Press.

———— Hickler, H. (1982), *Vivienne*. New York: Mentor Books, New American Library.

Maltsberger, J.T., & Buie, D.H. (1974), Countertransference hate in the treatment of suicidal patients. *Arch. Gen. Psychiat.*, 30:625.

———— ———— (1980), The devices of suicide. *Internat. Rev. Psycho-Anal.*, 7:61–72.

McIntosh, J.L., & Jewell, B.L. (1986), Sex difference trends in completed suicide. *Suicide & Life-Threat. Behav.*, 16:16–27.

Meissner, W.W. (1977), Psychoanalytic notes on suicide. *Internat. J. Psychoanal. Psychother.*, 6:415–447.

Miller, J.B. (1984), *The Development of Women's Sense of Self*. Stone Center Working Paper Series. Wellesley, MA: The Stone Center, Wellesley College.

———— (1986), *What Do We Mean by Relationships?* Stone Center Working Paper Series. Wellesley, MA: The Stone Center, Wellesley College.

Mostow, E., & Newberry, P. (1975), Work role and depression in women: A comparison of workers and housewives in treatment. *Amer. J. Orthopsychiat.*, 45:538–548.

National Center for Health Statistics, Unpublished data for 1979–1983. Washington, DC.

Neuringer, C. (1982), Suicidal behavior in women. *Crisis*, 3:41–49.

Ornstein, M.D. (1983), The impact of marital status, age, and employment on female suicide in British Columbia. *Can. Rev. Sociol. & Anthropol.*, 20:96–100.

Pearlin, L.I., Lieberman, M.A., Menaghan, E.G., & Mullen, J.T. (1981), The stress process. *J. Health & Soc. Behav.*, 22:337–356.

Petersen, A.C., & Craighead, W.E. (1986), Emotional and personality development in normal adolescents and young adults. In: *Suicide and Depression Among Adolescents and Young Adults*, ed. G.L. Klerman. Washington DC: American Psychiatric Press.

Pfeffer, C.R. (1982), Childhood and adolescent suicidal behavior with emphasis on girls. In: *The Woman Patient*, Vol. 3, eds. M. Notman & C. Nadelson. New York: Plenum Press, pp. 115–130.

Pokorny, A.D. (1965), On suicide and other forms of deviant behavior/human violence; a comparison of homicide, aggravated assault, suicide and attempted suicide. *J. Crim. Law, Criminal. Police Sci.*, 56:488–497.

Robins, E. (1981), *The Final Months*. New York: Oxford University Press.

Sassen, G. (1980), Success anxiety in women: A constructivist interpretation of its sources and its significance. *Harvard Ed. Rev.*, 50:13–25.

Shein, H.M., & Stone, A.A. (1969), Monitoring and treatment of suicidal potential within the context of psychotherapy. *Comprehen. Psychiat.*, 10:59–70.

Shneidman, E.S. (1975), Psychiatric emergencies. In: *Comprehensive Textbook of Psychiatry*, Vol. 2, eds. A.M. Freedman, H.I. Kaplan, & B.J. Sadock. Baltimore: Williams & Wilkins.

Sifneos, P.E. (1978), Patient management. In: *The Harvard Guide to Modern Psychiatry*, ed. A.M. Nicholi. Cambridge, MA: Harvard University Press.

Simpson, M.A. (1976), Self mutilation and suicide. In: *Suicidology: Contemporary Developments*, ed. E.S. Shneidman. New York: Grune & Stratton.

Stack, S. (1978), A comparative analysis. *Soc. Forces*, 57:644–653.

Stengel, E. (1964), *Suicide and Attempted Suicide*. Baltimore, MD: Penguin.

Stephens, B.J. (1985), Suicidal women and their relationships with husbands, boyfriends, and lovers. *Suicide & Life-Threat. Behav.*, 15:77–90.

Stiver, I.P. (1985), *The Meaning of Care*. Stone Center Working Paper Series. Wellesley, MA: Stone Center, Wellesley College.

Surrey, J. (1984), *The "Self-in-Relation": A Theory of Women's Development*. Stone Center Working Paper Series. Wellesley, MA: Stone Center, Wellesley College.

———— (1985), *Eating patterns as a reflection of women's development*. Stone Center Working Paper Series. Wellesley, MA: The Stone Center, Wellesley College.

Tishler, C.L. McKenry, P.C., & Morgan, K.D. (1981), Adolescent suicide attempts: Some significant factors. *Suicide & Life-Threat. Behav.*, 11:86–92.

Tronick, E.Z., & Gianino, A. (1986), Interactive mismatch and repair: Challenges to the coping infant. *Zero to Three. Bull. Nat. Center Clin. Infant Progr.* 6:1–6.

U.S. Department of Labor, Bureau of Labor Statistics, April, 1983. *Women at Work: A Chartbook*.

Warren, M. (1976), On suicide. *J. Amer. Psychoanal. Assn.*, 24:199–234.

Weissman, M.M. (1974), The epidemiology of suicide attempts. *Arch. Gen. Psychiat.*, 30:737–746.

———— Klerman, G.L. (1982), Depression in women: Epidemiology, explanations, and impact on the family. In: *The Woman Patient*, Vol. 3, ed. M. Notman & C. Nadelson. New York: Plenum Press.

Wilson, M. (1981), Suicidal behavior: Toward an explanation of differences in female and male rates. *Suicide & Life-Threat. Behav.*, 11/3:131–140.

Part **III**

Treatment Context and Considerations

A. Psychodynamic and Psychotherapeutic Strategies and Pitfalls

15

Common Errors in the Management of Suicidal Patients

John T. Maltsberger, M.D.
Dan H. Buie, Jr., M.D.

Suicide once provoked so much guilt and distress in hospital staffs that for many years the clinical facts usually were buried with the patient who died that way. It was simply too painful to subject the data to a critical examination and little appeared in the psychiatric literature reflecting close study of successful suicides.

The increasing interest in suicide of recent years has been accompanied by a more generous capacity to subject these tragic cases to a more critical and impartial analysis. Because of our continuing interest in this subject we have had the good fortune to be invited to discuss five or ten successful suicides or very serious attempts each year for the last ten years in a variety of clinical settings. A close examination of some forty successful suicides at a major clinical center between 1963 and 1968 further prepared the authors to discern a variety of difficulties that are likely to lead to fatal outcomes in suicide cases.

There seem to be seven common errors that contribute to suicidal outcome, and it is our purpose to review them here.

ERRORS ARISING FROM COUNTERTRANSFERENCE

The hate that suicidal patients arouse in psychotherapists and other caretakers, particularly when it remains out of awareness, is very likely to distort clinical judgment and lead to mishaps. We have described elsewhere the role that the different components of countertransference hate (malice and aversion) may play in promoting a suicidal outcome (Maltsberger and Buie, 1974).

Undesirable as malicious acting out against patients may be, it is the aversive component of countertransference hate that is most likely to precipitate suicide attempts. Suicidal patients have a much higher tolerance for sadomasochistic struggling than they have for deprivation of support systems. It is aversive affect that invites rejection. Operating under the sway of active but unconscious countertransference aversion, the psychotherapist may rationalize premature termination of a treatment or otherwise reject his patient.

Consider those cases in which the patient acts out in provocative ways so as to raise the therapist's anxiety to a high level. Some psychotherapists have a very low tolerance for wrist-cutting or sexual acting out, for example. The patient's self-destructive activity may be met after some time goes by with the issuing of an ultimatum: the therapist informs the patient that if such behavior is repeated the therapy will be terminated.

It is a rare patient who will be able to resist the temptation to put his therapist to a test. The issuing of such an ultimatum is usually met in fairly short order with a repetition of the forbidden behavior; if the therapist is true to his word, the patient will be dismissed.

We have encountered one recent example in which such a maneuver resulted in the immediate suicide of a patient whose interaction with the therapist for some time had been a struggle over the matter of who was in control of the patient's body.[1] Because the struggle between the patient and the therapist had for so long been at the center of attention neither had paid very much attention to the dynamic meaning of a scary behavior. In retrospect it seemed that the patient had needed to provoke a rejection from the therapist. Once satisfied that no one really understood or cared he could turn away from other people and destroy himself.

The issuing of ultimatums of this nature in the treatment of very disturbed patients is often a signal that the therapist's sense of helplessness has risen to an intolerable level (Adler, 1972). The demand that the patient control himself arises from the personal discomfort of the therapist and not from a quiet, well-conceived therapeutic design. Making an ultimatum says to the patient that certain parts of his sick self are intolerable and must be suppressed or controlled before they are understood. This is analogous to demanding of a drowning man that he stop struggling before he is towed to shore. Termination in the face of such an ultimatum makes it possible for unconscious countertransference aversion to be expressed and for the responsibility of the treatment's failure to be shifted to the patient.

Acting out of this sort requires selective neglect of specific aspects of the clinical formulation that can point to danger. The isolation of the patient, his lack of social resources, or the danger of earlier profound suicide attempts can all be overlooked in the heat of a struggle for control.

Countertransference malice may then express itself in a half-suppressed sense of righteous indignation; the more lethal wish to reject the patient finds its totally unconscious expression in the termination of treatment.

Similar selective inattention to the formulation in the service of countertrans-

---

[1]Although in this case no developmental data were available, we have observed repeatedly in other suicidal patients that a struggle of this nature frequently repeats a significant part of the childhood of patients who later become suicide prone.

ference acting out is found also in the hospital setting. Here the staff may support each other in minimizing the danger of discharge when the patient involved is tiring and pesty, perhaps not having shown much improvement over a long period of time.

Economic realities of the contemporary psychiatric department make it difficult to keep psychiatric patients in the hospital for a long time. There may be substantial pressures on those responsible for the care of suicidal individuals to abbreviate the hospital stay. The staff, overtaxed by weeks or months of effort on behalf of an annoying but unresponsive patient can easily overlook important aspects of the patient's history and circumstances in the service of labeling him manipulative, uncooperative, or otherwise unsuitable or unmeritorious for continuing investment. This is particularly likely to happen when the patient does not seem depressed or when there has been no suicidal threatening for some time. A fairly unalarming mental state examination can then be used to rationalize a discharge more motivated by hidden aversion than by a realistic evaluation of the patient's ability to sustain himself outside the ward.

ERRORS ARISING FROM THE MISAPPLICATION OF THE MENTAL STATE EXAMINATION

While the mental state examination is a fundamental and valuable tool that may guide the clinician in assessing the danger of suicide, it is insufficient in itself for coming to any definite conclusions. Patients may be seriously suicidal without appearing depressed, and some depressed patients with suicidal ideation may not be in a dangerous condition. Furthermore, certain aspects of the mental state examination may be overlooked which, if carefully scrutinized, will provide significant and serious information about the risk of suicide.

The clinical aphorism that says the depressed patient who is getting better may be especially likely to commit suicide is hoary with age. It is not a helpful adage, however, in making a decision about discharging a patient recovering from a depression. Obviously most people who have been depressed and are getting better are not actively suicidal. Nevertheless, depression sometimes lifts when a patient decides to do away with himself.

Most people who kill themselves are not, of course, clinically depressed. It has been known for years that schizophrenic individuals are suicide vulnerable, and so are other patients who show few if any of the classical marks of depression such as weight loss, retardation of motor activity and speech, sleeplessness, or other vegetative signs.

In some centers the decision to admit or to discharge from the psychiatric department is likely to be based almost entirely on the mental state examination, and when this is the practice, it is inevitable that a certain number of otherwise preventable suicides will take place. It is simply not true that the patient who looks better and talks better is necessarily out of danger for committing suicide.

Whether or not the patient seems depressed is a poor criterion for assessing danger of suicide. Zilboorg, for example, pointed out many years ago that a fair proportion of the individuals who committed suicide are spiteful and angry in emotional attitude, not depressed (Zilboorg, 1936). Other suicides take place when the patient is under the sway of a terrifying delusional system so that the predominating affect in the mental state examination is terror. One of two most profoundly suicidal individuals in our experience was a paranoid schizophrenic man who impaled himself because he felt that death was the only way to escape the relentless and terrifying persecutions of hallucinatory voices.

Other patients may kill themselves in turmoil at the onset of a psychotic disorganization or a delirium because death seems preferable to the agony of the subjective experience of a disintegrating self. Such patients may present a mental state examination that shows acute and gross disorganization of thought with pronounced lability of affect.

The patient with a "smiling depression" may also be in grave danger of suicide. These individuals may conceal underlying attitudes of despair out of a fierce sense of independence and a determination never to acknowledge a need for support. Only when the mental state examination is weighed against careful formulation of character organization and an assessment of who is available to help maintain a sense of personal worth can a realistic judgment be reached regarding the hazard of suicide (Havens, 1965).

As another example of the suicidal case whose mental state examination does not necessarily suggest danger, we cite those individuals who are emerging from a paranoid psychosis. It is clinically possible for such persons to move into severely suicidal states as paranoid, blaming attitudes give way to guilt and self-contempt.

Case Example

A 50-year-old widow, admitted to the hospital in an angry and paranoid state, seemed to respond well to treatment and after a short period was discharged. As the patient's anger at her family quieted, psychiatrists and the staff responsible for her care did not appreciate that she had moved into an attitude of quiet resignation and despair that led to her successful suicide a few days later. At no time in the course of her treatment had the patient seemed disturbingly depressed to anyone, and there had been no suicidal threatening or preoccupation that the patient had made known to any of her examiners. She destroyed herself shortly after discharge when her son announced his plans for marriage. Only in retrospect was it noticed that this dependent woman was without support in her social and family context.

Disorders of the mental state can not only be indicators of suicidal potential (though poor predictors) but can provoke suicide as well. Some such patients may be difficult to understand psychodynamically until a meticulous and systematic mental state examination is carried out. There are, for instance, tragic people who recognize that they are psychotic and who become suicidally depressed in reaction to the discovery. These may attempt to conceal secret hallucinations or delusions from the examiners. This they may succeed in doing, but cognitive disturbances can often be detected if the patient is painstakingly and expertly examined.

Others cannot endure the pain of acknowledging a thought disorder or some other defect of mind such as a mild dementia. Suicides can take place in those who prize highly and lose an intact and effective capacity for clear thought, just as other individuals, certain athletes, for example, may become suicidal because they lose some highly prized body function. It is obvious in such cases that the degree of suicide danger cannot be assessed without taking into account the subjective meaning to the patient of what has been lost.

Whenever a patient is being examined to assess suicide risk it is essential that the mental content be carefully surveyed for illusions or secret delusions that may lead the patient into lethal behavior in the false belief that death provides a passage into some kind of nirvana, reunion, or happier other life. Such fantasies are often preconscious or unconscious and may be difficult to detect, although they may be powerful motives to self-destruction. Because of their comparatively hidden nature, they are often overlooked (Maltsberger and Buie, 1980). In the course of the mental state examination an effort should be made to find out what the patient imagines it would be like to be dead.

ERRORS ARISING FROM EXCESSIVE RELIANCE ON CLINICAL INTUITION

Frequently one finds clinicians relying on an "intuitive sense" about how dangerous a suicide problem may be. While it is true that experienced clinicians sometimes develop a capacity to arrive at a correct decision about the comparative lethality of a given case without consciously working out a formulation, here it is easy to fall into a pit. Intuitive decisions, arising as they do out of preconscious processes are particularly likely to be influenced by preconscious or unconscious wishes and countertransference attitudes. It is always best to examine one's intuitions carefully in the context of carefully collected clinical data in order to avoid bad decisions arising from false intuition.

There would appear to be particular danger in relying on so-called "empathic" assessment in determining the suicide risk where schizophrenic and borderline cases are involved. This trap arises from two areas. The first one is that the subjective experience of such individuals is often so far from that of the psychotherapist that there is a generous margin in which empathic mistakes can take place. Most psychotherapists have not experienced the profound sense of aloneness or the devastating shame of worthlessness that is the daily lot of very disturbed patients. Even if the therapist is experienced and himself no stranger to such affects, to experience them even in an empathic way is very distressing. The tendency is always there to ward them off by denial, isolation, or some other defense.

A second empathic difficulty lies in the fact that the mental state examination of some patients will not betray the clues necessary to evoke a signal of alarm in the empathic observer that would enable him to recognize the subjective states that can accompany suicide. We have repeatedly encountered cases in which patients were examined frequently by competent and experienced clinicians and in which significant sectors of inner life pertaining to deep and lethal suicide preoccupation remained concealed.

ERRORS ARISING FROM FALSE BELIEFS

From time to time one meets the situation in which the psychotherapist has arranged a "contract" with the patient. In its usual form such a contract is an agreement entered into by both the therapist and the patient that no suicidal acting out will take place before the patient calls the therapist. While it is, of course, perfectly sensible and necessary for a therapist to make himself available outside the ordinary appointment time should the patient experience an upsurge of suicidal feelings, it is little more than magical thinking to credit such a contract with having any efficacy in preventing suicides from taking place.

Such contracts are particularly dangerous when they succeed in lulling the pscyhotherapist into a false sense of security. Trusting the contract can lead to premature hospital discharge or other unwise decisions which can deprive patients of life-sustaining supports.

Some patients may find the offering of a contract supportive, and for this reason the device may have some merit. The hazard lies in placing confidence in it as an effective prophylaxis against suicide.

Another common mistake that arises from clinical ignorance is the tendency to estimate the danger of a suicide attempt on the basis of external observable facts without taking into account the patient's intention or belief about the means chosen for the attempt. While the ingestion of a half-dozen aspirin tablets may not seem a particularly lethal attempt to a sophisticated examiner, the matter will take on a different complexion should he learn that the patient naively but sincerely believed that the small amount of aspirin would produce death.

Wrist-cutting, ordinarily treated by the medically trained examiner inured to such behavior as belonging to the "gesturing" (or not very serious) type of suicidal behavior must also be understood in terms of what it means to the patient. There are those individuals who are so anatomically naive as to believe that no terribly profound cuts of the superficial veins of the wrist can lead to a lethal hemorrhage.

By no means is all suicide "gesturing" benign in its significance. While it is true that most wrist-cutting and overdosing is not intended to produce a fatal result, every such gesture should be carefully assessed. Some patients almost ready for suicide but as yet undecided, betray their ambivalence through a minor attempt. Only a careful formulation of the case can provide reliable guidance. We know of one young schizophrenic woman who ingested six Stelazine tablets, an event misunderstood at the time as a negativistic gesture of little significance. A few days later, her indecision resolved, the patient fired her father's pistol through her head.

Neither should one assume because a patient has gestured repeatedly in the past that a fresh, seemingly minor attempt is but one more in an ugly but not lethal series. Each gesture has to be examined in the context of the patient's life circumstances; what was a spite overdose last week may become a dangerous overdose next week if there are significant shifts in the patient's sources of support and hope.

It is sometimes said that a pregnant woman will not commit suicide. One would think on a moment's reflection that because women from time to time murder their children before killing themselves that a suicide in pregnancy would not be out of the question. Some people nevertheless seem to believe that the contrary is the case: suicide in pregnancy definitely does take place. As always, any correct understanding of the dangers requires the psychiatrist to take into account the subjective meaning of all of the factors and events in the patient's life that bear upon questions of living and dying. While it might very well be the case, for instance, that one depressed woman would not take her life while pregnant because of a wish to spare her unborn child, for another pregnancy may be profoundly unwelcome. Although suicide in pregnancy does not lie within our immediate clinical experience it is by no means unthinkable that some pregnant women may develop repellent delusions respecting the nature and origin of the pregnancy that would promote and not hinder their suicides.

ERRORS ARISING FROM FAILURE TO TAKE INTO ACCOUNT THE SOURCES AND RELIABILITY OF EMOTIONAL SUPPORT

Very often a depressed patient is admitted to the hospital with suicidal ideation and almost immediately improves in mental state. The patient who once seemed so overwhelmed with despair may soon appear cheerful, speak hopefully, and be discharged in a few days. We have seen a number of such patients become dangerously depressed again following discharge from the hospital. Indeed, sometimes the situation is worse than before. The patient, having fallen ill again after what seemed to be a successful period of treatment, concludes he must be a failure. He does not return to the hospital for further treatment either because he thinks he has disgraced himself by falling ill again or because he has made up his mind that he is not treatable and the hospital has nothing to offer.

Many depressive relapses of this sort are obviously the result of the loss of the supportive hospital milieu, and, more specifically, the loss of specific supportive individuals within the hospital network. Socially isolated patients who have no one may often improve simply on the basis of the warmth and care made available to them in a good psychiatric center. If life circumstances outside the ward have not changed, hospital discharge simply means that the patient will be deprived of the sources of emotional support that enabled his initial improvement to take place.

Obviously no suicidal individual can safely be discharged from the hospital on the basis of this kind of improvement alone. As discharge planning proceeds, part of an intelligent formulation of a suicidal case lies in carefully taking into account what supports have become available to the patient in the community outside the ward that were not there before.

It seems worth emphasizing again that support withdrawal very commonly precipitates a suicidal crisis. Hospital discharge may be an occasion for loss of support if managed clumsily. Similarly, the vacation time of the therapist is a common occasion for suicide. Because vacations mean the loss of support and because such patients have a paranoid proclivity to experience absences of any nature as a rejection, such times are perilous. Those charged with the care of suicidal cases need to be sensitive to what meaning such ordinary ward events as the going and coming of medical students, psychiatric aides, or others may have to the patients' sense of security and support.

Even though some patients have the good fortune to be surrounded by family and friends who are genuinely loving and available for support, the examiner must not assume that the recovering patient can safely be discharged until he ascertains whether or not the patient can make use of such resources. Only a case formulation can show whether what is available will suffice; only a careful examination of the patient's mental state can disclose whether he has the will and the capacity to accept what is available. Some profoundly narcissistic patients, for instance, may repudiate others who wish to help.

SUICIDE ARISING IN THE CONTEXT
OF DISTURBED PROFESSIONAL RELATIONSHIPS

Stanton and Schwartz pointed out many years ago that when overt differences between the caretaking personnel of a psychiatric ward were not directly managed by frank discussion between the parties concerned, periods of disturbed patient behavior were likely to ensue (Stanton and Schwartz, 1954). It would seem that suicide is a form of such disturbed behavior that can be fostered during periods of unrest among psychiatric staff. We know of one suicide that took place when a much respected attending psychiatrist left a ward and was replaced by a younger man who had not yet won the full confidence and cooperation of the staff. Because of covert resentment about the change, some life-saving advice he gave was overlooked and a patient was lost.

On another occasion when several senior psychiatrists' vacations happened to coincide and the anxiety of the staff who remained behind was high, a number of suicides took place in rapid succession. Transitional times are likely to result in staff anxiety and conflict. It would appear that patients are likely to believe, correctly or not, that the care and support they need for survival is not available at such times and react accordingly.

Other kinds of staff relationships may contribute to successful suicide. We know of one instance in which the competitive attitude of a younger psychiatrist led him to dismiss with fatal results some critically important advice that an older colleague offered him.

Outside the hospital, ambiguity about who should undertake the assessment and possible care of a patient who threatens suicide can result in a series of rejections by reluctant caretakers, none of whom is willing to accept what might be an unpleasant task, especially at an inconvenient hour. The danger of such professional recalcitrance to a genuinely suicidal patient is obvious.

ERRORS ARISING FROM THE BELIEF THAT SUICIDE MAY BE PREVENTED BY IMPERSONAL MEANS

The grossest error of this category is probably the notion that suicide can safely be prevented by mechanically interfering with a patient's freedom. In this era of diminishing public support for psychiatric hospitals there is a tendency to turn more and more to mechanical restraint and seclusion than was heretofore the case. It may be that some of the lessons of the past will have to be relearned by bitter experience. Mechanical interference with the patient is a poor suicide preventative. While restraint of one kind or another may be necessary on rare occasions temporarily until a relationship is formed, it is impossible to keep people in restraint for very long without antagonizing them and heightening the suicidal hazard. A review of all the suicides at the Metropolitan State Hospital in Norwalk, Connecticut, over a period of 42 years, showed that more than half took place in seclusion rooms (Beisser and Blanchette, 1961).

Just as many years ago the value of taking away sharp objects and belts from psychiatric patients was found to be of limited usefulness, other impersonal means of treatment may infect the staff with a false sense of security out of a mistaken belief that something definitive has been done. Even though a patient has received a course of antidepressant medication followed by an improvement in mental state, he can remain dangerously suicidal. The same is true for those who have had a significant improvement following a course of electroconvulsive therapy. While suicide after eight or ten electroconvulsive treatments is extremely unusual, it nevertheless does occur.

The only possible way to arrive at a trustworthy assessment of suicidal vulnerability is to take all factors into account in a carefully worked out case formulation.

REFERENCES

Adler, G. (1972), Helplessness in the helpers. *Brit. J. Med. Psychol.*, 45:315–326.

Beisser, A.R., & Blanchette, J. (1961), A study of suicides in a mental hospital. *Dis. Nerv. Syst.*, 22:365–369.

Havens, L. (1965), The anatomy of a suicide. *N. Engl. J. Med.*, 272:401–406.

Maltsberger, J.T., & Buie, D. (1974), Countertransference hate in the treatment of suicidal patients. *Arch. Gen. Psychiat.*, 30:625–633.

——— ——— (1980), The devices of suicide: Revenge, riddance, and rebirth. *Internat. Rev. Psycho-Anal.*, 7:61–72.

Stanton, A.H., & Schwartz, M.S. (1954), *The Mental Hospital*. New York: Basic Books.

Zilboorg, G. (1936), Suicide among civilized and primitive races. *Amer. J. Psychiat.*, 92:1347–1369.

16

The Threat of Suicide in Psychotherapy

Norman E. Zinberg, M.D.

In the continuing treatment of patients who threaten to commit suicide but are not clearly psychotic, the therapist's choice of intervention makes a critical difference. Mention of suicide by a patient naturally stirs up considerable anxiety in all therapists; obviously, no one would want to minimize the seriousness of the threat. In fact, the assessment of suicidal risk is one of the rare occasions when the psychological practitioner, as opposed to the medical practitioner, is faced with a decision that is life threatening.

Acutely suicidal situations occur often enough to be menacing; at the same time, there is a group of patients whose characterological style is such that they must present themselves in the worst possible light, including talking of suicide. If these patients are accepted at their own weakest estimate of themselves as a result of the therapist's extreme concern about this one life-threatening syndrome, the continued unraveling of their repetitious and automatic mode of self-presentation may become extremely difficult. For if one part of the patient wishes to be accepted as weak and the therapist goes along with that wish, it will reduce the therapy to an empty struggle for such acceptance.

This chapter will spell out an approach to therapy that I have found useful in treating patients, including those threatening suicide. I shall refer to this approach as an ego psychological model, the characterological model, or the structural model (Gill, 1967, 1981; Klein, 1968; Zinberg, 1975, 1985; Schafer, 1976; Gill and Hoffman, 1982). Although it cannot be put forward as truth, it will offer an alternative way of thinking about therapy that other practitioners may care to work into their own framework of operation. The first section of the chapter will make very few direct references to suicide, but it will supply essential background by reconsidering the theories of technique that are available to psychotherapists today in differentiating between the "genuinely" suicidal person and the one who is desperate to be seen as desperate. In the second section, the characteristics of these two broad groups of patients threatening suicide will be elucidated through two case histories, and the clinical choices to be made in treating them will be described. The last section will explain and illustrate why the ego psychological or structural approach is more useful than the more traditional developmental approach in differentiating between and treating suicide-threatening patients as well as others.

RECONSIDERATION OF THE THEORY OF TECHNIQUE

Although there is little controversy today over the prevailing direction that psychoanalytic theory has taken in recent years, there is a powerful inertia against incorporating these theoretical changes into therapeutic presentations. This resistance is usually expressed as a fear that the baby will be thrown out with the bathwater (Brenner, 1979).

Freud's Structural Model

Freud made one great theoretical change when he abandoned his more mechanistic, topographic model of mental functioning and committed himself to the dynamic structural model of id, ego, and superego (Freud, 1923). Initially the power, according to this structural theory, belonged to the id, and the ego was considered the "rider of the id horse." The superego, divided between the "shalt not" conscience and the perfectionistic "shalt" ego-ideal, was seen as having great influence, an influence that resulted from the superego's easy alliance with the id impulses, which it consciously strove to control. The close relationship between law enforcers and criminals has for many years offered a facile analogy to this alliance.

According to that way of thinking, ego development was seen as a product of the conflict between the powerful inner forces of the id and the external civilizing but dominating superego (A. Freud, 1966). The ego's primary purpose was defensive: to control impulses, to delay discharge, to search for ways to achieve impulse gratification that would satisfy the superego, and then to reduce anxiety and activate responses to danger. Whether challenges came from within or without, the main emphasis was on the ego as reactive (Hartmann, 1939; Rapaport, 1958). This inherently embattled, negativistic view of mental functioning left little room for constructive, positive ego capacities. The responsibility for explaining human actions that were other than reactive fell on the concept of sublimation, and it was even conceptualized as a defense mechanism that used the energies of the impulses but transmitted them from an interest in simple, direct gratification to more complex, substantive, "higher" forms of gratification (A. Freud, 1966).

This model of mental functioning made it easy to see how things could and would go wrong. In any model of emotional conflict, battles must be lost to painful difficulties, but in this model emphasizing constant struggle it was hard to think about human emotional functioning as anything other than psychopathological or at least actively involved in coping with psychopathology. The term "psychopathology" itself was borrowed from the description of anatomical defects or of failure in anatomical functioning, and thus was a far cry from the notion of a wide range of emotional responses to complex life situations. In fact, in early writings the defenses themselves were seen as questionably "pathological" despite the absence of clear-cut ideas of "normal" functioning (Jahoda, 1965). Therefore, while physical medicine, including physiology and pathology, has been rapidly developing progressively clearer standards of normal body functioning, psychiatrists have been struggling hard but unsuccessfully to find a concept of normal emotional functioning. At the same time, psychiatry and psychoanalysis have not limited the definition of emotional "illness" to the severe disorders that readily differentiate a sufferer from his fellows (and may well turn out to be genetic or biochemical rather than emotional), but have insisted on using that label for what Thomas Szasz (1974) dubbed the "emotional problems of living."

Looking back, it is easy to understand the dilemma of the psychoanalytic pioneers for whom the great discoveries of the unconscious, the regularity of emotional functioning, the impact of early relationships on later functioning, and the problems of adapting and coping were new and fresh and could be developed into principles. Taken together these discoveries constituted the most comprehensive theory of mental functioning ever devised. Because explorations within this existing framework were available everywhere one looked, there was little need to reassess the framework. Yet the sense of certainty that the therapeutic task was intended to "cure" illnesses, as presented in Freud's famous case histories, soon began to slip (Freud, 1937). As the fame of psychoanalytic principles and the awareness of them spread, two things happened, one quickly, the other slowly. First, analysts began to be consulted by a far wider range of patients—by some whose disturbances were not so clear-cut and debilitating as those of Dora or the Wolf Man, and by others who were clearly suffering from major mental illness. Over time this enormously enlarged pool of consumers led to the second and more cumulative change: by the midtwentieth century all patients were coming to therapy with a lifelong exposure to the precepts of psychoanalysis.

Autonomous Ego Functions

With the publication of *The Ego and the Mechanisms of Defense* (A. Freud, 1966), "Analysis Terminable and Interminable" (Freud, 1937), and *Ego Psychology and the Problem of Adaptation* (Hartmann, 1939), came the formal recognition that a theory of emotional functioning based almost entirely on the drives and impulses as motivating and exploratory forces was insufficient. The defenses and other ego structures, which were gradually elaborated, began to be seen as vigorous in their own right. The ego was no longer regarded as the reactive rider of the powerful id horse. Following Heinz Hartmann, David Rapaport and many other theorists not only detailed the functions of the ego but also began to incorporate into basic psychoanalytic theory the hypothesis that the ego possessed its own energies, not derived from the id. In effect, this hypothesis allowed ego functions to be thought of as relatively autonomous from the id. Such functions as perception, discharge thresholds, memory, and attitude development began to be conceived of as autonomous genetic givens, but, of course, this autonomy was relative. The rest of the mental apparatus, as well as the external environment, was essential and influential both in maintaining relative autonomy and in shaping the directions that autonomy would take.

Although this theoretical direction was generally accepted when it was spelled out carefully by Rapaport in 1958, many analytic theorists remained cautious and fearful of the influence of these changes on the essential base of psychoanalytic theory. In 1959 Merton Gill stated this argument succinctly and precisely, concluding that the roots of the psychoanalytic theory tree remained in the cannibalistic, destructive, incestuous impulses, while the elaboration of ego functions, autonomous and otherwise, formed the branches and other secondary growth. A reading of Gill's recent work (Gill, 1981; Gill and Hoffman, 1982) makes it clear that he would no longer support that earlier conclusion, even though most of the authors writing on the theory of technique in the 1979 edition of the *Journal of the American Psychoanalytic Association* entitled "Psychoanalytic Technique and the Theory of Therapy" would (Blum, 1979). That collection, better than any other single body of work (with the exception of Gill's early paper in 1959), represents the strength of the wish within organized psychoanalysis to perceive psychoanalytic theory as basically unalterable. Any discussion should thus be aimed at categorizing details (such as the place of a therapeutic alliance in the transference neurosis, or the relationship of preoedipal to oedipal factors in development) rather than presenting the theory as a robust body of thought undergoing a slow but constant process of evolution.

Roy Schafer, one of the leading psychoanalytic theorists to recognize that psychoanalytic theory needs to change in order to remain vigorous, states, or rather warns, in a recent paper (1982) that the life history narrative expounded in the therapeutic situation is a product of that situation. He points out that different situations, that is, analysts with different points of view or elicitors from other disciplines, will produce different life history narratives. This extremely important point is often accepted as a truism, but its implications are not understood. The same thing can be said of another point made by Schafer in the same paper: that the life history used in each therapeutic situation is simply a series of hypotheses elaborated from a particular point of view within a particular situation. Anyone who has been in the business long enough knows this fact all too well, having learned that the history a patient recounted at age twenty, for example, is presented very differently by the same patient at age forty. This is one of those points that arouses casual agreement when stated in principle but that is not observed at case conferences. For example, a presenter of a case history may say that the mother of the patient was a cold, distant woman or the father a passive, angry man, and then assume, in reconstructing the development of a problem, that these perceptions were factual. It requires a great capacity for relativity to think of such judgments, made from memory, as simply the patient's assumption at that historical moment.

Importance of the Social Setting

Schafer's perceptions of the relativity of the case history accentuate the importance of the social setting in which the therapeutic interaction takes place. In one sense, the interaction between therapist and patient has long been regarded as basic, whether it is thought of purely as transference, as a therapeutic alliance, or as an interpersonal field; but implicitly or explicitly these views have stressed the relationship between therapist and patient. Schafer's elaboration brings in the potential that other social positions, such as the larger social setting, the culture, are influencing the direct therapy because the assumptions used to develop the hypothesis called a personal history are influenced by values and attitudes current in that social setting (Zinberg, 1984). Here Schafer puts his finger on one of the great weaknesses of psychoanalytic theory, one that becomes more evident with the passage of time. This is that the enormous emphasis in this theory on the unconscious (the id) and on the mastery of primitive impulses has clearly minimized the impact of the larger social setting throughout life. Certainly Erik Erikson (1950) has tried to put psychosocial development on center stage; and, in a different way, various object-relations theorists stress the socialization process inherent in the close relationships of early childhood (Kernberg, 1976; Greenberg and Mitchell, 1983). In both of these efforts, however, the thrust returns to a consideration of the inside, rather than the setting. Object-relations theorists become preoccupied with how these early relationships are introjected; and, once introjected, they are seen to embody aspects of the primitive impulses and are thought of as introjects, part of the inner life. There is then little necessity to expand on either the continuing relationships with those figures and a systematic understanding of how the continuing learning in the relationships affects the early introjects, or on the impact of a variety of social attitudes and values (acquired during growing up) on how the early experiences are used. It is assumed that once these early objects have been taken into the individual's psyche, everything that occurs subsequently is strained through these objects, leaving little room for autonomy.

Erikson has made the most sophisticated effort to fill the gap in psychoanalytic theory by delineating a coherent sense of the ego's relationship to the outside world, one akin to the coherent developmental structuring of the ego's relationship to the inner world, but he still puts the greatest emphasis on the impact of early relationships and early development. When we read Erikson's account of the life cycle, we get the impression that a child with a reasonable genetic inheritance and good parenting could develop the flexible inner capacity to weather whatever life stages the culture presents. The author certainly does not want to criticize Erikson's seminal work, but rather to suggest that even such inspired work as his has been able to move only slowly beyond its historical theoretical base. As Rapaport (1959) points out in his splendid introduction to *Identity and the Life Cycle,* Erikson returns again and again to instinctual impulses as the best hope for improving the lot of mankind. For example, in a paper summarizing his psychosocial contributions to psycho-analytic theory, Erikson (1980) indicates that "complete psychoanalytic theory may well demand that some instinctual drive toward a generative interplay with offspring be assumed to exist in human nature" (p. 31). That statement shows his fidelity to notions of instinct as well as his reliance on early development and the significant family as the wellspring from which flow the later psychosocial developmental phases he postulates.

Erikson's Concept of Psychosocial Development

If we examine Erikson's approach to psychosocial development, it is easy to understand his attraction to universal, basic human structures. He attempts to delineate stages of social development that are as universal as possible. Each of his eight stages from infancy to old age is matched by a psychosocial crisis ranging from basic trust–mistrust to integrity–despair, and all of the potential problems or resolutions, whether initiative–guilt or intimacy–isolation, refer to emotions and emotional alternatives that are absolutely universal; the same can be said for the basic relationships, the strengths and weaknesses, the principles of social order, and the ritualisms that he outlines. Of course, he recognizes that cultures differ and that in differing developmental situations one or another of these stages and their surrounding ego structures can be modified. He contends, however, that the stages are universal, even though the different cultures channel them differently. He applies to social development the same underlying criteria that he applies to all genetic or developmental constructs. "In the epigenetic sequence of development each organ has its time of origin and if the organ misses its time of ascendance it is not only doomed as an entity, it endangers at the same time the whole hierarchy or organ" (Erikson, 1980, p. 18). Here Erikson, in the distinguished company of Freud, clings to a biological model which he uses for both psychological and social development. This theoretical approach permits the inclusion of many postulates about psychologi-cal and social activities that spring from "improper" building blocks of devel-opment, thus retaining a rather idealistic view of the developmental sequence.

Such a theoretical approach is less applicable when it is used to explain how various ego structures, such as value or attitude formation, perceptual consistencies (for example, when looking at a tree a dendrologist, artist, soldier, and fugitive would have differing but internally consistent perceptions), and discharge thresholds, become relatively autonomous, often in very unfavorable developmental situations, and what factors in the average expectable environment interact with the individual in such a way as to either maintain or destabilize that autonomy. Not surprisingly, Erikson, unlike Rapaport, is not so interested in the differences in average expectable environment within the same culture, such as class or guild differences, as he is in large differences between cultures. In fact, he virtually dismisses the average expectable environment by saying that it "seems to postulate only a minimum of environmental conditions which make survival universally possible while putting aside the enormous variations and complexities of social life which are the source of individual and communal vitality—as well as conflict" (Erikson, 1980, p. 18). In other words, the concept of average expectable environment pays too little attention to what Erikson sees as universal and general social stages and endeavors.

As with most writers tortured by insight, vision, and the willingness to struggle with large objectives, Erikson's work presents the occasional paradox. Although he pays little attention to the average expectable environment when postulating universal social tasks, he shows in some of his writings how an idea, a theory, a technological advance, can change how people think (their ego structures) in ways that influence their lives and, in the author's view, their psyches.

> All revolutionary advances in the natural sciences, of course, have cognitive and ethical implications which at first seem to endanger the previously dominant world image and, with it, the very cosmic reassurances of the basic ego needs we listed. Thus, to give one example, Copernicus upset man's (as well as the earth's) centrality in the universe. But eventually, the very insight that comes with such a radical change in basic orientation also reaffirms the adaptive power of the human mind, even as it stimulates a new innovative ethos [Erikson, 1980, p. 57].

To those first few who were willing to consider the world round was assigned the role of deviant and probably heretic. To them also came a changed vision of man's potential, the possibility of adventure and diversity, that eventually changed the average expectable environment of everyone growing up in Europe at the time. It would not be too far-fetched to suggest that Copernicus' hypothesis opened up vistas that have influenced our thinking about the value of human life, the worth of childhood, and the importance of parenting as much as has any instinct seeking a generative interplay with offspring. All of the above, in turn, influence what may make a threat of suicide crucial to an understanding of our patients.

Effect of Social Learning on Ego Structure

Freud's work has brought about shifts in how the individual is experienced by his culture and by himself that are sufficient to have changed a variety of developing ego structures. By now few parents, in Western culture at least, whatever their social background (and that is a large contention), have grown up without knowing consciously that there are intense, conflicted, emotional interactions between parents and children, some of which are not directly available to consciousness. This awareness is conveyed to children by the content and tone of the interactions as well as by constant questions about their emotional state. These concerns continue in our social institutions, whether schools, clinics, or other agencies. The shock value elicited by Freud when he showed patients at the turn of the century that there were feelings inside of them that they did not know about, and that many of these feelings concerned their parents, is not available to modern psychotherapists. This is not to say that the modern sensibility allows people to know all about their less conscious conflicts; far from it. But to a certain extent it does support the hypothesis that the person is prepared for these "discoveries" so that the return of the repressed does not come to an unprepared ego ready and willing to assimilate a surprising but emotionally convincing flash of insight. Rather, discoveries of less conscious conflict, particularly surrounding childhood and parents, take place in the context of a prepared ego, wary and eager to defend against and restructure the discovery.

Frequently, therapists who are aware of the availability of much knowledge about relationships between parents and children dismiss it as intellectualization or think that such knowledge represents a genuine dissociation. The complex question of the intellectual versus the emotional is too great to be considered here. Suffice it to say that the result of social learning about psychoanalytic theory is not the awareness of any single item of childhood interactions but rather the understanding, which is both cognitive and emotional, that these interactions are emotionally loaded. In modern therapy all too many of the discussions centering on the past and relationships to parents are essentially intellectual and defensive. Often the patient's awareness of the impact of parent–child interaction is used to insist: "I feel or do this or that *because* my parent(s) said or did this or that," and this reductionism attempts to pass as awareness. Here it is useful to recall Schafer's perception that individual histories are partly hypothetical attempts to explain what now exists (Schafer, 1982). The choice by a person of what to retain and what to make central to his structure, from the innumerable possibilites in the parent–child interactions, is incremental, and it involves the continuation of such choices through many subsequent relationships and experiences. That is why the question: "Is that response characteristic of you?" which very often comes as a surprise to the patient, is such an interesting one for the therapist to ask.

Social learning refers to the acquisition of knowledge that is simply in the air and is so naturally accepted that it requires little formal conveyance (Zinberg, 1984). Learning about the telephone in our average expectable environment is one sort of social learning, as is evident to anyone who has visited a culture, such as that of the South American Indians, whose average expectable environment does not include such an instrument. A number of examples could be given of the way in which current social learning prepares an individual's ego to tolerate emotionally intense and confusing experiences. The difference in experience between a person taking LSD in the midsixties and a similar person taking the same drug in the early seventies is a good example that I have described at length elsewhere (Zinberg, 1984). In the sixties, in a social setting tense with concern about psychedelic drugs, attributing to them power to foment spirituality, mystical oneness, personal insight or personal disintegration, madness, and destructive acts, the users had profound experiences, both good and bad, that were filled with primitive and shaking visions. But after a decade of cultural immersion in psychedelic colors, clothing, philosophy, and music, the first-time user, once high, merely thought, "Oh, so that's what is meant by a psychedelic color." Although the drug experience could even then be very intense and sometimes quite unpleasant, the ego was prepared for it. Hence by 1973 most of the noxious sequelae, such as short- and long-term postdrug psychotic episodes, had virtually disappeared, even though more people with very dissimilar personality structures were taking LSD than ever before.

This example shows how information conveyed inchoately but consistently throughout the average expectable environment has led to changes in various aspects of specific ego situations. These changes have enabled the individual to tolerate a highly charged emotional experience that he could not have tolerated without this social learning. Obviously social learning can affect an ego structure only within certain boundaries defined by both the individual's character structure and the social reality. Some people's values and attitudes are such that they would never want to go near LSD, and if they did, they might well have a ghastly experience. Similarly, whatever messages social reality may send about the destructiveness of suicide are likely to have little impact on certain ego structures. A patient who wishes to be seen and accepted as weak for whatever secondary gains, would indeed use just such social messages as indicators of the necessity for his suicidal threats to be taken at face value. In contrast, a person who has given up, as part of the process of growing up, isolates himself from social messages of all kinds.

In his paper on life history narratives, Schafer offers a highly condensed case history in order to show the interdependent relationship between reconstructions of the infantile past and the transferential present. At the end of the case description he comments, almost as an aside, "He had to keep a low profile in analysis as in life, and a low profile for him was both defensive self-castration and non-individuation. One might say it was a living death that guaranteed survival" (Schafer, 1982, p. 80). Earlier in his paper Schafer had analyzed the patient's depressive reactions and his transference response to the analyst (as depressed) as constituting an identification with his depressed mother. The patient's reluctance to see the positive and active parts of his father was also seen as fear of his mother's response. This presentation is typical and traditional. The character style of low profile is seen as "bad" and as stemming more or less directly from the reconstruction of the infantile past. This approach conceives of character style as purely defensive. There is little in the tone of the discussion (as opposed to the actual treatment, where more character analysis was done than is presented) to indicate what aspects of that low-profile approach worked for the person, what values and attitudes he had developed to sustain that way of presenting and thinking about himself, and where and how, in his own view, it worked against him.

This is not to say that in each of our growings-up we do not *choose* a way of dealing with our external reality (largely our parents) and our internal reality. Our styles are forged in that crucible, but they are not exclusively of it. Genetic givens, birth order, gender, gender sequence, and small, virtually fortuitous experiences can affect the choice of profile. This way of thinking about the self is then buttressed by finding values and attitudes that support the perception and make it functional. Few, if any, hold on to these perceptions if they do not work for them. Dismissing as self-castration the subtle ways in which the mosaic of values and attitudes, discharge thresholds, and selective perceptions operate is an oversimplification that is all too typical. Although taking a "weak" position, that is, a low profile, may indeed mean to an individual a rejection or fear of a strength that symbolizes masculinity, its aim, developed over time through many experiences, is far more complex. Too often presentations give the impression that therapy works only with the big discoveries of mother transference, father transference, identification with the depressed mother, self-castration, and the powerful affects that go with these discoveries. In fact, in therapy as in life, the work and the affects emerge around trivia, such as the patient's fury over who had left the cap off the toothpaste. The threat of suicide, as we will see in our case examples, as important as it is in its own right, is also a message from that person to the external world couched in terms to elicit specific responses.

As Schafer (1976) shows, and Gill (1981) and Gill and Hoffman (1982) have stressed, it is within the transference that the patient reveals his repetitious, characteristic ways of perceiving himself within a social context. But Schafer quickly refers this revelation to mother–father rather than to the therapist's painstaking effort to think carefully about the automaticity and consistency of response and to understand what perceptions support that consistency. The shifting of emphasis in the therapy away from the parental figures and the parental transference to the low profile can sharply change the flow of the therapy. The dawning awareness of the patient that he is trying to make the therapy and the therapist something that it is not and is thereby distorting the therapeutic context in repetitious and consistent ways can be revealing of uniquely personal and deeply emotional responses that go far beyond ways of coping with early concerns about mother and father. Noticing the low profile, noticing that the patient does *not* notice it; pointing out how often the patient wants to know why the low profile is important to him and how to fix it, that is, to get "better," even before he is fully aware of how consistently he chooses this position; treating explanations that deal with early parental relationships as only emphasizing the consistency over time of the choice of a low profile; studying when this choice is made and when it is not made in the therapeutic situation—all make for a different process of therapy. In this process, the therapist is far more likely to ask the patient if he would *mind* if he felt a certain way (sad, mean, spiteful, gentle, close, sexy, fearful) than to ask if he felt a certain way. Asking if he minds his feeling or, conversely, if it pleases him, gets to the values, attitudes, and other ego structures that support the patient's characterological stance—in this case, a low profile.

Of course, this way of looking at the material must assume that the discovery by the person being studied that he might feel a certain way about a situation or a person that he had not thought of before will be prepared for, or discounted, by a post-Freudian ego that is ready to put discoveries back into the nexus of characterologically sustained attitudes and values. For example, a woman patient busily berating her mother for being selfish uses as an example her mother's statement, made after her divorce when the patient was a teenager, "I will do what I can for you kids, but I want you to know I am going to try to make something of my life." When asked whether she thought there was anything admirable in her mother's desire to take care of herself, the patient was stunned. After a few minutes of puzzling over her difficulty in even thinking about her mother in that light, she reverted to a characteristic post-Freudian complaint: "But she didn't do it. She didn't really take care of herself and provide a role model for me." By then, however, it was easier to show her that the important point was not what her mother had done or not done, but that her perception of her mother was rooted in her own complaint, and that she was inhibiting her capacity to look at her mother's statement and see the various possibilities in it, just as she might be similarly inhibited from "hearing" her therapist's comments.

When cases are discussed from this point of view, other therapists may wonder whether the practitioner who gently asks about a patient's attitude toward having a feeling rather than going after the affect itself is not conducting a therapy that is more cognitive than abstract, more intellectual than emotional. In practice, this is not so. The therapist who precisely and consistently goes after a person's way of perceiving the inside and outside worlds not only does not need to fear intellectuality but must watch out for too much emotion too soon. Most patients want their way of doing business fixed so that it is effective; they only very reluctantly, with much pain, annoyance, and often sadness (as well as pleasure in discovery and in increased awareness), accept the necessity of close study of their way of doing business. Some would much prefer, and would find it easier, to dissect their parents and their own troublesome past. A theory of technique that puts the emphasis on character style, relative autonomy of ego structures, and interference (both too much and too little) with those autonomies, tends to study the early forging of that style within the context of the awareness of the style and, more important, the awareness of how dear that style, such as a low profile, is to patients. To their surprise they discover how much they want to cling to it and to "make" it work as they want it to work, including concealing what they believe their style enables them to conceal. It would not be going too far to suggest that in this theory of technique the resistance is the therapy. For example, the threat of suicide by a patient who wishes to be accepted as weak is a way of "resisting" the therapy in the sense that the patient is insisting that the therapist do something other than think through with him the myriad but consistent efforts at self-deceit and its motivations.

This change toward an ego psychological approach has important precedents when dealing with depression and suicide. The earlier view based on instinct theory regarded depression as the turning of powerful aggressive impulses against the self. Suicide was seen as the murder of the hated introjected object, almost invariably a parent. Not until the publication of Edward Bibring's seminal paper on depression in 1953 did therapists begin to consider depression as an ego state. The sense of hopelessness and helplessness characterizing the perceptions of the depressed individual flooded the ego and was experienced as real by the person so affected. In terms of social learning, it is fascinating to see how Bibring's view now pervades discussions of depression at case conferences without most of the people present having any awareness of the extent to which this change in theoretical stance has changed the approach to therapy. Nor do they usually have much appreciation of the underlying theoretical positions involved.

A theory of technique that views hard affects (rage, sex, fear) as simply human and in which the interest in therapy revolves around how these very few affects are metabolized differently within each person leads to a type of practice that differs considerably from the more traditionally oriented therapies. In fact, the mere presentation of theoretical differences cannot convey the extent of the differences in practice. The best proof of that fact is to read the issue of the *Journal of the American Psychoanalytic Association* entitled "Psychoanalytic Technique and the Theory of Therapy," mentioned earlier (Blum, 1979), where almost all of the authors speak of illness—cure, show little self-consciousness about knowing what is "better," present cases "showing" how specific interactions with parents have "caused" specific forms of "psychopathology," and pay no attention to what patients know about themselves as a factor in the therapy. Surely such thinking would lead, as Schafer points out, to different "histories" even though certain aspects of them might be similar. In Schafer's case history the patient's passive longings had to be made conscious, as they would, in my view, in any productive therapy, but the route to consciousness might make a difference as to how those longings were conceptualized in the person's view of his own functioning.

TWO CLINICAL CASES

The clearest way to show how the ego psychological or structural approach affects therapeutic practice is to present two case histories, one of a "genuinely" suicidal person and the other of a person who insisted upon being seen as suicidal, and then to point out the clinical choices that are available to the therapist.

Case Example 1

The patient, David Brown, was a 26-year-old white, Protestant, slender male with glasses, light-brown hair, and regular features. He spoke slowly and precisely, with vigor but with a sense of calculation behind each word. He had come to see the therapist at the insistence of his mother, who was concerned about his growing isolation and difficulty in choosing between further schooling and work. During the previous four years of inactivity after graduation from an excellent, small New England college, Mr. Brown had consulted therapists on four separate occasions, none for more than five sessions. One had seemed to him aggressive and unintelligent, another too "psychoanalytic" and insistent upon examining his early childhood, another was seen principally for testing and vocational counseling (unsatisfactory), and the fourth was too silent. Yet in spite of these disappointments he admitted to having welcomed his mother's suggestion to try again.

Mr. Brown was the youngest of four children. His mother and father had been divorced when he was eight. The first-born son, 39, was currently a moderately successful computer engineer living in New Hampshire with his wife and three children. They were on good terms; Mr. Brown visited them occasionally and was particularly friendly with his brother's 14-year-old youngest son. His older sister, 35, was a divorced photographer living in New York whom he was not close to and who had been in psychoanalysis for more than five years. The other sister, 30, the sibling to whom he had been closest while growing up, was unmarried, an editor in a large publishing firm also living in New York, and was seen as living an odd existence. They were no longer close, and by odd he meant frequent but not compulsive use of illicit drugs and a social life that veered erratically between isolation and immersion in new groups of friends.

Mr. Brown's father was a corporate tax attorney practicing on his own. When just beginning law practice he had put together a very complex merger of interests (the therapist never understood it) from which he had benefited handsomely and which had remained virtually his only client. He had been married for 13 years to a divorced woman with three children, the oldest of whom was one year younger than Mr. Brown. The father and stepmother never went to bed sober, and indeed the father was rarely sober after lunch. Mr. Brown's mother, described as a nervous woman, anxious to please, was a teetotaler, had never seriously considered remarriage, and kept busy with many community activities. There was little doubt in Mr. Brown's mind that he was his mother's favorite, and he felt considerable concern over the anxiety he was causing her.

Money was not a problem. At the time of the divorce, his father had not only settled a sum comfortable enough for his mother to maintain her Beacon Hill and Peabody homes but had also provided each child with a trust producing $30,000 to $35,000 a year. Mr. Brown's one consistent activity over the last four years had been a study of the stock market. He had managed in a declining market to increase the value of his own trust by 50 percent, a fact of which he was quite proud.

The story was fairly straightforward. In his last years at college he had considered law school and graduate business degrees with a particular interest in administration and marketing. But he felt very strongly that he did not wish to pursue graduate studies just for the sake of a degree. He wished to make a far more definitive decision about what he wanted to do and then to follow through. In college, where contact with others was built into the dormitory arrangements and no special initiative was required of him, he made a number of friends. There had been some activity with women, especially when a woman who had taken a fancy to him had pursued him. When asked about his father and stepmother, he managed a laugh and said that she, in contrast to his mother, was a very active person, and that he was the one in his family most like his father. In the four years since college more and more of his contacts had stopped calling him and consequently his friendships had dried up. He often meant to initiate contacts but rarely did.

But lack of direct career activity did not mean idleness. His stock market research led him toward definitive management ideals concerning small companies that were developing new products, and in the one interchange he had managed with a company director he had been much encouraged but had not followed through. With questioning, it came out that there was a conscious awareness of his inhibition against activity unless conditions were absolutely right, but he became a little annoyed at the therapist's suggestion that waiting for one giant step could be a fallacy since decisions were made by a series of little steps. It took a series of gentle questions about his day-to-day life in his little house, located quite near but separate from a small town 40 miles from Boston, to elicit his feelings of loneliness and melancholy. Coming to see a therapist had cheered him up, but he suspected only momentarily. He felt he could not at this point act, but neither could he bear not to. Before the second interview ended, he thought it was necessary to report, in his quiet but punctilious fashion, that although he had had no active homosexual relationships, he thought that he had the potential for bisexuality under the right conditions. Without being prompted, he added that such feelings were not active in his close relationship to his nephew. He used alcohol (only wine) sparingly; in his last year of college he had smoked a lot of marijuana, but now he used it only very occasionally when he was with old college friends. He did not use any other drugs.

Then the therapy ran into difficulty. Mr. Brown had known before he came that this was only an evaluation–consultation, but when the discussion turned to the importance of continuing therapy, he acknowledged considerable disappointment that the evaluator could not continue with the therapy. Finally, after acknowledging the extent of his current discomfort, he agreed to accept a referral. After a few days he was offered two names, a man's and a woman's, and agreed to call. After a month or so the evaluator learned that Mr. Brown had not called either one. In response to a phone call he said that he was feeling somewhat better, had seen an apartment in an old, unfashionable section of Boston that he hoped to take, and was not going to follow through on therapy at this time. Nonetheless, he agreed to come and see the evaluator again one month later.

The change in Mr. Brown was obvious at once. The muscles in his face sagged; his voice was low; he spoke far more slowly and without his previous preciseness. Since he had last been seen, he had had a number of disappointments. First, his brother had had an elliptical talk with him which Mr. Brown thought, probably correctly, was intended to convey concern about the closeness between Mr. Brown and the younger son. The vagueness and mixed feelings apparent in this talk—since the older brother respected David Brown's intellect and wanted his 14-year-old to become interested in getting a good education—were particularly annoying to the patient. Then there was a complicated story about having to decide over a holiday weekend whether to be visited by a woman he had gone with in college or to go to California for the wedding of his stepbrother. He had chosen to go to California, in part because of pressure from his father, but in his heart he knew that he was also reluctant to resume with his old girl friend.

Although he was feeling painfully depressed, his appetite was fair and he was sleeping. In some measure he saw the depression as helpful because it was forcing him into activity. This comment was questioned by the evaluator as possibly indicating a punishing rather than a constructive activity. Mr. Brown thought it contained some of both. He had resolved to move back to the city and was looking hard for an apartment to rent or buy since the one he had wanted had fallen through. In response to questioning, he admitted, with difficulty, that the incident with his brother had brought to the fore his fears of being seen by himself and others as homosexual. Appearances meant a great deal to him, and the possibility that his brother might see him as being at the least sexually provocative had been extremely upsetting. It had raised gnawing doubts in him as to what others saw when they looked at him, despite his extreme care in trying to present exactly the "right" impression. Choosing not to see the girl with whom he had had an extremely active and satisfactory sexual relationship had also stirred up painful concerns within himself as to his sexuality. As a result of all this, his commitment to therapy had intensified, but he still wanted to work with the evaluator.

That was on Friday, and the therapist was to be away the following week, so that an appointment was made for about ten days later. At first glance Mr. Brown looked better. There was somewhat more energy in his step, and his speech was brisker. But after a moment that impression faded because the previous apathy had been replaced with a chilly sense of isolation and distance. It was as if the discussion were about someone else. Shortly after the previous appointment, after seeing many places he had hated and becoming very discouraged, he had found exactly the right apartment. He described it carefully, indicating how it provided a setting both in the building and the neighborhood that would arouse interest in people as to what he was doing there; in addition, once inside, the apartment itself would be a stunner. Old family furniture would be just right. He felt that it was a place he could ask people to in order to see it rather than him, and that would allow him to be socially vigorous.

Mr. Brown told the real estate agent of his wish to buy and outlined his terms, all of which seemed acceptable. He had already moved out of his house and was temporarily living with his mother. The real estate dealer called back that evening to say that unfortunately the apartment, which had not sold after some time on the market, had been rented that day for a year and he could not have it until then. That was the crowning blow. After that, for several days, he felt absolutely helpless, hardly able to get out of bed, possessed by a sense that his efforts could lead to nothing but, in his uncharacteristic word, *shit*.

After about a week of this, he said that he suddenly realized that he was not helpless, that he could do something about his life. "End it," was his response to the question, "What?" He was in possession of his grandfather's gun and knew how to use it. This week was to be spent tidying up various affairs, and he was very clear that he would never mess up his mother's house. All of this was said in a businesslike tone of voice without sadness, self-pity, or pain. The appointment had been seen as an obligation. Mr. Brown allowed that he had rather liked the therapist, although he too had proved, typically, to be a great disappointment by stirring up hope and then proving unavailable. Also, Mr. Brown said he had few people to whom he wished to say goodbye.

Case Example 2

The second patient, James Carter, was 36 years old, dark-haired, chunky but not fat, with quick, anxious movements, and a flow of speech. He was referred by a therapist in New York City whom Dr. Carter had seen for two years while a surgical resident. At that time he had recently become a full partner in a small (three doctors), lucrative, surgical group practice. In spite of his obvious professional success—he also had been granted privileges and sought-after teaching appointments at prominent hospitals—he was as tormented by career indecision as he had been when he had consulted a therapist previously.

It was a complex story. In brief, Carter had been running the family real estate business at the same time he was functioning as a surgical resident and busy surgeon. It is hard to determine exactly when, but at some point, his father, who clearly had begun to fail mentally, had turned to Dr. Carter for help. Both he and his father realized that his sister, two years younger, and her unambitious husband were incapable of managing the small but engrossing and profitable business. Dr. Carter had begun by helping his father on nights and weekends; but as his father continued to fail, he had assumed more and more responsibility. Finally, when he was "forced" to put both his mother and father in a nursing home, he took a few months off to organize the business, then brought in his father-in-law, retired and also unambitious, to do the routine work while he went on with his surgical career. He remained as deeply involved in the business as time allowed, retaining all the executive functions.

Both of his parents were the children of emigrés and had been born abroad. Father was English, mother German, and both had arrived in the United States while still very young. Yet neither set of grandparents or parents had lost a sense of strangeness in the United States. This feeling that they were different, did not quite belong, accompanied by both an underlying arrogance and an attitude of self-deprecation, had pervaded the households of both of his parents while they were growing up, and their own household during his youthful years. The families of origin had been poor and had come to the United States to improve their fortunes.

Dr. Carter's initial presentation of his parents depicted his father as a dour, overwhelmingly nervous man, who would call him up fifteen or twenty times to verify an opinion. His mother was seen as a frightened, withdrawn woman who had retained many European mannerisms, which appeared as affectations. Although she leaned heavily on his father, she did so with contempt. Dr. Carter felt that from infancy he had been not just his mother's favorite but virtually her whole life, to the exclusion of his father and sister.

Growing up, according to Dr. Carter, was pure hell. He described himself as a frightened, whiny, angry, uncomfortable child, teenager, and young man. There was some acknowledgment that others may not necessarily have seen him that way, if for no other reason than his academic success, but it was surely his experience of himself. The two years of therapy had been extremely useful, not toward resolving his career dilemma but toward helping him to see himself as less directly at the mercy of what he experienced as the powerful influences of his parents and other significant figures. He was frightened "because my mother had instilled in me her constant fears" and "because I had displaced my father and felt retribution to be inevitable." There were many other such comments that fitted his view of psychoanalytic explanations, placed his current dilemma's origins in early childhood and family, presented himself as the passive receptacle of others' feelings, and implicitly asked for more and deeper explanations of the same sort.

He had had some friends when he was growing up, but full participation in social life had been hampered by his mother's fearfulness. Dating was hard because he hated to make the initial phone calls, although he would force himself. He had had sexual experiences in which he was reluctant and the woman was forward. In retrospect, he saw that there were many sexual opportunities open to him; it was not that he chose not to take advantage of them, but that at the time he literally did not know the women were interested in him. He met his wife when he was in medical school in Chicago and she in law school. She was described as red haired (both his parents were dark), attractive, energetic, and very positive; that is, she had a definite opinion about everything in contrast to his sense of himself as being immediately susceptible to and searching for directions from others. A year and a half of stormy courtship followed, caused by his feeling that she saw herself as always right. Because of his uncertainty, he would give in by going along or apologizing, and then it would turn out that he had been right. She would never apologize, and he would be furious and sulk. This interaction has persisted to the present time.

At the time of initial consultation, Dr. and Mrs. Carter had one son, two-and-a-half years old, and at her insistence they were attempting to have another child. She had pursued her career actively, but, according to him, she was bitter at having been hampered in following up opportunities because of moving to Boston for his training. Despite her wish to become pregnant again and although the first pregnancy was planned and she continued to work, she expressed anger at the prospect of missed status, prestige, and income of her own. As for him, the prospect of greater responsibility and time demands resulting from another child when he already felt overwhelmed by his two jobs was terrifying. Yet Dr. Carter and his wife, in spite of their many disagreements and her complaints about his social ineptness, extreme rigidity, and meticulousness about what he saw as ethical issues, as well as his sparse sexual interest, sullenness, and career indecision, seemed tightly committed to each other. (He had had two or three instances of mutual masturbation with male friends at age thirteen, but no further homosexual activity.) The Carters drank moderately socially, used marijuana once a month or less, and about once a year took LSD together, which he reported as an extremely pleasurable and intimate experience for both of them. Yet he felt quite desperate about the need to make a decision as to his life. On the one hand, his efforts to become a surgeon, his interest in medicine, and the prestige attached to being a doctor meant a great deal to him. On the other hand, the money to be made in the business, the chances for a more leisurely life, the commitment to his parents and to his sister, all of whom derived incomes from the business, and the fact that disposing of it would bring only a fraction of its worth in generating income, operated as a constant pull away from surgery. But he felt he could not go on doing both, and his father-in-law wanted to get out. Because of his time constraints, he and the therapist agreed to meet just twice a week in spite of his agitation.

The concept, discussed during the evaluation, that in thinking about himself he insisted on seeing himself as weak and afraid of thinking about himself in any other way came as a surprise to him. As far as he was concerned, he did not think of himself as weak; he *was* undecided, easily influenced, and frightened. There was some grudging admission that others did not necessarily see him that way, but as far as he was concerned, that was because of his learned facade. This insistence was pointed out to him not only in his direct statements but also in one association after another. Whenever Dr. Carter said anything that indicated a direct wish on his part or a sense of himself as other than weak, he would quickly balance it by showing that the wish had come about because of his wife's (or someone else's) pressure, and thus the expressed view of himself as other than weak was ephemeral and quickly replaced by his more usual depiction.

Another facet of his personality structure emerged clearly in the early months of treatment. He had stern litigious rules for himself and others as to formal law-breaking or moral relaxation, and his rare show of direct anger and condemnation of others took place when he saw them flout his strictures. Nevertheless, and this was very important to him, when he saw himself as gulled, cheated, or pushed around, he resolutely turned the other cheek—much to his wife's consternation and outrage—feeling deeply that his moral superiority both punished the other person and gave him a sense of triumph. It should be remembered that in spite of his concerns about his inabilities—mostly as depicted to him by his wife—he was functioning well behaviorally in two extremely demanding situations, surgery and business, and was achieving at least a standoff on the home front.

After starting therapy, he began to assert himself here and there and to describe incidents in which he had resisted his wife's influence. This pleased him and he ascribed it to the therapy. He was continually taken aback when the therapist pointed out that these were behavioral changes and asked what impact they had on his insistence on seeing himself as weak. The idea that Dr. Carter wanted to see himself as getting "stronger" as a result of the influence of the therapy or the therapist, it was suggested, might be little different from his previous posture concerning his wife, his parents, and his senior partners. He was aware that this idea of the therapist's displeased him; he was also aware that he did not want to be displeased and saw no reason for annoyance at the therapist, who was "only doing your job."

Thus, seven or eight months passed in which Dr. Carter expressed pleasure with the therapy. He commented frequently that his wife, who had had many doubts about therapy and had only acceded to his decision to begin because she was at her wits' end with him, saw definite improvement. Then several external events occurred that sharply changed his mood. Even before these occurred, however, the therapist had begun to point out Dr. Carter's growing impatience with his inability to come to a decision about his life, and hence, his impatience, although unspoken, with the therapy. Dr. Carter experienced the impatience of being more with himself than with the therapy. He redoubled his efforts to find the answer in his attachments to his mother and father and the extent of their influence over him, although in fact his visits to them in the nursing home were rare. One further issue had begun to be talked about reluctantly. Dr. Carter was haunted by bizarre sexual fears, such as dentate vaginas, being demeaned or castrated, and being caught in humiliating pornographic situations.

The following external events sharply changed his mood: his father had a serious stroke in the nursing home, and his mother became increasingly disoriented; his father-in-law finally decided to retire; and his wife became extremely upset because she was not getting pregnant. He felt overwhelmed and desperate. At first he came to his hours prepared with questions about his mother's condition and his wife's state of mind that might help him out. He was reluctant to discuss any possibility that the desperateness of his plight allowed him to want "help" from the therapist. There were also questions about what he could do to make his own career decision, which elicited from the therapist the same clarification.

Then Dr. Carter's approach changed again, and though he continued to be agitated in the sessions, he began to express a level of desperation and hopelessness not heard before. He vowed to quit surgery, a decision, as he had earlier indicated, that he thought the therapist, as a doctor, would disapprove. And for the first time he discussed this as a possibility with his senior partner, much to that gentleman's surprise. The senior partner remained calm, however, and told Dr. Carter that he should give the matter further thought because it was too important a decision to be made hastily.

Somehow this response was seen by Dr. Carter as indicating that he, his dilemma, and the extent of his upset were not being taken seriously, a charge which he had been hurling constantly at the therapist. He could hardly imagine the possibility that not agreeing with his view of himself in all this was not the same as minimizing his plight and his discomfort. In fact, it was during such a discussion that he first brought up suicide. During the next few sessions he continued to elaborate on his sense of desperation. He was furious with his senior partner for not getting back to their discussion about his resignation. He felt he could not handle the complex arrangements concerning the situation with his parents, let alone the emotional implications, and his sister was useless (this seemed true). He felt responsible for his wife's agitation, blaming his own sexual perversity for the lack of conception. He felt he could neither prevail on his father-in-law to remain in the business nor could he let the business go. The therapy had been his last hope, but here too his difficulty in getting in touch with his emotions, another example of his essential weakness, had doomed it to failure. In these hopeless circumstances the only way out was somehow or other to do himself in. "My wife and child will be better off without me as a burden," was his cry.

THE CLINICAL CHOICES

All threats of suicide must be taken seriously (Farberow and Shneidman, 1961; Stengel, 1964). Even those that are patently aimed at getting attention or stirring things up rather than at self-destruction can lead to miscalculation and death (Motto, 1965). The clinical question is less whether a nonpsychotic patient has a genuine wish to kill himself than whether there is a genuine threat that a suicide attempt will be made. Those making suicide threats, and especially suicide attempts, can be located along a continuum. Although this continuum has two poles, every point on it partakes to some degree of an underlying sense of helplessness and hopelessness (Bibring, 1953).

Even if it seems that clinically a person may be suicidal, it is often difficult to decide what to do about it. The first consideration is usually whether hospitalization might be useful. This is a complex question. Hospitalization carries with it the possibility of great costs in money, time, dignity, hospitalitis, the establishment of a permanent, detrimental record, and the effect on others' views of the individual. Of even greater importance, it often does not work. Determined people can and do kill themselves in hospitals (Kahne, 1968). Hospitalization works best if some part of the patient can acknowledge its necessity and if his social network can be mobilized to encourage and support the experience and to interact effectively with the hospital community (Stengel and Cook, 1958).

As patients, Mr. Brown and Dr. Carter had much in common. Both of them, while certainly perceiving various aspects of their internal and external relationships through distorting lenses, had no trouble with reality relatedness to time, place, and person. Neither psychosis, hostile delusions, nor any of the other antecedents of suicide searched for in individual histories were present. Neither patient had had anyone close to him commit suicide or had experienced an early or traumatic loss of a significant other. There were no previous hospitalizations or suicide attempts, nor were the vegetative signs of depression, such as prolonged sleeplessness, overpowering. Although both men experienced various external events as traumatic and crushing, neither was in a genuinely destructive reality bind, as they both acknowledged. Dr. Carter contrasted his relatively minor difficulties with those of an acquaintance who had committed suicide before being indicted for embezzlement. The extent of Dr. Carter's reaction to his own dilemma was taken by him as an indication of his feeble intolerance to pain. And finally, both of these men, in the therapy as in the rest of their lives, had the capacity to be sufficiently convincing to frighten most therapists. This fact had to be taken into account because therapists, as some of the best known practitioners contend (Litman, 1959; Mintz, 1961; Motto, 1965), must rely on their gut feelings—their deep-seated intuitions, honed by experience—to help them delineate a genuine risk of suicide.

There were, however, differentiating factors in the two cases. Although neither patient had an actual problem with reality relatedness, Mr. Brown's sense that his external world had collapsed had the quality of belief rather than fear, and therefore it was qualitatively different from Dr. Carter's frantic feeling that he could not find in himself the strength to deal with his quandaries. And again, although neither had overwhelming vegetative signs of depression, Mr. Brown's report of waking at 3:00 A.M., staring hopelessly into the darkness, and praying for oblivion, conveyed the conviction of a wish for total surcease from sorrow. Mr. Brown also had a plan. Far from insisting in a general way that death might be better than life, he knew exactly what he wished to do and, even more to the point, once he had come to that decision, he no longer felt mired in the apathy of hopelessness and helplessness. His decision freed energy. He continued to feel hopeless but not helpless (Minkoff, Bergman, Beck, and Beck, 1973).

Besides having decided on a plan of action, which was in itself remarkable, Mr. Brown had the available energy to carry it out. Above all, he had achieved a dissociation so that affects other than those concerned with self-destruction were separated and repressed. It seemed to the therapist that those human feelings of connectedness and attachment to other human beings and to one's own hopes for oneself, or even to the mean, envious, spiteful, vengeful feelings that are part of everyone's motivation to continue living, were no longer directly available to Mr. Brown.

Under such circumstances a clinical decision was made to take steps beyond therapeutic clarification. The therapist felt that Mr. Brown's keeping of the appointment provided some leeway by suggesting that suicidal action was not intended to be precipitous. Mr. Brown was told that his mother would be contacted right away and that a period of hospitalization was necessary. The only choice offered to Mr. Brown was the small one of deciding whether he would collect his belongings with his mother or would let her do it alone. His mother came to the therapist's office while Mr. Brown waited, and arrangements were made. After making initial complaints and disclaimers of the necessity for all this, which were met with gentle but firm statements that right then he was in no position emotionally to make sound decisions, he relapsed into a stony, apathetic, monosyllabic state. It was in this condition that he was admitted to the hospital.

Although in the case of Dr. Carter the tempo of the treatment interaction was very intense, factors different from those evident in Mr. Brown's case seemed to be at work. Throughout the period of suicide threats (Basescu, 1965) and the agitation, he never missed work and seemed to be doing a satisfactory job—although the idea of a surgeon working in that state is enough to give any therapist gray hair! The greatest agitation seemed to be expressed to the therapist; much less spilled over at home. Dr. Carter's ability and willingness to compartmentalize his difficulties indicated a continuing capacity both to be aware of what was appropriate and to care enough to act on that awareness. Whatever sleep problems he had were similar to those he had occasionally had when he was in an anxious state.

The issue that made the clinical decision particularly tricky was Dr. Carter's insistence that the therapist must do something "helpful." That meant to do something other than point out that all this thunder and lightning represented convincing evidence of the extent to which Dr. Carter wanted something done by the therapist about his weakness. He wanted some concrete life direction rather than the therapeutic process of attempting to make sense of what made him see himself as so weak and desperate when he obviously was choosing not to use the emotional and intellectual capacities available to him. Showing him the extent of his belief that the therapist had splendid advice or succor that would lead him down the right path, but was withholding it out of some doctrinaire nonsense that the patient should find it for himself, was seen by Dr. Carter as not doing anything and certainly not as taking his pain seriously. It was hard for him even to think of the possibility that part of him could make good use of what was going on in the therapy by learning about himself rather than by getting from the therapist what he "wanted," which was not there to be gotten. Dr. Carter himself suggested hospitalization and medication (Kiev, 1975), and he offered potent interpretations about his identification with his weak father and equally potent interpretations about his castration fears—in fact, anything that would provide strength from the outside, rather than thinking about what made it important for him to see himself, and to be seen by others, as weak, impotent, and incapable both in the therapy and out of it. It would have been easy, of course, to show him that actually he was picking and choosing where he wanted to be seen as weak, and that in most of his outside life he was maintaining a very different image. But it was feared that he was so agitated that he might see this as a sort of dare or a demand that he had to give up appearances of "strength" on the outside before he could get what he wanted from the therapist.

In some respects that last possibility was the chief concern. The turmoil in the therapy was considerable, but the clinical evidence pointed less to suicide than to a struggle over what the therapy was about. The tyranny of this contention of weakness was evident in every interchange. The mutual observation of this display of power provided a very different view of Dr. Carter's claimed interactions with parents, wife, friends, colleagues, and therapist than the one he himself held to so firmly. Nevertheless, if the struggle were to become sufficiently bitter, a man with so fixed a view of himself could easily pull out all the stops. Thus, if he were challenged as to his sincerity, a symbolic threat of suicide (the desperation used as a weapon in the therapy) could lead to an actual suicide attempt with all of the frightening consequences of such an act. Articulating that concern to Dr. Carter, and recognizing together that the struggle about what the therapy had become was the central issue, would prevent escalation. Fortunately, during the early honeymoon phase of the treatment similar clarifications had been more or less accepted and could be referred to. In addition, it was possible to show Dr. Carter that similar struggles existed in situations outside the therapy: his marriage and his relationship with a live-in baby-sitter provided particularly rich and convincing counterpoints.

THE TREATMENT OF SUICIDAL PATIENTS

As anyone familiar with the histories presented in the professional literature will have anticipated, both of these cases had happy endings. When discussing them in a teaching situation it is relatively easy to show how the therapist was able to differentiate between the serious suicidal risk and the individual who wanted to be seen as suicidal. The criteria for identifying the genuinely suicidal patient can be presented in a reasonably straightforward manner in a lecture—although, of course, to list these criteria intellectually is quite different from putting them to use in the tense atmosphere of an interaction with a severely upset person (Stengel and Cook, 1958; Farberow and Shneidman, 1961).

It is much harder to convey to students two delicate balances that must be understood by the therapist. The first is the seesaw between the patient's positive and negative feelings toward the therapist and the therapy (the transference). The second is the balance between content and structure; that is, between the actual content of what the patient says (the expression of his desperation), and the underlying structural determinants of what he says (his sense that it is important to be seen as desperate).

Positive Versus Negative Feelings

The need to understand the balance between the patient's positive and negative feelings toward the therapist has been obscured by the belief, held by many analytically oriented therapists, that a split exists between the therapeutic alliance and the transference neurosis (Blum, 1979; Greenson and Wexler, 1969; Zetzel, 1970). The therapeutic alliance is seen as the more human or more "real" relationship between therapist and patient, and the transference neurosis is defined as the feelings and ideas derived from early relationships that are transferred to the therapist, thereby permitting the exposure, analysis, and reconstruction of the original infantile neurosis. From the ego psychological or structural viewpoint taken by this chapter, there is no such split, but neither does the transference consist entirely of the original "infantile neurosis." If one views the therapeutic situation from the standpoint of the consistent, relatively autonomous ego patterns of perceiving and reacting within relationships, then every aspect of the patient's interaction with the therapist, whether it concerns the wish to change an appointment, to report a death in the family, or to make a demand for advice, will be influenced by the patient's characteristic ways of responding. Thus the question to be decided by the therapist is not on which side of the so-called split the interaction is taking place, but rather what is the best, most appropriate moment in which to show the patient that a particular mode of interaction is characteristic and automatic.

The therapist recognizes the patient's style of interaction as ego-syntonic. By judiciously pointing out this style, the therapist attempts to call its unvarying nature into question so that the style of response will become, at least as far as the therapy goes, ego-dystonic. In becoming conscious about the unvarying style of response, the patient gains the ability to think more closely about when that style seems reasonable and useful and when it does not. This sort of investigation arouses the patient's curiosity, as well as often irritating him, and permits a more careful assessment of those instances or areas in which the response is relatively free of painful conflicts and of those in which it is not. For instance, although Dr. Carter's somewhat self-effacing manner had served him well throughout his school career and had made him a very popular surgeon among operating room staff, it served him poorly in close personal relationships and in his efforts to resolve inner conflicts about ambition. In therapy, this manner, shown by his difficulty in asking for a change in appointment time, led more directly to his worries about being pushy than did either his repetitive statements about acquiring his fears because of his father's weakness or his expression of anger at his senior partner.

The issue of whether the therapist should be "human" with his patient by expressing sympathy about a loss, for example, seems nothing more than a red herring. Therapy is by definition a human relationship and an equal one. The therapist and the patient are colleagues in the study of the patient. Hartmann (1939) accurately called therapy "the study of self-deceit and its motivations" (p. 57). In order for this study to be effective, these two experts—the patient concerning himself, the therapist on how people's psyches function—are assigned quite different tasks. This task differentiation does not imply inequality. But inequality would be implied if the therapist thought that his "human" expression of sympathy was so important to the patient that without it the whole therapeutic enterprise would collapse. Is it less human to say to the patient, "How upsetting this must be for you!" (if it was), than to formally state, "How sorry I was to hear about your loss"? To take one of the polar alternatives—saying nothing or immediately considering the event from the point of view of some deep-seated interpretation derived from the infantile neurosis—may miss the chance to establish an empathic awareness of what is going on within the patient without losing the potential for objectivity. It does not seem necessary or even advisable for the therapist to set himself up as a person with his own set of feelings about the event—the therapeutic alliance position—any more than it would be advisable to use the event to exhume unconscious associations at a time when conscious feelings are so pertinent—the reconstruction of the infantile neurosis position. As will be reiterated at the end of this chapter, to the greatest extent possible the therapist always wants to involve some part of the patient's observing ego in their interchanges (Zinberg, 1987).

Considering the balance between the patient's positive and negative feelings about the endeavor means to consider how the task is going as a whole; it has nothing to do with a presumed split between a positive, "real" relationship and a negative or positive transference relationship. The negative or positive transference reactions indeed occur, but these arise in connection with other factors that are active in the therapeutic process.

It is easy to understand what prompted such students of therapeutic technique as Ralph Greenson and Milton Wexler (1969) and Elizabeth Zetzel (1970) to promulgate the notion of a therapeutic alliance in the first place. Therapist and patient embark on the enterprise together. They both have decided that there is a credible job to be done, and the patient has decided that the therapist seems to be a reasonable person to work with. To the extent that the therapist demonstrates a capacity for empathy, maintains objectivity, indicates thoughtfulness and intelligence and a continuing good will, there is a positive bond. Because of this bond, the negative feelings about what is going on can be thought about and pointed out as coming from the patient's underlying wishes and preoccupations, often stemming from early life. From the transference neurosis point of view, the patient wants gratification from the therapist, and it is this hope for gratification that keeps him in treatment. The therapist must frustrate these wishes in order that they may be available for the reconstruction of their origins and thus may be worked through. Strict adherents of this transference neurosis, such as Charles Brenner (1979), see Greenson's stress on the real or human aspect of the patient–therapist relationship as gratifying these desires, and thus the argument about the complex relationship of therapist and patient is reduced to the question of "to gratify or not to gratify."

What seems to have been overlooked in the issue of the *Journal of the American Psychoanalytic Association* already referred to (Blum, 1979) is the patient's curiosity about himself. Few people would come to a therapist if they did not wonder about their ways of dealing with themselves and others. There is no denying the power of the desire for gratification as evidenced by Dr. Carter; nevertheless, what kept him in treatment was less the belief that the magical road to strength would be shown him than his dawning curiosity about what made it so important for him to deny, minimize, reduce, and fear his own active capacities. Without that curiosity there would have been no treatment. Yet the process of evoking this curiosity called into question much of what was habitual and therefore reliable in his responses—no easy experience for him! In spite of the patient's awareness that the therapist makes sense in showing up certain inflexibilities, therapy is a troublesome and irritating process. The therapist may be doing his job, but the patient finds it hard to like either it or the colleague therapist who was responsible for the self-consciousness about ways of thinking in the first place. That the colleague tries to be sure that both participants are keenly aware of what is being worked on is little help in alleviating the irritation. The state of the feelings active in the therapeutic relationship at this point is slightly negative at best. For the therapist to regard such feelings chiefly as the current representatives of frustrations arising from old longings and old frustrations is to miss a great deal of the nature of the job undertaken. Since the patient could not have known in advance where this undertaking might lead, it is not surprising that he finds self-consciousness about his automatic responses uncomfortable and irritating despite his growing curiosity and his pleasure in self-discovery.

It is the therapist's capacity for empathy that helps make the therapy bearable and consistently interesting. Empathy here does not mean just sympathy for the patient's discomfort. It means conveying not only an awareness of the discomfort but a clear and precise sense of how it is being experienced. The therapist must show the patient that he can understand, almost from the inside, the patient's feeling of desperation—in Dr. Carter's case, a feeling that he could not face the world (his wife) that was demanding a decision from him and his embarrassment at his "inability" to make one. The therapist's spoken awareness of Dr. Carter's irritation at the insistence that he had the capacity to make a decision but at the moment found it important to postpone making it was annoying enough. What was even more annoying was the therapist's insistence that the patient's metaphorical whipping of both the therapist and himself in order to force a decision was part of the patient's problem, not the solution. In this situation the precision of the therapist's understanding of what was going on in Dr. Carter had to be convincing. Conveying to him that the work of the therapy, by calling attention repeatedly to his ways of treating himself as issues to be studied, left Dr. Carter feeling helpless, particularly in relation to feeling justified in his struggle with the therapist. For only if Dr. Carter believed that the therapist had an empathic awareness of how he felt, could he consider that the therapist's objective disagreement with his perception of himself came from something other than insensitivity, hostility, or stupidity (Zinberg, 1987).

An excessively positive transference reaction must be handled with even greater empathy than a patient's negative feelings. Everyone is very delicate when it comes to rejection; feelings are easily hurt. Conveying to patients the awareness that their positive feelings are based on misperceptions runs the risk of distorting the underlying equality of the relationship. But not taking up excessive positive feelings would run the risk of the therapist's silence being seen as acceptance, which might be taken as proof of the validity of the feelings themselves or of the acceptance of the hopes that had prompted such feelings, whether of direct gratification, magical intervention, the importance of worship, or the minimization of the adorer. Raising such questions, asking someone to doubt positive feelings (which, at some level at least people like to have), if not done carefully, brings up the fear (a cliché but very real) that the therapy will show that only negative (bad) feelings are at the core of the individual's psyche and that positive feelings are false or inconsequential.

The most effective way to prevent the various transference feelings about the therapist and the therapeutic task from becoming an overwhelming issue is to prepare for them as early as possible. The earlier the therapist can point out to the patient that it might be hard for him to see himself as having wishes he would disapprove of, or that his habit of being an appreciator versus a critic could be an issue in therapy, or that it is painful to feel attached to someone whom one disapproves of or to find that the attachment is not requited, the better prepared the patient is when these issues come up. Also, the therapist can objectify the transference relationship by classifying the therapy itself as one of various life situations that lend themselves to the study of the patient's repetitious ways of thinking about interactions. In Mr. Brown's case, for example, it would be important at the right time to show that just as it was hard to be active enough to call up friends or to initiate a job search, so it might be hard to arrange appointments in therapy. In the same way a patient who is frightened unless she has a cache of vitamins or a potential supply of boyfriends should be warned early that concerns about the supply of therapy may well arise.

Relationship Between Structure and Content

Taking up the emotional reactions to the therapist and the therapy is, of course, part of the content of therapy. But just as there are patients with whom it is hard to have any discussion of the therapy itself, so there are those who are more than willing for that microcosm to occupy the entire space. The first rule of any therapy must be to meet the patient where he is. First, both therapist and patient must acknowledge the importance to the patient of his desperation. Second, the therapist must take the patient where he does not want to go. If the patient prefers to emphasize the transference, the therapist will wonder if the same emotions and points of view apply elsewhere, in both the past and the present. If the patient sticks to his present life, the therapist will wonder about the past and the transference. That search for content is not for the supposed "facts" of the content, as the patient often thinks, but in order to discover the extent to which the patient brings the same point of view to bear on every aspect of his life. As pointed out earlier, this can be difficult and irritating, as well as interest producing, so that the timing of these interventions is balanced by the therapist's awareness of the patient's emotional position vis-à-vis the therapist.

This is particularly true when approaching the patient from the structural or characterological standpoint, regarding the patient's current positions as the product of a consistent series of emotional choices. In Gill's terms (1981), the patient is seen as proactive rather than reactive. In using these terms Gill was distinguishing a psychological model of functioning from a medical model. In the medical model the doctor is in charge and the patient's reactive position is appropriate. The same holds true when a psychiatrist gives out medication (or advice). Gill visualizes the psychological model in its clearest form as proactive; that is, both therapist and patient have an inherent concept of responsibility for each other's part in the interaction. This responsibility has less to do with activity in the behavioral sense than with ego activity. Accepting advice can amount to an ego choice, of course, just as storming a machine-gun nest after receiving orders to charge can indicate ego passivity. Patients often speak of someone having "made me feel guilty." They are nonplussed when asked, "Is it important for you to respond to that with guilt?" Being asked instead the more automatic question, "What makes you feel guilty about that?" they are more likely to both justify their feelings of guilt and emphasize the guilt-evoker's intent. Although both questions are intended to stimulate interest in the patient's ego activity or proactivity, in regard to guilt, the question about importance places the issue more squarely within an ego hierarchy of values. It not only implies choice but also calls attention to those thoughts and feelings that might actively take exception—be in conflict—if guilt were not evoked. There can be enormous pain and self-loathing in guilt just as at other times there can be piety as well.

As much as possible, the therapist who works from the characterological point of view perceives the content of therapy as proactive. But to the therapist committed to the developmental standpoint, who sees a direct causal relationship between early childhood events and adult concerns, the proactivity of content is far less obvious. Certainly patients who come to therapists today believe in a reactive relationship between childhood and adult issues, and well they may. Consider, for example, the following statement in a feature article in *The New York Times Magazine* (Sass, 1982) on the new interest in borderline personalities, which is preceded by a description of a young man who had joined a cult because of difficulty in tolerating being alone: "A major cause of abandonment depression is the behavior of a mother who, threatened by separation from her baby, may become punitive or emotionally withdrawn when the child expresses his need for independence (for example, when he learns to walk)" (p. 66). Any patient who had read that statement might reasonably say, "I hate to be alone, and I feel empty and deserted because I was psychologically deserted by my bad mother at age one," and might feel at the same time that this reactive response was explanatory. In the developmental model this position, which is to a certain extent justified, presents the patient with a complex contradictory message. As stated at the beginning of this chapter, Freud's early insistence that patients had thoughts and feelings about these early interactions was shocking. For his first patients to permit recognition of these feelings was proactive, but for a modern patient to come to the therapist with such a statement is reactive.

If the therapist were to accept such a statement as explanatory, there would be no reason for therapist and patient to explore what had made it so important for the patient to hold on to the old wishes for mother to be there, even if the "history" was "true." Some questions would hardly need to be considered if the early view of mother–child interaction was seen as causal. For example: "Even today as an adult the absence of mother (or a reasonable facsimile thereof) is still experienced as terrifying or depressing; isn't that interesting?" or, "What perceptions of yourself would be active in conceptualizing the situation in that way?"

The suicidal threats seen in our case histories raise interesting questions about the proactive or ego active way of thinking about intent. Dr. Carter's case is fairly straightforward. He believed himself a reactive victim of both early childhood experience and current reality encounters. The task of the therapy was to show up the inhibitions against seeing himself as ego active in general—certainly in the present and, perhaps in a somewhat different way, in the past. With Mr. Brown the issue was more complex. He did not deny his responsibility; that is, he recognized his ego activity in his passive behavior. The decision to kill himself was experienced by him as both ego active and, if carried out, behaviorally active. At the same time, he saw himself, given his feeling state, as having no choice. Thus, though he saw himself as ego active by making the decision, in his dissociated state he felt that he had not made a proactive choice but was following the only road open to him, and to that extent he was ego passive. The therapist's job would be to show him at some point that this was a misperception of ego activity.

In fact, Mr. Brown's view of suicide came very close to a way in which the public perceives psychiatric therapy (Shneidman, 1971). There is a persistent belief in the curative power of abreaction; that is, getting one's feelings out. By killing himself, Mr. Brown hoped to discharge all the pent-up affects and find surcease from conflict. If death was the only way to do it, so be it. In a characterological model, the emphasis would be far less on the feelings pent up in Mr. Brown than on *what made him feel* that he could tolerate affects so poorly, whether rage, tenderness, envy, spite, or closeness. All of us have all of these feelings, and each of us tolerates some of them better than others. Asking Mr. Brown what factors made the occasional spitefulness hard for him to bear was different from the traditional cliché, "What did you feel about that?" or, "It made you angry, didn't it?" thereby asking for a discharge of affect. In the traditional view, that sort of discharge could as easily be reactive as proactive, particularly if the patient believed himself justified in having the feeling. Therefore the responsibility for the feeling could, in the patient's view, lie in the situation, not in himself.

Equally, a patient may believe that the expression of such affects is seen by the therapist as a good thing, and in that event the patient is reactively providing what the therapist wants. In an ego psychological model, affects are necessary but not sufficient. If the expression of those affects that are painful and poorly tolerated by the patient is to be proactive and clarifying of self-deceit, the patient must become aware of the ego structures that have made them so difficult to tolerate.

A similar issue arises in connection with the currently popular word "needs." "To have one's needs fulfilled" has become a freedom or entitlement virtually equivalent to freedom of religion, equality under the law, or the pursuit of happiness. Although the use of the word need rather than wish may represent only a semantic quibble, often it does not. When patients say they need affection or discharge, they frequently do not see themselves as having a choice. At the moment they do not realize that our needs are few—food, drink, sleep, and defecation— while our wishes are many. By calling a wish a need they are experiencing themselves as not ego active but as reactive and justified. Who could blame us, or even imagine we had a choice, for seeking and demanding water if we were dying of thirst in the desert? But to want something, no matter how badly or overdeterminedly, means that one has a choice and that, in choosing, one exhibits ego activity and takes responsibility for the choice. Thus, throughout the therapy the patient's choices, particularly in relation to the therapist and the therapy, are kept consistently in awareness. They are affected by the way in which the content, the patient's material, is approached. Although it is clearly recognized that at some times in life—for example, in early childhood, in extreme old age, and in certain situations, such as being drafted or being destitute—one's choices are limited and one's responses are overdetermined, some choice is virtually always possible. Looking at one's inner and outer life, and at the past in particular, from this point of view of making choices sharply changes one's view of one's interaction with the world.

During the work of the therapy, the therapist and patient have clearly differentiated but equal tasks. The one is an expert on himself and the other an expert on how people function psychologically. As awareness develops, what is done with that awareness is the job of the patient. One situation a therapist *never* wants to let develop is for the patient to ask: "Now that I know that, what good does it do me?" At all times it should be the therapist who asks the question: "Now that you know that, how will you use it?" In this view of therapy, there is no question of intellectual versus emotional awareness as there sometimes is in a more developmental view of therapy. What would stop the patient from putting to use the sense of himself gained in the therapy is seen as not only part of the therapy but part of the resistance to therapy. For example, Dr. Carter for a long time kept his growing awareness of his wish to be accepted as weak separate from his difficulty in making a career decision, which allowed him to continue his threats of suicide. It was important for the therapist to keep this separation in the forefront of the therapy. If he had not, Dr. Carter would surely have been one to belabor the futility of self-awareness (Zinberg, 1987).

This sense of choice, of proaction, carries with it a greater necessity to consider the relatedness of the choice to external social reality than if one relied on a more reactive, developmental model. From the structural viewpoint, initial choices concerning a mode of response in the family microcosm are not static responses based solely on early identifications or interactions, for instance, in the case of consistent and stubbornly refusing to give an inch, or of getting assistance easily through trying hard but ineptly. They are tested in a variety of social environments and must be effective—whatever that means to the individual—if they are to become increasingly independent of whatever prompted them in the first place. Even the primitive superego, which reflects the early childhood experience in total yes/no terms, without points in between, can quickly define what is to be a yes and what is to be a no, based on social experience. It is interesting to consider the effect of social change on ego development. In the past when, according to students of the history of science, knowledge doubled about every 100 years, most transmission of knowledge was vertical, from the older parental generation to the younger. With knowledge today doubling every twelve years, parents and children in many respects do not share the same average expectable environment. Such transmission of information, particularly around social mores but subtly around technology as well, is horizontal, through the peer group. Parents who are uncomfortable with computers see their children accepting them as easily as the telephone. Certainly, information about the technology as well as the mores of intoxicant use has been transmitted through peer groups with dispatch (Zinberg, 1975).

The importance of social learning is being emphasized here because it is a central element in the ego development of values, attitudes, and perceptual and discharge thresholds. But it is limited. The ego is adaptable and plastic, but only within limits. The task of therapy, as pointed out earlier, is to enable a person to become aware of his characteristic responses and the values and attitudes he has accepted to support these responses. Only through the recognition of elaborate skeins of rationalization and self-deception can it be determined where these habitual responses work for him and where they work against him. Potentially that recognition of areas of self-deceit opens up fresh choices, but again only within limits. Dr. Carter may develop sufficient awareness to recognize that his secret satisfaction at being holier than those about him may be costly to him in the world of social reality and to his own self-esteem, and he may then forgo that satisfaction in order to get something done in his business. But he will always be a careful person with a distaste for direct pushiness, preferring to achieve his goals through a low profile.

In this structural view the ego is seen as a coherent whole striving to maintain a homeostasis. There may be inhibitions against the use of what is available, and to each individual that leads to painful and destructive choices, but there are no defects. Certainly some people are inhibited against using such primitive emotions as rage and lust reasonably. But what has made it important for them to inhibit various stances either too much or too little can be thought through after they have begun to understand that they mind having ordinary human emotions such as rage or jealousy. The way this is usually phrased by patients is that although it is not bad to have such feelings, the way or the degree to which they have them is awful. It is surprising to what extent therapists tend to see the affect per se as "causing" the problem, rather than seeing how it has been managed by the ego. From the perspective of functioning in the world, the ego's homeostasis can be thought of as having various potential levels of functioning.

The concept of therapy is based largely on the ability of the ego to split and observe itself. If one considers the case of Mr. Brown in the light of the work of Otto Kernberg (1976), it is clear that the ego can proceed with its general functioning, where several activities, such as the executive, perceptual, and setting discharge thresholds, which go on simultaneously (in therapy, for example), provide not only content and affect but also a virtually simultaneous observing aspect. With Mr. Brown there was no lack of conscious awareness of his overall sense of purposelessness, but that awareness was separated from any desire to observe its origins and concomitants. A therapy aimed at revealing self-deceit and its motivations constantly calls upon that observing capacity of the ego. It is as if all of the therapist never addresses directly all of the patient, because the therapist, in the way he puts his remarks, always takes along with him some aspect of the patient's observing ego. Every question, every comment, approaches the material from the side, so to speak, asking the patient's observing ego to notice, to perceive, to be aware of the characteristic position from which the material emanated. In this view, with the exception of major mental illness, there is no illness, nor is there any becoming better; there is only awareness and choice.

CONCLUSION

It is necessary, in dealing with suicidal patients, to go beyond the attempt to relate their weak, depressed view of themselves to the emotional experiences of their early life (the developmental approach), in the expectation that the working out of those childhood affects will remove the desire for self-destruction. Proceeding from the basis of the structural model, in which the relatively autonomous ego is influenced by the social setting and social learning, the author has attempted to ask questions that will elicit not just an affect but the individual's attitude toward that affect. In this way the goal of the therapy has been to discover and make clear to patients the automatic, repetitious ways in which they view themselves and the world, and to show them that self-awareness (and the resulting ability to make responsible choices) rather than self-destruction is their goal.

REFERENCES

Basescu, S. (1965), The threat of suicide in psychotherapy. *Amer. J. Psychother.*, 19:99–102.
Bibring, E. (1953), The mechanism of depression. In: *Affective Disorders*, ed. P. Greenacre. New York: International Universities Press, pp. 13–48.
Blum, H.T. (1979), Psychoanalytic technique and the theory of therapy. *J. Amer. Psychoanal. Assn.* (Suppl.), Vol. 27.
Brenner, C. (1979), Working alliance, therapeutic alliance and transference. *J. Amer. Psychoanal. Assn.*, 27:137–158.
Erikson, E.H. (1950), *Childhood and Society*. New York: W.W. Norton.
——— (1980), Elements of a psychoanalytic theory of psychosocial development. In: *The Course of Life. Psychoanalytic Contributions toward Understanding Personality Development, Vol. 1, Infancy and Early Childhood*, eds. S.I. Greenspan & G.H. Pollock. Rockville, MD: National Institute of Mental Health.

Farberow, N.L., & Shneidman, E.S., eds. (1961), *The Cry for Help*. New York: McGraw-Hill.

Freud, A. (1966), The ego and the mechanisms of defense. In: *The Writings of Anna Freud*, Vol. 2. New York: International Universities Press.

Freud, S. (1923), The ego and the id. *Standard Edition*, 19:1–60. London: Hogarth Press, 1961.

———— (1937), Analysis terminable and interminable. *Standard Edition*, 22:209–255. London: Hogarth Press, 1964.

Gill, M.M. (1959), The present state of psychoanalytic theory. *J. Abnorm. Soc. Psychol.*, 58:62–71.

———— ed. (1967), *The Collected Papers of David Rapaport*. New York: Basic Books.

———— (1981), *Analysis of Transference: Theory and Technique*, Vol. 1. New York: International Universities Press.

———— Hoffman, I.Z. (1982), *Analysis of Transference: Studies of Seven Audio-recorded Psychoanalytic Sessions*, Vol. 2. New York: International Universities Press.

Greenberg, J.R., & Mitchell, S.A. (1983), *Object Relations in Psychoanalytic Theory*. Cambridge, MA: Harvard University Press.

Greenson, R.R., & Wexler, M. (1969), The non-transference relationship in the psychoanalytic situation. *Internat. J. Psycho-Anal.*, 51:143–150.

Hartmann, H. (1939), *Ego Psychology and the Problem of Adaptation*. New York: International Universities Press, 1958.

Jahoda, M. (1965), *Definitions of Normality*. New York: International Universities Press.

Kahne, M.J. (1968), Suicide among patients in mental hospitals: A study of the psychiatrists who conducted their psychotherapy. *Psychiatry*, 31:32–43.

Kernberg, O. (1976), *Object Relations Theory and Psychoanalysis*. New York: Jason Aronson.

Kiev, A. (1975), Symptoms, patterns and the acceptance of the "sick role" in attempted suicide. *Curr. Med. Res. Opinion*, 2 (Suppl.):34.

Klein, G.S. (1968), Psychoanalysis—II: Ego psychology. In: *International Encyclopaedia of the Social Sciences*, Vol. 13, ed. D.L. Sills. New York: Macmillan/Free Press.

Litman, R.E. (1959), Immobilization response to suicidal behavior. *Arch. Gen. Psychiat.*, 81:360–364.

Minkoff, K., Bergman, E., Beck, A.T., & Beck, R. (1973), Hopelessness, depression, and attempted suicide. *Amer. J. Psychiat.*, 130:455–457.

Mintz, R.S. (1961), Psychotherapy of the suicidal patient. *Amer. J. Psychother.*, 15:348–350.

Motto, J. (1965), Suicide attempts: A longitudinal view. *Arch. Gen. Psychiat.*, 13:916–920.

Rapaport, D. (1958), The theory of ego autonomy. In: *The Collected Papers of David Rapaport*, ed. M.M. Gill. New York: Basic Books, 1976, pp. 722–744.

———— (1959), Historical introduction. In: *Identity and the Life Cycle*, E.H. Erikson. Psychological Issues, Monograph 1. New York: International Universities Press.

Sass, L. (1982), The borderline personality. *New York Times Magazine*, August 22:66.

Schafer, R. (1976), *A New Language for Psychoanalysis*. New Haven, CT: Yale University Press.

———— (1982), The relevance of the "here and now" transference interpretation to the reconstruction of early development. *Inter. J. Psycho-Anal.*, 63:77–82.

Shneidman, E.S. (1971), On the deromanticization of death. *Amer. J. Psychother.*, 25:4.

Stengel, E. (1964), *Suicide and Attempted Suicide*. Baltimore, MD: Penguin Books.

———— Cook, N.G. (1958), *Attempted Suicide: Its Social Significance and Effects*. Maudsley Monograph 4. London: Chapman & Hall.

Szasz, T.S. (1974), *The Myth of Mental Illness: Foundation of a Theory of Personal Conduct*, rev. ed. New York: Harper & Row.

Zetzel, E.R. (1970), *The Capacity for Emotional Growth*. New York: International Universities Press.

Zinberg, N.E. (1975), Addiction and ego function. *The Psychoanalytic Study of the Child*, 30:567–588. New Haven, CT: Yale University Press.

———— (1984), *Drug, Set, and Setting: The Basis for Controlled Intoxicant Use*. New Haven, CT: Yale University Press.

———— (1985), The private versus the public psychiatric interview. *Amer. J. Psychiat.*, 142:889–894.

———— (1987), Elements of the private therapeutic interview. *Amer. J. Psychiat.*, 144:1527–1533.

17

Psychotherapy with Suicidal Patients: The Empathic Method

Douglas Jacobs, M.D.

Edwin Shneidman, one of the leading authorities on suicide, states that "working with a highly suicidal person demands a different kind of involvement. There may be as important a conceptual difference between ordinary psychotherapy (with individuals where dying or living is not the issue) and psychotherapy with acutely suicidal persons as there is between ordinary psychotherapy and ordinary talk" (Shneidman, 1981, p. 344).

There are many questions that a therapist must ask himself in relation to psychotherapy with suicidal patients: How active should I be? How available, how accepting? How much can I tolerate? How much can I monitor my own feelings?

The skills and techniques of the therapist are varied—the relevance of biology and diagnosis must be integrated. The utility of giving appropriate medication whether it be antidepressants or antipsychotics must be considered. It is *part* of the psychotherapy and should not be seen as an either/or phenomenon. Robins, in his recent book *The Final Months,* noted in a sample of 134 unselected suicides that over 47 percent had a diagnosis of affective disorders (Robins, 1981). Therapists should be familiar with demographics and clinical factors that have been shown to correlate with higher suicide risks. But, although one must be cognizant of the general statistics, it is the uniqueness of the individual that becomes paramount—the specific biological or genetic factors, the psychologic or personality development, and the social context (Motto, Heilbron, and Juster, 1985; Mack, in press).

Because suicide cuts across the whole spectrum of psychiatric illness, a therapist should be familiar with several theories as part of developing a therapeutic strategy. It is important to recognize that there are valuable contributions to the treatment of suicide from several different schools. It is not suggested that a choice be made between one school of thought or another, but rather an interweaving of perspectives, depending on the condition of the patient.

Dynamic theory, beginning from the time of Freud, has provided us with a framework for understanding suicide as a potential outcome of depression. The turning against oneself of hostile impulses and the splitting of the ego are psychologic mechanisms that occur in suicidally depressed persons (Litman, 1967). Although these mechanisms may have been overemphasized, they are still useful concepts for therapists to consider. Menninger talks about the elements of suicide: the wish to die, the wish to kill, and the wish to be killed. He stresses the breakdown of ego defenses and affect being out of control as part and parcel of a suicidally depressed patient. Treatment recommendations are based on these precepts. In *Man Against Himself,* Menninger (1938) discusses the necessity of establishing rapport. This is done through the transference, which allows the patient to better understand his problems and ultimately expand his ego.

From the development of ego and self psychology, there emerged a distinction between ego and self. The basis for understanding the mechanism of depression shifted from the loss of an ambivalently held narcissistic object to the vicissitudes of ego and self-esteem development. In recent years, John Mack has emphasized the crucial role of self-worth and the vulnerability to suicide when self-worth is in question (Mack and Hickler, 1981; Mack, 1983). Mack stresses that the therapist must constantly focus on the patient's self-worth, and in the process convey to the patient that he or she matters. To quote from Mack, "A trusting-caring relationship must be established which can provide the vehicle to repair the injury to self regard that dominates the clinical picture," (Mack, 1983, p. 87).

The difficult task for the therapist is the establishing of a trusting, caring relationship with patients who have been injured. Developmentally, these patients have not achieved autonomy. In being with or understanding the patient, the therapist must understand the basis for self-worth. Self psychologists refer to a lack of a sense of autonomy in suicide-vulnerable individuals who use external resources as self objects as a basis for their self-worth. Buie and Maltsberger (1983) speak of this in terms of the importance of acquiring self-soothing introjects—individuals who have not achieved this developmental task will suffer from "imperative dependency." This will make them vulnerable to ordinary losses. These patients will suffer from aloneness, which is the inability to experience any sense of connectedness or worth when one is alone; this leads to a subjective state of being vacant, cold, and isolated—without hope of comfort from within or without.

One important fact that must be recognized in beginning to treat suicidal patients is that there is a fine line between depression and despair—with depression frequently leading to despair. There is a crucial distinction between a despairing patient and a depressed patient. Therapists must recognize this distinction as it affects the kind of therapeutic stance taken with patients. In depression, there is a sense of loss, separation, anger, and protest. There is a predominant affective state that dominates the clinical picture. However, a person who has reached the state of despair has gone beyond an affective state in that there is an inability to maintain any human connection—the meaning of life is gone. There may be no sense of future, and in fact as Lifton (1979) has pointed out, their future may only be as a suicide. Complete despair probably results from the fact that alternatives have already been explored and found useless.

The relationship between depression and despair is complex and not mutually exclusive. Depressed patients may become despairing. When the clinical picture is primarily that of depression, we should employ all our knowledge and technique of biologic and dynamic theory. As the patient evolves into a despairing state, we should focus on self-worth and employ principles of existentialism. We must be willing to use ourselves to connect with the patient, to feel their despair (Havens, 1974). We must be prepared to utilize more than one perspective, but we must also be prepared to acknowledge which perspective we are most comfortable with. The capacity to understand the plight of our suicidal patients is a central ingredient for successful therapies. It is the author's contention that we are trained to do so when we are dealing with the depressed person, whether it be on the basis of loss or low self-esteem. However, we are less prepared to help the person who has reached the state of despair. The question for therapists becomes both a personal and professional one at the same time. Are we able and willing to accept the despair, are we willing to use more of ourselves in the course of therapy with patients, and can we employ both the psychodynamic and existential perspective in our therapies?

The elements that make working with suicidal persons so difficult are connected to the reasons many people enter the health professions: to cure disease, to master death. We all know what it feels like when we feel we have won the battle against disease or death. However, in the medical profession death is an accepted (though unwelcome) possibility. In most of psychiatry, death is not a common occurrence. In the treatment of suicide, however, the possibility of death is ever present. This can be a very difficult and discouraging condition to work under. We must not, however, avoid situations where people may seem beyond help or hope. When I was a resident at the Massachusetts Mental Health Center, the superintendent, Dr. Ewalt, used to say, "Hospitals that don't have suicides are turning away sick people." To truly accept death as a possible outcome is the only way to reach out to those patients whose despair seems overwhelming.

To be with a despairing person requires a degree of self-involvement and confrontation with utter misery that we may not want or be able to accomplish (Lifton, 1979). However, we must try. For it is in the trying that we may ultimately find ourselves and, most importantly, help our patients. To quote from Dr. George Murphy, a psychiatrist with a long-standing interest in the problem of suicide prediction: "Prediction must be done at close quarters and we can never know with certainty that we prevented a suicide. Our efforts must be designed to relieve the substrate of despair that is the proximate basis for most suicides. If we are successful in relieving that despair our accomplishment is considerable . . ." (Murphy, 1983, p. 344).

Our goal should be, as Havens has often said, "to be with the patient, in a sense to allow him or her to feel suicidal" (L. Havens, personal communication, 1983). So often there is this tendency to reject, to minimize, to make light of the seriousness of the situation—to deny death (Havens, 1967). Lifton refers to this as "psychic numbing" (Lifton and Falk, 1982). How often do we hear about families trying to cover up a suicide or feeling ashamed? By negating the patient's subjective experience, the therapist or family member will only serve to isolate the patient and intensify the feeling of being misunderstood. Suicidal people already feel an inordinate sense of isolation. The challenge for the therapist is to engage the isolated patient and not deny the despair and misery, even if it appears unrealistic. The patient must be allowed the freedom to feel his or her pain and to share it with another person, be it family, friend, or therapist. The therapist must call upon his or her empathic resources to feel the despair with the patient. Being able to sustain this empathic relationship and face the specter of death with the patient is the most difficult aspect of psychotherapy with suicidal patients. Being with suicidal persons challenges all human relationships. It is so difficult that even people very close to the suicidal person often cannot maintain an empathic connection to them.

An example of this kind of failed empathy comes from a clinical analysis of Hotchner's biography of Ernest Hemingway (Hotchner, 1983). In this biography, Hotchner recounts his last conversation with the great writer. Hotchner desperately wanted to be helpful but had difficulty hearing Hemingway. He asked Hemingway, "Papa, why do you want to kill yourself?" Hemingway responded, "What do you think happens to a man going on 62, when he realizes that he can never write the books and stories he promised himself. If I can't exist on my own terms, then existence is impossible. Do you understand?" (p. 297). The response to this question may have been as vital as insulin to the diabetic, as anticonvulsant medication to the seizure victim, and the Heimlich maneuver for someone choking. Let us listen to Hotchner's initial response: "But why can't you just put writing aside for now, you have always spent a long time between books. Ten years between *To Have and to Have Not* and *For Whom the Bell Tolls*. Take some time off. Don't force yourself." "I can't" replied Hemingway. This was followed by more protestations from Hotchner about how *good* a writer Hemingway *was*. Hemingway then laments over the fact that he is not the same writer, and no one can really accept that. He goes on to say, "But unlike a baseball player, a prize fighter, or a matador, how does a writer retire? No one accepts that his legs are shot, or the whiplash gone from his reflexes. Everywhere he goes he hears the same Goddamn question—what are you working on?" (p. 298).

From this passage you can see that Hemingway is trying to convey his misery. Each statement is progressively more despairing. Hotchner, in a reasonable human response tries to cheer him up, to make him forget his despair. A therapist would need to recognize the importance of connecting to the patient through his despair. Hotchner was merely making understandable efforts to be supportive in trying to lessen Hemingway's suffering when he said, "and you should work hard to think about the things you care about and like to do, and not about all those negative things. That's the best that can happen" (p. 299). He could not have known that Hemingway must have experienced what he was saying as—I don't hear you, I don't want to listen, I can't accept that you, a great man are so miserable. This is exemplified in Hemingway's response where he says:

"Sure, sure it is, the best things in life and other ballroom bananas. But what the hell? What does a man care about—staying healthy, working good, eating and drinking with his friends, enjoying himself in bed, I haven't got any of these, do you understand Goddamnit, none of them. And while I'm planning my good times and worldwide adventures, who will keep the Feds off my ass and how do the taxes get paid if I don't turn out the stuff that gets them paid. You've been pumping me and getting the goods but you're like Vernon Lord and all the rest, turning state's evidence, selling out to them" [p. 300].

Hotchner replied by lashing into Hemingway, "Papa, Papa damnit, stop it, stop it, cut it out." The biographer concludes this passage, "I stayed with him for a few hours in his room, he was pleasant but distant. We talked about books and sports, nothing personal. Later in the day I drove him back to Minneapolis. I never saw him again" (p. 300). One week later, Hemingway convinced the doctors to discharge him from the hospital. The next morning he killed himself with his shotgun.

It was clear that Hemingway did not feel understood and one response was to develop paranoid distrust. This makes empathy still more difficult, for the friends and family as well as the therapist. Hemingway was pleading for someone to share his misery. Hotchner did not understand what his friend needed (and he could not have been expected to). In *The Book of Laughter and Forgetting*, there is a Czech word, *Litost* (Kundera, 1981). It is a synthesis of many words: grief, sympathy, remorse, indefinable longing. The first syllable is long and stressed and, sounds like the wail of an abandoned dog. It is a state of torment caused by sudden insight into one's own miserable self. This insight is incompatible with life. Hemingway is a good example. He could see only misery. In the therapy situation, as with Hemingway, it becomes dangerous when we turn away from the despairing patient. Therapists must understand patients' need to share their misery and despair. As has been suggested, the best therapeutic tool for achieving this sharing state with a suicidal patient is empathy.

Empathy is defined as the emotional knowing of another person, rather than an intellectual understanding. Kohut states that empathy is a mode of data collection, a value-free tool that allows one to experience "vicarious introspection" (Kohut, 1978). It is a way of thinking oneself into the inner life of another. Existentialists rely heavily on the use of empathy to allow oneself to "see the world through the eyes of another." We often refer to the importance of making an empathic connection with a suicidal patient. However, several questions emerge from the above. First, can we, and how do we feel the despair of another person? Second, how does this empathic connection affect our clinical responsibility? And third, how does making this connection help turn despair around?

The technique of empathy was addressed by Margulies (1984) on the uses of wonder. He looks to literature to help us understand the process, particularly the work of the poet Keats, who coined the term *negative capability,* which refers to man's capability of being in uncertainty, of momentarily suspending judgment, and using imaginative projection of one's own consciousness into another being. But can we leave ourselves and enter into and feel the pain and despairing world of another?

In trying to achieve this state, it can be helpful to try to see oneself as an actor—to try to become the character. Maltsberger (1986) says that suicidal despair has two affective components, ". . . intolerable suffering (aloneness, murderous hate, and self-contempt) and an experience of 'recognition' in which the patient gives up on himself" (p. 16). Thus, we must use our creative (or imaginative, negative) capabilities if we are to be with patients as they are experiencing these affects. A therapist needs to try to find something from his or her own experience that he can imitate to bring forth the desired emotion. This is what actors do when, for instance, a role requires that they cry. With patients we do this by trying to make a connection. To feel ourselves into the despairing world of another we must momentarily imagine a joyless experience or one of persistent rejection. The question that emerges is, how do we do this? Recommendations emanate from the works of Leston Havens, Elvin Semrad, and Heinz Kohut.

Havens describes the technique of "going below" in which the therapist tries to engage the patient by deepening the awareness of painful experience (see chapter 21). This technique is challenging because it counters the natural human tendency to bolster the spirits of a despairing person. Futhermore, Havens has said on the subject of empathizing with the suicidal person to, "Remember two points. One, we cannot deny death, and two, we must acknowledge the desirability of death" (personal communication, 1983). It is the second point that I feel is the most critical. By acknowledging the possibility and desirability of death we make a connection with the patient. This is where they are and where we must strive to be. Connecting with patients in this way is critical to the success or failure of the psychotherapy of the suicidal patient.

Once you have imagined and felt the despair, Semrad would tell you that the work has just begun. For now, you must sit with that feeling and demonstrate to the patient that you can tolerate their pain (Semrad, 1984). Again, this counters our usual responses to painful situations, where we look for mechanisms to immediately alleviate pain.

The teachings and writings of Kohut (1978) offer additional advice on how to empathize—focusing more on the cognitive level. A brief example will illustrate this. A patient recently said to me, "Sometimes I feel like Humpty Dumpty, ready to crack." This metaphor is rich for us as we listen with psychological ears. But stop and try to imagine what it must be like to have the potential for self fragmentation. We have all experienced loss, pain, even severe disappointment. But can we imagine ourselves not being whole? Empathy means that we must find a way to get with this feeling. Kohut (1978) offers some suggestions on how to do this:

> We see a person who is unusually tall. It is not to be disputed that this person's unusual size is an important fact for our psychological assessment—without introspection and

empathy, however, his size remains simply a physical attribute. Only when we think ourselves into his place, only when we, by vicarious introspection, begin to feel his unusual size as if it were our own and thus revive inner experiences in which we had been unusual or conspicuous, only then do we begin to appreciate the meaning that this unusual size may have for this person . . . [p. 207].

Thus, we have the advice of three "masters" in the field of empathy. But how can the ordinary therapist learn to incorporate the empathic method into his or her practice? There is often this sense with empathy, that you have either "got it" or not, you are either in the "club" or out. My contention is that empathy is a technique that all therapists who deal with suicidal patients can and must learn in order to bring their patients back from the brink of disaster (Havens, 1984; Havens and Palmer, 1984). This is both the challenge and the dilemma. What is required of the therapist is that, like the actor, we must put ourselves into the "role"—some of you has to come through so that the emotion is real and believable. The therapist must be multidimensional; that is, getting into the role in a real way and yet maintaining enough distance to function as an effective clinician.

The question that remains is this: Is it possible to empathize with the desirability of death? The existentialist, Ernest Becker, states in his book *The Denial of Death*, "The fear of death must be present behind all our normal functioning, in order for the organism to be armed toward self-preservation (1973, p. 16). But the fear of death cannot be present constantly in one's mental functioning, else the organism could not function." Still, how do we know if we are achieving "vicarious introspection" as Kohut suggests? One way to enter the patient's world is by living through the crises with the patient and bearing some of the anxiety and uncertainty about his or her future. This can mean avoiding hospitalization, making oneself more available, and tolerating dependent behavior and increased appointments. Many questions emerge in the course of therapy with suicidal patients. Should more interpretation be used? Should the therapist be more supportive, hospitalize? How should the therapist approach the patient's defensive structure? Recommendations vary, for example, some suggest contracts as being useful, where others warn against them giving a false sense of security. Some say do anything you can to reduce the lethality of the patient—gratify dependency needs, be active. Yet one article warns about the potential for suicide to be precipitated by psychotherapy (Stone, 1961). This study warns against the symbiotic transference.

As we struggle with these issues and agonize over the decisions we make, knowing that we may hold the life of another in our hands, facing the possibility of death, we may begin to understand what our patients grapple with as they confront the option of whether or not they want to live or die. In chapter 23 Dr. Thomas Szasz maintains that we must allow patients to be free and responsible and not try to control their behavior. Although the empathic method allows one to see the despairing world of a patient, the ethical concerns of clinicians can be addressed by recognizing the importance of responding to what the patient *needs* rather than what will make the therapist feel comforted or reassured.

A question that emerges in this process, one that has been asked by clinicians and, in particular, Les Havens, is, How does empathy turn despair around? The mere act of being with another, of listening and sharing their pain conveys acceptance. "If this person can stand me, maybe I'm not so bad after all." John Mack has emphasized the central role that the notion of self-worth plays in the development of the suicidal state. Doubting one's value or feeling that one has no value is incompatible with life—death must follow. A role of the therapist is to convey to the patient that he or she matters. By accepting and understanding the patient, we affirm to the patient that he or she is understandable. In this way empathy offers validation to someone who may not be feeling valid. Another mechanism that occurs is empathic sharing. Sharing is defined as "dividing into portions"—you take some, I take some. We help the despairing person by momentarily accepting a portion of their miserable state, which reduces the intensity of the affect. In addition to sharing, empathy permits a connection to be established and maintained (Havens, 1976). It is this aspect of empathy that is the most crucial in turning despair around. By maintaining connections, suicidal patients who are on the verge of losing their sense of self can find themselves through their ability to find others. A case example highlights this mechanism.

The patient, a 30-year-old, single woman schoolteacher was referred to me five years ago because of depression. During the initial interview, the patient related that one month earlier, on the anniversary of her father's suicide, she had made a suicide attempt by driving her car off of a major roadway. She was headed toward a large rock formation, but at the last minute had turned away because, "my family had been through it once already." After one month of therapy she brought a suicide note into the session which revealed the seriousness of her despair.

If it is to end this way, as I think it must, please understand that I could not fight this dark cloud that kept invading my brain any longer. This way, I can finally sleep, and should I be able to wake up maybe in my sleep I will have gotten some peace. I stopped this foolishness before. It always helped to think of my family. I guess I understand Dad better now. I don't think he had any choice. The same way I don't have any choice. Please don't ever feel responsible. I know I did about Dad for years.

After reading this note that the patient had given me, I hospitalized her for two weeks; she and her family were able to talk about her depression and for the first time (after a nine-year silence), her father's suicide. Over the five-year period the patient has allowed me to enter her inner world, which is frighteningly morbid at times. Clearly a major conflict for her was her father's suicide. She told me in one session, "I felt it was my fate and I was responsible. I had been home when he went into the garage, I should have been able to smell the gas." During our sessions we discovered that because she was making breakfast for her family at the time and was cooking bacon (while they were at church) she could not possibly have detected the gas fumes. Since she had never gone over the details of the suicide, that fact was never made apparent to her. I believe this revelation was helpful to the ultimate resolution about her father's suicide.

The next year and a half were spent dealing with the patient's lack of a sense of future and purpose. While teaching class, she reported the intrusion of suicidal thoughts that have been classified as passive suicidal fantasies by the European suicidologist Erwin Ringel (1976). The patient was not frightened by these thoughts nor by death, sometimes I experienced a queasy feeling when she would discuss this with me. Sessions were sparse in terms of conversation; the patient repeatedly wondered whether or not she should be coming to therapy. I reinforced my interest and concern. Although we seemed to reach a stalemate I continued to be the only person, the only connection, in her life outside of her home. The patient decided to change jobs and located a teaching position at a school for the hearing impaired. The school was 90 miles away which meant that she would be moving away from home. Consequently our sessions were reduced to one a month. The suicidal fantasies continued. However, after being in the program for six months it was clear that the patient was becoming involved. She was talking about the future. Her life began to have a purpose. One day she appeared for her regular monthly appointment looking like a different person. Her face was alive with expression, her hair was permed, and she was talking spontaneously. When I commented on this she said, "I no longer understand my Dad. I don't feel connected to him. I feel separate." This struck me as profound. The patient had felt connected to her father as a suicide, but now she did not understand him. She had a purpose and future. Thus, it seemed that her therapy had been an opportunity to disconnect with death, but not before she had flirted with it.

I often wondered what had kept her going, her life being so empty. Perhaps it was my persistence in talking about the suicidal fantasies about death that helped. It was the vehicle for maintaining connections. In order to pursue this question of how empathy turns despair around, I decided to ask the patient in the hopes that she might provide some clues. Initially the patient talked about empathic acceptance in the following manner. She stated that her suicidal fantasies made her feel "weird— not normal." She said, "But you never said, 'That's ridiculous.' You provided me with a channel to let out these feelings. It's different when you talk out loud and hear it come back to you." She then proceeded to share with me what I find to be one of the most intimate and privileged experiences that I have had with a patient.

She described her view of herself which is shown in Figure 17.1. Her use of the term *connections* was startling to me—that she actually saw her world in these terms. Figure 17.2 depicts a disintegration of her world. Her losing connections with the different links in her world. On a separate sheet, she described the meaning of the diagrams:

"Depression" seems to happen when the arrows, normally going in both directions, are cut off one by one. No longer is it possible to look outside the "sphere"—all arrows point inward. The person (me) becomes withdrawn and self-centered, realizes that, but is caught up in the

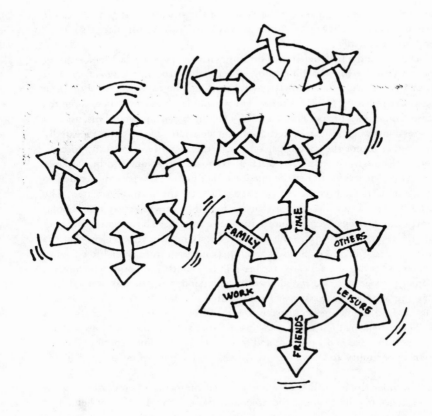

IDEALLY A PERSON MOVES IN HIS OWN SPHERE
AND HAS A VARIETY OF 'CONNECTIONS' TO
THE WORLD. EACH PERSON'S CONNECTIONS MAY
BE DIFFERENT, SOME MORE IMPORTANT THAN OTHERS,
BUT IDEALLY THERE IS BALANCE AND STABILITY
IN EACH PERSON'S SPHERE BECAUSE OF THESE
'CONNECTIONS' OR 'LINKS.'
THE INDIVIDUAL SPHERES MOVE MUCH LIKE THE
GEARS IN A MACHINE.

Figure 17.1

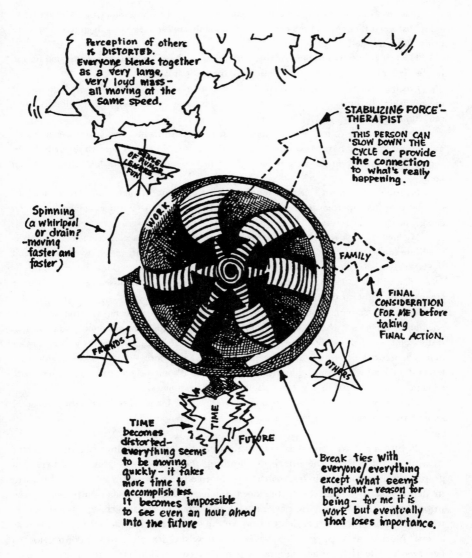

Perception of others
is DISTORTED.
Everyone blends together
as a very large,
very loud mass—
all moving at the
same speed.

'STABILIZING FORCE'—
THERAPIST
THIS PERSON CAN
'SLOW DOWN' THE
CYCLE or provide
the connection
to what's really
happening.

Spinning
(a whirlpool
or drain?
—moving
faster and
faster)

FAMILY

A FINAL
CONSIDERATION
(FOR ME) before
taking
FINAL ACTION.

WORK

FRIENDS

OTHERS

TIME
becomes
distorted—
everything seems
to be moving
quickly – it takes
more time to
accomplish less.
It becomes impossible
to see even an hour ahead
into the future

TIME

FUTURE

Break ties with
everyone/everything
except what seems
important – reason for
being – for me it is
work but eventually
that loses importance.

Figure 17.2

"whirlpool." It becomes difficult to hold onto any connection that would slow or stop the "whirlpool."

It seems I can operate with reasonable connections to the world for a time. My balance is easily disturbed though, and my connections suddenly appear superficial (if in fact they were really there in the first place).

The first connection to break is that with *friends*. (This is not a strong connection for me in the first place.) I start to avoid people ("friends") at all cost.

I then lose interest in *leisure activities*—they seem pointless. My *sense of humor* is gone—for me everything becomes very serious but everyone else seems to be laughing very loudly and I can't understand why.

Time is then distorted. Events from the past seem to haunt. Everything seems to be moving very quickly but it takes me longer and longer to do what I need to do. It becomes very difficult to concentrate on any one task. It becomes impossible to look ahead even an hour.

My connection with *others* no longer seems important to maintain. (For as long as possible it seems important to act the part of a "balanced sphere"—but it soon takes too much energy to continue acting.

My final is a link which fluctuates between connection and disconnection. For me this is a delicate connection and is hard to break (due to my family's history . . . w/my father, and the later experience w/me). This is not really a straightforward connection—but my family is aware that at times "I don't feel well" but beyond that it is not discussed because it doesn't seem fair or right to discuss.

The very last connection is one that not all people have—a "therapist" who can be the one stabilizing force—who can slow down the cycle and provide a strong connection to what is really going on. I think that most people find their own "stabilizing force" by using one or more connections or arrows. Some people never find that force—for whatever reason, my father didn't and was consumed by the "whirlpool." And some people, like me, are fortunate enough to have a "stabilizing force" built into their spheres.

I have to want to make this last connection, however. If and when I make that decision I know that eventually the cycle will stop (at least temporarily).

Figure 17.2 and the narrative highlights the critical vulnerable period. Her turning in on herself, the image of spinning one's wheels, of going nowhere is a graphic description of self-fragmentation. Notice her view of time, a typical feature in depression in which the future does not exist. Her view also emphasizes how important it is to know your patient, to know what matters to them. In her case it was family and work. In her description we can see the crucial role her family plays as a link. Notice the slip, *final* for *family,* and how she uses *final* in her connection to her *family*. Clearly, danger mounts when this connection is in jeopardy.

In terms of therapy, she refers to the therapist as a stabilizing force—a connection. Although we have not talked directly about what she means by this, I will offer my speculation. Kohut uses the term *empathic resonance* to refer to a reciprocal process that occurs between patients and therapists in which the patient has "an empathic grasp of the psychological state and activity of the therapist at the moment." Other people may refer to this as "being in the room with the patient" or "part of the real relationship." But what it accomplishes is the achievement of a connection with another person. *Webster's New Collegiate Dictionary* (1977) defines *connection* as a "relation of personal intimacy." *Connect* means to "unite or join." However, what I was most interesting was the definition of *connecting rod*—it is a rod that transmits power from one rotating part of a machine to another in reciprocating motion. This image conveys the back and forth aspect or exchanging of empathy that occurs between patient and therapist. Through this exchange, a self object tie is created. In addition, opportunities for identification with the therapist are opened up. As the patient graphically describes, suicidal states develop when self objects disappear. To quote from Ernest Wolf in talking about Kohut's contribution to the understanding of the self:

> Most important, increasing self structure does not mean an eventual independence from self objects, but an increased ability to find them and to use them. As obvious as this seems, particularly in the light of everyone's day to day experience of the world, it is one of the most controversial findings of psychoanalytic self psychology. Traditional psychoanalytic theory is not alone in its excessive stress on independent self sufficiency, self directiveness, and self responsiblity as the goal of human development. . . . I believe this view is grieviously mistaken because it is out of balance. It misunderstands the basic striving of the human soul which is not just to save itself in its capacity for individual distinctiveness, but to find a resonant response in the cosmos [Wolf, 1983, p. 504].

In summary, the empathic method in the treatment of the suicidal person integrates principles of dynamic and existential psychiatry, and self psychology. The challenge is to be where the patient is—a place where, under ordinary circumstances, we would not choose to go. But in a sense, this is our obligation, our responsibility. You have to acknowledge the potential for suicide in your patient. In so doing there will always be a degree of uncertainty as regards to safety. The issue of responsibility should not be confused with overprotectiveness nor omnipotence—it is merely being sensitive to and facing the gravity of the patient's situation. I used the analogy of the actor in the strictist sense—to get into the role and not pretend. We must be able to see death in its darkest moments to make it possible to see the light.

REFERENCES

Becker, E., (1973), *The Denial of Death*. New York Free Press/Macmillan.

Buie, D., & Maltsberger, J.T. (1983), *The Practical Formulation of Suicide Risk*. Cambridge, MA: Firefly Press.

Havens, L.L. (1967), Recognition of suicidal risks through the psychologic examination. *N. Eng. J. Med.*, 276:210–215.

———— (1974), Existential use of the self. *Amer. J. Psychiat.*, 131:1–10.

———— (1976), Existential therapy. In: *Current Psychiatric Therapies*, Vol. 16, ed. J.H. Masserman. New York: Grune & Stratton.

———— (1984), The need for tests of normal functioning in the psychiatric interview. *Amer. J. Psychiat.*, 141:1208–1211.

———— Palmer H.L. (1984), Forms, difficulties, and tests of empathy. *Hillside J. Clin. Psychiat.*, 6/2:285–291.

Hotchner, A.E. (1983), *Papa Hemingway, The Ecstasy and Sorrow*. William Morrow/Quill. New York.

Kohut, H., (1978), *The Search for the Self: Selected Writings of Heinz Kohut 1950–1978*, ed. P.H. Ornstein. New York: International Universities Press, pp. 205–232.

Kundera, M. (1981), *The Book of Laughter and Forgetting*. New York: Penguin Books.

Lifton, R.J. (1979), *The Broken Connection*. New York: Simon & Schuster, pp. 239–262.

———— Falk, R. (1982), *Indefensible Weapons: The Political and Psychological Case Against Nuclearism*. New York: Basic Books.

Litman, R.E. (1967), Sigmund Freud on suicide. In: *Essays in Self-Destruction*, E.S. Shneidman. New York: Science House.

Mack, J.E. (1983), Book Review: *The Journals of Sylvia Plath*, edited by Frances McCullough and Ted Hughes, Dial Press, New York, 1982. *N. Eng. J. Med.*, 308:107–108.

———— (in press), Adolescent suicide: An architectural model. In: *Youth in Despair: Preventive Aspects of Suicide and Depression Among Adolescents and Young Adults*, ed. G. Klerman. Washington, DC: American Psychiatric Press Associated.

———— Hickler, H. (1981), *Vivienne: The Life and Suicide of an Adolescent Girl*, Boston: Little, Brown.

Maltsberger, J.T. (1986), *Suicide Risk: The Formulation of Clinical Judgement*. New York: New York University Press.

Margulies, A. (1984), Toward empathy: The uses of wonder. *Amer. J. Psychiat.*, 141:1025–1033.

Menninger, K. (1938), *Man Against Himself*. New York: Harcourt, Brace, & World.

Motto, J.A., Heilbron, D.C., Juster, R.P. (1985), Development of a clinical instrument to estimate suicide. *Amer. J. Psychiat.*, 142/6:680–686.

Murphy, G. (1983), On suicide prediction and prevention. *Arch. Gen. Psychiat.*, 40:343–344.

Ringel, E. (1976), The presuicidal syndrome. *Suicide & Life-Threat. Behav.*, 6:131–149.

Robins, E. (1981), *The Final Months*. New York: Oxford University Press.

Shneidman, E. (1981), Psychotherapy with suicidal patients. *Suicide & Life-Threat. Behav.*, 11:341–347.

Semrad, E.V. (1984), Psychotherapy of the psychoses. *Samiska* (published by the Indian Psychoanalytic Society), 8/1.

Stone, A.A. (1961), Suicide precipitated by psychotherapy a clinical contribution. *Amer. J. Psychother.*, 25:18–26.

Tuckman, J., & Youngman, W.F. (1968), A scale for assessing suicidal risk in attempted suicide. *J. Clin. Psychiat.*, 24:17–19.

Wolf, E.S. (1983), Concluding statement. In: *The Future of Psychoanalysis*, ed. A. Goldberg. New York: International Universities Press.

18

Clinical Interview with a Suicidal Patient

Leston Havens, M.D.

EDITORS' NOTE

The following interview by Dr. Havens is of a middle-aged, divorced, and chronically depressed woman once addicted to amphetamines. The interview was conducted in order to help her therapist of five years better undertand and respond to the patient's recurrent suicidal thoughts and feelings.

The reader should note that Dr. Havens conceives of the interview as having three general phases:

(1) Engaging the Patient
(2) Replacing the Punitive Superego
(3) Building an Internal Ally

Important explanatory comments by Dr. Havens follow each phase, and the interview is discussed by two clinicians who observed it. These comments and the discussions paraphrase the original remarks made during one of the Harvard Medical School suicide symposia at which the interview was shown.

The patient's therapist is given the fictitious name "Ruth" in the transcript comments and discussion.

We understand that no single interview, no single patient, can illustrate all the considerations in working with suicidal people.

INTERVIEW

Phase One: Engaging the Patient

Dr. Havens: The interview is to provide some assistance to your therapist for the work that you and she have been doing. For how long?

Patient: Five years.

Dr. Havens: Five years? Five years. A long time, right?

Patient: Five years, yes.

Dr. Havens: So you're not newfound friends, no?

Patient: No, it's been five long years. She has been very helpful. But I am still a depressed person.

Dr. Havens: Well, I guess that's one of the reasons that I'm sitting here. How can we make that less true or not true at all?

Patient: I have no idea. I think you have to have the desire to want to live, and if you don't have that, you just stay depressed.

Dr. Havens: Those things are so often the same, aren't they? Being depressed and not caring to live. And there may not be anything more in your life now than there was five years ago. Maybe less in your life to live for.

Patient: That's true.

Dr. Havens: Some of the good things may have gone.

Patient: That's true too.

Dr. Havens: The children are getting older, moving along.

Patient: Oh, they're doing fine. That's what I wanted for them. One is married, just became a mother. The other one's going to be married. That's what I wanted for them. To be taken care of and take care of themselves. Make their own lives.

Dr. Havens: Where does that leave you?

Patient: (Sigh) Well, mainly what I think keeps me going is them. There are times when I've really wanted to do something and thought of them and wouldn't do it. I'd call my therapist and she'd talk to me and help me. And I just keep pushing myself.

Dr. Havens: Now they don't need their mother the way they once did, I guess eh?

Patient: No. And like I said, that's what I wanted for them.

Dr. Havens: It's what you wanted, right?

Patient: Yes, it's what I wanted.

Dr. Havens: So where are you supposed to find meaning in your life now?

Patient: I don't know.

Dr. Havens: I know. If you knew the answer to that question, you wouldn't be sitting here.

Patient: No. I wouldn't be here.

Dr. Havens: You wouldn't be sitting here, would you?

Patient: No, I wouldn't.

Dr. Havens: Nor is it a new thing. It may go back more than five years too, maybe ten, fifteen, twenty.

Patient: My God. I've been on drugs for 24 years. I stopped taking drugs five years ago, and tried to cope with life in a sense. Sometimes I seem to do all right, but then I think I was just pushing and trying too hard, and I just got tired of doing all that.

Dr. Havens: Your therapist may not know what to do either.

Patient: That's true.

Dr. Havens: Does she . . . does she want you to live?

Patient: Yes.

Dr. Havens: She does.

Patient: Yes. She does.

Dr. Havens: I have that impression too.

Patient: More than I do, I guess.

Dr. Havens: More than you do. So that you might be alive partly not to upset her, right?

Patient: No, I think it's mainly my children. I couldn't leave them with a hurt like having their mother commit suicide.

Dr. Havens: Umm-hmm. They so often feel to blame, or that they haven't done something.

Patient: Well, I don't know how they would feel.

Dr. Havens: Although that's not the case here, is it?

Patient: No.

Dr. Havens: It's really the other way around, isn't it? They've made your life as worth living as it has been. So that if you were to leave, you could say to them, you gave whatever I had that was good.

Patient: They have. They were everything I wanted them to be. They are two beautiful children inside and out.

Dr. Havens: That's unusual, isn't it. To have achieved that.

Patient: I've been lucky. I've been very fortunate, and they deserve a lot of the credit.

Dr. Havens: But that doesn't mean that you feel beautiful inside, does it?

Patient: No, I don't.

Commentary by Dr. Havens: The purpose of the first phase of the interview was to engage the patient, to find where she was. This was done historically, by sharing her past difficulties, her drug experiences, and in particular, the present absence of hope. Furthermore, there were the difficulties the therapist was having, difficulties anyone would have, as well as the imprisonment that her obligation to her therapist and the children to some extent represented. Here the temptation, the danger of reassuring her and seizing on some hope must be avoided. Instead, the historical review constantly seeks to "go below" her present mood and measure the depth of her despair. In this way, the engagement is extended and deepened, and we begin to find out who it is that we are engaged with.

Phase Two: Replacing the Punitive Superego

Dr. Havens: It may not even be possible to describe how you feel inside.

Patient: Empty, lonely, so many different feelings. Useless.

Dr. Havens: Useless too?

Patient: Hopeless.

Dr. Havens: Hopeless. Bad, maybe?

Patient: Bad.

Dr. Havens: You're bad too?

Patient: Yep.

Dr. Havens: So on that list you're not much good at all are you? Useless, hopeless, bad. Are there those who agree with you about that? People who say that about you?

Patient: No.

Dr. Havens: No? There are even friends who disagree with that?

Patient: Well, I don't really go around to my friends and tell them how I feel. I've told Ruth. But I know my friends wouldn't agree with my feelings.

Dr. Havens: They wouldn't? They wouldn't buy that picture of you.

Patient: No, they wouldn't.

Dr. Havens: They wouldn't. In fact they might say different things. But that probably doesn't affect what you feel about it.

Patient: It doesn't affect me at all.

Patient: I . . . I don't know how helpful I am to you, because I don't talk too much.

Dr. Havens: Oh, I have no complaints. I'm very appreciative that you put up with these circumstances in the first place. And then I'm also appreciative that you like to share what is obviously an awful feeling.

Patient: Well, it is. It's sharing, and to let other people know, it's not my style. I'm usually a very private person. I'm surprised I'm doing as well as I am. Maybe I have a little ham in me.

Dr. Havens: I hope so. I hope so. Because despite what you think about, what you say you think about yourself there may be some wonderful things to show the world. Certainly what you say about the children suggests that, doesn't it.

Patient: They are special.

Dr. Havens: That's not the way you feel about yourself, is it?

Patient: No, I feel differently.

Dr. Havens: You feel like you have hurt other people.

Patient: No, I feel I've hurt myself.

Dr. Havens: Hurt yourself?

Patient: I try not to hurt other people either.

Dr. Havens: But you felt like you deserved to hurt yourself, right? That you should be punished.

Patient: Umm-hmm. Well, I don't think I've been very good. Being a drug addict and all the other things.

Dr. Havens: That you've been this bad person that I mentioned.

Patient: Yeah.

Dr. Havens: That you have sinned.

Patient: Yeah, so to speak.

Dr. Havens: Other things too that give you this feeling about yourself that seems so different than what other people sense about you. You may live with much more bitterness than you show.

Patient: No, I'm not bitter.

Dr. Havens: No, I say you don't seem bitter at all, but I wonder if you don't live with it, inside no? Because you've had some hard . . . some very hard knocks sometimes, right?

Patient: Oh yeah. At times I think life has been unfair to me. But then I think other people have probably went through worse.

Dr. Havens: Well, there may be other people . . . but it may have been bad enough, right?

Patient: Mmm-hmmm.

Dr. Havens: But when you talk to me now, you talk more with sweetness than bitterness. Maybe bitterness towards yourself, but not towards the world, right?

Patient: While not towards the world really. Towards some people. But even then I try not to . . . I try not to allow hate into my life.

Dr. Havens: Mmm-hmm. Except in one place.

Patient: Towards myself, I know.

Dr. Havens: You make an exception there, don't you?

Patient: Yeah, I just can't pass that block, I guess.

Dr. Havens: Despite the fact that of the people that you've known, you are maybe one of the finest.

Patient: I consider myself a loser.

Dr. Havens: A loser? How do you mean, a loser?

Patient: I just can't gather my depression, my thoughts.

Dr. Havens: I see, so you blame yourself for that.

Patient: Mmm-hmm.

Dr. Havens: You feel that somehow you should be able to throw off this mood and love life more.

Patient: Yes, I think so.

Dr. Havens: So that part of the depression is really a feeling of being to blame for it, of being at fault because of it. That it's sort of your . . . another one of your crimes. Do you see any goodness in yourself?

Patient: Well, like I said, I don't go around hurting people. I try to help people if I can. But there's a lot of people like that.

Dr. Havens: Not so many as one thinks though, right?

Patient: Hmmm?

Dr. Havens: Not so many good people really.

Patient: No, there's a lot of good people.

Dr. Havens: Has that been your experience?

Patient: No, I mean that there are a lot of people, good people in the world though, that I'm talking about.

Dr. Havens: You've certainly tried very hard to be one of them, too, haven't you?

Patient: Mmm-hmmm.

Dr. Havens: But you feel that you've failed.

Patient: Yeah.

Dr. Havens: You feel that you've failed at that task of being good, right?

Patient: Well, I'm not good.

Dr. Havens: Maybe even as a little girl, you felt that way, did you? That you wanted to be good, but that somehow it didn't work out that way?

Patient: Well, I was kind of shut out and shut up, when I was being raised, so . . . and the way I was being raised, I made sure I didn't raise my kids.

Dr. Havens: Mmm-hmmm. You'd learned a very bitter lesson by that.

Patient: Mmm-hmmm.

Dr. Havens: Well the misery of those days may never have left you.

Patient: I should be able to bury the past.

Dr. Havens: Why should you be able to bury the past? Oh, I hope you'll tell me how to do that. A psychiatrist should know, shouldn't he?

Patient: I thought they knew everything.

Dr. Havens: Oh God, what we don't know. What we don't know. How does one bury the past? You've had some parts of it that you'd love to bury, right? Say good-bye to forever?

Patient: Yeah.

Dr. Havens: You wouldn't say that.

Patient: No.

Dr. Havens: It would be like lifting a mountain off your back I bet.

Patient: Yep.

Dr. Havens: How do you say good-bye to the misery, the bitterness, the disappointments, the horrors . . . horrors, too, right? . . . Of the past. Well, you know what the shrinks say? You've heard all that I'm sure a thousand times, right? You're supposed to talk about it. Oh, my God. You're supposed to tell, you're supposed to talk about it.

Patient: It doesn't make everything go away.

Dr. Havens: It sure doesn't. Sometimes it makes it seem to come back.

Patient: Right, right. It brings it all back.

Dr. Havens: That's one of the reasons it's so hard to do it, right? It brings it all back. You're supposed to talk about the horrors and then they are supposed to go away. And yet they don't go away, do they? Often they don't. And one of the things you've been saying, I think. Maybe . . . tell me if I'm all wet. Is that life . . . the horror is all there is to you? You're the sort of walking horror, right? You're the accumulation of all that experience, the mistakes, the bad things that have happened, right? And that's all there is to you. As if there wasn't anybody else.

Patient: Mmmmm. Well, misery I guess. Depression is also misery.

Dr. Havens: It's almost as if all those experiences and all that time had destroyed everything sort of cheerful and fun and good and hopeful about humans.

Patient: I don't know. It's hard to remember. I spent a lot of years on drugs. I can't remember the real me.

Dr. Havens: Where is the real you? Is it lost?

Patient: I believe so.

Dr. Havens: Can it ever be found again, huh? Or built up again? You're certainly not feeling very cheerful about that, are you? 'Cause you're not sweet sixteen anymore, either. It isn't like you can . . . it's easy to start over now.

Patient: Well, because I was so miserable I went to drugs, and I stayed on . . .

Dr. Havens: And that's one of the things that you blame yourself for right?

Patient: Well, it's true.

Dr. Havens: As if it, as if it was something that you chose. As if it was a fault.

Patient: Well, not everybody takes drugs. You have to be kind of weak I think to take drugs.

Dr. Havens: You have to be weak.

Patient: At least I was.

Dr. Havens: You were weak. Another one of your crimes. That wasn't the worst . . . was it? Of your crimes. You've got a list of them a yard long, I'm sure. So not only would you have the job of forgiving yourself, right? But you also have this job we talked about of forgetting the past, right? The miseries.

Patient: Right.

Dr. Havens: And is there enough energy left in you to do those things?

Patient: No.

Dr. Havens: To build up a new person and to say good-bye to at least part of the horrors.

Patient: Well, I had five years to do it, and I couldn't do it.

Dr. Havens: They couldn't do it.

Patient: I couldn't do it.

Dr. Havens: Oh, I see. You don't even put it down to the great psychiatric profession.

Patient: Well.

Dr. Havens: Well, you warned me about that. You said you didn't like to blame other people, right? Hmm?

Patient: Ruth was very good. You're very good. She helped me a lot. But if you're depressed, you're depressed. You just can't get out of it no matter what.

Dr. Havens: This too is a failing of yours. A weakness of yours. It shows you're not made of the right stuff or something right?

Patient: I think I'm tired of pushing.

Dr. Havens: You're tired of pushing?

Patient: Mmmm-hmmm. May I light a cigarette, or would that interfere?

Dr. Havens: By all means. There's not . . . there's little enough joy to your life without depriving you of that, for God's sake. Yeah, what would make the difference?

Patient: I don't know.

Dr. Havens: No, you don't. If you knew, you would already have done it right? You wouldn't . . . you're not enjoying your state of mind. You would have already done it, wouldn't you?

Patient: Right. If there was an answer. If I knew what to do. If somebody told me what to do, and I did, and it worked.

Dr. Havens: You'd do it. You'd work at it the way you worked with the children and all the other things, right?

Patient: I'd do it.

Dr. Havens: So it looks like it's up to us. How about that? That will give you no feeling of security, knowing that you're in these hands.

Commentary by Dr. Havens: In this second phase, as I understand it, the person's self-description and affects are reviewed. Here the temptation and the principal mistake is to collude with the patients' judgment about themselves. By expecting people to remember, by expecting them even to forget, we impose a demand that is yet another task at which they fail. In this way we reinforce their sense of inadequacy. I dealt with that by moving over beside her and talking about how difficult and impossible this situation can be. The struggle is to avoid reinforcing the attitude she has toward herself, confirming her self-image. I now make a pronounced effort to replace her punitive superego with an ego-ideal that is less judgmental, and provide a more empathic self-conception. At this point in the interview, the cigarette is a sign of the ending of her work. It is her way of saying "I'm finished now. Tell me what you are going to do about this." She has done her part of the interview. She told me the story, she is helpless, and now "the ball is in my court." I have to supply her with something that modifies this view of her, to remoralize or idealize her in some way. This has to come from the outside. She hasn't located anything within herself that would make that possible; therefore, in the last part of the interview, I take a very active responsibility. This is in part to offset her pathological tendency to assume too much of it herself for everything. I am essentially locating the next move, which will then be her therapist's responsibility.

Phase Three: Building an Internal Ally

Patient: Well, you seem like you're a very kind person.

Dr. Havens: You've worked at it, you've worked at it hard. And Jan has worked at it hard, and we have to think of something else.

Patient: Ruth's worked hard. Sometimes I think harder than I.

Dr. Havens: She seems very fond of you.

Patient: She's a very nice person.

Dr. Havens: Nice person, right? But notice how you say, well, you didn't work as hard as she did, maybe. It was all your fault.

Patient: Well, that's true. I think she . . . I imagine there were plenty of times I must have been an aggravation to her.

Dr. Havens: An aggravation. She'd just as soon get rid of you or something, dispose of you.

Patient: No, I know she doesn't feel that way.

Dr. Havens: No, I didn't have that impression that she thought that way.

Patient: No, I don't think so. Sometimes I feel like I'm a burden to her.

Dr. Havens: A burden.

Patient: That I can't get myself going. Because if she's putting a lot of time and energy into me. She has . . .

Dr. Havens: Well, she may actually be fond of you, you know. I think quite apart from any professional thing that she's supposed to be doing, right?

Patient: I think it's . . . I mean she's a friend, but she's also a therapist.

Dr. Havens: Well, those things are hard to separate often.

Patient: No, she has showed me that she cares. And she cares.

Dr. Havens: Well, it looks like the ball is in my court.

Patient: What are your plans?

Dr. Havens: Yeah, what are my plans? That's what seems to be the question of the moment anyway, then, because you're discouraged about it. She didn't want to lose you. And she knew how desperate you felt, right? How un . . . how un-in-love-with-life you were at the moment anyway, right? And she wanted to do something, so she asked me if I could suggest something.

Patient: Yep. I think it's a lost cause.

Dr. Havens: You don't think I've got a chance?

Patient: No.

Dr. Havens: Well that's . . . stimulating. It makes me challenged, right? But you think I'm barking up the wrong tree, whatever the expression is.

Patient: Banging your head against a stone wall.

Dr. Havens: Banging my head against a stone wall. I wouldn't have thought of you as a stone wall. I think you've got lots of courage and "stick-to-it-iveness," and kindness, but I wouldn't have thought of you as a stone wall.

Patient: Well, I have a lot of control. I don't burst out crying. I don't get real angry. I don't. . . .

Dr. Havens: You've needed a lot of control in your life, haven't you? You've had tough things to go through, right? Heartbreakers, right?

Patient: Mmm-hmmm.

Dr. Havens: You've needed a lot of control.

Patient: Well you learn to do something real well as you are growing up. And you become sort of a perfectionist at it.

Dr. Havens: You are a perfectionist at it?

Patient: I think I am.

Dr. Havens: Well, you probably need to be. Because I think what you had to face was very formidable. And you must have felt like you were throwing yourself at a stone wall often, right?

Patient: Oh yeah.

Dr. Havens: Life probably seemed like a terrible stone wall a lot of the time, huh? And one of the things that you didn't give way to, which impressed me so much is that you didn't give way to bitterness. You tried to keep going somehow, right? That may have been why you took the drugs, to try to keep going?

Patient: Well, they gave you that feeling of being able to cope.

Dr. Havens: That's right. They were your own treatment, right.

Patient: I used to call them my "happy pills."

Dr. Havens: Your happy pills, and God knows you needed them, right, because you were up against real stone walls, right. If I think I'm up against a stone wall, I should ask you about your stone walls, right. You know, I wouldn't think of you as a stone wall.

Patient: Well, you don't know me so well.

Dr. Havens: But you think I should be more discouraged than I seem.

Patient: I guess I just don't feel like anyone or anything can help me.

Dr. Havens: That it's all over now.

Patient: Well, I'm not going to go out and kill myself. If that's what you're thinking.

Dr. Havens: Well, I hope you don't. But if life is so miserable it certainly must be a temptation.

Patient: It is, but I have children. That would . . . I won't leave that with them.

Dr. Havens: Well, I admire you for that.

Patient: You don't have to admire me for it.

Dr. Havens: I don't have to. No, indeed I don't. No, I don't have to do anything.

Patient: I think any mother . . . excuse me, any mother would do the same.

Dr. Havens: No, I'm afraid you're not right about that. I wish you were. But meantime, you have your own life, right? And your own self to live with. This person that you describe so negatively.

Patient: And that's the part I don't like.

Dr. Havens: Well, who would like it, right? Nobody in their right mind would like it. Feeling that way about themselves, would they?

Patient: No, I guess not.

Dr. Havens: So really what this stone wall is, is changing how you feel about yourself, isn't it. So that you look for some kind of pleasure, or even excitement in yourself. How about that? That seems like a remote thing, doesn't it?

Patient: Yeah.

Dr. Havens: Could we . . . could we help you to love yourself? You wouldn't be very cheerful about that, would you?

Patient: I just don't think it's possible. It's hard to teach an old dog new tricks.

Dr. Havens: You're an old dog now, is that it? Among your other sins, you're an old dog?

Patient: No, not really, I just. . . .

Dr. Havens: No, I know the expression. But it would be a new trick you say, to love yourself.

Patient: Myself, and life, and wanting to live. Now that would be something.

Dr. Havens: Well, at least it gives us a nice thing to work for, doesn't it. It would be a nice way of knowing how successful we were, wouldn't it. But you told me not to be optimistic about that.

Commentary by Dr. Havens: The structure of the interview is fairly identifiable. It begins with what I call the attempt at engagement, which is to "find" the patient, with a detailing of what is found. In the first part the danger is to lighten the engagement by reassurance or grasping for hope. In the second phase the danger lies in colluding with the negative judgment that is very subtly presented as possible by the patient. One finally looks for "somebody new" to develop and reconstruct in terms of the relationship between the superego and ego-ideal. I want to emphasize that this really wholehearted effort to "make lovable" is necessary. The kind of advice we usually give in cases like this depends on there being a viable structure already in the patient, who is able to do, for example, the mourning work, the rejection of the hostile, remembered, ambivalently held figures. As with many of these cases, particularly the very downtrodden and supine people who accept the criticism of their agencies, there is essentially no person present in the patient with whom the therapist can ally to do the psychodynamic work. Therefore, before the work can go forward, there must be an often considerable period in which an ally of the work, and ally of the patient, is constructed internally.

DISCUSSION OF LESTON HAVENS'S INTERVIEW

Sheldon Roth, M.D.

There are several vantage points from which one can approach this interview: (1) the point of depression, its form and expression in this woman; (2) the role of suicide in this context; (3) her relation to her therapy and therapist, and perhaps the window on this provided by the development of the relationship with the substituting therapist–consultant, Dr. Havens. To this we would add (4) Dr. Havens's developing relationship with her; and (5) the impact of the pair on the reader through the course of the interview. Unfortunately, or fortunately, due to the usual realities of time we shall settle for shunting back and forth among these vantage points in commenting on this interview.

There is no doubt Dr. Havens engaged the patient—chatting, joshing, ironicizing, weaving and bobbing, reading into her comments, attributing goodness to her (not unwarrantedly), demonstrating himself as being as helpless as she is, allying himself with the frustration of the patient, always humanizing himself, evoking images of Sullivan with the paradoxes and challenging, outlandish hyperbole as when he states "despite the fact that of the people that you've known, you may be one of the finest," and especially with the slightly quizzical, "we're in this together—how about that!" attitude (recall Sullivan's comment, "we are all more human than othewise"). He is working so darned hard the patient would be hard put not to recognize a man attempting to be as caring, responsible, involved, and human as this strange technological event could allow for. The interview certainly demonstrates an essential in the interviewing of the depressed and suicidal patient: reaching through the gray web of depression and striking a personal relationship with the patient that contains support, and the possibility of hope, even while striking the stance of despair, and accepting the possibility of failure. Either one alone does not face the psychologically ambivalent realities of the depressed–suicidal patient who is still alive, and would leave the patient with the impression that the therapist, although delightfully charming, is a fool and not to be trusted. If the purpose of the first consultative interview is to have a second, I have no doubt this woman would grant it to Dr. Havens.

But the activity, the activity! I was reminded of Semrad's comment: "The purpose of depression is to get somebody else to do something they're not doing" (p. 15). So naturally we must appreciate that in this short stretch of time Dr. Havens unfolded this process to us, the countertransferential living out of the patient's transference needs, condensed for our observation and learning. Still, I was provoked to wish he'd quiet down a bit, particularly when the patient would begin to move to specific aspects of her life, as when she said in childhood she was "shut out and shut up." What a powerfully alliterative description! And, Dr. Havens to some extent then interrupted her, and perhaps recapitulated the shutting up and shutting out she had just begun to talk about. Being the stoic personality she has settled into, in a way a form of aggression against the talkative and shutting up and out environment, she kind of says, "go ahead and talk, I'll listen pleasantly, but you won't change a thing."

Suicide is a final common pathway—no if, ands, or buts, the patient no matter what the diagnosis is, is 100 percent dead. Suicidal thinking, on the other hand, is complex and runs through many avenues, and may have varied meaning and functions. This woman is chronically suicidal, and ironically, it seems as if *that* is part of what keeps her alive, just as the pills did. It provides her with solace, a final resting place, a way out, a feeling of control in a mind awash with a sense of helplessness. It attaches her to people like Ruth and helps her meet unusual minds like Dr. Havens. This is a partial list of its multiple uses. To replace this would require an enormous shift in her character and self-image, and bespeaks perhaps a never-ending therapeutic relationship of one sort or another. Given the life-sustaining place she accorded her children, I should think that as the grandchildren pile up in number, and increase in age, her role and function will again take on the mothering, altruistic surrender of self into the loving of the young. Undoing her own childhood (as for many people) has been the deepest form of loving growth for this woman. Indeed, given the range of defenses alloted to humans it is a rather highly civilized one. I felt Dr. Havens was struck by the same observation during his interview.

Chronic suicidal ideation as a way to remain alive and the chronic sense of depression leads us to ponder the state of chronicity and the therapeutic task deriving from it. Again, we turn to Semrad. Who knew more about depression than Elvin? "Chronicity follows when the precipitating factor in the original regression has not been worked through and resolved. This is what the therapist must go for" (p. 153). I return to the moment of her talking of "shut out and shut up." It seems *both* mother and daughter were shut up and shut out, at least from one another. Could this be one of the deep lures of the suicidal urge, the feeling of badness? When viewed from this perspective it is not totally badness, it is the sense of closeness and identity with this strange and abandoning mother. The patient is torn to be like her and not to be like her. I don't know the history, but I suspect that given this woman's warm qualities, her apparent good mothering (these are characteristics that don't drop from the sky), experiences with mother may have been possible other than the abandoning ones. Even so, the lure of final union, the fantasy of joining is a powerful motive in many suicidal people, but is often hidden due to terror of being subsumed and overwhelmed by the longing for such a strange and terrifying mother. Ralph Greenson felt that in all his clinical experience the deepest resistance in treatment for a woman was the earliest primitive love and longing for her mother. There is a great deal of submerged libido in what looks like naked rage and aggression. In this area, the vast realms of mourning are where the ultimate work with this patient must take place. This is a complicated mourning process whose thread of love for mother is woven not only through her childhood, and her iron fortress character developed to cope with it, but also in the warps and woofs of her own children, and now her grandchild. And, this brings me to my final point. For the question is, How does this process become initiated? Thus, we come to the therapist and the issue of the transference, ironically about which very little was said directly in a genetic, reconstructive fashion. What is this woman re-creating in her urge to lose Ruth as well as her family? Has Ruth become her as a child (reversing self and object), and the patient finally become the dread mother as she wishes to abandon all? This is a treacherously tempting psychic bait for a woman "shut up and shut out" from the sphere of mother as a child. What is the needed attitude of the therapist in this anxious matrix?

Perhaps an answer to this lies within the work itself as the artist might say as the problems of a painting are considered. The microcosm often reflects the macrocosm, and let us note the microglimpse offered by Dr. Havens. He responds openly, honestly, at times cynically, this both aids in his pent-up frustration with the stubborn and dangerously threatening event he is confronted with, and at the same time conveys a self-trust that he is working with integrity, applying himself to an important person with an important task. This frees him up to be in the same quandry that the patient is in, and yet convey a sense of *hope,* a continued desire to explore, search, think, pause, tread water until some reasonable idea comes to him, a sense of sustaining anxiety through patience. The net effect of this stance is that of a strong, *enduring, staying object* in the life of a person obsessed with a desire to drive all people out of their existence, while at the same time longing for them just as intensely. In the usually very long psychotherapeutic run, it is this element that initiates the patient's mourning process as it reawakens memories of tasted goodness. "I forgot who the real me is," says this woman, a suggestion of deeper wellsprings of good experience, hints of a forgotten little girl long since "shut out," whose love for herself was so deeply tied to a troubling mother it was best buried away, only to resurrect itself in the strange form of suicidal urges. Some may marvel at how much I might make of what may have been a traumatic childhood. How could so much longing exist for such an ambivalently held figure, and how could the power of the transference move the psyche in such a predicament? For both questions, for brevity's sake, I recall to you Semrad's comment: "A touch of love, is like a touch of pregnancy" (p. 33).

Reflecting the patient's ambivalence about living is the therapist's dual attitude that conveys that the patient has the power within her to end her life should that be the ultimate bottom line. We can only watch in somewhat of a stupified awe at such a decision. And at the same time, firmly experience him or her as an irrepressible, alive, and potentially lovable presence that bespeaks other opportunities for the patient's life, as it recalls earlier forgotten opportunities. On the whole, when treatment is successful with such a patient it is a long war of attrition. In this waning process one of the essentials is this irrepressible, enduring presence of the therapist, expressed through the varying styles of therapists, and a lovely, multimusing specimen of which we've been treated to by Dr. Havens. Recall what Dr. Jacobs's (see chapter 17) patient stated when he asked her what made the difference between the choice of suicide or not: it was your "stability and faith" she said, the irrepressible and enduring presence of the therapist.

Translating this to *consultative* advice to the therapist is to realize that the countertransference of the therapist is a receptacle for the projected transference of the patient. The therapist succumbs to the illness, a necessary occupational hazard, and becomes the blocked, helpless object the patient was, and is faced with losing the patient in a way the patient was faced with losing her own mother. Ironically, as Dr. Jacobs has unfolded in his candid and sensitive discussion of empathy, empathy plays a major role in forming the boundaries and pathways of the countertransference. What begins as a *trial identification* with the experience of the patient, in these troubling waters of the suicidal patient easily moves into *trial action* in the form of countertransference, and in a profound sense is necessary for a realistic idea of the patient's complicated feelings of helplessness, worthlessness, and resulting affectual turmoil. The consultant turns then to the therapist and becomes a holding environment, and acknowledges the pain of the therapist as the therapist is experiencing the projected pain of the patient. Hope is rekindled by nudging the therapist back into realistic pursuit (not blind optimism), of the lost libido and loves of this woman, realizing that she would never have lived this long without sufficient sustaining, supporting, and gratifying experiences, and helping her to acknowledge, bear, and put all this into realistic perspective.

DISCUSSION

John T. Maltsberger, M.D.

Some of the audience may have been eager to see how Dr. Havens would solve this therapeutic dilemma by a brilliant tour de force, and set the patient and her therapist on the right road with one or two brilliant strokes. But we have seen no fireworks. There is no penetrating interpretation, no uncovering of a subtle countertransference impasse, no discovery of a hitherto concealed loss. He seems oddly inactive, even self-deprecating at times. This extremely difficult patient makes her hoplessness plain, forceably keeps up her guard, gives him little to work with. Yet what has been accomplished by the interview's end? He has entered the patient's isolation, intruded a hope-giving relationship where one was not expected and hardly wanted, relieved, at least for a time, her distress. How does he manage these things?

He is first of all supportive of the patient's defenses. He does not crowd; he does not probe for history. She tells him, "I was shut out and shut up" in childhood. So very quietly he opens the closed door just a little in case she wants to remember and to explain, but when she chooses to keep her horrors to herself, her terrible memories, he does not press. He does not push in, throw open the shutters, rummage and bustle in her privacy. He just keeps respectfully still, waiting at the door, available, just in case.

He freely acknowledges and admits the real difficulties in her life, including the fact her treatment has been long, weary, and not very successful. Her children are leaving her. She has little to live for. But he makes no demands. "If you knew how to like yourself, you wouldn't be sitting here, would you?" He is careful to do nothing that would add to the patient's heavy burden of guilt, failure, self-blame, or to her profound sense of incompetence.

On the more active side, Dr. Havens tries to relieve the patient's self-scorn. He points out that she is kind to everyone but herself, calling herself an old dog, a loser. When she scorns herself for drug taking, for being bad, guilty of crimes, Dr. Havens gently apologizes for the patient to herself. He suggests that the drugs were her treatment, her tranquilizers, that she has reasons for keeping her thoughts and feelings to herself.

The only place he takes issue with the patient is over her willingness to surrender to her interior enemy—a hating, carping interior presence. Over the course of history this kind of interior enemy has been given a variety of names— demon, dybbuk, superego, hostile introject. Its names are legion. Against this enemy Dr. Havens exerts some pressure, explaining to the patient that the way it treats her is not kind, is not fair. He will not go along with this interior attack, but instead shelters her for a while from the artillery barrage.

An important aim in the psychotherapy of depression is to exorcise, as best we can, interior enemies of this sort. In the first place one must draw the patient's attention to a hostile self-attitude, then try to help the patient gain some distance from it. Ultimately we hope to pit the patient against it, to get the patient to see his critical self-aspect for the tinpot tyrant that it really is, to help the patient dethrone it. Sometimes this kind of maneuvering works, sometimes it does not, but it is usually at least partly successful, and it almost always lends the patient some comfort. Dr. Havens did a bit of this work today, and I think that is why the patient said he was kind.

We should notice, also, that Dr. Havens engages in a little gentle mockery of psychiatry. "Oh, what we [psychiatrists] don't know!" he exclaims. There are other such little deprecations of our profession. What he is doing, of course, is guessing what anger and disappointment the patient must somewhere feel against those caretakers who have raised her hopes and failed to deliver her from depressive suffering. He takes this anger up and validates it. He acknowledges that as a profession there is much that we do not know. Subtly he lets her know she has a right to feel angry and disappointed. He is sending her a message that she is not bad to hate the people who try to help her. He does not leave her alone with her guilt. This maneuver helps him join the patient in spite of herself.

He does not try to take her fortress by storm, but quietly creeps into it by joining her in the feeling of hopelessness, suggesting she is kind to everyone but herself, giving her permission to be angry at the psychiatrists who have failed her, letting her know she need not feel so guilty about her secret hostility. In the end when she is all too willing to hand over to him the responsibility for the dilemma of her life, he does not quail, but accepts it good humoredly and goes off to do his homework. He shows us how to get into a relationship with a person who, living on the edge of despair, doesn't much want one. There is no lecturing, no pep talk, but rather an acknowledgment of failure, of the patient's hopelessness, participation in the dilemma, willingness to accept the load of responsibility, a defense of the patient against her inner enemy, conscience, and no surrender.

What is not evident from this interview is that Dr. Havens would be prepared to go on like this, were the patient his, for hours and hours, not giving up hope, but waiting for some spontaneous movement. Elvin Semrad, speaking of Frieda Fromm-Reichman, said that that little old lady kept coming back and kept coming back and kept coming back and kept coming back until the patient could not stand it any longer. Something had to give. He used to say that if you will stay with a patient like this long enough without surrender one day the patient will say to himself, "If this doctor can care so much and be so interested in me, maybe I've got it wrong, maybe I've got something worthwhile that I can't see but he can." But one must wait. You cannot be in a hurry.

Sometimes some spontaneous movement will take place, after a long period of time, and the patient gains some capacity to hope. When the necessary internalization of the loving, patient, returning therapist has taken place, perhaps more conventional psychotherapeutic maneuvers will succeed and the patient can begin to grieve.

A strong argument can be made to the effect that suicidal despair arises from the patient's incapacity to bear two highly corrosive affects—worthlessness and aloneness. These have been discussed in chapter 2. They drive the patient to desperation and it is this that makes so many of them so demanding. They feel they must have relief or die. The relieving person is known in some quarters as a self object; I prefer to call such a person a self-sustaining object. Without some such resource the suicide-vulnerable person is in danger of self-collapse.

With great craft Dr. Havens has fashioned himself into exactly, specifically, the right kind of self-sustaining object this patient needs. He shields her from self-contempt, steals into her isolation. Pointedly he does not give up on her and does not leave her alone.

Such patients commonly evoke a strong countertransference wish to do something active, powerful, healing, so we will not have to endure the empathic pain of acknowledging the patient's hopelessness. We want them to get better fast to help ourselves. Hence our wish for fireworks from the consultant. Dr. Havens has offered no prescription for a magic cure in this interview, but he has offered the patient the best that there is available. He offers us no tour de force, but he offers her a tour d'amour. And he has offered us a chance to learn. He did not, as consultants are sometimes tempted to do when interviewing a patient with students or other colleagues, give in to a need to show us that he is not helpless, or to show the patient that he is not responsible for her dilemma, but that she is. Nowhere is there a hint that Dr. Havens is having to separate himself from the patient in order to reassure himself or us or the patient he is not hopeless, inept, inadequate.

The only inference possible is that Dr. Havens has the capacity to acknowledge, bear, and keep in perspective the suffering of this patient, her sense of worthlessness and aloneness, her possible death, our collective professional ineptitude, without abandoning her or burdening her, and without giving way to therapeutic despair. That is what we all must learn to do if we are to help very sick patients.

B. Treatment Settings

19

Evaluation and Care of Suicidal Behavior in Emergency Settings

Douglas Jacobs, M.D.

Suicide is currently the ninth leading cause of death in the United States, claiming 27,294 lives (12.5 per 100,000) in 1978 (National Center for Health Statistics, 1978; Frederick, 1978). In the decade from 1960 to 1970, visits to psychiatric emergency rooms tripled (Gerson and Bassuk, 1980). This was due in large part to the Community Mental Health Centers Act of 1963, which mandated emergency psychiatric care as one of five essential services. Concurrent with this development, the shift away from long-term state hospital care precipitated an influx of patients to community-based facilities. Community mental health centers, general hospital emergency rooms, and private practitioners are therefore increasingly called upon to evaluate suicidal behavior. It has been reported (Meyerson, Glick, and Kiev, 1976) that approximately 15 percent of psychiatric visits to general hospital emergency rooms are made by people who have at least a moderate degree of suicidal ideation and/or have made a recent suicide attempt. At facilities that accept police referrals and have ambulance services, the rate is even higher. For example, at the psychiatric emergency service of The Cambridge Hospital in Cambridge, Massachusetts, 40 percent of patients either present with suicidal ideation or have made a suicide attempt (National Center for Health Statistics, 1978). As previously noted by Perry and Jacobs, there has been a broadening of the functional roles of psychiatric emergency services to include diagnostic and treatment capabilities specific for dealing quickly with emergencies (Perry and Jacobs, 1982). It thus becomes essential for the emergency room clinician and clinic–office practitioner to be able to evaluate and care for suicidal behavior, as well as to be able to recognize certain frequent, negative reactions during encounters with suicidal patients that emerge in himself.

The aim of this chapter is twofold: (1) to proceed sequentially through the

This chapter was previously published in *Internat. J. Psychiat. Med.*, 12:293–307, 1982–1983.

assessment stages, from the perspective of the clinician confronted with suicidal behavior in an emergency setting, and (2) to discuss the clinical implications of these stages in various suicidal patient groups, presenting in this setting. Although some of the crucial factors in this sequence overlap, and are often not clinically discrete, the goal is to outline an approach to evaluating and caring for suicidal behavior that includes the following components:

1. A knowledge of some of the pitfalls in assessment and prediction related to clinical and demographic risk factors,
2. A willingness by the clinician to confront particular frequent negative reactions that may arise during the process of evaluating and caring for suicidal patients,
3. A schema for describing and grading suicidal behaviors that includes development of a vocabulary to describe and evaluate the seriousness of an attempt, as well as an understanding of patient characteristics based on the method of attempt chosen,
4. An understanding of chronic suicidal behavior,
5. A consistent, yet flexible treatment approach.

RISK ASSESSMENT AND PREDICTION

Traditional medical training emphasizes the importance of establishing a diagnosis before treatment is begun. In emergency settings, this is not always possible because of the rapidity required in decision making. Moreover, because suicide can be either a manifestation or an outcome of any psychiatric disorder, the issue of diagnosis is complex for the emergency clinician (Miles, 1977; Frederick 1978).[1] Thus the clinician must make assessments with the entire spectrum of mental illness in mind. As a diagnostician in the traditional sense, the clinician must be aware of those psychiatric illnesses that involve higher suicide risk (Frederick, 1978). The clinician must, however, go beyond formal diagnosis because many suicides occur in persons not psychologically ill. As Motto (1978) has pointed out, "suicidal behaviors may be generated in the presence of practically any diagnostic entity, and at times in the absence of pathological states" (p. 540). And, as Mack and Hickler (1981) have stated: "The problem of suicide cuts across all diagnoses. Many of those who take their lives are mentally ill, but some are not. Some are psychotic but most are not. Some act impulsively but most do not " (p. ix). Because the etiology of a suicidal state is so varied, persons must be diagnosed on the basis of how hard they have been hit, where they can obtain support, and why they want to live.

---

[1]The percentage of completed suicides by psychiatric diagnosis is as follows: depression, including all categories of affective disorders, from manic-depressive illness to depressive neurosis, 30 percent; alcoholism, 15 percent; schizophrenia, 10 percent; opiate addiction, 10 percent; personality disorder, 5 percent (Miles, 1977).

The second set of concerns regarding assessment and prediction relates to the application of demographic and clinical factors purported to affect risk. The clinician must be cognizant of the demographic factors that correlate with high suicide risk. Ten demographic and personal history risk factors have been correlated statistically with completed suicides. Patients among whom these factors are present are at 200 to 300 times the risk for suicide than the general population (Tuckman and Youngman, 1968). The demographic profile of individuals at greatest suicide risk is white, male, over age 45, separated, widowed, or divorced, living alone, and unemployed. Professional persons may also be at high risk; male physicians, for instance, are twice as prone to suicide as other professionals (Rose and Posow, 1973; Rich and Pitts, 1980). Historical factors include poor physical health, medical care within the last six months, positive psychiatric history, and a prior suicide attempt (Tuckman and Youngman, 1968). Any patient who makes an attempt, regardless of seriousness, and manifests all of these factors should be hospitalized immediately.

A positive psychiatric history and a history of previous suicide attempts place a person in a higher risk category; 20 to 25 percent of actual suicides have in fact made prior attempts (Robins, 1959; Maris, 1981). Reports in the literature on the ratio of attempted suicides to those completed vary. Some cite a ratio of 8 to 1, while others have seriously questioned this figure as low (Weissman, 1974; Wexler, Weissman, and Kasl, 1978); a Boston study, for example, supplies a ratio of 39 to 1 (O'Brien, 1977). Thus, although prediction of actual suicide from previous suicidal behavior may be extremely difficult, this should not deter clinicians from attempting to identify suicide risk.

Age has often been cited as a useful parameter for assessment of suicide risk (Weissman, 1974; Robins, West, and Murphy, 1977; National Center for Health Statistics, 1978) and to distinguish those who attempt from those who complete suicide. Epidemiological studies demonstrate that suicide attempters are younger, female, more likely to be married, and use pills (Weissman, 1975; Wexler et al., 1978), whereas the completers are older, male, single, and use violent means. In fact, 50 percent of all suicide attempters are under the age of 30. Because the suicide rate for this age group has more than doubled in the past two decades, evaluation of suicide risk in the young adult is particularly difficult. In 1978, 12 percent of all suicides were in the 20 to 24 age range and comprised the largest total number of completed suicides for any five-year birth cohort (National Center for Health Statistics, 1978). The increase in suicide among the young has begun to change the previously held relationship between age and suicide; as Peck and Litman have stated: "Suicide rates now generally increase rapidly in the teen years, reaching a peak sometime in the 20's, taper off and drop slightly in the 30's and 40's, and then rise again in the 60's and 70's" (Peck and Litman, 1974, p. 14).

Demographic risk factors are useful in identifying but not eliminating the possibility of suicide. These factors are useful only when coupled with examination of clinical issues. In identifying suicide risk, consideration of these issues is especially important (Fawcett, Leff, and Bunney, 1969; Murphy, 1972). Of particular significance are feelings of hopelessness and helplessness; presence of a detailed suicide plan; recent (within six weeks) loss (actual or threatened); development of passive suicidal fantasies; increasing social isolation and an inability to accept help (Motto, 1965, 1978; Ringel, 1976). Psychodynamic considerations that take into account the significance of the crisis and/or the patient's basis for self-worth are critical (Gerson and Bassuk, 1980). Thus the clinician must consider these clinical factors together with demographic risk factors when assessing risk.

In order to broaden the base from which a clinician can rapidly determine risk, Litman (1976) correlated risk with particular patient types. In reviewing over 26,000 cases at the Los Angeles Suicide Prevention Center, he was able to determine suicide rates for patient populations based on brief history and demographic data. Essentially he formulated suicide risk as a prediction of suicide probability based on past experience, and distinguished degrees of risk among potential suicidal patients. His categories range from nonrisk to high risk, with each successive category being ten times more lethal than the preceding one. For example, those at low risk are psychiatric patients in general, with a suicide rate of 100 per 100,000. The moderate risk group consists of suicide attempters who require hospitalization because of the attempt: the suicide rate for this group is 1,000 per 100,000 (1 percent). The highest risk group (with a mortality rate of 22 percent), are patients with major mental illness who have been hospitalized because of a high lethality attempt.

After careful consideration of clinical and demographic factors, the clinician is better able to assess where the patient is located along a suicide-risk continuum. As the clinician proceeds through this stage of the suicide assessment process, he or she is called upon to assemble, digest, and evaluate data of several kinds, including demographic, clinical, and patient history. However, the clinician is also confronted with his or her own responses and attitudes, which, in turn, become important factors in assessment as well as in deciding on treatment strategy for the patient.

CLINICIAN RESPONSES AND ATTITUDES

The second component of the evaluation process concerns the clinician's response in encounters with patients. The emergency room clinician is under acute pressures of time and available resources in evaluating and caring for the suicidal patient (Gerson and Bassuk, 1980). Is the patient really suicidal? Would crisis intervention be useful? Is admission necessary? Are there any beds? As these dispositional questions are being considered, the clinician often also notices that the patient is not very cooperative or is excessively demanding ("If you don't admit me, I will kill myself"). Maltsberger and Buie (1974) discuss the affects generated in clinicians treating and evaluating the suicidal patient—emotions which include hate, restlessness, hopelessness, fear, pity, and indifference. Clinicians must expect and be aware of these feelings. These authors stress that the more aware the clinician is of his own feelings in relation to these patients, the less is the potential for counterproductive interactions. Adler (1972) advises that the clinician use his own feelings as a guide to assess what the patient is experiencing; in so doing, the clinician attempts to "convert helplessness and fury into a force to help a patient understand what is happening" (p. 317). The process of assessing one's own feelings in regard to the patient can thus enable the clinician to focus on the patient's pain rather than to engage in a fruitless struggle over whether or not he or she should be admitted.

A related issue involves the clinician's attitude toward the phenomenon of suicidal behavior. A core feature of the suicidal person is his ambivalence—the wish to die oscillating with the wish to live and be helped (Menninger, 1938). Therapeutically, we must try to ally ourselves with the side of the patient that wants to live. If we view the suicide attempt as an attempt to continue living rather than an effort to die, we can help the patient focus on his or her distress (Dressler, 1975). This change of attitude can only occur if we have a rational and specific approach to evaluating and caring for suicidal behavior.

EVALUATING AND GRADING SUICIDAL BEHAVIOR

As noted in the prior section, negative affects are prominent and inevitable in the clinician encountering suicidal patients. In addition to acknowledging and accepting these negative feelings, the next assessment stage focuses on developing an objective approach for grading suicidal behavior. The components of this approach include a consistent vocabulary, a schema for determining the seriousness of the attempt, and an appreciation of the relation between method of attempt chosen and suicide risk.

Vocabulary

In order to evaluate suicidal behavior, one must develop a consistent, germane vocabulary. Many terms are currently used to describe suicide attempts; these include abortive suicides, gestures, histrionic suicide attempts, and parasuicides, just to name a few. Such labels are not clinically useful and may often be counterproductive. Two of those most commonly used are "gesture" and "manipulation." Webster defines "gesture" as something done as a symbol for the effect on the attitude of others. Clinicians use this term pejoratively to describe patients who have performed minor (rather than lethal) self-destructive acts. However, the fact that a self-destructive act is minor does not mean that the patient is not suicidal. "Manipulation" is an individual's attempt to control another person in order to get from that person what he wants but has been unable to achieve—such as trying to prevent a loved one from leaving (Sifneos, 1966). The clinician may often feel that she or he is being manipulated, and may then begin to focus on not being manipulated rather than on the suicide crisis.

Describing a nonlethal suicide attempt as a gesture is therefore not only vague, but also does not take into account that the patient may have been very serious about dying, but simply lacked knowledge for completion. Conversely, a manipulator may not have wanted to die, but has mistakenly chosen a highly lethal method. By using more objectifiable, less value-laden terms, clinicians can communicate more effectively with patients and each other to better understand and evaluate a particular suicidal act.

In addition, placing these labels on suicidal behavior may establish an atmosphere of rejection that will prevent the clinician from experiencing the distress and pain of the patient. In most instances labeling interferes with the kind of therapeutic engagement necessary in emergency room settings for making sound dispositional and intervention decisions, that is, the patient's assurance that someone cares and will listen.

The terms gesture and manipulation should be discarded from our vocabulary and be replaced by the classification system recommended by the National Institute of Mental Health (NIMH) in 1970 (i.e., completed suicides, suicide attempts, and suicide ideas). The major usefulness of this system lies in objectifying the suicide attempt (Pokorny, 1974).

Dimensions of Suicidal Behavior

The dimensions recommended to objectify the suicide attempt include intent, lethality, and mitigating circumstances. This objectification enables the clinician to separate a person's suicidal *intent* or purpose from the physical consequences or *lethality* of the suicidal act.

Intent Intent refers to the patient's subjective expectation that a particular self-destructive act will or will not end in his death. This expectation will vary from low to high; for example, patients who say: "I only take ten pills or cut my wrist not to die, but just to relieve the pain," illustrate the former. Evaluation of intent includes two components: (1) a patient's self-report about the purpose of the attempt—his or her conception of what is necessary to cause death and emphasis on the wish to die; and (2) the objective circumstances surrounding the attempt, such as the time of day, prevention against discovery, presence or absence of suicide note, and preparation (Beck, Beck, and Kovacs, 1975). The following questions are included in the Suicide Intent Scale developed by Beck (Beck, Schuyler, and Herman, 1974) to assess a patient's preparation regarding attempt.

1. When did you decide to kill yourself?
2. Did you make plans or do it impulsively?
3. Were any special arrangements made to be alone at the time of the suicide? (p. 46).

This scale is especially helpful in emergency settings because it provides specific questions that are clinically useful to a wide range of mental health personnel when exploring suicidal intent.

Lethality   The dimension of lethality refers to the danger to life in a medical, biological sense. This is considered separately from the patient's conception of what is medically dangerous. Also classified from low to high, lethality can be determined by assessing the seriousness of the method chosen and the actual damage sustained (the death potential), as well as the probability of rescue. Rescue factors are particularly germane and include choice of location of attempt, chances for discovery, and time interval from attempt to discovery. The Risk Rescue Rating Scale developed by Weissman and Worden (1972) describes in more detail the range of factors to consider—reversibility of method chosen, medical treatment required, and accessibility to rescue. The assessment of lethality is particularly useful for the care of the chronic suicidal patient where one can plot the above factors over time: Is the patient using a more toxic method? Are the clues and chances for discovery lessening?

Unfortunately there is not a linear relationship between intent and lethality (Beck et al., 1975). Patients may not wish to die but may make a life-threatening attempt. Correlation does exist, however, if the patient has an accurate conception of what is needed to produce a fatal outcome. Those patients who are serious about suicide and have an accurate knowledge of lethality are at the highest risk. Patients who are unclear about the danger to life of the particular method chosen are the most difficult to evaluate and care for. Evaluation of suicide risk is not complete without clarifying these issues with the patient—asking the patient, for example, what he knew about the potential lethality of the pills that he ingested.

Mitigating Circumstances   Another dimension in classifying a suicide attempt consists of the mitigating circumstances; that is, the demographic and clinical factors that might aggravate a patient's self-destructive impulse or alter awareness of the consequences of his actions. Acute alcoholic states, deliria, or acute depression would be some examples.

Methods of Attempt

What can the clinician learn from the way in which people try to hurt themselves? Another component in the schema for grading suicidal behavior includes an understanding and differentiation of patient characteristics based on the choice of method in the suicidal attempt. An examination of the two most common methods of suicide attempts—self-poisoning and wrist slashing—begin to provide some answers to this question.

Self-poisoning by pill ingestion is the most common method of suicide attempt, used by 70 to 90 percent of patients. (Weissman, 1974; Wexler et al., 1978). Those who choose this method have less serious psychiatric disturbances than wrist-cutters or those using more violent means (Morgan, 1979). In realizing the clinical importance of poor correlation between intent and lethality, we note that these patients with seemingly low suicidal intent may nonetheless often make an impulsive and yet serious suicide attempt (Fox and Weissman, 1975; Rosen, 1976). As mentioned previously, any suicidal behavior, regardless of severity, places a person at 10 to 100 times more than the normal risk for suicide.

Since most self-poisonings are impulsive, patients tend to ingest what is available. Thus, usually more than one substance or drug is involved, leading to several possible pharmacologic interactions. Simple additive effects occur when barbiturates and benzodiazepines are ingested simultaneously. More serious, synergistic effects (in which one drug potentiates the effects of another so that the combined effect is greater than simple addition of two drugs) occur with the simultaneous ingestion of alcohol and benzodiazepines, resulting in a 50 percent potentiation of the benzodiazepines. In fact, almost all cases of reported death from chlordiazepoxide or diazepam occur because of the simultaneous ingestion of barbiturates, hypnotics, or alcohol. Table 19.1 presents the types of pills most frequently taken and their approximate toxic levels (Sterling-Smith, 1974), the most dangerous drugs being barbiturates, tricyclics, and lithium, whether taken singly or in combination.

The precipitant for the pill ingester is usually interpersonal turmoil—the "cry for help" frequently referred to—with motivation directed at reestablishing the relationship. If the person does not require medical hospitalization, a crisis-intervention approach should be taken. Because of the importance of the interpersonal context in the ingester's act, attempts should be made to determine at whom the person is angry, evaluate the other party (if available), and attempt to interview both parties. If the patient is in treatment, the clinician should investigate the therapeutic relationship to determine if the patient is experiencing feelings of dissatisfaction or problems in the relationship. The clinician should then assume the role of consultant and offer to contact the therapist, discuss the disjunctions between patient and therapist, as reported from the patient's perspective, and encourage the patient to be more explicit about what he needs with the therapist (Skodol, Kass, and Charles 1979). The presence or absence of psychosis should also be determined. As Litman has noted, suicide attempters with major mental illness are at significantly higher risk than other suicide attempters.

A careful investigation of the relation between intent and lethality among pill ingesters can be helpful in determining disposition. The extent of the patient's knowledge about medication is useful information. Even though the threat to life may have been relatively minimal, the patient may need to be hospitalized because of high intent. An important goal here is to engage the person in treatment (Motto, 1965). This may, in fact, be the major purpose for hospitalization.

The second most common presenting suicidal behavior in emergency settings in wrist-cutting. Clinicians previously often held that wrist-cutters were a discrete group consisting of young attractive women with hysterical personalities

Table 19.1

Types of Pills Most Frequently Ingested[a]

Type	Estimated Lethal Amount
Barbiturates	
Short acting	2–3 gm (20–30 pills)
Long acting	6–9 gm (60–90 pills)
Aspirin	30 gm (90 pills)
Psychotropic agents	
Tricyclic antidepressants	2–2.5 gm (50 pills)
Phenothiazines (Chlorpromazine)	3–4 gm (30–40 pills)
Lithium carbonate (Toxicity)	2 meq/liter (10–20 pills)
Benzodiazepines[b]	
Chlordiazepoxide	2.25 gm (100 pills)
Diazepam	1.4 gm (140 pills)

[a]Usually there is multiple drug ingestion resulting in the problem of *synergism*.
[b]There are few case reports of fatalities by the ingestion of benzodiazepines as a sole agent. Most fatalities involve combinations of drugs.

(Grunebaum and Klerman, 1967; Rosenthal, Kinzler, Walsh, and Klausner, 1972). However, careful epidemiological research has revealed that wrist-cutters do not constitute a group with discrete characteristics; rather, they comprise a heterogeneous population (Clendenin and Murphy, 1971; Weissman, 1975). Wrist-cutters account for 11 percent of suicide attempts. Men, in fact, are more likely to cut their wrists than take pills. Wrist-cutters are less likely to be hospitalized than pill ingesters because lethality is generally low in this group. However, within this population, schizophrenics and psychotic depressives are at high risk and will usually require hospitalization (Simpson, 1976).

A subgroup of repeated wrist-cutters, described as "delicate cutters," tend to be female and frequently display certain dynamic or motivational similarities. These patients are particularly sensitive to loss and have an inability to tolerate particular affects. They describe a state of depersonalization as tension and anger mount and will cut their wrists (usually reporting the absence of pain) to provide relief from the tension (Simpson, 1976). In her poem *Cut,* the poet Sylvia Plath graphically describes this state as "the thin papery feeling" (1965).

In assessing the wrist-cutter, intent and lethality should be evaluated. Patients who are psychotic, including some borderline patients, should be hospitalized. Intoxicated patients must be carefully evaluated, especially when there is significant tissue damage. If the patient does not require hospitalization, the management in the emergency room should focus on helping the patient verbalize angry feelings and review the situation that has created the tension. This can be extremely difficult and requires a careful monitoring of countertransference feelings. One should keep in mind that the anger generated in the clinician by the patient is a reflection of "what is going on inside the patient" (Adler, 1972). As with pill ingesters, wrist-cutters have an increased risk for suicide, and every effort should be made to engage them in treatment.

SPECIAL POPULATIONS

Alcoholic and chronic suicidal patients comprise two of the largest groups seen in emergency room settings. The assessment dimensions appropriate for other categories of suicidal patients apply with these groups, perhaps with even intensified scrutiny.

The Alcoholic Patient

Alcoholics constitute a very high risk group as well as a serious management problem: 15 percent die by suicide, a number equal to a suicide rate per year of 270 per 100,000 alcoholics (Mayfield and Montgomery, 1972). Although there is some overlap between alcoholism and depression, the suicide rate reported for alcoholics does not appear to be inflated by this overlap (Miles, 1977). When suicide does occur, it tends to occur later in life or as a late complication of alcoholism (Mayfield and Montgomery, 1972). This is in contrast to depression and schizophrenia, which show a high incidence of suicide occurring close to the onset of the illness.

Two separate groups seem to comprise the alcoholic suicidal population. The first group consists of the abreactive type, in which suicidal behavior usually occurs at the onset of drinking and in the context of severe interpersonal turmoil. The typical example is a suicide attempt that follows an argument or angry outburst with a loved one. These attempts are unpredictable, which makes intervention very difficult. Moreover, suicidal behavior does not occur with every intoxication.

Assessment of this population must include factors of intent, lethality, diagnosis, and interpersonal context. Treatment should be based on a crisis intervention model focused on mobilization of support and crisis containment. In particular, every effort should be made to involve the significant other. If the significant other has left or died (especially within six weeks), the patient should be considered at higher risk and hospitalized, regardless of lethality (Murphy, Armstrong, and Hermele, 1979).

The second group of alcoholic suicide attempters has been described as the depressive syndrome of chronic intoxication (Mayfield and Montgomery, 1972, p. 349). This syndrome has been borne out by recent research on the chronic effects of alcohol by Mendelson in which he demonstrated an increase rather than a reduction of anxiety and depression (Mendelson and Mello, 1979). Suicide attempts occur at the end of a binge, as opposed to the beginning, and depressive symptoms will appear days prior to the attempt. These individuals are more likely to be diagnosed as chronic alcoholic, and the treatment for these patients is the treatment for alcoholism. Depression will usually remit upon the cessation of alcohol intake; abstinence should be the goal of intervention.

Chronic alcoholics in the middle of a binge who display signs of depression and lack social support should be considered at high risk. Hospitalization should be implemented, even if involuntary, despite the belief that mental status is difficult to assess in the intoxicated patient. Behaviorally, these patients are withdrawn and may not appear to be in a crisis state, a presentation that could mislead a clinician.

The Chronic Suicidal Patient

The chronically suicidal patient is defined here as one for whom self-harm has become a way of life. Diagnostically, these patients often suffer from severe character disorders, most frequently borderline or schizophrenia. Dynamically, these individuals frequently have a poor sense of self and have incorporated suicidal behavior into their psychic structure so that it has become ego syntonic (Schwartz, 1979). Vaillant (1979) characterizes this type of suicidal behavior as a manifestation of an immature defense mechanism which is called into use for the purpose of obtaining care. These patients may be very similar to the hypochondriac who only wants to talk about his back pain and yet can seemingly never be comforted. The chronically suicidal patient will cut his wrists or take pills to gain nurturance from care givers or those around him.

How does the clinician approach a patient who presents on a weekly basis with cut wrists or having taken a small overdose? Are these patients really suicidal? What sort of treatment is most useful? When is hospitalization indicated? When is it counterproductive? These patients present particular management problems in emergency room settings. Unlike acutely suicidal patients, these persons may neither be involved in a crisis nor demonstrate signs of stress. In a study that examined clinician attitudes toward suicide attempters, extremely angry staff feelings were reported toward patients evidencing suicidal behavior in the absence of precipitating events (Dressler, 1975).

Management of these patients requires an understanding of the dynamics involved. The author's own experience suggests an approach that has been successfully used for hypochondriacal patients; namely, encouraging them to talk about the pain in their lives (Brown and Vaillant, 1981). This may help avoid power struggles that occur, as well as allow the patient to feel understood. By not focusing solely on the suicidal behavior, one permits the patient to talk about his chronic distress. Hospitalization decisions are always difficult with these patients. If hospitalization is decided on, it should be kept brief.

The clinician should be aware of some of the adverse effects of the usual crisis approach to suicide (Schwartz, 1979). Providing nurturance does not necessarily reduce the suicide potential. An important question is whether an individual will accept help. If refused, involuntary treatment may be necessary. A care plan should be devised for the emergency room or clinic that allows for frequent but short visits because continued contact is essential for these patients. Intervention, however, should focus on the patient's assuming more and more responsibility for his life.

It is with these patients that staff education and communication must be effective. Once suicide behavior has become a way of life, the road to suicide may be inevitable; staff must be prepared for this inevitability in some patients. However, communication among emergency room staff about these patients can be helpful: Are the visits increasing? Are the risk and rescue factors changing? Is the staff becoming more hopeless and helpless? Affirmative answers to these questions are all signs that suicide is near and that a more acute crisis approach is necessary.

TREATMENT APPROACH

The treatment approach for the patient presenting with suicidal behavior in emergency settings should be aimed at providing relief and determining what the patient needs. Providing relief can be achieved by assisting the patient to clarify his emotional state in a manner that generates a sense of "relatedness," permitting the patient the opportunity to feel understood and accepted (Motto, 1975). Both the manifest behavior and less readily perceived attitudes of clinicians toward their suicidal patients are of crucial importance. This group of patients is particularly sensitive to rejection and recognizes staff annoyance easily. Clinicians must therefore avoid expressing the fear or anger generated by the patient's suicidal behavior. Staff must also be willing to accept the dependent behavior of these patients.

Intervention should be aimed at defining the suicide crisis. This may consist of contacting a significant other, calling a therapist, dispensing medication, or breaching confidentiality. Because of the complexity of predicting suicide, safety cannot always be guaranteed. Emergency room clinicians are not omnipotent and cannot prevent all suicides. However, they should offer what assistance and support they have available. Litman (1966) refers to this process as maintaining a "medical attitude." By having a sense of where the patient is along the suicide-risk continuum, the clinician can proceed to offer a disposition directed at what the *patient* needs rather than what the *situation* demands. This is another way of saying that every self-destructive act is not intended to be suicidal.

CONCLUSION

The assessment of suicidal behavior in emergency settings is a complicated matter. The patients with this behavior constitute a heterogeneous group, ranging across the full spectrum of psychiatric illness. Particular diagnostic groups, such as depressives and alcoholics, comprise the largest number of completed suicides, which means that patients with these diagnoses are at highest risk. But how does one accurately assess suicide risk? Certain demographic profiles that include age, sex, race, living situation, marital state, and employment factors become important, and when these are present in combination with a suicide attempt, suicide potential is increased. However, since most persons who attempt suicide do not manifest every factor in the high risk profile, prediction can be difficult. Prediction should not be the focus of suicide assessment; the goal should be the treatment of distressed persons. Although some will need more protection than others, all need and deserve treatment.

Recognition and management of the clinician's own feelings is essential for effective treatment of patients with suicidal behavior. These patients will generate negative affects in clinicians, which have to be acknowledged.

One cannot expect to prevent suicide in the high risk population seen in emergency settings, but this does not mean that we stop trying. As Freud wrote in 1926: "What weighs on me in his case is my belief that unless the outcome is very good it will be very bad indeed, what I mean is that he would commit suicide without any hesitation. I shall therefore do all in my power to avert that eventuality" (Freud, 1926, p. 101).

REFERENCES

Adler, G. (1972), Helplessness in the helpers. *Brit. J. Med. Psychol.*, 45:315–326.

Beck, A.T., Beck, R., & Kovacs, M. (1975), Classification of suicidal behaviors: I. Quantifying intent and medical lethality. *Amer. J. Psychiat.*, 132:285–287.

——— Schuyler, D., & Herman, I. (1974), Development of suicidal intent scales. In: *The Prediction of Suicide*, eds. A.T. Beck, H.L.D. Resnik, & D.J. Lettieri. Bowie, MD: Charles Press, pp. 45–56.

Brown, H.N., & Vaillant, G.E. (1981), Hypochondriasis. *Arch. Internat. Med.*, 141:723–726.

Clendenin, W.W., & Murphy, G.E. (1971), Wrist cutting. New epidemiological findings. *Arch. Gen. Psychiat.*, 25:465–469.

Dressler, D. (1975), Clinician attitudes toward the suicide attempter. *J. Nerv. Dis.*, 160:146–155.

Fawcett, J., Leff, M., & Bunney, W.E. (1969), Suicide: Clues from interpersonal communication. *Arch. Gen. Psychiat.*, 21:129–137.

Fox, K., & Weissman, M. (1975), Suicide attempts and drugs: Contradiction between method and intent. *Soc. Psychiat.*, 10:31–38.

Frederick, C. (1978), Current trends in suicidal behavior in the United States. *Amer. J. Psychother.*, 32:172–201.

Freud. S. (1926), *Psychoanalysis and Faith*. New York: Basic Books, pp. 101–102, 1963.

Gerson, S., & Bassuk, E.L. (1980), Psychiatric emergencies: An overview. *Amer. J. Psychiat.*, 137:1–11.

Grunebaum, H., & Klerman, G.L. (1967), Wrist Slashing. *Amer. J. Psychiat.*, 124:527–534.

Leff, S., Senger, M., & Jacobs, D. (unpublished), *Staff Judgements of Service Needs in a Psychiatric Emergency Service*, 1981.

Litman, R.E. (1966), Acutely suicidal patients: Management in a general medical practice. *Calif. Med.*, 104:168–174.

——— (1976), Prediction models of suicidal behaviors. In: *The Prediction of Suicide*, eds. A.T. Beck, L.O.P. Resnick, & D.J. Lettieri. Bowie, MD: Charles Press.

Mack, J.E., & Hickler, H. (1981), *Vivienne: The Life and Suicide of an Adolescent Girl*. Boston. Little, Brown.

Maltsberger, J.T., & Buie, D.H. (1974), Countertransference hate in the treatment of suicidal patients. *Arch. Gen. Psychiat.*, 30:625–633.

Maris, R.W. (1981), *Pathways to Suicide: A Survey of Self-Destructive Behaviors.* Baltimore, MD: Johns Hopkins University Press.

Mayfield, D.G., & Montgomery, M.D. (1972), Alcoholism, alcohol intoxication and suicide attempts. *Arch. Gen. Psychiat.*, 27:349–353.

Mendelson, J., & Mello, N. (1979), Biologic concomitants of alcoholism. *N. Engl. J. Med.*, 301:912–921.

Menninger, K. (1938), *Man Against Himself.* New York: Harcourt, Brace & World.

Meyerson, A.I., Glick, R.A., & Kiev, A. (1976), Suicide. In: *Psychiatric Emergencies*, eds. R.A. Glick, A.I. Meyerson, E. Robbins, and J.A. Talbott. New York: Grune & Stratton.

Miles, C.P. (1977), Conditions predisposing to suicide: A review. *J. Nerv. & Ment. Dis.*, 164:231–246.

Morgan, H.G. (1979), *Death Wishes? The Understanding and Management of Deliberate Self Harm.* New York: John Wiley.

Motto, J.A. (1965), Suicide attempts: A longitudinal view. *Arch. Gen. Psychiat.*, 13:516–520.

———— (1975), The recognition and management of the suicidal patient. In: *The Nature and Treatment of Depression,* eds. F.F. Flach and S.C. Draghi. New York: John Wiley.

———— (1978), Recognition, evaluation, and management of persons at risk for suicide. *Personnel & Guid. J.*, 26:537–543.

Murphy, G.E. (1972), Clinical identification of suicidal risk. *Arch. Gen. Psychiat.*, 27:356–359.

———— Armstrong, J.W., Hermele, S.L., Fischer, J.R., & Clendenin, W.W. (1979), Suicide and alcoholism: Interpersonal loss confirmed as a predictor. *Arch. Gen. Psychiat.*, 36:64–69.

National Center for Health Statistics (1978), *Vital Statistics of the United States, 1978*, Vol. 29(6), Suppl. 2, Final Mortality Statistics. Hyattsville, MD: National Center for Health Statistics.

O'Brien, J.P. (1977), Increase in suicide attempts by drug ingestion: The Boston experience, 1967–1974. *Arch. Gen. Psychiat.*, 34:1165–1169.

Peck, M.L. & Litman, R.E. (1974), Current trends in youthful suicide. In: *Suicide in Blacks* (A monograph for continuing education in suicide prevention), ed. J. Bush, Fenton Research Development. Los Angeles: Charles R. Drew Postgraduate Medical Center, pp. 13–27.

Perry, C.J., & Jacobs, D. (1982), Clinical applications of the amytal interview in psychiatric emergency settings. *Amer. J. Psychiat.*, 139:552–559.

Plath, S. (1965), *Ariel.* New York: Harper & Row.

Pokorny, A.D. (1974), A scheme for classifying suicidal behaviors. In: *The Prediction of Suicide*, eds. A.T. Beck, H.L.P. Resnik, and D.J. Lettieri. Bowie, MD: Charles Press.

Rich, C.L., & Pitts, F.W. (1980), Suicide by psychiatrists: A study of medical specialists among 18,730 consecutive physician deaths during a five-year period, 1967–1973. *J. Clin. Psychiat.*, 4:261–263.

Ringel, E. (1976), The presuicidal syndrome. *Suicide & Life-Threat. Behav.*, 6:131–149.

Robins, E. (1959), The communication of suicidal intent: A study of 134 consecutive cases of successful (completed) suicide. *Amer. J. Pychiat.*, 115:724–733.

Robins, L.W., West, P.A., & Murphy, G.E. (1977), The high rate of suicide in older white men: A study testing ten hypotheses. *Soc. Psychiat.*, 12:1–20.

Rose, D.K., & Posow, I. (1973), Physicians who kill themselves. *Arch. Gen Psychiat.*, 29:800–805.

Rosen, D. (1976), The serious suicide attempt: Five-year follow-up study of 886 patients. *J. Amer. Med. Assn.*, 235:2105–2109.

Rosenthal, R.J., Kinzler, L., Walsh, N., & Klausner, E. (1972), Wrist cutting syndrome: The meaning of a gesture. *Amer. J. Psychiat.*, 128:1363–1368.

Schwartz, D.A. (1979), The suicidal character. *Psychiat. Quart.*, 5:64–70.

Sifneos, P.E. (1966), Manipulative suicide. *Psychiat. Quart.*, 40:525–537.

Simpson, M.A. (1976), Self-mutilation and suicide. In: *Suicidology: Contemporary Development,* ed. E. Shneidman. New York: Grune & Stratton.

Skodol, A.D., Kass, F., & Charles, E. (1979), Crisis in psychotherapy: Principles of emergency consultation and intervention. *Amer. J. Orthopsychiat.*, 49:585–597.

Sterling-Smith, R.S. (1974), A medical toxicology index: An evaluation of commonly used suicidal drugs. In: *The Prediction of Suicide*, eds. A.T. Beck, H.L.D. Resnick, & D.J. Lettieri. Bowie, MD: Charles Press.

Tuckman, J., & Youngman, W.F. (1968), A scale of assessing suicidal risk in attempted suicide. *J. Clin. Psychol.*, 24:17–19.

Vaillant, G.E. (1979), *Adaptation to Life*. Boston: Little, Brown.

Weissman, A.D., & Worden, W. (1972), Risk-rescue rating in suicide assessment. *Arch. Gen. Psychiat.*, 26:553–560.

Weissman, M.W. (1974), The epidemiology of suicide attempts, 1960–1971. *Arch. Gen. Psychiat.*, 30:737–746.

——— (1975), Wrist cutting: Relationship between clinical observations and epidemiological findings. *Arch. Gen. Psychiat.*, 32:1166–1171.

Wexler, L., Weissman, M., & Kasl, S.V. (1978), Suicide attempts 1970–75: Updating a United States study and comparisons with international trends. *Brit. J. Psychiat.*, 132:180–185.

20

Hospital Treatment of
the Suicidal Patient

Rohn S. Friedman, M.D.

Clinicians are well aware of the ubiquity of suicidal phenomena on inpatient psychiatry units. Suicidal patients frequently get hospitalized, and hospitalized patients frequently get suicidal. Dangerousness to self is the single most frequent determinant of the decision to admit a patient to a psychiatric unit (Friedman, 1983), and the frequency of suicide in patients with a history of psychiatric hospitalization may be nearly fifteen times that in the general population for men, and forty times that in the general population for women (Black, Warrack, and Winokur, 1985). In addition to dealing with patients who initially present as suicidal and to considering suicidal risk in deciding privileges and discharge for any patient, the staff of the inpatient unit must deal with the relatively continuous presence of suicidal thoughts, threats, and gestures in the milieu.

Despite the ubiquity of suicidal phenomena on inpatient units, there are relatively few extended discussions in the literature of the inpatient treatment of suicidal patients. A textbook of inpatient psychiatry does not have a chapter on, or sustained discussion of, this subject and indexes only twenty brief references to suicidality in the context of other topics (Sederer, 1983). This oversight is more the rule than the exception. With the arrival of *The Diagnostic and Statistical Manual of Mental Disorders* (DSM-III-R) and its new diagnostic precision, phenomena like suicide that cross diagnostic classes may be in danger of being relegated to the status of subsidiary topics. Yet there has been a large rise in suicide attempts (Khuri and Akiskal, 1983), and an increase in the number of completed suicides by inpatients and recently discharged patients (Shaw and Sims, 1984). Under such circumstances a discussion of the inpatient treatment of the suicidal person is timely.

ASSESSMENT OF THE SUICIDAL INPATIENT

The inpatient assessment of the suicidal person is directed toward understanding what underlies the patient's current suicidal behavior and under what circumstances the patient is at what degree of risk for what specific type of suicidal behavior. In attempting to explore these questions, the clinician must avoid the kind of psychological intuitionism that seeks the answers in a vaguely defined empathic sense of what the patient is experiencing (Buie, 1981). Such empathic communications are subject to interference from a host of countertransference reactions. In addition, there are patients who do not form an alliance that allows accurate empathy. It is necessary to reflect on empathic intuitions and to compare them with objective information about suicide risk, a careful history, diagnostic precision, and a thorough psychodynamic formulation.

Overreliance on the objective suicide rating scales may be just as misleading as overreliance on an unquestioned empathy. Despite the large areas of overlap between studies that suggest some validity to such rating scales, one must beware of a wishful overconfidence in mechanical prediction of suicide risk. The base rate of suicide is low, and these scales have a low sensitivity as well as a low specificity in predicting suicide. Under these conditions, as one recent study found:

> [T]he conclusion is inescapable that we do not possess any item of information or any combination of items that permit us to identify to a useful degree the particular persons who will commit suicide, in spite of the fact that we do have scores of items available, each of which is significantly related to suicide [Pokorny, 1983, p. 257].

These statistical complexities only underline the complexity of suicide phenomena and the fact that clinical judgment based on training and experience will remain an essential element in the evaluation of suicide risk. The task is one of integrating what is known of statistical risk factors, biological factors, and psychodynamic factors into an overall assessment of the patient.

We shall here follow the format of a standard case history.

Identifying Data

Certain demographic factors correlate with suicidal behavior.

Age   In the general population age constitutes a risk factor for suicide, with persons over age 45 being at particularly high risk. On the other hand, younger age (20–30) constitutes a risk factor for a failed suicide attempt (Khuri and Akiskal, 1983; Pattison and Kahan, 1983). Among psychiatric patients, older age does not appear to correlate with suicide risk in a number of studies (Roy, 1982; Morrison, 1984; Black et al., 1985), although others continue to find the association (Motto,

Heilbron, and Juster, 1985). Among suicide attempters, age greater than 45 correlates with eventual suicide (Pallis, Gibbons, and Pierce, 1984). Finally, schizophrenic suicides tend to be young (Breier and Astrachan, 1984). A possible interpretation of this data is that there are several distinct populations to be aware of as suicide risks, such as young schizophrenics or elderly depressed patients.

Sex   There is a preponderance of males among completed suicides, and of females among suicide attempters (Khuri and Akiskal, 1983). The predominance of males is present among psychiatric patients who have suicided (Copas and Robin, 1982), though it is less prominent than in the general population (Black et al., 1985).

Marital Status   There is a great overrepresentation of single, widowed, separated, or divorced individuals among suicides. This is true of the general population (Sletten and Barton, 1979), psychiatric patients (Roy, 1982), and schizophrenic patients (Breier and Astrachan, 1984).

Race   Caucasians show high rates of suicide, while nonwhites show higher rates of attempt (Khuri and Akiskal, 1983).

Socioeconomic Status and Social Network   Unemployed or retired individuals and professionals show high rates of suicide. All classes are represented in suicidal phenomena. Persons living alone and without a network of social supports are at highest risk (Pallis, Barraclough, Levey, Jenkins, and Sainsbury, 1982; Khuri and Akiskal, 1983).

History of Present Illness

Phenomenology   A detailed phenomenological examination of suicidal thoughts, feelings, and acts is central to the history of the present illness. It is important to explore exactly what thoughts and events led up to and followed the suicidal ideation or attempt. Was the patient psychotic or intoxicated at the time? Was the patient's conscious intent to kill himself, to hurt himself, or to produce a particular response in others?

Did the patient have a well-worked-out plan or only a vague notion of killing himself? Did he have access to, or already obtain, the pills or gun specified in his plan? Did he attempt self-harm under circumstances in which there would be a high probability of discovery, did he call someone to report what he had done, or did he take steps to insure that he would not be found? What was the mode of suicide attempt or plan? More violent plans or attempts, such as those via gunshot or asphyxiation, carry both a higher risk of death in an attempt and higher risk of eventual suicide. Less violent and idiosyncratic or bizarre modes, such as overdose or wrist-cutting, carry less ominous prognostic import for eventual completion.

How did the patient react to a suicide attempt? Did he feel pain? Was there a feeling of relief of tension following the plan or attempt? Did it take the sight of blood to feel relief?

Various rating scales may be helpful in evaluating these details, including the Beck Suicide Intent Scale (Beck, Schuyler, and Herman, 1974) and the Weisman and Worden Risk–Rescue rating (Weisman and Worden, 1972).

Another important factor in the precipitating circumstances has to do with the somewhat magical significance of dates in suicidal ideation.

A 28-year-old married professional had been hospitalized for depression in the context of marital turmoil and threatened divorce. He steadily improved, participated in individual and couples' treatment, and successfully negotiated initial passes off the unit. He was given a pass to spend Valentine's Day with his wife. The unit was notified by the police that he had jumped to his death on his way home.

Holidays (especially those associated with loved ones like Christmas or Thanksgiving); anniversary dates (birthdays, deaths, or other important events); and self-imposed deadlines ("I'll give therapy a chance, but if I'm not feeling better by the time my insurance runs out   . . .") must be carefully followed in the evaluation and treatment of the suicidal patient.

Therapists are often reluctant to insist upon so vivid a retelling for fear of precipitating further suicidal behavior, as well as from their horror and shock at some of the details. For their part, patients are sometimes reluctant to provide details, while at other times they flood the interviewer with details in a show of bravado designed to shock or repel. An air of clinical objectivity combined with an insistence on a detailed understanding of the circumstances of suicidal thought or behavior can establish therapeutic rapport.

A 25-year-old single woman with a long history of wrist-cutting severe enough to produce tendon damage, extensive ugly scars, and numerous surgical and psychiatric admissions had fended off several interviewers with gory details of her past attempts. Staff members avoided her and were reluctant to confront the intense affects of anger, fear, violence, and repulsion she experienced and inspired. A major therapeutic advance occurred when a consultant, being regaled by the patient with the usual details, insisted on knowing exactly what kind of razor the patient habitually used and why, exactly what her blood looked like to her, and how much was necessary for a feeling of relief, how she knew when to stop, and so on. The patient was overtly shocked and uneasy about being pressed for further details, the gaps in what she had reported became evident, and her bravado gave way to a more engageable depressive affect. It was only when she felt that someone could withstand and contain her intense affects and experiences that she felt safe enough to participate in treatment.

The usual considerations of tact and timing apply to the pursuit of a detailed history of the suicidal phenomenon, but this information is crucial and cannot be safely ignored.

Psychosocial Context   A second aspect of the history of present illness is the elucidation of the life context for the suicidal behavior or thought. Stressful life events such as loss of job, loss of significant other, and poor health have all been correlated with lethality and frequency of suicidal behavior (Khuri and Akiskal, 1983). Narcissistic losses and wounds may be more subtle and subjective, such as the abandonment of dearly held aspirations.

It is important to know whether there are "objects"—whether people, pets, or ideals—for which the patient still wishes to live. Does the patient *have* something to offset threatened or actual losses?

While stressful life events, particularly financial or personal losses, appear to precipitate suicidal phenomena in a population of depressed and suicidal patients (Motto et al., 1985), this may not be true of schizophrenic patients (Breier and Astrachan, 1984).

Neurovegetative Signs and Substance Abuse   A final aspect of taking the history of present illness relevant to suicidal patients is to inquire specifically about the presence of drug or alcohol abuse and the presence of neurovegetative signs of depression (sleep disturbance, weight change, or alteration of libido). Both substance abuse and depression are important elements in assessing and treating the suicidal patient.

Medical History

One must review carefully the patient's medical history. Items of particular note include any serious illness or recent deterioration in health, recent visits to a physician, and any prescribed medications (especially those that can produce depression, such as alpha-methyldopa; those that can produce psychosis, such as steroids; those that can produce confusional states, such as minor tranquilizers; and those that can easily be used in a lethal overdose, such as tricyclic antidepressants). Poor physical health and concern for one's health are risk factors for suicide (Sletten and Barton, 1979).

Psychiatric History

It is important to note the detailed history of past suicidal thoughts, feelings, and behavior. Most patients who commit suicide have a prior history of some suicidal ideation or behavior. Knowing under what circumstances the patient has been suicidal in the past will help both to evaluate the current level of suicidal risk and to determine circumstances that might ameliorate or increase the risk. The chronicity or acuteness of the suicidal impulses is also relevant. Some patients chronically present to inpatient units for admission every six weeks and may safely be sent home on these routine visits, unlike a patient with the new onset of suicidal impulses, who requires more thorough evaluation. On the other hand, if there is a change in pattern even for one of these repeaters, such as showing up on three consecutive nights, this acute change in a pattern must be evaluated seriously. Finally, one must investigate whether there is a crisis in the current psychiatric treatment, such as a vacation separation or a messy transference–countertransference impasse.

Family History

In the family history it is important to pay close attention to any history of depression or suicidal behavior. Whether on the basis of genetic factors or shared environment, a family history of suicide is a powerful risk factor. In one study of hospitalized psychiatric patients, nearly 50 percent of those with a family history of suicide attempted suicide themselves, and 2.8 percent of them eventually suicided (Roy, 1983). A family history of response to a particular treatment modality, such as a particular drug or electroconvulsive therapy (ECT), may be helpful in predicting treatment response and choosing a modality.

Personal History

A thorough personal history is essential to clarifying the unique meaning of suicidal thought and behavior in the life of a particular individual. A thorough review should include childhood experiences, academic and professional careers, and interpersonal relationships. It is important to know what persons, ideas, or values have been passionately held by the patient. Experiences of loss, especially early parental loss (Adams, Bouckoms, and Streiner, 1982), and the patient's reaction to them are relevant to understanding the meaning of suicidal ideation.

Physical and Laboratory Examinations

It is important not to overlook the examination of the patient. Old scars and even current bleeding wounds not reported by the patient have been noted in suicidal patients. Coarse nystagmus or cardiac arrhythmia may be evidence of an unreported overdose attempt.

A 26-year-old young man, recently jilted by his lover, was brought to the hospital by his friends after tearfully confessing his suicidal feelings to them. After a brief interview he was left on a hospital cot in the corridor of a busy emergency service while another patient was seen. A medical student found the patient unresponsive. Intubation, gastric lavage, and intensive care prevented his death from a large barbiturate overdose.

Laboratory exam can reveal evidence of toxic substances or medical problems of relevance either to the suicidal behavior or its treatment.

Specific laboratory findings in suicidal patients are controversial. Investigators have reported increased urinary corticosteroids (Ostroff, Giller, Bonese, Ebersole, Harkness, and Mason, 1982), and some suggestive work on suicide completers has found low levels of cerebrospinal fluid serotonin metabolites as well as low monoamine oxidase levels (Traskman, Asberg, Bertilsson, and Sjostrand, 1981). This work is still at the experimental stage and not yet of demonstrated clinical utility. A more useful test may be the dexamethasone suppression test (DST) which has been reported to be positive in a higher rate in suicide attempters than in nonsuicidal patients (Targum, Rosen, and Capodanno, 1983). More intriguingly, in this study three of five attempters and the one completer had positive DSTs that failed to normalize with treatment. Thus, serial DSTs in patients who initially fail to suppress may distinguish a high risk suicidal group among those who fail to normalize.

Mental Status Examination

The appearance and behavior of the suicidal patient may show psychomotor retardation, but an agitated state is more typical. One noteworthy presentation involves a state of intense anxiety and irritability with a restless demand for relief in any form. Such an initial presentation often alienates caretakers and is misperceived as manipulative when it is in fact highly ominous.

A middle-aged married man was admitted in an intensely agitated, anxious, and irritable state. He demanded constant attention and immediate relief from the vague but intolerable state of tension he experienced. He had made one previous major suicide attempt, resulting in extensive litigation against the physicians treating him. After several days his demanding behavior was unchanging and seemed to be aggravated by attention. Suicide precautions were relaxed from a constant companion to fifteen-minute checks. The patient was found in his room, unresponsive, after cutting both wrists and his neck with a piece of broken glass. After emergency surgery and a course of ECT, he showed a prompt and dramatic recovery.

In retrospect it seemed clear that the patient suffered from a treatable major depression, but his provocative behavior and the predominance of irritability masked the depression in the cloak of a hostile and manipulative character disorder.

Higher cognitive functioning is a much-overlooked element in suicidal behavior. Organic brain syndromes of delirium, dementia, or intoxication all increase the risk of suicide. First, the capacity to make sense of their surroundings is reduced in such patients, and often only a paranoid construction seems to restore a distorted sense of comprehensibility to their world. In such a fearful and confused state, suicidal behavior may seem the only escape from a terrifying persecutor. Second, in the case of actual cerebral damage, a "catastrophic reaction" may ensue in response to the profound narcissistic loss of cognitive capacity (Goldstein, 1948). A patient suddenly coming to grips with a loss of cognitive capacity, whether from dementia or a more localized lesion, may be an acute suicide risk. Third, as a final common pathway to suicide in these states, impulse control is reduced, so what might be a suicidal thought in other circumstances may be acted on with tragic consequences.

A 65-year-old woman with a long history of alcohol abuse was admitted for depression. She had multiple somatic complaints, appeared medically ill, and was very irritable and provocative. After a course of antidepressant medications, she was cheerful and outgoing, although the occupational therapist reported that she was unable to complete even very simple tasks. At the patient's insistence, she was given passes to prepare for discharge. She was found drowned in her bathtub.

While the cause of death in this case was not clear, patients in disordered cognitive states, whether from organic pathology or as a manifestation of psychosis, are at high risk of both suicide and accidental death.

The most common affective state in suicide is depression, though anxiety, irritability, and manic euphoria may also be danger signals. Anxious and irritable states are often diagnostic and countertransference dilemmas, as in the example above. Hopelessness has been repeatedly found to be a most powerful correlate of suicide (Minkoff, Bergman, Beck, and Beck, 1973; Beck, Steer, Kovacs, and Garrison, 1985).

The presence of psychosis is itself a marker for suicide risk, whether in the form of delusions (Roose, Glassman, Walsh, Woodring, and Vital-Herne, 1983), hallucinations (such as the classic command suicidal hallucinations), or disordered thought.

Diagnosis

Although some have suggested a categorization of suicide along such dimensions as contemplated, attempted, or completed, impulsive or planned, acute or chronic, and have even suggested some new diagnostic entities such as the deliberate self-harm syndrome (Pattison and Kahan, 1983), for diagnostic and treatment purposes, suicidal behavior does not exist as a separate entity. It is essential to consider those psychiatric disorders that may underlie the suicidal impulse. Diagnosis should follow DSM-III-R.

The most obvious diagnostic category of relevance is major depression. Paykel and Dienelt (1971) found a 10 percent annual rate of suicide attempts in a depressed population. Up to 65 percent of suicides are suffering from a major affective disorder at the time of their deaths (Roy, 1982). Schizophrenic and bipolar disorders also may involve suicidal behavior. Morrison (1984) found that these diagnoses accounted for 50 percent of the suicides in psychiatric patients, and as many as 10 percent of schizophrenic patients may ultimately suicide (Miles, 1977). An organic brain syndrome may be associated with suicidal behavior, and alcoholism is present in a quarter of suicides (Robins, Murphy, and Wilkinson, 1959).

Among Axis II diagnoses, borderline personality is perhaps the diagnosis most clearly associated with suicidal ideation and actions.

Axis III diagnoses may also bear a relationship to suicidal evaluations: as many as 51 percent of suicides have a history of significant physical illness (Robins et al., 1959).

Formulation

A formulation is a systematic psychological explanation of behavior. As such it is distinct from the diagnosis, which is more a descriptive shorthand than an explanation, and from empathic intuition, which is not systematic.

First of all, it is important to consider the role of aggression in the patient. Individuals with a history of violent behavior directed toward self or others—tantrums, fights, head-banging—demonstrate prominent aggressive trends that can power suicidal behavior. Paradoxically an exaggerated avoidance of aggressive expression, seen in an overly passive and inhibited patient, may reflect rigid and brittle attempts to contain concealed but powerful aggressive trends that create as much suicidal risk as more overt aggression. It is important to keep in mind that suicide is both a violent and an aggressive act.

Second, it is important to consider impulse control and frustration tolerance. Individuals with poor impulse control, as evidenced by impulsive behavior, job instability, or substance abuse are also vulnerable to impulsive self-destructive behavior.

Impaired reality testing is another factor related to suicide risk. The extreme forms of impairment are delusional beliefs or hallucinations, but even more subtle alterations in the sense of reality such as depersonalization and derealization experiences may predispose to suicide.

Superego factors in suicide relate both to critical, self-punitive functions and to self-esteem (narcissistic or ego ideal) functions. Individuals with a harsh, self-punitive superego are vulnerable to suicide insofar as self-criticism can escalate into a demand for self-annihilation. In some individuals, self-esteem is so precariously dependent on external success or approval that under the impact of a narcissistic injury such as job loss or sexual rejection they may feel helpless, worthless, and suicidal.

One key developmental factor to assess in the formulation is how an individual has experienced and coped with separation throughout his life. Early failures and difficulties in the separation–individuation process produce a regressive tendency in subsequent relationships that may be connected to suicidal tendencies. When there are primitive types of object relationship that involve merger, poorly defined ego boundaries, or an undiscriminating type of identification, a close relationship with someone who died or attempted suicide may form the basis for suicide. Sadomasochistic elements in object relationships may also eventuate in suicidal behavior.

A thorough understanding of the meaning of death and suicide to the patient is essential to arriving at an adequate formulation. Five central fantasies involved in suicide are revenge, rescue, reparation, reunion, and respite. Revenge fantasies involve picturing suicide as an attack on someone else. Such suicidal individuals are enraged. Their affect typically impresses the observer as more angry than depressed. The revenge may be aimed at others directly and expressed in fantasies of the guilt and suffering of loved ones after the patient's death. Alternatively the target may first come to reside within the patient himself by processes of identification and internalization, so that in fantasy the patient is killing the hated (or loved-and-hated) other in killing the hateful and hated part of himself. The attack on the hostile introject is often united with the attack on the hostile object in a complex fantasy:

A 23-year-old woman had a history of depression. When suicidal, however, her anger was considerably more marked than her depression. She was hospitalized and developed a very hostile relationship with her caretakers. She was desperately afraid of becoming a chronic mental patient like her mother and was unconsciously furious at her consciously idealized father for not rescuing her from the mother. She attempted suicide on her first pass from an open unit which she could easily have left at any time, creating a great deal of anger and guilt in the milieu. Eventually she suicided in her father's house.

In analyzing this patient's motives, it seems likely that the fantasy of killing off her introjected sick mother while punishing her father and other caretakers who had failed her were joined in her final act. It is perhaps also true that she secretly hoped for rescue from those she sought to punish, since she always left clues or warnings. Revenge and rescue may both be present within such a complex fantasy.

Reparation is the fantasy that suicide or self-injury will atone for some act, propitiate some person, and restore some relationship threatened by the patient's wishes or actions. The predominant affect of patients for whom this is a central theme is guilt.

The wish for reunion is prominent in cases where a loved one has died and there are overt fantasies of reunion with that person after death. More complex are the cases in which the desire is to return not just to lost person but to an earlier relationship and an earlier state of existence. Such wishes are evident in fantasies of a return to a womblike symbiotic state after death.

The wish for respite is another common underlying fantasy. Here death signifies an end to intolerable suffering. Such patients show a quiet determination and often see suicide as the one alternative to a passive helplessness. Most typically this fantasy is linked to the wish for reunion with an omnipotent, comforting caretaker.

ASSESSMENT OF THE SUICIDE MILIEU

It is important to assess the status of the inpatient milieu in evaluating suicide risk for an inpatient. The milieu produces powerful social forces that impact on all of its members, not always for the better. A striking finding is that suicidal behavior tends to occur in rashes or epidemics on inpatient units (Walsh and Rosen, 1985), strongly implicating elements of the ward milieu. There are three circumstances that increase the risk of suicidal behavior: change, conflict, and collusion.

All inpatient units experience periods of change: staff turnover, trainee turnover, and patient turnover. At any of these periods both patients and staff show varying degrees of uncertainty about what to expect. The anxiety level of the ward rises, staff and patients alike feel inadequately tended, and risk of suicidal behavior rises. Suicide in this context may express the sense of helplessness, the anger at caretakers, the demand for attention, or any combination thereof.

Circumstances of staff conflict are endemic on inpatient units. The surface expression of the conflict is usually a clinical disagreement: should a patient have privileges, should medication be changed, should a patient be discharged or transferred? Underlying the specific disagreement there may be a philosophical disagreement: how flexible should rules be, how much acting out should be tolerated, how restrictive should the environment be? Finally there are typically even deeper-lying power struggles and personality conflicts. In these circumstances nonspecific excitement appears, and patients become increasingly symptomatic. Suicidal behavior is likeliest to occur at such times. Amidst conflict the collective reservoir of aggression and guilt is increased, and unconscious fears and wishes that the staff "opponent" in the clinical or personal struggle be proved wrong may be communicated to the patient. The patient's suicidal enactment may be the final word in the staff debate over who is right or wrong.

Finally, circumstances of collusion may exist on the inpatient unit. Collusion on the unconscious level includes the kind of indirect communications during staff conflicts discussed above. More conscious collusion also goes on, one form of it being the suicide pact. One or more patients may make an overt pact or may challenge and goad one another into a progressively more serious series of self-destructive acts. Often one or more patients knows of a fellow patient's suicidal intent. A conspiracy of silence emerges in which the victim may feel "honor-bound" to carry out his intention and the guilty coconspirators may subsequently be at risk to act out self-destructive impulses. Such suicidal contagions can be remarkable.

> This form of response to tension [epidemic suicidal behavior] can be learned and propagated in a hospital or institution and is often sustained by the widespread conflict and guilt such acts tend to arouse in the staff. The author had encountered an

epidemic occurring in a general hospital psychiatric ward, which eventually involved twelve patients and two nurses, who were so disturbed by the sequence of events that they felt compelled to cut themselves [Simpson, 1975, pp. 431–432].

Such epidemics strongly implicate the milieu and point to the need to include an evaluation and monitoring of the milieu in the assessment of suicidal thought and behavior.

PREVENTION

The prevention of suicide in the inpatient context has both secondary and tertiary aspects.

Tertiary Prevention

Tertiary prevention involves the reduction of morbidity and mortality in patients who are actively suicidal. Hospitalization itself is often the first step in prevention. The simple removal from a toxic, stressful environment may be adequate to insure the patient's safety. At times, however, the hospital must employ more restrictive measures such as a locked door, seclusion, physical restraints, chemical restraints, and ECT. Less restrictive preventive measures that should be available include one-to-one special duty nursing, restriction to common areas where the patient can be observed, and restriction to wearing bedclothes to discourage leaving an open unit.

Architectural considerations in the design of inpatient units should emphasize the crucial importance of maintaining unobstructed lines of vision between the nurses' station and all patient areas. Windows should not open to the point where a patient could jump out, electric outlets should have protective covers that prevent electrocution, curtain and clothing rods or hooks should give way at a low weight to prevent hangings, and flammable materials and breakable glass should be avoided in the unit design.

Consideration of the safety of the patient himself, other patients, and staff must preempt worries about being overly intrusive. All new admissions and their possessions must be examined for dangerous objects and substances. Despite their explicit denials, patients have brought razor blades and toxic substances onto inpatient units. Sharp objects such as razors and scissors may be banned, but it is probably not feasible to avoid all potentially dangerous materials.

An important area for prevention is the assessment of privileges. Privileges must be assigned and monitored carefully rather than routinely. One-third to one-half of inpatient suicides occur on pass, suggesting the clinical importance of such decisions (Crammer, 1984). It is important to see rules and privileges not only as restraints but as avenues of communication. Suicidal patients often have great difficulty communicating their thoughts, feelings, or intentions verbally in the face of conflicting wishes to live and die. Ward policies and privileges constitute an arena for nonverbal communication that may be the only chance for any kind of communication.

The 23-year-old woman mentioned in a previous example was eager to get privileges to leave the hospital. She had made several prior suicide attempts, was quite labile, and told several staff and patients that she intended to kill herself and was concealing that intent from the staff. She had shown some improvement and seemed more involved on the unit. After much consideration and with realization that it involved the acceptance of considerable risk, the patient was given privileges to leave the floor and go to the hospital cafeteria. On her first departures from the floor she recurrently failed in minor ways to follow the usual sign-in and sign-out procedures. Nevertheless, she appeared improved and began demanding time out of the hospital. A decision was made to allow a pass. The morning of the pass she went to the cafeteria for a protracted period without permission. In response to this infraction, staff made her pass conditional on her signing a contract that she would observe the rules and would not hurt herself on pass. She signed, left, and jumped in front of a subway train.

This example points out several important principles of inpatient management. First of all, it is necessary at times to accept risk. One cannot ever prevent all suicide, but must be prepared to make difficult decisions that involve real risk. For this patient in particular, there never would have been a point imaginable at which she would not be a serious suicide risk. The crucial decision is whether the risk is acceptable if the alternative is an unending hospitalization and if there is not a point in the foreseeable future when there would be less risk. Thus the initial decision to advance her privileges, even in the face of her lability and suicidality, may well have been the best one available.

Second, the case illustrates the principle of using privileges as a mode of communication. The patient advanced stepwise from one-to-one observation, to common area restriction, and to ward restriction without difficulty. The next step to hospital cafeteria privileges was accomplished only with infringements. Such infringements on the part of a patient very familiar with the rules constitute a presumptive message and a request for intervention that could not be made more directly. Not only did the patient deny any suicidal intent, she browbeat the staff about their violations of her liberty and demanded further privileges. Here a message was missed, and the calculated risk was *mis*calculated.

Finally, one must consider the overall context of a contract and not assume magically that because a contract has been made that the patient will desire or be able to fulfill it. A contract with a patient who has consciously withheld information in the past, who has been unable to carry out the implicit contract over the last step of privileges, and who is wildly impulsive may provide reassurance for the staff but it provides little protection for the patient.

Secondary Prevention

Secondary prevention seeks to avoid the development of suicidal behavior in patients at high risk. In the case of suicide, the entire inpatient ward constitutes a population at risk.

The milieu plays a central part in preventing the appearance of suicidal thought and behavior. Well-functioning inpatient units share certain factors: clarity in role definition, unambiguous lines of authority, and openness of communication. It is important to recognize that units will differ in the specifics of role definition (on one unit nurses will do certain tasks that social workers or psychiatric residents perform on another unit), distribution of power and authority (who reports to whom will vary with setting), and channels of communication (formal and informal, vertical and horizontal lines of communication will differ). Yet whatever the specifics, clarity in role definition makes everyone's work clear, lack of ambiguity in power structure makes it clear to whom to turn for a given decision, and openness in communication eliminates blocks in the formal channels of communication. Under these ideal circumstances, the problems of change, conflict, and collusion discussed above are least disruptive.

Three more specific milieu attitudes are also important in the prevention of suicide: openness in the discussion of suicidal thoughts and actions, sharing of information, and acknowledgment of both countertransference and the realistic limits of therapeutic responsibility. Patients and staff alike can be intimidated by a suicidal patient. Fears that open questioning or discussion will lead to suicide can lead to avoidance of this crucial topic. A subtle variation on this theme occurs when the patient protests that if he or she talks about suicidal feelings, restrictions or longer hospitalization will ensue. It would be equally mistaken either to avoid discussing suicide or to avoid responding appropriately to the clinical information produced. Neither suicide nor restrictions are *caused* by talking about suicide. They are related to what is said, not the mere fact of its being said. The ward culture should encourage open discussion of suicidal thoughts, feelings, and actions. In this process important clinical information is conveyed, and patients can obtain the support of realizing they are not alone. The more such discussions are expected rather than extraordinary events, the more comfortable they will be for all.

The sharing of information between staff is crucial. Typical of many suicidal patients is the desire to obtain the collusive silence of a confidant among staff or patients. Therapist, milieu worker, or ward director may be enticed with the offer of special confidences. The risk of suicidal behavior rises when such requests for collusive silence or confidentiality are honored, for such secrecy may induce the patient to act out the suicide in order to produce guilt in the confidant, to be rescued by the secret friend, and to produce staff or milieu conflict.

Acknowledgment of countertransference is also vital to both prevention and treatment of suicidal behavior. The acknowledgment is to oneself, and to some extent to one's colleagues. Acknowledgment to the patient is an issue of tact and timing we shall not discuss here.

Suicidal behavior produces feelings of sadness, guilt, anger, and betrayal, as well as wishes to retaliate, blame, withdraw, and rescue. In the absence of milieu acceptance and discussion of such feelings, they are denied, projected, or displaced. Such unacknowledged countertransference feelings interfere with the realistic appraisal of therapeutic responsibility, and often lead to unrealistic and omnipotent notions of the therapist's role.

The therapist and the staff are responsible for the patient's treatment, not for the patient's life. The best available treatment includes the acceptance of an inevitable element of risk and uncertainty in one's clinical decisions. If one cannot accept the fact of risk and recognize the patient's responsibility for his own life, one is at risk of colluding with the patient's fantasies of omnipotent rescue by his caretakers, as well as his fantasies of sadistic retaliation through inducing guilt in them. Such circumstances raise the likelihood of suicidal behavior. Acknowledgment of the limits of one's omnipotence leads to a sounder assessment of responsibility and a more effective therapeutic milieu.

In difficult situations of high risk and ward tension, a particularly useful technique to make clear both the best clinical decision and the limits of therapeutic responsibility is the ward consultation. A consultant's role in this circumstance is both to make specific recommendations and to facilitate the process of defining and sharing responsibility. With the consultant's support, uncomfortable countertransference feelings can be identified with a sense of relief. Once these feelings are identified, there is less tendency to act on them; and the staff is able to resume the work with the patient.

A word of warning is in order: sometimes the admonition to acknowledge limitation and risk openly leads to a kind of therapeutic bravado. In such a mood the therapist may acknowledge as inevitable and acceptable a risk which is in fact unacceptable or preventable. It *is* the responsibility of the staff to assess risk accurately, to decide whether there is any intervention that would alter that risk, and to provide that intervention. It is only the acceptance of excessive and inappropriate responsibility for the patient's life decisions that must be avoided.

When is it legally and morally acceptable, as well as clinically indicated, to shoulder the risk of suicide without restricting or committing a patient at risk? There are two circumstances that call for a conservative attitude. The first is in the situation of initial evaluation of admission or an acute clinical change in the course of an admission. Until a patient can be thoroughly assessed, extreme care must be exercised, and one should err on the side of caution. Sometimes a patient will, for example, arrive in the emergency room for suturing of a wrist laceration and then deny any suicidal ideation or wish for psychiatric intervention. In such a situation, until adequate information to assess the attempt has been obtained, coercive measures such as commitment are appropriate.

The second set of circumstances demanding a conservative attitude involve those in which the patient is at high risk for suicide, there is a treatment that can be provided even under coercive circumstances (such as ECT) that would be likely to alter that risk significantly, and there are the acute circumstances that provide legal justification for coercive measures.

The circumstances that lead one to accept a risk without restrictions, commitment, or other coercive measures are those in which no treatment could reasonably be expected to alter the level of risk in a foreseeable period or in which a thorough assessment has been made and the indicated treatment could not be provided under coercive circumstances (such as in a case where coercion would undermine the psychotherapeutic alliance irreparably or where essential vocational or family work could not be provided in the coercive setting).

A 25-year-old borderline woman was admitted for impulsive assaultive and suicidal behavior in the context of the loss of a lover. She made minimal contact with staff or therapist, was generally uncooperative, and ultimately signed out when the immediate feeling of crisis passed. She did not follow through with outpatient referral for continuing therapeutic work. Several days later she reappeared in the emergency room in crisis because of tension with the lover, insisting she had nowhere else to go, and strongly suggesting that if she were not admitted, she would have little alternative to suicide.

She was told that she was correct: there was a real risk that she might hurt or kill herself. The staff wished to help her; and after a thorough assessment on her last admission, they had recommended outpatient treatment. Nothing had changed to alter that recommendation, and there was no clear reason to think that further inpatient treatment had anything to offer her, even in this crisis, since crises were weekly if not daily events in her life. If she needed a place to stay, a list of shelters or other safe places could be provided.

In this way both her responsibility and capacity to take care of herself were supported, risk was openly acknowledged in a way that undercut fantasy, and the staff's continued commitment to and responsibility for the treatment were underlined.

The patient dramatically pulled herself together, "remembered" several places she could stay which she had not been able to suggest earlier, and asked how to proceed with the outpatient referral.

In these cases it is helpful to share the risk openly with the patient, staff, and family. Such a strategic collaboration and sharing of risk both minimizes the risk of later litigation by encouraging the family's participation in the decision not to employ more coercive measures and actually lowers the risk of suicidal enactments by reducing fantasies of omnipotent rescue or retaliation.

TREATMENT

Inpatient treatment demands an intensive multidisciplinary and multimodal approach. In dealing with suicidal patients, like any other inpatients, somatic therapy, sociotherapy, and psychotherapy must be integrated in a unified treatment plan.

Biological Treatment

Biological treatment of the suicidal patient does not exist as such. Suicide is not a unitary diagnostic or therapeutic entity. Biological treatment is directed toward the underlying diagnosable entity. The most common underlying entities for which biological treatments are well established are bipolar and unipolar affective disorders, schizophrenia, and organic brain syndromes (including intoxications, dependencies, medical illnesses, and other states that reduce impulse control).

It is clearly not possible to review fully biological treatments for such a wide range of disorders, but a few points of special applicability in the case of suicidal patients are noteworthy.

It is important to remember that the period of greatest risk may be after initial response to somatic treatment. A depressed patient may emerge from psychomotor retardation with enough energy to make a suicide attempt that was only contemplated before (Slater and Roth, 1977). Similarly, a schizophrenic may be at greatest risk as his acute symptoms remit, and he faces the integration of the psychotic episode. The suicide risk is highest *after* the abatement of psychotic symptoms (Farberow, Shneidman, and Leonard, 1965).

After successful treatment of the acute episode, follow-up is of the utmost importance with suicidal patients. One recent study of psychiatric outpatients who committed suicide demonstrated that 81.3 percent of them had recently been discharged from the hospital and that 71.1 percent of those with a diagnosis of depression were not receiving adequate antidepressant or lithium treatment at the time of their suicide (Roy, 1982). While a low rate of compliance may be one problem, it is also the case that clinicians are often wary of giving medications to potentially suicidal patients. Priority must be given to providing necessary treatment. If this cannot be done safely outside of the hospital, the patient must be hospitalized rather than withholding the treatment.

Finally, it is essential to avoid dogmatic either/or decisions between biological and psychosocial treatments. Major psychiatric illnesses may be conceptualized as reducing the threshold of vulnerability to psychosocial stress. Treatment is logically directed simultaneously to raising that threshold by means of somatic treatment while reducing the stress and expanding coping capacities by means of psychosocial treatments. Weissman, Prusoff, DiMascio, Neu, Goklaney, and Klerman's study (1979) of the synergy of pharmacotherapy and psychotherapy in the treatment of depression supports such a view.

Sociotherapy

There is no specific sociotherapy of suicidal patients, insofar as suicidality crosses diagnostic classes and social circumstances. Sociotherapy addresses the underlying social stressors that can produce suicidal behavior. In the hospital sociotherapy addresses the patient's needs for social interaction and social skills (milieu therapy) and to maintain connection and resolve problems with family and community (family therapy, occupational therapy, and social work).

Milieu Therapy Milieu therapy plays an important role in the treatment of the suicidal patient. Gunderson (1978) has defined five essential functions of the milieu: containment, support, structure, involvement, and validation. All of these functions are relevant to the suicidal patient. The inpatient unit must first contain the patient in a safe environment, then provide support and validation to help the patient bear unbearable affects and to enhance his self-esteem. Involvement in interpersonal relationships and activities on the unit combats social isolation, and structured activities strengthen organically or psychotically impaired cognitive processes.

There are at the same time numerous ways in which the milieu can be an antitherapeutic environment (Sacks and Carpenter, 1974). Conditions of change, conflict, and collusion promote the development of suicidal behavior on the unit, as do low staff morale, unclear policies, and poor training. Morgan and Priest (1984) report a process of "malignant alienation" in which a patient suicided after alienating staff with behavior construed as provocative, manipulative, or dependent. Establishing consistent policies and stable administration on the ward, fostering staff attitudes and morale conducive to effective treatment, and a calm but vigilant monitoring of the milieu with regular discussions among staff of the "state of the milieu" are ways of preventing the appearance of these antitherapeutic forces.

Social Work and Occupational Therapy An important risk factor in the development of suicidal behavior is the absence of social and financial resources. Social isolation, unemployment, and impoverishment accentuate the kind of helplessness and hopelessness that can eventuate in a suicide. Inpatient treatment seeks to expand and weave more securely the individual's network of social resources. Housing, financial stability, and a job are all important parts of the effective treatment and prevention of suicidal behavior.

Another goal of sociotherapy is to secure outpatient follow-up and to establish a secure after-care link prior to discharge. Such a link should be both institutional, with therapists and social workers in close coordination, and personal, with opportunity for the patient to meet new therapists and to visit new settings prior to discharge. After-care arrangements must be within financial and geographical reach and acceptable to the patient. The importance of adequate after care is evident in the fact that 44 percent of hospitalized patients who suicide do so within a month of discharge (Roy, 1982).

Family Therapy The inpatient unit can also enlist the family's help. A psychoeducational emphasis makes the family an ally rather than a scapegoat by viewing the patient and family as victims rather than perpetrators of an illness. The shared task of combatting the illness replaces combatting each other. Staff, patient, and family also share the risk of suicide, making it more manageable. By clarifying the nature of the patient's illness and fostering appropriate expectations of him or her, such an approach can maximize the likelihood of a supportive home environment. After establishing this kind of supportive, psychoeducational alliance, clinicians can more easily initiate structural family therapy to address family problems related to the patient's suicidal behavior.

Psychotherapy

As with pharmacotherapy and sociotherapy, there is no specific psychotherapy of suicide. There is only psychotherapy with patients, each of whom is a complex and unique amalgam of fantasies and experiences.

Focal Therapy Inpatient psychotherapy exists under constraints. In most cases it is a time-limited intervention, since most insurers cover only relatively brief inpatient stays. Often the inpatient therapist is not able to continue as the outpatient therapist. Under these circumstances it is especially important for the therapist to be clear about the goals and limitations of therapy in each case (Waltzer, 1982).

The initial sessions with the patient serve to foster a sense of rapport and to develop a detailed history, diagnosis, and initial formulation. Given the constraints discussed above, it becomes critical at this point to establish a focus for the inpatient psychotherapy. In the case of suicidal patients some typical foci are the suicide attempt itself with its surrounding circumstances and fantasies, some experience of present or past loss central to the depressed affect and suicidal ideation, or a transference–countertransference impasse in the outpatient therapy connected to the current suicidality. The establishment of a discharge date at the start of treatment can be a powerful tool in accelerating the psychotherapeutic work on this focus, similar to the model of time-limited, short-term dynamic psychotherapy advanced by Mann (1973).

Deficit Model There are two major components in the conceptualization of inpatient psychotherapy, the experiential and the analytic. The experiential aspect of therapy addresses structural and developmental deficits such as ego weaknesses, failures of empathy, and pathologic object relations. The approach is to create circumstances more conducive to adaptive internalization and structuralization. This approach implicitly assumes a "deficit model," and treatment involves a kind of reparenting and repair. Parental unempathic behavior, inconsistent limit-setting, and ambivalence are replaced with the experience of a consistent empathic therapist. Specific therapeutic techniques emphasized in this model include nonjudgmental empathic listening, encouragement, and tolerance of the expression of painful affects, flexible responsiveness to the patient's needs, and consistent limit-setting. It is important to remember that the absence of limits, allowing a patient to endanger himself or others, is neither empathic nor therapeutic.

Conflict Model   The analytic aspect of therapy focuses on the identification of conflicts and the fostering of insight. It is a "conflict model." In the suicidal patient, such an approach requires listening for the fantasies associated with the suicidal behavior, such as fantasies of revenge, rescue, reparation, reunion, or respite. Wishes for dependency, admiration, and erotic or aggressive gratification and the accompanying fears of loss of self, abandonment, punishment, or guilt are explored. Specific techniques include confrontation, clarification, and interpretation.

Transference and Countertransference   Many of these fantasies, wishes, and fears appear in the transference and elicit countertransference feelings of anger, guilt, or helplessness. These countertransference feelings may mirror the patient's own subjective experience or reproduce attitudes of significant others in the patient's past. Recognition of these feelings provides important information, avoids enacting the feelings, and prevents defensive reactions on the therapist's part such as denial or indifference, which may be the most dangerous kind of countertransference with a suicidal patient (Maltsberger and Buie, 1976).

THE AFTERMATH OF SUICIDE

Despite thorough assessment and the best available treatment, suicide occurs. The survivors of a suicide—family and friends, fellow patients, and ward staff—are also its victims.

> Survivor-victims of suicides are invaded by an unhealthy complex of disturbing emotions: shame, guilt, hatred, and perplexity. They are obsessed with thoughts about the death, seeking reasons, finding targets, and often punishing themselves. There is a marked increase in dependency needs, with regressive behavior and traumatic loss of feelings of identity, and, overall, a kind of affective anesthesia, an unhealthy docility, a cowed and subdued reaction [Friedman, Kaplan, and Sadock, 1976, p. 873].

In the wake of a successful suicide or major suicide attempt by an inpatient or recently discharged patient one frequently sees suicidal behavior by other patients who feel guilty at not preventing the suicide. One may also see litigation against the hospital by a guilt-ridden family: one-third of inpatient suicides result in lawsuits

(Litman, 1982). Finally, guilt, anger, and frustration can lead to a rash of blame-trading among the staff.

Family

Family and involved friends of the patient should be contacted by staff, preferably by staff who have already established a relationship with them. Most often the family and friends appreciate the contact and will accept an offer of a chance to talk directly with the staff. It is important to tolerate negative emotions directed toward the patient (anger or relief), toward the staff (devaluating or blaming), and toward themselves (inadequacy or guilt), without empty reassurance or defensive self-justification. Once aired and shared, such feelings can usually be integrated with feelings of love, esteem, and sadness.

Ward

An emergency ward meeting should be held as soon as possible. The basic facts should be set before the community as simply and clearly as possible. Patients should be given a chance to air feelings of guilt, fear of their own suicidal impulses, and anger at the staff's inability to prevent the suicide. The staff should listen empathically, acknowledge their lack of omnipotence while implicitly maintaining their professional competence, and model the sharing of feelings such as those of shock, sadness, anger, and fear. Daily meetings should continue for a week to insure adequate opportunity to express reactions openly, to provide mutual support, and to monitor the state of the therapeutic community. At the initial meeting passes and privileges should be canceled. Such privileges should be reevaluated when the state of the ward can be more adequately assessed in a couple of days.

Staff

Staff are also profoundly affected by an inpatient suicide. When the helpers are helpless, the caretakers abandoned, and the partners in a therapeutic alliance betrayed, powerful feelings often erupt. One study found that after a suicide.

> The reactions of therapists as therapists emphasized fears concerning blame, responsi-
> bility, and inadequacy. . . . Therapists expressed fears of being sued, of being vilified
> in the press, of being investigated, and of losing professional standing. They were
> afraid that others among their patients would be adversely affected by the news, or ask
> embarrassing questions, or that there might be reproaches from the relatives.
> Sometimes therapists felt marked and exposed [Litman, 1965].

What is true of therapists is also true of other staff members. A suicide sends ripples through the entire staff.

It is important to provide formal opportunities such as a staff meeting as well as informal opportunities to talk about the suicide. The ward director, head nurse, and other senior staff can model by sharing their reactions and their past experiences.

A more specialized technique is the ward consultation. A week or more after the suicide a consultation is scheduled with a senior clinician, expert in dealing with suicide and without administrative relationship to the ward. The case is reviewed from the standpoint of learning from it. The task of the consultant is in part to provide clinical teaching, in part to validate staff reactions, and to counter fantasies of harsh criticism. The consultation provides a forum for working through countertransference feelings without the kind of denial, repression, and projection that can wreak havoc following an inpatient suicide. At times individual private consultation to the therapist or other staff member closely involved with the patient may be helpful to deal with more personal and difficult to bear reactions. In both individual and ward consultation the goal is to provide some closure and to facilitate a return to the work of the ward.

SUMMARY

This chapter has reviewed the inpatient assessment, prevention, and treatment of suicidal behavior. While suicidal phenomena are ubiquitous on inpatient wards, each patient must be approached individually from the standpoint of diagnosis, formulation, and treatment planning. The milieu is of key importance, and therapeutic and antitherapeutic possibilities are discussed. Despite the best available treatment, suicides do occur; and ways of coping with the effect of a suicide on an inpatient unit are described.

REFERENCES

Adams, K.S., Bouckoms, A., & Streiner, D. (1982), Parental loss and family stability in attempted suicide. *Arch. Gen. Psychiat.*, 39:1081–1085.
Beck, A.T., Schuyler, D., & Herman, R. (1974), Development of suicidal intent scales. In: *The Prediction of Suicide*, eds. A.T. Beck, H.L.P. Resnick, & D.J. Lettieri. Bowie, MD: Charles Press, pp. 45–56.
———— Steer, R.A., Kovacs, M., & Garrison, B. (1985), Hopelessness and eventual suicide: A 20-year prospective study of patients hospitalized with suicidal ideation. *Amer. J. Psychiat.*, 142:559–563.
Black, D.W., Warrack, G., & Winokur, G. (1985), The Iowa Record-Linkage Study I: Suicide and accidental deaths among psychiatric patients. *Arch. Gen. Psychiat.*, 42:71–75.
Breier, A., & Astrachan, B.M. (1984), Characterization of schizophrenic patients who commit suicide. *Amer. J. Psychiat.*, 141:206–209.
Buie, D.H. (1981), Empathy: Its nature and limitations. *J. Amer. Psychoanal. Assn.*, 29:281–307.
Copas, J.B., & Robin, A. (1982), Suicide in psychiatric inpatients. *Brit. J. Psychiat.*., 141:503–511.
Crammer, J.L. (1984), The special characteristics of suicide in hospital inpatients. *Brit. J. Psychiat.*, 145:460–463.

Farberow, N.L., Shneidman, E.S., & Leonard, C.V. (1965), Suicide among schizophrenic mental hospital patients. In: *The Cry for Help*, eds. N.L. Farberow & E.S. Shneidman. New York: McGraw-Hill, pp. 78–109.

Friedman, A.M., Kaplan, H.I., & Sadock, B.T. (1976), *Modern Synopsis of Comprehensive Textbook of Psychiatry*, Vol. 2. Baltimore, MD: Williams & Wilkins, p. 873.

Friedman, R.S. (1983), Hospital treatment of psychiatric emergencies. *Psychiat. Clin. N. Amer.*, 6:293–303.

Goldstein, K. (1948), *Language and Language Disturbances*. New York: Grune & Stratton.

Gunderson, J.G. (1978), Defining the therapeutic processes in psychiatric milieus. *Psychiatry*, 41:327–335.

Khuri, R., & Akiskal, H.S. (1983), Suicide prevention: The necessity of treating contributory psychiatric disorders. *Psychiat. Clin. N. Amer.*, 6:193–207.

Litman, R.E. (1965), When patients commit suicide. *Amer. J. Psychother.*, 19:570–576.

——— (1982), Hospital suicides: Lawsuits and standards. *Suicide & Life-Threat. Behav.*, 12:212–220

Maltsberger, J.T., & Buie, D.H. (1976), Countertransference hate in the treatment of suicidal patients. *Arch. Gen. Psychiat.*, 30:625–633.

Mann, J. (1973), *Time-Limited Psychotherapy*. Cambridge, MA: Harvard University Press.

Miles, C.P. (1977), Conditions predisposing to suicide: A review. *J. Nerv. & Ment. Dis.*, 164:231–246.

Minkoff, K., Bergman, E., Beck, A.T., & Beck, R. (1973), Hopelessness, depression, and attempted suicide. *Amer. J. Psychiat.*, 130:455–459.

Morgan, H.G., & Priest, P. (1984), Assessment of suicide risk in psychiatric inpatients. *Brit. J. Psychiat.*, 145:467–469.

Morrison, J. (1984), Suicide in psychiatric patients: Age distribution. *Suicide & Life-Threat. Behav.*, 14:52–58.

Motto, J.A., Heilbron, D.C., & Juster, R.P. (1985), Development of a clinical instrument to estimate suicide risk. *Amer. J. Psychiat.*, 142:680–686.

Ostroff, R., Giller, E., Bonese, K., Ebersole, E., Harkness, L., & Mason, J. (1982), Neuroendocrine risk factors of suicidal behavior. *Amer. J. Psychiat.*, 139:1323–1325.

Pallis, D.J., Barraclough, B.M., Levey, A.B., Jenkins, J.S., & Sainsbury, P. (1982), Estimating suicide risk among attempted suicides: I. The development of new clinical scales. *Brit. J. Psychiat.*, 141:37–44.

——— Gibbons, J.S., & Pierce, D.W. (1984), Estimating suicide risk among attempted suicides: II. Efficiency of predictive scales after the attempt. *Brit. J. Psychiat.*, 144:139–148.

Paykel, E., & Dienelt, M. (1971), Suicide attempts following acute depression. *J. Nerv. & Ment. Dis.*, 153:234–243.

Pattison, E.M., & Kahan J. (1983), The deliberate self-harm syndrome. *Amer. J. Psychiat.*, 140:867–872.

Pokorny, A.D. (1983), Prediction of suicide in psychiatric patients. *Arch. Gen. Psychiat.*, 40:249–257.

Robins, E., Murphy, G., & Wilkinson, R.H. (1959), Some clinical observations in the prevention of suicide based on a study of 134 successful suicides. *Amer. J. Pub. Health*, 49:888–899.

Roose, S.P., Glassman, A.H., Walsh, B.T., Woodring, S., & Vital-Herne, J. (1983), Depression, delusions, and suicide. *Amer. J. Psychiat.*, 140:1159–1162.

Roy, A. (1982), Risk factors for suicide in psychiatric patients. *Arch. Gen. Psychiat.*, 39:1089–1095.

——— (1983), Family history of suicide. *Arch. Gen. Psychiat.*, 40:971–974.

Sacks, M.H., & Carpenter, W.T. (1974), The pseudotherapeutic community: An examination of antitherapeutic forces on psychiatric units. *Hosp. Comm. Psychiat.*, 25:315–318.

Sederer, L.I., ed. (1983), *Inpatient Psychiatry*. Baltimore, MD: Williams & Wilkins.

Shaw, S., & Sims, A. (1984), A survey of unexpected deaths among psychiatric in-patients and ex-patients. *Brit. J. Psychiat.*, 145:473–476.

Simpson, M.A. (1975), The phenomenology of self-mutilation in a general hospital setting. *Can. Psychiat. Assn. J.*, 20:429–433.

Slater, E., & Roth, M. (1977), *Clinical Psychiatry*. London: Balliere-Tindall.

Sletten, I.W., & Barton, J.L. (1979), Suicidal patients in the emergency room: A guide for evaluation and disposition. *Hosp. Comm. Psychiat.*, 30:407–411.

Targum, S.D., Rosen, L, & Capodanno, A.E. (1983), The dexamethasone suppression test in suicidal patients with unipolar depression. *Amer. J. Psychiat.*, 140:877–879.

Traskman, L., Asberg, M., Bertilsson, L., & Sjostrand, L. (1981), Monoamine metabolites in CSF and suicidal behavior. *Arch. Gen. Psychiat.*, 38:631–636.

Walsh, B.W., & Rosen, P. (1985), Self-mutilation and contagion: An empirical test. *Amer. J. Psychiat.*, 142:119–120.

Waltzer, H. (1982), The biopsychosocial model for brief inpatient treatment of the schizophrenic syndrome. *Psychiat. Quart.*, 54:97–108.

Weisman, A.D., & Worden, J.W. (1972), Risk-rescue rating in suicide assessment. *Arch. Gen. Psychiat.*, 26:553–560.

Weissman, M., Prusoff, B.A., DiMascio, A., Neu, C., Goklaney, M., & Klerman, G.L. (1979), The efficacy of drugs and psychotherapy in the treatment of acute depressive episodes. *Amer. J. Psychiat.*, 136:555–558.

C. Aftermath

21

Guidelines for Dealing with Suicide on a Psychiatric Inpatient Unit

Paul G. Cotton, M.D.
Robert E. Drake, M.D., Ph.D.
Anne Whitaker, M.D.
Jenny Potter, M.D.

One of the most difficult tasks a psychiatric inpatient unit must face is to cope with the suicide of one of its patients. The tragic occurrence on our unit of four suicides within sixteen months produced a cumulative stress that amplified the painful experiences of staff, and placed their attempts to adjust in bold relief. Based on this experience, we have developed a framework for understanding staff reaction patterns and guidelines for helping staff during the postsuicide period.

Suicide is a catastrophic but inevitable occurrence that affects inpatient psychiatric units (Schwartz, Flinn, and Slawson, 1975). Over the past 75 years, the frequency of inpatient suicides has been remarkably constant despite a wide diversity of therapeutic ideologies and methodologies (Lonnquist, 1974). Studies of the epidemiology, predictions, prevention, and understanding of inpatient suicides are abundant, but few guidelines for the postsuicide management of a unit are available. Most of the work on caring for the survivors of a suicide focuses on family rather than on caregivers (Resnik, 1969; Silverman, 1972; Shneidman, 1975).

The impact of suicide on an inpatient staff can be devastating. In one poignant discussion, an anonymous author described how disorganized and demoralized the staff was by a series of three suicides (1977). Staff meetings that focused on these feelings appeared to exacerbate rather than to ameliorate guilt and blame. The author concluded that a more effective resolution of the postsuicide period should involve turning away from staff issues and consciously focusing on patient treatment issues such as improved treatment plans.

Kayton and Freed (1967) studied a hospital's reaction to a single suicide.

An earlier version of this chapter was published in *Hospital & Community Psychiatry* (1983), 34:55–59.

Patients who had a history of suicidal behavior were severely affected. To stabilize a ward after a suicide, Kayton and Freed suggest holding a patient–staff meeting to convey information to create an atmosphere that permits further discussion.

Olin (1980) offers a series of helpful precautions for working with surviving patients after a ward suicide. These precautions include a staff meeting, a patient–staff meeting, a review of privileges, a memorial service, and a psychological autopsy.

CRISIS INTERVENTION

Efforts to understand and intervene in the postsuicide period have generally neglected the important theoretical and empirical perspective of crisis intervention (Thomas, 1909; Lindemann, 1944; Tyhurst, 1951; Erikson, 1959; Caplan, 1964; Darbonne, 1968; Schulberg and Sheldon, 1968; Brandon, 1970; Eastham, Coates and Allodi, 1970; Raphael, 1971). In a crisis, a brief phase of impact, during which individuals are stunned and bewildered, is followed by a prolonged period of turmoil, during which a flood of intense emotions predominates. As an individual slowly regains his equilibrium, his personality often undergoes significant changes, and a dual potential for maturational growth or prolonged disability exists (Thomas, 1909; Tyhurst, 1951; Caplan, 1964).

Several works, including Freud's writing on mourning (1917) and Lindemann's studies of acute grief (1944), have emphasized the association between appropriate expression of strong feelings and good outcomes. Our interview data support this phasic sequence of response to suicide. We have also found the interventions are effective only to the extent that they address the specific needs of each phase.

THE INTERVIEWS

Approximately one year after the four suicides occurred on our inpatient unit, two of us (Cotton and Drake) conducted individual interviews with 23 staff members who were involved with at least one of the patients who had committed suicide. Interview subjects were selected on the basis of availability and included psychiatrists, psychiatric residents, social workers, nurses, and mental health workers. Our inpatient unit is a 22-bed psychiatric service in a general hospital that is affiliated with a university. The unit provides training for a variety of young, entry-level mental health professionals.

We told each interview subject that the purpose of the study was to learn more about successful coping techniques after a suicide and that his suggestions would be incorporated into the unit's program for staff education. Interviews were open-ended and lasted for approximately one hour. They focused on a description of events on the unit after the suicide; personal reactions to the suicide, from the moment of hearing the news to the present; and impressions of which activities and administrative decisions were or were not helpful throughout this time.

STAFF RESPONSE

Most of the individuals interviewed experienced suicide as a personal crisis. Habitual patterns of coping were disrupted, a period of prolonged distress and attempts to reestablish equilibrium followed, and ultimately a new level of adjustment was reached. A few staff members were relatively unaffected, however, usually because they had little close contact with any of the patients who had committed suicide. Nevertheless, everyone we interviewed vividly recalled the lengthy, painful malaise of the group.

We will present an overview of the staff's response rather than a statistical count of the individual interviews. The individual reactions may vary widely according to the circumstances of the specific suicide and the particular individuals involved, but the sequence of events that the staff described as helpful and the implications for intervention were remarkably consistent. As we describe staff responses, we will also present some guidelines, based on the interviews, that senior clinical or administrative staff can make.

Although the individual's experiences were continuous, we have divided the postsuicide period into three phases: the first few days after the suicide while the ward was closed to new admissions; the next one to two months ending with the suicide-review conference; and the first several months after the conference. These intervals correspond to predominant staff coping patterns and to suggested administrative interventions.

PHASE 1: WORKING IN SHOCK

No matter how suicidal a patient becomes, the initial staff response to a suicide is shock. Immediate reactions of disorientation, distractability, disbelief, and even denial occur. A staff member stated: "When we met and discussed the hour of Mr. A.'s death, it became clear that he walked directly from the hospital to the subway station. I think he decided to jump before he left the unit. It seemed more real when I realized that."

Although the need to care for patients brings staff back to reality, the state of shock persists for several days. Our staff worked a full schedule after suicides but reported feeling confused, bewildered, and helpless.

Staff members stated that strong feelings began to well up almost immediately, but remained undifferentiated or suppressed until the shock mitigated. During this interim, staff feared they would be considered inadequate and be blamed for the suicide. Certainly suicide represents a repudiation of the mental health professional's work and, even in the first few hours, strikes at the core of feelings about professional competence and esteem. Many staff members recalled a general sense of loss of control during the first few hours, as well as the specific fear that other suicides would occur immediately.

During this period of maximal vulnerability and minimal coping capacity, the crucial tasks for the entire staff are to provide information, protection, and support. The first step is for unit staff who know the deceased patient's family to inform these relatives of the suicide. Next a staff meeting should be held to discuss the death. Staff are reminded of the deceased patient's right to confidentiality and the need to protect patients who remain on the unit. The ward is closed to admission and passes are canceled.

The unit leadership, such as the director or the nursing supervisor, assume responsibility for dealing with the world outside of the unit—medical examiner, police, reporters, and hospital administrators—and support the patient's treatment team in their work with the deceased patient's family and in completing the medical record.

The next step is to inform the entire ward. During a ward meeting, staff members provide factual information to patients and again stress the deceased patient's continuing right to confidentiality. Questions are answered in a straightforward manner, while patients are assured that they will be safe and that staff will be available. One staff person who knew the suicided patient well stated: "I felt so bad in the community meeting. I wanted to tell everybody what had been going on with the patient during the past few days. It took a few minutes to remember that Mr. A. still deserved the confidentiality and respect due everyone." Another staff member remembered a patient in the meeting who said: "I'm sorry. I really didn't know Mr. A. I was admitted just yesterday."

Since some patients regress immediately and severely and others react minimally, the ward meeting should be brief. Treatment plans should be reviewed so that patients can be dealt with individually. Staff agreed that one of our worst experiences was with a manic patient who had improved through a program of minimal stimulation; when we allowed him to participate in the ward discussion of the suicide, the experience precipitated another manic crisis. The next step in protection is to call in additional staff to help with ward coverage.

Providing Team Support

The team that treated the deceased patient needs the most support during the time when shock gives way to a flow of intense feelings. The unit leadership, including the director and discipline chiefs, should review details of the treatment and suicide with the treatment team. They can then ask the treatment team to describe their work with the patient. The unit leaders can share personal experiences with suicide and listen to the treatment team's concerns, fears, and feelings. One staff person said: "The chief resident made it easier for me to talk to others and feel more in control. She stayed in the evening just sitting in the day room chatting informally with patients; she also told us that there would be no new admissions until the nursing staff thought the ward was stable."

The strength of an inpatient unit is the combined emotional capacities of its members. It is no surprise, therefore, that staff cited informal peer contact as the most valuable support of their initial attempts to cope. Those who coped well made use of peer supports during the first few postsuicide days.

Another source of support came from participation in the common rituals of death. Staff, as well as patients who were able and interested, visited the funeral home, sent flowers, expressed condolences, and attended the funeral. Staff reported that sharing the process of grieving with the family helped them to express feelings that had remained closed off in their hospital work. Many inpatient staff members were young and had never experienced death and the rituals surrounding it. One said: "I was nervous about going to the wake and seeing the body. I'd never seen a dead person. It was a good thing because I think it helped his family know we cared. Also, this might sound silly, but I wondered if they thought we were embarrassed about his death, ashamed to show ourselves. I think this showed we weren't." Several staff members cited the funeral as a turning point when the numbness ended and feelings returned.

Expressions of sympathy should not be limited to the family. Since a patient's suicide is a profound trauma for any therapist who treated the patient in outpatient practice before their inpatient admission (Litman, 1965), he should be invited to meet with the inpatient treatment team. Both staff and the individual therapists found these meetings helpful. An outside therapist, however, might perceive an open-ended invitation to meet with the inpatient team as a threat, meaning that he must submit to questioning during a sensitive time. The mutually supportive purpose of the meeting and the meeting's utility on previous similar occasions need to be emphasized.

When staff have recovered from the initial shock, treatment plans have been reconsidered, and the rituals of death have been observed, protective precautions can be relaxed. Opening the ward to new admissions symbolizes this change. No single event, however, should obscure the gradual nature and individual variance in the process of recovery. A few staff may feel devastated, and many patients will continue to require extra protection.

PHASE 2: EMERGENCE OF OVERWHELMING FEELINGS

As the days pass and the spontaneous outpouring of energy, support, and comradeship decreases, staff appear exhausted, demoralized, and overwhelmed by intense feelings. Everyone we interviewed agreed that the flood of rage, guilt, anxiety, and depression makes this phase the most difficult and dangerous period. One staff person said: "I seemed so tired during those first few weeks. I thought it was all depression until a colleague pointed out how many extra hours of work I was spending dealing with Mr. A.'s death." A second remembered: "Staying late all the time. I felt like all my charts were sloppy." Another said: "It seemed so hard to go to staff meetings. Everything Dr. C. [the unit director] said sounded critical." A third noted: "I really couldn't do my job. I guess others just picked up for me."

The expression of feelings is a central part of adjusting to any crisis. Yet, we noted staff either avoided these feelings or allowed them to interfere with clinical work during the second phase. What Vaillant (1977) has termed *immature* coping strategies predominated. Thus, anger toward the deceased patient was expressed covertly as neglect of work and tardiness or was displaced onto fellow staff members.

Staff members manifested severe self-doubt and masochism by questioning their own judgment and by inefficient, unproductive overwork. Sick calls and absenteeism increased as some staff developed illness and others psychologically withdrew from work. Guilt frequently took the form of attributing blame for suicide, usually disguised as sophisticated psychological analysis. Increased drinking and other self-destructive activities outside of work complicated all of these maladaptive responses.

These staff feelings may affect patients in dangerous ways. Suicidal patients may be treated too restrictively because of staff's pervasive fear of another suicide. Anger may be turned against patients in the form of unwise discharges or other punitive actions. Self-doubt may paralyze decision making about patient treatments. Thus, the depression and pessimism that infect the staff may be transmitted directly to patients.

Meetings and Conferences

During this phase, it becomes essential to cope with feelings by providing channels of expression and limiting destructive manifestations. Ward and team meetings, supervision sessions, and informal staff discussions can serve as arenas for expression. Staff must be encouraged to face the painful elements of the experience but at the same time to accept necessary limits on emotional reactions. Excessive self-blame, overwork, emotional withdrawal, and critical remarks toward colleagues should be discouraged. Treatment plans must be carefully monitored. Good staff relations and high levels of self-respect should be modeled by ward leaders who encourage other staff members to do the same.

If these maneuvers are successful, most staff gradually adopt more sophisticated coping strategies. Although much of the pain remains, negative effects diminish or can be contained so that they do not intrude into patient care.

At this point, staff should hold a suicide-review conference. The review conference is intended to reconstruct and understand the suicide, an approach that Shneidman (1969) terms the *psychological autopsy*. Staff members agreed that the chance to talk about their work and their feelings in the presence of an expert from outside the unit was as important as reconstruction of the suicide. For this reason, the staff who were most closely involved with the suicide should be encouraged to plan the conference and present the material.

The conference chairperson can play a crucial role in this process. One chairperson performed the psychological autopsy competently, but then proceeded to talk about the problems of deinstitutionalization. Because he ignored the staff's efforts and pain, he was remembered one year later as being unhelpful. Another chairperson clarifed many issues that led to the patient's suicide and then said, "I suppose I could add intellectual background, but it seems out of place; let me say instead that I think the staff here did a fine job caring for the patient." His comments addressed the staff's injury and helped the staff to put their painful feelings behind them.

PHASE 3: NEW GROWTH AROUND EMOTIONAL SCARS

In the months after the review conference, the staff moved toward a renewed commitment in their work. Although the staff's idealism has been tempered by tragedy and the emotional scars from the suicide remain, the overwhelmingly intense feelings and the bitterness have passed. As one staff member said, "For two months I thought about quitting. Finally, I realized that I had to become less negative and to get to work again." Another staff person noted: "I was annoyed when I was asked if my patient was in a similar situation to Mr. C. [a suicided patient] at the time of admission. I thought, 'enough already.' But I suppose it was helpful to compare their clinical conditions. It alerted me to the possibility of suicide and to consider further the hopelessness a patient can feel."

With this renewed commitment, staff transform their concerns about their professional competence into broad questions regarding policy, treatment, and training. For instance, is the unit treating too many suicidal patients? What is the effect of deinstitutionalization?

In answering these questions, staff reveal a healthy recovery marked by more mature coping strategies, such as sublimation, anticipation, and altruism. For example, our staff organized a seminar to review the literature on suicide. They also helped to train new staff in suicide-assessment techniques.

Training newly hired staff to assess suicidal patients provides another opportunity for the unit to further consider the impact of the suicides. Issues learned from the completed suicides should be reviewed with newly hired staff and the unit leadership should include as many old staff as is practical in the teaching process. One staff person said: "I really appreciated hearing about this patient. The review taught me something about the patient, about how the unit reacted to his death, and it certainly helped me when Ms. B. committed suicide."

Most staff members recognized these signs of maturation in themselves one year later. Many described the process as gaining mastery over the anxiety that attends working with suicidal patients. One staff member stated that "adjusting to the suicide was the most difficult part of my training, but I feel that the fear of suicide and of my reaction to a suicide no longer inhibits my work the way it did previously." Increased competence was the legacy of their painful experience.

For other staff members, the suicide led to more prolonged disability. A few individuals were never able to invest themselves in their work on our unit and gradually found new jobs or new careers. When we interviewed these staff members, similar patterns emerged. They avoided group meetings on the inpatient service after the suicide and failed to use peer supports; they were relatively unable to express their feelings after the suicide. One year after the suicides, most of them had apparently recovered and were functioning well in new jobs, but at least one former staff member continued to experience painful, intrusive recollections of suicide.

THREE CONCLUSIONS

Although our impressions in this report are necessarily subjective, we drew three conclusions from our interviews, based both on frequency of response and on staff members' emphasis on aspects of their reactions. First, workers came to psychiatric inpatient units with very different professional backgrounds. Physicians and many nurses had previous medical experience acquainting them with death. They suffered less and experienced less prolonged disability than had workers from other disciplines, such as mental health workers.

Some of the most severe staff reactions to the suicides occurred among mental health workers who had no professional background and only inservice training. Individuals who try to help staff cope after a suicide must remember that for some young staff the suicide may be their very first experience, or one of their first experiences, with death.

Second, any effort to help must appreciate and correspond to the sequence of staff reactions. For example, confronting the denial of feelings is inappropriate when staff are in shock and need protection. Similarly, a grand rounds on suicide is more effective when staff have passed through the phase of intense feelings and are in the phase of new growth.

Third, interaction among staff members on an inpatient ward is crucial. A psychiatric inpatient unit provides a unique social setting with fellow staff members who can provide support and insight. Staff who attended meetings, drew strength from peer supports, and talked easily with others recovered more quickly than did those who behaved in a more solitary way.

The potential interventions we have suggested are ideals. The staff members we interviewed described successful interventions that became clear only after many failures. Frequently the need for such interventions became clear only during our interviews held one year after the suicides. Thus, a suicide is another facet of the developmental life of an inpatient service—uneven, often painful, and best evaluated by a careful retrospective review.

REFERENCES

Anonymous (1977), A suicide epidemic in a psychiatric hospital. *Dis. Nerv. Syst.*, 38:327–331.

Brandon, S. (1970), Crisis theory and possibilities of therapeutic intervention. *Brit. J. Psychiat.*, 117:627–633.

Caplan, G. (1964), *Principles of Preventive Psychiatry*. New York: Basic Books.

Darbonne, A. (1968), Crisis: A Review of theory, practice, and research. *Internat. J. Psychiat.*, 6:371–379.

Eastham, K., Coates, D., & Allodi, F. (1970), The concept of crisis. *Can. Psychiat. Assn. J.*, 15:463–472.

Erikson, E. (1959), Growth and crisis of the health personality. In: *Identity and the Life Cycle*. Psychological Issues, Monograph, 1:50–100. New York: International Universities Press.

Freud, S. (1917), Mourning and melancholia. *Standard Edition*, 14:237–258. London: Hogarth Press, 1957.

Kayton, L., & Freed, H. (1967), Effects of a suicide in a psychiatric hospital. *Arch. Gen. Psychiat.*, 17:187–194.

Lindemann, E. (1944), Symptomatology and management of acute grief. *Amer. J. Psychiat.*, 101:141–148.

Litman, R.E. (1965), When patients commit suicide. *Amer. J. Psychother.*, 19:570–576.

Lonnquist, J. (1974), Suicide in psychiatric hospitals in different eras. *Psychiat. Fennica*, 265–273.

Olin, H.S. (1980), Management precautions for surviving patients following a ward suicide. *Hosp. & Commun. Psychiat.*, 31:348–349.

Raphael, B. (1971), Crisis intervention: Theoretical and methodological considerations. *Austral. & NZ J. Psychiat.*, 5:183–190.

Resnik, H. (1969), Psychological resynthesis: A clinical approach to the survivors of suicide. *Internat. Psychiat. Clin.*, 6:213–224.

Schulberg, H., & Sheldon, A. (1968), The probability of crisis and strategies for preventive intervention. *Arch. Gen. Psychiat.*, 18:553–558.

Schwartz, D.A., Flinn, D.E., & Slawson, P.F. (1975), Suicide in the psychiatric hospital. *Amer. J. Psychiat.*, 132:150–153.

Shneidman, E. (1969), Suicide, lethality, and the psychological autopsy. *Internat. Psychiat. Clin.*, 6:225–250.

——— (1975), Postvention: The care of the bereaved. *Consult. Liaison Psychiat.*, ed. R.O. Pasnau. New York: Grune & Stratton.

Silverman, P. (1972), Intervention with the widow of a suicide. In: *Survivors of Suicide*, ed. A.C. Cain. Springfield, IL: Charles C Thomas.

Thomas, W. (1909), *A Source Book of Social Origins*. Boston: R.G. Gadger.

Tyhurst, J.S. (1951), Individual reactions to community disaster: The natural history of psychiatric phenomena. *Amer. J. Psychiat.*, 107:764–769.

Vaillant, G.E. (1977). *Adaptation to Life*. Boston: Little, Brown.

22

Patient Suicide and Therapists in Training

Herbert N. Brown, M.D.

> Consideration for the dead, who, after all, no longer need it, is more important to us than truth, and certainly for most of us, than consideration for the living (Freud, 1915, p. 290).

This attitude toward death has changed since Freud criticized it in 1915. Now, those left following a death, even one by suicide, receive greater consideration (Cain, 1972). With suicide this is in part because we have come to appreciate that one of its many unfortunate legacies is the increased risk of suicide by the dead person's survivors (Resnik, 1969a, b). In addition, the enormous shame and psychological pain suffered by so many following a suicide has been increasingly recognized.

Building on the concept of "preventive intervention" introduced by Lindemann (1944) in his work with the grieving survivors of the Coconut Grove fire disaster, Shneidman (1969a, 1971) coined the term *postvention* to describe "working with survivor–victims of a committed suicide to help them with their anguish, guilt, anger, shame and perplexity" (p. 453). Postvention emphasizes that suicide is not an isolated personal tragedy. It is recognized, also, as an interpersonal event of disastrous proportions. Many individual health practitioners, suicide prevention centers, and community mental health agencies have begun as a matter of general policy to reach out to the survivors of suicide. But what of these professionals themselves? What is the impact of patient suicide on them? Who reaches out to them?

Everyone knows that work with suicidal patients is intense and demanding. The stakes feel higher than with nonsuicidal patients, and the work proportionally harder. Most therapists strictly limit the number of suicidal patients they will work with at one time, and more than a few find reasons for not accepting the referral of any patient known to be suicidal. Of course some of this is attributable to the "logistics" of the work: predictably difficult telephone calls (often at particularly inopportune moments), requests and sometimes the need for unscheduled emergency appointments, and the requirement for a backup inpatient hospital unit (including, sometimes, the necessity of working with an unfamiliar or even uncomplementary team of other professionals), and so on. These are certainly the issues that are mentioned most frequently and most readily. And these considerations are properly relevant as each practitioner decides which patients he or she is really prepared to treat. But I think most of the avoidance stems directly from anxiety about the real possibility of the patient's death by suicide during treatment.

When such an unwelcome event does occur the therapist reacts strongly. Litman (1965) seems to have been among the first to describe these reactions in detail, while simultaneously providing data that such an occurrence is probably not unusual for therapists. Indeed, 14 of the 50 patients (that is about 28 percent) whose suicides he systematically reviewed were in treatment or recently discharged. He observed in his total study of over 200 therapists that they reacted to the suicide both personally ("as human beings") and professionally ("according to their special role in society"). Among the prominent personal reactions were a sense of guilt that replicated the experience of relatives of people who had committed suicide, defeat, anger, denial, and repression. As therapists, there were prominent concerns about blame, responsibility, and inadequacy. Some therapists decided thereafter to avoid suicidal patients in the future, while others tried to use the experience to improve their professional judgment and actions. More recently, Goldstein and Buongiorno (1984) reported on their interviews with 20 psychotherapists who had a patient commit suicide. Their findings were largely consistent with those of Litman, while they emphasize that it is normal for the experience to remain vividly on the therapist's mind.

As the director of a residency training program, a particular feature of this situation has struck me in recent years. I have been surprised that the impact of patient suicide on therapists in training has received so little attention. Given the apparent analogy to differences between the impact of suicide on a developing child and the impact on a grown adult, this relative inattention seems as inappropriate as it is remarkable. Suicide is never easily understood or accepted by anyone, yet the impact on the less-formed individual will, in general, be more profound. I suggest the same is true for the developing therapist in training. Certainly this situation has not yet received adequate recognition or attention. Once noticed, it is compelling to think that there must be reasons we have tended to look the other way.

AVOIDANCE OF THE PROBLEM

Training experiences are deeply etched in the memories of most mental health professionals. Patient suicide has strong and unforgettable impact also. When the two coincide—when suicide occurs in the context of treatment by a student who is intensely involved in the formative years of early training—the trainee's development as well as the experience of training itself may be profoundly influenced. This, in and of itself, should not seem surprising. But, given such potential importance, it is surprising that neither the incidence of this experience nor its effect on trainees has been thoroughly investigated. In fact, there seems to be a reluctance to explore the subject. I believe that, among the possible explanations for this avoidance, the following influences should be considered:

1. While sounding cynical, it is merely realistic to recognize that trainees are "used" in the usual academically affiliated clinical setting. The "system" tends to rely on inexperienced newcomers to cover not only routine clinical services and emergencies, as well as nights and holidays, but also, along the way, to treat many very difficult patients. Faculty are proportionally free to pursue their academic responsibilities and they have more protected time to treat selected patients. In return, trainees are paid rather well these days (including good fringe benefits), they learn their profession, and, importantly, they buy into the system in the sense that they will not again be required to do trainee-level work. Other new recruits will come along to do so. There is a complicated and understandable rationale for this system. That it has evolved at all, and then persisted in relatively stable form, speaks to some level of "fit." The point here is not that the system is either wrong or correct, only that discussion of its merits will predictably engender resistance because it disrupts the current equilibrium. It may become convenient not to notice how frequently patients of trainees commit suicide or what the impact on trainees is.

2. Some training directors may either minimize the issue or experience a guilty defensiveness about it, stemming from their role in administering programs that assign the care of extraordinarily sick patients to inexperienced trainees. We may assume that such resistance is often not conscious. The result, however, may be that awareness of the potential problem remains low.

3. Many programs may not be eager to discuss or report the incidence of suicide of patients treated by trainees for fear that such information may adversely affect recruitment or morale. Politically speaking, it is a good subject to avoid if possible, and there isn't much of a constituency pressing for deeper probing.

4. Perhaps patient suicide is truly rare in some training programs or at some sites. This, of course, would make it no less important to those affected.

5. It has been said that there are two kinds of mental health professionals: those who have had a patient commit suicide and those who will. Those professionals and trainees who have not yet had a patient suicide generally treat the subject like a hot

potato. (Actually, as discussed later in this chapter, they only require a reasonably confidential setting and encouragement by program leaders to overcome this reluctance.) Sometimes there appears to be a kind of survivor guilt operating to suppress discussion, as well as what can only be termed a superstitious sense that not talking about it will ensure that they continue to be spared the experience. On the other hand, those who have had a patient suicide often experience it as a failure they would prefer to forget, even though it lives on vividly in their thoughts and feelings.

6. In a larger sense, maybe the issue of accepting death—recently made so much more complicated in general medical practice due to technological advances, and never simple with regard to self-destruction—is particularly hard for mental health professionals because of the relative inexactitude of diagnosis, dynamic formulation, treatment, and prognosis. When outcome is uncertain, endings are proportionally difficult to acknowledge or to accept. No one could be expected to be more confused and more reluctant about this than trainees, thus contributing to the general lack of exploration.

7. Perhaps the impact of suicide is actually more stressful for those who are beyond formal training. After all they no longer have the "protective advantage" or "explanation" following a suicide of still being in training. This consideration might explain and even justify greater emphasis and concern about graduated professionals.

These factors, perhaps along with others, seem to have synergized to reduce exploration of the impact of patient suicide on trainees. One result is that little is known about the scope of this problem for trainees.

THE SCOPE OF THE PROBLEM

We don't have a good sense of how common this experience is for trainees. The sparse information currently available can be summarized all to quickly. Kahne (1968) reported (as part of his study of an "epidemic" of suicides in the McLean Hospital) that 14 percent of psychiatric residents having from one to four years of training had a patient commit suicide. Rosen (1974) reported a comparable rate of 16 percent for residents in a different setting. And recently Schnur and Levin (1985) reported that five of 33 residents (15 percent) had experienced a suicide when surveyed, thus tending to confirm the one-in-seven residents figure over nearly a 20-year period. The most radical assessment comes from Henn (1978), who reported data in support of his contention that "patient suicide is a common, if not universal, part of psychiatric residency" (p. 745) (even though most of the residents in his study were unaware of the suicide because he counted all patients who ever had "professional contact" with a resident).

In reviewing stress factors in psychiatric residency training, Kelly (1973) prominently cites the care of suicidal patients. He does not, however, comment explicitly on the incidence or the effect of some of these patients actually ending their own lives. Despite Litman's (1965) other important contributions, he too does not focus on the special situation of the therapist in training. And Goldstein and Buongiorno's (1984) recent study of 20 psychotherapists as suicide survivors makes no differentiated comment about trainees, even though they do note that six of the 20 affected therapists were residents in training. (I find this particularly interesting both because these data indicate that 30 percent of those studied were trainees, and because the possibility appears to exist that although reported by graduated professionals even more of the suicides might actually have occurred during training.) Finally Kolodny, Binder, Bronstein, and Friend (1979) provide an outstanding description of how a group of four trainees from varied mental health disciplines understand and work through their reactions to patients' suicide. While it is clear that several trainees experienced a patient's suicide relatively early in the year within this one training setting, the authors make no direct statement about overall incidence.

Recently I reported a study of 55 graduates of the psychiatric residency training program at the Cambridge Hospital during the ten-year period from 1974 through 1983 (Brown, 1987a). I found that 33 percent of these psychiatrists had experienced the suicide of one of their patients during training—indicating that the experience may be much more common than generally recognized. In addition I offered several considerations to bolster this finding in the face of the lower incidence reported in the few earlier studies. Among these considerations I note that both Rosen and Kahne conducted studies that did not follow their group of residents through graduation, so that their results also must be considered underestimates.

To make explicit something that is probably already entirely evident, most reports about the impact of patient suicide on trainees refer to psychiatric residents. In fact I have found no study relating directly to other disciplines except for the Kolodny report mentioned previously which includes reference to one psychology and one doctor of mental health trainee in addition to two residents. Perhaps this is both justified and understandable because residents are in clinical training longer than other mental health professionals and because they may care for more severely ill (including suicidal) patients. Yet other trainees are not immune from or spared this problem. [It is of interest that Kolodny et al. (1979) explicitly observed that having gone to medical school and having already had the experience of caring for patients who died in no way gave the residents an advantage in dealing with suicide.]

In the hope of learning more about the scope of this problem among all mental health disciplines, in August 1983, I surveyed 155 staff and trainees in the Department of Psychiatry at the Cambridge Hospital. [For those interested, the Department is described in Brown (1987b).] Among other questions, I asked each professional: "Did a patient of yours commit suicide during your training years?" The results of this survey were recently reported (Brown, 1987a) and are outlined in Table 22.1. As noted, all nonresponders in this survey were counted as negative, an assumption that probably leads to underestimates of incidence. This is particularly relevant for the results regarding mental health workers and nurses, who

Table 22.1

Incidence of Suicide by Trainees' Patients (According to Discipline)

	Total Surveyed	Total Responders	Patient Suicide During Training
Mental health workers	23 (15%)	1 (4%)	1 (4%)[a]
Nurses & students	21 (13.5%)	6 (28.5%)	2 (9.5%)[a]
Psychiatrists & residents	62 (40%)	60 (97%)	23 (37%)[a,b]
Psychologists & interns	35 (22.5%)	25 (71%)	5 (14%)[a]
Social workers & students	14 (9.0%)	10 (71%)	2 (14%)[a]
Totals	155	102 (65%)	33 (21%)

[a]Percent based on total surveyed (nonresponders assumed to be negative).
[b]Although counted as a single positive response, two responders reported two suicides and one reported four suicides while in training.

tended not to respond to the questionnaire as frequently as those in the fields of social work, psychology, and psychiatry. I sensed, with mental health workers especially, that they are sometimes sheltered just enough from direct responsibility for patients to be relatively overlooked after the suicide, but involved enough with the patient to feel the impact deeply. With a response rate of 97 percent, the figures for psychiatrists in training are likely to be highly accurate. A further consideration regarding the accuracy of these results is that the survey was conducted rather early in the training year (August). First-year trainees would therefore have only two months of clinical experience, thus again tending to produce underestimates. This factor would obviously have no effect on graduated practitioners who were asked to recall their experience during training.

It is interesting that social workers and psychologists report the same incidence of experience of patient suicide during training (14 percent). Moreover, the 37 percent figure for psychiatric residents is remarkably consistent with my ten-year study mentioned previously, thus adding a bit more credence to those results— especially since 60 percent of the faculty members trained elsewhere than Cambridge.

One overall implication of these results is that patient suicide during training is certainly not a rare event for many mental health professionals. The experience of mental health workers and nurses must be regarded as essentially unknown, and this may be an important area for further investigation by others. It should be noted that three of the 33 positive responders (9 percent of all psychiatric residents) had multiple experiences with patient suicide, and this group too deserves closer attention. Unfortunately I did not ascertain the total number of patients each trainee had seen.

IMPACT ON TRAINEES

Even casual observation of virtually any therapist following the suicide of a patient confirms that the experience is powerfully shocking and disturbing. In the case of trainees there are several explanations for this reaction.

First, while their specific motivations may vary, trainees have a uniformly deep investment in being helpful. Simultaneously, they feel uncertain about how to go about accomplishing this—caught in the swirl of complex, unfamiliar, and sometimes conflicting approaches to psychiatric diagnosis and treatment. To complicate matters further, particularly in the early training years, they are often assigned and/or with supervision choose among a general population of severely disturbed inpatients. Moreover, as hospital stays continue to shorten, trainees increasingly care for these same patients in less structured and less secure ambulatory settings. For a while, therefore, the development of a reasonably sound sense of how to do a good job rides on the trainee's perception of how they and a relatively small number of very difficult patients fare.

Second, some supervisors take the position with trainees that working with suicidal patients is like doing cardiac surgery: it is normal (currently unavoidable and expectable) that a certain number of patients will not survive the treatment. Or the clinical situation may be portrayed as analogous to surgery for appendicitis, in that a certain number of mistakes (comparable to the removal of a normal appendix) actually indicates that patients are being treated with appropriate vigor. Without risk there can be no growth or change. While perhaps reassuring and even apt, the obvious problem with such analogies is that psychological practice is not exactly like doing surgery. Perhaps one of the greatest differences is that the mental health professional brings more of himself or herself as a person to the clinical encounter, in addition to purely technical skills. This is especially true for trainees, who in the beginning know so little about psychological practice that it often feels as if they bring *only* themselves to the encounter with the patient. No matter how much trainees know intellectually about psychotherapeutic practice they tend to put near total emphasis on helping the patient through their own personal qualities. Consequently, when a patient commits suicide the trainee feels that he or she has failed as a person. It takes time and supervision to work out the complex amalgam of true personal intimacy and objective professional skill that must characterize effective psychotherapeutic practice. Trainees usually have not yet had time to do this.

Third, trainees may lack adequate skill to understand and help seriously suicidal patients. Or, in parallel fashion, some of these patients may not be able to make use of what *any* therapist has to offer. In either case the trainee is likely to feel that he or she has failed if suicide occurs. In Edward Bibring's (1953) terms, the trainee is shockingly confronted with his or her limitations in achieving deeply held narcissistic aspirations. It is then difficult for the trainee to avoid concluding either that he or she is no good or that the patient is no good ("She was the worst borderline we've had on the unit for years"). Discouragement and depression become inevitable out of guilt for the rejecting hatefulness felt toward the patient and/or out of a sense of narcissistic failure.

Finally, it is instructive to consider the enormous difference between the threat and the actuality of patient suicide. The suicide of a patient is a dramatically extreme and violent version of what goes on during day-to-day psychotherapy in general. In work with patients who threaten suicide but do not kill themselves (as well as in the psychotherapeutic work with patients who do not include suicidal feelings or impulses as part of their response to internal conflict or interpersonal predicament), trainees learn gradually to understand these patients, themselves, and the process of therapy. During even the most productive work there are numerous experiences with feeling lost, or being confused, or making mistakes, or being unable to formulate accurately what is going on. There must be periods of discouragement. All therapists, whether accomplished or still in training, have the experience of misunderstanding their patients in the sense of not appreciating the key dynamic issues at any given moment. Failures in empathy occur regularly because of transference distortions and because it is, indeed, a tall order to get into the world of someone else. Yet, in usual circumstances, both patient and therapist can learn and grow despite—and surely sometimes because of—the limitations or imperfections in their interaction. In the case of patient suicide, the opportunity for growth together is suddenly obliterated. There is instead a sudden and shocking confrontation with loss and what often feels like failure. The earlier this experience occurs in training, the more shocking and the more problematic it tends to be. In addition, the countertransference hatred engendered by many suicidal patients, as described by Havens (1965) and Maltsberger and Buie (1974), can make understanding and accepting the suicide all the more difficult—especially for trainees not yet comfortable or familiar with such reactions.

The experience of a patient suicide during training may alter the development of mental health professionals. Because training experiences are so complex and varied it is, of course, difficult to assess this. One of the interesting findings in my ten-year study of psychiatric residency graduates was that 62 percent felt the experience of patient suicide had a "major effect" on their development. When asked if the effect was "for the worse" or "for the better," no graduate answered "for the worse." Is this mere denial? Is it just another example of the superficial adjustment of young, ambitious, and capable professionals?

My impression from talking with many of these graduates (as well as from about a dozen interviews with other psychiatrists who had the experience of patient suicide in training) is that the experience was deeply emotional for each of them. Despite the inhibiting influence of a study setting these interviews were often very poignant. Remarkably detailed memories of the situation were readily available, as if preserved in encapsulated form. Every graduate remembered the name of his or her patient. In interviews with faculty I found the details and names remained vivid even after 20 or 30 years. Simple forgetting or putting on rose-colored glasses does not seem to explain the "for the better" response. Nor does this ultimate conclusion mean that residents or trainees in any mental health discipline avoid a phase of feeling "for the worse." Rather, two kinds of reactions to patient suicide during training seem to emerge. From the affected trainee's point of view, both could be experienced as growth and positive adjustment and thus reported as "for the better."

The psychiatric residents seemed to take "lessons" away from the experience. Some gained a sense of both their rescue aspirations and their limitations. They developed an appreciation for how little actual control they have with regard to another individual's life, without becoming discouraged about the psychotherapeutic process in general. Conversely, others reacted by redoubling efforts to be more careful and to assume greater responsibility for patients. It was encouraging to note that several seemed to integrate both lessons: relatively comfortable acceptance of their limitations along with the undenied awareness that, for example, some people really do intend to kill themselves and require active intervention. The following are examples of responses volunteered by the graduates in this study:

> It took me a good two years before I began to feel comfortable working with suicidal patients. Through the combination of personal treatment and continued training I found my sense of competence again and established it on a much firmer footing. I believe a key lesson for me was how little real control we have over another's life. This helped me to move from a more controlling active stance to a more passive and empathic one.

> I had to face many personal and professional issues—i.e., a sense of failure, the inability to prevent death, rescue fantasies, etc. The outcome was to be more realistic and stronger. I had lots of group support and support in supervision.

> I learned about the limits of responsibility as well as how to assess dangerousness more realistically.

These considerations regarding trainee development apply to all mental health disciplines, although expectations or aspirations to work with suicidal patients and/ or their families may vary among the professions and individual trainees. Certainly the experience of a patient suicide might influence career direction for any mental health professional. While graduating trainees may choose for many reasons not to devote much, if any, of their future professional lives to the care of seriously ill patients, it would be undesirable for any individual trainee (and for society) if such work was avoided on the basis of an unworked-through experience. One of the graduates in my study, who reported a "very strong grief reaction" to the suicide of a patient but who did not feel the experience had a major effect on his development, was candid enough to pose the following unanswered dilemma: "I would qualify this [his indication that the experience did not have a major effect on his professional development] by saying that I do not choose to carry chronically suicidal patients in my caseload. I am not sure whether this is due to this one experience or to my overall practice/personal experience.

PROGRAM RESPONSE

In his discussion of schizophrenia and the inevitability of death, Searles (1965) states that "we might say that every human faces this dilemma: He cannot face death unless he is a whole person, yet he can become a truly whole person only by facing death" (p. 501). We might also say that every mental health trainee faces a comparable dilemma. He or she will have great difficulty facing the suicide of a patient until professional development is complete, and yet the completion of this development may only grow out of an experience like patient suicide. The core of the dilemma is that the encounter with suicide may occur so very early in professional development. I take the position myself that programs have an obligation to expose most trainees to closely supervised work with seriously ill and "risky" patients. They have, as well, a corresponding obligation to provide the emotional support and intellectual context for bearing and understanding the sequelae of such work.

Trainees must, in particular, learn that clinical failures do not make them failures. Yet, when there is a clinical failure, there may be something to learn. Every mental health professional must eventually develop an appropriate sense of personal limitation (both with regard to themselves and their patients), without losing therapeutic hope and without falling victim to excessive self-doubt or self-satisfaction. Yet how can trainees know this with so little experience and so little self-exploration under their belts? Usually this large lesson is learned little by little in the day-to-day work with a variety of patients. Progress and regression are encountered over and over again. Often a patient's motive in producing stalemate or failure is an important discovery, and one of the sort that every dynamic therapist must learn to make and to bring usefully into treatment. Moreover, there is the enduring need to become familiar with those particular issues that patients bring to the work that are difficult for the therapist to hear or to understand—something that is usually achieved only through years of personal analysis/psychotherapy and supervision.

Such perspective is hard to come by when a trainee is suddenly confronted by a patient's death by suicide. That event is more profound than the usual ups and downs of clinical work. In fact, the trainee is usually unable to come to terms with it on his or her own. Special programmatic sensitivity and effort are required to help the trainee work through this experience.

The outstanding account by Kolodny et al. (1979) already referred to on page 419 should be mentioned again here as an example of how trainees—apparently with little program interference or encouragement—can help each other to work through the experience of a patient suicide in a self-help group setting. However, in smaller programs, or in situations where trainees do not "connect" as this group did, or in the absence of a relative rash of suicides early in the training year, this specific approach may not be readily applied elsewhere. Marshall (1980) has also outlined a method that promotes the orderly working through of a patient's suicide by involved treatment personnel. He puts emphasis on the thorough expression of feelings in the context of the involved staff member not being left alone. Marshall does not make reference to the needs of trainees, although the presumption seems reasonable that similar principles apply to them as well.

Helen Resnik's interest in the suicides of adolescent children and the resultant effects on their parents and families led her to formulate a process of "psychological resynthesis" as an approach to the survivors of suicide. As she put it: "Psychological resynthesis differs [from the psychological autopsy] in that it is primarily therapeutic. A dynamic approach to the survivors of suicides can be established that will revive them. Otherwise, survivors have a great likelihood of becoming psychological walking wounded" (p. 213). She describes this approach as having three component parts: "resuscitation" (breathing life into the survivors who have serious psychological wounds), "rehabilitation" (helping survivors work through their mourning), and "renewal" (giving up grief and the bondage to the suicide) (Resnik, 1969b). Borrowing somewhat from her approach (and similar to the phasic approach discussed by Cotton, Drake, Whitaker, and Potter in chapter 21 of this book), I have suggested a way of conceptualizing this process in guiding a program's response to the suicide of a trainee's patient. This program approach derives from my experience with current residents, as well as from questionnaire responses and interviews with graduates and members of our multidisciplinary faculty who had the experience of patient suicide during training. I will describe the five-phase system (see Table 22.2) that evolved, including several representative questionnaire responses or interview quotations to convey some of the qualities of each phase. I use this approach in the psychiatry residency training program at the Cambridge Hospital (Brown, 1987b).

The suggested time frames are given in terms relevant to psychiatric residents and are, of course, only rough estimates that will vary with individual trainees and situations. This approach differs from Resnik's not so much because of the minor modifications in naming the phases, but, rather, because it is focused on professionals in training (not families), and because it incorporates specific anticipation and preparation for posttraining phases.

Anticipation

Instead of conveying the impression that the experience is unlikely, training directors and supervisors should take the initiative in encouraging trainees (individually and as a group) to anticipate the real possibility that one or more of them may have a patient commit suicide during training. In our program the residency director discusses the available data about this subject in an introductory

Table 22.2

Phases of Trainee and Program Responses to Patient Suicide

Phase 1:	Anticipation (PGY1 or early PGY2)
Phase 2:	Acute impact (hours to about 8 weeks)
Phase 3:	Clarification and working through (about 2 to 6 months)
Phase 4:	Reorganization: Relative resolution versus ongoing doubt (about 6 to 18 months)
Phase 5:	Preparation for reactivation and posttraining practice (mid-PGY4)

seminar early in PGY2. Residents are encouraged to imagine what they might think and feel should a patient of theirs or of a colleague commit suicide. In her discussion of suicidal patients and therapists in training, Fuchs (1982) suggested that it might be helpful for trainees to "rehearse" how it might feel for a patient to commit suicide. Resident response to this kind of anticipation has been very positive. Anxiety is actually allayed rather than heightened.

The training program and responsible department can collaborate to establish policies that aid in the preparation for a suicide by a trainee's patient. These policies, which essentially provide a kind of structural context, should ensure that suicidal and seriously ill patients are treated by faculty members as well as by trainees, and also that there is a review of case assignments for trainees. When faculty are known to treat sick and difficult patients, trainees identify this work as important and valuable. They are also helped to avoid the bitterness that can understandably result if they perceive themselves as the only ones in a department who are called upon to work with the most difficult patients. Moreover, a department's commitment to excellent clinical care is served by this arrangement. For example, many suicidal patients are extremely sensitive to changes in therapists (Oldham and Russakoff, 1984). Such repeated changes are predictable with trainees and can eventually become a burden greater than these patients can bear. They deserve, if possible, a chance to work consistently with a staff-level therapist who is likely to be available for the many years often required for effective treatment. Trainees do bring great advantages to their work with patients (including hopeful enthusiasm, lower cost, and sometimes the capacity to continue with their patients after graduation), but from a patient's point of view they can often be experienced as a kind of unstable blur among many transient trainee therapists. In the Cambridge Hospital program, a "patient at risk rounds" (like the "impossible case conference" suggested by Kolodny et al., 1979) has been established for staff and trainees' patients alike. These rounds permit trainees to present their own cases and to observe how all mental health professionals struggle with the dilemmas raised during the treatment of suicidal and other difficult patients.

Although the nature of psychotherapeutic responsibility is complex, certain aspects of this concept as it relates to suicidal patients must be introduced early with trainees. "Team responsibility" for patients particularly must be clarified. Of course there is a place for team-oriented crisis work with suicidal patients, but this must be contrasted to the trainee's individual therapeutic endeavors with these patients.

Suicidal patients frequently do place heavy or near impossible demands on their therapist. These demands may feel unbearable, and sometimes they may be impossible to meet. Sharing this burden within the structure of a team is commonly recommended and enormously valuable, including provision for clinical coverage when the trainee is unavailable or on vacation. But any diffusion of responsibility as the patient's therapist must be avoided, no matter how tempting. There can be only one therapist at a time, who must integrate the available support, advice, and supervision. Indistinct responsibility (the defensive feeling that someone else is really responsible) must be contrasted with the difficult, but preferable, stance of explicit responsibility within a realistic, highly supportive, and nonisolated context ("I am responsible, but help is available"). Such help includes the rare transfer of the patient to another therapist if needed. Trainees often feel responsible following a suicide. They are only set up for confusion and irresolution by indistinct clinical responsibility. It must be clear whether the patient is or is not theirs. Exactly what they are responsible for within that clear context is also critically important, but cannot be the focus here ("The patient is yours, but let's think through what that means").

Although routinely provided by most programs (and therefore not emphasized here), trainees are indeed aided in their anticipation of understanding a patient's suicide by having adequate didactic instruction about the epidemiology and dynamics of suicide. Supervisors play an important role in this process, in addition to formal seminars.

Comments relevant to this phase include: "I wish there was a way of preparing people. Programs should say: This is probably going to happen to some of you, and force people to fantasize and free associate about this." "I felt I must do something to save her". "It caught me by surprise. No one prepared me for this."

Acute Impact

The training director, preceptor, supervisors, and others should reach out to the affected trainee. The only required procedure relating to the suicide of a resident's patient in our program calls for the director and preceptor to meet with the resident, at the resident's convenience, within 24 hours of a suicide. It is crucial at this time that the resident not feel alone, either in the sense that this experience is terribly unique or that he or she must bear it completely on their own. Such reaching out can and should be accomplished without descending upon or crowding the trainee.

The trainee's characteristic adaptive style should be respected and supported during this phase. Resnik (1969) has referred to this as a period of "resuscitation" during which the survivor of a suicide needs to be provided with active support ("psychological first-aid").

The trainee should be encouraged (not forced) to meet with the significant relatives of the deceased patient. This not only offers the trainee an opportunity to observe the reactions and needs of family members, but also allows him the opportunity to help others who are in a position somewhat similar to his own. Close supervision and support should be provided for this, sometimes including a supervisor or appropriate clinical director actually being present during the family meeting. (It is also my impression that such attention to the relatives minimizes, in most cases, the likelihood of malpractice action.)

If a training group experience is part of the program, it can provide highly effective support during this phase. This depends, however, on the general nature and current psychological posture of the group. Competitive, hostile, or scapegoat-ing attitudes periodically dominate such group experiences, and the leader's sensitivity to the impact of a suicide on the trainee is critical. When groups work well, they offer the enormous advantage that some trainees can listen passively, internally noticing their own reactions to the suicide.

Quotations applicable to this phase have included:

> I felt I was unlucky. But maybe I'm just incompetent and should go into Pediatrics.

> I felt that I had failed . . . that this happened to me because I was not as good as my fellow trainees.

> It was helpful when a supervisor reminded me that when someone dies one does not process it all acutely.

> It's a trauma. You have to allow it to hurt.

> At first I felt like I was the only one this had ever happened to.

Clarification and Working Through

Although the highly visible acute reaction has passed, preceptors and supervisors should actively look for ways to help the trainee think through possible influences of his or her patient's suicide on present attitudes and work. This should not, of course, take the form of intrusive or anxious hovering over all of the trainee's work. Nonetheless, there are opportunities to keep an eye on the way the experience with the suicide may be affecting the trainee's ongoing work. Particular emphasis should be put on any other currently suicidal patients, but generalizations to psycho-therapeutic work with nonsuicidal patients should not be neglected.

This is the optimal time for a "review" or "psychological autopsy" (Shneidman, 1969b, 1981). The trainee is now generally able to go back over what happened. This is the time to try to apply the advice often attributed to Semrad (1980): "Try to keep your mind open about it and see what you can learn". Such reviews should address at least three aspects of the suicide, with proportional emphasis varying from case to case: (1) trying to understand why the death occurred, (2) evaluating the quality of care provided, and (3) dealing with the effect on the development of the therapist. In my experience, those faculty who are involved in these reviews must adroitly steer a course between the twin dangers of participating in either a whitewash or a witchhunt. Trainees have very sensitive antennae for detecting both of these activities.

If the trainee appears either "struck" or as though he or she might benefit from a further, perhaps "more neutral" review, an outside consultant for the trainee should be provided. This need may reflect the trainee's state or the state of the clinical area in which the suicide occurred. Our program facilitates, and pays for, such voluntary consultation.

Trainees themselves should use their own therapy to explore the meaning of the suicide to them personally and professionally, as well as to explore relevant countertransference issues.

Comments pretaining to this phase have included:

> I had to get over my anger at my supervisors for not knowing—for not protecting me.

> My own therapy helped the most.

> It helped to go to the funeral, and then in later months to talk with the family.

> The review felt somewhat like a whitewash.

> It's hard not to feel blamed when possible mistakes are explored.

Reorganization

A meeting with the program director toward the end of this phase is often useful, both so that the director can assess how the trainee is doing in general and also as a specific opportunity to take up issues of "failure" and blame. The director is in a somewhat difficult, but particularly useful, position for working this through with a trainee because he or she is vested with establishing standards in the program.

The trainee should be encouraged to offer to meet with the family again at the first anniversary of the suicide. Perhaps this meeting will supplement or bring to a natural close a series of regular meetings that may have occurred at intervals since the suicide.

If a state of chronic doubt is evident, the program should actively encourage further processing by the trainee. This can involve providing an outside consultant, encouraging therapy if it has thus far not been available, and more active attention by supervisors.

Statements which typify this phase include:

> This experience produced a very great change in my work. I realized that love alone is not enough.

> I still avoid suicidal patients.

> It's something like getting the "red badge of courage." Now I'm different. I've seen something bad and been touched by it. I'm not worse and not better, but larger—I've gained perspective. That's positive.

> I have avoided clinical practice ever since. Sometimes I think of private practice but then I think of the suicide and decide against it. This was not the only influence, but a very strong one.

> I am still affected, but I am resolved about it.

> The experience has made me a better therapist, but as a person, I'd just as soon pass on it.

Preparation for Reactivation and Posttraining Practice

Prior to graduation from formal training, a context for anticipating the transition to posttraining practice should be provided by training programs. Borus (1978) has described a transition-to-practice seminar for psychiatric residents, aptly nicknamed "Reality Rounds." As part of such preparations some attention should also be devoted to future work with suicidal patients. Residents who have experienced a suicide in training would benefit from reconsideration of how this experience has affected them, including the inevitable reactivation of memories and feelings when other suicidal patients are encountered. Trainees not yet directly affected need to be reminded that such clinical experience may be rather likely for them or colleagues in many future clinical practice settings.

The value of ongoing learning, consultation, and nonisolation from colleagues should be emphasized. Ideally, such an approach to clinical work will have been naturally internalized during the program.

The importance of reaching out empathically, nonjudgmentally, and constructively to fellow professionals in difficulty should be stressed.

Statements relevant to this phase include: "I have never forgotten the experience." "I wish there was some way of preparing people." "While in training, I'm not supposed to know everything."

This discussion of programmatic responses to the suicide of a trainee's patient may seem to imply that the only thing on the trainee's mind is the suicide experience. This is not, and should not be, the case. Life goes on, and programs should convey this to affected trainees. Yet a program should have an effective method for recognizing and dealing with the extensive meaning of these experiences for trainees. In practice, multiple programmatic approaches are required. What is supportive and useful for one trainee may be considerably less so for another. Moreover, the suggestions made here are not meant for recipelike implementation. This chapter aims only to provide a chart of some of the psychological territory, something like a topographical map as opposed to a detailed road map.

The expectation following the suicide of a trainee's patient is of an adaptive, yet painful, response. No program or personal intervention by a training director, supervisor, or colleague can entirely alleviate the distress. The basic hope is that despite the shock and pain, and to some extent because of them, the trainee might grow and learn something new about themselves and about patients from the experience. Kolodny and her group (1979) put it very well:

> We found that as we worked through our mourning, we felt we had been through a rite of passage. While we did not feel immunized against having to reexperience this painful process in the future, we felt we had undergone something which had transformed and matured us and increased our sense of what we could withstand. We became more able to give up magical expectations and fantasies of therapeutic omnipotence. We had undergone a process during which we had realized a profound sense of isolation, a painful sense of having betrayed our patients' and our institution's trust in us and having felt connectedness with one another in our group and with other therapists with similar experiences. Further, we became more willing to accept our own limitations and to forgive ourselves [pp. 44–45].

Programs should not attempt to remove entirely the stress of possible or actual patient suicide. Working with suicidal patients—including the unfortunate actual suicide of the patient—is an acceptable and an important aspect of training. I conclude that attempting to protect trainees from this experience would be something like attempting to arrange that medical students and medical interns and residents never have a patient die.

Finally, it must be acknowledged that litigation and learning do not mix well in this context. A malpractice suit can be the worst thing that can happen. Protectionism tends to set in and exploration tends to be displaced by ass-covering. Programs can resist this. Something can be learned, but it is much more difficult in a legalized context. In addition to covering up, there can be a great urge to stay clear of the situation when a lawsuit is involved. Faculty must consciously resist that understandable tendency because it leaves the affected trainee isolated. Programs also have the responsibility to clarify local legal practices and precedents for trainees, and, obviously, to provide secure insurance coverage.

CONCLUSIONS

Even if the suicide of a trainee's patient was a rare event (an assumption refuted in this chapter), training directors and others interested in the development of mental health professionals would still be concerned about the ramifications for those affected. Beyond this, it is clear that we need more information from larger and more diverse studies about the incidence of this experience for trainees. Our knowledge is particularly limited about nonpsychiatrists.

The primary purpose of this chapter will have been accomplished if those interested in and responsible for the education of mental health professionals have become more aware that this experience may be more common than previously thought and may have important effects on the emotional quality and direction of professional development. Perhaps this awareness will even be of importance to those mental health professionals who had this experience in training themselves several, or even many, years ago.

We must recognize that programs make a difference in the outcome of this crisis for trainees. The suicide rate is not declining in our country, and the experience of having a patient commit suicide is obviously unavoidable for a certain number of trainees. Moreover, if we decide that training systems that assign to trainees the care of seriously ill patients are educationally sound, or simply inevitable, then it becomes all the more imperative to anticipate patient suicide as one consequence of that arrangement and to appreciate its human, programmatic, and developmental impact for trainees. Growth can be fostered or, undesirably, trainees can be left to cope in relative uncertainty and isolation. Included here should be a willingness within programs to consider seriously whether they are avoiding self-evaluation about the use of trainees in particular settings.

Certainly programs must take seriously the hope and expectation that trainees might learn something of value from these unwelcome situations. There is some comfort in the knowledge that, while inexperienced and vulnerable, trainees do have the enormous protective advantage of being "in training." This perspective can facilitate the open examination of suicide from a clinical, professional, and personal vantage point. And there is a significant group effect as well; that is, in the unfortunate event of a patient suicide, the attitude a training program establishes will influence all trainees (whether they were directly involved themselves or not). Directly or indirectly trainees can thus begin to internalize an approach to this experience should they encounter it later in their own professional career or in a colleague's.

George Vaillant's (1977) first conclusion about the men of the Grant Study is germane:

> [I]solated traumatic events rarely mold individual lives. That is not to say that the premature death of a parent, the unexpected award of a scholarship, the chance first encounter with a future spouse or a heart attack will not result in sudden change in

life's trajectory. Unexpected events affect our lives, just as a wrong or a fortuitous turn might affect a cross-country journey. But the quality of the whole journey is seldom changed by a single turning. The life circumstances that truly impinge upon health, the circumstances that facilitate adaptation or that stunt later growth—in contrast to fame—are not isolated events. What makes or breaks our luck seems to be the continued interaction between our choice of adaptive mechanisms and our sustained relationship with other people [p. 368].

So it is with the major crisis of patient suicide in a trainee's life. Growth through this crisis will be strongly influenced by the trainee's preparation and reactions, plus important sustaining relationships within the training program. To facilitate both such preparation and interactions, every training program should have a consciously conceived perspective and approach to this crisis.

REFERENCES

Bibring, E. (1953), The mechanism of depression. In: *Affective Disorders*, ed. P. Greenacre. New York: International Universities Press.

Borus, J.F. (1978), The transition to practice seminar. *Amer. J. Psychiat.*, 135:1513–1516.

Brown, H.N. (1987a), The impact of suicide on therapists in training. *Comp. Psychiat.*, 28:101–112.

———— (1987b), Patient suicide during residency training: Incidence, implications, and program response. *J. Psychiat. Ed.*, 2:201–216.

Cain, A.C., ed. (1972), *Survivors of Suicide*. Springfield, IL: Charles C Thomas.

Freud, S. (1915), Our attitude toward death. *Standard Edition*, 14:289–300. London: Hogarth Press, 1957.

Fuchs, R. (1982), Suicidal patients and the therapist-in-training. In: *Lifelines,* eds. E.S. Bassuk, S.C. Schoonover, & A.D. Gill. New York: Plenum.

Goldstein, L.S., & Buongiorno, P.A. (1984), Psychotherapists as suicide survivors. *Amer. J. Psychother.*, 38:392–398.

Havens, L.L. (1965), The anatomy of a suicide. *N. Engl. J. Med.*, 272:401–406.

Henn, R.F. (1978), Patient suicide as part of psychiatry residency. *Amer. J. Psychiat.*, 135:745–746.

Kahne, M.J. (1968), Suicide among patients in mental hospitals: A study of the psychiatrists who conducted their psychotherapy. *Psychiatry*, 31:32–43.

Kelly, W.A. (1973), Suicide and psychiatric education. *Amer. J. Psychiat.*, 130:463–468.

Kolodny, S., Binder, R.L., Bronstein, A.A., & Friend, R.L. (1979), The working through of patients' suicides by four therapists. *Suicide & Life-Threat. Behav.*, 9:33–46.

Lindemann, E. (1944), Symptomatology and management of acute grief. *Amer. J. Psychiat.*, 101:141–148.

Litman, R. (1965), When patients commit suicide. *Amer. J. Psychiat.*, 19:570–576.

Maltsberger, J.T., & Buie, D.H. (1974), Countertransference hate in the treatment of suicidal patients. *Arch. Gen. Psychiat.*, 30:625–633.

Marshall, K.A. (1980), When a patient commits suicide. *Suicide & Life-Threat. Behav.*, 10:29–39.

Oldham, J.M., & Russakoff, M.L. (1984), Suicide at a training center. *J. Psychiat. Ed.*, 8:97–104.

Resnik, H.L.P. (1969a), The neglected search for the suicidococcus contagiosa. *Arch. Environ. Health*, 19:307–309.

———— (1969b), Psychological resynthesis: A clinical approach to the survivors of a death by suicide. In: *Aspects of Depression*, ed. E.S. Shneidman & M. Ortega. Boston: Little, Brown.

Rosen, D.H. (1974), Mental stresses in residency training and opportunities for prevention. Paper

Herbert N. Brown

presented at the 12th annual meeting of the American Psychiatric Association, May, Detroit, Michigan.

Schnur, D.B., & Levin, E.H. (1985), The impact of successfully completed suicide on psychiatric residents. *J. Psychiat. Ed.*, 9/2:127–136.

Searles, H.F. (1965), Schizophrenia and the inevitability of death. In: *Collected Papers on Schizophrenia and Related Subjects.* New York: International Universities Press.

Semrad, E. (1980), *The Heart of the Therapist,* eds. S. Rako & H. Mazer. New York: Jason Aronson.

Shneidman, E.S., ed. (1969a), *On the Nature of Suicide.* San Francisco: Jossey-Bass.

———— (1969b), Suicide, lethality, and the psychological autopsy. *Internat. Psychiat. Clin.*, 6:225–242.

———— (1971), Prevention, intervention, and postvention in suicide. *Ann. Intern. Med.*, 75:453–458.

———— (1981), The psychological autopsy. *Suicide & Life-Threat. Behav.*, 11:325–340.

Vaillant, G.E. (1977), *Adaptation to Life.* Boston: Little, Brown.

Part IV

Philosophical and Larger
Perspectives

23

A Moral View on Suicide

Thomas S. Szasz, M.D.

I

My views on the ethics of suicide were first set forth in an essay written some years ago (Szasz, 1971). Arguing from individualistic–libertarian premises, I there maintained that suicide was a basic human right: in other words, that the real or assumed danger of a person's committing suicide did not justify coercive interventions in his life.[1]

While the theme of this book addresses some of the issues discussed in that essay, its focus is not on the ethical nature of suicide but rather on the psychiatrist's responsibility for the suicide of a person considered to be his patient. This topic raises certain questions that I have not formally addressed before. Among such questions, the following are especially important: What do we mean when we assert that a psychiatrist is responsible for preventing, or trying to prevent, a patient's suicide? How do we ascertain or define when or whether a person is a patient, is suicidal, or has died as a result of suicide? If, as I suggest, we reject coercive methods of suicide prevention, what is our responsibility, as professionals concerned with helping suffering individuals, toward so-called suicidal persons? Finally, and most important, how should we, as intelligent citizens who want to maximize individual liberty and responsibility and minimize the power of the state to coerce persons innocent of crime, foster laws, social policies, and professional practices consonant with such a goal?

I suggest that we entertain the possibility that the question of the "clinician's" responsibility for suicide has little, if anything, to do with either medicine or treatment. Why ask about the psychiatrist's responsibility for suicide, and not about the "patient's"? Because, unless he wanted to risk being branded a heretic, the psychiatrist would say, indeed, he would insist, that suicide is an illness. "We are

---

[1]For the sake of economy and clarity, throughout this essay, the terms *psychiatrist* and *patient* will be used to refer to all mental health professionals and their clients.

now . . . in agreement," declared Stanley Yolles when he was the director of the National Institute of Mental Health, "that this [suicide] is a public health matter and that the state should combat the disease of suicide" (Yolles, 1967). This, of course, is a claim for more psychiatric territory rather than a demonstration that suicide conforms to certain criteria that qualify it as a disease. But even if suicide were an illness, psychiatrists would still, correctly speaking, not be responsible for it. Cancer is an illness but oncologists are not responsible for it. Moreover, even if suicide were, or were considered to be, an illness, the patient himself might be partly or wholly responsible for it, as for example an alcoholic is for his hepatic cirrhosis. And even if suicide were an illness for which the patient is completely blameless, for example, lupus or Hodgkin's disease, he would still be responsible for its management. Although it is obvious, perhaps I should add that if suicide is not an illness (or the symptom of an illness) but the act of a moral agent, then the only person ultimately responsible for it is the actor himself. This does not mean that psychiatrists or others, inside or outside the medical profession, may not assume specific moral or legal responsibilities vis-à-vis certain persons deemed to be suicidal. It means only that the psychiatrist has no more responsibility for preventing other people's suicidal behavior than any ordinary person has for preventing the lawful behavior of total strangers.

That, of course, is not the prevailing view today. It is now conventional psychiatric wisdom, never questioned by "rational" persons, that the psychiatrist must intervene in the lives of persons who might commit suicide. All that is left to debate is when and how the psychiatrist should intervene. This presumption prejudges the "problem" of suicide. In his attitude toward suicide, the modern psychiatrist thus displays an ethical provincialism typical of a medieval priest: only *his* views on suicide are valid, only *his* policies for preventing suicide are moral (compassionate, humane, therapeutic).

II

Before we can even begin to examine the question of the psychiatrist's responsibility for the so-called "suicidal patient," we must clarify what we mean when we speak of one person's responsibility for another, and more specifically of a professional person's for his client or patient. We use the term "responsible" to describe a person's accountability for the conduct and welfare of another person or himself. For example, parents are responsible for their children (especially when the children are young); whereas competent adults are responsible for themselves.

The idea of responsibility is intertwined with two other concepts: liberty and control. Liberty and responsibility are, in fact, two sides of the same coin. Ordinarily, we assume that adults are moral agents endowed with free will; that is, they choose their behavior from among a range of options, large or small. We also assume that they are responsible for their actions; that is, they are praised or blamed, rewarded or punished, depending on whether their conduct is judged to be good or bad.

Where there is no freedom, there is no responsibility: we do not hold infants responsible for their behavior; duress is a complete excuse in the criminal law, and so forth. And where there is no control, there can be no responsibility: a person cannot be held responsible for something he does not control. (This is the flip side of the commonsense notion that a person can, and should, be held responsible for what he can control.) Asserting that "X is responsible for Y" (for Y's welfare, health, not committing suicide, etc.) is thus tantamount to asserting that X can, and indeed must, have enough control over Y to bring about the desired condition of Y. This is why persons who want to assume control over others typically claim to be responsible for them (called "paternalism"); and why persons who want to reject responsibility for their own conduct typically claim to have no control over themselves (called "mental illness").

These principles are recognized in countless contractual arrangements, for example, when a bank trustee is empowered to manage someone else's money or an anesthesiologist to put someone else to sleep. Such experts undertake to exercise a specific responsibility, for the proper discharge of which they are granted control over specific objects or functions (money, respiration, and so forth). In every such situation, the controller becomes responsible for what he controls, and only for what he controls. It follows, then, that anyone who assumes the task of preventing another person from committing suicide must assume the most far-reaching control over that person's capacity to act. Since, in fact, it is virtually impossible to prevent the suicide of a person determined on killing himself, and since forcibly imposed interventions to prevent suicide deprive the patient of liberty and dignity, the use of psychiatric coercion to prevent suicide is at once impractical and immoral. It should, of course, be noted that because children have neither the rights nor the responsibilities of adults, and because, unlike adults, children are typically treated coercively by the medical (as well as the educational) system, we must always clearly distinguish between policies aimed at children and policies aimed at adults. The principle of coercive paternalism obliterates precisely this basic distinction.[2] In this discussion, we shall be concerned with *adults* only; and among adult "suicidal patients" especially with those subjected to *involuntary (coerced)* psychiatric interventions.

---

[2]The extension of the principles and practices of coercive paternalism to adults—because they are, or are said to be, disabled, impaired, or suicidal—lies at the heart of most contemporary problems of political philosophy and civil rights.

III

Why are physicians, especially psychiatrists, concerned with suicide? There are two basic reasons. First, because the physician's seemingly narrow concerns with the diagnosis and treatment of diseases actually serve a broader purpose, namely, the preservation of life. Second, because there is a rich historical and philosophical connection between suicide and the idea of mental illness. I wrote in my essay on *The Ethics of Suicide:*

> The physician is committed to saving lives. . . . He thus reacts, perhaps "unconsciously" (in the sense that he does not articulate the problem in these terms), to the suicidal patient as if the patient had affronted, insulted, or attacked him. The physician strives valiantly, often at the cost of his own well-being, to save lives; and here comes a person who not only does not let the physician save him but, *horrible dictu,* makes the physician an unwilling witness to that person's deliberate self-destruction. That is more than most physicians can take. Feeling assaulted in the very center of their spiritual identity, some take flight, while others counterattack [Szasz, 1971, p. 74–75].

By and large, it is the nonpsychiatric physician who takes flight, and the psychiatrist who counterattacks. The psychiatrist does so by trying to "save the patient from himself"; or, what comes to the same thing, by trying to save the patient from his mental illness. Without going into further details, this means that insofar as the psychiatrist views (severe) mental illness as a condition that renders its "victim" incompetent (so that he resembles a young child), or as a condition that renders him unfree (so that he resembles a person subjected to duress), he regards and treats the mental patient as if the patient did not possess his full powers as a human agent. This psychiatric matrimony between mental illness and suicide is held firmly together, in a virtually indissoluble union, by a long legal tradition distinguishing between sane and insane suicides (with a powerful presumption favoring insanity in cases of self-inflicted death). This is a tradition now combined with and supported by a popular predisposition to viewing suicide as a "symptom" of mental illness, and mental illness as a "cause" of suicide. In short, because we tend to assume that the suicidal person is mentally ill, or because we attribute such an illness to him, we inject psychiatrists and psychiatry into the drama of suicide (to excuse or prevent it). I object to the psychiatrization of suicide—as I do to the psychiatrization of personal conduct generally—because I believe that psychopathological explanations are empirically false, and that the coercive interventions based on them are ethically undesirable.

The modern psychiatric approach to suicide and suicide prevention betrays important but unarticulated value judgments, exemplifying Sir James Fitzjames Stephen's important insight that "Men have an all but incurable propensity to try to prejudge all the great questions which interest them by stamping their prejudices upon their language" (Stephen, 1873, p. 176). A Ghandi starving himself is not counted as suicidal, nor is a Bobby Sands (the IRA "terrorist" who starved himself to death in prison) counted as a suicide; on the contrary, such men are considered to be religious leaders, patriots, or martyrs. The very term "suicide," having the same linguistic structure as, and resonating with, "homicide," not only identifies but also condemns the act. The claims of psychiatrists and suicidologists that they are scientists seeking an understanding of suicidal behaviors are thus every bit as absurd as would be the claims of right-to-lifers (who call abortion "murder of the fetus") that they are scientists seeking an understanding of feticidal behavior.

The very concern of clinicians with suicide and the idea that someone other than the suicidal person himself might be responsible for his act is at once typically Western (Judeo-Christian) and modern (Fedden, 1938; Sprott, 1961). Until as recently as 200 years ago, suicide was, de facto, considered to be a crime—similar to, but even worse than, homicide—for which the person committing the act was "obviously" responsible. Suicide continued to be classified, de jure, as a criminal act well into the twentieth century in many jurisdictions in the United States. The now fashionable belief that suicide is a phenomenon for which the suicidal person is not responsible is thus simply an inversion of the belief it displaced. Both beliefs are symptomatic of our predecessors' skittishness toward this subject, and our continued reluctance to view suicide as we view other morally heavily freighted acts—like divorce or killing—as good or bad, depending on the circumstances in which they occur and on the criteria by which they are judged.

IV

It is inevitable that insofar as suicide is perceived as an undesirable act or event, people will insist on holding someone or something responsible for it. In the history of Western civilization, the end of the Enlightenment, or roughly the year 1800, marks a dramatic change in the perception of suicide. Before that time, suicide was considered to be both a sin and a crime for which the actor himself was responsible; since then, suicide has increasingly been regarded as a manifestation of madness. This is why mental illness is now considered to be the cause of suicide with psychiatrists and psychiatric institutions viewed as responsible for preventing it. Exemplifying both views, and the transformation of the former into the latter, are the records of two suicides in the Louisiana colony in the eighteenth century. A man named Jean Baptiste, who killed himself in 1765, was punished by having his corpse tied to the back of a cart and dragged to the public square, where it was hung upside down from the scaffold for 24 hours. Another man, named André Sauvinien, who killed himself in 1752, was sentenced to similar degradations as well as to the seizure of all of his property. Probably because of the latter penalty, Sauvinien's family succeeded in having the superior council of the colony overturn the sentence on the ground that Sauvinien was insane when he killed himself (*Parade*, 1982).

While the history of suicide is not germane to our present concerns, it is important to keep in mind that the idea of suicide as self-murder originates from a specifically Judeo-Christian cosmology in which God is viewed as both "giving" and "taking" each human being's life: hence, taking one's own life is a most grievous offense against Him. The modern medical–psychiatric view on suicide represents a secularized version of the same belief concerning the impermissibility of this act. The idea that anyone who kills himself is crazy at one fell swoop reinforces this moral valuation, exonerates the suicide from wrongdoing, and excuses the survivors from punishing the deed. In my view the belief that suicide is a sickness is thus basically similar to the belief that suicide is a sin, and both are similar to basic religious beliefs, such as that the Jews are the Chosen People or that Jesus is the Son of God. As everyone knows, such views are regarded as the profoundest truths by those who believe them, and as the most absurd untruths, follies, or delusions by those who do not.

V

Why do we now give psychiatrists special privileges and powers to intervene vis-à-vis suicidal persons? Because, as I have noted, in the psychiatric view, the person who threatens or commits suicide is irrational or mentally ill, allowing the psychiatrist to play doctor and thereby, like other doctors, to save lives. However, there is neither philosophical nor empirical support for viewing suicide as different, in principle, for other acts, such as getting married or divorced, working on the Sabbath, eating shrimp, or smoking tobacco. These and countless other things people do are the result of personal decisions. Insofar as people believe that mental illness or irrationality robs a person of his capacity to make sane (rational, responsible, self-protective) decisions, mental illness or irrationality must, perforce, have such an effect across the board, on behaviors of all kinds, not just on suicide (or homicide).

To put it differently: If suicide is always something bad—like working on the Sabbath—then why should abstaining from or preventing it, and promoting and enforcing abstinence from it, not be everyone's duty instead of only the psychiatrist's? Similarly, if the coercive prevention of irrational suicide is something good—like the coercive prevention of homicide—then why is the coercive prevention of a host of other irrational acts not also a good? The fact that the psychiatrist plays such a decisive and distinctive role in the contemporary policies and practices of suicide prevention points to a hidden agenda, namely, to our general reliance on psychiatric explanations of disturbing behavior and on psychiatric control of disturbing persons.

The phrase "suicide prevention" is itself a misleading slogan characteristic of our modern therapeutic age. Insofar as suicide is a physical possibility, there can be no suicide prevention; insofar as suicide is a fundamental human right, there ought to be no such thing. If the psychiatrist is to prevent a person intent on killing himself from doing so, he clearly cannot, and should not, be expected to accomplish that task unless he can exercise complete control over the capacity of the suicidal person to act. But it is either impossible to do this or it may require reducing the patient to a social state beneath that of a slave: for the slave is compelled only to labor against his will, whereas the suicidal person is compelled to live against his will. Such a life is not the life of a person or human being, but only that of a human organism or living human thing.

This does not mean that individuals troubled by suicidal ideas or impulses should not be able to secure the assistance they seek, provided they can find others willing to render such assistance. It only means that expressions of so-called suicidal behavior—in any of their psychiatric forms or shapes, such as suicidal ideation, suicidal impulse, suicide attempt, and so forth—would no longer qualify as a justification for coercing the so-called patient. Were such a policy adopted, people would have to make do with noncoercive methods of preventing suicide, just as they must now make do with noncoercive methods of preventing other forms of (self-harming) actions—such as warnings from the Surgeon General on packages of cigarettes or diet soda.

No one can deny that policies aimed at preventing suicide by means of legal–psychiatric coercion imply a paternalistic attitude toward the patient and require giving certain privileges and powers to a special class of protectors vis-à-vis a special class of victims. Clearly, all such solutions of human or social problems are purchased at the cost of creating the fresh problem of "Who shall guard the guardians?" The demonstrable harms generated by the mistakes and misuses of the powers of psychiatrists and judges (delegated to them on the grounds that they are protecting suicidal persons from themselves) must be balanced against the alleged or ostensible benefits generated by coercive policies of suicide prevention. Inasmuch as we have no generally agreed upon criteria for adjudicating controversies concerning such a trade-off, our acceptance or rejection of coercive suicide prevention is perhaps best viewed as a manifestation of our moral–political (existential, religious) beliefs in certain ideas and their practical implications—such as free will and personal responsibility on the one hand, mental illness and psychiatric paternalism on the other hand.

The fact remains that psychiatrists now stigmatize suicide much as priests did before them, but with one important difference: the theory and practice of coercive suicide prevention also stigmatizes the psychiatrists. By assuming control over persons who want to kill themselves, psychiatrists patronize their patients and promise more than they can deliver, doubly compromising their integrity. By actually trying to prevent suicide, psychiatrists ally themselves with the police powers of the state and resort to coercion, thus defining themselves as foes rather than friends of individual liberty and responsibility. It is no wonder that policies of coercive suicide prevention are at once an indispensable source of prestige and power for psychiatrists and an embarrassing emblem of the fateful antagonism lurking in their relationship to mental patients. That such policies should now also constitute a vast reservoir of complex legal problems for psychiatrists should not surprise us.

VI

What then, you might ask, is my answer to the question "What is the clinician's responsibility for suicide?" I shall offer two answers. First, interpreting the question literally, I would answer that the clinician's responsibility for his patient's suicide *is* whatever the law and social custom say it is. Interpreting the question more broadly—asking, in effect, what I believe *should be* the psychiatrist's responsibility vis-à-vis the suicidal patient—I would answer that it should be the same as any other physician's vis-à-vis his competent adult patient, for example, the ophthalmologist's vis-à-vis the person with a refractive error of the eye. If the patient wants or is willing to accept psychiatric help for being suicidal, the psychiatrist has a moral obligation—and, depending on circumstances, may have a legal obligation—to provide some sort of help for that person; but if the patient does not want such help and actively rejects it, then the psychiatrist's duty ought to be to leave him alone (or to try to persuade him to accept help).

In short, my position on coercive suicide prevention is similar to the abolitionist position on the death penalty. If a person says, as many people now do, that he is morally opposed to the judicial system killing anyone, then it would be inconsistent for that person to inquire into a defendant's criminal deeds, to ascertain whether or not he should be executed. In addition, it would be pointless and absurd for an interlocutor to try to change the speaker's mind by emphasizing the depravity of any particular criminal. I am similarly opposed, as a matter of principle, to coercive interventions vis-à-vis suicidal persons. The contention that the patient is psychotic or treatable is thus irrelevant to this argument.

However, inasmuch as this overview on suicide contains an interview by Dr. Havens, with a so-called suicidal patient, I want at this point to further clarify my position on suicide by comparing it to Justice Hugo Black's on pornography. Before deciding whether to permit or prohibit the distribution of a particular item deemed, by lower courts, to be pornographic, it was the custom of the Justices of the Supreme Court to view the evidence. Hugo Black refused to participate in such collective acts of judicial voyeurism. Why? Because he believed that it did not matter whether a particular book or film was or was not pornographic; all that mattered was whether or not the Constitution—as he understood or wanted to interpret it—authorized the government to prohibit the sale of such materials because, in the opinion of law enforcement authorities, they were prurient. Having concluded that the First

Amendment protects the sale of pornographic and nonpornographic materials alike, Justice Black felt that there was no point in his viewing an allegedly pornographic film before deciding whether or not the Supreme Court should make its distribution illegal (Dunne, 1977).

In other words, there is a fundamental difference between deciding what sort of social policy vis-à-vis pornography we approve or disapprove, and deciding whether a particular film is or is not pornographic. Mutatis mutandis, there is a difference between deciding what sort of social policy vis-à-vis suicide we approve or disapprove, and deciding whether or not a particular suicidal person is psychotic. Accordingly, if on moral and political grounds we decide that we oppose a social policy authorizing coercive psychiatric interventions vis-à-vis so-called suicidal persons, then the mental state of any particular suicidal person becomes irrelevant to judging whether, in that specific case, such a policy should or should not be implemented. This does not mean that a suicidal person's mental state is irrelevant for other purposes; on the contrary, it is highly relevant for an intelligent pursuit of certain other tasks; for example, determining how best to help him noncoercively, what such help might entail or require, and whether or not we (as particular moral agents in a universe or many such agents) want to participate in efforts to help him.

As it must be clear by now, I object to our present policies of suicide prevention because they downgrade the individual's (patient's) responsibility for the conduct of his own life and death. Since I value individual liberty very highly and am convinced that liberty and responsibility are indivisible, I want to enlarge the scope of both liberty and responsibility: in the present instance, this means opposing policies of suicide prevention that minimize the patient's responsibility for killing himself and supporting policies that maximize his responsibility for doing so. In other words, we should make it more difficult for the suicidal patient to reject responsibility for his own life, and for the psychiatrist to assume responsibility for such a patient's life. To achieve such a goal, we would have to hold every adult responsible for his behavior, and, temporarily at least, make use of a "psychiatric will" (a legal–psychiatric instrument I have described elsewhere) (Szasz, 1982). The adoption of such a will would symbolize the presumption that every adult is responsible (when sane) for deciding how he wants to be treated should he be deemed (because of mental illness, however diagnosed) to require coercive, psychiatric methods of suicide prevention. Such a mechanism would protect the patient from being coercively paternalized by psychiatrists (unless he himself wanted, under certain future circumstances, to submit to specific involuntary interventions), and the psychiatrist from being held responsible for the action of another person (unless he chose to assume such an obligation). Adopting such a mechanism would shift our policies of suicide prevention from coercive to contractual methods, restoring self-responsibility to all of the parties involved in the drama of suicide and its prevention.

VII

Inquiry into the psychiatric perspective of suicide probes some of our most passionately held, but not universally shared, beliefs about ending our own lives. Is such an act like homicide and accordingly properly called suicide? Or is it more like birth control and accordingly more properly termed *death control?* In this connection, we should recall the familiar distinction between *ritual observances within one's own faith,* such as abstaining from work on the Sabbath, and *universal moral obligations recognized by people of many faiths,* such as abstaining from the unprovoked killing of innocent persons. The behavior of countless successful and prominent persons shows us unmistakably that most Americans view suicide ambivalently, as a dreaded enemy as well as a trusted friend. This is why there is no controversy in America about using coercion to make people abstain from murder, but there is endless controversy about using coercion to make them abstain from suicide. And this is why although psychiatrists pretend that not committing suicide is like a universal moral obligation, they in fact treat it as if it were *their* sectarian religious belief: hence their special powers to interfere with the suicidal behavior of others and their blatant hypocrisy in engaging in such behavior themselves.

The belief that it is the legitimate function of the state to coerce a person because he might kill himself is a characteristically modern, quasi-medical idea, catering at once to our craving for dependency and omnipotence. The result is an intricate web of economic, legal, and psychiatric interventions and institutions that have themselves become powerful engines of hypocrisy and seemingly indispensable mechanisms for satisfying human needs now buried in hidden agendas.

It has taken a long time to get psychiatrists so deeply and singularly engaged in the suicide business, and, most likely, it will take a long time to get them out of it. In the meantime, psychiatrist and patient are both lost in the existential–legal labyrinth generated by treating suicide as if it constituted a psychiatric problem, indeed a psychiatric emergency. If we refuse, however, to play a part in the drama of coercive suicide prevention, then we shall be sorely tempted to conclude that the psychiatrist and his suicidal patient richly deserve one another and the torment each is so ready and eager to inflict on the other.

REFERENCES

Dunne, G.T. (1977), *Hugo Black and the Judicial Revolution.* New York: Simon & Schuster, p. 356.

Fedden, H.R., (1938), *Suicide: A Social and Historical Study.* London: Peter Davies.

Parade (1982), Convicted of killing themselves (editorial). September 19, p. 23.

Sprott, S.E. (1961), *The English Debate on Suicide: From Donne to Hume.* Lasalle, IL: Open Court.

Stephen, J.F. (1873), *Liberty, Equality, Fraternity.* Cambridge, UK: Cambridge University Press, 1967, p. 176.

Szasz, T.S. (1971), The ethics of suicide. In: *The Theology of Medicine.* New York: Harper Colophon, 1977, pp. 68–85.

———— (1982), The psychiatric will: A new mechanism for protecting persons against "psychosis" and psychiatry. *Amer. Psychol.*, 37:762–770.

Yolles, S.F. (1967), The tragedy of suicide in the United States. In: *Symposium on Suicide*, ed. L. Yochelson. Washington, DC: George Washington University, pp. 16–17.

24

Suicide Intervention: The Existential and Biomedical Perspectives

Ronald W. Maris, Ph.D.

> Everywhere there were people living out their lives using aspects of suicide against themselves. They did not even have the authenticity of the final act to speak for them. Suicide is, in short, the one continuous, everyday, ever-present problem of living. It is a question of degree. I've seen them all in varying stages of development and despair. The failed lawyer, the cynical doctor, the depressed housewife, the angry teen-ager . . . all of mankind engaged in the massive conspiracy against their own lives that is their daily activity. The meaning of suicide, the true meaning, had yet to be defined, had yet to be created in the broad dimensions it deserved.
>
> *The Suicide Academy,* Daniel Stern (1968)

For the most part suicide is poorly understood (Maris, 1982). The essence of suicide is not that life has gone awry, needs healing or repair, but that life under the best of circumstances is inane, pointless, not worth the effort. We tend to believe that suicides are suicidal because they are depressed, schizophrenic, cancerous, terribly lonely, without economic viability, have suffered an unacceptable reversal, have become gripped and consumed by alcohol, cannot work effectively, and so on. Accordingly, we conclude that if we could "only" remedy those life defects, life would be pleasurable, plausible, and worth the struggle.

However, the typical suicide feels utter despair, is devoid of hope, life is a psychotic nightmare endurable only by subhumans or the anesthetized. Everything is wrong, and it cannot get better. Suicide is the solution to the problem of life—of having to eat, to breathe, to work, to get up each morning, to shave, to move about, to go to school, to sleep, to cope with other humans, to experience pain, anxiety, and so on. The heart of the unacceptability of suicide is that it symbolizes that *all* life (life itself) is at bottom not worth the trouble, not possible, ultimately comes to ruin, a world devoid of gods or heroes, a world without redemption, except in the void of extinction.

At the same time suicide is not one thing, nor does it have one cause (Shneidman, 1985). Although I do not agree with him completely, Edwin Shneidman's definition of suicide comes closest to my argument. He writes: "suicide is a conscious act of self-induced annihilation, best understood as a multidimensional malaise in a needful individual who defines an issue for which suicide is perceived as the best solution" (p. 291). Most of the suicides (about three-fourths) I have known in 25 years of clinical and research work were *escape suicides* (Maris, 1981, pp. 294–311). They simply wanted the pain to stop and realized that they probably had to die for the depression, the loneliness, the failure, rejection, shame, anxiety, illness, and anger, to be finally over. These suicides tended to be older males (around 50 years old), with a progressive constriction of their adaptive repertoires over long "suicidal careers." Examples would include Ernest Hemingway, the New York Bowery pariah, or the terminal cancer patient.

A second major general type of suicides is aggressive or revenge based—what Menninger (1938), following Freud, called "murder-in-the-180°." Aggressive suicides occur more commonly among young people and are more likely to have interpersonal dynamics. Often such suicides wish to effect a life-change or to manipulate others, not especially to die. Still other suicides are self-sacrificing or self-altering (Baechler, 1979, p. 157, "oblative suicides"). Such people may kill themselves or others, because their culture requires it [e.g., Eskimos, in Leighton and Hughes (1955)]. Durkheim labeled such suicides "altruistic" and cited hara-kiri and early Christian martyrs as examples. Finally, suicides can be risk-takers (Baechler, 1979, p. 175, "ludic suicides"; Klausner, 1968) who are willing to die to enhance the quality of life, intensify life experiences, live more fully, or recharge the stimuli of routine life experiences. Other factors that further differentiate *ideal* types of suicides include age, race, occupation, religion, mental illness, marital status, culture, physical illness, anomie, isolation, anger, hormones, brain chemistry, genetics, alcohol and drugs, and suicidal models.

To anticipate some of my conclusions, *if* the suicide is right about life, suicide may be rational, especially for certain types of suicide in some specific circumstances. We all can think of suicides that seem justifiable, in which our interventions might have even been supportive of suicide. Of note are the suicide of Mr. Peusey, former President of Union Theological Seminary in New York City, and his wife, or seventy-six-year-old Dutch suicidologist Dr. Nico Speijer in 1981 (Diekstra, 1985). Speijer argued that suicide among the terminally ill should be allowed, if (1) it is a free decision, (2) if the physical or mental condition is painful and irreversible, (3) the wish to suicide is persistent over time, (4) the suicide minimizes hurt to others, (5) the suicide helper is a qualified professional, and (6) helping decisions are group professional decisions (Humphrey, 1981). The great majority of suicides do *not* satisfy these conditions and, thus, are not rational.

THE EXISTENTIAL VIEW OF SUICIDE

Life is, in fact, a battle. Evil is insolent and strong; beauty enchanting but rare; goodness very apt to be weak; folly very apt to be defiant; wickedness to carry the day; imbeciles to be in great places, people of sense in small, and mankind generally unhappy. But the world as it stands is no illusion, no phantasm, no evil dream of a night; we wake up to it again for ever and ever; we can neither forget it nor deny it nor dispense with it [Henry James quoted by Alvarez, 1970, p. 285].

To be more fully empathic with suicides, to make our dilemmas of intervention real, we must be honest about our attempt to understand their world view, to try to see how life looks and feels to them. Much of what presuicides experience fits into a rich tradition of what we may loosely call "existentialism." (The less generous may call such thinking clinically depressed, confused, or cynical.) What is referred to here primarily is the work of Ernest Becker (1973), Norman O. Brown (1959), and myself (1981), Battin and Maris (1983), Kierkegaard (1843, 1849), Tolstoi (1899), Poe (1902), Nietzsche (1927), Camus (1945), Tillich (1951, 1952), Sartre (1956), Plath (1963, 1965).

Existentialists basically ask: "What does it mean to be a *human* being?" What is the uniquely *human* condition (Maris, 1981, pp. 291–296; 1982, p. 5)? For openers it means living in tension, with heightened self-awareness, and experiencing an irreconcilable essential duality. In the words of Becker (1973) "we are gods who defecate" and "death is the worm in the apple of life." Life is a fragile parenthesis between the pain of birth and the pain of decline and death. Kierkegaard writes:

Listen to the newborn infant's cry in the hour of birth—see the death struggles in the final hour—and then declare whether what begins and erodes in this way can be intended to be enjoyment . . . we human beings do everything as fast as possible to get away from these two points [Kierkegaard quoted in Becker, 1973, pp. 67–92].

Even Freud saw an irreconcilable conflict between eros seeking to preserve and enrich life, and the death instinct, seeking to return life to the peace of death (Brown, 1959, p. 80).

From the existential perspective under the *best* conditions life is short, painful, fickle, often lonely, and anxiety generating (Maris, 1981, pp. xviii–xix). The human condition requires constant struggle and adaption (Henry James cited in Alvarez, 1970). Nothing short of death can truly end the problems associated with being human. All nonsuicidal alternatives are relatively inadequate, short-term adaptations to the human condition. Yet, not everyone suicides. In fact only 1 to 3 in 10,000 do. Why do relatively few of us ever suicide? For most a troubled, conflicted, and painful life is generally more valuable than no life at all. Suicidal resolution of the human condition tends to occur: (1) when one's life is and has been exceedingly harsh; (2) when nonsuicidal alternatives are blocked or used up (what are referred to previously as "constriction of the adaptive repertoire"); (3) when suicide is positively valued, prescribed, encouraged by suicidal role models, and so on; (4) when tolerance thresholds for coping with the human condition have been breached repeatedly; (5) when individuals are male and/or aged or otherwise unfit to cope with life's struggles; and (6) when individuals are isolated from love, meaningful work, and support (Freud's *Lieben und Arbeiten*).

To repeat, for existentialists the major life problem is life itself (not life "gone wrong"). Thus, only death truly resolves the life problem. Suicide is self-killing deriving from one's inability or unwillingness to accept the terms of the human condition. Many suicides are relatively unfit (in the Darwinian sense) for life, I mean genetically, hormonally, intellectually, vocationally, physically, socially, emotionally, and so on. For them life is not really viable. For other relatively fit individuals (a much smaller group), death can still be chosen. Why is it self-evident that we should do something, rather than nothing? The reason this second group is relatively small is that life is all we have (there is no afterlife) and that it is often pleasurable. From the existentialist perspective suicide is the rejection of what it means to be human. Suicides refuse to allow tension, uncertainty, conflict, failure, dependence, replacing them all with the icy resolution of nothingness.

THE BIOMEDICAL VIEW OF SUICIDE

To argue that suicide is an illness or a disease implies that it is biologically based (but not completely determined by biological factors); has specific organic causes and known symptoms; has known causes of development, expected outcomes, durations, and responds (if at all) to technical treatments (like psychotropic drugs or ECT) (Kety, 1976; Snyder, 1980; Tsuang and Vandermey, 1980). Given this definition, it is contended that suicide is an illness. Suicides have "careers" that are predictable, have known causes and courses, and admit to technical (usually chemical) interventions—psychotherapy alone is not very effective with suicides (Maris, 1981; Beck, Resnik, and Lettieri, 1974). However, and this is important, to claim that suicide is an illness does not on that ground alone give us a right to intervene to prevent it, any more than we have a right to prevent, say, heart disease. Suicides can have biomedical causes without being pathological.

Without getting into the intricacies of cause and effect, there is no doubt that on the whole the biology of most suicides is different from that of most nonsuicides. In an edited work (Maris, 1986), it is claimed that there are a dozen or so broad types of major biological differences in suicides compared to nonsuicides. These include (1) a lower capacity to promote one's own genes (deCatanzaro, 1981, p. 27); (2) higher rate of alcoholism (Robins, 1981); (3) neurochemical factors in depression (Stanley, Virgilio, and Gershon, 1982), (4) more lutenizing hormones (Dietz, Mendelson, and Ellingboe, 1982), (5) endocrinological indicators (especially dexemethasone suppression and cortisol (Rich, 1986), (6) menstrual cycle effects (Young, 1986), (7) ECT effects (Tanney, 1986), (8) irregular EEGs (Struve, 1986), (9) monozygotic twin suicides and genetic differences (Lester, 1986), and (10) differences suggested by animal studies (deCatanzaro, 1981; Lester, 1983).

Of course the most popular model of suicide as an illness attempts to link suicide with depression (and sometimes with alcoholism and minor tranquilizers as well: Hughes and Brewin, 1979; Snyder, 1980; Robins, 1981). Some (Rubinstein, 1985) argue that stress causes an increased demand for neurotransmitters like norepinephrine and serotonin. When demand for norepinephrine and serotonin exceeds supply, a depletion of both substances occurs, which in turn is related to the development of clinical depressions.

Regardless of the etiology, the "biogenic amine hypothesis" posits that some depressions may be associated with an absolute or relative deficiency of catecholamines (particularly of norepinephrine) at functionally important receptor sites in the brain, while manias are associated with an excess of such monoamines (Kety, 1976, p. 181; Kaplan, Sadock, and Freedman, 1975). Furthermore, there may be complex reciprocal effects of norepinephrine with serotonin. Postmortems of suicides show a constant diminution of serotonin or its metabolite. Recent research has shown that binding sites for imipramine were 45 percent lower in suicides than in nonsuicidal controls (Stanley et al., 1982; Brown, Elbert, Goyer, Jimerson, Klein, Bunney, and Goodwin, 1982; Greenberg, 1982). All this suggests particular neurochemical substrates in suicides. Still, two caveats are in order. First, the relationship of suicide and depression can vary widely with culture (which it should not, if biology is constant). Second, neurotransmitters may not be the key to suicide, if suicide occurs when we "are at our best."

Probably, except in rare instances (e.g., the "Lysch-Nyhan Syndrome" in infants; Berman, Blais, and Dancis, 1969), biology alone does not cause suicide. Suicide is, as Shneidman claims, multidimensional. We can all think of individuals with the supposed biological profile of suicides who in fact were not suicidal. Nevertheless, few suicides do not have the usual biological antecedents—depression, alcoholism, agedness, maleness, aggressiveness, and so on.

SOME ETHICAL AND EMPATHETIC DILEMMAS FROM THE EXISTENTIAL AND BIOMEDICAL PERSPECTIVES

Existential philosophers and physicians are usually not thought to have very much in common. But even though the two perspectives are distinct, they do share some essential traits. For example, both tend to see life problems as empirical, not definitional. Suicides really are sick, not just labeled so or created by doctors and medical care ("iatrogenesis"). Second, existentialists and physicians both tend to be skeptical about how much we can do to help would-be suicides, since certain understandable irresolvable problems inhere in life itself. For example, we all age, wear down and out, are not infinitely perfectable, cannot live forever, and so on. Finally, life and existence are the issues, not just the well-being of one individual's life. Both the existential and biomedical perspectives look at our obligations to enhance and maintain what we may call the "life-force." In this concluding section I will suggest about a half-dozen dilemmas in suicide and its intervention as seen from the existential and biomedical perspectives.

Are We Morally Required to Suffer Without Hope to Please Others or Should We Kill Ourselves?

We do not have to suffer great pain, if the prospect of cure is miniscule and others' preferences are whimsical (Regan, 1983). As Wittgenstein reminds us (1953) our pain is our own. No one else literally feels our pain, nor lives our lives. Of course, we should care about the well-being of our family and friends. Each responsible suicide must be assured that their survivors can survive and consider the meaning of their suicide for those who love and depend upon them (actually discuss it with them). Although it would take a lot for me to abandon my family, others who care about me have no compulsion to model their lives after mine. Usually others can decide in *themselves* about their lives. Indeed, their lives or their perception of the human condition may be quite different from mine.

But then are we obligated to live for God or for the state (Durkheim, 1912)? If you do not accept God's existence, then obviously you do not have to live for God. Although we do have obligations to the state (this is a complex issue), most of the time society gets along very well without particular individuals.

Is Life Worthwhile or Not?

> It will generally be found that as soon as the terrors of life reach the point where they outweigh the terrors of death a man will put an end to his life. But the terrors of death offer considerable resistance; they stand like a sentinel at the gate leading out of this world. Perhaps there is no man alive who would not have already put an end to his life, if this end had been of a purely negative character, a sudden stoppage of existence. There is something positive about it; it is the destruction of the body; and a man shrinks from that, because his body is the manifestation of the will to live [Schopenhauer, quoted in Alvarez, 1970, p. 138].

As Schopenhauer suggests, probably on balance most lives are more pleasurable than painful. Otherwise there would be more suicides than there are. Also, even a painful life may be better than death, especially if something short of death (e.g., psychoactive drugs, alcohol, religion, therapy, divorce, a new job, and so on) would have produced the same effect, by easing the pain.

Just because we must die eventually, does not invalidate the process or products of our lives. People erroneously see death as failure; as if something that ends like that cannot be worthwhile. Actually the opposite is true. Death makes life valuable. Furthermore, the life of an individual in a specific situation can be not worthwhile and yet life itself can be worthwhile.

A related question is Is there anything we are supposed to do with our lives that suicide thwarts (Regan, 1983)? Certainly we cannot do anything we want to with our lives. Each death has implications for the life-force and the viability of society.

Are Individuals Autonomous or Part of a Larger Collectivity (e.g., Society, the State, God)?

The ultimate "sin" of suicide has nothing to do with the fact that someone dies. What we cannot accept is the hubris of the suicidal act; that someone dared to defy God or the state. Of course, social order is not possible if we indulge our natural urges capriciously or become narcissistically preoccupied (Hobbes [1651]; however, see Durkheim [1893], on "organic solidarity").

And yet, to be too collectively oriented (Huxley, 1939) is to run the risk of sacrificing human creativity, spontaneity, and freedom. "Cheerful robots" may never suicide, but never be fully human either. It has to be remembered that "my" death is different from the death of others. Still, it is also true that many suicides occur because we take our own individual lives too seriously (i.e., are overly involved with our individual projects).

Does the Individual Never or Always Know What He or She Wants?

Brandt claims (1975) that under conditions of severe depression we are unlikely to be *able* to consider our best alternatives to suicide; that is, most suicides do *not* know what they themselves want and, thus, are, not rational. Second, almost every suicide is ambivalent (Shneidman, 1973; 1985). Suicides both want to die *and* live (actually we suspect they mainly want to live under changed circumstances). A major therapeutic problem is which side of the suicide's ambivalence do we respond to and under what conditions? Finally, some suicidal patients never know that they are killing themselves. Should we not elucidate the probabilities of suicidal death for such people?

Is Suicide Prevention Indefensible Coercion or Justifiable Intervention?

Of course, suicide prevention often *is* coercion (Szasz, 1976). We suicidologists and physicians have a strong compulsion to meddle with other people's lives, to save their souls, to tell them how to live (and die), even if it makes them miserable (the "Jiminy Cricket" syndrome). Suicide prevention often tells us more about the needs of the helper, than about the needs of the suicidal individual. Nevertheless, if someone is sick and wants help, we ought to provide it. One can always suicide tomorrow, next week, next year. If a life is not salvageable, you can count on suicide eventually in one form or another.

Is Suicide Rational (Moral, etc.) or Insane?

Whether or not suicide is rational, right, or morally appropriate usually gets two broad types of responses, those of utilitarians and Kantians (Battin and Maris, 1983). Utilitarians (Narveson, 1983) examine the consequences of suicide acts. Suicide is rational or moral if it produces pleasure or happiness for the suicide and others. For classical Kantians suicide is always seen as a violation of duty to oneself. Suicide is seen as deviating from some ideal (Hill, 1983); for example, what if *everyone* suicided?

Certainly, insane, psychotic people do suicide. On the other hand, suicide is not prima facie evidence for mental illness. Also, decisions to suicide can be charged with affect and still be rational. In fact affect may weigh against a "reasonable" suicide, because suicide still does not "feel" appropriate.

Is Length or Quality of Life More Important?

Life is impoverished, it loses in interest, when the highest stake in the game of living, life itself, may not be risked. It becomes as shallow and empty as, let us say, an American flirtation. . . . It is evident that war is bound to sweep away [the] conventional treatment of death. Death will no longer be denied; we are forced to believe in it. People really die; and no longer one by one, but many, often tens of thousands, in a single day . . . Life has, indeed, become interesting again; it has recovered its full content [Freud quoted in Alvarez 1970, p. 263].

Obviously, most of us would like to live both long and well, but that is not always possible. Given a choice, the object is not to live forever, but rather to live well. Curiously, suicide rates are often highest in quality settings where excellence is sought with passion (e.g., among Harvard students, San Francisco residents, top business executives, elite soldiers, and so on.).

The optimum suicide rate is not zero. It was virtually zero in Huxley's fictitious "brave new world" (1939), but Shakespeare's writings were kept in a safe. We could easily have a zero suicide rate, but I suspect none of us would want to live in such a world. Many things are far worse than suicide.

REFERENCES

Alvarez, A. (1970), *The Savage God*. New York: Random House.

Baechler, J. (1979), *Suicides*. New York: Basic Books.

Battin, M.P., & Maris R.W., eds. (1983), *Suicide and Ethics*. New York: Human Sciences Press.

Beck, A.T., Resnik, H.L.P., & Lettieri, D.J. (1974), *The Prediction of Suicide*. Bowie, MD: Charles Press.

Becker, E. (1973), *The Denial of Death*. New York: The Free Press.

Berman, P., Blais, M., & Dancis, J. (1969), Congenital hypericemia. *Arch. Neurol.*, 20:44–53.

Brandt, R.B. (1975), The morality and rationality of suicide. In: *A Handbook for the Study of Suicide*, ed. S. Perlin. New York: Oxford University Press, pp. 61–76.

Brown, N.O. (1959), *Life Against Death*. Middletown, CT: Wesleyan University Press.

Brown, G.L., Elbert, M.H., Goyer, P.F., Jimerson, D.C., Klein, W.J., Bunney, W.E., & Goodwin, F.K. (1982), Aggression, suicide, and serotonin: Relationships to CSF amine metabolites. *Amer. J. Psychiat.*, 139/6:741.

Camus, A. (1945), *The Myth of Sisyphus*. London: Hamish Hamilton.

deCatanzaro, D. (1981), *Suicide and Self-Damaging Behavior: A Sociobiological Perspective*. New York: Academic Press.

Diekstra, R. (1985), The significance of Nico Speijer's suicide. *Suicide & Life-Threat. Behav.*, 15/4:13–16.

Dietz, E.P., Mendelson, J.H., & Ellingboe, J. (1982), Postmortem plasma lunteinizing hormone levels and antemortem violence. *Pharmacol., Biochem., & Behav.*, 17:171–173.

Durkheim, E. (1893), *The Division of Labor in Society*. New York: Free Press, 1947.

———— (1897), *Suicide: A Study in Sociology*. New York: Free Press, 1951.

———— (1912), *The Elementary Forms of the Religious Life*. New York: Free Press, 1954.

Greenberg, J. (1982), Suicide linked to brain chemical deficit. *Science News*, 121(22):335.

Hill, T.E. (1983), Self-regarding suicide: A modified Kantian view. In: *Suicide and Ethics*, eds. M.P. Battin & R.W. Maris. New York: Human Sciences Press. pp. 254–275.

Hobbes, T. (1651), *Leviathan*. New York: Macmillan, 1947.

Hughes, R., & Brewin, R. (1979), *The Tranquilizing of America*. New York: Harcourt, Brace, Jovanovich.

Humphrey, D. (1981), *Let Me Die Before I Wake*. Glendale, CA: Economy Self-Publishing.

Huxley, A. (1939), *Brave New World*. New York: Harper.

James, H. (1973, 1979), *Tales of Henry James, 1864–1874*, Vols. 1 & 2. New York: Oxford University Press.

Kaplan, H.I., Sadock, B.J., & Freedman, A.M. (1975), The brain and psychiatry. *Comprehensive Textbook of Psychiatry*, 2nd ed. Baltimore, MD: Williams & Wilkins.

Kety, S.S. (1976), Biochemistry of the major psychoses. In: *Comprehensive Textbook in Psychiatry*, 2nd ed., eds. A.M. Freedman, H.I. Kaplan, & B.J. Sadock. Baltimore, MD: Williams & Wilkins, p. 1785.

Kierkegaard, S. (1843), *Fear and Trembling*. Princeton, NJ: Princeton University Press, 1941.

———— (1849), *The Sickness Unto Death*. Princeton, NJ: Princeton University Press, 1941.

Klausner, S.Z. (1968), *Why Men Take Chances*. Garden City, NY: Doubleday/Anchor Books.

Leighton, A.H., & Hughes, C.C. (1955), Notes on Eskimo patterns of suicide. *Southwestern J. Anthropol.*, 11:327–328.

Lesch, M., & Nyhan, W.L. (1964), A familial disorder of uric acid metabolism and central nervous system function. *Amer. J. Med.*, 36.

Lester, D. (1983), *Why People Kill Themselves*. Springfield, IL: Charles C Thomas.

———— (1986), Genetics, twin studies, and suicide. In: *The Biological Aspects of Suicide*, ed. R.W. Maris. New York: Human Sciences Press.

Maris, R.W. (1981), *Pathways to Suicide*. Baltimore, MD: Johns Hopkins University Press.

———— (1982), Rational suicide: An impoverished self-transformation. *Suicide & Life-Threat. Behav.*, 12/1:4–16.

———— ed. (1986), *The Biological Aspects of Suicide*. New York: Human Sciences Press.

Menninger, K. (1938). *Man Against Himself*. New York: Harcourt, Brace & World.

Narveson, J. (1983), Self-ownership and the ethics of suicide. In: *Suicide and Ethics*, eds. M.P. Battin & R.W. Maris. New York: Human Sciences Press, pp. 240–253.

Nietzsche, F.W. (1927), *The Philosophy of Nietzsche*. New York: Modern Library.

Plath, S. (1963), *The Bell Jar*. New York: Harper & Row, 1971.

———— (1965), *Ariel*. London: Faber & Faber.

Poe, E.A. (1902), *Complete Tales and Poems*. New York: Random House, 1975.

Regan, D.H. (1983), Suicide and the failure of modern moral theory. In: *Suicide and Ethics*, eds. M.P. Battin & R.W. Maris. New York: Human Sciences Press, pp. 276–292.

Rich, C. (1986), Endocrinology and suicide. In: *The Biological Aspects of Suicide*, ed. R.W. Maris. New York: Human Sciences Press.

Robins, E. (1981), *The Final Months*. New York: Oxford University Press.

Rubinstein, D.H. (1985), A stress-diathesis theory of suicide. *Suicide & Life-Threat. Behav.*, 15/4:122–197.

Sartre, J.-P. (1956), *Being and Nothingness: An Essay on Phenomenological Ontology*. New York: Philosophical Library.

Schopenhauer, A. (1964), *The Pessimist Handbook*, ed. H.E. Barnes. Lincoln: University of Nebraska Press.

Shneidman, E.S. (1973), *Deaths of Man*. New York: Quadrangle Books.

———— (1985), *The Definition of Suicide: An Essay*. New York: John Wiley & Sons.

Snyder, S.H. (1980), *Biological Aspects of Mental Disorder*. New York: Oxford University Press.

Stanley, M., Virgilio, J., & Gershon, S. (1982), Tritiated imipramine binding sites are decreased in the frontal cortex of suicides. *Science*, 216:1337.

Stern, D. (1968), *The Suicide Academy*. New York: McGraw-Hill.

Struve, F. (1986), Electroencephalographic correlates of suicide attempts. In: *The Biological Aspects of Suicide*, ed. R.W. Maris. New York: Human Sciences Press.

Szasz, T. (1976), *Heresies*. Garden City, NY: Anchor Books.

Tanney, B. (1986), ECT and suicide. In: *The Biological Aspects of Suicide*, ed. R.W. Maris. New York: Human Sciences Press.

Tillich, P. (1951), *Systematic Theology*. Chicago: University of Chicago Press.

———— (1952), *The Courage to Be*. New Haven, CT: Yale University Press.

Tolstoi, L. (1899), *Death of Ivan Ilyitch*. New York: Bantam, 1981.

Tsuang, M.T., & Vandermey, R. (1980), *Genes and the Mind*. New York: Oxford University Press.

Wittgenstein, L. (1953), *Philosophical Investigations*. New York: Macmillan.

Young, D. (1986), The menstrual cycle and suicide. In: *The Biological Aspects of Suicide*, ed. R.W. Maris. New York: Human Sciences Press.

25

Suicide: The Quest for a Future

Robert Jay Lifton, M.D.

A great deal of attention has been paid recently to the dangers of collective suicide, that of our species. Nuclear war would be a form of mass murder and suicide, reminiscent in some ways, though on an extraordinarily greater scale, of the People's Temple episode in Guyana in 1978.

Yet however global our concern, we have to return to the individual, in this case to individual self-destruction, in order to retain a proper perspective, both experientially and morally. It is, after all, the person, the individual human being, who must concern us. At the same time we must recognize that each individual suicide, or prospective suicide, has a larger context that directly affects the seemingly paradoxical quest I speak of in my title, "The Quest for a Future." With that recognition we ask in turn: How is that context affected by serious doubts about whether a society or a civilization or a species has a future? How do those doubts influence decisions about suicide and its relationship to that quest for an individual future? Answers to such questions are at best elusive, but we learn a great deal in seeking them.

My discussion can be divided into three parts. In the first portion, I want to suggest some general principles about suicide that may slightly clarify what is probably the most confused and confusing psychological literature that we have. Second, I want to suggest three basic psychic components of suicide. And third, I want to illustrate the operation of its principles and components in a celebrated public suicide, that of the Japanese novelist, Yukio Mishima, in 1970 (Scott-Stokes, 1974). Finally I will return to the larger theme that I addressed in my introduction.

GENERAL PRINCIPLES

The first larger principle to note is that suicide is not a psychiatric problem per se. The psychiatric profession cannot claim to be the exclusive authority on or guardian against suicide. Yet any psychiatry can be judged by its approach to suicide as a touchstone for its sensitivity and humanity.

Second, there is a back-and-forth swing, a polarity between the traditional Judeo-Christian horror and condemnation of suicide, and a critical view of this stance in the form of affirmation of suicide and even romantic idealization. As psychiatric physicians and at the same time advocates of human rights, we need to find our way between the principle of autonomy in suicide and our concern about human life and commitment to its perpetuation.

The third theme I wish to stress, one that is not very popular right now, is what I would call the unitary principle in suicide. Recent study of differentiating details in suicide has stressed its varied forms, and rightly so. I would insist, however, that there is common ground to suicide, no matter who carries it out, as a violent statement about human connection, broken or maintained. Whatever the differences between the suicide of Socrates as an affirmative act of a healthy, mature man and that of the most regressed schizophrenic person, each is an absolute act of the killing of the self. That is why Menninger (1959) could describe suicide as "a peculiar form of death which entails three elements: the element of dying, the element of killing, and the element of being killed" (p. 332), while stressing that "the death penalty is self-inflicted." Menninger also spoke of ordinary forms of suicide as "prototypes of acute, generalized, total self-destruction" (p. 338). Any suicide under any circumstances harkens back to this principle of "generalized, total self-destruction" as a broad human capability (p. 346).

The fourth principle concerning suicide is its universality. It is difficult to find a culture, or a mythology, in which suicide does not play a significant role. One must in fact assume that individual suicide is in some way compatible with the perpetuation of the human species. We may say that when man discovered death, began to symbolize, and created culture when man became man—he realized that he could kill others and kill himself. More simply, in learning that we die, we learn that we can inflict our own death. Eissler (1955) states that "the potentiality of such an action rests in every person" (p. 64) and "in every analysis we have to grapple with suicidal tendencies in the patient" (p. 67). One could say that to be human is to be exposed to the possibility of killing oneself.

A fifth principle is the paradoxical attitude toward suicide on the part of cultures and religions. Frazer (1936) speaks of the "dread and fear" of the spirits of those who have taken their own lives, spirits or ghosts considered dangerous because of being rendered restless and homeless by the deviant and unacceptable form of death that produced them. Yet Zilboorg, after an extensive survey of primitive suicide, concluded that the majority of primitive cultures "idealize . . . rather than condemn . . . suicide" (1936). The problem lies in the either/or assumption that a particular culture prohibits or else honors suicide: All cultures do both (Campbell, 1964). The Greeks accepted certain forms of suicide as appropriate to particular situations (again that of Socrates, but also of Jocasta, mother of Oedipus) (Choron, 1972), yet also had the custom of cutting off the right hand of a suicide and burying it apart from his body as a means of disarming a dangerous ghost (Frazer, 1936). There is a similar impulse in the medieval custom of putting a stake into the corpse of the suicide and burying him at the crossroads. Indeed in various expressions of Christian doctrine suicide is rendered a crime without possibility of repentence, or even a form of murder in which man becomes "his own assassin" [Browne cited in Alvarez (1972)]. Yet, Christianity, from its beginnings, reveres a particular form of suicide, that of martyrdom, as an ultimate spiritual principle and even a life goal.

There is a similar dichotomy in non-Christian Japanese tradition. We often think of the Japanese as idealizing suicide, as in the ritual act of hara-kiri or seppuku, in which one ends one's life voluntarily in order to reassert eternal cultural principles. But behind ritual suicides there could be considerable pressure, even coercion. Moreover, no such ennobling act was expected of ordinary people, who were in fact subject to prohibitions against suicide.

Reverend Tuke, the seventeenth-century English preacher, captured this overall duality of suicide by contrasting two forms, "the one lawful and honest" (that of martyrs, modeled on Jesus himself) and the other "dishonest and unlawful" (in which men without divine sanction take it upon themselves to end their own lives) (cited by Farber, 1966). The general principle here is that all cultures have a place for suicide, but bring to it a mixture of awe, terror, and prohibition. The fear lies in the threat suicide poses to existing definitions and rules concerning human connection. But for the same reason cultures, religions, governments, and political movements embrace certain forms of suicide when they can be performed specifically on behalf of their immortalizing principles. Everything depends on which way the winds of immortality are blowing.

Involved in all of this is, of course, a form of death management that cultures take on. The designation of who may or should kill himself, and under what circumstances, is the essence of a group's relationship to and control over life and death. One could say much about war and suicide, and about terrorism and suicide—the designation of suicide missions of one form or another for the ostensible purpose of maintaining the life of the larger group. Even nuclear holocaust could be seen by some, at whatever level of consciousness and illusion, as some such "life-enhancing" suicide mission.

The sixth principle involves another dialectic: the suicide wants both to die and to live, desiring literally to bring his or her life to an end but wishing also to assert a form of vitality in the act of self-destruction. There is fundamental truth to the insight, beginning with Freud, that one may kill oneself to deny the fact of death. But when Freud (1915) insists that the suicide wishes to kill an "internalized object" (p. 252) rather than the self, I would modify that assumption by insisting that it is that "object"-dominated *self*—the self still suffering from unresolved relationships and experiences—that the suicidal person does indeed seek to kill (Litman, 1967). Yet the vitality sought in suicide, I would maintain, goes beyond a "cry for help" and is more on the order of a demand for unending recognition and life-power.

A PARADIGM

In order to carry forth this narrative I need to present a model or a paradigm from which I view suicide and all else in psychological matters. One can trace a sequence from the classical psychoanalytic paradigm of Freud, that of instinct and defense, to Erikson's paradigm, that of identity and the life cycle. And more recently there has been a general tendency toward a paradigm of death and the continuity of life or, as I now prefer, the symbolization of life and death. This is a generally useful paradigm, but particularly so for suicide.

This model or paradigm is not meant to be a thanatology, but rather a psychology of life that gives death its due. There are two levels on which the paradigm exists: an immediate or proximate level and an ultimate one. The immediate dimension has to to with three polarities or dialectics: connection and separation, movement and stasis, and integrity and disintegration. The negative poles—separation, stasis, and fear of disintegration—are what I call death equivalents. What begins as a physiological experience (the newborn's separation from the mother at birth and during moments of neonatal experience), gradually becomes an image (that of separation and loss), and then becomes highly symbolized over the course of childhood and adulthood (inner constructs of loneliness, lack of intimacy, and alienation). But that very early experience of separation contributes to the emerging idea of death itself, which can begin to appear as early as the latter part of the second year of life. All through one's life there is an interplay between a death equivalent, such as separation, and death itself. If you encounter death, if someone close to you dies, you experience not only that death and direct death imagery but also have reactivated within you a general imagery of separation. Similarly, when undergoing separation of a meaningful kind, you are likely to have called forth actual death imagery.

The ultimate dimension in this model or paradigm involves the symbolization of one's larger connectedness—to those who have gone on before and those who will go on after one's finite life span. This is the way we symbolize our connection to our history and even to our biology. We experience a sense of human continuity as a symbolic form of immortality: whether through a biological mode, that of the family (or biosocial mode, one's group); through one's work, or human influences; through a spiritual attainment or a religious mode; or through one's attachment to eternal nature. Finally, there is the mode that depends on a direct form of experience, that of transcendence. It is what Freud called the oceanic feeling, the psychic state so intense that time and death disappear.

In this paradigm or model, the stress is not on this symbol or that but on continuous symbolization, on the constant creation and recreation of images and forms, that is, on a formative process. The self becomes both the overall coordinator of symbolization and the inclusive symbol of one's own organism. We distinguish proximate and ultimate levels only for intellectual convenience: in actuality they merge in a struggle for vitality and larger connectedness, a struggle that is in no way limited to the time of anticipated dying but goes on through all of one's life.

With suicide, there are questions about death equivalents—about separation, stasis and the fear of disintegration—and about death itself. It is amazing how often death can be left out of suicide in at least many of our constructs or concepts. But then, death can be left out of almost anything. Though death has recently become a popular subject, there is still great difficulty in thinking about it rigorously in relation to psychological theory—a failure we may look on as our conceptual denial of death. That conceptual denial bedevils our thought in general; in the case of suicide it becomes ludicrous. Yet suicide is concerned not only with death but with the quest for life continuity. Indeed suicide is concerned with questions of meaning on all levels.

ELEMENTS OF SUICIDE

Now I would like to consider what I take to be the fundamental elements of suicide. One is the issue of entrapment and despair. Another is a quest for meaning, that is, for a future, especially an immortalizing future. The last is what I call the suicide construct.

Evidence is well recorded on the subject of entrapment and despair. There is a sense that there is no way out other than killing oneself. What I want to stress here is the distinction between depression and despair. The two are treated as though they were the same; they are not. In terms of the preceding paradigm, depression tends to involve loss and a sense of separation, and the experience of the other two death equivalents, stasis and the fear of disintegration, as well. It also brings out elements of anger and protest. Despair functions more on that ultimate level that I described. In despair, there is a sense of inability to maintain or envision any larger human connections of significance—any ongoing connection to the great chain of being. And there is now some interesting research that shows that people can be depressed, and exhibit the very symptoms that we know to be true of depression, without despairing of their future. These people can feel helpless without feeling futureless (Beck, 1963). While depression and despair tend to merge, it is the element of despair that is central to suicide. The most difficult situation is one in which both of these elements are strong. But the despair is the critical element, with or without manifestations of depression.

In terms of despair and the sense of impaired larger human connection, one can say that the suicide can create a future only by killing himself. That is, he can reawaken a sense of psychic action and imagine vital elements beyond the present only by deciding on and carrying through that suicide. Although this may appear to be a paradox, and observers have called it irrational or a psychosemantic fallacy, such judgments may obscure the matter. At issue is the individual experience of the symbolizing process, within which radically negative expectations of the future call forth a desperate, indeed deadly, assertion of self and future. One kills the "dead self" in order to break out of the despair.

The other two fundamental elements of suicide that I wish to stress have been largely neglected: they are the quest for future-oriented meaning, and what I call the suicide construct. On the issue of meaning, Farber (1966) has written that the suicide is a sadly deluded figure, because instead of finding his life, he ends it. But for some, the act of ending one's life is the only way of finding it. For instance, Binswanger (1958) wrote of the suicide of his famous patient, Ellen West: "Only in her decision for death did she find herself and choose herself" (p. 298). And Antonin Artaud, the revolutionary dramatist wrote: "If I commit suicide, it will not be to destroy myself but to put myself back together again. . . . By suicide I reintroduce my design in nature, I shall for the first time give things the shape of my will . . ." [quoted in Alvarez (1972 p. 131)]. While Binswanger had more than a touch of the romantic, and Artaud was mad as well as gifted, they articulate the powerful theme of suicide as self-completion, as the only means of appropriately locating oneself in the "design" of the cosmos. This theme is present in every suicide, however agonizing or demeaning the circumstances. That is why Hillman (1964) could speak of suicide as an "urge for hasty transformation . . . the late reaction of a delayed life which did not transform as it went along" (pp. 73, 454). One can observe this quest for meaning most clearly in what Durkheim called altruistic suicide. We shall find Yukio Mishima to be a case in point. Mishima asserted publicly his intent to kill himself in order to revitalize the martial principles of Japanese culture, immortalized from eary days but increasingly abandoned in the face of what he considered harmful modern and contemporary influences. We shall see that Mishima combined this quest for larger meaning with elements of personal despair, and that both are likely to be present in every suicide. Where the one— either the despair or the larger meaning—seems to predominate, there are likely to be quiet manifestations of the other.

The third principle, that of the suicide construct, addresses the question of why some people kill themselves and others with similar psychological motifs in their lives do not. One beginning answer is the existence, often from early life, of the concrete possibility of killing oneself as an active ingredient of psychological experience. The suicide construct can be culturally transmitted, as in the case of the premodern samurai instilled from early childhood with imagery of meeting certain kinds of situations honorably by killing oneself in specific ritual fashion. The Christian missionary's anticipation of martyrdom could entail a parallel suicide construct.

There can also be family transmission of a suicide construct, as in the clinical impression on the part of many that suicide is more of a danger where parents or close relatives have in the past committed suicide. This is sometimes seen as hereditary influence, but psychological transmission is probably much more important. Contained in the suicide construct is a central idea: "Suicide is an option—something I can do in my life, something I've seen done, a possibility for me."

Alvarez, in his interesting study of suicide, tells of his personal experience with a suicide construct. As a child he had become aware that both parents had on some occasion put their heads in the gas oven, which seemed to him "a rather splendid gesture. . . . something hidden, attractive and not for the children, like sex." Over the course of his life, when things would go badly, he would say to himself, "I wish I were dead"—muttering it "unthinkingly," as automatically as a Catholic priest tells his rosary. . . . "IwishIweredead . . . IwishIweredead . . . IwishIweredead." And then one day, in a moment of illumination, "I heard the phrase as though for the first time," and shortly afterward made a serious suicide attempt" (Alvarez, 1972, pp. 267–269).

In the case of Ellen West there is also a powerful suicide construct. Binswanger pointed out that two of her uncles had committed suicide, and a third was "severely ascetic"; a younger brother was briefly hospitalized for "a mental ailment with suicidal ideas"; and both of her parents were subject to severe depressions (including, in all probability, significant suicidal ideation). Ellen West herself grew up with a romanticized feeling about death itself, and as a child would be disappointed when a fever would go down. She wrote poetry extolling death, and was entranced by the sentence: "Those whom the Gods love die young" (Binswanger, 1958). She killed herself at the age of 32, after a number of unsuccessful attempts—including pills, jumping out of a window and in front of cars, and self-starvation.

She had previously been hospitalized and was considered a suicide risk. Binswanger explained to her husband that he could assume responsibility for his patient if they agreed to put her on a closed ward. But Ellen West did not want to be on a closed ward and her husband refused to put her there. She wanted to leave the hospital and to kill herself, which, when a decision was made to release her, was what she did. Shortly after leaving, she became calm for the first time in thirteen years and ate a hearty breakfast. She seemed happy and even in a celebratory mood. She was, according to her husband, as if transformed.

One can say that by taking hold of her death in this way, Ellen could experience, however briefly, a sense of vitality. She found a larger sense of meaning in her violent conquest of the despairing meaninglessness in which she had lived. So all-consuming had been her suicide construct that killing herself was the *only* meaning toward which her life could strive.

The suicide construct can have a certain situational importance, as in a pattern of suicidal contagion that has sometimes been noted. In one important study (Kahne, 1966) there was virtual epidemic of suicide in a group of mental hospital patients, after a disturbing series of upheavals and turnovers among the staff. There was surely a breakdown in imagery of connection and intensification of despair among these patients. But we may also postulate a spreading intensification of the suicide construct, of the idea in each mind that one might actually kill oneself.

Yukio Mishima is worth returning to here because he illustrates, in the most vivid way, all of these elements at work. In fact his suicide was so vivid and flamboyant that it had strong elements of caricature. Mishima was a highly talented novelist, considered on more than one occasion for the Nobel prize, who in November 1970 performed a florid version of ritual Japanese self-immolation or seppuku. Gaining entrance to a Self Defense Force (Army) headquarters in Tokyo under a pretense, Mishima kept the General there hostage; and after making an abortive speech to the men below, he retired to an inner room and disemboweled himself. He was then beheaded by one of his followers in the Shield Society, a group he had formed as a private army whose name derived from the traditional Japanese concept of serving as a shield for the Emperor. Mishima's suicide note was his manifesto, in which he exorted the Japanese to take up arms against contemporary Western and commercial influences on Japan, in the name of ancient forms of Emperor-centered military and cultural glory. He wrote, "Let us restore Nippon to its true state, and let us die" (Scott-Stokes, 1974, p. 43).

At first view Mishima's actions seem to exemplify suicide in the service of larger, prospective meaning; certainly the immortalizing reach is loud and clear. Yet when you look more closely you can also find strong elements of despair, and above all a lifelong suicide construct.

There is a quality of absurdity in the sequence of events: the "Kitsch" uniforms (patterned after those of the Meiji era), the mocking responses to his balcony speech, and a good deal of difficulty with the beheading. The absurdity reflected Mishima's own inner chaos, including long-standing sexual conflict as a bisexual, increasing feelings of emptiness, and mounting despair over declining creative power and diminishing appreciation of his work by the Japanese public. The greater his sense of decline, the more he engaged in external display—in what some have called public stunts—including death-dominated theatrical literalism, display of his body [he had taken up body-building, Japanese fencing (kendo), as well as Western boxing], acting in films, melodramatic rightist political stances, and so on.

But all along Mishima was bound by his extraordinarily powerful suicide construct. He had spent most of his early childhood, until the age of twelve, in the sickroom of his elderly grandmother. For many years she was considered to be dying and would depend on only the young Mishima to give her medicine and tend to her needs. In an autobiographical novel she becomes a love object—she and death itself. Mishima also tells how, instead of fantasizing about little people, about elves and gnomes (kappas in Japan), he fantasized about little diseases that went about. He wondered which disease creature was more fatal than the others.

Mishima's most persistent fantasy from early childhood was that of the martyrdom of St. Sebastian, in which there is both the homoerotic attraction and an erotic attraction to death. As an adolescent and young adult during World War II, Mishima embraced the death-dominated aesthetics and politics of the Japanese romantic school of literature and equally romanticized right-wing militarized politics. Yet when called up to serve in the military—synonymous with expectation of death—it turned out that he did not want that death after all. His actions in fact could be called a form of malingering in his encouragement of doctors' suspicion of tuberculosis, when he had nothing more than a temporary cold. He spent the rest of his life seeking the romantic, immortalizing death he had lacked the courage to embrace as a late adolescent during World War II. He eventually staged the suicide he had been seeking over the course of his adult life. His immortalizing commitment to Japanese glory was very real to him, even as it combined with elements of despair and his lifelong suicide construct.

SUICIDE AND CONTEMPORARY THREAT

After this exploration of individual suicide in a social and historical context, can we now say something more about historical or social suicide from the standpoint of what we know about the individual tendency? Here one must start with the increasingly documented recognition, at least on the part of Americans, of the threat of extermination (Yankelovitch, 1984). The widespread experience of what I call the imagery of extinction. I call my general conceptual study "The Broken Connection" because I view this imagery of extinction as a source of a major rent in our psychic tissues (Lifton, 1983, chapters 17 and 18). To be sure we do not consciously entertain possibilities of our extinction during most of our waking hours. But that image is now with us at differing levels of awareness and with periodic waves of intensity—with us in ways we are just beginning to grasp. Does that broken connection between life and death affect our relationship to suicide?

Alvarez thinks it does and speaks of a sharp increase in suicide among artists and writers. He draws on my Hiroshima material to construct a thesis that the artist has become entrapped in the threat of meaningless mass death, and can find no language, no imagery, with which to express that existential state or escape from that entrapment. Alvarez speaks of the overwhelming "pressure to discover a language adequate to this apparently impossible task. . . . an artistic language with which to grasp in the imagination the historical facts of this century . . . the dimension of unnatural, premature death." In struggling to break out of the shared suppression of feeling, the collective psychic numbness, the artist, Alvarez tells us, becomes a "scapegoat" who "puts himself at risk and explores his own vulnerability . . . testing out his own death in his imagination" (1972, pp. 445–446). They move toward "a suicide of the imagination" if not toward the act itself in their Sisyphean struggle to create (and here Alvarez quotes a Hiroshima survivor, Keisuke Harada, from *Genbaku no kioku*): "language which can comfort guinea pigs who do not know the cause of their death" (1972).

But we must also ask What about the rest of us? What about the shared struggle with imagery of radical futurelessness, precisely the struggle that so haunts the artists Alvarez discusses. What does that fear of literal human end, of nothingness, do to our overall relationship to suicide?

We do not know the answer to that question. It is hard to tell whether there is an actual increase of suicide in our time; and if there is, whether this imagery of extinction plays a significant part. The variables involved are, in every sense, difficult

to control. But we can and should raise questions. Does perceived nuclear futurelessness contribute to the kind of despair and impaired human connection that we know
to be part of individual suicide? Does the image of collective nuclear murder/suicide
contribute, however indirectly, to the formation and the broad or even "contagious"
dissemination of suicide constructs?

These questions contribute to our uneasy fascination with the mass suicide-
murder of about 950 people in Guyana in 1978. Jim Jones, the leader of the People's
Temple movement, who set the process in motion, looked at the event as a form of
"revolutionary suicide," that is, collective suicide for an immortalizing purpose that
the group could not achieve in life. There was also deep underlying despair: people
leaving the group, a threatening investigation by congressmen, a sense of increasing
criticism, and pressure from every side. And the group's own apocalyptic impulses
were associated by Jones with parallel images of nuclear threat, undoubtedly used
manipulatively but at the same time genuinely experienced. What was most peculiar
to this group was a collective suicide construct, really a suicide theology formulated
by Jones. Hence the rehearsals of collective suicide in readiness for the occasion of its
enactment, should a situation arise in which that enactment became the best or only
expression of the group's immortalizing mission. Yet these elements of suicide were
not originally visible in a movement that called forth, at least at its beginning,
considerable idealism concerning racial harmony and communal living.

What haunts us about the Guyana episode is our fear that it prefigures a more
massive nuclear suicide/murder that could result from a sequence of events, partly
initiated by what is perceived as idealism, but increasingly out of human control.

Finally, can we make life-enhancing use of this recognition of potential
influence between suicide and nuclear threat? The death-related psychological issues
raised by nuclear threat could help us considerably in our continuous struggle to
grasp and cope with the elements of individual suicide. Still more important, what
we learn in our explorations of individual suicide, if applied wisely, might well
contribute to the desperately needed imaginative efforts to confront the imagery of
nuclear extinction, on behalf of rejecting and preventing that fate.

Finally, then, the words of poets who assert life rather than succumb to the lore
of suicide in our time. First Stanley Kunitz (1971):

> The sands whispered, *Be separate*,
> the stones taught me, *Be hard*.
> I dance, for the joy of surviving,
> on the edge of the road.

And Philip Levine (1979):

> Let me begin again as a speck
> of dust caught in the night winds
> sweeping out to sea. . . .
> a tiny wise child who this time will love
> his life because it is like no other.

REFERENCES

Alvarez, A. (1972), *The Savage God*. New York: Random House.

Beck, A.T. (1963), Thinking and depression. *Arch. Gen. Psychiat.*, 9:324–333.

Binswanger, L. (1958), The case of Ellen West: An anthropological–clinical study. In: *Existence: A New Dimension in Psychiatry and Psychology*, eds. R. May, E. Angel, & H.F. Ellenberger. New York: Basic Books.

Browne, T. (———), *Religio Medici*. Quoted in A. Alvarez (1972), *The Savage God*. New York: Random House.

——— (1613), *A Discourse of Death*. Quoted in M.D. Faber (1967), Shakespeare's suicides: Some historic, dramatic and psychological reflections. In: *Essays in Self-Destruction*, ed. E.S. Shneidman. New York: Science House.

Campbell, J. (1964), *The Masks of God: Primitive Mythology*. New York: Viking Press.

Choron, J. (1972), *Suicide*. New York: Scribner.

Eissler, K.R. (1955), Psychoanalytic aspects of suicide. In: *The Psychiatrist and the Dying Patient*. New York: International Universities Press.

Farber, L. (1966), *Ways of the Will*. New York: Basic Books.

Frazer, J.G. (1936), *The Fear of the Dead in Primitive Religion*. London: MacMillan.

Freud, S. (1915), Mourning and melancholia. *Standard Edition*, 14:237–258. London: Hogarth Press, 1957.

Hillman, J. (1964), *Suicide and the Soul*. New York: Harper & Row/Colophon Books, 1973.

Kahne, M.J. (1966), Suicide in mental hospitals. *J. Health & Soc. Behav.*, 12:177–186.

Kunitz, S. (1971), Excerpts from an old cracked tune. In: *The Poems of Stanley Kunitz 1928–1978*. Boston: Little, Brown.

Levine, P. (1979), Excerpt from lost and found. In: *Ashes*. Phillip Anthony Publishers.

Lifton, R.J. (1979), *The Broken Connection*. New York: Basic Books, 1983.

Litman, R.E. (1967), Sigmund Freud on suicide. In: *Essays in Self-Destruction*, ed. E.S. Shneidman. New York: Science House.

Menninger, K. (1959), Psychoanalytic aspects of suicide. In: *A Psychiatrist's World: Selected Papers of Karl Menninger*. New York: Viking.

Scott-Stokes, H. (1974), *The Life and Death of Yukio Mishima*. New York: Farrar, Straus & Giroux.

Yankelovitch, D. (1984), The public mood: Nuclear weapons and the U.S.S.R. *For. Aff.*, Fall:33–46.

Zilboorg, G. (1936), Suicide among civilized and primitive races. *Amer. Psychiat.*, 92:1361.

26

The Conditions of Collective Suicide and the Threat of Nuclear War

John E. Mack, M.D.

> It is the exhibitionistic drunken gesturing of two suicidal giants that may result, not in war or even battle, but in group suicide inaugurated by a handful of men in two different countries who will not speak to each other in any other terms.
>
> Karl Menninger (1983)

> The emigration may last from one to three years according to the route taken and the distance to be traversed before they reach the seacoast, and notwithstanding the destructive influences to which they are exposed, lemmings breed with such prodigality as actually to increase their numbers during the journey. Their ultimate goal is either the Atlantic Ocean or the Gulf of Bothnia, depending on whether their emigration begins from the west or the east side of the central elevated plateau. Those that finally perish in the sea, committing what appears to be a voluntary suicide, are only acting under the same blind impulse which had led them previously to cross shallower pieces of water with safety.
>
> *Encyclopaedia Britannica* (1962)

The human species stands now on the brink of extinction. Should we actually succeed in destroying ourselves, this will not occur as a result of some climatic catastrophe, like the advance of glaciers, or through overwhelming infection by an epidemic disease, such as bubonic plague. Rather, it will be done by man's own hand: a collective suicide through the detonation of nuclear devices of mass

Reprinted with permission from the *Bulletin of the Menninger Clinic*, 50(5):464–479, copyright 1986, The Menninger Foundation.

destruction. Yet when one considers the importance of this matter, or its urgency, it is remarkable to discover how little we understand about the phenomenon of group self-destruction, or how little effort has been made to apply to our present peril insights which can be derived from experiences in this area.

Before proceeding further I will set down what will not be emphasized in this essay. Appealing, for example, as the model of lemmings plunging en masse into the sea may be as an existing case in nature of collective suicide, it has little value for us here except in a metaphoric sense. For the "blind impulse" of these small rodents, however mysterious its origins, serves a biologically valuable, population-regulating function from the standpoint of that species, necessitated perhaps by crowding or scarcity of food. Although some have seemed to welcome nuclear war as a population-reducing device, or as an apocalyptic purging of the species through which good people will be saved and evil ones killed off, such views need not be taken seriously except insofar as they are symptomatic of the emotionally intolerable quality of the nuclear threat and the odd, dangerous ideas it has spawned. Nor is there any evidence that the human species is acting under its own "blind impulse" in the narrow sense of a simple, self-destructive, biological impulse or death wish. Rather, the threat of nuclear self-destruction will be considered as an outgrowth of humankind's group life, especially the extraordinary difficulty we have had as a species in getting along safely within the framework of the self-governing institutions called nations.

First, we may consider epidemiological variations in suicide rates, such as the marked increase in completed suicide among adolescents in the United States and other countries in the past several decades, since these differences reflect community or social determinants of suicide. Increased rates of suicide have been associated with unemployment, the disintegration of family structures, the loss of freedom, and other social afflictions (Baechler, 1975). Suicide rates have been shown to differ among countries (Hendin, 1978) or among major religious groupings. In Japan rashes of suicide have been associated with examination failures among students applying to leading universities, and in West Germany large numbers of high school suicides have been related to a punitive system of preselection for higher education and scarcity of jobs for those under eighteen (Wiseman and Nater, 1976).

"Epidemics" or "clusters" of suicides are found in local communities and school districts. A "suicide belt" has been described in an affluent lakefront area north of Chicago (*Time*, 1980). A string of deaths in 1979, some unexplained, alarmed school administrators and guidance counselors at West Morris High School in New Jersey (Hanley, 1979), and the death of a seventeen-year-old youth in a drag-racing accident in a Dallas, Texas suburb was followed by a string of six suicides (Thomas, 1984). The media carry frequent reports of such clusters, or pairs, of suicide in which the suicide or death of one adolescent seems to permit or inspire similar behavior among other vulnerable teenagers.

But such miniepidemics, or seemingly related suicides, are difficult to document statistically, and the cause and effect connections between or among the deaths cannot be established with certainty except by the kind of intensive case study approach that has been rare in this field. Furthermore, such instances, in which suicide rates are influenced by group dynamic or epidemiological factors, or the apparent "epidemics" of suicide, are still, in essence, instances of individual self-destruction. By this I mean that the group element resides in the effect of social determinants, group processes, or the influence of other individuals upon single persons, who choose, by themselves, to end their lives. They are not situations, like the examples to be considered next, in which varying sized groups of people elected simultaneously to end their lives en masse.

The best known historical instance of a mass suicide occurred in 73 A.D. at Masada, a high granite rock in the Judean hills overlooking the Dead Sea. The mass deaths at Masada, in which 960 Jewish defenders perished, was the final act in a war against the oppressive Roman procurators that had begun seven years before. Under the leadership of Eleazar ben Shimon, the resistors, who were known as Zealots, had retreated to Masada and maintained a desperate defense for two years. Rather than be captured and enslaved by the Romans these last survivors chose collective suicide. Eleazar's oration to the Zealots was recorded by the historian Flavius Josephus, a former Roman Commander in Galilee who defected to the enemy in 67 (Perlin, 1975). Josephus, arguing that the "darker regions of the Netherworld" (p. 5) would receive the souls of the suicides, opposed self-destruction. Eleazar's speech contained the following passages:

Long since, my brave men, we determined neither to serve the Romans nor any other save God, for He alone is man's true and righteous Lord; and now the time is come which bids us verify that resolution by our actions. At this crisis let us not disgrace ourselves; we who in the past refused to submit even to a slavery involving no peril, let us not now, along with slavery, deliberately accept the irreparable penalties awaiting us if we are to fall into Roman hands . . . [p. 595].

Let our wives thus die undishonoured, our children unacquainted with slavery; and, when they are gone, let us render a generous service to each other, preserving our liberty as a noble winding-sheet. But first let us destroy our chattels and the fortress by fire; for the Romans, well I know, will be grieved to lose at once our persons and the lucre. Our provisions only let us spare; for they will testify, when we are dead, that it was not want which subdued us, but that, in keeping with our initial resolve, we preferred death to slavery . . . [p. 597].

But outrage and servitude and the sight of our wives being led to shame with their children—these are no necessary evils imposed by nature on mankind, but befall, through their own cowardice, those who, having the chance of forestalling them by death, refuse to take it . . . [p. 599].

Who then can fail to foresee their wrath if they take us alive? Wretched will be the young whose vigorous frames can sustain many tortures, wretched the more advanced in years whose age is incapable of bearing such calamities. Is a man to see his wife led

off to violation, to hear the voice of his child crying "Father!" when his own hands are
bound? No, while those hands are free and grasp the sword, let them render an
honourable service. Unenslaved by the foe let us die, as free men with our children and
wives let us quit this life together! [Josephus, c. 79, p. 613].

Self-destruction, based on honor and religious conviction, and to avoid capture,
humiliation, and murder at the hands of the enemy, appears to have been quite
frequent in the conflicts among the Greeks, Romans, and their neighbors (Perlin,
1975, p. 5).

Baechler (1979) has provided several examples of collective suicide among
oppressed Jews in the Middle Ages in which rabbis urged death on their followers
rather than succumb to anti-Semitic persecution or apostasy. Baechler (1975) quotes
the chronicler, Albert of Aix, concerning a mass suicide at Mainz in Germany in
1096.

The Jews, seeing the Christians rise as enemies against them and their children, with
no respect for the weakness of age, took arms in turn against their coreligionists,
against their wives, their children, their mothers, and their sisters, and massacred their
own. A horrible thing to tell of—the mothers seized the sword, cut the throats of the
children at their breast, choosing to destroy themselves with their own hands rather
than to succumb to the blows of the uncircumcised [Baechler, p. 93].

In our own century there are documented examples of mass suicides occurring
in anticipation of defeat or fear of capture, especially in the closing months of World
War II. With the dissolution of the Third Reich there were recorded instances of
group suicides among high ranking Nazis who feared reprisal, and several examples
of mass suicide in Germany under conditions of panic as Russian troops approached
from the East. According to Baechler, "During the months and weeks that preceded
the collapse of the Third Reich, the press, radio, and cinema news willingly
described the unprecedented horrors that Russian occupation would bring with it,
and launched the slogan "Lieber todt als rot (Better dead than red)" (p. 329). One
thousand suicides took place at Stolp in Pomerania the night before the Russian
troops arrived, 100 at Drossen in Brandenberg, 100 at Oderberg in Landskron, and
300 in Brux in Bohemia. In the taking of Saipan in the Marianas Islands over 1,000
Japanese soldiers and civilians are reported to have killed themselves by walking off
cliffs, wading into the ocean, blowing themselves up with grenades, or surrendering
voluntarily to decapitation rather than face capture and dishonor (Meerloo, 1962).

On November 18, 1978 the most dramatic instance of a mass suicide in
modern times occurred when over 900 members of a religious sect called the People's
Temple took their lives in South America upon the instructions of their minister, the
Reverend James Jones. Jones, a messianic religious leader, had feared nuclear
holocaust from the early 1960s, if not before. He had read a magazine article that
listed the nine safest spots in the event of nuclear war, and, in April, 1962 had

moved his family to one of them, Belo Horizonte, a Brazilian city about 250 miles north of Rio de Janeiro. One neighbor in Brazil said Jones was so terrified of nuclear war, "There were times when just the sound of an airplane flying overhead would start him crying" (*Newsweek*, 1978, p. 56). In 1965, back in California, Jones announced to his congregation that the world would be engulfed by a devastating thermonuclear war on July 15, 1967, and he led about seventy familes to a rural setting among the redwoods in Mendocino County.

In 1976, affected apparently by growing criticism in California of his political and financial dealings, Jones moved with many members of his congregation to a 27,000-acre tract of land in Guyana, which he had scouted in the 1960s and had begun to develop in 1974. In Guyana, Jones said, he hoped to create a Christian, socialist paradise, a commune in which all the races (many members of the congregation were black) could mix in peace and work for the common good. Substantial, plain houses were built, a school was started, and there were some medical facilities that were advanced by Guyanese standards. Brochures for Jonestown said that every day "the laughter of children rings through the air. Our children are our greatest treasure" (*Newsweek*, 1978, p. 62). And the children do seem, at least at first, to have been happy there.

Jones's ability to inspire loyalty in his followers evidently was extraordinary. One disciple who worked with him for several years said, "I've never seen anyone relate to people the way he could. He would build them up, convince them that anyone as intelligent and sensitive as they were ought to do whatever it was that he wanted them to" (*Newsweek*, 1978, p. 55). Jones seemed also to inspire intense love among his followers and a willingness to surrender personal authority. A black woman, who was a church member from 1972 until 1976 said, "I loved him. . . . The way he sang in such a beautiful voice, 'It Ain't Necessarily So' was lovely. But he changed; he turned from a beautiful Christian man to a Jekyll and Hyde, a monster" (Lindsey, 1978, p. 20). A 71-year-old woman in Jonestown wrote to Jones, "You practice the highest principle of Socialism-Communism than anyone else in the entire universe. We should emulate you and Mother [presumably Jones's wife, Marcie] because you are the best Father anyone can have. Mother is the best Mother that we can have . . . I have given material things, money and time to the cause, but I will not betray my trust to the cause knowingly. I do not have a commitment to anything but the cause . . . I know that one is due to obey authority and respect authority. I try daily to be obedient and respectful" (*Newsweek*, 1978, p. 66).

Reverend Jesse Jackson, noting how many of those who died at Jonestown were black, related the tendency of his people to obey a white leader unquestioningly to the psychological legacy of slavery. Blacks in America are "trained to believe in whites," Jackson said. "We are trained to believe in their beauty, their brains and their power. . . . Our following white leaders is not altogether new. . . . The effects of slavery are still deep in our minds, in our everyday lives. We reject black authority even when we have the options" (*The New York Times*, 1978, p. A14).

The combination of personal and social forces that caused Jones's rapid deterioration and the emergence of a frankly paranoid set of ideas is poorly understood. About two years before the mass suicide occurred—soon after he arrived in Guyana—Jones seems to have preached increasingly about "dark forces," external enemies that were seeking to shut down his experiment in communal living. His methods of domination became increasingly threatening and violent (Lindsey, 1978, p. 20). At least seven months before the mass suicide Jones was quoted as saying that "it is better to die than to be constantly harassed from one continent to the next" (Lindsey, 1978, p. 20). In preparation for the real thing Jones began a series of "White Nights," suicide rehearsals through which he sought to overcome the fear of death in the community. He would summon the residents from sleep and harangue them over loudspeakers about "the beauty of dying" (*Time*, 1978, p. 20). Liquid that was not actually poisonous was drunk as a loyalty test. The arrival of an investigating team headed by a California Congressman (whom Jones's followers killed) seems to have confirmed in his mind that threatening forces were closing in on him. Shortly before the carnage, commune guards said, "It's a great moment—we all die." They told the communards that Jones was ordering a revolutionary suicide "to protest racism and facism" (*Newsweek*, 1978, p. 51). According to Larry Shact, a medical school graduate who prepared the vat of cyanide, painkillers, and tranquilizers mixed in strawberry flavor Kool-aid that killed the 900 communards, Jones told his followers, "The GDF [Guyanese Defense Forces] will be here in 45 minutes . . . we must die with dignity" (*Newsweek*, 1978, p. 52). Then he urged them frantically to drink the lethal mixture. Almost all obeyed and died. When the dying was nearly over Jones shot himself in the head. Witnesses said that his last words were "Mother—Mother" (Lindsey, 1978, p. 20).

Diane Johnson, in a 1979 review of four books published within six months of the Jonestown "massacre," based largely on the accounts of survivors, remarked upon how little understanding these studies provided about "the duped and sad people who died there" (1979, p. 3). What seemed to characterize the survivors as a group, Johnson noted, was "the lack of self-inquiry. None (at least to judge from their published statements) appears to have examined his assumptions about politics, groups, religions, or leaders" (Johnson, 1979, p. 5). Complete credulity, lack of self-responsibility, and total surrender of individual will to the authority of Jones and the congregation was the core experience of the Jonestown communards.

On Memorial Day, 1977, eighteen months before the Jonestown deaths, Reverend Jim Jones delivered an extemporaneous speech at an antisuicide rally at the Golden Gate Bridge in San Francisco. The speech, which was taperecorded by an alert journalist, provides an ironic twist. "Suicide," Jones said on this occasion, "is a symptom of an uncaring society. The suicide is a victim of conditions we cannot tolerate, and, I guess that was a Freudian slip because I meant to say which *he* cannot tolerate, which overwhelms him for which there is no recourse" (Seiden, 1979, p. 118).

Let us consider now the common elements in these examples of collective suicide. First, in each instance the group must exist as some sort of community, with sufficient cohesiveness or unity to be able to act with a degree of simultaneity, or at least for its members to feel that they share a common danger.

Second, the group needs to be strongly under the influence of a powerful elite or a single leader, who is either a religious figure or someone to whom Godlike rights and powers are attributed. Will and personal authority are surrendered to the leadership, which can command obedience, even to the point of gaining the acquiescence in self-destruction of virtually every member of the group.

Third, the leader represents to the group a vision—an ideology, a cause, the possibilities of a better life or social system to whose promise the group members become totally committed. Psychologist Philip Dwyer, noting the similarities between Masada and Jonestown, writes of a "totalistic milieu," an environment in which there is a "reordering of values to such a degree that life itself is subordinated to the group's values. Not only one's own life, but also the lives of loved ones and strangers. That is to say, murder as well as suicide is sanctioned by the group ethic" (Dwyer, 1979, p. 121). Dwyer describes further how the totalist leader indoctrinates members of the community into a "philosophy of death" by a barrage that combines social pressure and continuous propagandizing through which the polarized group ideology becomes the dominant reality. "This polarization leads to a gradual yielding of the individual's conscience, old values, and decision-making process to the group" (Dwyer, 1979, p. 122).

Fourth, the situation in which the group finds itself is perceived, or represented by the leader, to be hopeless and extremely threatening. Fear of an outside danger grows until the group's panic makes it particularly susceptible to the leader's solution of suicide to escape the unbearable affect associated with the desperate situation. Captivity and a fate worse than death confront the community—enslavement at Masada, the horrors of Russian occupation in eastern Germany, loss of honor in Saipan, or a takeover by ill-defined enemies at Jonestown. As Dwyer has pointed out, as far as the community's self-destruction is concerned, it does not matter whether the external threat is real, or, as at Jonestown, largely imagined. What is essential is that the group members, and probably also the leader himself if he is to be persuasive, believe that it is real.

Fifth, the leader(s) must be capable from a purely technical standpoint of bringing about the mass self-killing in a relatively short period of time. This requires a combination of determinants, which include tight organizational control by the leader and command of the group's loyalty, an efficient and rapid method of killing, and an emotional climate in which the final passive surrender to death is experienced as itself a positive act or a relief from unbearable future suffering. In earlier historical periods, when such technologically advanced agents of mass death as cyanide or nuclear devices were not available, the lack of technical proficiency might be compensated for, as at Masada, by the intense determination, cohesion, and ideological or religious commitment of the group members.

Let us return now to the nuclear arms race and consider the extent to which the conditions of collective suicide described above may or may not be currently present or developing.

When one observes the superpower competition, and the apparent rush or drift toward nuclear annihilation (the perception depending on how stable the current international balance of terror seems to be, or how imminent one thinks nuclear destruction may be) our species does appear to be set on a course leading to its destruction. Yet this fact, if it is a fact, does not by itself confirm, let alone locate, any *intention* to commit collective suicide as a species. Yet within the international nuclear system (it is hard to know what to call the collective structures that perpetuate or advance the arms race) some force, *some* sort of intentionality, or at least failure of the will to prevent the destruction, must be operating. Otherwise it seems impossible to account for behaviors on the part of the nuclear adversaries that are so maladaptive from a species standpoint.

One possibility is that the human race, as a whole, is possessed by some sort of death wish. Something like this possibility has been suggested by Brandeis sociologist Gordon Fellman. Fellman (submitted) suggests that humankind harbors a secret, unacknowledged self-hatred that is directed most intensely against the institutions of civilization we have created. He finds evidence for this collective rage in our popular culture, especially postnuclear films like *Road Warrior, Testament,* and *The Day After,* which offer "quasi-romantic images of struggle, self-sufficiency, and survival, amidst the ruins," in the apocalyptic religious prophecy that seems to welcome the end of life on earth, and in various writings that look to a nuclear holocaust, a "total homicide and collective suicide," as a welcome relief from the unbearable tensions of living in the nuclear age (Fellman, submitted). When we look about us, Fellman's view does not seem far-fetched. Yet it is difficult to make the connection between such a broadly defined collective impulse and the manifest world of the superpower conflict.

The American Committee on East–West Accord explains the nuclear danger through a different universal impulse. "It is," the Committee says "the *convergence* of human pride and ambition, joined with the geo-political resources to carry them out, that seem to propel the great powers toward collision" (Homet, 1985, p. 1). But here too there is the problem of locating more accurately and relevantly "human pride and ambition," and of connecting these emotions to the actualities or manifestations of the nuclear reality. In this effort, the outline of conditions for collective suicide described above, derived from historical examples, may prove to have some value.

Consider first the matter of community cohesiveness. The sovereign groupings we call nations, through which mankind now organizes much of its communal life, are certainly not connected together as a single, collective organism. But for the purposes of nuclear mass suicide this does not matter, as the instruments of destruction are now so powerful that a single nuclear nation can, by itself, destroy virtually all of humanity and its own people with no cooperation from another country.

Similarly, the leaders of the nuclear powers may initiate the final holocaust with a minimum of obedience on the part of their populations. For initiating nuclear war is such a technically remote activity that it can be undertaken by a few men who may be almost totally out of touch with the wishes or fears of the citizenry. No supporting "home front," not even armies, are needed. A small elite can arrogate Godlike powers to themselves and proceed with a nuclear showdown without obtaining the acquiescence of the world's population in their self-destruction. The would-be victims are manipulated into believing the present direction is the only one that is possible in view of the enemy's intentions and behavior, and experience themselves as largely powerless to divert the leaders from their course.

In relation to our third condition of collective suicide, the representation by the leader to his followers of an ideology, a preferred social system, or a vision of a better sort of group life, the nuclear competition shows a clear resemblance to the previously described instances of mass suicide. For each superpower has repeatedly expressed its willingness to risk the destruction of life on earth as we know it in the defense of its values or way of life, often crudely defined as "freedom," "socialism," "democracy," "human rights," or "Marxism-Leninism." Ideological propagandizing has been undertaken with such intensity that each nuclear superpower has come to equate its cause with absolute goodness, and to view the opposing power's system as so totally evil that risking global murder/suicide in the service of these proclaimed values can then be justified. As Dwyer wrote of the instances of collective suicide described above, this continuous propagandizing and polarization "leads to a gradual yielding of the individual's conscience, old values, and decision-making process to the group" (Dwyer, 1979, p. 122).

The fourth condition—fear of takeover or of terrible suffering at the hands of a dangerous enemy—is even more clearly demonstrated in the nuclear deadlock. In the mid-1980s the mutual fear that the people of the United States and the Soviet Union came to experience in relation to the adversary nation reached an intensity out of proportion to any actual, or at least intended, threat. Visitors to the Soviet Union have reported a fear that it might be forced to launch a preemptive nuclear strike, as increasingly advanced American nuclear devices seemed to threaten the Soviet heartland beyond the point of toleration and to jeopardize the survivability of the Soviet deterrant system. Recent American films, such as *Red Dawn, Invasion-U.S.A.,* and an ABC miniseries, *Amerika* (Smith, 1985), which depict actual "Russian" military attacks and occupation of the United States by Soviet forces, both reflect and whip up terror of a dehumanized Soviet enemy.

The sources of this fear are complex and go beyond the real differences, historical and ideological, that separate the two countries. It is caused in part by the extraordinary destructiveness of the weapons themselves and the helplessness that we feel in relation to them—a helplessness that no form of purely military protection can offset. The need of each government to exaggerate to its poeple the threatening intentions of the other power in order to justify a giant, nuclear weapons-based, military establishment, also contributes to the fear that the United States and the

Soviet Union have of each other. Furthermore, the knowledge deep within us that we cannot resort to the historic option of actual war to express our political will, or to satisfy our national interests, may contribute to the tension, especially when no constructive alternative for addressing our differences has yet been derived.

Fear of harm at the level of intensity that the nuclear threat has inspired brings about among some people a "get it over with" attitude, a kind of showdown mentality that seeks relief in a cleansing apocalyptic discharge. Our newspapers not infrequently carry statements of individuals who seem unable to bear the tension of living in the nuclear age. Fellman (1985) quotes a letter to the *San Francisco Chronicle* in which the writer says he would be "proud to push the button" if that is what it would take to prevent mankind from being "domesticated into acceptance of coerced conformity." "The surgery of carnage heals," the writer says (*San Francisco Chronicle*, 1982, cited in Fellman, submitted). What the get-it-over-with approach tends to overlook is the fact that, should a nuclear exchange occur, far more people will suffer agonizing, prolonged deaths with unimaginable suffering than will be blessed by painless instant extinction.

The fifth condition, the technical capacity of national leaders to bring about the mass killing in a short period of time, hardly requires discussion. For more than two decades the leaders of the nuclear superpowers have had at their disposal sufficient destructive power to eliminate life on the planet as we know it in just a few minutes. As has been stressed above, the populations of human beings (not to mention the other species which will perish) will have little participation in their own self-destruction.

In summary, the conditions of collective suicide seem now to be present for all of mankind: national communities of potential victims, seemingly helpless to direct their leaders from taking such a course; polarized ideological positions that mobilize public opinion and are used to justify the coming holocaust; terror of succumbing to a fate worse than death that drives the self-destroying machinery; and advanced technology that would enable the leaders to carry out the mass destruction with relative ease.

The collective suicide/homicide with which humankind now threatens itself can and must be prevented. There are several steps in this process. The first, which is largely diagnostic, was recognized by the Norwegian Nobel Committee in awarding the 1985 Nobel Peace Prize to International Physicians for the Prevention of Nuclear War. In announcing their choice the Committe said that the physicians had "performed a considerable service to mankind by spreading authoritative information and by creating an awareness of the catastrophic consequences of atomic warfare" (Butterfield, 1985, p. 1).

The steps of preventive treatment follow from the diagnostic work of the physicians and relate to the dynamics of collective suicide that have been identified. This process has already begun. In addition to becoming aware of the danger we face, it is important for leaders and citizens to acknowledge together the deep and intense fear that nuclear instruments of mass destruction occasion and the paralysis of action, the polarization of thinking, and the distortions of reality that this terror can bring about. Only then can we begin to address and to modify the dichotomizing and separating ideologies that perpetuate the dangerous states of enmity and distrust that drive the nuclear arms race and prevent a sober approach to genuine serious international political differences. Once this process is underway it may be possible to create a new vision that can replace the anachronism of dividing nationalisms— the possibility of a global community in which annihilation of one part of humankind by another becomes unthinkable.

As individuals and groups of people in the nuclear and nonnuclear countries come to recognize fully the danger that mankind has created through instruments of mass destruction, they often refuse to participate in their own destruction. Gradually we are seeing now the overcoming of passivity, increasing resistance to psychological manipulation, and the development of a worldwide movement of protest directed at the leaders of the nuclear powers. Responsible public action is beginning to replace mass acquiescence in the progress toward self-annihilation that has characterized the nuclear age.

Finally, our preventive therapy requires that we direct attention to the unique problems of nuclear technology itself. Because of the highly technical nature of nuclear devices and the sophisticated delivery systems that bring them to their targets, a gigantic gulf has been created between those who create and administer the weapon systems and the rest of humankind. An elite group—scientists and technicians possessing special knowledge and supported by a seemingly impenetrable bureaucratic structure—has become separated from the citizenry for whose security it bears responsibility. Nuclear weapons are researched, developed, and even deployed with little or no accountability to anyone, or at least not to persons who grasp fully the self-destructive implications of a continuing arms race for the fate of our planet. An essential step in the prevention of our collective suicide will be the establishment of nuclear accountability, a breaking down of the arcane and remote mystique that surrounds nuclear technology, and, finally, our overcoming of the distance that now separates the nuclear decision makers from the billions of human beings for whose protection they bear the ultimate responsibility.

REFERENCES

Baechler, J. (1975), *Suicides*, trans. B. Cooper. New York: Basic Books, 1979.

Butterfield, F. (1985), Nobel Peace Prize given to doctors opposed to war. *New York Times*, October 12, pp. 1, 14 (Late edition).

Dwyer, P.M. (1979), An inquiry into the psychological dimensions of cult suicide. *Suicide & Life-Threat. Behav.*, 9:120–127.

Fellman, G. (submitted). *Immortal Adversaries: Eros, Violence, and the Threat of Nuclear Death.*

Hanley, R. (1979), Series of Mendham student deaths troubles classmates. *New York Times*, June 16, p. 23. (Late city edition.)

Hendin, H. (1978), Suicide: The psychosocial dimension. *Suicide & Life-Threat. Behav.*, 8:99–117.

Homet, R.S., Jr. (1985), Ideologies and inevitabilities. *East–West Outlook*, 8/5:1.

Johnson, D. (1979). Heart of darkness. *New York Review of Books*, April 19, 26/6:3–7.

Josephus, F. (c. 79), *The Jewish War*, trans. H. St. J. Thackeray. New York: G.P. Putnam's Sons. 1928.

Lindsey, R. (1978), Jim Jones—from poverty to power of life and death. *New York Times*, November 26:1, 20 (Late city edition).

Meerloo, J. (1962), *Suicide and Mass Suicide*. New York: Grune & Stratton.

Menninger, K. (1983), The suicidal intention of nuclear armament. *Bull. Menn. Clin.*, 47:325–353.

Newsweek, (1978), The cult of death. December 4:38–44, 49–56, 59–60, 62, 65–66, 71–72, 74, 77.

New York Times (1978), Rev. Jackson ties U.S. to deaths in Guyana. November 29:A14.

Perlin, S., ed. (1975), *A Handbook for the Study of Suicide*. New York: Oxford University Press.

Seiden, R.H. (1979), Reverend Jones on suicide. *Suicide & Life-Threat. Behav.*, 9:116–119.

Smith, S.B. (1985), Film shows U.S. after takeover. *New York Times Television*, October 7:C18.

Thomas, P. (1984), Multiple teen suicides: Copycat behavior? *Clin. Psychiat. News*, 12/6:3, 19.

Time (1978), Nightmare in Jonestown. December 4:16–21.

Time (1980), Suicide belt. September 1:56.

Wiseman, C.S., & Nater, T. (1976), West Germany: Suicide course. *Newsweek*. March 8:28 (Pacific edition international).

Afterword: Reflections on Suicide

Karl Menninger, M.D.

I have been asked by the editors to reflect on the problem of suicide, after devoting more than 60 years to its study. Suicide is a great mystery, isn't it? Why do some of our fellow earth dwellers seem not to want to live any longer, when others of us think it's great to be alive and want life to go on as long as possible because we're enjoying it?

Some want to quit right now. Why? Freud is being accused at present of having changed his mind about some of his early observations and information about human nature, and the destructiveness, the self-destructiveness of people. He thought suicide was a most mysterious thing, and he finally attributed it to an instinct.

We keep asking ourselves why do some people want to quit what most of us want so much to continue? How can people be that different from us? "Well," someone says, "last year, I did feel a little suicidal, when I was having all that trouble, but I was ashamed of it and after a while it went away. I don't know why I took it so seriously." Some people do take it seriously.

Some people commit suicide to escape from pain. I know of a situation in which a son left a note to his mother. "Mother, don't look at this as suicidal," it said. "It is a great escape. I have [had] so much pain that I can't tell you about that I'm simply going to have to get away from it, and you must be glad because I'm going to be free from it." His mother read the note to me over the telephone. One wonders whether she was comforted by that note.

Suicides do more to us than get rid of somebody. They hurt people—other people than the victim. They shock, they grieve, they dismay, they disappoint. This pain that the suicide causes people other than the victim is a peculiar aspect of the phenomenon. Sometimes it *seems* to have been a fantasy, a wish, or intention of the deceased that he *wanted* to grieve and wound someone—was willing to pay for his cruel enactment against someone with his own life. What other possible motives could there be for a piece of violence like this, besides that of *killing* and wanting to escape further suffering? What else is achieved by an act that costs so much?

In a case of suicide, a combination of at least three things seems to happen.

Somebody gets killed that other people didn't want killed. Somebody does some killing despite what other people wanted. And in the midst of all this commotion, somebody dies; a life goes away out of somebody.

Now what is this thing "life" which has disappeared? We don't exactly know, you know, even we biological and medical people. We see it come and go; we've studied aspects of it; we think we can sometimes influence it. But we don't know what it is.

I have been asked if I have changed my mind about the triad of motives mentioned above: to kill, to escape, to inflict injury. I am no longer an active student of the subject. It is for current and future students to change or add to my theoretical proposal. But I do have one addition to suggest: I think there is one more unconscious motive to add to the triad. I think some love gets into suicide motivation. I really believe that some degree of positive intent gets into the determination to put oneself out.

For example, in Thomas Hardy's book, *Jude the Obscure,* the family has to move away, and in their new quarters, the children are hungry and cold and poor and sad. A new child comes to the family. One day the parents are both out trying to find a job, and come home to find the oldest boy hanging in the closet. On his coat was a note in his handwriting, saying, "Because we are too menny [many is spelled childishly]": Maybe that was a suicide in which there was a love factor.

There are some psychological pains that are pretty severe, almost unendurable—like huge burns. But are they severe enough alone to evoke this act? Well, I don't know. I think that it's important that we continue the study of suicide, and the emphasis should be on how to persuade somebody to try life a while longer, or dissuade somebody from impulsively ending it. One has to be a very strong persuader to dissuade people set on suicide because it is a strong impulse. That's why Freud thought it was an instinct.

In my final words to the attendees of the conference where I made these remarks, I said, "All of us are really encouraging each other to 'hang on,' try it a little longer. When we ask each other every day 'How are you?,' don't we mean how are you holding up? Try to stick it out. Hold on! The situation looks pretty dark, but let's not give up. Cling to hope."

Concluding Remarks

Herbert N. Brown
Douglas Jacobs

We thought it fitting to end with Karl Menninger's comments. Not only has his thinking and writing about suicide been enormously helpful to clinicians and influential with theoreticians throughout much of the midportion of this century, but even as he claims to be "no longer an active student" he continues to offer new directions for our efforts to understand and to respond to suicide. Perhaps "some love" (p. 484) is embedded in the motivation for some suicides, despite the difficulty many of us may have in seeing it that way. Certainly there can be no doubt that Menninger's well-articulated fear about nuclear self-destruction pervades our thinking and living these days. The forces of love and hatred that have occupied so many psychologically attuned clinicians and writers are, indeed, now being played out by individuals and groups on a global, species-relevant level. As we face this, it is also worth recalling Menniger's final comments about hope which echo the conclusion of *The Vital Balance* in the early sixties (K. Menninger, M. Mayman, and P. W. Pruyser, New York: Viking Press, 1963):

> Where there is life there is, usually, hope. Earlier we considered giving this book the title Where There Is Life. But we felt that in one sense the implication was misleading; it was as if to say that *only while* there is life is there hope, that hope is sustained by life. Our point is rather that life is sustained by hope—that where there is hope there is life! [pp. 416–417].

Here Menninger's observation about hope recalls Erikson's thoughts about activity and continuity in this volume's Foreword. The emphasis that "everybody has to recover his own sense of actuality" (Erikson, this volume, p. xiv) fits with "Hold on! . . . Cling to hope" (Menninger, p. 484). The clinical challenge is to find, and to foster, such healthful direction and staying power in the suicidal person.

485

It is impossible to summarize a book of this breadth. We do, however, offer three concluding remarks:

1. To respond to the dilemma of human suicide we must understand suicide as fully as possible.
2. The best chance for full understanding of both the general phenomenon of suicide as well as particular clinical cases comes from an approach that includes and, where possible, integrates biological, psychological, and social perspectives: The "Eriksonian" point of view, Havens's "knot of circumstances," Mack's "architectural" model, etc.
3. Not everyone needs to do the clinical work with suicidal people. Those who are drawn to the work enter into clinical waters that are inadequately charted and that have the potential to become hurricane-level rough. It is wise not to set out alone on such waters. Even the best prepared and experienced will sometimes need consultation and support. Others may appropriately, wisely, and even bravely decide not to do the work. There will inevitably be clinical failures and deaths, and their meaning for those involved must be included in the preparation for the work. There is also the opportunity to comfort and even to help those caught up in suicide.

Finally, we hope to have captured some of the lively theoretical richness and clinical relevance that has characterized the annual Suicide Symposia. We make no claim that this book completely covers the subject of suicide, only that we have attempted to present a reasonably organized and authoritative, thought-provoking, and forward-looking resource for those concerned with this enduring human dilemma.

Name Index

Subject Index

DATE DUE

9 3 99			
OC 23 '02			
DE 3 '02			
NY 17 04			
GAYLORD			PRINTED IN U.S.A.